VIRTUAL CURRENCIES

# VIRTUAL CURRENCIES

## A Legal Framework

Niels Vandezande

intersentia
Cambridge – Antwerp – Portland

KU LEUVEN CiTiP
CENTRE FOR IT & IP LAW

Intersentia Ltd
Sheraton House | Castle Park
Cambridge | CB3 0AX | United Kingdom
Tel.: +44 1223 370 170 | Fax: +44 1223 370 169
Email: mail@intersentia.co.uk
www.intersentia.com | www.intersentia.co.uk

*Distribution for the UK and Ireland:*
NBN International
Airport Business Centre, 10 Thornbury Road
Plymouth, PL6 7 PP
United Kingdom
Tel.: +44 1752 202 301 | Fax: +44 1752 202 331
Email: orders@nbninternational.com

*Distribution for Europe and all other countries:*
Intersentia Publishing nv
Groenstraat 31
2640 Mortsel
Belgium
Tel.: +32 3 680 15 50 | Fax: +32 3 658 71 21
Email: mail@intersentia.be

*Distribution for the USA and Canada:*
International Specialized Book Services
920 NE 58th Ave. Suite 300
Portland, OR 97213
USA
Tel.: +1 800 944 6190 (toll free) | Fax: +1 503 280 8832
Email: info@isbs.com



ISBN 978-1-78068-675-2
ISBN 978-1-78068-696-7 (pdf)
D/2018/7849/48
NUR 827

GPRC
Guaranteed
Peer Reviewed
Content

British Library Cataloguing in Publication Data. A catalogue record for this book is available from the British Library.

# FOREWORD

Dear Reader,

This book could not have been published at a better moment. Basically every day, newspapers report about bitcoin and other cryptocurrencies. Earlier this year, the Guardian labeled 'blockchain' – the open-source ledger behind bitcoin – as the buzzword of 2018.1

Also policymakers and industry seem to be gearing up for the FinTech future. End of February 2018, the European Commission organized a roundtable in Brussels on "Cryptocurrencies – Opportunities and Risks" with key authorities, industry representatives and experts.[2] In his speech following the roundtable, Valdis Dombrovskis, Commission Vice-President in charge of Financial Stability, Financial Services and Capital Markets Union, pointed to the opportunities of cryptocurrencies, but also – and perhaps mainly – to the substantial risks for consumers and investors associated with their use. Not only is the value of most cryptocurrencies extremely volatile,[3] crypto-assets also present risks relating to money laundering and the financing of illicit activities, and Initial Coin Offerings expose investors to substantial risk because of the lack of transparency regarding the identity of the issuers and underlying business plans.[4] Mr. Dombrovskis also pointed out that they *"need to assess further under what circumstances crypto-currencies and related services are covered by existing regulation"*.

The need for a better understanding of the risks and opportunities that go with the use of crypto-assets, and a better understanding of the applicability of EU

1 M. Busby, "Blockchain is this year's buzzword – but can it outlive the hype?", The Guardian, 30 January 2018, https://www.theguardian.com/technology/2018/jan/30/blockchain-buzzword-hype-open-source-ledger-bitcoin.

2 Https://ec.europa.eu/commission/news/roundtable-cryptocurrencies-2018-feb-26_en

3 As John Oliver (the presenter of HBO's popular show "Last Week Tonight with John Oliver") phrased it recently in an episode dedicated to cryptocurrencies and bitcoin: *"if you choose to invest in the cryptocurrency space, just know that you're not investing, you're gambling..."* https://www.youtube.com/watch?v=g6iDZspbRMg.

4 Recent reports show that on average USD 9 million per day is lost to crypto-scams – and that is without taking into account larger incidents such as the hacking of an exchange such as the Japanese Coincheck (https://www.bloomberg.com/news/articles/2018-03-08/coincheck-to-start-paying-back-victims-of-500-million-heist).

regulation – such as the rules on anti-money laundering and on e-money – was equally stressed in the European Commission's FinTech Action Plan that was released shortly after the roundtable, on March 8th of this year: "*An assessment of the suitability of the current EU regulatory framework with regard to Initial Coin Offerings and crypto-assets more generally is necessary*".[5] Indeed, a fair and transparent framework that can appropriately address the associated risks seems a *sine qua non* in order to ensure that EU firms, investors and consumers can take advantage of the technical innovations in the financial sector, while also appropriately addressing the risks.

This book offers an important contribution to that objective. It explores the concept of virtual currencies and guides you through the maze of European financial law. Starting with a conceptual analysis of virtual currencies in light of traditional notions like 'money' and 'trust', and looking at useful typologies to classify a wide range of virtual currencies, it continues with an in-depth legal analysis of the applicability of the current EU frameworks for e-money, payment services, anti-money laundering and financial instruments to virtual currencies. It also offers a normative perspective by formulating recommendations for revision, taking inspiration – where relevant – from experiences outside the EU (in particular the United States). It is therefore not only relevant for the academic community, but also for policy makers and industry.

Despite the highly specialized nature of the topic (and its typical jargon), the book reads fluently and is also accessible to non-experts in the field. It contains the results of the doctoral research that the author carried out at the Centre for IT & IP Law (CiTiP) at KU Leuven in the period 2014–2018. Throughout the text, though, it becomes clear that he masters the topic not only from a theoretical perspective, but that he also understands the practical implications of his findings. Undoubtedly, this is to a large extent due to the fact that the author could carry out his research in the context of interdisciplinary and industry-driven iMinds (now imec) projects dealing with mobile payment platforms and blockchain (like CoMobile, SoLoMIDEM, TRU-BLISS, and BoSS). In these projects, he frequently interacted with technical and economic experts, as well as industry representatives and practitioners.

Combining various projects and tasks at our research group, which he joined in 2009 (at that time called 'ICRI'), the author has shown to be a very tech-savvy and versatile researcher. He has acquired a very broad but also deep knowledge of many areas where new technologies pose challenges for existing legal frameworks (including also digital archiving, identity management,

---

5 Https://ec.europa.eu/info/publications/180308-action-plan-fintech_en and http://europa.eu/rapid/press-release_IP-18-1403_en.htm.

eGovernment, eHealth, privacy & data protection, security and trust in the Internet of Things, and public information availability). With his research, he gained international visibility and won important prizes, such as the SWIFT Institute research grant and a ticket to present at the prestigious SIBOS conference in Singapore in 2015.

This book lays the foundation for a promising new research track at KU Leuven that brings together the expertise of CiTiP and the Jan Ronse Institute for Company and Financial Law. For me personally, it has been a rewarding experience and a true pleasure to serve, together with Prof. Veerle Colaert, as the promoter of this research. We have confidence in our trustworthy guide, Niels, that he will show us the way through this fascinating emerging field of FinTech and help us distinguish between hype and reality.

In the meantime, we wish you, dear Reader, a rewarding intellectual journey through this book!

Prof. Dr. Peggy Valcke
imec – KU Leuven – CiTiP
16 May 2018

# ACKNOWLEDGMENTS

This book marks the publication of my doctoral thesis, which I defended on 13 March 2018. Having arrived at the end of my PhD journey, I can only confirm what those who went before me already said: a PhD thesis is in the first place an individual work, but it can never be done without the help of others. Here, I would like to express my gratitude to at least some of those others.

First of all, I would like to thank my promotor, prof. dr. Peggy Valcke, for immediately believing in my project to conduct research on 'this bitcoin-thing', for her inspiring guidance and feedback throughout the journey, and for always keeping faith in that I would one day finish it. It is her careful balancing between giving me the freedom to pursue my own research interests and guiding me towards the finish line that resulted in this thesis.

Second, I would like to thank my co-promotor, prof. dr. Veerle Colaert, for accepting the co-promotorship of a 'CiTiP PhD', for reminding me to take the necessary time away from other projects to focus on my PhD research, and for sharing her invaluable knowledge in the often highly technical domain of financial law.

Third, I would like to thank the members of my doctoral guidance committee, prof. dr. Leo Van Hove, prof. dr. Matthias Edward Storme, and prof. dr. Wim Decock, for their feedback throughout the writing process and at the occasion of my doctoral seminars. I also thank prof. dr. Antonella Sciarrone Alibrandi, for joining the examination committee, and em. prof. dr. Frans Vanistendael, for chairing the examination committee.

I have the pleasure to be working at the KU Leuven Centre for IT & IP Law (CiTiP) – formerly the Interdisciplinary Centre for Law & IT (ICRI) – since 2009. The centre's broad variety of research projects has enabled me to learn about so many of the issues encountered at the crossroads between law and technology, and has allowed me to have a taste of several of these issues before settling on the topic of my PhD research. Its highly interdisciplinary outlook can only serve as an example for the legal professional of the future. The centre's unique culture is of course only made possible by the work and dedication of its members, with whom I have had the pleasure to collaborate and discuss throughout the years.

Throughout my project research, I have had the pleasure to meet and collaborate with many inspiring people from several disciplines. In particular, I would like to thank our close colleagues at the COSIC and DistriNet research groups, as well as the CoMobile project team – as it is that project which first set me on the path that eventually resulted in this thesis.

Writing a PhD thesis is not a purely professional endeavor, as it tends to invade all aspects of life. I am therefore indebted to my parents, for providing me with the opportunities to undertake my studies, and for listening to my talking about practically nothing else these past few years. Last, but certainly not least, I owe my eternal gratitude to Nathalie, for putting up with me at all times – and not just during the course of my doctoral research. Without her love and support, this thesis or any of my other endeavors could not have been possible.

Niels Vandezande

# CONTENTS

# ACRONYMS

| | |
|---|---|
| AML | Anti-Money Laundering |
| AMLD1 | First Anti-Money Laundering Directive |
| AMLD2 | Second Anti-Money Laundering Directive |
| AMLD3 | Third Anti-Money Laundering Directive |
| AMLD4 | Fourth Anti-Money Laundering Directive |
| ATM | Automated Teller Machine |
| BaFin | Bundesamt für Finanzdienstleistungen |
| BCDR | Business Continuity and Disaster Recovery |
| CA | Certificate Authority |
| CDD | Customer Due Diligence |
| CEPS | Common Electronic Purse Specifications |
| CESR | Committee of European Securities Regulators |
| CFTC | Commodity Futures Trading Commission |
| CFPB | Consumer Financial Protection Bureau |
| CJEU | Court of Justice of the European Union |
| COREPER II | Committee of Permanent Representatives |
| DAO | Decentralized Autonomous Organization |
| DNS | Domain Name System |
| DRM | Digital Rights Management |
| EBA | European Banking Authority |
| ECB | European Central Bank |
| EFT | Electronic Funds Transfers |
| EFTPOS | Electronic Funds Transfer at Point of Sale |
| EMD1 | First E-money Directive |
| EMD2 | Second E-money Directive |
| EMI | European Monetary Institute |
| EMU | Economic and Monetary Union |
| EPC | European Payments Council |
| ESMA | European Securities and Markets Authority |
| ETF | Exchange-Traded Fund |
| EU | European Union |
| EULA | End-User License Agreement |
| FATF | Financial Action Task Force on Money Laundering |
| FinCEN | Financial Crimes Enforcement Network |
| FIU | Financial Intelligence Unit |

| | |
|---|---|
| FSMA | Financial Services and Markets Authority |
| GDP | Gross Domestic Product |
| ICO | Initial Coin Offering |
| IRS | Internal Revenue Service |
| ISD | Investment Services Directive |
| KYC | Know-Your-Customer |
| LETS | Local Exchange Trading System |
| MiFID1 | First Markets in Financial Instruments Directive |
| MiFID2 | Second Markets in Financial Instruments Directive |
| MiFiR | Markets in Financial Instruments Regulation |
| MMORPG | Massively Multiplayer Online Role-Playing Games |
| MTF | Multilateral Trading Facility |
| MVNO | Mobile Virtual Network Operator |
| NASAA | North American Securities Administrators Association |
| NIS | Network and Information Security |
| NFC | Near Field Communication |
| OCSP | Online Certificate Status Protocol |
| OJ | Official Journal of the European Union |
| OTF | Organized Trading Facility |
| P2P | Peer-to-peer |
| PKI | Public Key Infrastructure |
| PSD1 | First Payment Services Directive |
| PSD2 | Second Payment Services Directive |
| PSP | Payment Service Provider |
| RFID | Radio-Frequency Identification |
| SEC | Securities and Exchange Commission |
| SegWit | Segregated Witness |
| SEPA | Single Euro Payments Area |
| TFEU | Treaty on the Functioning of the European Union |
| TLD | Top-level domain |
| TTP | Trusted Third Party |
| UCC | Uniform Commercial Code |
| VAT | Value added tax |

# INTRODUCTION

## 1 BACKGROUND OF THE RESEARCH

RISING TECHNOLOGY – The influence of the Internet on commercial transactions is undeniable. More and more purchases are concluded at electronic commerce, or e-commerce, websites such as Amazon. Currently, the main focus of developments in the e-commerce sector is on mobile payments[1] – or m-payments, framed within the broader rise of financial technologies or fintech.[2] On the one hand, m-payments could be conducted using technologies that allow for contactless payments, such as near field communication (NFC). Such technologies are already implemented in most major credit and debit cards.[3] On the other hand, service providers can develop mobile wallets[4], which can store online cash balances, bank cards, loyalty cards, or even boarding passes and tickets. Most major banks and established alternatives such as PayPal have already deployed mobile banking applications.[5] However, the growth of fintech means that such services are no longer the exclusive domain of traditional players in the financial services industry. Also predominantly technology-oriented companies, such as Google and Apple, are becoming significant players in this field, and have developed their own mobile wallets.[6]

VIRTUAL CURRENCIES – Another significant development here is the use of virtual currencies.[7] Some virtual currencies are deployed within a closed system – for instance a game such as World of Warcraft – and serve a single purpose, or are limited-purpose at most. Others, however, could theoretically serve unlimited purposes. That is, for instance, the case when a classic loyalty scheme is combined with the issuing of a virtual currency.[8] Another example are so-called cryptocurrencies, such as bitcoin, which are distinct in not being

---

1 With the notion 'mobile' to be understood as referring to the use of devices such as smartphones and tablets, as used in: European Commission (2012) "Green Paper Towards an integrated European market for card, internet and mobile payments", *COM(2011) 941 final.*

2 *Ibid.*, 5.The total global value of mobile payments exceeded USD 1 trillion in 2014.

3 E.g. *visa.co.uk/products/visa-contactless.*

4 Such as Google Wallet or Apple Passbook.

5 For instance, Google Play lists applications for all major Belgian banks. *play.google.com/store/apps/category/FINANCE/collection/topselling_free.*

6 I.e. Google Pay and Apple Wallet (used with Apple Pay).

7 The notion of virtual currencies will be more clearly defined in chapter I.

8 As was the case for the CityLife pilot project. *leveninleuven.be/2013/12/15/citylife-een-gezamenlijke-klantenkaart-van-20-handelaars-in-leuven.*

issued by a central authority.[9] The adoption of cryptocurrencies has grown exponentially over the last few years, despite their often volatile exchange rates. For instance, in 2017, 7.500 physical stores and 100.000 online businesses accepted bitcoin, including Microsoft, Expedia, and Overstock.[10]

Legal uncertainty – While there are economic benefits to the aforementioned developments in virtual currencies, they also raise important legal questions. Given the rising use of virtual currencies and virtual currency services, there is a clear need to establish whether there is a legal framework governing such services and the providers thereof, both to ensure that issuers and professional service providers are working in compliance with such a legal framework and to ensure that the consumer of virtual currency services is provided with the applicable legal protection, or can at least be certain of the presence or absence of such protection.

# 2 PROBLEM STATEMENT AND STATE OF THE ART

## 2.1 LEGAL UNCERTAINTY

Unclear legal framework – In the current state of the art, there is no comprehensive legal framework regulating all aspects of virtual currencies.[11] From the perspective of economic and financial law, there are a few EU legal frameworks that are of particular relevance here: the Second E-money Directive[12] (EMD2), the Second Payment Services Directive[13] (PSD2), the Fourth Anti-Money Laundering Directive[14] (AMLD4), and the Second Markets

9 Examples include bitcoin, dogecoin, litecoin and peercoin. Cryptocurrencies record and timestamp all transactions in a public ledger, called the 'blockchain', to prevent double spending. This recording and timestamping requires the calculation of cryptographic hash functions to confirm a transaction. When confirmed transactions are bundled into a new block to be added to the blockchain, an activity known as 'mining', new units of the cryptocurrency are created and rewarded to the creator of the block. This creation of new units is completely determined by the algorithms underlying the network, without control of a central person or entity.

10 *Coinmap.org; coinbase.com; bitpay.com.*

11 A single transaction could, for instance, elicit legal concerns relating to financial regulations, fiscal laws, data protection legislation, consumer protection, etc.

12 Directive 2009/110/EC of the European Parliament and of the Council of 16 September 2009 on the taking up, pursuit and prudential supervision of the business of electronic money institutions amending Directives 2005/60/EC and 2006/48/EC and repealing Directive 2000/46/EC, *OJ* L 267 of 10 October 2009, 7–17 (hereinafter: EMD2).

13 Directive 2015/2366 of the European Parliament and of the Council of 25 November 2015 on payment services in the internal market, amending Directives 2002/65/EC, 2009/110/EC and 2013/36/EU and Regulation (EU) No 1093/2010, and repealing Directive 2007/64/EC, *OJ* L 337 of 23 December 2015, 35–127 (hereinafter: PSD2).

14 Directive 2015/849 of the European Parliament and of the Council of 20 May 2015 on the prevention of the use of the financial system for the purposes of money laundering or terrorist financing, amending Regulation (EU) No 648/2012 of the European Parliament and of the

in Financial Instruments Directive[15] (MiFID2). However, the application of these existing legal frameworks to virtual currencies is unclear. This was the case at the onset of this research in 2014, and remains true in 2018. In its March 2018 FinTech Action Plan, for instance, the European Commission stated that an "*assessment of the suitability of the current EU regulatory framework with regard to Initial Coin Offerings and crypto-assets more generally is necessary*".[16] Moreover, it is uncertain what other legal framework could apply.

Broader view from financial and economic law needed – One potential reaction is to reduce the question regarding the legal qualification of virtual currencies to the payment obligation underlying the transaction in which they are used and to interpret this strictly according to civil law. Such an approach, however, does not fully take into account the aspects of virtual currencies as digital representations of value that can be used as instruments for concluding payment transactions.[17] As a result, it is necessary to also consider financial and economic law, with aspects of private law added where needed, in order to gain a full understanding of the matter.[18] The research conducted here focuses mainly on those aspects of financial and economic law surrounding the matter of virtual currencies. Such a narrowing down of the scope of the research ensures the feasibility of the study.

EU and fundamental research – Moreover, the clear international nature of virtual currencies necessitates a more EU-oriented approach for legislative action. The approach maintained here builds forth on research conducted within the framework of applied research projects in which the KU Leuven Centre for IT & IP Law participated.[19] It is in those projects that the need for a more fundamental approach toward the subject of virtual currencies was identified.

Council, and repealing Directive 2005/60/EC of the European Parliament and of the Council and Commission Directive 2006/70/EC, *OJ* L 141 of 5 June 2015, 73–117 (hereinafter: AMLD4).

15 Directive 2014/65/EU of the European Parliament and of the Council of 15 May 2014 on markets in financial instruments and amending Directive 2002/92/EC and Directive 2011/61/EU, *OJ* L 173 of 12 June 2014, 349–496 (hereinafter: MiFID2).

16 European Commission (2018) "FinTech Action plan: For a more competitive and innovative European financial sector", *COM(2018) 109 final*, 6.

17 As defined by the European Banking Authority (EBA). The EBA also clearly references the need to examine whether virtual currencies could or should be subjected to the framework on payment service providers. EBA (2014) "EBA Opinion on 'virtual currencies'", *EBA/Op/2014/08*, 7–8.

18 For instance, cryptocurrencies such as bitcoin have two components: the virtual currency itself and the payment system in which that currency is used. Citing security, low transaction costs and short transaction processing time, this payment system has, according to UBS, the potential to "*reduce systemic costs, and provide faster, secure, transfers – particularly in the international arena*". Rizzo, P. (2014) "UBS: Banks Could 'Absorb the Benefits' of Bitcoin", *coindesk.com*, 28 March 2014. This further demonstrates the need to approach that matter from a financial and economic perspective.

19 Such as NFC-Voucher (2008–2009), CoMobile (2012–2013), SoLoMIDEM (2013–2014), Media ID (2013–2014) and TRU-BLISS (2014–2016). Working in interdisciplinary groups –

## 2.2 REGULATORY INACTION

Diverse reactions – Actions undertaken by lawmakers in the field of virtual currencies have been fragmented and incomplete at best, with many conflicting opinions adding to the uncertainty.[20] For instance, in the US the Internal Revenue Service (IRS) considers virtual currencies as property[21], whereas a Texas District Court ruled that cryptocurrencies are money.[22] In Europe, the European Central Bank (ECB) stated that cryptocurrencies are not e-money, without providing a potential positive assessment.[23] The German Federal Financial Supervisory Authority (BaFin) considers virtual currencies as financial instruments[24], as being units of account similar to foreign currencies but without the status of legal tender.[25] Several countries have issued warnings against the use of cryptocurrencies, though some expressed interest in taxing their gains.[26] The current situation of regulatory uncertainty and inaction may also raise the issue of jurisdiction and forum shopping. For instance, several virtual currency service providers are already establishing themselves in countries with clearer or less stringent rules regarding the matter.[27]

Limited initiative – In 2012, the ECB advocated to wait with regulatory initiative until virtual currencies gain sufficient economic impact.[28] In 2017, ECB President Mario Draghi found virtual currencies insufficiently mature

including industry partners – CITIP has in those projects conducted research on the scope of the existing legal frameworks regarding payment services and e-money, and has advised partners on how the services they planned to develop would be influenced by those legal frameworks. Be it in the form of vouchers, mobile wallets or loyalty schemes, these projects all raised questions that could be boiled down to the same underlying issue: the uncertainty regarding the legal status of virtual currencies.

20 At the present moment, only the New York State Department of Financial Services has adopted a comprehensive legal framework for virtual currency businesses. In the EU, some suggestions toward action have been made by the European Commission and the European Banking Authority, yet with thus far only legislative action in the anti-money laundering field.

21 IRS (2014) "Virtual currency guidance", *irs.gov*, Notice 2014–21.

22 *Securities and Exchange Commission v. Trendon T. Shavers and Bitcoin Savings and Trust*, 4:13-CV-416 (Texas, 6 August 2013).

23 The ECB even points out the lack of a legal framework: European Central Bank (2012) "Virtual Currency Schemes", *ecb.europa.eu*, 42.

24 With 'financial instrument' to be understood as a form of unit of account pursuant to section 1 (11) sentence 1 of the German Banking Act (Kreditwesengesetz – KWG).

25 Münzer, J. (2013) "Bitcoins: Aufsichtliche Bewertung und Risiken für Nutzer", *www.bafin.de*; Deutscher Bundestag, Schriftliche Fragen, *17/14530*, 41. Here, the German Federal Minister of Finance compared virtual currencies to a *Tauschring*, a form of LETS.

26 Law Library of Congress (2014) "Regulation of Bitcoin in Selected Jurisdictions", *loc.gov.*

27 As virtual currencies are mainly used online, the place of establishment of a service provider is not important.

28 European Central Bank (2012) "Virtual Currency Schemes", *ecb.europa.eu*, 44.

to regulate.[29] It was, however, also the ECB that called for early regulation of e-money[30] to raise consumer and merchant confidence in that technology, precisely due to the lack of economic impact at the time.[31] Some authors have argued virtual currencies to be a bubble, but such predictions have proven only partially true.[32] Moreover, new virtual currencies are launched continuously.[33] The downfall of one example, or even an entire type of virtual currencies, would therefore not derogate from the importance of the problems stated here, but serves as a reminder of the risks posed by legal uncertainty, amongst other factors.[34]

## 2.3 STAKEHOLDER RISKS

Risk for the consumer... – The lack of regulatory clarity has significant risks.[35] For instance, uncertainty regarding the legal status of bitcoin in China caused crashes of the cryptocurrency's value in 2014 and 2017, bearing clear similarities to a bank run.[36] While lawmakers and public institutions do recognize the risks of virtual currencies, such risks are mainly held to relate to speculative investments by consumers.[37]

... as well as for businesses and service providers – It can be argued, however, that the risk is not only on the consumer. Given the competitive pressure in the emerging virtual currency market, businesses and service

29 Sundararajan, S. (2017) "ECB President: Bitcoin Not 'Mature' Enough to Be Regulated", *CoinDesk*, 20 October.

30 To be understood in the meaning of the EDM2. In practice, this refers to e-purses such as Proton, and network money such as offered in the services of PayPal.

31 European Central Bank (1998) "Report on Electronic Money", *ecb.europa.eu*, 20–21.

32 Kearns, J. (2013) "Greenspan Says Bitcoin a Bubble Without Intrinsic Currency Value", *Bloomberg*, 4 December 2013; Quiggin, J. (2013) "The Bitcoin Bubble and a Bad Hypothesis", *The National Interest*, 16 April 2013; Schiller, R. (2014) "In Search of a Stable Electronic Currency", *New York Times*, 1 March 2014. While Schiller does consider the current situation to be a bubble, he also acknowledges that cryptocurrencies could serve broader future purposes, be it in the function of money as unit of account.

33 Amazon launched Amazon Coins, an alternative payment unit for its own store, in 2013.

34 Also Bank of America Merril Lynch points out the potential benefits of cryptocurrencies and warns for the dangers caused by the situation of regulatory uncertainty. Bank of America Merril Lynch (2013) "Bitcoin: a first assessment", *Bank of America*, 5 December 2013.

35 European Central Bank (2012) "Virtual Currency Schemes", *ecb.europa.eu*, 42. The ECB finds that the "*non-existence of a clear legal basis for virtual currency schemes is an illustration of the overall existing lack of understanding about virtual economies and their impact on the real economy*" and that the lack of a legal basis for virtual currencies is one of the most critical aspects of their instability.

36 Rizzo, P. (2014) "BTC Price Declines Following False Report of Bitcoin Ban in China", *coindesk.com*, 21 March 2014.

37 Mersch, Y. (2014) "Efficient retail payments: key in strengthening the competitiveness and growth potential of the EU", Speech at the ECB/Banca d'Italia Workshop on Interchange Fees, Rome 24 March 2014, *ecb.europa.eu*.

providers may feel compelled to join in.[38] This exposes them to an unavoidable risk, or a catch-22. On the one hand, they risk falling behind on their competitors by failing to adapt to emerging technologies. On the other hand, if they do adapt, they are exposed to the associated risks. Both the risks on consumers and on businesses and service providers could have an effect on economic growth.

## 3 RESEARCH OBJECTIVE

CORE OBJECTIVE – The main objective of this research is to provide an assessment from the perspective of financial and economic law of the extent to which virtual currencies can be considered as money, e-money, payment services, or financial instruments, the gaps and shortcomings identified there and the potential way forward. That objective will be achieved by first analyzing whether virtual currencies can already be included under the existing legal frameworks regarding e-money, payment services, anti-money laundering and markets in financial instruments, and by assessing whether such would provide stakeholders with legal certainty. If gaps are found to exist within those frameworks, the aim is to explore whether there is a need for the amendment of those existing legal frameworks or for the adoption of specific regulation for virtual currencies.

RESEARCH FOCUS – The main focus is therefore the legal assessment of virtual currencies under financial and economic law. Such an assessment is necessary to provide stakeholders with legal certainty regarding their rights and responsibilities. Additionally, aspects of trust services are considered, as trust[39] is imperative for virtual currencies to succeed.[40]

INTERNATIONAL OUTLOOK – As virtual currencies are generally not bound to a particular jurisdiction, it is important to take into account international aspects. Such is necessary, for instance, for the international coordination in efforts against money laundering and fraud, for which virtual currencies have already been used.

---

38 As evidenced in the growth of both online and brick and mortar merchants accepting cryptocurrencies as payment, as well as in the growing number of cryptocurrency service providers.

39 To be taken in the literal sense of the word. Apart from looking at the abstract concept of trust itself, the research will also refer to the implementation of this notion through the figure of trust services, or Trusted Third Party (TTP). Examples of this in law are the Certificate Authority (CA) or qualified certification-service-provider in the sense of Annex II to the Electronic Signatures Directive (1999/93/EC, *OJ* L 13 of 19 January 2000), the trust service provider under the so-called eIDAS Regulation (910/2014, *OJ* L 257of 28 August 2014), or even the public notary.

40 As evidenced by the low uptake of e-money after the adoption of the EMD1, the establishment of a legal framework alone may not be sufficient to make a market develop itself.

Output – The main output is an analysis of the need and potential for legal regulation of virtual currencies, with accompanying assessments of whether such an assessment can provide legal certainty and whether it can augment stakeholder trust in these developments. Where needed, this assessment is supplemented with recommendations for further legislative initiative.

## 4 RESEARCH QUESTIONS

First research question – There are two main research questions to answer. The first question is to what extent can virtual currencies be considered as money, e-money, payment services, or financial instruments under the currently applicable relevant legal frameworks, and what gaps and incompatibilities can be identified from this analysis? The aim of this first question is to assess whether virtual currencies can be considered as money, and whether the frameworks set by the EMD2, the PSD2, the AMLD4, or the MiFID2 can apply to the development of virtual currencies. In doing so, it also aims to expose whether gaps and incompatibilities can be identified in those legal frameworks regarding such an application.

Supportive questions 1 – In support of the first research question, a number of sub-questions are formulated. As virtual currencies can take a number of forms, this research first analyzes how different types of virtual currencies can be classified. To this end, a typology will be formulated. Second, the research must verify whether the current roles and functions of money can be fulfilled by virtual currencies. This serves to identify whether virtual currencies can be considered as money. Third, it must be assessed to what extent the current legal frameworks regarding e-money, payment services, anti-money laundering, or markets in financial instruments can apply to virtual currencies. This will serve to expose the potential gaps and incompatibilities in those legal frameworks in relation to virtual currencies.

Second research question – As preliminary research[41] shows that there may indeed be barriers to the implementation of virtual currencies in the frameworks regarding money, e-money, payment services, anti-money laundering and markets in financial instruments, a second more normative main research question rises: *should virtual currencies be regulated in order to provide stakeholders with legal certainty, and, if so, should such regulation be the subject of a separate legal framework or should it be integrated in existing financial and economic law?*

Supportive questions 2 – Also the second main research question finds support in a number of sub-questions. First, the *ratio legis* behind e-money must be

41 As conducted in the framework of the applied research projects mentioned in footnote 19.

identified in order to verify whether the demarcation line between this regulated form of immaterial currency and unregulated virtual currencies can be upheld. This exposes the potential for legislative amendment of the legal framework regarding e-money in relation to virtual currencies. Second, the research assesses whether the services developed around virtual currencies should be considered as payment services, thus making the providers of these services payment service providers. This could serve to regulate the behavior of market players and their services in the payment services field, rather than the virtual currencies themselves. Third, the consequences of the application of anti-money laundering rules on virtual currencies must be identified. Fourth, it must be established whether virtual currencies qualify as financial instruments in the sense of the legal framework on markets in financial instruments. Fifth, inspiration for legislative coherence between virtual currencies, e-money, payment services, and financial instruments is sought in the US. A functional comparison with a country where the matter of virtual currency regulation is more developed aims to provide more clarity on whether legislative initiative is needed at all. Last, it must be analyzed whether trust mechanisms can support the reliability of virtual currencies. If no legislative initiative is taken, the notion of trust could serve to augment the trustworthiness of virtual currencies. Therefore, trust measures could play an integral role supporting the trustworthiness of virtual currencies if specific regulation would not be found necessary.

Normative criteria – As the second main research question is normative in nature, criteria must be formulated to support the analysis. For the sake of delineating this research, the following serve as the primary normative criteria.

The first criterion is legal certainty. In order to remedy the current situation of uncertainty, the outcome of this research should be able to provide the stakeholders involved with legal certainty on the position of virtual currencies under financial and economic law. Regardless of the outcome – implementation of virtual currencies under an existing legal framework, separate regulation or no regulation at all – it must be clear to all parties to a transaction what their legal position is *re* the virtual currencies they use. Also, where legislative initiative was taken throughout the course of this research, it was analyzed whether such an initiative indeed resulted in a situation of legal certainty.[42]

Second, proportionality must be considered, as potential legislative measures to provide legal certainty must be (1) suitable to achieve their legitimate aim, (2) use the least restrictive means available, and (3) may not have excessive effect on

[42] Meaning that the resulting rule must be precise and clear, with foreseeable legal implications. As will be discussed further on (footnote 45), the EMD1 did not result in legal certainty. The mere adoption of legislation is therefore not a guaranteed or automatic fulfillment of the criterion of legal certainty. See also section 5.

the interests at stake.[43] In the particular context of virtual currencies, conflict could arise between, *inter alea*, the interests of providing for market stability, of protecting consumers, and of fostering economic growth through innovation in virtual currencies. Striking the right balance between these interests is by no means an easy exercise, as the precise impact of a legislative measure in the field of virtual currencies on stakeholders may be difficult to quantify. As this research is mainly legal conceptual in nature – rather than empirical or policy-oriented – it is explicitly chosen to approach such analysis in a neutral manner. Therefore, the different interests at stake will be accorded equal weight, as establishing the criteria by which one interest were given more importance than another interest would in itself already constitute a policy decision. This position of neutrality corresponds to the open outlook of the research, whereby it is not *a priori* assumed that regulation of virtual currencies is a necessary outcome.[44] Moreover, such a neutral position prevents regulatory difficulties that could result from early position-taking.[45]

A third criterion is trust. As virtual currencies are not accepted as legal tender, their whole lifecycle of issuance and acceptance depends on trust between the parties involved.[46] The outcome of this research should therefore be able to raise the trustworthiness of virtual currencies. As the matter of trust plays an important role in the subject of virtual currencies – whether the outcome is to regulate virtual currencies or not – it has therefore been included as a primary normative criterion.

Last, regulatory coherence must be considered. Given the potential for virtual currencies to be deployed at an international scale, there is a clear need to approach the matter with an international regulatory view. This means that the outcome of the research should have the potential to be implemented in a coherent manner, at least at across the EU Member States. Moreover, there must be compatibility with other applicable legal frameworks.

---

43 Tridimas, T. (1999) "Proportionality in Community Law: Searching for the Appropriate Standard of Scrutiny", In: Ellis, E. (ed.) *The Principle of Proportionality in the Laws of Europe*, Oxford: Hart Publishing, 68.

44 If, for instance, it were decided that market protection is the most important interest at stake, the result would be that any development with potential impact on the market – or rather on monetary policy in this case – requires regulation. In that case, the need to regulate virtual currencies would be unavoidable, given the policy decision thus taken.

45 Here reference can be made to the EMD1. The ECB decided from the very beginning that a strict regime was needed to protect financial stability. This strict position was irreconcilable with the EC's desire to open up the e-money market in order to support its growth. The resulting directive was a compromise plagued by inconsistencies and dubious terminology, leading to difficulties in its implementation by the Member States. The directive ended up at least contributing to the limited development of the e-money market. European Commission (2008) "Commission Staff working document – Accompanying document to the proposal for a Directive of the European Parliament and of the Council amending Directive 2000/46/EC on the taking up, pursuit of and prudential supervision of the business of electronic money institutions – Summary of the Impact Assessment", *ec.europa.eu*, SEC(2008)2572, 3.

46 Especially in the case of cryptocurrencies, where there is not even a single central issuer, trust in the blockchain – the public ledger – is essential to their functioning.

Other criteria considered – In considering certain other applicable legal frameworks, the following core principles of those frameworks were identified. However, as they do not play a capital role serving the particular purposes of this research, they will not be considered as primary normative criteria. While their value is certainly acknowledged, they will therefore only play an auxiliary role where their application would prove necessary.

For instance, while privacy is naturally a concern within the context of payment transactions using virtual currencies, it should also be noted that the privacy concern relates mainly to the processing of the personal data of the parties involved in such transactions. Personal data processing operations are already covered by an EU-wide legal framework[47], which will be applicable here in any case. Therefore, for the sake of legislative coherence, it can be argued that a legal framework regarding virtual currencies could best refer to the existing framework on personal data protection. Another element that has been considered is security.[48] As with privacy, security is imperative to the functioning of schemes in which virtual currencies are deployed, given the often sensitive nature of the data processed.[49] Also here, reference can be made to existing principles, rather than advocating the adoption of separate security principles for virtual currencies.[50]

Expected outcome – The output of the research does not aim to result in direct policy initiatives, but to provide an assessment of whether a need and potential can be found for the application of a legal framework under financial and economic law to virtual currencies in a manner that is coherent, proportionate and that provides legal certainty and trustworthiness to all stakeholders. However, where it is found that existing legal frameworks are not suited to that end, the research will analyze whether there is a need to propose avenues for legislative development.

## 5 RELEVANCE OF THE RESEARCH

Need for fundamental approach – As noted in section 2.1, applied research projects made it clear that a more fundamental approach toward the topic of virtual

47 As set by the Data Protection Directive (95/46/EC, *OJ* L 281 of 23 November 1995) and its national transpositions. This framework is to be replaced by the General Data Protection Regulation (2016/679, *OJ* L 119 of 4 May 2016).

48 Given the recent developments in terms of data breaches, network and information security (NIS) is more and more considered as an essential principle underlying the information society. This is evidenced by its inclusion and operationalization in recent legislation, such as the eIDAS Regulation (910/2014, *OJ* L 257of 28 August 2014) and the General Data Protection Regulation (2016/679, *OJ* L 119 of 4 May 2016).

49 Note: while financial data can be sensitive to certain persons, it is not sensitive personal data within the scope of article 8 of the Data Protection Directive.

50 For instance, Directive (EU) 2016/1148 of the European Parliament and of the Council of 6 July 2016 concerning measures for a high common level of security of network and information systems across the Union, *OJ* L 194 of 19 July 2016, 1–30.

currencies is needed. While such projects did lead to findings that could apply within their project-specific context, they did not serve to answer the more abstract and fundamental questions regarding the precise legal status of virtual currencies and their place in the framework set by the EMD2, the PSD2, the AMLD4, and the MiFID2. Although virtual currencies do receive broad attention, there exists to the best of our knowledge no ongoing fundamental research covering the scope of the proposed research. While there is scientific literature on virtual currencies, existing research does not go further than confirming regulatory uncertainty, or suggesting the application of money laundering or taxation rules.[51]

NEED FOR COHERENT SOLUTION – As explained in the problem statement, also lawmakers have not managed to propose a coherent solution to end the current situation of uncertainty, nor appears an initiative thereto – beyond anti-money laundering rules – to be on the cards.[52] It is therefore the hope for this research to weigh in on the legislative discussions, using its findings to support the legislative process. Thereto, this research aims to serve as a guide to potential legislative initiatives, for instance by assessing whether such an initiative would indeed result in a situation of legal certainty.

BROADER CONTEXTUALIZATION – A fundamental approach allows this research to surpass project-specific results, to raise the findings to a more abstract level than what can be provided by legislative initiatives, and to provide broader

51 See, for instance: OECD (2012) "Report on Consumer Protection in Online and Mobile Payments", OECD Digital Economy Papers, No. 204, *dx.doi.org/10.1787/5k9490gwp7f3-en*; Stokes, R. (2012) "Virtual money laundering: the case of Bitcoin and the Linden dollar", *Information & Communications Technology Law*, vol. 21, nr. 3, 221–236; Jacobs, E. (2011) "Bitcoin: A Bit Too Far?", *Journal of Internet Banking and Commerce*, vol. 16, nr. 2, *arraydev.com/commerce/jibc;* De Filippi, P. (2014) "Bitcoin: a regulatory nightmare to a libertarian dream", *Internet Policy Review*, vol. 3, nr. 2, DOI: 10.14763/2014.2.286; Grinberg, R. (2012) "Bitcoin: An Innovative Alternative Digital Currency", *Hastings Science & Technology Law Journal*, vol. 4, 158–208; Bollen, R. (2013) "The Legal Status of Online Currencies: Are Bitcoins the Future?", *Journal of Banking and Finance Law and Practice*, vol. 24, nr. 4, 272–293; Trautman, L. (2014) "Virtual Currencies: Bitcoin & What Now after Liberty Reserve, Silk Road, and Mt. Gox?", *Richmond Journal of Law and Technology*, vol. 20, nr. 4; Kien-Meng Ly, M. (2014) "Coining Bitcoin's 'legal-bits': examining the regulatory framework for Bitcoin and virtual currencies", *Harvard Journal of Law & Technology*, vol. 27, nr. 2, 587–608; Smith, D. (2012) "More Money, More Problems: The Bitcoin Virtual Currency and the Legal Problems that Face It", *Case Western Reserve Journal of Law Technology & The Internet*, vol. 3, 427–442; Pflaum, I., Hateley, E. (2014) "A bit of a problem: National and extraterritorial regulation of virtual currency in the age of financial disintermediation", *Georgetown Journal of International Law*, Vol. 45, 1169–1215.

52 As one of the first European authorities, the EBA called for action regarding virtual currencies: European Banking Authority (2014) "EBA Opinion on 'virtual currencies'", *eba.europa.eu*, EBA/Op/2014/08. While the European Commission has hinted at following the developments regarding virtual currencies in view of its review of the PSD1 and the EMD2, this has not resulted in a legislative proposal. Payment Systems Market Expert Group (2013) "Minutes of the meeting of 24 October 2013, Brussels", *ec.europa*.eu, 5. Thus far, legislative action has been limited to an inclusion of virtual currencies under anti-money laundering rules.

contextualization of the issues at hand. Thus, this research presents a novel approach to the subject of virtual currencies and aims to valorize its output through usable recommendations for all stakeholders. Broader conclusions also serve to raise awareness in policymakers regarding the matter of virtual currencies.

Potential economic benefits – Apart from contributing to legal certainty in the matter of virtual currencies, the research could also result in economic benefits by addressing one of the core barriers in the market for virtual currencies. As the online economy – including virtual currencies – is only expected to continue to grow[53], the topic of this research also demonstrates clear practical relevance, having potential economic and societal value.

# 6 METHODOLOGY AND STRUCTURE

## 6.1 TYPOLOGY, TERMINOLOGY, AND INTERDISCIPLINARY RESEARCH

Scope and terminology – The first three chapters form Part I of the book. These chapters provide more conceptual analyses. Chapter I further demarcates and refines the scope of the research by establishing a typology of the different types of virtual currencies, identifying their inherent differences and commonalities. In doing so, chapter I will also provide an explanation for the at times confusing terminology encountered when approaching the subject of virtual currencies.[54] Such will clarify the scope of the terms as they are to be understood for the purposes of this research to a broader audience. The establishment of a typology and terminology will serve the later research in assessing whether all virtual currencies can be subjected to the same principles, or whether differentiated approaches are needed. Given the economic and technical aspects of virtual currencies, a certain level of interdisciplinary outlook needs to be taken into account alongside the legal aspects, using

53 See, for instance: Boston Consulting Group (2014) "The Internet Economy in the G-20", *bgc.com*, 57p; HM Government (2013) "UK Government Information Economy Strategy", *gov.uk*, BIS/13/611, 13; European Commission (2013) "Europe's digital challenge", *ec.europa.eu*, 27p.

54 For instance, virtual currencies can also be addressed as digital currencies. While to some, these terms might be synonymous, others see clear differences. Bradbury, D. (2014) "Is Bitcoin a Digital Currency or a Virtual One?", *Coindesk.com*, 19 March 2014. Also, as the term 'e-money' can be used freely in the US since no specific regulation using this term exists there, the context in which it is used may not necessarily correspond to what is understood as e-money in the EU. Moreover, while the notion 'prepaid' could be applied to certain types of virtual currencies, it also plays a clear role in e-money in the form of multi-purpose prepaid cards. These cards – or e-purses – such as Proton have their value embedded on them should be distinguished from account access devices such as debit and credit cards.

literature stemming from economics and computer science.[55] For instance, while cryptocurrencies are used for payments and investments, it is unsure what their use is for fractional-reserve banking.[56] As fractional-reserve banking is mainly an economic matter, this requires certain economic aspects to be considered together with regulations in this field.[57]

Typology – Using the ECB's[58] typology as starting point, the eventual typology to emerge from this research incorporates an identification of specific risks – relating to, for instance, market stability and stakeholder protection – posed

---

55 Castronova, E. (2002) "On Virtual Economies", CESifo Working Paper Series No. 752, *ssrn.com/abstract=338500*; Irwin, D., Chase, J., Grit, L., Yumerefendi, A. (2005) "Self-recharging virtual currency", *P2PECON '05 Proceedings of the 2005 ACM SIGCOMM workshop on Economics of peer-to-peer systems*, 93–98; Guo, J., Chow, A. (2008) "Virtual Money Systems: A Phenomenal Analysis", *Proceedings of the IEEE Joint Conference on E-Commerce Technology (CEC'08) and Enterprise Computing, E-Commerce and E-Services (EEE'08)*, 267–272; Lehdonvirta, V., (2009) "Virtual item sales as a revenue model: identifying attributes that drive purchase decisions", *Electron Commer Res*, Vol. 9, 97–113; Salomon, M., Soudoplatoff S. (2010) "Why Virtual-World Economies Matter", *Journal of Virtual Worlds Research*, Vol. 2, 14p; Heeks, R. (2010) "Understanding "Gold Farming" and Real-Money Trading as the Intersection of Real and Virtual Economies", *Journal of Virtual Worlds Research*, Vol. 2, 27p; Luther, W. (2013) "Cryptocurrencies, Network Effects, and Switching Costs", *George Mason University Mercatus Center Working Paper 13-17*, 37p; Surda, P. (2012) "Economics of Bitcoin: is Bitcoin an alternative to fiat currencies and gold?", *Thesis WU Vienna University of Economics and Business*, 90p; Surda, P. (2014) "The Origin, Classification and Utility of Bitcoin", *papers.ssrn.com/sol3/papers.cfm?abstract_id=2436823*, 28p; Yermack, D. (2013) "Is Bitcoin a Real Currency? An economic appraisal", *NBER Working Paper No. 19747*, 22p; Bergstra, J.A., Weijland, P. (2014) "Bitcoin: a Money-like Informational Commodity", *University of Amsterdam Theory of Computer Science Electronic Report Series TCS1402*, 32p; Nakamoto, S. (2008) "Bitcoin: a peer-to-peer electronic cash system", *bitcoin.org/Bitcoin.pdf*; Barber, S., Boyen, X., Shi, E., Uzun, E. (2012) "Bitter to Better – How to Make Bitcoin a Better Currency", *Financial Cryptography (FC 2012), volume 7397 of Lecture Notes in Computer Science*, 399–414; Brito, J., Castillo, A. (2013) *Bitcoin: A Primer for Policymakers*, Arlington: George Mason University Mercatus Center, 43p; Eyal, I., Gün Sirer, E. (2014) "Majority is not Enough: Bitcoin Mining is Vulnerable", Presented at the 18th International Conference on Financial Cryptography and Data Security (FC), Barbados, March 2014, *diyhpl.us/~bryan/papers2/paperbot/Majority%20is%20not%20Enough:%20Bitcoin%20Mining%20is%20Vulnerable.pdf*, 17p; Zarifis, A., Efthymiou, L., Cheng, X., Demetriou, S. (2014) "Consumer Trust in Digital Currency Enabled Transactions", *Business Information Systems Workshops Lecture Notes in Business Information Processing*, Vol. 183, 241–254; Ahamad, S., Nair, M., Varghese, B. (2013) "A Survey on Crypto Currencies", *Proc. of Int. Conf. on Advances in Computer Science, AETACS*, 42–48.

56 Sankowski, for instance, argues that this does not seem feasible given the current acceptance of cryptocurrencies. Sankowski, M. (2013) "Bitcoins, Fractional Reserve Banking, and Private Currencies", *monetaryrealism.com*, 2 May 2013.

57 For instance, Rothbard's theory on money supply seems to support Sankowski's argument. Rothbard, M. (1978) "Austrian Definitions of the Supply of Money", In: Spadaro, L. (ed.) *New Directions in Austrian Economics*, Kansas City: Sheed Andrews and McMeel, 145.

58 European Central Bank (2012) "Virtual Currency Schemes", *ecb.europa.eu*, 13–14. This typology includes closed schemes (where virtual currency and physical-world currency cannot be exchanged for one another), unidirectional schemes (where physical-world currency is used to obtain virtual currency, but not vice versa), and bidirectional schemes (where virtual currencies and physical-world currencies are interchangeable).

by different virtual currencies. Practical examples – including examples from cryptocurrencies[59], in-game currencies[60], gift card currencies[61] and loyalty schemes[62] – are analyzed from a legal, economical and technical viewpoint to support and refine the further analysis of core concepts and the typology of virtual currencies used in this research. This practical analysis therefore serves to identify key issues at stake and to contextualize the concepts at hand. In doing so, chapter I also establishes the definitions for the purposes of this research of the core terms used, and explains the concepts and notions of the topic of virtual currencies to a broader audience. The source material for such an analysis includes results of national and international research and scholarly papers of the different scientific disciplines selected for this research, namely law, economics and computer science.[63]

Goal of the chapter – The main goal of chapter I is to identify whether there are core elements common to different types of virtual currencies. Such serves the further research as those elements determine their potential for regulation under the relevant legal frameworks. In doing so, chapter I provides the basic contextualization and conceptualization of the topic of the research.

## 6.2 SUPPORTIVE TRUST ANALYSIS

Trust as supportive concept – Chapter II provides a descriptive analysis of a particular element underlying the wider adoption and implementation of virtual currencies, namely trust. As none of the identified types of virtual currencies are backed by a central government, nor tied to valuable assets, they rely strongly on trust between the parties involved in a virtual currency scheme. Without these parties trusting each other and the underlying system, the scheme would fail. Therefore, trust is an imperative facilitator for the further development and implementation of virtual currencies. As evidenced by the slow uptake of e-money after the EMD1, regulation on its own may prove inadequate to foster such trust.[64]

Abstract analysis – In chapter II, the concept of trust will be analyzed at its abstract level, in order to understand what it constitutes and what the

59 See footnote 9.

60 Currencies used in video games, such as World of Warcraft. Here, the game character controller by the player can obtain the in-game currency by performing tasks within the game, and can in turn use that currency to obtain in-game objects.

61 Such as Microsoft Points and Amazon Coins, these currencies are an alternative currency to be used within a particular platform (here being the Microsoft Xbox platform or Amazon's store). Being single-purpose, or limited-purpose at most, these currencies are not considered as e-money and can therefore be considered as virtual currencies.

62 Such as the aforementioned CityLife.

63 Building forth on the basic sources identified in footnote 55.

64 As referenced in footnote 45.

implications thereof are to virtual currencies. While the concept of trust is well-known, clear definitions are sparse and dependent on the scientific discipline from which it is approached. For instance, in sociology, trust is perceived as a social construct that serves as a bet for future possibilities, therefore inherently constituting a risk.[65] Also in economics theory, trust is perceived as enabling new possibilities, which could be leading to new business opportunities or lower transaction costs.[66] Trust could therefore lead to economic growth, yet conferring a too high level of trust on transactions with a lower level of trustworthiness could in turn lead to exploitation.[67] Trustworthiness here should then be understood as being the "*characteristics and actions of the trustee* [that] *will lead that person to be more or less trusted*".[68] The level of trust invested in a transaction by the trustor should therefore be at the same height as the level of trustworthiness of the trustee. To that end, the second chapter will utilize a critical study of literature of legal science and related social sciences such as sociology and economics to analyze how the trustworthiness of virtual currencies should be enhanced in order to correspond to the trust required from its stakeholders to adopt their use.[69] If, for instance, the outcome of the research were to regulate virtual currencies, certain aspects of trust could be included

---

65 Luhmann, N. (1979) *Trust and Power*, New York: John Wiley & Sons Ltd., 1–103; Gambetta, D. (2000) "Can We Trust Trust?", In: Gambetta, D. (ed.) *Trust: Making and Breaking Cooperative Relations*, Department of Sociology, University of Oxford, 217–218; Lewis, J. D., Weigert, A. (1985) "Trust as a social reality", *Social Forces*, Vol. 63, 968.

66 Andreoni, J. (2005) "Trust, Reciprocity, and Contract Enforcement: Experiments on Satisfaction Guaranteed", *econ.ucsd.edu/~jandreon/WorkingPapers/verify.pdf*, 33p; Pollitt, M. (2002) "The Economics of Trust, Norms and Networks", *Business Ethics: A European Review*, Vol. 11, 120; Jones, K. (2001) "Trust: philosophical aspects", In: Smelser, N.J., Baltes, P.B. (eds.) *The International Encyclopedia of the Behavioural and Social Sciences*, Oxford: Pergamon Press, 15917.

67 On the specific issue of exploitation in trust relationships: James, H.S. (2002) "The trust paradox: a survey of economic inquiries into the nature of trust and trustworthiness", *Journal of Economic Behavior & Organization*, Vol. 47, 291–307.

68 Mayer, R.C., Davis, J.H., Schoorman, F.D. (1995) "An integrative model of organizational trust", *Academy of management review*, Vol. 20, 717.

69 Initial results of this study were published as: Dumortier, J., Vandezande, N. (2012) "Trust in the proposed EU regulation on trust services?", *Computer Law and Security Report*, vol. 28, nr. 5. This initial result will serve as the basis for the further research. Literature consulted for the initial study will serve as the basis for the further work. This includes: McKnight, D. H., Choudhury, V., Kacmar, C. (2002) "The impact of initial consumer trust on intentions to transact with a web site: a trust building model", Journal of Strategic Information Systems, Vol. 11, 297–323; Mayer, R.C., Davis, J.H., Schoorman, F.D. (1995) "An integrative model of organizational trust", *Academy of management review*, Vol. 20, 717; James, H.S. (2002) "The trust paradox: a survey of economic inquiries into the nature of trust and trustworthiness", *Journal of Economic Behavior & Organization*, Vol. 47, 291–307; Luhmann, N. (1979) *Trust and Power*, New York: John Wiley & Sons Ltd., 1–103; Gambetta, D. (2000) "Can We Trust Trust?", In: Gambetta, D. (ed.) *Trust: Making and Breaking Cooperative Relations*, Department of Sociology, University of Oxford, 217–218; Lewis, J. D., Weigert, A. (1985) "Trust as a social reality", *Social Forces*, Vol. 63, 968; Andreoni, J. (2005) "Trust, Reciprocity, and Contract Enforcement: Experiments on Satisfaction Guaranteed", *econ.ucsd.edu/~jandreon/WorkingPapers/verify.pdf*, 33p; Pollitt, M. (2002) "The Economics of Trust, Norms and Networks", *Business Ethics: A European Review*, Vol. 11, 120; Jones, K.

in such regulation. If the outcome were to not regulate virtual currencies, other avenues for enhancing stakeholder trust in this development should be considered.

Operationalization – In doing so, it is also examined how the abstract concept of trust is currently operationalized in practice in law. This entails a descriptive analysis of trust services at the level of the EU[70] to assess whether virtual currency service providers could become trusted third party (TTP) service providers. The goal is to critically analyze the potential for additional measures that could raise the overall trustworthiness of virtual currencies. Such measures could support the legal assessment of these developments and assist in providing legal certainty.

## 6.3 MONEY AND VIRTUAL CURRENCIES

Relation between virtual currencies and money – In chapter III, parallels between money and virtual currencies will be sought. The goal of that analysis is to provide a clear assessment of whether the different types of virtual currencies can be supported by different theories on money, or whether they can fulfill the economic functions expected from money.

Search for differences and commonalities – In chapter III, the seminal work of the legal scholar Mann[71] will be analyzed as a basis to identify the core theories underlying the current understanding of money. That work will include, for instance, an analysis of the credit and state theories of money, as well of the role of the state – and the development thereof – in money creation.

Analysis of economic functions – As discussion on money is inherently economic in nature, such legal research will be supplemented with the works of economic scholars from different schools of thought. Moreover, this research critically analyzes whether the different types of virtual currencies can fulfill the basic functions of money as a store of value, medium of exchange and unit of account. Those analyses will ascertain whether certain legal or economic principles applicable to money could apply to the different types of virtual currencies. The sources for the analysis conducted here will include economic

(2001) "Trust: philosophical aspects", In: Smelser, N.J., Baltes, P.B. (eds.) *The International Encyclopedia of the Behavioural and Social Sciences*, Oxford: Pergamon Press, 15917.

70 For instance the inclusion of trust services in Regulation 910/2014 of the European Parliament and of the Council of 23 July 2014 on electronic identification and trust services for electronic transactions in the internal market and repealing Directive 1999/93/EC, *OJ* L 257 of 28 August 2014, 73–114.

71 Proctor, C., Kleiner, C., Mohs, F. (2012) *Mann on the legal aspect of money [6th edition]*, Oxford: Oxford University Press.

literature, focusing on the basic theories of money as proposed by scholars such as Knapp, Innes, Hayek, Rothbard and von Mises.[72]

## 6.4 FUNDAMENTAL ANALYSIS AND CRITICAL ASSESSMENT

VIRTUAL CURRENCIES, E-MONEY, PAYMENT SERVICES, ANTI-MONEY LAUNDERING, AND MARKETS IN FINANCIAL INSTRUMENTS – Part II of the book provides the main legal analyses. The first three chapters of this part focus on EU law, with the last chapter focusing on US law. The EU chapters analyze whether the existing legal frameworks regarding e-money and payment services (chapter IV), anti-money laundering (chapter V) and markets in financial instruments (chapter VI) in the EU can be applied to virtual currencies, or whether they display gaps and incompatibilities. The chapter on US law (chapter VII) will analyze whether virtual currencies are caught under the scope of comparable legal frameworks regarding money, payments, anti-money laundering, and securities under US law. The methodology for that chapter will be further elaborated in section 6.5.

CAN CURRENT LEGAL FRAMEWORKS BE APPLIED? – A descriptive analysis is conducted of the fundamental scope of the legal frameworks on e-money, payment services, anti-money laundering and markets in financial instruments in the EU, using a study of legal sources – relying on the work from national and international scholars and institutions.[73] Supplementing that legal source

---

72 Knapp, G. F. (1924) *The State Theory of Money*, London: Macmillan & Co.; Innes, M. A. (1913) "What is Money?", *Banking Law Journal*, Vol. 30, 377–408; Hayek, F.A. (1990) *Denationalisation of Money – The Argument Refined*, London: The Institute of Economic Affairs; Rothbard, M. (1978) "Austrian Definitions of the Supply of Money", In: Spadaro, L. (ed.) *New Directions in Austrian Economics*, Kansas City: Sheed Andrews and McMeel; Von Mises, L. (1981) *The Theory of Money and Credit*, Indianapolis, IN: Liberty Fund, Inc.

73 For instance, the European Commission and the ECB provide extensive resources on the legal frameworks discussed here. Other institutions with noteworthy work on the matter are the European Banking Authority, the European Payments Council, as well as the Bank for International Settlements. Sources identified in preliminary analyses include: Alter, C. (2010) *Droit bancaire général*, Brussels: Larcier; Athanassiou, P., Mas-Guix, N. (2008) "Electronic money institutions", ECB Legal Working Paper Series nr.7, *ssrn.com/abstract_id=1000855*; European Banking Authority (2014) "EBA Opinion on 'virtual currencies'", *eba.europa.eu*, EBA/Op/2014/08; European Central Bank (1998) "Report on Electronic Money", *ecb.europa.eu*; European Central Bank (2012) "Virtual Currency Schemes", *ecb.europa.eu*; Halpin, R., Moore, R. (2009) "Developments in electronic money regulation – the Electronic Money Directive: A better deal for e-money issuers?", *Computer Law & Security Review*, vol. 25, 563–568; Jacobs, E. (2011) "Bitcoin: A Bit Too Far?", *Journal of Internet Banking and Commerce*, vol. 16; Krueger, M. (2002) "E-money regulation in the EU", In: Pringle, R., Robinson, M., (eds.), *E-Money and Payment Systems Review*, London: Centralbanking, 239–251; Vandezande, N. (2014) "Between Bitcoins and mobile payments: will the European Commission's new proposal provide more legal certainty?", *International Journal of Law and Information Technology*, vol. 22, 295–310.

analysis is a critical assessment of the scopes of the selected legal frameworks. A critical view determines whether the e-money, payment services, anti-money laundering or markets in financial instruments frameworks can apply to the different types of virtual currencies identified here, whether such an application can comply with the normative criteria of legal certainty, proportionality, trust, and coherence, or whether gaps remain. For instance, the demarcation line between regulated e-money and unregulated virtual currencies must be identified in order to analyze whether that demarcation should or even can be upheld. This analysis shows whether the legal framework on e-money could or should be amended to include certain or all types of virtual currencies. Alternatively, the legal framework on payment services could provide an anchor to subject virtual currency service providers to certain regulation. Even absent a clear regulation of virtual currencies as e-money or payment services, certain providers of virtual currency services could still be brought within the scope of the EU's anti-money laundering framework. Moreover, given the rising use of virtual currencies for investment purposes, such investment virtual currencies could come under the scope of the legal framework on markets in financial instruments.

Normative question of regulation – The normative aspects of the research become apparent here, as potential regulation of virtual currencies would need to serve the normative criteria formulated earlier.

EU-focused legal literature study – This critical assessment uses a study of relevant legal sources, including legislative instruments, case law and literature. Legislative instruments mainly serve the descriptive task of establishing the scope of the relevant legal frameworks.[74] For case law, the lack of decisions by higher state or international courts necessitates the inclusion of case law by lower national courts of the EU Member States. Cases will be selected on their inclusion of the particular elements of the legal frameworks discussed here relevant to the topic of virtual currencies.[75] However, as case law is expected to be only sparsely available or to provide insufficient insight, the main focus of the research will be put on the literature study. For literature, the focus is put on legal work from scholars and law- and policymakers with a geographic focus on sources relating to the EU, given the focus on EU legal frameworks.[76] National sources within the EU can be taken into consideration when a notable deviation from EU law can be identified.

74 Other relevant legislation at the level of the EU – or as transposed by Member States – are consulted where needed.

75 For e-money, for instance, the focus will be put on cases that particularly address the scope of the e-money legal framework, or its redeemability requirement. Also for payment services, cases focusing on the scope are relevant to this research. See, for instance: CJEU, T-Mobile Austria GmbH *v* Verein für Konsumenteninformation, C-616/11.

76 Including, for instance, some of the earlier analyses on the EMD1 and its inception by Manfred Kohlbach, Malte Krueger, Simon Lelieveldt and Hugo Godschalk. Lelieveldt, S. (1997) "How

## 6.5 FUNCTIONAL COMPARISON

International outlook – As the global scope of virtual currencies necessitates an international outlook, chapter VII incorporates methods of functional comparative legal research. The focus of such a comparison is put on the US, being the lead market in virtual currencies, the main actor regarding legislative initiative in the field of virtual currencies, and for its practical and linguistic accessibility of sources.

Functional comparison between EU and US – A functional comparison allows to focus on the effects of law as a response to real-life situations, rather than focusing on doctrinal structures and arguments.[77] Therefore, while the financial sectors of the EU and US are intrinsically different, a functional comparison between elements of these different laws and institutions can be made in light of their societal function in response to the types of virtual currencies identified here.[78] The aim is not to analyze the differences between both systems as a whole, but to identify the points of commonality and divergence between their respective responses to functionally equivalent situations. The goal is to analyze the particular elements that resulted in the current legal treatment of the different types of virtual currencies and their related services, to compare whether similar elements can be found and whether similar conclusions could be drawn from that for the EU. As a result, the comparison must be directly contributive to the research questions. The normative criteria selected earlier serve as basis for the evaluation of the comparison.

Legal literature study – Given the focus of the functional comparison on the effect of the US legal system on the EU notions of virtual currencies, e-money, payment services, anti-money laundering and markets in financial instruments, the main source material is legal literature focused on the US federal and state

---

to regulate electronic cash: an overview of regulatory issues and strategies", *The American University Law Review*, vol. 46, 1173–1174; Lelieveldt, S. (2006) "Impact of the E-Money Directive – Its application to 'hybrid' operators issuing e-money", presented at the E-Money Directive (2000/46/EC) – Round Table Meeting, Brussels, 8 March 2006, *simonl.org;* Lelieveldt, S. (2001) "Why is the Electronic Money-Directive Significant?", *EPSO Newsletter*, 7, May 2001; Godschalk, H., Krueger, M. (2000) "Why e-money still fails – chances of e-money within a competitive payment instrument market", Presented at the Third Berlin Internet Economics Workshop, Berlin, May 26–27, 2000; Godschalk, H. (2013) "Can an overseer overlook some basics? – The ECB on e-money and virtual currencies", *DGC Magazine*, 11 August 2013; Kohlbach, M. (2004) "Making Sense of Electronic Money", *Journal of Information, Law and Technology*, 19p; Krueger, M. (2002) "E-money regulation in the EU", In: Pringle, R., Robinson, M. (eds.), *E-Money and Payment Systems Review*, London: Centralbanking, 239–251; Van Hove, L. (2004) "Electronic purses in Euroland: why do penetration and usage rates differ?", *SUERF Studies 2004/4*; Weber, R. (2001) "The European E-Money Directive: Background, Problems, and Prospects", *Y.B. Int'l Fin. & Econ. L.*, Vol. 5, 293–309.

77 Michaels, R. (2006) "The Functional Method of Comparative Law", In: Reimann, M., Zimmermann, R. (eds.) *The Oxford Handbook of Comparative Law*, Oxford: University Press, 342.

78 *Ibid.*, 369.

levels.[79] Such sources are expected to lead to the further consultation of relevant case law – with preference to cases at the federal level where available[80] – and primary sources where needed.[81] One example here is the regulation of virtual currency services in the state of New York.[82]

## 6.6 INTEGRATION, FINAL ASSESSMENT AND RECOMMENDATIONS

Integration and assessment against normative criteria – Part III of the book forms the conclusions. The final chapter, chapter VIII, will integrate the previous findings for further critical analysis and processing. Here, assessments for the different types of virtual currencies identified in previous chapters are weighed against each other to the normative criteria. In doing so, the goal is to assess the need and potential for a balanced regulation of virtual currencies in terms of legal certainty, proportionality, trust and coherence. The findings of chapter II provide the possibilities for trust measures in order to support that balance. The final assessment of chapter VIII follows a deductive process, assessing whether the results of the previous steps lead to the conclusion that legislative initiative is needed to regulate virtual currencies and – where such is found to be the case – how such an initiative is to be approached. The functional comparison will provide additional inspiration to such an analysis, by demonstrating what results can be achieved under a different approach.

Recommendations for regulation, if needed – Where need and potential for the regulation – of all or some types – of virtual currencies under a currently

---

79 Initial literature that was identified includes: Bank of America Merril Lynch (2013) "Bitcoin: a first assessment", *Bank of America*, 5 December 2013; Brito, J., Castillo, A. (2013) *Bitcoin: A Primer for Policymakers*, Arlington: George Mason University Mercatus Center; Bollen, R. (2013) "The Legal Status of Online Currencies: Are Bitcoins the Future?", *Journal of Banking and Finance Law and Practice*, vol. 24, 272–293; Claxton, N. (2011) "Progress, Privacy, and Preemption: A Study of the Regulatory History of Stored-Value Cards in the United States and the European Union", *Ariz. J. Int'l & Comp. L.*, vol. 28, 501–538; Geva, B. (2009) "Payment Transactions under the EU Payment Services Directive: A U.S. Comparative Perspective", *Penn St. Int'l L. Rev.*, vol. 27, 713–755; Grinberg, R. (2012) "Bitcoin: An Innovative Alternative Digital Currency", *Hastings Sci. & Tech. L.J.*, vol. 4, 159–208; Kien-Meng Ly, M. (2014) "Coining Bitcoin's 'legal-bits': examining the regulatory framework for Bitcoin and virtual currencies", *Harvard Journal of Law & Technology*, vol. 27, nr. 2, 587–608; Pflaum, I., Hateley, E. (2014) "A bit of a problem: National and extraterritorial regulation of virtual currency in the age of financial disintermediation", *Georgetown Journal of International Law*, Vol. 45, 1169–1215.

80 For instance: *Securities and Exchange Commission v. Trendon T. Shavers and Bitcoin Savings and Trust*, 4:13-CV-416 (Texas, 6 August 2013). As in the previous section focusing on EU law, where case law provides insufficient insight, the literature study will be deepened.

81 Primary sources here include the Electronic Fund Transfer Act and its implementation through the Federal Reserve's so-called Regulation E.

82 As noted in footnote 20.

existing legal framework is found, recommendations to such an inclusion are formulated. Where existing legal frameworks are found not to provide legal certainty, proportionality, trust, and coherence regarding the inclusion of virtual currencies, recommendations toward amendments or toward new legislative initiatives can be formulated if such proves necessary.

Recommendations for stakeholders – The final conclusions will take the form of recommendations that will address three specific stakeholders. First, they aim to address merchant and consumer users of virtual currencies to help raising legal certainty in the use of such schemes. Second, the recommendations address virtual currency service providers and issuers. Those providers need to clearly establish what legal framework they operate under, in order to provide their customers with the necessary protection and information. Last, the recommendations aim to address legislators and policymakers, as they need to be made aware of gaps and incompatibilities in the current legal framework that could relate to virtual currencies.

# PART I

# CONCEPTUAL ANALYSIS

# CHAPTER I

# TYPOLOGY AND TERMINOLOGY OF VIRTUAL CURRENCIES

## 1 INTRODUCTION

OBJECTIVES OF THE CHAPTER – The main objectives of this first chapter are to provide more background to the topic of the research, and to further demarcate its scope. This chapter will attain those objectives by first addressing some of the concerns underlying the core terminology used in this research. Second, the aim is to establish a typology for the different kinds of virtual currencies that can be found in practice. In doing so, this chapter provides further explanation and guidance concerning those types of virtual currencies in order to ensure readability of the research to a broader audience.

USE IN FURTHER RESEARCH – The typology decided upon in this chapter will serve the further research. The broad range of virtual currencies already in existence poses clear difficulties from a regulatory perspective. On the one hand, the principle of rule of law requires legislation to be sufficiently precise and clear. On the other hand, legislation that focuses on one type of virtual currency would risk being outdated rapidly, as technological developments in the field of virtual currencies tend to move faster than legislators. As a result, if conclusions were drawn that propose the adoption of legislation for virtual currencies, such a legislative initiative would need to take into account the broad range of types of virtual currencies and their inherent differences, while at the same time ensuring sufficient precision in its scope.

TERMINOLOGY – First, this chapter will focus on the term of virtual currencies itself. While 'virtual currencies' is the most broadly used term to address the particular developments covered by the scope of this research, that term is by no means without adversaries. By clearly addressing the matter of terminology and by stating why a particular term was chosen above others, the terminology analysis will aid to better understand the precise scope of this research.

TYPOLOGY – Second, this chapter proposes a typology for virtual currencies. In seeking alignment with research already conducted in the field of virtual currencies, the basic typology formulated by the European Central Bank (ECB) will serve as the starting point. Before presenting that typology, this chapter will identify a number of practical examples of virtual currencies. Such practical framing will further clarify the particular elements and terminology of this research to a non-expert audience. Moreover, the practical case analyses will serve to assess whether and to what extent those cases can fit into the typology formulated by the ECB. If conflicts were to arise in that analysis, the ECB's typology could be amended or fully replaced by a new typology. The end result of the analysis will be the final typology agreed upon for the purposes of this research, as well as further identification of the inherent differences between virtual currencies, and the need to recognize those differences in potential legislative steps.

# 2 TERMINOLOGY OF VIRTUAL CURRENCIES

Background – This section will provide a brief overview of the background of virtual currencies, along with a discussion of the core terminology that will be used throughout this research. More in particular, this section will focus mainly on the term 'virtual currencies' itself, as well as on the scope thereof and its definition. The following sections of this chapter will further analyze and define more practical terms – such as cryptocurrencies.

## 2.1 VIRTUAL CURRENCIES IN THE EU

Developments in payment methods – Historically, money has mostly been considered as being a physical good. However, with the rise of the information society, it is clear that the use of physical coins and banknotes would be highly undesirable when conducting, for instance, e-commerce transactions. After all, the ease of purchasing goods or services online requires that such transactions can also be paid for without requiring the simultaneous physical presence of the parties involved to conduct a monetary exchange. As a result, e-commerce transactions generally rely on electronic funds transfers (EFT) where debit or credit cards linked to accounts at financial institutions can be used to facilitate money transfers. Such electronic funds transfers and their reliance on commercial bank deposits have since long made the use of non-physical money transfers a daily reality. Also for purchases made at 'brick-and-mortar' stores, customers are more and more relying on the use of card payment instruments than on the use of physical currency.[83] The rising developments of the

[83] Facilitated through, for instance, electronic funds transfer at point of sale (EFTPOS). In 2012, the number of non-cash payments in the EU totaled 94.5 billion, an increase of 4.2% compared with the previous year. Card transactions were conducted with a total value of more than EUR 2 trillion. European Central Bank (2013) "Payment statistics for 2012",

information society have, however, not halted at the mere process of 'connecting' existing banking processes to the online realm. Such developments have given rise to the development of new payment methods, for instance making use of technologies such as Near Field Communication (NFC).[84]

Regulation of different types of money – When considering the use of dematerialized money or currencies at large, many different concepts can come to mind.[85] One of the more notable of those concepts is the notion of electronic money, or e-money. While in the broad sense of the word e-money could be interpreted as referring to a whole range of different kinds of non-physical currency services, the EU has adopted a specific legal framework to regulate what it considers to be e-money.[86] That regulation resulted in a demarcation of different kinds of digital or non-physical currencies. The ECB summarizes the whole range of types of money in the following matrix:

**Table 1: Money matrix**[87]

| | Physical | Digital |
|---|---|---|
| **Unregulated** | Certain types of local currencies | Virtual currencies |
| **Regulated** | Banknotes and coins | E-money, Commercial bank money (deposits) |

Unregulated virtual currency – In the physical regulated field, there are of course the well-known government-issued banknotes and coins. Also electronic money is regulated in the EU, for as far as the scope of the e-money legal framework goes. Bank transfers are as noted also mainly being conducted

Press release 10 September 2013, *ecb.europa.eu*. Also in the US it is acknowledged that cash payments are decreasing in favor of other payment methods, while paradoxically the amount of circulating cash keeps increasing. Williams, J.C. (2012) "Cash Is Dead! Long Live Cash!", *Federal Reserve Bank of San Francisco 2012 Annual Report*, 7–15.

84 Building forth of earlier standards such as Radio-Frequency Identification (RFID), NFC is a set of standards that allows for two-way communication between close-range endpoints. These standards can be implemented in, for instance, contactless payment transactions. The NFC standards can be found in, amongst others, ISO/IEC 18092:2013 and ECMA-340. In practice, an NFC-equipped smartphone could be used to perform a payment transaction simply by waving the phone by a terminal. However, as of 2017, uptake of the NFC technology in the EU remains fairly low.

85 For instance, some local exchange trading systems (LETS) utilize electronic transactions. Also mobile micro-financing services such as the Kenyan M-Pesa are strictly non-physical. On the Internet, many different non-physical alternative currencies have risen and fallen over the years, including Beenz, Flooz and E-gold. The current primary example of non-physical currencies are cryptocurrencies such as bitcoin.

86 See chapter IV.

87 European Central Bank (2012) "Virtual Currency Schemes", *ecb.europa.eu*, 11.

electronically nowadays, yet are still bound to the amount of money in a user's account, connected to physical regulated currency. While local physical money is generally unregulated, it poses relatively small risks due to its physical and local nature.[88] On the digital level, however, virtual currencies have the potential to reach a much broader audience precisely due to their non-physical nature. Virtual currencies are therefore for those purposes characterized by the ECB as being digital – meaning that they do not exist in physical form – and being unregulated, as opposed to the regulated e-money.

QUESTION OF E-MONEY'S SCOPE – However, considering the rising number of services and developments relating to non-physical currencies, it may be questioned whether the EU's legal framework regarding e-money is sufficiently inclusive by regulating what it currently regulates, or whether it is too narrow by leaving a large group of other non-physical currencies unregulated. That particular question will be considered in chapter IV of this research.

ECB DEFINITION OF VIRTUAL CURRENCY – In defining virtual currencies, the ECB originally proposed that a virtual currency is *"a type of unregulated, digital money, which is issued and usually controlled by its developers, and used and accepted among the members of a specific virtual community"*.[89] The three elements that made up that definition each posed particular difficulties. The notion that virtual currencies are issued and usually controlled by a central developer cannot easily apply to cryptocurrencies. As will be discussed further on in this chapter, cryptocurrencies are decentralized and are therefore not under the control of a single entity. Second, the notion of virtual currencies serving a specific virtual community has been surpassed already, with certain virtual currencies being accepted in the physical world. Last, the notion of virtual currencies as a type of unregulated digital money essentially defines virtual currencies in the negative sense, being every non-physical currency that is not commercial bank money or e-money.

PLACE IN EUROPEAN CONTEXT – That last remark of course only makes sense within the EU, where the term 'e-money' has been given a particular scope due to its definition in the EMD2.[90] Outside the EU, there exists very few specific regulation on the matter of e-money, meaning that the term 'e-money' can

---

88 An example are *Torekes*, a local currency used in a Ghent municipal district. This currency, a type of LETS, is obtained by performing certain community services and can be used for small purchases at local vendors, such as bakeries. *www.torekes.be*.

89 European Central Bank (2012) "Virtual Currency Schemes", *ecb.europa.eu*, 13.

90 Article 2(2) Directive 2009/110/EC of the European Parliament and of the Council of 16 September 2009 on the taking up, pursuit and prudential supervision of the business of electronic money institutions amending Directives 2005/60/EC and 2006/48/EC and repealing Directive 2000/46/EC, *OJ* L 267 of 10 October 2009, 7–17 (hereinafter: Second E-money Directive or EMD2).

be used more freely.[91] Consequently, when discussing e-money at a global level, the precise scope of that notion can be very different from what the EU's definition includes. Such would of course also affect the understanding of virtual currencies if their scope is defined in comparison to the notion of e-money. What is considered as a virtual currency elsewhere could in the EU fall under the scope of e-money, and what is regarded as e-money elsewhere could – under the ECB's money matrix – be considered as a virtual currency in the EU.

More global outlook needed – Therefore, for the purposes of giving this research a global outlook, a more universally applicable definition would need to be proposed. In a 2015 update to its report, the ECB acknowledged the limitations of its original definition and proposed amendments.[92] However, before going into the specifics of that new definition, the notion of 'virtual currencies' itself should be examined.

## 2.2 WHY 'VIRTUAL CURRENCIES'?

Deconstructing the notion – This section further explores the notion of 'virtual currencies'. The broad range of monetary developments covered by the scope of this research could, for instance, also be addressed as 'digital currencies' or 'electronic currencies'. The term 'currency' could substitute for 'money', although it could also be argued that both terms are not particularly suited for application to the matter of this research.

### *2.2.1 'Digital', 'electronic', or 'virtual'?*

Dictionary research – For the purposes of this research, 'digital' can be considered as relating to technologies that involve digital data, or make use of digital computers or devices; something that involves or relates to digital or computer technology; or something relating to a computer-mediated counterpart of objects in the physical world.[93] Also definitions for digital money

91 One example of a non-EU state that has specific e-money regulation is longtime EU-Membership candidate Turkey. Law No. 6493 on payment and security settlement systems, payment services and electronic money institutions of 20 June 2013 (original Turkish: Ödeme ve menkul kiymet mutabakat sistemleri, ödeme hizmetleri ve elektronik para kuruluşlari hakkinda kanun), *Resmî Gazete* 27 June 2013, Sayı 28690. That legislation is clearly modeled after the EU's EMD2. While Switzerland does not have a specific regulation of e-money, it does refer to the terminology used by the EU. Hess, M., Weiss Voigt, A. (2014) "E-money, e- and m-payments according to Swiss law", *clearit.ch*; Swiss National Bank (2014) "Glossary", *www.snb.ch/en/system/glossary.*

92 European Central Bank (2015) "Virtual Currency Schemes – a further analysis", *ecb.europa.eu*, 25.

93 "digital, n. and adj." (2014), *OED Online*, Oxford University Press; "digital" (2014), *Merriam-Webster.com*, Merriam-Webster.

can be found, such as "*money represented and held in a digital form which can be transferred electronically from one party to another*"[94] or "*money or a money substitute that is transformed into information stored on a computer or computer chip so that it can be transferred over information systems such as the Internet*".[95] Similarly, electronic can be considered as something involving electronic means for information storage or transmission; or conducted using electronic devices or computers.[96] Consequently, 'electronic money' or 'electronic cash' could in that sense be defined as "*money represented, held, and exchanged in electronic form*".[97] Virtual can be considered as something that is "*established or conducted using computer technology rather than more traditional means*".[98]

COMMONALITIES – From that brief dictionary research, it appears that the three terms analyzed here are very closely related and to significant extent cover similar meanings. Especially for legal purposes, as evidenced by Black's Law Dictionary, the notions of 'digital' and 'electronic' can for the purposes of this research be considered as synonyms, at least in theory.

DIFFERENCES – The practical application of those terms, however, could become more difficult. As noted before, the term 'e-money' has been defined in EU law, making its application to what is considered under the scope of this research problematic and potentially confusing.[99] To avoid that issue, it can for the purposes of this research be decided to refrain from using the adjective 'electronic' when not specifically addressing the EU's legal framework on e-money.

LIMITATIONS TO INTERCHANGEABILITY – Also the interchangeability of the terms 'digital' and 'virtual' could be questioned. For instance, the US Secret Service considers virtual currencies as alternative currencies which are not "*legal*

---

94 "digital, n. and adj." (2014), *OED Online*, Oxford University Press.

95 "e-money" (2014), *Black's Law Dictionary* (9th ed.), West. Note that "digital cash" refers to the definition of "e-money", thus considering 'electronic' and 'digital' as synonyms here.

96 "electronic, adj." (2014), *OED Online*, Oxford University Press; "electronic" (2014), *Merriam-Webster.com*, Merriam-Webster.

97 "electronic, adj." (2014), *OED Online*, Oxford University Press. Likewise, that dictionary considers electronic banking as transactions that do not require physical money exchange. The earlier mentioned Black's Law Dictionary definition of e-money provides a similar broad field of application.

98 "virtual, adj. and n." (2014), *OED Online*, Oxford University Press; "virtual" (2014), *Merriam-Webster.com*, Merriam-Webster. While 'virtual' can also be understood as referring to something unreal, or a derivative from what is considered real, it is clear that for the purposes of this research the focus is to be put on understanding 'virtual' in the sense of a computer-mediated entity. See: Lehdonvirta, V. (2010) "Virtual Worlds Don't Exist: Questioning the Dichotomous Approach in MMO Studies", *Game Studies*, Vol. 10, nr. 1.

99 It is, after all, unclear as of yet whether the virtual currencies considered in this research can be subjected to the scope of the EU's EMD2. Therefore, the application of the term 'e-money' to these virtual currencies at this stage would be unwise.

*tender or administered by a national government or central bank*".[100] In that understanding, digital currencies are considered as a subset of virtual currencies that only exist in electronic form.[101] On the other hand, authors such as Andrew Wagner posit that 'digital' may also be considered as being the broader term, referring to all currencies that are stored and exchanged electronically, where 'virtual' then refers to digital currencies that are used within a specific non-physical reality.[102] Another reasoning comes to a similar conclusion – namely that 'virtual' should only be used when referring to currencies confined to a particular non-physical system – yet without considering one type as the subset of the other.[103] That reasoning essentially makes a distinction between non-physical currencies that can be exchanged into and from legal tender currencies (digital), and those who cannot be freely exchanged (virtual).[104] Yet another reasoning holds that virtual currencies are decentralized, whereas digital currencies are centralized.[105]

Reconciliation with ECB definition – The earlier mentioned definition proposed by the ECB[106] seems to agree with some of the definitions found in practice in the sense that it considers virtual currencies to only be used within a specific virtual community. Moreover, in holding that virtual currencies are a type of digital money, the ECB seems to follow Wagner's interpretation that 'digital' is the broader term and that 'virtual' currencies are a subset thereof. That position is, however, difficult to reconcile with the ECB's classification of bitcoin as a virtual currency, as the use of bitcoin is not restricted to a particular virtual community. Here, it should be remarked that the ECB acknowledged that its definition may have to be revised in light of future developments, and also did propose such an update in 2015.[107]

---

100 US Senate Committee on Homeland Security and Governmental Affairs (2013) "Beyond Silk Road: Potential Risks, Threats and Promises of Virtual Currencies – Testimony of Edward Lowery III", *hsgac.senate.gov*, 1.

101 *Id.*

102 Wagner, A. (2014) "Digital vs. Virtual Currencies", *Bitcoin Magazine*, 22 August 2014. This interpretation seems to be supported by: Grinberg, R. (2012) "Bitcoin: An Innovative Alternative Digital Currency", *Hastings Science & Technology Law Journal*, vol. 4, 159–208.

103 Bradbury, D. (2014) "Is Bitcoin a Digital Currency or a Virtual One?", *CoinDesk.com*, 19 March 2014.

104 The exchangeability of virtual currencies is a matter that will be addressed in the typology. See section 4.1 of this chapter.

105 Münzer, J. (2014) "Bitcoins: Supervisory assessment and risks to users", *BaFin Expert Articles*, 17 February 2014.

106 See footnote 89.

107 European Central Bank (2012) "Virtual Currency Schemes", *ecb.europa.eu*, 5. As bitcoin was at the time of the ECB's research still practically confined to use within a small online group of enthusiasts, the then proposed definition could have fit the bill. However, given the growth of this phenomenon beyond that group and even beyond the online realm, it is clear that a new definition had to be sought. European Central Bank (2015) "Virtual Currency Schemes – a further analysis", *ecb.europa.eu*, 25.

No perfect synonyms – The previous paragraphs demonstrate that the terms 'electronic', 'digital', and 'virtual' may in practice not always be synonymous. However, as the wide range of different interpretations presented here demonstrates, the establishment of a definition can be considered more as a matter of convention and preference, rather than one of precision. Also, as demonstrated by the ECB's example, the lines between different terms may begin to blur as developments in the field of virtual currencies continue. Moreover, a brief literature overview shows that most authors – especially within the public sector – seem to prefer the term 'virtual' or do not make a clear distinction between the different terms proposed here.[108]

Selection of 'virtual' – Therefore, the term 'virtual' is selected for the purposes of this research, as it is the more widely used term to address the specific developments considered here, regardless of the particular reasoning behind its use. As a reminder, 'virtual' serves here as referring to Internet-mediated technologies, rather than providing an opposition of something unreal or non-existent versus something real.

### *2.2.2 'Cash', 'currency', 'money', or none of the above?*

Dictionary research – Having decided on the use of the adjective 'virtual', this section assesses which noun is most suited for application to the research matter. As already evidenced in the previous subsection, some dictionaries seem to find no difference between electronic, digital or virtual 'cash', 'money', or 'currency'.[109] 'Cash' can be defined as money or its equivalent; ready currency

---

108 The notion of 'virtual' currencies is, for instance, used by the ECB, the US Internal Revenue Service (IRS), US Congress, the US Government Accountability Office, and in academic literature. European Central Bank (2012) "Virtual Currency Schemes", *ecb.europa.eu*; IRS (2014) "IRS Virtual Currency Guidance: Virtual Currency Is Treated as Property for U.S. Federal Tax Purposes; General Rules for Property Transactions Apply", *irs.gov*; US Senate Committee on Homeland Security and Governmental Affairs (2013) "Beyond Silk Road: Potential Risks, Threats and Promises of Virtual Currencies – Hearing of 18 November 2013", *hsgac.senate.gov*; US Senate Committee on Banking, Housing and Urban Affairs (2013) "The present and future impact of virtual currency – hearing of 19 November 2013", *banking.senate.gov*; GAO (2013) "Virtual Economies and Currencies", *GAO-13-516*; Smith, D. (2012) "More Money, More Problems: The Bitcoin Virtual Currency and the Legal Problems that Face It", *Case Western Reserve Journal of Law Technology & The Internet*, vol. 3, 427–442; Pflaum, I., Hateley, E. (2014) "A bit of a problem: National and extraterritorial regulation of virtual currency in the age of financial disintermediation", *Georgetown Journal of International Law*, Vol. 45, 1169–1215; Kien-Meng Ly, M. (2014) "Coining Bitcoin's 'legal-bits': examining the regulatory framework for Bitcoin and virtual currencies", *Harvard Journal of Law & Technology*, vol. 27, nr. 2, 587–608; European Banking Authority (2014) "EBA Opinion on 'virtual currencies'", *eba.europa.eu*, EBA/Op/2014/08; De Filippi, P. (2014) "Bitcoin : A Regulatory Nightmare to a Libertarian", *Internet Policy Review*, Vol. 3, nr. 2, 1–11.

109 Black's Law Dictionary (9th ed.), for instance, refers to its definition of 'e-money' for 'electronic cash', 'digital cash', and 'electronic currency'.

or coin.[110] 'Currency' could generally be understood as referring to a circulating medium of exchange.[111] 'Money', in turn, could be understood as a generally accepted medium of exchange – often with the status of legal tender[112] – that represents purchasing power, or assets that can be easily converted into cash.[113] In general, all three notions refer to a medium of exchange that is readily usable in practice. Such a medium of exchange could, for instance, also refer to checks or demand deposits.[114] 'Money', however, could be considered as a more strict term, given the reference to legal tender found here.[115]

ELIMINATION – From the previous paragraph it can be gathered that the virtual currencies covered by the scope of this research should not be referred to as 'money', as they do not hold the status of legal tender in any particular jurisdiction. Strictly speaking, a distinction could be made between government-issued public money and privately-issued alternative money, but such a distinction could risk further confusion at this stage of the research.[116] Here, it is thus recommendable to rely on the use of 'cash' or 'currency'. The use of 'cash' in the particular field of

---

110 "cash" (2014), *Black's Law Dictionary* (9th ed.), West; "cash, n.1" (2014), *OED Online*, Oxford University Press; "cash" (2014), *Merriam-Webster.com*, Merriam-Webster; "cash" (2014), *OED Online*, Oxford University Press; "cash" (2014), *collinsdictionary.com*, HarperCollins Publishers.

111 "currency" (2014), *Black's Law Dictionary* (9th ed.), West; "currency, n." (2014), *OED Online*, Oxford University Press; "currency" (2014), *Merriam-Webster.com*, Merriam-Webster; "currency" (2014), *collinsdictionary.com*, HarperCollins Publishers. Note that while currency can also refer to the legal tender of a state, it does not solely refer to legal tender only.

112 Note that Black's Law Dictionary (9th ed.) considers 'money' as equalizing legal tender in reference to Uniform Commercial Code §1-201(b)(24). Also Collins Dictionary makes the direct connection to legal tender: "money" (2014), *collinsdictionary.com*, HarperCollins Publishers.

113 "money" (2014), *Black's Law Dictionary* (9th ed.), West; "money, n." (2014), *OED Online*, Oxford University Press; "money" (2014), *Merriam-Webster.com*, Merriam-Webster.

114 At least in the US: Scott *v.* Vandor, 671 S.W.2d 79 (Tex. App. Houston 1st Dist. 1984).

115 Black's Law Dictionary (9th ed.), for instance, considers 'money' to be adopted by a government as part of its currency. For the US, legal tender is defined in 31 USC §5103 as "*United States coins and currency (including Federal reserve notes and circulating notes of Federal reserve banks and national banks)*". For the EU, article 128 of the Treaty on the Functioning of the European Union (TFEU) holds that "*the banknotes issued by the European Central Bank and the national central banks shall be the only such notes to have the status of legal tender within the Union*". For coins, a similar provision is found in article 11 Council Regulation (EC) No 974/98 of 3 May 1998 on the introduction of the euro, *OJ* L 139 of 11 May 1998, 1–5. That view on legal tender was confirmed in: Commission Recommendation of 22 March 2010 on the scope and effects of legal tender of euro banknotes and coins, *OJ* L 83 of 30 March 2010, 70–71. However, also 'currency' has already been used in reference to legal tender, though that appears to be a minority case. Article 2(a) Directive 2014/62/EU of the European Parliament and of the Council of 15 May 2014 on the protection of the euro and other currencies against counterfeiting by criminal law, and replacing Council Framework Decision 2000/383/JHA, *OJ* L 151 of 21 May 2014, 1–8.

116 As used by the European Commission: *ec.europa.eu/economy_finance/euro/cash/legal_tender/index_en.htm*. Note also that the correspondence of the virtual currencies covered by the scope of this research to money will be analyzed in chapter III.

non-physical currencies can be considered to be somewhat outdated. References to 'digital cash' or 'electronic cash' are mainly found in literature dating back to the 1990's, when the digitalization of payment systems and means was still mostly understood as creating a non-physical equivalent to the well-known physical elements.[117] Under that reasoning, the use of 'currency' is preferred as some of the developments that will be covered by the scope of this research are going further than what the original 'digital cash' varieties could offer.

Alternative view – It has, however, also been proposed that none of these terms should apply. The European Banking Authority (EBA), for instance, considers virtual currencies as "*digital representation*[s] *of value* [...] *neither issued by a central bank or public authority nor necessarily attached to a FC, but* [...] *accepted by natural or legal persons as a means of exchange and* [...] *transferred, stored or traded electronically*".[118] One argument here is that the use of the term 'currency' could insinuate that those virtual currencies are exchangeable for other currencies, which – following further on in this chapter – is not always the case.[119] Also the range of acceptance of virtual currencies may be limited, which could limit the use of such 'currencies' as circulating media of exchange.[120] In defining virtual currencies, the EBA therefore breaks down their essence into a number of constitutive elements, the most important of which being that virtual currencies are a digital representation of value.[121]

Selection of 'currency' – However, while it can be agreed that all the here proposed terms may hold their own shortcomings and that maybe none of them is perfectly applicable to what is considered under the scope of this research, it is also clear that particular terminology must be agreed upon as a matter of convention. Here, it is therefore decided to follow the EBA's reasoning that – reflecting its common public usage – the notion of 'virtual currency' is best suited.[122]

117 Tucker, for one, explicitly considers 'digital cash' as an electronic representation of cash: Tucker, G. (1997) "Some Legal Issues Relating to Digital Cash on the Information Highway", *Journal of Law and Information Science*, Vol. 8, 46–67. See also: Froomkin, A.M. (1996) "Flood control on the information ocean: living with anonymity, digital cash, and distributed databases", *Journal of Law & Commerce*, Vol. 15, 395–507; Anderson, C., Butler, C., Kirch, A., et al. (1997) "Exploring Digital Cash", *courses.ischool.berkeley.edu/i204/f97/GroupE*; Maurer, B. (1998) "Cyberspatial Sovereignties: Offshore Finance, Digital Cash, and the Limits of Liberalism", Indiana Journal of Global Legal Studies, Vol. 4, 493–519; Akindemowo, O.E. (1998) "The Fading Rustle, Chink and Jingle: Electronic Value and the Concept of Money", *University of New South Wales Law Journal*, Vol. 21, 466–488; Hoffman, C.D. (1998) "Encrypted Digital Cash Transfers: Why Traditional Money Laundering Controls May Fail without Uniform Cryptography Regulations", *Fordham International Law Journal*, Vol. 21, 836–860.

118 EBA (2014) "Opinion on 'virtual currencies'", *eba.europa.eu*, EBA/Op/2014/08, 7.

119 *Id.* In the 2015 update to its earlier opinion, the ECB adopts the EBA's reasoning: European Central Bank (2015) "Virtual Currency Schemes – a further analysis", *ecb.europa.eu*, 25.

120 EBA (2014) "Opinion on 'virtual currencies'", *eba.europa.eu*, EBA/Op/2014/08, 12.

121 *Ibid.*, 11.

122 *Id.*

## 2.3 DEFINING VIRTUAL CURRENCIES

NEED FOR A BROAD DEFINITION – In searching for the most suited terminology for the purposes of this research, a number of elements that can support the definition of the notion of virtual currencies were already identified. As noted before, the goal here is to establish a broad and universally acceptable definition. At the same time, however, the notion of virtual currencies must be sufficiently demarcated from other forms of non-physical money, such as bank account balances. While such forms of money are not necessarily designated as legal tender, it is clear that they are different from virtual currencies, given their close relation to legal tender.[123] Naturally, the definition will to some extent resemble – but not necessarily overlap with – that of e-money as regulated within the EU. Chapter IV will assess to what extent the current EU legal framework on e-money can be applied to virtual currencies.

NON-PHYSICAL FORM ONLY – First, it must be understood that virtual currencies principally exist only in non-physical form, which sets them apart from physical money. Such corresponds to the EBA's view of virtual currencies as digital representations of value.[124] While it is possible to 'physicalize' virtual currencies, such a physical form holds little value. For instance, cryptocurrencies can be stored in a paper wallet, which is essentially a print-out of the unique identifier of the virtual wallet that holds the virtual currency. That paper wallet in itself will not serve as money, but is merely an access medium to the virtual wallet that holds the actual value. Similarly, online stores can issue physical prepaid cards that can be purchased at brick-and-mortar stores. Those cards are not money in their own right, but provide access to a certain value.

UNIT OF ACCOUNT – Second, virtual currencies should be able to serve as their own unit of account.[125] This element distinguishes virtual currencies from other forms of non-physical money, as the latter are digital representations of state-issued fiat currency, which virtual currencies are not.[126] Even though for some virtual currencies it may be debatable whether or not they fulfill that function well, the presence of a unit of account – stable or not – is necessary to be considered as a functioning currency.[127]

USED AS MEANS TO CONCLUDE PAYMENTS – Third, virtual currencies are intended to serve as means to conclude payments. While it is possible that a virtual currency will only serve within a closed online community or system – such as a game – it is clear that virtual currencies can also enjoy wider acceptance. Some virtual currencies

---

123 This point will be further elaborated in section 5.1 of chapter III.

124 EBA (2014) "Opinion on 'virtual currencies'", *eba.europa.eu*, EBA/Op/2014/08, 11.

125 *Id.*

126 *Id.*

127 See, for instance, Bal, A. (2014) "Taxation of virtual currency", *PhD Thesis Leiden University*, 62.

have grown beyond their initial community or even beyond acceptance confined to the virtual realm.[128] As a result of the first element identified here, virtual currencies are in principle created and exchanged within virtual worlds, but that does not preclude their use in acquiring physical goods or services. The ECB's original limited view on the acceptance of virtual currencies must therefore be rejected in favor of a broader view.[129] A specific reference to the conclusion of payments aims to include the finality of payments in the definition. After all, when parties agree to conduct a payment in virtual currencies, the transaction should be final.

WITHOUT EXCLUDING INVESTMENTS – Fourth, while virtual currencies clearly developed within the field of payments, the last few years have seen the development of a new class of virtual currencies – particularly within the field of cryptocurrencies – that serve mainly or even solely as means of investment. For the purposes of this research, the main focus will be put on virtual currencies serving as means of payment. However, a few cases regarding virtual currencies serving as means of investment must be taken into account – particularly in chapter VI. As a result, while the definition established here focuses on virtual currencies serving as means to conclude payments, the existence of virtual currencies serving as means of investment should not be excluded.

NO LEGAL TENDER – Last, virtual currencies do not have the status of legal tender.[130] The direct consequence thereof is that creditors of payment obligations are not obliged to accept virtual currencies as a means for payment. This is in line with what is considered under the EMD2 as e-money within the EU, which does not have the status of legal tender either.[131]

---

128 As is the case for bitcoin.

129 EBA (2014) "Opinion on 'virtual currencies'", *eba.europa.eu*, EBA/Op/2014/08, 12; Pflaum, I., Hateley, E. (2014) "A bit of a problem: National and extraterritorial regulation of virtual currency in the age of financial disintermediation", *Georgetown Journal of International Law*, Vol. 45, 1173; Kien-Meng Ly, M. (2014) "Coining Bitcoin's 'legal-bits': examining the regulatory framework for Bitcoin and virtual currencies", *Harvard Journal of Law & Technology*, vol. 27, nr. 2, 589.

130 EBA (2014) "Opinion on 'virtual currencies'", *eba.europa.eu*, EBA/Op/2014/08, 11–14; GAO (2013) "Virtual Economies and Currencies", *GAO-13-516*, 3; Pflaum, I., Hateley, E. (2014) "A bit of a problem: National and extraterritorial regulation of virtual currency in the age of financial disintermediation", *Georgetown Journal of International Law*, Vol. 45, 1172; Financial Crimes Enforcement Network (FinCEN (2014) "Application of FinCEN's Regulations to Persons Administering, Exchanging, or Using Virtual Currencies", *FIN-2013-G001*, 1; Kien-Meng Ly, M. (2014) "Coining Bitcoin's 'legal-bits': examining the regulatory framework for Bitcoin and virtual currencies", *Harvard Journal of Law & Technology*, vol. 27, nr. 2, 589; IRS (2014) "IRS Virtual Currency Guidance: Virtual Currency Is Treated as Property for U.S. Federal Tax Purposes; General Rules for Property Transactions Apply", *irs.gov;* US Senate Committee on Homeland Security and Governmental Affairs (2013) "Beyond Silk Road: Potential Risks, Threats and Promises of Virtual Currencies – Testimony of Edward Lowery III", *hsgac.senate.gov*, 1.

131 As noted in footnote 115, only the coins and banknotes issued by the ECB are legal tender within the Eurozone.

While it is in principle possible that a virtual currency is adopted by a government as legal tender, that possibility is not covered by the definition as it raises the question of whether such is compatible with the nature of virtual currencies.[132] The mere reference to virtual currencies not being legal tender does leave open the situation where a public authority issues a virtual currency. One example is the government of Estonia, which in September 2017 voiced the idea of launching a national cryptocurrency.[133] While such a cryptocurrency would be government-issued, it could not become legal tender as Estonia is part of the Euro Area – whose members are bound to only the euro as legal tender.

Establishment of a definition – Combining the core elements established in the previous paragraphs, virtual currencies can for the purposes of this research be defined as "*digital representations of value, which are not legal tender, which serve as a unit of account, separate from existing state- or central bank-issued currencies, and which can serve as a means to conclude payments*". This definition adopts the core elements found in the definitions currently used in literature.[134] Moreover, the definition follows the broad lines of the definition proposed by the EBA in its 2014 opinion, as well as of the new definition proposed by the ECB in the 2015 update to its report. In that report, the ECB now defines virtual currencies as "*a digital representation of value, not issued by a central bank, credit institution or e-money institution, which, in some circumstances, can be used as an alternative to money*".[135]

---

132 After all, the one element that all definitions found in literature seem to agree upon is that virtual currencies are an alternative to government-issued currency – regardless of the form thereof. If a virtual currency were adopted by a government as legal tender, this would inevitably result in a certain level of government control, which in turn would contradict the very nature of virtual currencies.

133 Haig, S. (2017) "European Central Bank Criticizes Estonian National Cryptocurrency Plans", *bitcoin.com*, 18 September.

134 For instance, the ECB's inclusion of limited acceptance of virtual currencies has proven outdated. Also, the New York State Department of Financial Services' license for virtual currency business activities includes a reference to whether the virtual currency is centralized or decentralized. However, as both options are possible, that reference can be considered as obsolete. Those rules furthermore exclude virtual currencies that only serve a virtual economy and virtual currencies used in loyalty programs from their scope. In aiming to adopt a broad and universal definition for virtual currencies, such scope limitations are not adopted in the present research. New York State Department of Financial Services (2015) "Regulation of the Conduct of Virtual Currency Businesses", *NYS Register*, 24 June 2015, 7–8; 23 CRR-NY s200.2(p). Another element that has been proposed to define virtual currencies is anonymity. However, since anonymous transactions are not possible for all virtual currencies – it would for instance be impossible to anonymously book a flight to spend virtual currencies in a frequent-flyer program – that element should be rejected as well. Karlstrøm, H. (2014) "Do libertarians dream of electric coins? The material embeddedness of Bitcoin", *Distinktion: Scandinavian Journal of Social Theory*, Vol. 15, 27.

135 European Central Bank (2015) "Virtual Currency Schemes – a further analysis", *ecb.europa.eu*, 25.

# 3 PRACTICAL EXAMPLES

FOUR CASES – Virtual currencies span a wide range of different forms, with new developments constantly arising. In order to provide a better understanding of the breadth of those forms, this section presents four use cases of virtual currencies. Those particular cases were selected because they, when taken together, are representative for the broad field of virtual currencies, and because they are the cases most regularly encountered within the literature consulted for this research.

## 3.1 LOYALTY PROGRAMS

MARKETING TOOL – Loyalty programs have since long been used as a competitive marketing tool. By rewarding consumer behavior, such programs aim at fostering brand or store loyalty, and at providing an incentive for further consumption.[136] Moreover, they can provide valuable insight in consumer behavior patterns, which can be used in future marketing campaigns.[137]

POINTS AND REDEMPTION – A classic loyalty program rewards certain consumer behavior with points. Those points can be saved up and redeemed for a reward. Such loyalty points can for the purposes of this research be considered as virtual currencies. After all, they are representations of value – and increasingly so in digital form – which are not recognized as legal tender, that have their own unit of account, and serve as a form to conclude payment for the reward.

NO DIRECT EXCHANGE – Loyalty points are a particular kind of virtual currency in the sense that the party obtaining the loyalty points – in this case the consumer – does not directly exchange legal tender or similar instruments for virtual currency. That does, however, not mean that such an exchange does not take place at all. In most loyalty programs there are multiple parties, such as the operator who sells points to retailers, who in turn reward those points to consumers upon their purchase behavior. The consumers can redeem the points for rewards at a redeemer – who in broader schemes can also be a different retailer from the one who granted the points to the consumer.[138] That redeemer is then reimbursed for the goods or services provided to the consumer by the operator. Such a reimbursement, in turn, is to be understood as "*consideration,*

---

136 European Central Bank (2012) "Virtual Currency Schemes", *ecb.europa.eu*, 18; Labbozzetta, C. (2007) "A principles approach to reward loyalty: an argument for code of conduct principles to remedy the contractual unfairness and legislative confusion in loyalty programs", *Macquarie Journal of Business Law*, Vol. 4, 124.

137 European Central Bank (2012) "Virtual Currency Schemes", *ecb.europa.eu*, 18.

138 Note that redeemer and scheme operator can also be the same entity. In a more limited scheme, the retailer can even be both operator and redeemer.

*paid by a third party, for a supply of goods to those customers or, as the case may be, a supply of services to them"*.[139] In other words, there is an exchange from legal tender or similar instruments into virtual currency in such a four party scheme, be it that it is not the consumer who conducts that exchange.

### *3.1.1 Classic loyalty point programs*

HIGH ADOPTION RATE – Classic loyalty programs have been around for a while and their adoption rate keeps growing.[140] While no generally accepted definition seems to exist, loyalty programs are widely considered as offering benefits to customers based on their consumer behavior, with the offering retailer's aims being to provide incentive for more consumer spending, to gain consumer insight and to increase consumer retention.[141] Despite their popularity – or perhaps rather because of their popularity – the effectiveness of loyalty programs is still debated.[142]

EXAMPLES – One example of a classic loyalty point program is Balance Rewards, offered by US pharmacy Walgreens.[143] Upon making purchases, customers are awarded points.[144] Those points can be saved up and redeemed as a discount.[145]

---

139 CJEU, Commissioners for Her Majesty's Revenue and Customs *v* Loyalty Management UK Ltd and Baxi Group Ltd, C-53/09 and C-55/09, consideration 66.

140 Zhang, J., Breugelmans, E. (2012) "The impact of an item-Based loyalty Program on Consumer Purchase Behavior", *Journal of Marketing Research*, Vol. 49, 50.

141 Breugelmans, E., Bijmolt, T.HA., Zhang, J., Basso, L.J., Dorotic, M., Kopalle, P., Minnam, A., Mijnlieff, W.J., Wünderlich, N.V. (2014) "Advancing Research on Loyalty Programs: A Future Research Agenda", *Marketing Letters,* 3; Evanschitzky, H., Ramaseshan, B., Woisetschläger, D.M., Richelsen, V., Blut, M., Backhaus, C. (2012) "Consequences of customer loyalty to the loyalty program and to the company", *Journal of the Academy of Marketing Science*, Vol. 40, 626; Zhang, J., Breugelmans, E. (2012) "The impact of an item-Based loyalty Program on Consumer Purchase Behavior", *Journal of Marketing Research*, Vol. 49, 50–51; Greenlee, P., Reitman, D. (2005) "Distinguishing Competitive and Exclusionary Uses of Loyalty Discounts", *Antitrust Bulletin*, Vol. 50, 442; Labbozzetta, C. (2007) "A Principled Approach to Reward Loyalty: An Argument for Code of Conduct Principles to Remedy the Contractual Unfairness and Legislative Confusion in Loyalty Programs", *Macquarie Journal of Business Law*, Vol. 4, 125.

142 For instance, consumers are generally part of several loyalty programs, raising the question whether such programs truly augment brand loyalty. Moreover, as many loyalty programs are not bound to a particular brand but span several – possibly competing – brands, there may be more program loyalty than brand loyalty. Selldahl, S. (2013) "Virtual currencies – Real opportunities?", *Master thesis KTH Industrial Engineering and Management*, 24; Zhang, J., Breugelmans, E. (2012) "The impact of an item-Based loyalty Program on Consumer Purchase Behavior", *Journal of Marketing Research*, Vol. 49, 50; Breugelmans, E., Bijmolt, T.HA., Zhang, J., Basso, L.J., Dorotic, M., Kopalle, P., Minnam, A., Mijnlieff, W.J., Wünderlich, N.V. (2014) "Advancing Research on Loyalty Programs: A Future Research Agenda", *Marketing Letters,* 3; Evanschitzky, H., Ramaseshan, B., Woisetschläger, D.M., Richelsen, V., Blut, M., Backhaus, C. (2012) "Consequences of customer loyalty to the loyalty program and to the company", *Journal of the Academy of Marketing Science*, Vol. 40, 626.

143 *Walgreens.com/topic/balancerewards/balance-program-details.jsp.*

144 For instance, when a customer has selected to automatically refill prescriptions, 500 points are awarded for every fill. *walgreens.com/topic/s/automatic-refill.jsp.*

145 5.000 points will provide a USD 5 discount.

Similar single-brand programs are operated by a wide range of companies such as the Intercontinental Hotels Group[146], The Body Shop[147], Tesco[148], HMV[149], and Carrefour.[150] Broader loyalty programs that span several brands include Flybuys[151], Nectar[152], Payback[153], Trumf[154], and American Express Membership Rewards.[155]

### 3.1.2 *Mobile platforms*

Mobile platforms – One recent development in terms of loyalty programs using mobile technology are platforms such as ShopKick that provide consumers with loyalty points for checking in at affiliated stores.[156] After consumers install the ShopKick application on their mobile phones, affiliated retailers can automatically detect those consumers when they enter their stores.[157] Upon a check-in, or by scanning items within the store, consumers are rewarded loyalty points, called kicks.[158] Those points can later be redeemed for gift cards and credit at stores that include, amongst others, iTunes, Target, and Starbucks.[159] This example is a form of location-based marketing, which grants rewards upon the participating retailer learning more about the consumer's shopping behavior and location in its store.[160]

Affiliate marketing – Another development mainly situated within the realm of mobile technologies is that of affiliate marketing. Here, consumers are awarded loyalty points on their completed activities, which can include survey taking, clicking on advertisements, playing games, or referring other people. Examples of affiliate marketing include Swagbucks[161] and FeaturePoints.[162]

146 *Ihg.com/rewardsclub/gb/en/home.*
147 *Thebodyshop-usa.com/loveyourbody.*
148 *Tesco.com/clubcard.*
149 *Purehmv.com/gb.*
150 *Bonuscard.carrefour.eu.*
151 *Flybuys.com.au.*
152 *Nectar.com/NectarHome.nectar.*
153 *Payback.de.*
154 *Trumf.no.*
155 *Global.americanexpress.com/rewards/landing.*
156 *Shopkick.com.*
157 ShopKick recently adopted the so-called iBeacon technology – trademarked by Apple – which uses a Bluetooth Low Energy proximity sensor to transmit a unique retailer identification code to consumers' mobile phones. The ShopKick application on those mobile phones will then register the consumers as having checked in at a particular retailer, thus awarding loyalty points. *shopkick.com/shopbeacon.* An older version of the application worked by having each affiliated retailer transmitting an inaudible sound unique to that retailer. Consumers' mobile phones would register that sound and identify the retailer where the consumer just checked in. Milian, M. (2012) "Aaron Emigh: Rewarding Shoppers With a Silent Signal", *Bloomberg,* 30 August 2012.
158 *Shopkick.desk.com/customer/portal/articles/1327298-what-is-shopkick-.*
159 Participating redeemers are announced on: *facebook.com/SHOPkick.*
160 Clifford, S. (2010) "Aisle by Aisle, an App That Pushes Bargain", *New York Times*, 17 August 2010. For instance, by rewarding consumers with extra kicks for actions such as scanning an item in a store, or trying out clothes, retailers are awarding specific consumer behavior.
161 *Swagbucks.com.*
162 *Featurepoints.com.*

### *3.1.3 Frequent-flyer programs*

HISTORY AND EXAMPLES – Another type of loyalty programs are frequent-flyer programs. Those are programs in which airline travelers generally receive points based on the distance they traveled. The first of such programs was inaugurated by Texas International Airlines in 1979, as a consequence of the broader deregulation of the US domestic air transport market in 1978.[163] That program was followed by American Airlines' AAdvantage program in 1981, which to this day remains one of the largest frequent-flyer programs in the world.[164] Other airlines worldwide followed suit, with the launch of programs such as Air Miles[165], Mileage Plus[166], LANPASS[167], Miles & More[168], Qantas Frequent Flyer[169], EuroBonus[170], Flying Blue[171], and British Airways Executive Club.[172]

CHANGING SCHEMES – Over the years, the details of such programs have changed significantly. Originally, the intention was to allow travelers to use their saved mileage points to purchase flights.[173] Now, saved points in frequent-flyer programs can also be used to obtain cabin upgrades, premium airport services, car rentals, or hotel reservations.[174] Many programs allow the points to be spend in participating shops, or to be exchanged for gift cards.[175] Moreover, due to the cooperation between airlines in airline alliances, points can often be redeemed at airlines other than the emitting airline.[176]

MOVE TO SPENDING-BASED PROGRAMS – Also the means by which the frequent-flyer points are earned have changed drastically. Since the introduction of co-branded credit cards, travelers have been able to gain frequent-flyer points

---

163 Rowell, D.M. (2010) "A History of US Airline Deregulation – Part 4: 1979 – 2010: The Effects of Deregulation – Lower Fares, More Travel, Frequent Flier Programs", *The Travel Insider*, 13 August 2010; De Boer, E.R., Gudmundsson, S.V. (2012) "30 years of frequent flyer programs", *Journal of Air Transport Management*, Vol. 24, 18.

164 *Aa.com/i18n/AAdvantage/programInformation/main.jsp.*

165 *Loyalty.com/coalition-loyalty/air-miles.*

166 *United.com/web/en-US/content/mileageplus/default.aspx.*

167 *Lan.com/en_ue/sitio_personas/lanpass/index.html.*

168 *Miles-and-more.com/online/portal/mam_com/de/homepage.*

169 *Qantas.com.au/fflyer/dyn/program/welcome.*

170 *Flysas.com/en/EuroBonus.*

171 *Klm.com/travel/nl_nl/flying_blue/index.htm.*

172 *Britishairways.com/en-be/executive-club.*

173 De Boer, E.R., Gudmundsson, S.V. (2012) "30 years of frequent flyer programs", *Journal of Air Transport Management*, Vol. 24, 18–19; Selldahl, S. (2013) "Virtual currencies – Real opportunities?", *Master thesis KTH Industrial Engineering and Management*, 25.

174 De Boer, E.R., Gudmundsson, S.V. (2012) "30 years of frequent flyer programs", *Journal of Air Transport Management*, Vol. 24, 19.

175 For instance the Eurobonus and AAdvantage programs.

176 Eurobonus points, for instance, are operated by SAS and can be redeemed at all other Star Alliance members, including Brussels Airlines, Lufthansa and United Airlines. *flysas.com/en/be/eurobonus/spend-points/airlines.*

based on their spending using such co-branded credit cards. That has proven to be a lucrative source of income for airline companies, as the affiliated financial institutions regularly spend over USD 1 billion per year to acquire the loyalty points they will distribute amongst their card-bearing travelers.[177] In doing so, frequent-flyer programs are increasingly becoming spending-based programs, rather than travel-based programs.[178] Moreover, consumers can often directly buy frequent-flyer points from the emitting airline companies.[179]

## 3.2 IN-GAME CURRENCIES

VIRTUAL WORLD – In-game currencies are virtual currencies that exist primarily within the confines of a virtual game world. As such, their main goal is to serve the virtual economy within that game.

### *3.2.1 Pay-to-play*

MMORPG – Massively Multiplayer Online Role-Playing Games (MMORPGs) are a form of video games in which players take control over characters – also referred to as avatars – and their actions within the game.[180] Such games are set in what is referred to as persistent worlds, meaning that the game world, its characters and events continue to exist and evolve, even in the absence of a particular player.[181] While classic video games accommodate just one player or a small group of players, MMORPGs can in theory accommodate an infinite number of players from all over the world.[182]

VIRTUAL ECONOMIES – Because of their persistent worlds, MMORPGs are known to have developed their own virtual economies and social structures. As part of such

177 De Boer, E.R., Gudmundsson, S.V. (2012) "30 years of frequent flyer programs", *Journal of Air Transport Management*, Vol. 24, 19. American Airlines, for instance, reported USD 2,6 billion other revenues in 2013, mostly consisting out of the sale of frequent-flyer mileage credits. American Airlines (2014) "2013 Form 10-K: annual report", *phx.corporate-ir.net/phoenix.zhtml?c=117098&p=irol-reportsannual*, 60.

178 Delta Airlines has already fully converted its SkyMiles program away from travel-based earning: *news.delta.com/index.php?s=20295&item=124381.*

179 E.g.: *buymiles.aa.com/en/buygift?c=AAC_MPG_EN,US_BUY*; *flysas.com/en/be/eurobonus/earn-points/buy-points.*

180 The origins of the notion of 'avatar' in games is explored in: Castronova, E. (2002) "On Virtual Economies", *CESifo Working Paper 752*, 6–13.

181 Castronova. E. (2001) "Virtual Worlds: A First-Hand Account of Market and Society on the Cyberian Frontier", *The Gruter Institute Working Papers on Law, Economics, and Evolutionary Biology*, Vol. 2, Nr. 1, 6.

182 Selldahl, S. (2013) "Virtual currencies – Real opportunities?", *Master thesis KTH Industrial Engineering and Management*, 29–30; Papagiannidis, S., Bourlakis, M., Li, F. (2008) "Making real money in virtual worlds: MMORPGs and emerging business opportunities, challenges and ethical implications in metaverses", *Technological Forecasting & Social Change*, Vol. 75, 611.

virtual economies, many MMORPGs utilize an in-game virtual currency, allowing players to trade amongst each other or to obtain the in-game goods and services needed to advance within the game. The game developer in such case does not allow in-game currency to be obtained by means of legal tender or similar instruments, nor can in-game currency be converted into legal tender or similar instruments. Furthermore, the in-game currency can only be used to obtain virtual goods and services within the game, thus having no direct value in the physical-world economy.

WoW Gold – One example of such an in-game currency is the unit 'Gold' used within World of Warcraft (WoW).[183] Overall, the supply of Gold is controlled by the collective players of the game, as it are their actions – such as completing a quest or defeating an enemy – that result in the creation of new units of Gold.[184] The developer of that game, Blizzard Entertainment, explicitly forbids players to "*buy or sell for "real" money or exchange gold, weapons, armor, or any other virtual items that may be used in World of Warcraft outside the World of Warcraft platform*".[185] If a player is found to engage in that practice, the developer can terminate the service – 'ban' the player's account.[186] Nevertheless, a black market has developed where so-called 'gold farmers' – often based in low-wage countries – employ players to collect in-game currency, which is subsequently sold to other players against legal tender or similar instruments.[187]

Physical-world implications – However, the principal lack of direct interaction between the virtual in-game economy and the physical-world economy does not mean that those game worlds and the actions performed by the players within them have no inherent economic value. It has, for instance, already been argued that the move of productivity to online worlds rather than conducted in the physical world could impact physical-world economies, if such occurred on a sufficiently massive scale.[188] Moreover, the black market trade described earlier inherently results in legal tender value being accorded to virtual goods and services.

EverQuest – Another example of an MMORPG using virtual currency is EverQuest, which reached its peak popularity in the early 2000's, before World

183 *Warcraft.com*. With over 100 million accounts created, World of Warcraft can be considered as one of the most popular MMORPGs. Sarkar, S. (2014) "Blizzard reaches 100M lifetime World of Warcraft accounts", *Polygon*, 28 January 2014.

184 Castronova, E. (2008) "Effects of botting on World of Warcraft – expert report filed for US District Court of Arizona case CV06-02555-PHX-DGC", *virtuallyblind.com/2008/03/23/mdy-blizzard-motions*, 7.

185 *Eu.blizzard.com/en-gb/company/legal/wow_tou.html.*

186 *Eu.blizzard.com/en-gb/company/legal/wow_termination.html.*

187 Lehdonvirta, V., Ernkvist, M. (2011) *Knowledge Map of the Virtual Economy*, Washington, DC: InfoDev/World Bank, 20–21.

188 Castronova, E. (2002) "On Virtual Economies", *CESifo Working Paper 752*, 30.

of Warcraft.[189] Also there, the game's developer considered all items within the game to be its own intellectual property, thus prohibiting the trade of such items against legal tender or similar instruments.[190] Black market trade did flourish nevertheless, even allowing the estimation of the virtual world's per capita gross national product to be equal to that of Russia at the time.[191]

Opening to interchangeability – While World of Warcraft and EverQuest are examples of MMORPGs that like to keep their virtual currencies locked within the virtual economy, there are, however, also examples of MMORPGs that have embraced – to various extents – interaction between the virtual and physical-world economy. Perhaps in realization that illicit transactions between the virtual and physical economy are unavoidable, a number of newer MMORPGs include trade markets operated by the game developer. Those markets allow players to trade amongst each other, but can also serve as a point to exchange legal tender or similar instruments into the in-game virtual currency.

EVE Online – One example is EVE Online, where developer CCP Games sells 'game time' for legal tender or similar instruments, which within the game can be converted to virtual currency.[192] While that does allow players to essentially convert legal tender or similar instruments into the game's virtual currency, conversions from the virtual currency to legal tender or similar instruments are still not allowed.[193] EverQuest has in recent years adopted a similar scheme.[194] Also Blizzard Entertainment tried its hand at the concept through the Real-Money Auction House originally included in Diablo III.[195] There, the concept was taken even further, allowing players to sell in-game items for legal tender or similar instruments.[196] That system thus allowed players to exchange legal tender or similar instruments for virtual currency, and *vice versa*.[197] However, feeling that such an economic interaction between the virtual and physical world was

189 *Everquest.com*.

190 Castronova. E. (2001) "Virtual Worlds: A First-Hand Account of Market and Society on the Cyberian Frontier", *The Gruter Institute Working Papers on Law, Economics, and Evolutionary Biology*, Vol. 2, Nr. 1, 25.

191 *Ibid.*, 28.

192 *Eveonline.com*. In order to play the game, players must have a paying subscription. One month of playing time equals one unit of PLEX (Pilot License Extension). Players buying PLEX can use it for themselves, or re-sell it to other players through the market place for the in-game currency ISK.

193 According to the EVE Online EULA: *community.eveonline.com/support/policies/eve-eula*.

194 *Everquest.com/krono*.

195 *Blizzard.com/diablo3*.

196 Onyett, C. (2011) "Get rich playing Diablo III", *IGN*, 1 August 2011.

197 Strictly speaking, the auction house allowed players to buy or sell in-game items for legal tender or similar instruments. The in-game currency, Gold, could also be obtained or sold this way, thus amounting to full currency convertibility.

hampering the game experience, the auction house was closed.[198] Consequently, Diablo III reverted to a closed model, where interaction between its in-game currency and legal tender or similar instruments is prohibited.[199] Blizzard Entertainment has, however, not given up on that model and introduced a game time token similar to that used in EVE Online in World of Warcraft.[200] Users can buy a game time token against legal tender or similar instruments and use it as game time, or sell it in the in-game auction house for the in-game currency Gold. Later, Blizzard Entertainment would also allow users to exchange that token for account balance, to be used in the developer's other games.[201]

### *3.2.2 Free-to-play*

FREEMIUM MODEL – The MMORPGs discussed in the previous subsection had one important element in common: the business model behind those games revolved around players paying to play the game. Such could be achieved through a one-time purchase fee, a recurring subscription fee, or a combination of both.[202] In more recent years, a rising number of video games utilizes the free-to-play model, also referred to as freemium. In that model, the full video game can be obtained and played for free.[203] However, players can be charged legal tender in order to advance quicker through the game, to obtain in-game objects, etc.

LOL – One example here is League of Legends (LoL).[204] That game can be played for free, but is supported by microtransactions – micropayments that

198 McWhertor, M. (2013) "Blizzard president Mike Morhaime on razing Diablo 3's auction house, rebuilding Titan", *Polygon*, 9 November 2013.

199 *Us.blizzard.com/en-us/company/about/termsofuse.html.* While services that sell the in-game currency Gold for legal tender or similar instruments still exist, the developer actively campaigns against players using such services, and discontinuing the accounts of players who are found to engage in such activity. *eu.battle.net/wow/en/shop/anti-gold.* As of 2015, Blizzard Entertainment announced it would introduce microtransactions in Diablo III – where players can buy in-game items for legal tender or similar instruments – be it only in the Asian market. Tassi, P. (2015) "Blizzard's 'Diablo 3' Will Start Dabbling In Microtransactions Again", *Forbes*, 22 February 2015.

200 *Eu.battle.net/wow/en/blog/18141101/introducing-the-wow-token-02-03-2015.*

201 *Us.battle.net/shop/en-gb/product/world-of-warcraft-token.*

202 In the examples used, Diablo III has a one-time purchase fee, while World of Warcraft and EVE Online combine a purchase fee with a recurring subscription fee. EverQuest uses a combination of the aforementioned strategies by providing a free download for the base game, with expansion packs being subjected to a one-time purchase fee, and recurring subscriptions required for all players.

203 Free-to-play is therefore not to be confused with the shareware or demos popular during the 1990's. Shareware constituted limited versions of a computer program that required a paid key to unlock the full abilities.

204 *Leagueoflegends.com.* With an average of 27 million daily active players and over 1 billion of playing hours logged per month, this game is by far the most popular MMORPG. Evangelho, J. (2012) "'League of Legends' Bigger Than 'WoW,' More Daily Players Than 'Call of Duty'", *Forbes*, 10 December 2012; Purchese, R. (2014) "LOL: 27 million people play it every day!", *eurogamer.net*, 28 January 2014.

allow the player to obtain virtual goods.[205] Overall, within the gaming market segment of MMORPGs, revenues from free-to-play games in 2014 were almost three times higher than those of traditional pay-to-play games.[206] As a result, many developers have made the leap to the free-to-play business model, or combine both models. While it is perfectly possible that a majority of players will never conduct any legal tender-denominated transaction, even the financial contributions of a small group of players have proven highly lucrative.[207]

Mobile games – Another example is the game Smurf's Village, available on the Android and iOS platforms.[208] Again, the game itself is available for free. The game uses an in-game currency – Smurfberries – that can be purchased for legal tender or similar instruments, and which can be used to advance gameplay.[209] Game developer Zynga is one of the main examples of a company that has embraced the free-to-play business model. Its popular games FarmVille and CityVille all offer in-app purchases to obtain the virtual currency necessary to advance within the game.[210]

Commonality – The common element in those free-to-play games is that all examples here use in-game virtual currencies that can be obtained through the players' actions within the game, as well as through purchase against legal tender or similar instruments. Those virtual currencies, however, cannot be exchanged

205 One of the in-game currencies – Riot Points – can be purchased with legal tender or similar instruments. In 2014, the total amount of microtransactions in League of Legends was expected to surpass USD 1 billion. Chalk, A. (2014) "League of Legends has made almost USD 1 billion in microtransactions", *PC Gamer,* 24 October 2014. By 2016, revenue had grown to USD 1,6 billion. Mueller, S. (2016) "Report: League of Legends made $1.6 billion in revenue last year", *dotesports.com,* 26 January. In-game goods can, however, not be sold for legal tender: *leagueoflegends.com/en/legal/eula* and *leagueoflegends.com/en/legal/termsofuse.*

206 SuperData Research (2014) "2014 Digital Games Year in Review", *superdataresearch.com,* 3 December 2014.

207 For instance, League of Legends has a reported conversion rate – meaning the percentage of players who actually conduct microtransactions against legal tender – of only 3,75%: Leigh, A. (2014) "Don't monetize like League of Legends, consultant says", *Gamasutra,* 11 August 2014. Selldahl, S. (2013) "Virtual currencies – Real opportunities?", *Master thesis KTH Industrial Engineering and Management,* 27.

208 *Beeline-i.com/product.php?id=59.*

209 The simplicity with which those Smurfberries can be purchased – a process known as in-app purchasing – resulted in at least one parent being confronted with a USD 1,400 bill amassed by her unsuspecting daughter. Kang, C (2011) "In-app purchases in iPad, iPhone, iPod kids' games touch off parental firestorm", *The Washington Post,* 8 February 2011. The practice of in-app purchasing has come under scrutiny from the European Commission, which proposed action: European Commission (2014) "In-app purchases: Joint action by the European Commission and Member States is leading to better protection for consumers in online games", *IP/14/187.*

210 For 2014, the company reported a revenue of almost USD 700 million. Zynga (2015) "Zynga Announces Fourth Quarter and 2014 Financial Results", *investor.zynga.com,* 12 February 2015.

back into legal tender or similar instruments.[211] Moreover, the in-game currencies can only be used to obtain in-game virtual goods and services.

### 3.2.3 *Second Life*

SOCIAL PLATFORM – A particular case is Linden Lab's Second Life.[212] While Second Life demonstrates a number of similarities to the MMORPGs discussed before, it is not technically a game as it has no set objectives or scripted actions.[213] Instead, Second Life is a free-to-play platform for social interaction between participants through their digital counterparts – also there referred to as avatars.[214] Using their avatars, participants can explore the virtual world and engage in activities together. One of the defining characteristics of Second Life is that participants are not bound in their activities to what the game developer provides, but can actively contribute to the virtual world by creating new objects and interactions.[215]

USER-GENERATED CONTENT – As a result of the amount of freedom given to participants to customize their experience, Second Life quickly attracted entrepreneurial endeavors. Participants opened shops where their creations – digital clothes, real estate and items – were sold, or created role-playing communities.[216] Also established physical-world brands, institutions and governments joined the hype.[217] All of that activity resulted in Second Life

211 One exception is Zynga Poker Plus, an online poker game in which players can bet and win legal tender-denominated money. ThT game is offered only in the UK, through a Gibraltar licensed gambling operator.

212 *Secondlife.com.*

213 Shelton, A.K. (2010) "Defining the lines between virtual and real world purchases: Second Life sells, but who's buying?", *Computers in Human Behavior*, Vol. 26, 1223.

214 Papagiannidis, S., Bourlakis, M., Li, F. (2008) "Making real money in virtual worlds: MMORPGs and emerging business opportunities, challenges and ethical implications in metaverses", *Technological Forecasting & Social Change*, Vol. 75, 611.

215 Through the Second Life Creator: *go.secondlife.com/landing/creator.* While MMORPGs generally also provide a number of customization options, players are limited to the options provided by the developer and generally cannot contribute their own creations.

216 User-created items can be bought and sold through the Marketplace: *marketplace.secondlife.com.* An example of a role-playing community in Second Life is a recreation of Weimar Berlin: *1920sberlin.com.* Shelton, A.K. (2010) "Defining the lines between virtual and real world purchases: Second Life sells, but who's buying?", *Computers in Human Behavior*, Vol. 26, 1224.

217 The British Broadcasting Company joined Second Life: Fildes, J. (2006) "BBC starts to rock online world", *bbc.co.uk*, 12 May 2006. Universities such as Harvard used Second Life for education purposes and library services: Community Virtual Library, *infoisland.org*; Wong, G. (2006) "Educators explore 'Second Life' online", *CNN*, 14 November 2006. Companies on Second Life include Dell, American Apparel, and Starwood Hotels: Krazit, T. (2006) "Dell sets up 'Second Life' shop, offers PCs to residents", *CNET*, 14 November 2006; American Apparel, *americanapparel.net/presscenter/secondlife;* Starwood Hotels, *virtualaloft.com.* A number of countries opened an embassy in Second Life, including Sweden and Estonia: *secondhouseofsweden.wordpress.com; saatkond.typepad.com.*

having a real functional economy.[218] In recent years, however, the popularity of Second Life has greatly waned, with most brands terminating their involvement with the platform.

Full interchangeability – Second Life's virtual economy is driven by a virtual currency – Linden dollars – which are unique in the sense that they are fully convertible: participants can exchange legal tender or similar instruments for Linden dollars and *vice versa*.[219] The exchange rate between legal tender-denominations and Linden dollars is controlled by Linden Labs.[220] Such convertibility sets the Linden dollar apart as a virtual currency with a complete two-way flow between the virtual and physical world. However, as with the other virtual currencies considered in this section, the Linden dollar can only be used to obtain goods and services within a virtual world and is not accepted as payment in the physical world.

Physical-world implications – Regardless, its full convertibility has allowed participants active on the Second Life Marketplace to earn substantial legal tender conducting virtual world transactions.[221] Therefore, while the economy of Second Life is mainly limited to its virtual world, the convertibility of its virtual currency does allow negative consequences to affect the physical-world participants. For instance, a bank founded in Second Life promised unrealistically high interest rates, similar to what would be found in a classic Ponzi scheme.[222] When the scheme collapsed in the virtual world – with the bank defaulting on its ability to pay back debtors – participants suffered the loss of their legal tender investments into the virtual scheme.[223]

---

218 As also acknowledged by the ECB: European Central Bank (2012) "Virtual Currency Schemes", *ecb.europa.eu*, 28–29.

219 Through the Linden Labs operated LindeX: *secondlife.wikia.com/wiki/LindeX.*

220 Papagiannidis, S., Bourlakis, M., Li, F. (2008) "Making real money in virtual worlds: MMORPGs and emerging business opportunities, challenges and ethical implications in metaverses", *Technological Forecasting & Social Change*, Vol. 75, 612.

221 Boyes, E. (2006) "Second Life realtor makes $1 million", *GameSpot*, 27 November 2006; MacMillan, D. (2007) "Big Spenders of Second Life", *Bloomberg*, 16 April 2007; Mitchell, J. (2011) "Second Life Makes $100M A Year in Revenue", *ReadWrite*, 8 August 2011. In 2010, monthly transactions of over USD 45 million were recorded: Jay, A. (2014) "Second Life, Second Remedies", In: Lakhani, A. (Ed.) *Commercial Transactions in the Virtual World*, Hong Kong: City University Press, 310.

222 European Central Bank (2012) "Virtual Currency Schemes", *ecb.europa.eu*, 31; Gardiner, B. (2007) "Bank Failure in Second Life Leads to Calls for Regulation", *Wired*, 15 August 2007; Semuels, A. (2008) "Virtual bank's Second Life scheme raises real concerns", *Los Angeles Times*, 22 January 2008; Talbot, D. (2008) "Second Life Closes Banks", *MIT Technology Review*, 10 January 2008.

223 European Central Bank (2012) "Virtual Currency Schemes", *ecb.europa.eu*, 31; Talbot, D. (2008) "Second Life Closes Banks", *MIT Technology Review*, 10 January 2008.

## 3.3 PREPAID VALUE CURRENCIES

Gift cards and store credit – Another popular use of virtual currencies is a prepaid value currency. Such a virtual currency can, for instance, be found in the form of a gift card as a type of store credit. The value of that store credit is recorded within the retailer's database, with the physical card given to the consumer displaying an identifier – such as a barcode or a unique code – that is linked to the recorded value.[224] As those prepaid value currencies are digital representations of value, not recognized as legal tender, having their own unit of account, and can serve as means of concluding payments, they can be considered as virtual currencies for the purposes of this research.

Difference from loyalty programs – Prepaid value currencies differ from the earlier discussed virtual currencies in loyalty programs in the sense that they are not offered as a reward or incentive for consumer spending. In the case of gift cards, they can be freely obtained by the consumer, either for personal use or as a gift to another person.

Microsoft Points – One example of a prepaid currency is Microsoft Points. That virtual currency was issued by Microsoft for use within its Xbox Live platform. Users could obtain the virtual currency against legal tender or similar instruments online or through gift cards bought at physical stores. The virtual currency could subsequently be spent on Xbox Live by buying games, music or additional digital content for Microsoft's Xbox gaming platform.[225] However, Microsoft's other online platforms – such as the Windows Store and the Windows Phone Store – allowed users to pay their purchases directly in their local legal tender. In an effort to integrate its services, Microsoft therefore phased out Microsoft Points, allowing users to buy content on Xbox Live using legal tender or similar instruments.[226]

Other examples – A similar story can be told of Facebook Credits. Like Microsoft Points, Facebook Credits were issued – by Facebook in this case – to make purchases on an online platform in order to obtain games or other content.[227] The virtual currency could be obtained for legal tender or similar instruments either online or through the purchase of physical gift cards. The

224 An example here are gift cards for Apple's iTunes Store. Consumers can buy these cards – with varying values – in physical stores. Each card has a unique identifier, which once entered into the iTunes Store will add the associated value to the user's account. *apple.com/gift-cards*.

225 The virtual currency was sometimes criticized for obscuring the purchase value. Gans, J.S., Halaburda, H. (2014) "Some Economics of Private Digital Currency ", In: Goldfarb, A., Greenstein, S., Tucker, C. (Eds.) *Economic Analysis of the Digital Economy*, Chicago: University Press, 4; X. (2010) "Microsoft Points Draw Class Action Suit", *Informationweek*, 22 January 2010.

226 *Support.xbox.com/en-US/billing/microsoft-points/microsoft-points-retire-faq*.

227 Courtland, R. (2012) "Virtual currency gets real: Will Facebook Credits and other social scrip challenge government-backed currencies?", *IEEE Spectrum*, Vol. 49, 52.

main goal of Facebook Credits was to provide a single virtual currency for use within all applications on the Facebook platform.[228] For instance, Facebook Credits could be used within the Zynga games developed for Facebook, such as FarmVille, despite such games also using their own internal virtual currency.[229] As part of its business model, Facebook kept 30% of the revenue earned through Facebook Credits, thus allowing it to profit from the use of the virtual currency.[230] However, like Microsoft Points, Facebook Credits have been phased out with Facebook now accepting payments in local legal tender.[231]

Amazon Coins – Another similar case are Amazon Coins. That virtual currency is issued by Amazon initially for use on its Kindle platform, which was later expanded to the whole Amazon website, before becoming confined to Amazon's App Store.[232] The currency can be obtained for legal tender or similar instruments through Amazon. While the virtual currency does not seem to have gained much following, it is still active.[233]

## 3.4 CRYPTOCURRENCIES

New development – Cryptocurrencies are a relatively recent form of virtual currencies, yet have quickly become their most prominent example. Their surge in popularity is mainly spurred by the prime example, bitcoin, and its many competitors and derivatives. This section will briefly introduce the phenomenon of cryptocurrencies. It also provides a more technical analysis of the underlying system – also referred to as blockchain technology.[234] That technology is what sets cryptocurrencies apart from other forms of virtual currencies and has

228 Castronova, E. (2014) "Digital Value Transfer Systems", *Washington & Lee Law Revue Online*, Vol. 71, 16.

229 See section 3.2.2 for Zynga's in-game currency. Jacobs, A., Nakata, K. (2010) "Evolving the social business: a look at stages of growth for Web 2.0 integration with business activities", presented at *First Interdisciplinary Workshop on Communication for Sustainable Communities (IWCSC '10)*, 26 September 2010, S.Carlos, Brazil, 4.

230 Whereas Facebook would not profit from each developer operating its own virtual currency. Castronova, E. (2014) "Digital Value Transfer Systems", *Washington & Lee Law Revue Online*, Vol. 71, 18; Fowler, G., Wingfield, N. (2011) "Facebook 'Credits' To Rule for Games", *Wall Street Journal*, 25 January 2011.

231 Thus silencing concerns on its growth potential. Gans, J.S., Halaburda, H. (2014) "Some Economics of Private Digital Currency ", In: Goldfarb, A., Greenstein, S., Tucker, C. (Eds.) *Economic Analysis of the Digital Economy,* Chicago: University Press, 6; Sengupta, S. (2012) "On Facebook, A Way to Use Real Money", *New York Times*, 20 June 2012.

232 *Developer.amazon.com/appsandservices/support/faq#AmazonCoins.*

233 Launched in the US in 2013, it was expanded to Amazon's EU stores in 2014.

234 For clarity purposes, lower-case words – e.g. 'bitcoin' – will be used to address the units of a cryptocurrency, while upper-case words – e.g. 'Bitcoin' – will refer to the underlying cryptographic system. Parliamentary Office of Science & Technology (2014) "POSTNote: Alternative Currencies", *POST-PN-475*, 2.

also become a speculation point for future applications, such as smart self-executing contracts. Last, this section explores the economic underpinnings of cryptocurrencies.

### *3.4.1 Background*

ROOTS IN CRYPTO-ANARCHISM – Cryptocurrencies can be considered as the spiritual successors to 1990's crypto-anarchism and developments in virtual alternative currencies. Like many crypto-anarchist developments, cryptocurrencies are construed around the use of public-key encryption, in part to allow their users to utilize pseudonymous identifiers.[235] Early alternative currencies that originated on the Internet – thus being virtual currencies for the purposes of this research – focused mainly on bringing existing schemes such as loyalty programs and prepaid cards online as a means of transferring money.[236] Other early forms of Internet-mediated virtual currencies are digital gold currencies, in which a virtual currency was backed by gold bullion[237], and centralized virtual currency transfer systems.[238]

DIGITAL CASH – One of the earliest systems to provide anonymous money transfers utilizing cryptography was David Chaum's DigiCash.[239] The core of DigiCash was later further expanded into Wei Dai's b-money, where a proof of work function was used to create a virtual currency.[240] A further step toward cryptocurrencies was made by Nick Szabo, who proposed a distributed proof of work string as ownership title, which he called 'bit gold'.[241] That development, together with other cryptographic developments such as Adam Back's Hashcash[242] and Hal Finney's Reusable Proofs of

235 Pseudonymity and anonymity being the core elements of May's crypto-anarchism: May, T.C. (1994) "Cyphernomicon", *spinnaker.com/crypt/cyphernomicon/CP-FAQ*.

236 InternetCash.com, for instance, used prepaid cards with a unique identifier as a means to top up an online balance that could be spend at participating online merchants. Flooz.com established an Internet-mediated currency that worked similarly to frequent-flyer programs. Beenz.com was an early form of an online affiliate marketing loyalty program. None of these currencies survived the early 2000's dot-com-bubble crash.

237 Precisely due to the fact that those currencies were backed by a tangible asset such as gold, they survived throughout the early 2000's before being closed down due to various legal issues. Examples include e-gold and e-Bullion.

238 Such as Liberty Reserve.

239 Based on the idea of blind signatures: Chaum, D. (1983) "Blind signatures for untraceable payments", *Advances in Cryptology Proceedings of Crypto*, Vol. 82, 199–203.

240 Dai, W. (1998) "B-money", *weidai.com/bmoney.txt*.

241 Szabo, N. (2005) "Bit gold", *unenumerated.blogspot.com/2005/12/bit-gold.html*. The core idea behind bit gold is that the effort – in terms of computing power – to establish a proof of work can make the solution valuable.

242 Originally intended as a denial-of-service countermeasure, Hashcash is now used in cryptocurrency mining. Back, A. (1997) "A partial hash collision based postage scheme", *hashcash.org/papers/announce.txt*.

Work[243] laid the groundwork for the development of the first cryptocurrency, Bitcoin.

Rise of bitcoin – Bitcoin was originally proposed in a paper by Satoshi Nakamoto in 2008.[244] The main focus of the paper was to establish an electronic payment system that relies on cryptographic proof, rather than on trust in third parties such as financial institutions.[245] As such, it can be considered as a product of its *zeitgeist* amidst the global financial recession then unfolding. While the concrete technical foundations of Bitcoin will be explored in the next section, it can be stated here that Nakamoto's paper proposes the use of timestamps in a peer-to-peer (P2P) network to determine the earliest transaction as a solution to the double-spending problem.[246] Early 2009, the Bitcoin network was released.[247] The announcement by Nakamoto also outlined a few core principles of Bitcoin: users that help maintain the network by lending their computer's calculating power are rewarded through the automatic generation of new units of bitcoin, the amount of new units generated is halved every four years, and no new units will be generated once 21 million units of bitcoin have been distributed.[248] Throughout 2009 and 2010, the value of bitcoin remained virtually zero, with no entities accepting bitcoin as a means of payment.[249] Further in 2010, Nakamoto left the project to some of its earliest adopters and disappeared.[250] The Bitcoin code is freely accessible to everyone, but is maintained by a small group of core developers. In order for a new version of Bitcoin to be adopted, a majority of the network must accept the changes.[251] More importantly, the first bitcoin exchanges were founded in 2010, allowing users to trade bitcoins for legal tender or similar instruments.[252] Late 2010, the value suddenly started going up as bitcoin became

---

243 Finney, H. (2004) "RPOW – Reusable Proofs of Work", *cryptome.org/rpow.htm.*

244 Nakamoto, S. (2008) "Bitcoin: A Peer-to-Peer Electronic Cash System", *bitcoin.org/bitcoin.pdf.*

245 *Ibid.*, 1.

246 *Ibid.*, 2.

247 *Mail-archive.com/cryptography@metzdowd.com/msg10142.html.*

248 *Id.*

249 *Blockchain.info/nl/charts/market-price?timespan=all.*

250 It is generally accepted that Satoshi Nakamoto was a pseudonym for the actual developer – or collective of developers – behind Bitcoin. The many theories regarding the true identity behind the cryptocurrency range from plausible ("it is one of the cryptographers who provided the groundwork for Bitcoin, such as Nick Szabo"), over speculative ("it is one of the earlier adopters of Bitcoin, such as Hal Finney or Gavin Andresen"), to downright paranoid ("Bitcoin is actually a secret surveillance project by the National Security Agency"). See also: Smith, D. (2012) "More Money, More Problems: The Bitcoin Virtual Currency and the Legal Problems that Face It", *Case Western Reserve Journal of Law Technology & The Internet*, vol. 3, 433.

251 Turpin, J. (2014) "Bitcoin: the economic case for a global virtual currency operating in an unexplored legal framework", *Indiana Journal of Global Legal Studies*, Vol. 21, 337.

252 The first exchange was Mt. Gox, which handled over 70% of all bitcoin trades before collapsing late 2013. McMillan, R. Metz, C. (2013) "The rise and fall of the world's largest bitcoin exchange", *Wired*, 6 November 2013. Mt. Gox was soon followed by other exchanges such as OKCoin, BitInstant, Bitstamp, BTC China, and Coinbase.

more widely known, first achieving parity with the US dollar early 2011.[253] 2011 also brought the first market bubble, with the value of one bitcoin going up to USD 32, before falling down again for the remainder of the year and throughout 2012.[254] 2013 saw two major price rallies, with one bringing the value of bitcoin up over USD 200, and the second one briefly bringing the value over USD 1.000, resulting in a total value of the bitcoin system at that point of USD 13 billion. It is also at that stage that bitcoin gained traction in being accepted as a means of payment at online and brick-and-mortar retailers.[255] The main growth factor was the development of Bitcoin payment services, which allow retailers to use an intermediary that accepts payments in bitcoin and immediately converts those bitcoins into legal tender or similar instruments – thus limiting retailers' exposure to value fluctuations.[256] Throughout 2014 and 2015, the value of bitcoin seemed in a gradual decline, with hiccups up and down caused in part by positive and negative news reports on the cryptocurrency. Despite the lower value, the acceptance of bitcoin as a means of payment continued to increase.[257] Throughout 2016, the value again appeared to be in a upwards trend, before dramatically rising up throughout 2017, when it even briefly breached the USD 20.000 mark.[258] Since early 2018, however, the value of bitcoin again went into a downward trajectory.[259]

Further developments – As the technical components behind Bitcoin are open source, other cryptocurrencies have started to emerge since 2011. Some of those cryptocurrencies are largely a copy of the Bitcoin ecosystem – some even being a fork of the latter – such as Bitcoin Cash.[260] Other cryptocurrencies use a different hash algorithm, such as Litecoin and Dogecoin.[261] Most of those alternatives, however, try to provide their own unique angle. Namecoin, for instance, acts

253 Wallace, B. (2011) "The rise and fall of bitcoin", *Wired*, 23 November 2011.

254 *Blockchain.info/nl/charts/market-price?timespan=all.*

255 For instance, bitcoin has at some point been accepted by Overstock, Dell, Expedia, Newegg, Time, and Microsoft. Vaishampayan, S. (2014) "Bitcoin now accepted on Overstock.com through VC-backed Coinbase", MarketWatch, 9 January 2014; Biggs, J. (2014) "Expedia Now Accepts Bitcoin For Your Crypto-Vacations", *TechCrunch*, 11 June 2014; Flacy, M. (2014) "Dell, Newegg start accepting bitcoin as payment", *DigitalTrends*, 19 July 2014; Ember, S. (2014) "Time Inc. Begins Accepting Bitcoin Payments", *New York* Times, 16 December 2014; Warren, T. (2014) "Microsoft now accepts Bitcoin to buy Xbox games and Windows apps", *The Verge*, 11 December 2014.

256 The two major bitcoin payment processors, BitPay and Coinbase, collectively serve over 90,000 businesses. *Bitpay.com, coinbase.com.*

257 As evidenced in footnote 255. However, although the number of retailers accepting bitcoin is increasing, the volume of retail purchases in bitcoin does not seem to grow: Orcutt, M. (2015) "Is Bitcoin Stalling?", *MIT Technology Review*, 18 February 2015.

258 Suberg, W. (2017) "Bitcoin Hits $20,000 Per Coin, Capping Year of Enormous Growth", *Coin Telegraph*, 17 December.

259 Higgins, S. (2018) "Bitcoin's Price Drops Below $10,000 for First Time Since Early December", *CoinDesk*, 17 January.

260 *Coinmarketcap.com/currencies/bitcoin-cash.*

261 *Litecoin.org, dogecoin.com.*

as a decentralized Domain Name System (DNS) server for the .bit top-level domain (TLD).[262] Peercoin does not have a predefined number of units that can be emitted and aims to keep a steady inflation of 1% per year.[263] Dogecoin is considered as a community-based currency, which can be used to tip social media users for worthwhile posts, while also having served for charity purposes.[264] Auroracoin was intended as an alternative to the Icelandic Króna.[265] Darkcoin aims to provide stronger privacy protection than Bitcoin.[266] Ripple aims to act as a bridge between different currencies – legal tender and cryptocurrencies – and commodities, while also offering its own cryptocurrency.[267]

### *3.4.2 Technical aspects*

Step-by-step analysis – Cryptocurrencies differ from the other virtual currencies discussed here by using a particularly advanced cryptographic technology, known as blockchain technology. The following paragraphs will facilitate a correct understanding of that technology, by conducting a step-by-step analysis of how the system functions.[268]

#### 3.4.2.1. Wallets and addresses

Wallets – Cryptocurrencies are managed through online wallets, which can be accessed via web browsers, computer applications or smartphone apps.[269] Those wallets are connected to the P2P network that supports the cryptocurrency, and store unique addresses, each holding a balance of units of cryptocurrency.[270] Such addresses are different from classic bank account identifiers in the sense that users can create a new address for each unique transaction.[271] The reason for this is that cryptocurrency transactions rely on the use of public-key cryptography, also known as asymmetric cryptography.[272] In public-key cryptography, a pair of corresponding

262 *Bit.namecoin.info.*
263 *Peercoin.net.*
264 *Dogecoin.com.*
265 *Auroracoin.org.*
266 *Darkcoin.io.*
267 *Ripple.com.*
268 Based on: Peck, M. (2012) "The cryptoanarchists' answer to cash", *IEEE Spectrum*, June 2012, 51–56.
269 For a list of wallets, see: *bitcoin.org/en/choose-your-wallet.*
270 While there are many different wallets, they all abide by the same underlying source code, lest the Bitcoin network not recognize them. Smith, D. (2012) "More Money, More Problems: The Bitcoin Virtual Currency and the Legal Problems that Face It", *Case Western Reserve Journal of Law Technology & The Internet,* vol. 3, 430; Grinberg, R. (2012) "Bitcoin: An Innovative Alternative Digital Currency", *Hastings Science & Technology Law Journal,* vol. 4, 163.
271 Peck, M. (2012) "The cryptoanarchists' answer to cash", *IEEE Spectrum*, June 2012, 54.
272 Surda, P. (2012) "Economics of Bitcoin: is Bitcoin an alternative to fiat currencies and gold?", *Thesis WU Vienna University of Economics and Business*, 7; Farmer, P. H. Jr. (2014)

keys – one being public and the other being private – is issued, allowing the recipient of a signed message to use the public key to determine that the message was signed by the holder of the corresponding private key.[273] Within a cryptocurrency ecosystem, the addresses function as public keys, with the corresponding private keys stored in the users' wallets.[274] In that sense, the private key attests ownership of the units of cryptocurrency, as a transaction cannot occur without the originating user applying the private key corresponding to the public key that is the address.[275] Also important to note is that most cryptocurrencies can be divided into sub-units. One unit of bitcoin, for instance, can be divided into 100 million satoshis.

Loss – While cryptocurrencies are maintained electronically, it is possible to lose control over units of cryptocurrency. Given the reliance on a private key to use and spend cryptocurrency, the loss of this private key effectively means that the units of cryptocurrency in the wallet associated with that private key become inaccessible. Because these private keys are mostly stored on breakable storage media – such as a hard-drive or USB-drive – the break-down of the storage medium may also result in the loss of the key and thus the associated units of cryptocurrency. One Dutch data recovery company already noted a sharp rise in customers seeking to recover private keys from broken storage media.[276]

### 3.4.2.2. Transactions

Asymmetric cryptography – To transfer a given amount of units of cryptocurrency from party A to party B, party B will first submit the address – being the public key – where he wants to receive the balance of the transaction

"Speculative Tech: The Bitcoin Legal Quagmire & the Need for Legal Innovation", *Journal of Business & Technology Law*, Vol. 9, 89–90.

273 While both keys are different, they are mathematically linked in the sense that a message encrypted by a particular key can only be decrypted by its corresponding key in the pair. This provides non-repudiability. Moreover, it is considered unfeasible to derive a private key from its corresponding public key. That allows public keys to be widely distributed without compromising the security of the key pair. Bollen, R. (2013) "The Legal Status of Online Currencies: Are Bitcoins the Future?", *Journal of Banking and Finance Law and Practice*, vol. 24, nr. 4, 272–293, *papers.ssrn.com/sol3/papers.cfm?abstract_id=2285247*, 6; Plassaras, N. (2014) "Regulating digital currencies: bringing Bitcoin within the reach of the IMF", *Chicago Journal of International law*, Vol. 14, 385.

274 Dion, D. (2013) "I'll gladly trade you two bits on Tuesday for a byte today: Bitcoin, regulating fraud in the e-conomy of hacker-cash", *Journal of Law, Technology & Policy*, 168; Turpin, J. (2014) "Bitcoin: the economic case for a global virtual currency operating in an unexplored legal framework", *Indiana Journal of Global Legal Studies*, Vol. 21, 338.

275 This also means that if a private key is lost, the user can no longer manage the units of cryptocurrency allocated to the corresponding address. Stokes, R. (2012) "Virtual money laundering: the case of Bitcoin and the Linden dollar", *Information & Communications Technology Law*, vol. 21, nr. 3, 224; Surda, P. (2012) "Economics of Bitcoin: is Bitcoin an alternative to fiat currencies and gold?", *Thesis WU Vienna University of Economics and Business*, 7.

276 Data Recovery Nederland (2017) "Data Recovery Nederland haalt voor klant 115 bitcoins terug", *Nieuwsbank*, 18 December.

to party A.[277] Party A will use his wallet to set up the transaction of the agreed balance from one of his own addresses to the address received from party B.[278] The transaction is signed using the private key corresponding to the public key of the originating address.[279] Using that public key, and following the aforementioned principles of asymmetric cryptography, all parties on the cryptocurrency network can verify that the transaction must have been signed by the corresponding private key.

OTHER MEANS OF OBTAINING CRYPTOCURRENCY – Apart from receiving units of cryptocurrency through transactions, there are several other ways to obtain cryptocurrency.[280] One way is to participate in mining operations. As will be explained more elaborately further on, miners that successfully mine a block are automatically rewarded newly created units of cryptocurrency. Cryptocurrency can also be purchased through specialized online exchanges. People could even meet face-to-face in order to electronically transfer cryptocurrency upon physical transfer of cash.

#### 3.4.2.3. Confirmation and blockchain

CONFIRMATION AGAINST DOUBLE-SPENDING – Transactions must be confirmed to prevent double-spending, ensuring that units of cryptocurrency leave the wallet of the sender and are added to the wallet of the receiver.[281] Double-spending is one of the core issues of electronic transactions.[282] While with physical transactions there is a clear and final transfer – thus ending the possession of one party and bringing the transferred item into possession of the other party – this is not the case for electronic transactions. When electronic information is transferred – for instance when e-mailing an electronic document

277 Peck, M. (2012) "The cryptoanarchists' answer to cash", *IEEE Spectrum*, June 2012, 54; Brito, J., Castillo, A. (2013) *Bitcoin: A Primer for Policymakers*, Arlington: George Mason University Mercatus Center, 7.

278 Pflaum, I., Hateley, E. (2014) "A bit of a problem: National and extraterritorial regulation of virtual currency in the age of financial disintermediation", *Georgetown Journal of International Law*, Vol. 45, 1174; Peck, M. (2012) "The cryptoanarchists' answer to cash", *IEEE Spectrum*, June 2012, 54.

279 Pflaum, I., Hateley, E. (2014) "A bit of a problem: National and extraterritorial regulation of virtual currency in the age of financial disintermediation", *Georgetown Journal of International Law*, Vol. 45, 1177.

280 Kaplanov, N. (2012) "Nerdy Money: Bitcoin, the Private Digital Currency, and the Case Against its Regulation", *Loyola Consumer Law Review*, Vol. 25, 121–123; Dion, D. (2013) "I'll gladly trade you two bits on Tuesday for a byte today: Bitcoin, regulating fraud in the e-conomy of hacker-cash", *Journal of Law, Technology & Policy*, 168.

281 Künnapas, K. (2016) "From Bitcoin to Smart Contracts: Legal Revolution or Evolution from the Perspective of de lege ferenda?", In: Kerikmäe, T., Rull, A. (Eds.), *The Future of Law and eTechnologies*, Cham: Springer, 113.

282 Brito, J., Castillo, A. (2013) *Bitcoin: A Primer for Policymakers*, Arlington: George Mason University Mercatus Center, 6.

– the information is essentially copied. Both sender and receiver will then have a copy of the transferred information. This is, of course, an issue for payment transactions, where there should be a final transfer of the electronic currency, and not just a copy. Bitcoin achieves this by recording the earliest transaction and by ignoring subsequent contradicting transactions.[283] Cryptocurrencies timestamp and record all transactions in a public ledger, called the blockchain.[284] As can already be derived from that term, transactions are bundled into blocks, which are subsequently added to the blockchain.[285] Once a transaction has been recorded in the blockchain, it can be considered as confirmed.[286] In the case of Bitcoin, new blocks are added approximately every 10 minutes. Other cryptocurrencies have established faster rates, for instance Litecoin's 2,5 minutes or Dogecoin's 1 minute.

Public ledger and anonymity – The reason why cryptocurrencies are often considered anonymous, or at least pseudonymous, is that while all transactions are publicly recorded, there is principally no verifiable bond between an address and the person behind it.[287] It should be noted, however, that such anonymity is not absolute, and it is possible to derive the identity of the person operating a particular address from its transaction history, or even through that person's public appropriation of an address.[288]

---

283 All transactions are timestamped. Turpin, J. (2014) "Bitcoin: the economic case for a global virtual currency operating in an unexplored legal framework", *Indiana Journal of Global Legal Studies*, Vol. 21, 340; Plassaras, N. (2014) "Regulating digital currencies: bringing Bitcoin within the reach of the IMF", *Chicago Journal of International law*, Vol. 14, 385.

284 Kien-Meng Ly, M. (2014) "Coining Bitcoin's 'legal-bits': examining the regulatory framework for Bitcoin and virtual currencies", *Harvard Journal of Law & Technology*, vol. 27, nr. 2, 590; Pflaum, I., Hateley, E. (2014) "A bit of a problem: National and extraterritorial regulation of virtual currency in the age of financial disintermediation", *Georgetown Journal of International Law*, Vol. 45, 1174.

285 Surda, P. (2012) "Economics of Bitcoin: is Bitcoin an alternative to fiat currencies and gold?", *Thesis WU Vienna University of Economics and Business*, 7.

286 Bollen, R. (2013) "The Legal Status of Online Currencies: Are Bitcoins the Future?", *Journal of Banking and Finance Law and Practice*, vol. 24, nr. 4, 272–293, *papers.ssrn.com/sol3/papers.cfm?abstract_id=2285247*, 10; Dion, D. (2013) "I'll gladly trade you two bits on Tuesday for a byte today: Bitcoin, regulating fraud in the e-conomy of hacker-cash", *Journal of Law, Technology & Policy*, 168.

287 Dion, D. (2013) "I'll gladly trade you two bits on Tuesday for a byte today: Bitcoin, regulating fraud in the e-conomy of hacker-cash", *Journal of Law, Technology & Policy*, 168.

288 For instance, many cryptocurrency users display one of their public keys in e-mail signatures, or in presentations. De Filippi, P. (2014) "Bitcoin: a regulatory nightmare to a libertarian dream", *Internet Policy Review*, vol. 3, nr. 2, 1–2; Turpin, J. (2014) "Bitcoin: the economic case for a global virtual currency operating in an unexplored legal framework", *Indiana Journal of Global Legal Studies*, Vol. 21, 338–339. Moreover, research has shown that an attack aimed at linking Bitcoin addresses to IP addresses is possible even when anonymization techniques are used. Biryukov, A., Khovratovich, D., Pustogarov, I. (2014) "Deanonymisation of Clients in Bitcoin P2P Network", Presented at *ACM Conference on Computer and Communications Security*, 3 November 2014, Scottsdale, Arizona, 15p; Brito, J., Castillo, A. (2013) *Bitcoin: A Primer for Policymakers*, Arlington: George Mason University Mercatus Center, 10–12.

Decentralization – Another important element of the public ledger is that it is not stored centrally, or even administered by a single central entity. In principle, all participants on the network will store a copy of the entire ledger, thus ensuring that it cannot be controlled by a single entity.[289] This makes the blockchain a distributed database, whereby new transactions – once bundled into blocks – are propagated to the entire network. As a result, the blockchain relies on computational trust, rather than on trust in a central party. This notion has been called 'trustless trust', meaning that participants in the network trust in the technology, rather than in other participants.[290] Its lack of a need for a central party is what makes blockchain technology such an interesting innovation.[291] However, the rising interest in so-called private or permissioned blockchains takes away much of that decentralization, as it effectively puts the system under centralized control.[292] Moreover, recent research has shown that also in a public or permissionless blockchain – such as bitcoin or Ethereum – there is a clear move towards centralization, with a very small group of miners controlling over 50% of those networks' hashrates.[293]

Blockchain – As will be explained in the following paragraph, the process of adding a new block to the blockchain requires mathematical computations that imply that altering or withdrawing a transaction recorded in the blockchain requires a re-computation of all subsequently added blocks.[294] As such is unfeasible, transactions are considered as irrevocable once recorded in the blockchain.[295]

---

289 Kaplanov, N. (2012) "Nerdy Money: Bitcoin, the Private Digital Currency, and the Case Against its Regulation", *Loyola Consumer Law Review*, Vol. 25, 117.

290 Finck, M. (2017) "Blockchain Regulation", *Max Planck Institute for Innovation and Competition Research Paper No. 17-13*, 4; Bayern, S. (2014) "Of Bitcoins, independently wealthy software, and the zero-member LLC", *Northwestern University law Review Online*, Vol. 108, 1489.

291 Bayern, S. (2014) "Of Bitcoins, independently wealthy software, and the zero-member LLC", *Northwestern University law Review Online*, Vol. 108, 1487.

292 Finck, M. (2017) "Blockchain Regulation", *Max Planck Institute for Innovation and Competition Research Paper No. 17-13*, 6.

293 Gencer, A. E., Basu, S., Eyal, I., van Renesse, R., Gün Sirer, E. (2018) "Decentralization in Bitcoin and Ethereum Networks", *arxiv.org/pdf/1801.03998.pdf*.

294 See footnote 304.

295 Moreover, if two competing blocks are formed, the system will automatically proceed with the more authoritative block, being the block that is adopted by more nodes in the network than the other block. Bollen, R. (2013) "The Legal Status of Online Currencies: Are Bitcoins the Future?", *Journal of Banking and Finance Law and Practice*, vol. 24, nr. 4, 272–293, *papers.ssrn.com/sol3/papers.cfm?abstract_id=2285247*, 10; Turpin, J. (2014) "Bitcoin: the economic case for a global virtual currency operating in an unexplored legal framework", *Indiana Journal of Global Legal Studies*, Vol. 21, 340; Plassaras, N. (2014) "Regulating digital currencies: bringing Bitcoin within the reach of the IMF", *Chicago Journal of International law*, Vol. 14, 385.

#### 3.4.2.4. Mining

CRYPTOGRAPHIC PROCESS – The process of bundling transactions into a new block to be added to the blockchain is referred to as mining.[296] Miners are cryptocurrency users who use their computer hardware for the purpose of mining.[297] In essence, miners calculate hash values.[298] A cryptographic hash function can derive an alphanumeric string – the hash value – from any given data. Even the slightest change in that data will result in a completely different hash value.[299] Cryptocurrencies use that characteristic to add a specific random number – called a nonce – to the data that is to be hashed.

DIFFICULTY TARGET – Every new block's hash value is the product of the network's hash function applied to the hash value of the previous block, together with the transaction data to be included in the new block and a nonce.[300] This creates what is called a Merkle tree. While hash calculation is a simple task to modern computers, cryptocurrencies require that the resulting hash values must have a specific format. In the case of bitcoin, for instance, the resulting hash value must begin with a predefined number of zeroes.[301] Finding the hash value that corresponds to that format serves as proof-of-work. In practice, this means that miners must try out a different nonce until they have found that particular nonce that will result in the hash value corresponding to the required format. That format is the difficulty target, which can be adjusted to make finding the right nonce easier or harder.[302] In the case of Bitcoin, the difficulty target is

---

296 De Filippi, P. (2014) "Bitcoin: a regulatory nightmare to a libertarian dream", *Internet Policy Review*, vol. 3, nr. 2, 1; Pflaum, I., Hateley, E. (2014) "A bit of a problem: National and extraterritorial regulation of virtual currency in the age of financial disintermediation", *Georgetown Journal of International Law*, Vol. 45, 1175.

297 Kien-Meng Ly, M. (2014) "Coining Bitcoin's 'legal-bits': examining the regulatory framework for Bitcoin and virtual currencies", *Harvard Journal of Law & Technology*, vol. 27, nr. 2, 590; Pflaum, I., Hateley, E. (2014) "A bit of a problem: National and extraterritorial regulation of virtual currency in the age of financial disintermediation", *Georgetown Journal of International Law*, Vol. 45, 1175.

298 Peck, M. (2012) "The cryptoanarchists' answer to cash", *IEEE Spectrum*, June 2012, 56; Twomey, P. (2013) "Halting a shift in the paradigm: the need for Bitcoin regulation", *Trinity College Law Review*, Vol. 16, 68.

299 Implying that every hash value is unique to the precise data from which it was derived. Moreover, hash calculations must be irreversible, meaning that despite having the hash value and knowing the hash function used, it should be impossible to reverse the calculation to derive the original data.

300 Note that different cryptocurrencies may use different hash functions. Bitcoin, for instance uses the SHA-256d algorithm, while Dogecoin uses scrypt.

301 Pflaum, I., Hateley, E. (2014) "A bit of a problem: National and extraterritorial regulation of virtual currency in the age of financial disintermediation", *Georgetown Journal of International Law*, Vol. 45, 1178; Twomey, P. (2013) "Halting a shift in the paradigm: the need for Bitcoin regulation", *Trinity College Law Review*, Vol. 16, 69.

302 The resulting hash value must be smaller than the set difficulty target, hence the number of zeroes. The accomplishment of finding that smaller value serves as proof of work that

adjusted to maintain that a new block is added every 10 minutes.[303] As noted, it is precisely such calculation that provides security to the network: as each new block includes the hash value of the previous block, changing or withdrawing a transaction included in an earlier block requires that and all subsequent blocks to be recalculated.[304] The result of this is that the further back in the blockchain a particular block is located, the more secure it becomes. After all, any subsequent block added makes it more difficult to alter the blocks that came before it.

PROFITABILITY – The speed at which miners can calculate the right hash value determines the profitability of their mining activities. When a miner has successfully calculated a new block, a predefined number of new units of cryptocurrency is created and awarded to that miner.[305] This means that the creation of new units of cryptocurrency is not subject to a policy decision by a central government – as is the case for fiat currency – but hardcoded into the underlying algorithm of the blockchain. The amount of that reward generally decreases over time. For instance, in the case of bitcoin there was an original reward of 50 units, later halvened to 25, and again to 12,5. The Bitcoin protocol dictates that this halving of rewards occurs after every 210.000 blocks.[306] Of course, if the value of the cryptocurrency rises, the lower amount of units issued to miners should still be more valuable than what they received before. For instance, 50 units of bitcoin received in 2010 were – at that time – not worth quite as much as 12,5 units received in 2017. The reward of new units of cryptocurrency may even be scrapped altogether. In the case of bitcoin, for instance, there is a built-in cap of 21 million units, meaning that no new units are created after those 21 million have been distributed. Furthermore, it is possible to give a tip to miners, as a form of transaction fee. Such transaction fees are swiftly becoming a major source of income to miners. When a cryptocurrency

---

the required calculations have been conducted. Pflaum, I., Hateley, E. (2014) "A bit of a problem: National and extraterritorial regulation of virtual currency in the age of financial disintermediation", *Georgetown Journal of International Law*, Vol. 45, 1178; Turpin, J. (2014) "Bitcoin: the economic case for a global virtual currency operating in an unexplored legal framework", *Indiana Journal of Global Legal Studies*, Vol. 21, 341.

303 Plassaras, N. (2014) "Regulating digital currencies: bringing Bitcoin within the reach of the IMF", *Chicago Journal of International law*, Vol. 14, 385; Surda, P. (2012) "Economics of Bitcoin: is Bitcoin an alternative to fiat currencies and gold?", *Thesis WU Vienna University of Economics and Business*, 8; Brito, J., Castillo, A. (2013) *Bitcoin: A Primer for Policymakers*, Arlington: George Mason University Mercatus Center, 9.

304 Pflaum, I., Hateley, E. (2014) "A bit of a problem: National and extraterritorial regulation of virtual currency in the age of financial disintermediation", *Georgetown Journal of International Law*, Vol. 45, 1178.

305 Peck, M. (2012) "The cryptoanarchists' answer to cash", *IEEE Spectrum*, June 2012, 56; Pflaum, I., Hateley, E. (2014) "A bit of a problem: National and extraterritorial regulation of virtual currency in the age of financial disintermediation", *Georgetown Journal of International Law*, Vol. 45, 1179.

306 Farmer, P. H. Jr. (2014) "Speculative Tech: The Bitcoin Legal Quagmire & the Need for Legal Innovation", *Journal of Business & Technology Law*, Vol. 9, 87–88.

has a built-in cap, as is the case for bitcoin, transaction fees will at one point even become the sole income of miners. Transaction fees will be further discussed in the next section, on the economic aspects of cryptocurrencies.

MINING COSTS – As mining activity increases – and rewards decrease – the mining difficulty of many cryptocurrencies has gone up to a level unattainable for consumer hardware. Purchasing more advanced hardware specifically suited for mining operations is therefore needed to participate in this activity. Most miners have therefore opted to pool their resources, in order to conduct mining operations as a single mining pool. In such case, the computing operations can be broken up in more manageable chunks and rewards are shared by all participants in the mining pool.[307] Moreover, such mining operations consume a lot of energy to both power and cool the hardware. By one estimate made late 2017, the bitcoin network was well on its way to consume as much energy annually as the entire country of Denmark.[308] The large costs of hardware and energy have resulted in many mining operations moving to countries where such operations are cheaper, such as China or Iceland.[309] An additional cost concerns data. In principle, all participants on the network store a copy of the entire blockchain, which means that a lot of data is moved between all nodes on the network. In the case of bitcoin, the blockchain size as of early 2018 is almost 150 GB.[310] With net neutrality rules still under debate in some parts of the world, that data could become more costly, or even be throttled.[311]

#### 3.4.2.5. Other applications

PRIVATE CORPORATE BONDS – The core application of the blockchain technology is of course cryptocurrencies. As noted before, the success of bitcoin has spawned several imitations – some more successful than others. Another form of implementation is the issuance of a private corporate bond using this technology.[312] Essentially, such allows blockchain technology based security markets to compete with traditional exchanges such as NASDAQ and NYSE. NASDAQ itself has also been exploring the use of blockchain technology for

307 Kaplanov, N. (2012) "Nerdy Money: Bitcoin, the Private Digital Currency, and the Case Against its Regulation", *Loyola Consumer Law Review*, Vol. 25, 120.

308 Lee, T. B. (2017) "Bitcoin's insane energy consumption, explained", *Ars Technica*, 6 December.

309 China has a fast-growing market in cheap electronics, as well as access to cheap hydroelectronic energy. Iceland has cheap geothermal energy and a cold climate that makes cooling costless.

310 *Blockchain.info/nl/charts/blocks-size.*

311 Pearson, J. (2017) "The End of Net Neutrality Means ISPs Could Crack Down on Cryptocurrencies", *Vice*, 27 November.

312 As planned by Overstock: Metz, C. (2015) "Overstock Will Issue a Private Bond Powered by Bitcoin Tech", *Wired*, 5 June 2015. In essence, the bond will be broken up into different tokens, which can be traded over a blockchain powered platform.

private trading platforms[313], while NYSE developed a bitcoin index.[314] Also traditional banks have been experimenting with the technology.[315]

Record-keeping – The core functionality of the blockchain technology in recording its transactions could also be applied to other purposes. The blockchain could, for instance, store interests in particular assets, or encrypted records.[316] Moreover, as existing cryptocurrency protocols support the inclusion of text within their transactions, it can be argued that such could be used to include identification numbers relating to securities or commodities – such as gold – thus allowing cryptocurrency networks to trade securities, or enact other complex financial transactions.[317]

Turing-complete contracts – It can even be argued that the blockchain system could be further developed into an autonomous business entity, managed not by people but by its underlying software.[318] One of such implementations focuses on self-executing smart contracts, drafted in a Turing-complete programming language.[319] In essence, such a platform allows users to apply the blockchain technology to register contracts, enact voting systems, etc.[320] One notable use case is The DAO, which will be discussed more elaborately in chapters VI and VII.

Going beyond finance – In recent years, blockchain technology has become one of the biggest buzzwords in the technology sector. New use cases for the technology are developed on almost a daily basis. Most of those use cases also go beyond blockchain's origins in the financial sector. By now, it has become difficult to imagine a single sector in which blockchain use cases are not being developed. To give a few examples: Air France is testing the technology for supply chain tracking[321]; the use of blockchain in issuing university degrees[322]; applications

---

313 Metz, C. (2015) "Bitcoin May Never Make It to Wall Street, But Its Tech Will", *Wired,* 12 May 2015; Hern, A. (2015) "Nasdaq bets on bitcoin's blockchain as the future of finance", *The Guardian,* 13 May 2015.

314 Intercontinental Exchange (2015) "NYSE to Launch NYSE Bitcoin Index, NYXBT", *Business Wire,* 19 May 2015.

315 Biggs, J. (2015) "Citibank Is Working On Its Own Digital Currency, Citicoin", *TechCrunch,* 7 July 2015.

316 Pflaum, I., Hateley, E. (2014) "A bit of a problem: National and extraterritorial regulation of virtual currency in the age of financial disintermediation", *Georgetown Journal of International Law,* Vol. 45, 1181.

317 *Ibid.*, 1180.

318 Bayern, S. (2014) "Of Bitcoins, independently wealthy software, and the zero-member LLC", *Northwestern University law Review Online*, Vol. 108, 1485–1500.

319 *Ethereum.org.*

320 *Github.com/ethereum/wiki/wiki/White-Paper.*

321 Higgins, S. (2017) "Air France Tests Blockchain for Supply Chain Tracking", *CoinDesk,* 5 October.

322 Haig, S. (2017) "MIT to Issue Diplomas Using Bitcoin Blockchain", *Bitcoin.com,* 22 October.

are being developed to manage IP rights on blockchains[323]; blockchain could support firms in complying with maritime insurance requirements.[324] Blockchain technology could then be considered as a foundational technology, having the potential to create new paradigms in existing fields.[325] However, given the focus on virtual currencies, other blockchain use cases remain outside the scope of this research.

### *3.4.3 Economic aspects*

USES AND RISKS – Apart from understanding the technicalities of cryptocurrencies, it is also worthwhile to look at cryptocurrencies from a more economic perspective. Apart from a few more general economic concerns regarding cryptocurrencies, this section will also address the potential for the use of cryptocurrencies in a fractional-reserve banking system, as well as the potential future risk posed by mining activities.

#### 3.4.3.1. Economics of cryptocurrencies

NO SINGULAR PURPOSE – Cryptocurrencies are different from the other forms of virtual currencies discussed here in the sense that they do not necessarily serve a singular purpose. While virtual currencies in loyalty programs serve as a reward for consumer behavior and an incentive for future purchases, cryptocurrency users often obtain their virtual currencies for no particular reason.[326] While virtual currencies in games serve to advance within the virtual world in which they operate, cryptocurrencies could be used to obtain goods and services, but are just as likely to be stored without purpose.

ALTERNATIVE PAYMENT METHOD – More fundamentally, cryptocurrencies are conceived as a potential alternative to legal tender and the institutionalized payment systems in which legal tender operates. However, while the issuance of legal tender is subjected to strict monetary policies – which in turn operate subject to various economic theories and indicators – the supply of cryptocurrencies is controlled by nothing else than what the person that wrote its source code decided upon. While the question of whether cryptocurrencies constitute that what is generally referred to as 'money' will be examined more closely in chapter III, it can be stated here that cryptocurrencies have succeeded

323 Del Castillo, M. (2017) "Fight for Your Right: Universal Music Veteran Launches Ethereum IP Platform", *CoinDesk*, 5 October.

324 O'Leary, R. R. (2017) "Shipping Giant Maersk to Deploy Blockchain Maritime Insurance Solution", *CoinDesk*, 6 September.

325 Iansiti, M., Lakhani, K. R. (2017) "The Truth About Blockchain", *Harvard Business Review*, January-February, 118–127.

326 For instance, in the case of dogecoin, units of this cryptocurrency are often donated as tips.

in functioning as a form of payment. As noted, the acceptance of bitcoin continues to spread, both in the physical world and in virtual worlds.

Inelasticity – One particular aspect of certain cryptocurrencies – such as bitcoin – is their supply inelasticity.[327] That can be argued to result in inherent deflation, whereby the value of the cryptocurrency increases due to its scarcity, for as long as the cryptocurrency's economy keeps growing.[328] It can, however, also be argued that the fact that such inelasticity is known on beforehand could offset the adverse consequences of deflation.[329]

No inherent value – Another criticism of cryptocurrencies is that they have no inherent value. After all, they are not backed by valuable assets or commodities – such as gold – nor are they backed by a central government – as fiat money is. That point is puzzling because it is unclear why anyone would accept cryptocurrencies as payment if they have no value, yet the relative success of cryptocurrencies demonstrates that somehow those virtual currencies have managed to secure actual value.[330] Ludwig von Mises, for instance, found that anything that is used as if it were money should have "*an objective exchange-value based on some other use*" prior to it being used as money.[331] That theory, also referred to as Mises' Regression Theorem, holds that there should always be a source of value, generally in the form of a commodity, thus refuting the application of a fictitious value on things that are intrinsically valueless.[332] An important part of the theory is that von Mises views money's purchasing power over time: people know that their money had value before and therefore currently expect their money to still hold value in the future.[333] Here, it can be argued that the original demand for cryptocurrencies stems from their link with legal tender: a demand for cryptocurrencies "*created from a non-exchange demand by employing established fiat monies*".[334] However, while it can indeed be said that such a demand has given way to the growth of cryptocurrencies, it does not provide an origin of value in the sense of Mises' Regression Theorem. As a result, cryptocurrencies seem to defy that theory, thus spurring further confusion.[335]

---

327 Bitcoin is capped at 21 million units.

328 R.A. (2014) "Bitcoin's deflation problem", *The Economist*, 3 April 2014.

329 Simonite, T. (2011) "What Bitcoin Is, and Why It Matters", *MIT Technology Review*, 25 May 2011.

330 Dowd, K. (2014) *New Private Monies*, London: The Institute of Economic Affairs, 44–45.

331 Von Mises, L. (1953) *The theory of Money and Credit*, New Haven: Yale University Press, 110.

332 *Id.*

333 *Ibid.*, 111.

334 Ólafsson, Í. (2014) "Is bitcoin money? An analysis from the Austrian school of economic thought", *Thesis University of Iceland Department of Economics*, 37.

335 *Ibid.*, 38. Here, Ólafsson attempts to reconcile the position of cryptocurrencies and the Regression Theorem by holding that if a medium of exchange has price and liquidity, it can sustain itself in its form as medium of exchange. In the case of cryptocurrencies, price could be determined by their link to legal tender, as this fits under the Regression Theorem.

Calculating value and cost – How can the value of cryptocurrencies be determined? One argument is that the value of cryptocurrencies can be determined as being the marginal production cost of one unit of cryptocurrency, with added value for its general credibility on the market.[336] Under that reasoning, the production cost would be considered as referring to the cost of mining – namely the purchase of the right equipment and the energy used.[337] As the cost of mining grows due to increasing mining difficulty, the value of cryptocurrencies grows correspondingly. However, this argument would effectively create a distinction between units of cryptocurrency depending on where they were mined. For instance, bitcoin mined in the US would be more valuable – given the higher equipment and energy costs – than bitcoin mined in China. This is, of course, not reflected in reality. It has, for instance, been argued that cash has a higher social and private cost than debit cards, but this does not mean that EUR 5 in cash is more valuable than EUR 5 on a debit account.[338] More closer to the truth is then perhaps that we still do not really know what exactly drives the value of cryptocurrencies. On the demand side, the last few years have regularly seen growing media attention resulting in a significant rise in cryptocurrency values. Negative reports on cryptocurrencies – the shutdown of a cryptocurrency exchange, theft of cryptocurrencies, or negative opinions from government actors – have often, but not always, resulted in dramatic value losses.[339] While the supply of most cryptocurrencies is fairly constant or at least predictable, their demand remains the unpredictable factor that makes future market developments unclear.[340] Moreover, inelastic supply, relatively low adoption, and bubble-bust cycles remain three possible causes of price instability.[341]

Volatility – The price volatility of cryptocurrencies has also raised the criticism that cryptocurrencies are Ponzi schemes.[342] While it is true that the volatility of cryptocurrency prices presents a particular investor risk, such does

---

336 Iwamura, M., Kitamura, Y., Matsumoto, T. (2014) "Is Bitcoin the Only Cryptocurrency in the Town? Economics of Cryptocurrency and Friedrich A. Hayek", *Hitotsubashi University Institute of Economic Research Discussion Paper 602*, 5.

337 Ólafsson, Í. (2014) "Is bitcoin money? An analysis from the Austrian school of economic thought", *Thesis University of Iceland Department of Economics*, 40.

338 Schmiedel, H., Kostova, G. L., Ruttenberg, W. (2012) "The Social and Private Costs of Retail Payment Instruments: A European Perspective", *ECB Occasional Paper No. 137.*

339 For an overview of price flows in bitcoin's first years and their link to outside events: Grushack, J. (2014) "Currency 3.0: examining digital crypto currency markets", *Master thesis Union College*, 10–14.

340 Dowd, K. (2014) *New Private Monies*, London: The Institute of Economic Affairs, 58–59.

341 *Ibid.*, 59.

342 Roubini, N. (2014) "Bitcoin isn't a currency", *Twitter*, 9 March 2014; European Central Bank (2012) "Virtual Currency Schemes", *ecb.europa.eu*, 27; Trugman, J. (2014) "Welcome to 21st-century Ponzi scheme: Bitcoin", *New York Post*, 15 February 2014; Ummelas, O., Seputyte, M. (2014) "Bitcoin 'Ponzi' Concern Sparks Warning From Estonia Bank", *Bloomberg*, 31 January 2014; Bennington, A. (2017) "Bitcoin Bear Peter Schiff Doubles Down: Even at $4,000 It's Still a 'Bubble'", *CoinDesk*, 17 August.

not necessarily indicate the presence of an actual Ponzi scheme. Alternatively, it has been argued – for instance by JP Morgan Chase CEO Jamie Dimon[343], Nouriel Roubini[344], and Warren Buffet[345] – that the volatility of cryptocurrency prices are typical of speculative bubbles.[346] In that sense, cryptocurrencies could be compared to a *"collective delusion"*, rather than fraud.[347] Moreover, cryptocurrencies do not inherently promise positive returns on investments, as is the case in Ponzi schemes.[348] Furthermore, Ponzi schemes typically rely on a central operator, who is absent in decentralized systems such as cryptocurrencies.[349] Also services relying on cryptocurrencies can come at a risk. Early 2018, news broke that Visa had terminated its collaboration with card-issuer WaveCrest.[350] As a result, all cards issued by the latter company became unusable. WaveCrest-issued cards were used by several cryptocurrency service providers that convert their users' cryptocurrency balances into e-money values, which are loaded onto prepaid Visa cards. However, in this particular case, WaveCrest assured its clients that – being a registered e-money institution – all funds were safeguarded against losses.[351] Moreover, Visa confirmed that the termination of its collaboration with WaveCrest was due to WaveCrest's violations of Visa's operating rules, rather than being targeted specifically at cryptocurrency services.[352]

#### 3.4.3.2. Cryptocurrencies and fractional-reserve banking

FRACTIONAL-RESERVE BANKING – While the supply of legal tender is principally controlled by the emitting state, there are also other ways in which the money supply has come to grow. One of those is fractional-reserve banking. Fractional-reserve banking occurs when banks use the deposits they receive from their clients – minus the part they are required to keep as reserve – to create new

343 Higgins, S. (2017) "Jamie Dimon: Bitcoin Is a 'Fraud'", *CoinDesk*, 12 September. See also: Rogoff, K. (2017) "Bitcoin's price bubble will burst under government pressure", *The Guardian*, 9 October.

344 Zhao, W. (2017) "'Dr. Doom' Roubini Joins Wall Street Chorus Calling Bitcoin a Bubble", *CoinDesk*, 8 November.

345 De, N. (2017) "'A Real Bubble': Billionaire Warren Buffett Doubles Down on Bitcoin Doubt", *CoinDesk*, 26 October.

346 Basu, K. (2014) "Ponzis: the science and mystique of a class of financial frauds", *World Bank Policy Research Working Paper WPS6967*, 6–7.

347 Posner, E. (2013) "Fool's Gold", *Slate*, 11 April 2013.

348 Swiss Federal Council (2014) "Report on virtual currencies in response to the Schwaab (13.3687) and Weibel (13.4070) postulates", *news.admin.ch*, 25 June 2014, 21.

349 Mather, J. (2013) "Ponzi logic: debunking Gary North", *The Libertarian Standard*, 1 December 2013.

350 Nova, A. (2018) "Some cryptocurrency-backed debit cards dropped from Visa network, leaving users scrambling", *CNBC*, 5 January.

351 *Id.*

352 Hughes, M. (2018) "Multiple Bitcoin debit card providers suspend service under orders of Visa", *TheNextWeb*, 5 January.

credit or to make loans.[353] The main principle behind that practice is that it is unlikely that all clients would come to withdraw their full deposits at the same time, and that therefore banks do not need to keep those deposits in full.[354] The depositor will hold a claim on the bank – in the form of a demand deposit – for the total amount of his deposit. The bank's action of putting part of that deposit back into circulation can therefore essentially increase the total money supply.[355]

No deposits – Fractional-reserve banking has since long been a common practice in banking, but it is less clear whether the practice could be applied to cryptocurrencies. At its most basic form, it could be argued that fractional-reserve banking would be unlikely to develop for cryptocurrencies, as those virtual currencies inherently have no direct need for depositing.[356] Without constant and stable deposits, banks would not be able to conduct fractional-reserve banking.

Need for secondary system – Moreover, as all cryptocurrency transactions are principally recorded in a public ledger, it would essentially require banks to create a separate transfer system in which all secondary transactions – being the loans and investments made against the cryptocurrency deposits – are recorded.[357] Additionally, the substitutes resulting from that practice would need to be widely accepted in order to have practical use.[358] Here, reference can be made to the economic theories of von Mises and Rothbard, holding that demand deposits can be considered as part of the money supply, for as long as they are accepted as if they were functionally equivalent to money.[359] Therefore, it can be held that the debt instruments based on cryptocurrency deposits that result from fractional-reserve banking would need to be widely accepted as if they were legal tender in order to be considered as affecting the money supply.[360] Given

---

353 Clients' accounts are credited with the amount of the deposit, with the bank guaranteeing that the full amount of that deposit can be withdrawn at any time.

354 When such event does happen – what is referred to as a 'bank run' – the bank in question will likely default on its obligations.

355 Murphy, R. (2010) "The fractional-reserve banking question", *Mises Daily*, 14 June 2010.

356 Unlike legal tender, cryptocurrencies have no direct need for safekeeping, nor do they need to be converted into balances on bank accounts for usability purposes. Surda, P. (2012) "Economics of Bitcoin: is Bitcoin an alternative to fiat currencies and gold?", *Thesis WU Vienna University of Economics and Business*, 46.

357 Sankowski, M. (2013) "Bitcoins, Fractional Reserve Banking, and Private Currencies", *monetaryrealism.com*, 2 May 2013. The main reason why such separate network would be needed is because no individual can create cryptocurrencies at will, as their emission is fully controlled by the network's underlying algorithm.

358 By existing separately from the core cryptocurrency network, these substitutes cannot be used within that network. They can therefore only be traded on their own separate network.

359 Rothbard, M. (1978) "Austrian Definitions of the Supply of Money", In: Spadaro, L. (ed.) *New Directions in Austrian Economics*, Kansas City: Sheed Andrews and McMeel, 145. In his work, Rothbard expands on the works of von Mises.

360 Ólafsson, Í. (2014) "Is bitcoin money? An analysis from the Austrian school of economic thought", *Thesis University of Iceland Department of Economics*, 61.

the current relatively limited acceptance of cryptocurrencies, it would therefore from a practical viewpoint seem unlikely for cryptocurrency fractional-reserve banking to occur at this point in time.

Regulatory limitations – Moreover, upcoming legislative initiatives to regulate cryptocurrencies may just downright prohibit this practice.[361] Imposing a 100% reserve requirement would effectively preclude the development of cryptocurrency fractional-reserve banking.

### 3.4.3.3. Mining risk

Importance of mining – One potential risk inherent to cryptocurrencies lies in their very foundation: mining. As noted in discussing the technicalities of cryptocurrencies, mining is what drives the blockchain technology. It is this activity that processes the transactions into blocks, thus confirming them and providing proof of said transactions, as well as protection against double-spending.

Risks – However, as the difficulty of mining increases, more advanced and expensive hardware is required, as well as energy to power and cool that hardware. Second, while the value of cryptocurrencies continues to fluctuate, it is not unimaginable that the value would become stuck in a downward trend.[362] Third, the reward for mining – the issuance of new units of cryptocurrency – continues to decrease by definition, and may in some cryptocurrencies even cease altogether.[363] The result is that the cost of mining continues to grow, whereas its returns inherently continue to decrease. The seeming lack of long-term profitability of the mining activity could therefore pose an existential threat to cryptocurrencies.[364]

Transaction fees – In theory, cryptocurrencies have a solution for the issue: transaction fees. Already now, it is possible to provide a small fee, or tip, to the miner who processes the transaction.[365] It is clear that such transaction

---

361 For instance, the New York State Department of Financial Services rules on virtual currency businesses (see footnote 134) require the persons licensed to engage in virtual currency business activities (licensees) to "*hold virtual currency of the same type and amount as that which is owed or obligated*", and prohibits licensees from otherwise encumbering customer assets. 23 CRR-NY s200.9. See also: Levine, M. (2014) "Bitcoin Banking Will Be Boring", *Bloomberg*, 17 July 2014.

362 See, for instance, the chart for bitcoin on *coinmarketcap.com/currencies/bitcoin*. Between 2014 and 2016, the value of bitcoin remained fairly stable at a lower price point.

363 Bitcoin has a build-in cap of 21 million units, meaning that no new units of bitcoin are issued when that cap is reached. Peercoin, on the other hand, does not have a hardcoded cap, but is designed to maintain a 1% inflation per year. Also dogecoin does not have a hardcoded cap.

364 Kroll, J., Davey, I., Felten, E. (2013) "The Economics of Bitcoin Mining, or Bitcoin in the Presence of Adversaries", Presented at *The Twelfth Workshop on the Economics of Information Security (WEIS 2013)*, Washington, DC, 11–12 June, 8.

365 *Bitcoin.org/en/faq#how-much-will-the-transaction-fee-be.*

fees will only become a more important incentive for miners. The reason is that, as miners can choose which transactions they will process into a block, they are likely to cherry-pick the transactions rewarding the highest transaction fees.[366] Especially if a particular miner were to hold a significant percentage of the total mining power, it would essentially gain the power to determine which transactions are to be processed.[367] That means that miners could theoretically start imposing transactions fees, with users risking that their transactions will not be picked up if they do not comply.[368] In December 2017, that practice resulted in users having to pay an overage transaction fee of over USD 20 per transaction in order to ensure processing of their transaction.[369]

Invalid blocks – Another risk posed by the practice of mining is the creation of invalid blocks. As the Bitcoin protocol is continuously maintained and further developed, there is a possibility of some miners using outdated software. The result is that a fork could occur, in which two concurring networks are established that each recognize different blocks. That already occurred in 2013 and caused a market panic with a significant drop in bitcoin trading prices.[370] It occurred again in 2015, when a small miner using outdated software mined an invalid block and subsequent blocks were added to that block, thus causing a risk for double-spending.[371]

---

366 Pflaum, I., Hateley, E. (2014) "A bit of a problem: National and extraterritorial regulation of virtual currency in the age of financial disintermediation", *Georgetown Journal of International Law*, Vol. 45, 1179.

367 This has become a concern as miners are increasingly combining their computing power into mining pools. One of such pools, GHash.IO, has already reached over 51% of all Bitcoin mining power on several occasions, thus essentially centralizing the control over the decentralized network. While GHash.IO has pledged to take measures to prevent its mining power to go over 40% of the Bitcoin network's total, the blockchain technology does not provide a reliable verification of whether such pledge is honored, nor any means to enforce it. Bershidsky, L. (2014) "Trust Will Kill Bitcoin", *Bloomberg*, 17 July 2014. The problem of such so-called 51%-attack is also discussed in: Kroll, J., Davey, I., Felten, E. (2013) "The Economics of Bitcoin Mining, or Bitcoin in the Presence of Adversaries", Presented at *The Twelfth Workshop on the Economics of Information Security (WEIS 2013)*, Washington, DC, 11–12 June, 11–12.

368 While Kroll *et al.* do not directly fear such scenario to unfold under the Bitcoin system's current rules, they do find that new rules would need to be agreed upon to preserve the system's viability. Kroll, J., Davey, I., Felten, E. (2013) "The Economics of Bitcoin Mining, or Bitcoin in the Presence of Adversaries", Presented at *The Twelfth Workshop on the Economics of Information Security (WEIS 2013)*, Washington, DC, 11–12 June, 16–17.

369 *Bitinfocharts.com/comparison/bitcoin-transactionfees.html;* Lee, T. B. (2017) "Bitcoin fees are skyrocketing", *Ars Technica*, 11 December.

370 Lee, T. (2013) "Major glitch in Bitcoin network sparks sell-off; price temporarily falls 23%", *Ars Technica*, 12 March 2013.

371 Rizzo, P. (2015) "Double Spending Risk Remains After July 4th Bitcoin Fork", *Coindesk*, 6 July 2015.

# 4 TYPOLOGY

Need for a typology – In acknowledgment of the broad range of rather divergent virtual currencies currently in the market, this research will adopt a typology. Grouping different virtual currencies into a limited number of basic types can easier identify and accommodate their inherent differences as well as commonalities. For instance, when later on in this research assessing whether the current EU legal frameworks on e-money or payment services can apply, it could be possible that those frameworks can apply to certain types of virtual currencies, but not to others. Establishing a typology therefore allows to adopt a differentiated approach where needed, as it may not be possible or even desirable to subject all virtual currencies to the same principles.

The ECB's typology – The ECB has already established a typology of virtual currencies.[372] The determining principle behind that typology is the money flow between virtual currencies and legal tender or similar instruments in the physical-world economy, which occurs through currency exchanges and through the possibility to use the virtual currencies to obtain physical goods and services.[373]

Applying the typology – This section will first present the ECB's typology as the starting point for the typology analysis. Subsequently, it will analyze whether the ECB's typology can cover the range of practical examples of virtual currencies analyzed in the previous section.

## 4.1 THE ECB'S TYPOLOGY OF VIRTUAL CURRENCIES

### *4.1.1 Closed schemes*

No interaction with physical-world economy – The first type identified by the ECB concerns closed scheme virtual currencies. Those virtual currency schemes principally have no interaction with the physical-world economy.[374] In essence, this means that (1) the virtual currency cannot be obtained with legal tender or similar instruments, (2) the virtual currency cannot be exchanged into legal tender or similar instruments, and (3) the virtual currency cannot be used to obtain physical-world goods and services. Consequently, there is no money flow between the physical-world economy and the virtual realm in which the

---

372 European Central Bank (2012) "Virtual Currency Schemes", *ecb.europa.eu*, 13–16.

373 *Ibid.*, 13. The ECB makes a clear distinction between the online virtual realm and the physical reality. That distinction will be followed here as the interaction between those two realms provides the basis for the typology.

374 *Id.*

virtual currency operates. This type of virtual currency is also referred to as a fictional currency.[375]

CONFINED TO VIRTUAL ECONOMY – Generally, those closed scheme virtual currencies are regarded as being confined to a virtual economy, often in the context of a game. In that case, players obtain the virtual currency through their actions within the game. Participation in the game itself can be either free or paid, but legal tender or similar instruments cannot be used for financial gain within the game.[376] Likewise, the virtual currency can only be used to obtain goods or services within the virtual economy of the game.[377]

#### 4.1.2 *Unidirectional schemes*

NO FULL INTERCHANGEABILITY – The second type of virtual currency schemes defined by the ECB concerns unidirectional schemes. Those schemes are characterized by the fact that their virtual currency can be obtained with legal tender or similar instruments, yet without full interchangeability between those two. As a result, under unidirectional schemes (1) virtual currency can be obtained with legal tender or similar instruments, (2) the virtual currency cannot be exchanged back into legal tender or similar instruments, and (3) the virtual currency can be used to obtain physical-world goods and services as well as virtual goods or services. In this case, there is a possible money flow from the physical-world economy into the virtual economy. There is, however, no direct money flow from the virtual currency to legal tender or similar instruments. Because of that, virtual currencies operating under this type of scheme are also referred to as closed loop virtual currencies.[378] Moreover, those virtual currencies are not necessarily confined to use within a closed virtual economy.

NEED FOR AN EXCHANGE RATE – In order to allow the exchange of legal tender or similar instruments into virtual currency, there must be an exchange rate defined. Normally, it is the operator of the virtual currency scheme who

---

375 Korolov, M. (2012) "Virtual currency 101", *hypergridbusiness.com/2012/07/virtual-currency-101*; as referenced in: Selldahl, S. (2013) "Virtual currencies – Real opportunities?", *Master thesis KTH Industrial Engineering and Management*, 19–21. The GAO has referred to these as 'closed flow' schemes. GAO (2013) "Virtual Economies and Currencies", *GAO-13-516*, 4.

376 As was further elaborated on in section 3.2, there is a possibility that a black market is created that allows players to use legal tender or similar instruments to obtain the in-game virtual currency. Such practices, however, are generally not condoned and are a violation of the end-user license agreements (EULA).

377 Also here, where a player accepts legal tender or similar instruments for in-game virtual currency, such would be in violation of the EULA.

378 Korolov, M. (2012) "Virtual currency 101", *hypergridbusiness.com/2012/07/virtual-currency-101*; as referenced in: Selldahl, S. (2013) "Virtual currencies – Real opportunities?", *Master thesis KTH Industrial Engineering and Management*, 19–20. The GAO refers to these as 'hybrid systems'. GAO (2013) "Virtual Economies and Currencies", *GAO-13-516*, 4–5.

determines such an exchange rate.[379] Also in the unidirectional type of scheme, in-game currencies are a prime example.[380] The ECB also considers certain loyalty schemes to fall under the scope of the unidirectional type of virtual currency scheme. More in particular, the ECB held that air miles in frequent flyer programs can be considered as a unidirectional virtual currency as they can be purchased directly with legal tender or similar instruments – apart from being earned by booking flights – but cannot be exchanged back into legal tender or similar instruments, and because they can be used to obtain physical-world goods and services.[381]

#### *4.1.3 Bidirectional schemes*

Fully interchangeable – The last type of virtual currency schemes identified by the ECB are the bidirectional schemes, which allow full interchangeability. As a result, under a bidirectional scheme (1) virtual currency can be obtained with legal tender or similar instruments, (2) the virtual currency can also be exchanged back into legal tender or similar instruments, and (3) the virtual currency can be used to obtain physical-world goods and services as well as virtual goods or services. Here, there is a perfect monetary flow from legal tender or similar instruments into virtual currencies and *vice versa*. This can also be referred to as an open loop scheme.[382] The virtual currency is also not confined to use within a virtual economy.

Need for an exchange rate – Also here an exchange rate is established between the virtual currency and legal tender or similar instruments. As both are fully interchangeable, the virtual currency acts as if it were a foreign currency with floating exchange rates. Here, trading platforms – exchanges – can be set up, with the exchange rate generally being determined by supply and demand in an auction market. The main example here are cryptocurrencies, which are fully convertible and can be used to obtain physical-world and virtual world goods and services.

Rejection of a narrow definition – Important to note at this stage is that the ECB's consideration of unidirectional and bidirectional schemes – in which virtual currencies can be used to obtain virtual and physical-world goods and services – may be difficult to reconcile with its original definition of virtual

379 European Central Bank (2012) "Virtual Currency Schemes", *ecb.europa.eu*, 14.

380 A significant evolution here are the so-called free-to-play games. Such games can be obtained and played for free – unlike the one-time purchase price and/or recurrent subscription fees charged by other games – yet charge players legal tender or similar to obtain the virtual currency necessary to advance in the game.

381 European Central Bank (2012) "Virtual Currency Schemes", *ecb.europa.eu*, 15.

382 Korolov, M. (2012) "Virtual currency 101", *hypergridbusiness.com/2012/07/virtual-currency-101*; as referenced in: Selldahl, S. (2013) "Virtual currencies – Real opportunities?", *Master thesis KTH Industrial Engineering and Management*, 20. The GAO refers to these as 'open flow' schemes. GAO (2013) "Virtual Economies and Currencies", *GAO-13-516*, 4–6.

currencies as being bound to a specific virtual community. After all, a broader acceptance of virtual currencies – as is already happening in practice – does not correspond to acceptance within a specific community, nor does acceptance in the physical-world economy correspond to acceptance within a virtual community.

## 4.2 APPLICATION OF TYPOLOGY TO PRACTICAL EXAMPLES

Four cases – The ECB's typology divides virtual currencies into different types based on three main characteristics: (1) flow of legal tender or similar instruments into the virtual currency, (2) flow of the virtual currency into legal tender or similar instruments, and (3) the ability of the virtual currency to obtain virtual and/or physical-world goods and services. This section will assess to what extent the four cases of practical examples of virtual currencies discussed in section 3 can fit within the ECB's typology.

### *4.2.1 Loyalty programs*

Classic loyalty point programs – In loyalty programs, there is an exchange from legal tender or similar instruments into the virtual currency that are the loyalty points.[383] However, the loyalty points in those programs can generally only be redeemed in the form of a good or service, mostly being a discount at the next purchase. There is principally no possibility to directly exchange the loyalty points into legal tender or similar instruments. The loyalty points can generally be used to obtain physical-world goods or services, most often in the form of discounts. Those three points make that classic loyalty programs can be considered as unidirectional virtual currencies under the ECB's typology.

Mobile platforms – Despite their use of the latest in mobile technologies, the virtual currencies in mobile platform programs are very similar to those found in classic loyalty programs. First, there will principally be an exchange from legal tender or similar instruments into virtual currency, regardless of the party making that exchange. Second, there is no possibility to exchange the virtual currency back into legal tender or similar instruments. Third, the virtual currency can mostly be used to obtain physical-world goods and services. As a result, loyalty programs utilizing mobile platforms can also be considered as unidirectional schemes under the ECB's typology.

Frequent-flyer programs – Under the ECB's typology, frequent-flyer programs are to be considered as a form of unidirectional virtual currencies.[384]

383 As noted, it is principally not directly the consumer who makes that exchange.
384 European Central Bank (2012) "Virtual Currency Schemes", *ecb.europa.eu*, 15–16.

First, there is a clear exchange from legal tender or similar instruments into the virtual currency – either by the consumer himself, or by entities affiliated to the frequent-flyer program such as co-branded card-issuing financial institutions. Second, there is principally no flow back from virtual currency into legal tender or similar instruments. The virtual currency can only be redeemed in kind. Third, redemption can be for virtual and physical-world goods and services.

Unidirectional currencies – Despite the seemingly diverse way in which loyalty programs and their virtual currencies can be set up, the main finding here is that such a virtual currency in all cases constitutes what is under the ECB's typology considered as unidirectional schemes. This means that (1) there is a flow of legal tender or similar instruments into the virtual currency – be it that it may on the surface not immediately be clear who conducts that exchange – (2) there is no flow of virtual currency back into legal tender or similar instruments, and (3) the virtual currencies used in loyalty programs can in all of the cases examined here be used to obtain goods and services in the virtual and physical world.

### *4.2.2 In-game currencies*

Changing business models – While in-game currencies could traditionally mostly be understood as closed scheme currencies, the advent of the free-to-play business model is changing that position.[385] As noted, all free-to-play games identified in this research offer the possibility for the player to obtain in-game currency with legal tender or similar instruments. Also the more traditional pay-to-play games were found to move in such direction. The original intent of game developers aiming to prevent any interaction between the physical-world economy and the in-game virtual economy therefore seems to become increasingly abandoned.

Limited full interchangeability – The exchange of virtual in-game currency into legal tender or similar instruments, however, is still a more contentious topic. Overall, game developers still maintain the position that in-game goods – including the virtual currencies used within the game – are part of their intellectual property and as such cannot be sold for legal tender or similar instruments by the players. Consequently, in-game currencies are generally not fully interchangeable. Notable exceptions are Diablo III's short-lived Real-Money Auction House and Second Life's Linden dollars.

385 Selldahl proposes to consider virtual currencies in free-to-play games as a different type of virtual currencies, namely monetization currencies. Such serves to keep pay-to-play in-game currencies under the closed scheme type, leaving the monetization currencies as unidirectional schemes. However, as pay-to-play games are also evolving toward unidirectional scheme virtual currencies, such distinction would have little practical use and is therefore not adopted here. Selldahl, S. (2013) "Virtual currencies – Real opportunities?", *Master thesis KTH Industrial Engineering and Management*, 23.

Limited acceptance – Also in terms of what can be obtained with in-game currencies, it is found that in-game virtual currencies are still overall limited to use within their closed virtual economy. That means that those virtual currencies can in principle only be used to obtain virtual goods and services within their specific virtual world. In all of the examples studied here, the virtual currency – like everything else in the virtual world – remains the intellectual property of the developer of the virtual world, who can thus prohibit the use of the virtual currency for the purchase of goods and services outside of that virtual world. While black markets do exist, developers firmly continue to crack down on such practices.

Need for re-assessment – The general finding here is therefore that the traditional position of considering in-game virtual currencies as what is defined by the ECB as closed schemes is increasingly becoming incorrect. Free-to-play games are at the least unidirectional, with some exceptions such as Second Life even being bidirectional. Also pay-to-play games are moving more into unidirectional ways, meaning that the definition of a closed scheme can no longer be applied to the in-game currency category as a whole. Given the range of different approaches identified here, a case-by-case assessment of the precise nature of the in-game virtual currency is required.

#### 4.2.3 *Prepaid value currencies*

Prepaid currencies – While the most prominent examples of prepaid value currencies are no longer active, the example of Amazon Coins shows that this is a form of virtual currency that is still being explored by companies as a potential element in their business model. The examples discussed here can be considered as unidirectional virtual currencies under the ECB's typology. There is an exchange of legal tender or similar instruments for virtual currency, yet not the other way around, and the virtual currency can be used to obtain goods and services, both in the physical and virtual realm.[386]

Unidirectional currencies – The prepaid value currencies discussed here are clear examples of unidirectional virtual currencies. They can be obtained with legal tender or similar instruments, yet there is no exchange back from virtual currency into legal tender or similar instruments. Moreover, they can be used to obtain virtual-world and physical-world goods and services.

#### 4.2.4 *Cryptocurrencies*

Bidirectional currency – Overall, cryptocurrencies can under the ECB's typology be considered as a prime example of a bidirectional virtual currency. That is

386 While Facebook Credits and Microsoft Points were used to obtain virtual-world goods and services, the temporary broader use of Amazon Coins allowed the user to obtain physical goods as well.

because (1) there is a clear possibility to exchange legal tender or similar instruments for cryptocurrencies, and (2) cryptocurrencies can be exchanged for legal tender or similar instruments. Moreover, (3) cryptocurrencies have already proven to be useful for obtaining goods and services, both in the physical and virtual worlds.

No central authority – Important to note is that, due to the decentralized nature of cryptocurrencies, it is not a central emitting authority that determines those characteristics. Cryptocurrencies have only achieved their characteristics as a result of their widening acceptance. In turn, it is also possible that a diminishing popularity could reverse that process. Unlike the other virtual currencies discussed here, there is no central instance that – to varying degrees – guarantees the future acceptance and convertibility of cryptocurrencies. At the same time, however, the absence of a central authority does not necessarily mean that cryptocurrencies cannot achieve financial stability. A central authority, as typically found in the form of a central bank, can be a highly politicized organ, subject to risks such as devaluation imposed by politics. Moreover, even a central bank can suffer systemic distrust from the public.[387]

## 4.3 ALTERNATIVE TYPOLOGY

Matryoshka model – Another classification proposed for payment instruments is the matryoshka model developed by Bleyen, Van Hove and Hartmann, consisting of multiple nested layers.[388] The first layer of such a model identifies the type of money used, with the second layer defining the core payment mechanism, the next two layers determining the channels and networks involved and the form factor and authentication device used, and the final layer containing seven generic payment methods.[389] The following paragraphs will determine whether that model could apply to virtual currencies.

Type of money – The first layer determines the type of money used. The matryoshka model allows for the inclusion of cash, scriptural money, e-money and privately issued currencies.[390] Of the different virtual currencies presented in section 3 of this chapter, it is clear that all examples are considered as privately issued currencies. That means that all of the virtual currencies discussed here could be placed under the matryoshka model's first layer.

387 Tonkiss, F. (2009) "Trust, Confidence and Economic Crisis", *Intereconomics*, Vol. 44, 198; Roth, F. (2009) "The Effect of the Financial Crisis on Systemic Trust", *Intereconomics*, Vol. 44, 203–208.

388 Bleyen, V.-A., Van Hove, L., Hartmann, M. (2010) "Classifying Payment Instruments: A Matryoshka Approach", *Communications & Strategies*, Nr. 79, 73–94.

389 *Ibid.*, 74.

390 *Ibid.*, 76.

Core payment mechanism – In terms of payment mechanisms, the second layer of the matryoshka model distinguishes between push and pull models.[391] The core difference is that a push transaction is initiated by the payer, whereas a pull transaction is initiated by the payee. The examples of virtual currencies discussed here could all be considered as involving push transactions, given that those virtual currencies can be pushed instantly to the beneficiary.

Channels and networks – The third layer of the matryoshka model identifies the different channels or networks through which payments are initiated, processed, and possibly cleared.[392] 'Channels' indicate the technology used for device-terminal communication, whereas 'networks' denote the infrastructure used in later stages. Possible channels include contact-based technologies – such as smartcard chips – contactless technologies – such as RFID and NFC – and wireless technologies – such as Bluetooth and mobile networks. Examples of networks include bank and non-bank networks, and proprietary schemes such as Visa, MasterCard or Bancontact. In terms of channels, most of the virtual currencies discussed here are transmitted over the Internet. However, a wide variety of channels – including card-based products – could be utilized. In terms of networks, all virtual currencies discussed here use non-bank schemes.

Form factor and authentication – Layer four of the model denotes the form factor of the payment instrument and the method of authentication used, if any.[393] The notion of form factor takes into account that most payment instruments are mere access products that do not carry money themselves. Several of the virtual currencies discussed here are held in server-based wallets. Those can be maintained centrally – as is the case for in-game currencies – or decentralized – in the case of cryptocurrencies. Physical form factors can be used as well, such as card-based products. Authentication methods vary greatly between the virtual currencies discussed here. Some examples may require no authentication, while others rely on username-password protection. Cryptocurrencies, on the other hand, use public-key cryptography.

Payment methods – The fifth and final layer identifies seven generic payment methods: "*banknotes or coins, cheques, credit transfers, direct debits, credit cards, debit cards and e-money (in all its forms)*".[394] The idea is that, in principle, all payment instruments utilize one of those generic payment methods. Some of the virtual currencies discussed here could be considered under the generic payment methods of layer five. For instance, cryptocurrencies and in-game currencies

391 *Ibid.*, 79–80.
392 *Ibid.*, 80–81.
393 *Ibid.*, 82.
394 *Ibid.*, 82–83.

could be likened to banknotes and coins. However, some virtual currencies are more difficult to place. Loyalty-based currencies, for instance, cannot readily be placed under this layer.[395]

Transcending layer – A sixth transcending layer was added to the matryoshka model for service providers that are difficult to place. That layer also includes a couple of specific cases, such as money transmitters, loyalty schemes, and collection/billing services.[396] From the virtual currencies discussed here, loyalty-based currencies therefore have to be included in this layer.

Conclusions – From the previous concise overview, it becomes clear that the virtual currencies discussed in this chapter could indeed fit within the different layers of the matryoshka model. That model could therefore serve as an alternative typology for virtual currencies, next to the payment instruments already included in the model. Could that model then replace the ECB's typology, set out in the previous sections? The main shortcoming of the matryoshka model for the purposes of this research is that it does not indicate the flow of legal tender or similar instruments to virtual currencies or the other way around. As will be shown in chapters IV to VI, precisely that monetary flow can be pivotal in the consideration of virtual currencies and the services developed around them under the legal frameworks on e-money, payment services, anti-money laundering, and financial instruments. The matryoshka model can consider virtual currencies as private currencies for the purposes of its first layer, but it does not indicate whether or not they could, for instance, be considered as e-money.[397] As a result, the ECB's typology seems more adapted to the purposes of some of the core research questions established here. However, the matryoshka model could prove useful for the later stages of the research, in questioning the need for regulation of virtual currencies and their services. If, for instance, a virtual currency service could be classified in the model in the same way that an existing and regulated payment instrument is classified, it raises the question whether they should not be subjected to the same or similar regulation. In that sense, the model could help to indicate a certain regulatory expectation. For that purpose, the final stages of this research will revisit the matryoshka model.

## 5 RISK ANALYSIS

Four-way risk analysis – While the ECB's basic typology has proven useful, it is clear that the typology only takes into account the specific exchange flows

[395] *Ibid.*, 89.
[396] *Ibid.*, 83.
[397] Moreover, the model uses the notion of e-money in its broadest sense, going beyond the strict legal definition of the EU's legal framework.

between virtual currencies and legal tender or similar instruments. In doing so, it does not take into account the specific risks that could follow from such exchanges, such as for instance the risks posed to stakeholders and relating to market stability. Therefore, this section provides a virtual currency risk analysis, in order to assess whether the typology to be used in this research could incorporate specific risks emanating from the use of virtual currencies. This section analyzes the risks posed by virtual currencies from four angles: (1) users, which include consumers that use virtual currencies in their private capacity and businesses that use virtual currencies in their professional capacity; (2) the market, where virtual currencies could pose risks to overall stability; (3) investors, who may hold some of their assets in virtual currencies; and (4) service providers, who provide virtual currency services.

## 5.1 USER RISKS

RISK OF GROWTH – One risk relates to the growth of virtual currencies. As noted in the discussion of in-game currencies, many virtual world currencies are evolving from being closed scheme virtual currencies toward unidirectional or even bidirectional virtual currencies. Consequently, it can be argued that such exposes the users of such virtual worlds to risks that would not have been present if the virtual currencies used there existed completely isolated from the physical world.[398] In the most classical sense, it could involve people conducting physical-world actions as repercussion for actions conducted in a virtual world.[399] Also, unidirectional and bidirectional virtual currencies generally involve a clear level of financial investment from their users – who will likely have to exchange legal tender or similar instruments for virtual currency. Where closed scheme virtual currencies could generally be obtained without the user investing legal tender or similar instruments, they therefore pose lesser risk.

FRAUD AND THEFT – Another important risk to users relates to losses incurred due to fraudulent or non-genuine exchanges, losses due to wallet or exchange theft or hacking, or identity theft. In its opinion on virtual currencies, the EBA conducts a risk assessment exercise, where it highly ranked those types of risks.[400] This means that, according to the EBA, those risks have a high

---

398 Thorpe, C., Hammer, J., Camp, J., Callas, J., Bond, M. (2007) "Virtual Economies: Threats and Risks", *Proceedings of Financial Cryptography and Data Security '07*, 2–3. For instance, it is argued that it would be impossible to sell forged items in a virtual world unless the developer of that virtual world specifically coded such possibility. However, virtual economies can also pose their own unique risks: most games allow players to murder an adversary and steal his assets without the risk of repercussion.

399 *Ibid.*, 4–5.

400 European Banking Authority (2014) "EBA Opinion on 'virtual currencies'", *eba.europa.eu*, EBA/Op/2014/08, 21–22 and 31.

probability to materialize and, should they materialize, have a high impact. Also a risk assessment conducted for the Bitcoin Foundation addressed those issues[401], as did a similar exercise by the Financial Action Task Force (FATF).[402] While those risks are of course also present in the traditional financial system, they can be regarded as higher for virtual currencies as virtual currency service providers are currently not bound to the licensing and security requirements imposed on traditional financial actors. That effectively opens the virtual currency market to opportunistic or even downright fraudulent service providers.

Instability and volatility – Like legal tender, virtual currencies can experience value fluctuations, which can result in the user incurring losses. The EBA ranks that risk as high, since virtual currency markets are relatively opaque, and prices can more easily be manipulated than on regulated legal tender markets.[403] Also the ECB pointed out the risks following from the high volatility of virtual currencies.[404] A risk assessment conducted for the Bitcoin Foundation expects the matter to resolve itself once cryptocurrency adoption increases.[405]

Risk posed by the counterparty – While virtual currency service providers could of course commit fraud and theft, also other behavior could pose risks to users. For instance, the user could incur losses due to delays in virtual currency recovery, due to intermediaries or counterparties failing to meet contractual settlement obligations, due to lack of acceptance or convertibility of virtual currencies[406], due to incorrect debiting, due to inability to access wallet or exchange services, and due to price manipulation.[407] The ECB also points out a couple of elements posing particular risks to users of virtual currencies: lack of transparency, lack of continuity, potential illiquidity, and high IT and network dependence.[408] As with fraud and theft, those risks can at least to some extent be attributed to the lack of clear regulation of virtual currency service providers, who are currently not bound to the behavioral rules imposed on traditional

401 Harper, J. (2014) "Removing Impediments to Bitcoin's Success: A Risk Management Study", *Bitcoin Foundation Research Brief 1*, 25.

402 Financial Action Task Force (2014) "Virtual Currencies: Key Definitions and Potential AML/CFT Risks", *fatf-gafi.org*, 9.

403 European Banking Authority (2014) "EBA Opinion on 'virtual currencies'", *eba.europa.eu*, EBA/Op/2014/08, 23.

404 European Central Bank (2015) "Virtual Currency Schemes – a further analysis", *ecb.europa.eu*, 23. See also: Kiran, M., Stannett, M. (2014) "Bitcoin Risk Analysis", *nemode.ac.uk*, 13.

405 Harper, J. (2014) "Removing Impediments to Bitcoin's Success: A Risk Management Study", *Bitcoin Foundation Research Brief 1*, 23.

406 *Ibid.*, 22.

407 European Banking Authority (2014) "EBA Opinion on 'virtual currencies'", *eba.europa.eu*, EBA/Op/2014/08, 22 and 32; Kiran, M., Stannett, M. (2014) "Bitcoin Risk Analysis", *nemode.ac.uk*, 13–14.

408 European Central Bank (2015) "Virtual Currency Schemes – a further analysis", *ecb.europa.eu*, 20–22.

financial actors.[409] Another element of that risk is that virtual currencies often allow counterparties to a transaction to operate anonymously, or at least pseudonymously.[410] Such would prevent the parties suffering the losses described here from claiming redress. At the same time, however, decreasing the privacy of virtual currency transactions has also been called a risk on its own.[411]

## 5.2 MARKET RISKS

Money laundering and other crimes – A potential threat to financial integrity is the money laundering risk posed by virtual currencies due to anonymous and rapid transfers. That also includes a risk of the use of virtual currencies for terrorist financing, a risk of control of virtual currency markets by criminals, illegal trade using virtual currencies, hindering of restorative justice of victims due to criminal use of virtual currencies, extortion, and criminal creation or use of virtual currency schemes.[412] Those concerns mainly stem from the relative degree of anonymity virtual currencies can offer their users.[413]

Risk to price stability – The ECB has warned that virtual currencies could have an effect on price stability and monetary policy. Here, the ECB references its earlier analyses regarding e-money, noting that virtual currencies could influence prices if they substantially modify the quantity of money, have an impact on velocity of money, and interact with the physical world economy.[414] The ECB found that the quantity and velocity of money are not impacted yet, but that the interaction between virtual currencies and the physical-world economy may warrant further

409 Kiran, M., Stannett, M. (2014) "Bitcoin Risk Analysis", *nemode.ac.uk*, 15. Although it must be noted that poorly executed regulation could also pose a risk to the further development of virtual currencies. Harper, J. (2014) "Removing Impediments to Bitcoin's Success: A Risk Management Study", *Bitcoin Foundation Research Brief 1*, 25–26.

410 European Central Bank (2015) "Virtual Currency Schemes – a further analysis", *ecb.europa.eu*, 22; Financial Action Task Force (2014) "Virtual Currencies: Key Definitions and Potential AML/CFT Risks", *fatf-gafi.org*, 9.

411 Harper, J. (2014) "Removing Impediments to Bitcoin's Success: A Risk Management Study", *Bitcoin Foundation Research Brief 1*, 23–24.

412 European Banking Authority (2014) "EBA Opinion on 'virtual currencies'", *eba.europa.eu*, EBA/Op/2014/08, 32–35; HM Treasury (2015) "UK national risk assessment of money laundering and terrorist financing", *gov.uk*, 82–83; Kiran, M., Stannett, M. (2014) "Bitcoin Risk Analysis", *nemode.ac.uk*, 7. Though Europol reported not to have concrete indications regarding the actual use of virtual currencies with regard to terrorist financing. Europol (2016) "Changes in modus operandi of Islamic State terrorist attacks", *europol.europa.eu*, 7.

413 Irwin, A., Slay, J., Choo, K.K., Liu, L. (2013) "Are the financial transactions conducted inside virtual environments truly anonymous? An experimental research from an Australian perspective", *Journal of Money Laundering Control*, Vol. 16, 7; Financial Action Task Force (2014) "Virtual Currencies: Key Definitions and Potential AML/CFT Risks", *fatf-gafi.org*, 9.

414 European Central Bank (2012) "Virtual Currency Schemes", *ecb.europa.eu*, 34.

monitoring.[415] The ECB does not consider virtual currencies a major risk for overall financial stability, noting that virtual currencies may be inherently unstable, and given their limited acceptance and low trade volume.[416] In the 2015 update to its opinion, the ECB maintains its view regarding the low current risk of virtual currencies, considering their transaction volume as still insignificant compared to that of traditional non-cash payment methods such as Visa, MasterCard and PayPal.[417] Therefore, the ECB confirms its earlier position that virtual currencies have not yet reached sufficient traction to have a meaningful impact.[418] In 2017, the president of the ECB, Mario Draghi, confirmed that virtual currencies had not yet reached sufficient traction for such market risks to materialize.[419]

Risk to payment systems' stability – On payment systems' stability, it is remarked that virtual currency payment systems could face the same risks as classic payment systems – more in particular risks regarding credit, liquidity, and operations, while also noting the unclear legal framework regarding virtual currencies – yet are not subjected to the same regulatory oversight.[420] In 2015, the ECB confirmed its earlier position that virtual currencies have not yet reached sufficient traction to have a meaningful impact.[421]

Risk to central banks – The ECB warns that the reputation of central banks could be damaged through negative evolutions in virtual currencies, if their use were to grow considerably.[422]

## 5.3 INVESTOR RISKS

User risks – As investors using virtual currencies are at the same time also users of virtual currencies, the risks discussed in section 5.1 apply to them as well.

Volatility – While a risk to all users, the volatility of certain virtual currencies – and in particular cryptocurrencies – weighs heavier on investors, as they may see the value of their virtual currency assets evaporate due to such volatility.[423] Here, reference can be made to the existing legal frameworks protecting investors

415 *Ibid.*, 37.
416 *Ibid.*, 39.
417 European Central Bank (2015) "Virtual Currency Schemes – a further analysis", *ecb.europa.eu*, 17.
418 *Ibid.*, 26–27.
419 *Ecb.europa.eu/pub/pdf/other/ecb.mepletter170720_bermejo_viegas.en.pdf.*
420 European Central Bank (2012) "Virtual Currency Schemes", *ecb.europa.eu*, 40–42.
421 European Central Bank (2015) "Virtual Currency Schemes – a further analysis", *ecb.europa.eu*, 26–27.
422 European Central Bank (2012) "Virtual Currency Schemes", *ecb.europa.eu*, 45.
423 Kiran, M., Stannett, M. (2014) "Bitcoin Risk Analysis", *nemode.ac.uk*, 17.

in securities.[424] Those frameworks impose rules of conduct on those offering securities to the public, and require them to fulfill information duties – such as the duty to publish a prospectus. While risk is inherent to investments, the legislator has thus made a clear choice to implement such protection mechanisms to at least ensure that the non-institutional investor is properly informed about the corresponding risks. However, chapter VI will point out whether the protection mechanisms mentioned here can apply to investments using virtual currencies.

Legality – While the overall legality of virtual currencies and their transactions is of course a concern for all stakeholders, it must be mentioned here that legislators have already taken steps to prohibit trade in financial products dependent on virtual currencies.[425] The legality of virtual currencies as a means for investment may therefore be questioned.

Deflation – A last risk applies specifically to certain cryptocurrencies – such as bitcoin. As those cryptocurrencies have a built-in cap on the number of units that can be in circulation – in the case of bitcoin the cap has been put at 21 million units – they are inherently deflationary. Once the maximum number of units has been put into circulation, no new units will be created anymore. That means that the value of each unit will increase, which in turn encourages users to save their units rather than spending them. The result of such increasing scarcity is that even less units are in circulation, thus further driving up the value, which could result in a deflationary spiral.[426]

## 5.4 SERVICE PROVIDER RISKS

Regulation – One of the main risks on service providers currently offering virtual currency services is that new regulation may impede their business model or may impose strict requirements that are unattainable for smaller service providers. That could effectively push smaller service providers out of the market or limit access to the market for new players. While, given the other risks discussed

424 Such as: Directive 2003/71/EC of the European Parliament and of the Council of 4 November 2003 on the prospectus to be published when securities are offered to the public or admitted to trading and amending Directive 2001/34/EC, *OJ* L 345 of 31 December 2003; Directive 2013/36/EU of the European Parliament and of the Council of 26 June 2013 on access to the activity of credit institutions and the prudential supervision of credit institutions and investment firms, amending Directive 2002/87/EC and repealing Directives 2006/48/EC and 2006/49/EC, *OJ* L 176 of 27 June 2013; or Directive 2004/39/EC of the European Parliament and of the Council of 21 April 2004 on markets in financial instruments amending Council Directives 85/611/EEC and 93/6/EEC and Directive 2000/12/EC of the European Parliament and of the Council and repealing Council Directive 93/22/EEC, *OJ* L 145 of 30 April 2004.

425 In Belgium: Royal Decree of 24 April 2014 approving the regulation of the Financial Services and Markets Authority concerning the commercialization prohibition of certain financial products to non-professional clients, *Belgian State Gazette* 20 May 2014.

426 Kiran, M., Stannett, M. (2014) "Bitcoin Risk Analysis", *nemode.ac.uk*, 16.

here, regulation of virtual currency service providers may prove necessary, such regulation would have to try to balance the need of a nascent market to develop with the need of stakeholders in the market to be provided adequate protection.

Virtual currency risk – Virtual currencies themselves may pose risks to the service providers who have built their business model around them. In the case of centralized virtual currencies, service providers who are not the issuer themselves are fully dependent on the central issuer. That issuer may implement substantial changes to the virtual currency scheme, or may even decide to end the scheme altogether. In the case of decentralized virtual currencies, questions may be raised regarding the long-term sustainability of the scheme. It has already been remarked in section 3.4.3 that cryptocurrencies are fully dependent on miners in order to validate transactions. Those miners may, for instance, collude to raise transaction fees or the value of the virtual currency, which could be an impediment to the development of other service providers.

## 5.5 RISKS AND TYPOLOGY

Risk allocation – Following the risks analyzed in this section, the ECB's basic typology can be supplemented with an understanding of the nature of the risks posed by the different types of virtual currencies. Taking into account the findings of the risk analysis, the following risk allocation can be proposed.

Closed scheme virtual currencies – Closed schemes generally pose little to no risk to the physical-world economy as interaction between virtual economy and physical-world economy is explicitly avoided or even prohibited. Other than the time spent within the virtual world by its participants – and thus their unavailability for physical-world productivity – there is no interaction between the two economies. From a financial perspective, there is no exchange between legal tender or similar instruments and virtual currency in any direction, black market activities notwithstanding. That limits the risks posed to the user by anonymity, lack of clear regulation, or fraudulent market participants. Also for the service providers themselves, there is little risk. Given the lack of interaction between the virtual and physical-world economy, closed schemes are not relevant to investors or the market. From a regulatory perspective, there seems little incentive to regulate the closed scheme type of virtual currency due to its limited impact.

Unidirectional scheme virtual currencies – Unidirectional schemes can be considered to pose an intermediate risk, mainly to users and other market participants. As there is an exchange of legal tender or similar instruments into virtual currency, there is a direct link between the physical-world economy and the virtual economy. While such does raise the risk level, the overall risk can still be considered as moderate since unidirectional schemes are controlled by a central entity.[427] For users, there is of course a risk of fraudulent market participants, anonymity and lack of clear regulation. For investors, the lack of full convertibility may limit the usability of the unidirectional type of virtual currencies for their intentions. For service providers, there is a risk that new regulation may impede their business models. Last, the risk for the overall price and financial stability and regulators is negligible, as unidirectional virtual currencies generally serve a specific purpose, thus mostly lacking the general propensity to develop into an all-purposes legal tender competitor. In terms of regulation, the unidirectional type of virtual currency would therefore only warrant regulation from the perspective of stakeholder protection.

Bidirectional scheme virtual currencies – Bidirectional schemes have the highest risk potential, precisely due to their fully convertible nature. That allows bidirectional virtual currencies to gain broader acceptance, beyond the more limited range typically found in closed and unidirectional schemes. The bidirectional type of virtual currency can also be developed in a decentralized manner – as found in cryptocurrencies – thus lacking the central authority that controls emission and conversion rates. As a result, bidirectional virtual currencies can pose added risks to users and other market participants such as investors, for instance in the forms of volatility, anonymity, and fraudulent market participants. If adoption and transaction volume of a bidirectional virtual currency were to grow, it could also gain the ability to threaten overall market and price stability, thus posing a risk to markets and their regulators. While that risk potential should therefore be taken into account when analyzing the need or potential for regulation of the bidirectional type of virtual currencies, it should also be taken into account that most of those risks have not yet materialized and could be avoided precisely through regulation, according to both the EBA and ECB. Incentive for regulation of the bidirectional type of virtual currency can be found in both stakeholder protection and market protection.

## 6 INTERIM CONCLUSIONS

Establishment of a definition – A first conclusion that can be drawn following the previous analysis is that there is no generally accepted definition of the term 'virtual currency'. More so, it was found that there is even little consensus about the use of the term 'virtual currency' itself. Therefore, the terminology and the definition proposed here should be read in light of its purposes within this particular research, and not be understood as a generalization of the different opinions on this matter.

427 In the analysis conducted here, no decentralized unidirectional scheme was found.

Wide range of practical examples – In analyzing a number of practical cases, it became clear that virtual currencies can be found in a wide range of different forms. That analysis has highlighted some of their differences, for instance in terms of adoption, issue, and government. Apart from establishing the inherent differences between forms of virtual currency, it was also attempted to identify their commonalities.

Typology can be applied – Overall, the typology proposed by the ECB was found to apply to all forms of virtual currencies analyzed in this chapter. As a result, it can be concluded that the ECB's typology does manage to cover all the forms of virtual currencies relevant for the purposes of this research. It could, however, be suggested that the third characteristic used to assign the ECB-defined types – namely that of whether the virtual currency can be used to obtain goods and services in either the physical realm, virtual realms, or in both – appears to be less pertinent than the other two elements and could therefore be abandoned. In the analysis conducted here, it was found that the elements of (1) flow of legal tender or similar instruments into virtual currency, and (2) flow of virtual currency into legal tender or similar instruments are sufficient in assigning the three types. The final element – (3) ability of the virtual currency to obtain virtual and/or physical-world goods and services – was not found to provide additional guidance in determining the type of virtual currency.[428] Moreover, it was found that the third element is more determined by convention between virtual currency users (*i.e.* whether they accept the virtual currency as payment amongst each other) or by the issuer of the virtual currency (*i.e.* whether the issuer restricts the use of the virtual currency to a particular realm), rather than by elements inherent to the virtual currency. For instance, the current usability of some forms of cryptocurrencies to obtain goods or services in the physical world is a consequence of their growth, but not an inherent trait of cryptocurrencies.[429]

Risk drivers and mitigation – The risk assessment conducted in this chapter identified a number of risks to different stakeholders regarding virtual currencies, as well as to the market. Overall, two main elements can be identified that are the basis for the risks presented here: anonymity and lack of clear regulation.

428 See also: Godschalk, H. (2013) "Can an overseer overlook some basics? – The ECB on e-money and virtual currencies", *DGC Magazine,* 11 August 2013.

429 For instance, the decision of a game developer to incorporate real-money transfer technologies – thus moving the in-game virtual currency from a closed scheme to a unidirectional scheme, or possibly even a bidirectional scheme – can be considered as an internal change to the nature of the virtual currency used in the virtual world, being under the sole and full control of that game developer. The rise in acceptance of a virtual currency – such as cryptocurrencies – is an external factor, unforeseeable and under no-one's control. A typology where virtual currencies switch from one type to another solely on the range of their acceptance is therefore rejected. Such typology is proposed in, for instance: Bal, A. (2013) "Stateless Virtual Money in the Tax System", *European Taxation*, 351–356.

Regarding anonymity, it was found that this element is a major factor in allowing untrustworthy actors to enter the market. Moreover, anonymity poses a significant risk of the use of virtual currencies for money laundering, terrorist financing, or other criminal activities. Here, reference could be made to existing customer due diligence (CDD) obligations as found in anti-money laundering legislation. Those obligations ensure that all parties to a transaction are properly identified, thus facilitating redress where needed and helping to discourage criminal intent. It could therefore be suggested that the application of those or similar obligations to virtual currency transactions could help mitigating the anonymity risk driver.

Regarding the lack of clear regulation, it was found that virtual currencies and their service providers at the present moment appear to operate outside the scope of legal frameworks protecting markets and market actors. Where a specific risk to a stakeholder or the market is identified, and a legal framework is identified that aims to protect that stakeholder or the market from such a risk, it could be interpreted as an indication that the legal framework should be extended to virtual currencies and related services. Overall, regulation should then allow for the auditability of virtual currency systems and users; ensure transparency of the system; provide a clear legal position and regulatory framework for all different actors involved; provide security standardization; provide a party to allow for stabilization, redress, and complaints; and ensure equal information distribution.[430] Here, reference can be made to the EBA, which as part of its mitigation strategy proposes the adoption of clearer legislation regulating virtual currency scheme governance, their transparency and customer due diligence, with the establishment of capital requirements and payment guarantees, amongst others.[431] More in particular, it must be identified which legal frameworks already exist to mitigate the risks identified here. For instance, where the current free access to the market regarding virtual currencies poses a risk of fraudulent services providers entering that market, reference can be made to legal frameworks that subject entry to a market to strict licensing requirements, as is the case for payment services and e-money. Where a risk is posed to investors, reference can be made to legal frameworks aimed at protecting these parties, such as MiFID or the Prospectus Directive.[432]

---

430 European Banking Authority (2014) "EBA Opinion on 'virtual currencies'", *eba.europa.eu*, EBA/Op/2014/08, 38.

431 *Ibid.*, 39–43.

432 Directive 2004/39/EC of the European Parliament and of the Council of 21 April 2004 on markets in financial instruments amending Council Directives 85/611/EEC and 93/6/EEC and Directive 2000/12/EC of the European Parliament and of the Council and repealing Council Directive 93/22/EEC, *OJ* L 145 of 30 April 2004, Directive 2003/71/EC of the European Parliament and of the Council of 4 November 2003 on the prospectus to be published when securities are offered to the public or admitted to trading and amending Directive 2001/34/EC, *OJ* L 345 of 31 December 2003.

Risks and typology – In section 5.5, the risks identified here were allocated to the typology. Regarding closed scheme virtual currencies, it can be said that these pose little, if any risk, to the four actors analyzed here. Unidirectional schemes pose moderate risks to users and service providers, but principally do not involve investors or the market. Bidirectional virtual currencies, however, affect all four actors identified here, and pose a more pronounced risk. It are therefore especially bidirectional virtual currencies, and to lesser extent unidirectional virtual currencies, that form candidates for the regulation identified in the previous paragraph.

# CHAPTER II
# ELEMENTS OF TRUST

## 1 INTRODUCTION

A COMMON NOTION... – The notion of trust is widely used in everyday language. Interpersonal relationships – be it friendship or romance – are in great part based on mutual trust. When parties enter into a legal relationship, they will have to trust each other at least to certain extent. While contracts can be used to ensure that all parties will duly carry out their responsibilities under such a legal relationship, it is clear that most parties like to avoid having to turn to the contract and potential litigation as a means of enforcing performance. When new services are introduced – such as e-commerce services or a new social media platform – one of the core questions potential users face is whether they trust the underlying service provider. The matter of trust has especially become important in the era of so-called Big Data, where service providers maintain a myriad of their users' personal data. The same is true for virtual currency services. As noted in the previous chapter, one driver behind the development of cryptocurrencies was distrust in traditional financial system market players – such as banks. In the case of cryptocurrencies, the decentralized blockchain technology provides cryptographic proof of its operations, rather than requiring users to trust one particular party. In turn, cryptocurrencies do require their users to trust the underlying technology. Such trust may not come automatically, as it has already been proven that the blockchain technology could be abused. As a result, cryptocurrencies – and virtual currencies at large – will have to prove worthy of their users' trust. Trust, in other words, is imperative yet must be earned.

... YET POSING CONCEPTUAL DIFFICULTIES – Despite the seeming familiarity with the notion of trust, it may prove difficult to clearly define this notion. Even in scientific discourse on trust, the concept has been described in terms ranging from "*elusive notion*", over "*confusing potpourri*", to "*conceptual morass*".[433] Different scientific disciplines employ a variety of interpretations

---

433 Gambetta, D. (2000) "Foreword", In: Gambetta, D. (ed.) *Trust: Making and Breaking Cooperative Relations, electronic edition*, Oxford: Basil Blackwell, vii; Shapiro, S. P. (1987) "The Social Control of Impersonal Trust", *American Journal of Sociology*, Vol. 93, 625; Barber, B. (1983) *The logic and limits of trust*, New Brunswick: Rutgers University Press, 1; Carnevale,

of the trust notion. In order to gain a clear understanding of what precisely constitutes trust and what the implications of that constitution are to virtual currencies, this chapter will first focus on analyzing the notion of trust on an abstract level. This analysis will provide a critical study of literature of legal science and other scientific disciplines to analyze the trust concept and to understand how the trustworthiness of virtual currencies should be enhanced in order to correspond to the trust required from their stakeholders to adopt their use.

Application of trust – In second order, this chapter will analyze how the abstract trust notion is operationalized in practice in law. To this end, this chapter will conduct a descriptive analysis of trust services at the level of the EU to assess whether virtual currency service providers could become trusted service providers. In second order, this chapter will analyze other forms of trust operationalization, be it in the form of trusted service providers at the level of certain EU Member States, or through other mechanisms in law.

Goal of this chapter – The goal of this chapter is to critically analyze the potential for additional legal measures that could raise the overall trustworthiness of virtual currencies. Such legal measures could support the legal assessment of these developments and assist in providing legal certainty.

## 2 THE ABSTRACT NOTION OF 'TRUST'

Abstract view on trust – This section will first analyze the notion of trust from an abstract viewpoint. This analysis will serve to understand how this concept is to be understood from an interdisciplinary scientific view. Second, this section will briefly analyze what the place of trust in modern society is. This will help to better understand to what degree society relies on trust.

Cross-disciplinary view – As noted in the introduction to this chapter, trust can be interpreted in a myriad of different ways, depending on the specific viewpoint of its interpreter. Therefore, this section approaches trust from a number of different scientific disciplines, in order to establish how their conceptualizations on trust overlap and differ. For each of these scientific disciplines, the scholarly definition and understanding of trust will be sought.

---

D. G., Wechsler, B. (1992) "Trust in the public sector: Individual and organizational determinants", *Administration & Society*, Vol. 23, 473; McKnight, D. H., Chervany, N. L. (2001) "Trust and Distrust Definitions: One Bite at a Time", In: Falcone, R., Singh, M., Tan, Y.-H. (Eds.) *Trust in Cyber-societies, LNAI 2246*, Berlin: Springer, 28.

Selected disciplines – The scientific disciplines selected for this analysis include the following:

- Philosophy, for providing the basic thinking used in many a scientific discourse;
- Psychology, for its insight in how relations affect the human psyche;
- Sociology, for its understanding of interpersonal relations;
- Economy, for its understanding of risk-based relations;
- Computer science, for its importance in modern relations; and
- Law, for its endeavors to regulate interpersonal relations.[434]

## 2.1 PHILOSOPHY

Philosophic origins – The concept of trust was already debated in philosophy as early as Plato's *Republic*. In Plato's work, it is argued that the fear of detection and punishment is what prevents humans from acting only in their self-interest.[435] Therefore, someone can only be trusted if it is clear that this person's fear of detection and punishment will persuade that person to act just.[436] In state matters, Plato advocates a state ruled by philosophers, the only humans worthy of their subjects' unconditional trust.[437] Hobbes presents a similar argument in his *Leviathan*, namely that humans have an inherent tendency not to act in each other's best interests. Therefore, a sovereign is needed who is trusted to impose the necessary rules to preserve peace and order.[438] Other philosophers, such as Hume, present a more optimistic view in that humans do seek cooperation and agreement. Trust, therefore, revolves around the assurance that if we contribute to a mutual interest, we will not be exploited.[439] Kant goes even further in his assessment of trust, considering it as the fundamental principle underlying human relations.[440] His categorical imperative forms the basis of rational behavior in a moral community.

Attribute to interpersonal relations – From these rather divergent philosophical views on the nature of the state and human relations – be it personal,

---

434 This analysis expands on research first conducted as part of the uTRUSTit project: Dumortier, J., Vandezande, N. (2011) "uTRUSTit D7.1 – Legal Requirements for Trust in the IoT", *utrustit.eu*, 7–11. See also: Dumortier, J., Vandezande, N. (2012) "Trust in the proposed EU regulation on trust services?", *Computer Law & Security Review*, Vol. 28, 573–574; Döbelt, S., Busch, M., Hochleitner, C. (2012) "uTRUSTit – Defining, Understanding, Explaining TRUST within the uTRUSTit Project", *utrustit.eu*, 29p.

435 Bailey, T. (2006) "On trust and philosophy", *open.edu*.

436 *Id.*

437 Price, C. (2006) "Trust in Plato's Republic", *open.edu;* Baier, A. (1986) "Trust and antitrust", Ethics, Vol. 96, 232–233.

438 Wolff, J. (2006) "Trust and the state of nature", *open.edu*.

439 Matravers, M. (2006) "Hume on trust", *open.edu*.

440 Hills, A. (2006) "Kantian trust", *open.edu*.

professional, social or economic[441] – it follows that trust can be considered as a critical attribute to these relations.[442] Trust is an elementary requirement in forming relations.[443] Given the nature of humanity, such trust requires a belief that another person will act a certain way, as well as a risk of that person not acting in that way.[444] Although there is an inherent uncertainty of the trustee acting as expected, trust generally implies a high degree of probability.[445] While such a situation can be described as one of reliance, it has been remarked that a breach of trust constitutes betrayal, whereas a breach of reliance only leads to disappointment.[446] While we are free to decide whom to trust, we are not always free to decide whom to rely on.[447]

Element of expectation – Trust can be seen from a narrow viewpoint – in the sense of trusting a person to perform a particular task – or from a wider viewpoint – constituting complete confidence.[448] It requires a certain attitude of optimism toward the trustee's goodwill and competence.[449] At the same time, it requires a more affective expectation that the trustee will be moved to act as expected.[450] The presence of expectation can be viewed as a central component of trust.[451]

441 Jones, K. (2001) "Trust: Philosophical Aspects", In: Smelser, N., Bates, P. (eds.) *International Encyclopedia of the Social and Behavioral Sciences*, Amsterdam: Elsevier Science, 15917.

442 McLeod, C. (2011) "Trust", In: Zalta, E. (ed.) *The Stanford Encyclopedia of Philosophy*, plato.stanford.edu.

443 Jones, K. (2001) "Trust: Philosophical Aspects", In: Smelser, N., Bates, P. (eds.) *International Encyclopedia of the Social and Behavioral Sciences*, Amsterdam: Elsevier Science, 15917; O'Neill, O. (2002) *A Question of Trust*, Cambridge: University Press, 4; Hardin, R. (2004) *Trust and Trustworthiness*, New York City: Russell Sage Foundation, 3–4.

444 Jones, K. (2001) "Trust: Philosophical Aspects", In: Smelser, N., Bates, P. (eds.) *International Encyclopedia of the Social and Behavioral Sciences*, Amsterdam: Elsevier Science, 15917.

445 Jones, K. (1998) "Trust", In: Craig, E. (ed.) *Routledge Encyclopedia of Philosophy*, Abingdon: Taylor & Francis, 467; McLeod, C. (2011) "Trust", In: Zalta, E. (ed.) *The Stanford Encyclopedia of Philosophy*, plato.stanford.edu.

446 Baier, A. (1986) "Trust and antitrust", *Ethics*, Vol. 96, 235; Jones, K. (1996) "Trust as an Affective Attitude", *Ethics*, Vol. 107, 14–15; McLeod, C. (2011) "Trust", In: Zalta, E. (ed.) *The Stanford Encyclopedia of Philosophy*, plato.stanford.edu; Jones, K. (1998) "Trust", In: Craig, E. (ed.) *Routledge Encyclopedia of Philosophy*, Abingdon: Taylor & Francis, 467; Jones, K. (2001) "Trust: Philosophical Aspects", In: Smelser, N., Bates, P. (eds.) *International Encyclopedia of the Social and Behavioral Sciences*, Amsterdam: Elsevier Science, 15918. As Jones notes, one can, for instance, rely on technology even when not necessarily trusting that technology.

447 For instance, in daily life we need to rely on doctors and pilots, even though we may not necessarily trust them.

448 Horsburgh, H. J. N. (1960) "The Ethics of Trust", *The Philosophical Quarterly*, Vol. 10, 343.

449 Jones, K. (1996) "Trust as an Affective Attitude", *Ethics*, Vol. 107, 7; McLeod, C. (2011) "Trust", In: Zalta, E. (ed.) *The Stanford Encyclopedia of Philosophy*, plato.stanford.edu; Hardin, R. (2004) *Trust and Trustworthiness*, New York City: Russell Sage Foundation, 8.

450 Jones, K. (1996) "Trust as an Affective Attitude", *Ethics*, Vol. 107, 8; O'Neill, O. (2002) *A Question of Trust*, Cambridge: University Press, 6; Möllering, G. (2001) "The Nature of Trust: From Georg Simmel to a Theory of Expectation, Interpretation and Suspension", *Sociology*, Vol 35, 404.

451 Jones, A. J. I. (2002) "On the concept of Trust", *Decision Support Systems*, Vol. 33, 225–232; Hardin, R. (2004) *Trust and Trustworthiness*, New York City: Russell Sage Foundation, 13.

## 2.2 PSYCHOLOGY

ROOTS IN PSYCHOSOCIAL DEVELOPMENT – From the philosophical understanding of trust it becomes clear that trust requires a certain attitude and expectation from the trustor. From a psychological perspective, however, trust can be considered as rooted firmly in the human mind, even being one of the core elements of psychological development. In Erikson's seminal work on the different stages of psychosocial development, he considers basic trust to be the very first characteristic learned by a newborn infant.[452] If that infant is exposed to warmth and affection in a secure environment, it will learn to establish a sense of basic trust in its parents. Failing to provide this primary care or a secure environment will result in the newborn infant to begin its life with a sense of mistrust against the world.[453]

TRUST AND MISTRUST – The sense of basic trust or mistrust will form the basis for the development of future social relationships throughout the individual's lifespan. Here, a lack of trust in certain situations has even been found to result in a lesser performance on a social, academic and professional level.[454] Bowlby, in formulating his Attachment Theory, found a clear link between early infant separations and later relational maladjustment.[455] The Attachment Theory has become the basis for further and current evolutions in developmental psychology.[456]

## 2.3 SOCIOLOGY

TRUST AS COMPLEXITY REDUCTION – While psychologists have focused on the importance of trust in the development of the individual, sociologists focus on the role of trust in the dynamic of interpersonal relationships.[457] The foundation for sociological thinking about trust was laid out by Luhmann, who considers trust to be a device to reduce the complexity of interpersonal relationships, and thus to cope with uncertainty.[458] Such relationships are inherently fraught with an endless

---

452 Erikson, E. H. (1959) *Identity and the lifecycle*, New York City: International Universities Press, 57–58.

453 *Ibid.*, 64–65.

454 On the correlation between social capital and academic achievement: Goddard, R. D. (2003) "Relational Networks, Social Trust, and Norms: A Social Capital Perspective on Students' Chances of Academic Success", *Educational Evaluation and Policy Analysis*, Vol. 25, 59–74.

455 Bowlby, J. (1969) *Attachment and Loss: Vol. 1 Attachment*, New York City: Basic Books, 399p.

456 Bretherton, I. (1992) "The origins of Attachment Theory: John Bowlby and Mary Ainsworth", *Developmental Psychology*, Vol. 28, 759–775.

457 The sociological foundation for the understanding of trust was posited mainly by Lewis and Weigert: Lewis, J. D., Weigert, A. (1985) "Trust as a social reality", *Social Forces*, Vol. 63, 967–985. It is their positioning of trust as a property of collective units – rather than of the isolated individual – that resulted in the current sociological understanding of trust.

458 Luhmann, N. (1979) *Trust and Power*, Chichester: John Wiley & Sons, 4–8; Levi, M. (2001) "Trust, sociology of", In: Smelser, N., Bates, P. (eds.) *International Encyclopedia of the Social*

number of uncertain variables which we cannot begin to process. Therefore, a certain level of rational prediction is applied to reduce the number of possible outcomes. However, as rationality alone cannot suffice[459], humans rely on trust to reduce the complexity of their relationships more quickly, economically and thoroughly.[460]

BET FOR FUTURE POSSIBILITIES – As a result, trust is perceived as a social construct serving as a bet for future possibilities.[461] It is based on both an expectation regarding the technical competence of the trustee and an expectation regarding what is referred to as the 'fiduciary obligation and responsibility'.[462] As no accurate predictions can be made about the future, nor can it be efficiently controlled, trust functions as a strategy to cope with an uncertain, unpredictable and uncontrollable future.[463] It is the finding that one person can decide to trust another person – thus with some probability[464] – but still requiring a certain leap of faith[465] – that the trustee will act as expected – that enables the trustor to engage in activities that would have been inconceivable absent that trust.[466]

---

*and Behavioral Sciences*, Amsterdam: Elsevier Science, 15923; Misztal, B. A. (1996) *Trust in Modern Societies: The Search for the Bases of Social Order*, Cambridge, MA: Polity Press, 73; Möllering, G. (2006) *Trust: Reason, Routine, Reflexivity*, Amsterdam: Elsevier, 8.

459 Here, it is argued that human rationality is inherently limited: Pixley, J. (1999) "Impersonal Trust in Global Mediating Organizations", *Sociological Perspectives*, Vol. 42, 652–653. Moreover, the limits of what can be explained by rationality can be regarded as producing the "*space for accidental events at the margins of its explanatory reach*". Green, J. (1995) *Risk, rationality and misfortune: towards a sociology of accidents*, PhD Thesis United Medical and Dental Schools of Guy's and St. Thomas's Hospitals, 231.

460 Lewis, J. D., Weigert, A. (1985) "Trust as a social reality", *Social Forces*, Vol. 63, 968–969.

461 Gambetta, D. (1988) "Can We Trust Trust?", In: Gambetta, D. (ed.) *Trust: Making and Breaking Cooperative Relations*, Oxford: Basil Blackwell, 217–218; Jalava, J. (2001) "Trust or confidence?", *presented at the 5th Conference of the European Sociological Association, 'Visions and Divisions'*, 28 August – 1 September 2001, Helsinki, Finland; Smith, C. (2005) "Understanding Trust and Confidence: Two Paradigms and their Significance for Health and Social Care", *Journal of Applied Philosophy*, Vol. 22, 300; Möllering, G. (2001) "The Nature of Trust: From Georg Simmel to a Theory of Expectation, Interpretation and Suspension", *Sociology*, Vol 35, 404.

462 Yamagishi, T. (2011) *Trust: The Evolutionary Game of Mind and Society*, Tokyo: Springer, 23–24.

463 Sztompka, P. (2001) "Trust: Cultural Concerns", In: Smelser, N., Bates, P. (eds.) *International Encyclopedia of the Social and Behavioral Sciences*, Amsterdam: Elsevier Science, 15913; Möllering, G. (2006) *Trust: Reason, Routine, Reflexivity*, Amsterdam: Elsevier, 23. Seligman finds trust to be the opposite of confidence, something we resort to when there is no predictability: Seligman, A. B. (1998) "Trust and Sociability: On the Limits of Confidence and Role Expectations", *American Journal of Economics and Sociology*, Vol. 57, 393.

464 In trying to reconcile the broad range of definitions and of possibilities between compete trust and distrust, Gambetta specifically focuses on the element of probability lying in between those extremes. Gambetta, D. (2000) "Can We Trust Trust?", in Gambetta, D. (ed.) *Trust: Making and Breaking Cooperative Relations*, Oxford: Basil Blackwell, 217–218.

465 Möllering, G. (2001) "The Nature of Trust: From Georg Simmel to a Theory of Expectation, Interpretation and Suspension", *Sociology*, Vol 35, 403–420.

466 Lewis and Weigert describe this as the cognitive leap of trust: we can trust because we expect the other to trust as well. This has also been described as 'trust in trust'. Lewis, J. D., Weigert, A. (1985) "Trust as a social reality", *Social Forces*, Vol. 63, 970; Zaltman, G.,

While such a situation has been construed as supposing cooperation, it must be noted that cooperation is also possible without trust.[467]

INHERENT RISK – At the same time, trust is mired in uncertainty, and inherently includes risk.[468] In other words, trust necessitates a willingness to take risk, and to become vulnerable to potential undesired outcomes to that risk.[469] As noted in philosophical literature, trust can be betrayed. Such a betrayal of trust has the potential to leave the trustor off worse than he was before the trust relationship.[470] It is in the possibility of breach of trust that the inherent risk of trust lies. Though the presence of such a risk cannot be avoided, the latter half of the 20th century has seen the rise of literature on risk management.[471]

---

Moorman, C. (1988) "The importance of personal trust in the use of research", *Journal of Advertising Research*, 17; McKnight, D. H., Chervany, N. L. (2001) "Trust and Distrust Definitions: One Bite at a Time", In: Falcone, R., Singh, M., Tan, Y.-H. (Eds.) *Trust in Cyber-societies, LNAI 2246*, Berlin: Springer, 36; Misztal, B. A. (1996) *Trust in Modern Societies: The Search for the Bases of Social Order*, Cambridge, MA: Polity Press, 74–75; Good, D. (2000) "Individuals, Interpersonal Relations, and Trust", In: Gambetta, D. (ed.) *Trust: Making and Breaking Cooperative Relations*, Oxford: Basil Blackwell, 33; Dasgupta, P. (2000) "Trust as a Commodity", In: Gambetta, D. (ed.) *Trust: Making and Breaking Cooperative Relations*, Oxford: Basil Blackwell, 55–56.

467 Mayer, R. C., Davis, J. H., Schoorman, F. D. (1995) "An Integrative Model of Organizational Trust", *The Academy of Management Review*, Vol. 20, 712–713. Good argues that cooperation could also be by chance rather than by design, and that a lack of cooperation does not necessarily constitute a breach of trust. Good, D. (2000) "Individuals, Interpersonal Relations, and Trust", In: Gambetta, D. (ed.) *Trust: Making and Breaking Cooperative Relations*, Oxford: Basil Blackwell, 33; Gambetta, D. (2000) "Can We Trust Trust?", in Gambetta, D. (ed.) *Trust: Making and Breaking Cooperative Relations*, Oxford: Basil Blackwell, 214.

468 Luhmann, N. (1979) *Trust and Power*, Chichester: John Wiley & Sons, 13 and 71; Lewis, J. D., Weigert, A. (1985) "Trust as a social reality", *Social Forces*, Vol. 63, 968; Levi, M. (2001) "Trust, sociology of", In: Smelser, N., Bates, P. (eds.) *International Encyclopedia of the Social and Behavioral Sciences*, Amsterdam: Elsevier Science, 15922; Misztal, B. A. (1996) *Trust in Modern Societies: The Search for the Bases of Social Order*, Cambridge, MA: Polity Press, 73; Gambetta, D. (2000) "Can We Trust Trust?", in Gambetta, D. (ed.) *Trust: Making and Breaking Cooperative Relations*, Oxford: Basil Blackwell, 218–219; Möllering, G. (2006) *Trust: Reason, Routine, Reflexivity*, Amsterdam: Elsevier, 8. Aligning the risk inherently associated with trust with Luhmann's notion of trust as a complexity reducing strategy, Yamagishi puts forward the notion of trust as an aspect of risk management. Yamagishi, T. (2011) *Trust: The Evolutionary Game of Mind and Society*, Tokyo: Springer, 168.

469 Mayer, R. C., Davis, J. H., Schoorman, F. D. (1995) "An Integrative Model of Organizational Trust", *The Academy of Management Review*, Vol. 20, 712; Nikolova, N., Möllering, G., Reihlen, M. (2015) "Trusting as a 'Leap of Faith': Trust-building practices in client–consultant relationships", *Scandinavian Journal of Management*, Vol. 31, 233.

470 McKnight, D. H., Chervany, N. L. (2001) "Trust and Distrust Definitions: One Bite at a Time", In: Falcone, R., Singh, M., Tan, Y.-H. (Eds.) *Trust in Cyber-societies, LNAI 2246*, Berlin: Springer, 34; Smith, C. (2005) "Understanding Trust and Confidence: Two Paradigms and their Significance for Health and Social Care", *Journal of Applied Philosophy*, Vol. 22, 300.

471 As part of what is referred to as the 'probabilistic revolution', aiming to control and manage risks and accidents. Green, J. (1995) *Risk, rationality and misfortune: towards a sociology of accidents*, PhD Thesis United Medical and Dental Schools of Guy's and St. Thomas's Hospitals, 232.

Application to information society – While most sociological research on trust focuses on classic interpersonal trust, the basic concepts employed there can also be applied to developments of the information society, such as e-commerce.[472]

## 2.4 ECONOMY

Trust and transaction risk – Trust is also an important concept within economics. It has even been remarked that "*virtually every commercial transaction has within itself an element of trust*".[473] The findings of economic scholars on trust are fairly similar to those of sociologists. Therefore, trust is also here perceived as a form of risk-taking. Such a risk is taken in order to enable new possibilities, which in turn could result in new business opportunities, lower transaction costs, and higher overall market efficiency.[474] In more concrete terms, research has demonstrated that an increase in trust can influence a state's growth in terms of Gross Domestic Product (GDP).[475]

Risk of betrayal – While trust could therefore serve to yield economic growth, the inherent element of risk also entails that trust could be betrayed. In that case, for instance when too much trust is conferred onto transactions with a low level of trustworthiness, the trustor risks being exploited.[476] Therefore, a balance must be struck in which the level of trust invested into a transactions by the trustor is at the same height as the level of trustworthiness of the

472 See, for instance: McKnight, D. H., Choudhury, V., Kacmar, C. (2002) "The impact of initial consumer trust on intentions to transact with a web site: a trust building model", *Journal of Strategic Information Systems*, Vol. 11, 297–323.

473 Arrow, K. (1972) "Gifts and Exchanges", *Philosophy & Public Affairs*, Vol. 1, 357. Pollitt concurs in finding that every economic handover involves "*vulnerability and the threat of appropriation*". Pollitt, M. (2002) "The economics of trust, norms and networks", *Business Ethics: A European Review*, Vol. 11, 120.

474 Andreoni, J. (2005) "Trust, Reciprocity, and Contract Enforcement: Experiments on Satisfaction Guaranteed", *econ.ucsd.edu/~jandreon/WorkingPapers/verify.pdf*, 3–4; Pollitt, M. (2002) "The Economics of Trust, Norms and Networks", *Business Ethics: A European Review*, Vol. 11, 120; Jones, K. (2001) "Trust: Philosophical Aspects", In: Smelser, N., Bates, P. (eds.) *International Encyclopedia of the Social and Behavioral Sciences*, Amsterdam: Elsevier Science, 15917.

475 Knack, S., Keefer, P. (1997) "Does Social Capital Have an Economic Payoff? A Cross-Country Investigation", *The Quarterly Journal of Economics*, Vol. 112, 1251–1288; Huang, H., Keser, C., Leland, J., Shachat, J. (2003) "Trust, the Internet, and the digital divide", *IBM Systems Journal*, Vol. 42, 508; Pollitt, M. (2002) "The economics of trust, norms and networks", *Business Ethics: A European Review*, Vol. 11, 122–123.

476 Arrow, K. (1972) "Gifts and Exchanges", *Philosophy & Public Affairs*, Vol. 1, 357. On the specific issue of exploitation in trust relationships: James, H.S. (2002) "The trust paradox: a survey of economic inquiries into the nature of trust and trustworthiness", *Journal of Economic Behavior & Organization*, Vol. 47, 291–307; Macy, M., Skvoretz, J. (1998) "The Evolution of Trust and Cooperation between Strangers: A Computational Model", *American Sociological Review*, Vol. 63, 643.

trustee.[477] Similar to what was found in sociological literature, trustworthiness is understood as the "*characteristics and actions of the trustee* [that] *will lead that person to be more or less trusted*", meaning a reliance on the trustee's competence and intention.[478]

TRUST MODELS AND METRICS – The main contribution of economics to trust research has been the development of the models and theories used to measure and build trust. The effects of strategic decision-making are the core topic of the field of game theory. The most well-known example here is the Prisoner's Dilemma, in which two prisoners are given the option to defect or to cooperate. The game is designed so that both prisoners seemingly have a personal incentive to defect, even though both gain a worse outcome from mutual defection than from mutual cooperation.[479] Here, it is posited that if the game is played indefinitely, cooperation could even form without trust.[480] However, in a single instant of the game, there is a high probability of defection precisely due to these personal incentives. The exposure to defection is where the risk element of trust lies.[481] However, while rational economic behavior in a single-instance Prisoner's Dilemma game should lead to actors defecting, it has – as stated before – also been found that trust is essential to economic development.[482] Therefore, research is conducted on how to measure and increase trust.[483] Given the close similarities

---

477 When considering 'levels' of trust and trustworthiness, it is indicated that there are limits to both trust and trustworthiness. A 'level of trust' is then the maximum amount of trust that is conferred upon a relationship, e.g. the maximum amount of money the trustor would lend to someone. Hornák, Z., Nyilas, I., Petró, D., Schrammel, J., Wolkerstorfer, P., Ellensohn, L., Geven, A., Kristjansdottir, K., Fritsch, L., Schultz, T., Abie, H., Pürzel, F., Wittstock, V. (2010) "uTRUSTit D.3.1 – Technology and Standard Report", *utrustit.eu*, 12–13; Möllering, G. (2006) *Trust: Reason, Routine, Reflexivity*, Amsterdam: Elsevier, 43.

478 Mayer, R. C., Davis, J. H., Schoorman, F. D. (1995) "An Integrative Model of Organizational Trust", *The Academy of Management Review*, Vol. 20, 717; Yamagishi, T. (2011) *Trust: The Evolutionary Game of Mind and Society*, Tokyo: Springer, 23–24.

479 Axelrod, R. (1988) "The Evolution of Cooperation", In: Gromyko, A., Hellman, M. (Eds.) *Breakthrough: Emerging New Thinking*, New York City: Walker and Co., 185.

480 Axelrod uses the arms control between the US and the USSR in the 1980's as an example: as both sides know they have to continue dealing with each other, they may adopt a mutual policy of arms control, even if they do not trust each other. It is therefore the durability of the relationship, not trust, which forms the basis of cooperation. Axelrod, R. (1988) "The Evolution of Cooperation", In: Gromyko, A., Hellman, M. (Eds.) *Breakthrough: Emerging New Thinking*, New York City: Walker and Co., 189.

481 Guerra, G., Zizzo, D., Dutton, W., Peltu, M. (2003) "Economics of Trust in the Information Economy: Issues of Identity, Privacy and Security", *Oxford Internet Institute, Research Report No. 1*, 4.

482 *Ibid.*, 6; Möllering, G. (2006) *Trust: Reason, Routine, Reflexivity*, Amsterdam: Elsevier, 46–47.

483 For instance, Huang *et al.* argue that solid and enforceable legal frameworks – such as regarding contracts and property rights – are imperative to foster trust. Huang, H., Keser, C., Leland, J., Shachat, J. (2003) "Trust, the Internet, and the digital divide", *IBM Systems Journal*, Vol. 42, 508. Knack and Zak focused on civil liberties, reducing income inequalities and raising educational levels. Knack, S., Zak, P. (2003) "Building Trust: Public Policy, Interpersonal Trust, and Economic Development", *Supreme Court Economic Review*, Vol. 10, 91–107.

between economics research on trust and trust research in sociology, there are numerous instances in which sociologists have adopted methods of game theory – particularly the Prisoner's Dilemma – in their research.[484] At the same time, economists also implement social thinking in their research.[485] Much of such research is focused on trust-building, for instance in consulting services.[486]

## 2.5 COMPUTER SCIENCE AND ENGINEERING

UNCERTAINTY IN THE INFORMATION SOCIETY – More and more interactions and transactions are conducted through the use of technologies such as computers, smart-devices and the Internet. However, at the same time the countless reports on hacks, security breaches and information leaks have resulted in a growing awareness of the risks associated with such practices.[487] The result is a situation where the trustworthiness of the devices and technologies of the information society may be questioned, even though at the same time their use can often no longer be avoided.[488]

---

484 See, for instance: Macy, M., Skvoretz, J. (1998) "The Evolution of Trust and Cooperation between Strangers: A Computational Model", *American Sociological Review*, Vol. 63, 638–660; Pixley, J. (1999) "Impersonal Trust in Global Mediating Organizations", *Sociological Perspectives*, Vol. 42, 647–671; Levi, M. (2001) "Trust, sociology of", In: Smelser, N., Bates, P. (eds.) *International Encyclopedia of the Social and Behavioral Sciences*, Amsterdam: Elsevier Science, 15925; Dasgupta, P. (2000) "Trust as a Commodity", In: Gambetta, D. (ed.) *Trust: Making and Breaking Cooperative Relations*, Oxford: Basil Blackwell, 49–72; Gambetta, D. (1988) "Can We Trust Trust?", In: Gambetta, D. (ed.) *Trust: Making and Breaking Cooperative Relations*, Oxford: Basil Blackwell, 213–237; Good, D. (2000) "Individuals, Interpersonal Relations, and Trust", In: Gambetta, D. (ed.) *Trust: Making and Breaking Cooperative Relations*, Oxford: Basil Blackwell, 31–48.

485 Research on trust modelling and measuring often includes social aspects. See, for instance, the research on how different social and policy strategies can raise trust, as referenced in footnote 483. Pollitt refers to such thinking as the economics behind social capital: Pollitt, M. (2002) "The economics of trust, norms and networks", *Business Ethics: A European Review*, Vol. 11, 119.

486 E.g.: Nikolova, N., Möllering, G., Reihlen, M. (2015) "Trusting as a 'Leap of Faith': Trust-building practices in client–consultant relationships", *Scandinavian Journal of Management*, Vol. 31, 232–245; May, M. (2004) "From consultant to courtier", *Consulting to Management*, Vol. 15, 17–34.

487 Major data breach incidents include the following:
- Yahoo (2013-2016): a US web services company, 3 billion accounts affected by data breach.
- Anthem (2015): a US health insurance provider, 80 million healthcare records leaked.
- Home Depot (2014): a US home improvement retailer, 56 million credit card numbers leaked.
- Target (2013): a US discount retailer, 40 million credit and debit card numbers leaked, affecting over 70 million customers.
- Sony PlayStation Network (2011): a Japanese video game service, 77 million user records leaked.

Krebs, B. (2015) "Data Breach at Health Insurer Anthem Could Impact Millions", *krebsonsecurity.com*, 4 February 2015; Backman, M. (2014) "Home Depot: 56 million cards exposed in breach", *CNN Money*, 18 September 2014; Perez, S. (2014) "Target's Data Breach Gets Worse: 70 Million Customers Had Info Stolen, Including Names, Emails And Phones", *TechCrunch*, 10 January 2014; Quinn, B., Arthur, C. (2011) "PlayStation Network hackers access data of 77 million users", *The Guardian*, 26 April 2011.

488 See, for instance, on trust building for consumer transactions in electronic commerce: McKnight, D. H., Choudhury, V., Kacmar, C. (2002) "The impact of initial consumer trust on

TRUST BETWEEN HUMANS AND TECHNOLOGY – While the previous scientific disciplines discussed here mainly focus on the interpersonal aspects of trust, there is a growing body of research on the aspects of trust in interactions between humans and the devices of the information society.[489] One particular area where the notion of trust in human interaction with information society devices, services and technologies has become a key focal point is that of Human-Computer Interaction (HCI).[490] Here, information society devices, technologies and services are regarded as the object of trust.[491] A related field, computer ethics, traditionally focuses on the ethics of computer use, but could also be seen from the perspective of the effect of ethics on computers.[492]

TRUSTED TECHNOLOGY – Within the scientific field of information security – a field comprising both computer scientists and electrical engineers – trust research is referred to as computational trust.[493] In the field of computational

---

intentions to transact with a web site: a trust building model", *Journal of Strategic Information Systems*, Vol. 11, 297–323; Shaker, L. (2006) "In Google we trust: Information integrity in the digital age", *First Monday*, Vol. 11; Patton, M. A., Jøsang, A. (2004) "Technologies for Trust in Electronic Commerce", *Electronic Commerce Research*, Vol. 4, 9–21. Harwood considers security and trust as some of the basic elements to be considered by computer scientists. Harwood, W. T. (2012) *The Logic of Trust*, PhD Thesis University of York, 21; Raab, C. (2004) "The future of privacy protection", *UK Department for Business, Information and Skills Foresight Project*, 15–16; Grabowskia, M., Sanborn, S. D. (2003) "Human performance and embedded intelligent technology in safety-critical systems", *Int. J. Human-Computer Studies*, Vol. 58, 639. Castelfranchi, for instance, underlines the importance of trust-building for IT systems: Castelfranchi, C. (2006) "Why We Need a Non-reductionist Approach to Trust", In: Stølen, K., Winsborough, W. H., Martinelli, F., Massacci, F. (Eds.) *iTrust 2006*, Berlin: Springer, 1–2.

489 Collins, B., Mansell, R. (Eds.) (2004) "Cyber Trust and Crime Prevention: A Synthesis of the State-of-the-Art Science Reviews", *UK Department for Business, Information and Skills Foresight Project*, 31–32.

490 Riegelsberger, J., Sasse, A., McCarthy, J. D. (2005) "The mechanics of trust: A framework for research and design", *Int. J. Human-Computer Studies*, Vol. 62, 382–383; Sasse, M. A. (2004) "Usability and trust in information systems", *UK Department for Business, Information and Skills Foresight Project*, 12–13; Castelfranchi, C. (2006) "Why We Need a Non-reductionist Approach to Trust", In: Stølen, K., Winsborough, W. H., Martinelli, F., Massacci, F. (Eds.) *iTrust 2006*, Berlin: Springer, 1–2.

491 Corritorea, C., Krachera, B., Wiedenbeck, S. (2003) "On-line trust: concepts, evolving themes, a model", *Int. J. Human-Computer Studies*, Vol. 58, 739.

492 Coleman, K. G. (2001) "Android arete: Toward a virtue ethic for computational agents", *Ethics and Information Technology*, Vol. 3, 247–265. Within information security, trust in information sciences has been described as comprising questions of person-to-person trust, person-to-system trust and system-to-system trust. Collins, B., Mansell, R. (Eds.) (2004) "Cyber Trust and Crime Prevention: A Synthesis of the State-of-the-Art Science Reviews", *UK Department for Business, Information and Skills Foresight Project*, 31.

493 One example includes Trusted Computing, in which cryptography is used to ensure that a computer will behave consistently in expected ways. Overall, trust in an information technology (IT) context can be considered as trust in the correct functioning of the IT system. Quirin, T., Fritsch, L., Husseiki, R. (2010) *Ergänzende und alternative Techniken zu Trusted Computing (TC-Erg./-A.) – Teil 1*, Bonn: Bundesamtes für Sicherheit in der Informationstechnik (BSI), 11. On Trusted Computing's impact on privacy: Hansen, M. (2004) "A Double-Edged Blade", *Datenschutz und Datensicherheit*, 525–528. Also the

trust, user trust in information technologies or trust in authorities using such technologies is aided by cryptography. While cryptography was originally devised as a tool to ensure information confidentiality between parties, it has also proven its use in ensuring entity authentication, data integrity, and non-repudiation.[494] In doing so, cryptography can therefore help establishing whether a party is truly who he purports to be, whether the information has been unaltered between sending and receiving – meaning that it has not been intercepted and altered with malicious intent – and that actions undertaken cannot be denied. Cryptography is also one of the core elements of what is referred to as trusted computing.[495] Here, a combination of specific hardware – such as the standardized Trusted Platform Module[496] – and software is used to ensure the reliable working of the computing platform.[497]

Trust in the Internet of Things – It could, however, be argued that security alone is not sufficient and that additional layers of trust are needed.[498] The importance of user trust in information society devices, services and technologies can only be expected to rise as computational connections and networks become ever more pervasive and ubiquitous. For several years now,

---

Article 29 Working Party has adopted a working document on Trusted Computing: Article 29 Working Party (2004) "Working Document on Trusted Computing Platforms and in particular on the work done by the Trusted Computing Group (TCG group)", *WP 86*. Jøsang has argued that in information security, trust should be knowledge-based. Jøsang, A. (1996) "The right type of trust for distributed systems", In: Haigh, T., Hosmer, H. (Eds.) *Proceedings of the 1996 New Security Paradigms Workshop (NSPW)*, New York: ACM, 119–131; Houmb, S. H., Ray, I., Ray, I. (2006) "Estimating the Relative Trustworthiness of Information Sources in Security Solution Evaluation", In: Stølen, K., Winsborough, W. H., Martinelli, F., Massacci, F. (Eds.) *iTrust 2006*, Berlin: Springer, 138–139.

494 Menezes, A. J., Van Oorschot, P. C., Vanstone, S. A. (2001) *Handbook of Applied Cryptography*, Boca Raton: CRC Press, 1–5.

495 While computer and network security have been around for a while, research into trust and the information society was still nascent just a decade ago. Dutton, W. H., Shepherd, A. (2004) "Confidence and risk on the Internet1", *UK Department for Business, Information and Skills Foresight Project*, 4–5.

496 Standardized as ISO/IEC 11889.

497 Brandl, H., Rosteck, T. (2004) "Technik, Implementierung und Anwendung des Trusted Computing Group-Standards", *Datenschutz und Datensicherheit*, Vol. 28, 529–530. Note, however, that the practice of trusted computing has also received criticism. It has been said to take control away from the user and to impose potentially privacy-invasive technologies such as Digital Rights Management (DRM). Hansen, M. (2004) "A Double-Edged Blade: On Trusted Computing's Impact on Privacy", *Datenschutz und Datensicherheit*, Vol. 28, 525–528; Kuhlmann, D., Gehring, R. A. (2003) "Trusted Platforms, DRM and Beyond", In: Becker, E., Buhse, W., Günnewig, D., Rump, N. (Eds.) *Digital Rights Management: Technological, Economic, Legal and Political Aspects*, Berlin: Springer, 193–195.

498 For instance, user and agent trust is needed as well. Falcone, R., Castelfranchi, C. (2001) "The Socio-cognitive Dynamics of Trust: Does Trust Create Trust?", In: Falcone, R., Singh, M., Tan, Y.-H. (Eds.) *Trust in Cyber-societies: Integrating the Human and Artificial Perspectives*, Berlin: Springer, 55–56.

the coming of the so-called Internet of Things has been heralded.[499] Essentially, the Internet of Things would allow the interconnection of virtually every object in life, ranging from thermostats and refrigerators to the most mundane object such as a sock.[500] Such interconnections are then expected to assist various tasks, such as home automation, automatic shopping or simply locating items. Given the enormous amounts of often sensitive data those interconnections transfer, it goes without saying that the Internet of Things requires a significant amount of trust from its users.[501] As learned from the previous scientific disciplines analyzed here, trust inherently constitutes a risk and conferring trust upon a new and uncertain relationship may lead to benefits, but could also result in exploitation.[502] To avoid exploitation, the Internet of Things has to display a level of trustworthiness equaling the level of trust required from its users. Factors that can augment trust include credibility, ease of use, and the perception of risk reduction.[503]

Application of trust models and metrics – As noted, scholars within the fields of economy and sociology have developed trust management strategies such as trust metrics to measure how trust should be conferred.[504] Such trust metrics could also be applied in computer science, thus guiding the process of augmenting the trustworthiness of a device, service or technology to correspond to the required level of user trust.[505] However, with trust being a very complex

499 Schulz, T. (2014) "Creating Universal Designed and Trustworthy Objects for the Internet of Things", In: Zaphiris, P., Ioannou, A. (Eds.) *Learning and Collaboration Technologies 2014, Part II*, Berlin: Springer, 207.

500 For instance, a smart thermostat would learn when homeowners arrive and leave and adjust the home's temperature accordingly, or it could be controlled from a distance. A smart fridge would learn when stock on certain products – e.g. milk or cheese – runs low and add those items to a digital grocery list. Tiny radio-frequency identification (RFID) chips could be embedded into clothes – such as socks – allowing their owner to track them. While the technologies needed to achieve such goals are widely available, they have yet to reach a wider audience.

501 As with all information processes, it must be assessed whether these processes are trustworthy. O'Hara, K., Shadbolt, N. (2004) "Knowledge technologies and the semantic web", *UK Department for Business, Information and Skills Foresight Project*, 1.

502 Riegelsberger, J., Sasse, M. A., McCarthy, J. D. (2003) "The researcher's dilemma: evaluating trust in computer-mediated communication", *Int. J. Human-Computer Studies*, Vol. 58, 761; Corritorea, C., Krachera, B., Wiedenbeck, S. (2003) "On-line trust: concepts, evolving themes, a model", *Int. J. Human-Computer Studies*, Vol. 58, 742; Marsh, S. P. (1994) *Formalising Trust as a Computational Concept*, University of Sterling PhD thesis, 32.

503 Corritorea, C., Krachera, B., Wiedenbeck, S. (2003) "On-line trust: concepts, evolving themes, a model", *Int. J. Human-Computer Studies*, Vol. 58, 750–752; Fogg, B. J., Tseng, H. (1999) "The elements of computer credibility", In: Williams, M., Altom, M. (Eds.) *Proceedings of the SIGCHI conference on Human Factors in Computing Systems (CHI '99)*, New York: ACM, 80–87.

504 The idea of measuring trust and trustworthiness to find the right balance can also be referred to as trust management: Jøsang, A., Keser, C., Dimitrakos, T. (2005) "Can we manage trust?", In: Herrmann, P., Issarny, V., Shiu, S. (Eds.) *Trust Management: Proceedings of the third international iTrust conference 2005*, Berlin: Springer, 93–107.

505 For a game theoretic approach of information science trust: Collins, B., Mansell, R. (Eds.) (2004) "Cyber Trust and Crime Prevention: A Synthesis of the State-of-the-Art Science

matter – as well as being subject to personal circumstances – it may be argued that trust management can never be fully accurate.[506]

TRUSTED THIRD PARTY – A significant development within the fields of computer science and engineering is the position of the trusted third party (TTP). Essentially, it allows two parties in a transaction that do not fully trust each other to instead confer their trust upon a third party they do trust.[507] The third party then vouches for the trustworthiness of both parties to the transaction, thus providing supporting trust that helps the user in establishing his final level of trust into a system.[508] A notable example of the trusted third party in practice is the figure of the qualified electronic signature found in EU law.[509] Here, a trusted third party – the Certificate Authority – provides a digital

---

Reviews", *UK Department for Business, Information and Skills Foresight Project,* 32–36. Moreover, research is needed on why people trust certain entities and the services they offer. It has, for instance, been posited that trustworthiness may in part relate to how such entity handles its counterparty's privacy. Raab, C. (2004) "The future of privacy protection", *UK Department for Business, Information and Skills Foresight Project,* 15–16. Another element to raise trustworthiness is the establishment of an entity's identity: O'Hara, K., Shadbolt, N. (2004) "Knowledge technologies and the semantic web", *UK Department for Business, Information and Skills Foresight Project,* 13–14; Ramchurn, S. D., Jennings, N. R. (2004) "Trust in agent-based software", *UK Department for Business, Information and Skills Foresight Project,* 4–5. For a trust model for e-health websites, see: Sillence, E., Briggs, P., Harris, P., Fishwick, L. (2006) "A framework for understanding trust factors in web-based health advice", *Int. J. Human-Computer Studies,* Vol. 64, 697–713. On trust requirements in e-business, see: Jones, S., Wilikens, M., Morris, P., Masera, M. (2000) "Trust Requirements in E-Business: A conceptual framework for understanding the needs and concerns of different stakeholders", *Communications of the ACM,* Vol. 43, 81–87.

506 Apart from risk identification and assessment, trust management also requires the adoption of strategies to cope with risk. The combination of all these elements is a difficult balancing act. O'Hara, K., Shadbolt, N. (2004) "Knowledge technologies and the semantic web", *UK Department for Business, Information and Skills Foresight Project,* 20–21; Ramchurn, S. D., Jennings, N. R. (2004) "Trust in agent-based software", *UK Department for Business, Information and Skills Foresight Project,* 2–3.

507 A more elaborate discussion regarding the importance of the TTP for trust in information systems can be found at: Jøsang, A., Van Laenen, F., Knapskog, S.J., Vandewalle, J. (1997) "How to trust systems", In: Yngström, L., Carlsen, J. (Eds.) *Information Security in Research and Business, Proceedings of the IFIP TC11 13th International Conference on Information Security (SEC '97),* London: Chapman & Hall, 241–252.

508 Jøsang, A. (1996) "The right type of trust for distributed systems", In: Haigh, T., Hosmer, H. (Eds.) *Proceedings of the 1996 New Security Paradigms Workshop (NSPW),* New York: ACM, 119–131; European Telecommunications Standards Institute (1997) "Telecommunications Security; Trusted Third Parties (TTP); Requirements for TTP Services", *EG 201 057,* 12.

509 First created at the level of the European Union by Directive 1999/93/EC of the European Parliament and of the Council of 13 December 1999 on a Community framework for electronic signatures, *OJ* L 13 of 19 January 2000, 12–20. This directive is to be replaced by a regulation: Regulation (EU) No 910/2014 of the European Parliament and of the Council of 23 July 2014 on electronic identification and trust services for electronic transactions in the internal market and repealing Directive 1999/93/EC, *OJ* L 257 of 28 August 2014, 73–114. See also: Gobert, D. (2004) "Commerce électronique: vers un cadre juridique général pour les tiers de confiance", *Revue du Droit des Technologies de l'information,* nr. 18, 33–34.

certificate of ownership of the cryptographic keys used to generate the electronic signature. When used in a transaction, the opposing party will then rely on the trustworthiness of the trusted third party to assure that the digital certificate is valid and thus that the person to whom the cryptographic keys belong is truly who he purports to be.[510]

## 2.6 LAW

COMMON THREADS ON TRUST – While the previous scientific disciplines discussed here demonstrate diverging understandings of the concept of trust, a few common threads could already be identified. For instance, it is clear that trust is generally accepted as constituting a risk undertaken by one person in confiding in another person, and in doing so hoping to benefit from that trust relationship. While trust is then understood as holding the potential for mutual benefit, it is also commonly accepted that there is a possibility for a negative outcome, for instance due to exploitation. Such a negative outcome could be the result of conferring too high a degree of trust onto an untrustworthy relationship. In order to level the chances for a positive outcome, a balance should therefore be struck between trust and trustworthiness.

DIVERGENCE IN LAW – Law, however, does not appear to follow this path identified in other scientific disciplines. Though many different incarnations of trust can be found in legal systems all over the world, there is a clear divergence from how trust is defined in other disciplines. In the following paragraphs, a number of different applications of the notion of trust in law will be presented.

TRUST LAW – A first reference to the trust notion found in legal systems is that of trust law, which governs the legal figure of the trust.[511] A trust is established by the intention of a settlor, who confides certain property to a trustee of his appointing.[512] Once the trustee has accepted his duties, he is bound to manage said property to the benefit of a beneficiary appointed by the settlor.[513] The governance of the relationship between settlor, trustee and beneficiary, as well

---

510 Poullet, Y. (1996) "Les transactions commerciales et industrielles par voie électronique: de quelques réflexions autour du droit de la preuve", In: X, *Le droit des affaires en évolution: le juriste face à l'invasion informatique*, Brussels: Bruylant, 64–65.

511 Despite its name, trust law does not bear a particular connection to antitrust law, which will be discussed further on.

512 The settlor's intent and the property (*res*) are two of the constitutive elements of a trust. "trust" (2015), *Black's Law Dictionary* (9th ed.), West; Restatement (Third) of Trusts §3 (Am. Law Inst. 2003); 76 Am. Jur. 2d Trusts §2 (2015).

513 The beneficiary being the third and final constitutive element of the trust. "trust" (2015), *Black's Law Dictionary* (9th ed.), West; Restatement (Third) of Trusts §3 and §76 (Am. Law Inst. 2003); 76 Am. Jur. 2d Trusts §2 (2015).

as the division of duties and liabilities between them, is governed by a deed of trust or through a will establishing the trust.[514] Upon establishment of the trust, the property is transferred, with the trustee gaining legal ownership and the beneficiary gaining equitable title.[515] A trust creates a fiduciary relationship between the parties involved.[516] The trustee is bound to observe the highest standard of care in his management of the trust property in benefit of the beneficiary.[517] It is in that notion of conferring trust upon another person in order to gain benefit – even though that benefit in this case is not to oneself but to another – that similarities are found to the trust concept found in social sciences. However, while social sciences mainly look at non-contractual interpersonal trust relationships, the fiduciary relationship under trust law is strictly regulated by law or equity, depending on the legal system. The origins of the trust, however, remain unclear. While it was at some point believed that English law developed in relative isolation from the European *ius commune*, more recent authors argue that English law was in fact influenced by Roman law as well.[518] It could then be possible, yet unproven, that the notion of trust finds its origins in the Roman notion of *fideicommissum*.[519, 520]Alternatively, in the late 19th century, the origins of trust became linked to the Germanic concept of *Salman* or *Treuhand*.[521] The fiduciary relationship in the *Treuhand* is indeed

514 In the latter case, a testamentary trust is established. Langbein, J. H. (1995) "The contractarian basis of the law of trusts", *Yale Law Journal*, Vol. 105, 636–637.

515 Moore v. Moore, 111 S.W.3d 530 (Mo. App. S.D., 2003); Jewish Community Ass'n of Casper v. Community First Nat. Bank, 6 P.3d 1264 (Wyo., 2000); Faulkner v. Bost, 137 S.W.3d 254 (Tex. App.–Tyler, 2004); 76 Am. Jur. 2d Trusts §1 (2015).

516 This establishes a set of duties, which include a duty of loyalty, honesty, and good faith. In re S & D Foods, Inc., 144 B.R. 121 (Bkrtcy. D. Colo., 1992). See also: Restatement (Third) of Trusts §77 (Am. Law Inst. 2007).

517 "fiduciary" (2015), *Black's Law Dictionary* (9th ed.), West. Those bound to a fiduciary duty cannot personally profit from their management of the trust property, all benefits belong to the beneficiary. 37 C.J.S. Fraud §7 (2015); In re Bender, 844 N.E.2d 170 (Ind. App., 2006); Restatement (Third) of Trusts §78 (Am. Law Inst. 2007); 76 Am. Jur. 2d Trusts §331 (2015).

518 For an overview of this: Van Rhee, C. H. (2000) "Trusts, Trust-like Concepts and Ius Commune", *European Review of Private Law*, Vol. 3, 454–455; Zimmermann, R. (2004) "Roman Law and the Harmonization of Private Law in Europe", In: Hartkamp, A., Hesselink, M., Hondius, E., Joustra, C., du Perron, E., Veldman, M. (Eds.) *Towards a European Civil Code – Third edition*, Nijmegen: Kluwer, 37–38.

519 As found, for instance, in the Institutiones of Gaius, 2.23.

520 Helmholz, R., Zimmermann, R. (1998) "Views of Trust and Treuhand. An Introduction", In: Helmholz, R., Zimmermann, R. (Eds.) *Itinera Fiduciae: Trust and Treuhand in Historical Perspective*, Berlin: Duncker & Humblot, 31; Van Rhee, C. H. (2000) "Trusts, Trust-like Concepts and Ius Commune", *European Review of Private Law*, Vol. 3, 457. Currently, UK trust law is governed by principles of common law and equity, as well as through specific statutes such as: Act to amend the law relating to trustees and persons having the investment powers of trustees; and for connected purposes of 23 November 2000 (Trustee Act 2000), 2000 ch. 29.

521 Helmholz, R., Zimmermann, R. (1998) "Views of Trust and Treuhand. An Introduction", In: Helmholz, R., Zimmermann, R. (Eds.) *Itinera Fiduciae: Trust and Treuhand in Historical Perspective*, Berlin: Duncker & Humblot, 33; Van Rhee, C. H. (2000) "Trusts, Trust-like Concepts and Ius Commune", *European Review of Private Law*, Vol. 3, 460.

similar to that in today's trust. However, thus far there is no convincing evidence that the *Treuhand* did indeed develop into the trust.[522] Whatever the origins of the trust, the concept has been adopted by other common law states and civil law states, be it that the precise scope of the trust figure in those countries may differ significantly from the trust found in UK law.[523]

Antitrust law – In the field of antitrust law, laws were originally enacted against the so-called corporate trust, which was a legal device used to consolidate power in large corporations.[524] Those corporate trusts gained particular infamy due to the late 19th and early 20th century monopolies or quasi-monopolies caused by corporations such as Standard Oil[525], U.S. Steel[526], and the American Tobacco Company.[527] Early examples of such antitrust laws include the US Sherman Act[528] and the US Clayton Act.[529] Despite its seeming relationship to trust law, antitrust law therefore concerns a different matter altogether, and

522 Van Rhee, C. H. (2000) "Trusts, Trust-like Concepts and Ius Commune", *European Review of Private Law*, Vol. 3, 461; Helmholz, R., Zimmermann, R. (1998) "Views of Trust and Treuhand. An Introduction", In: Helmholz, R., Zimmermann, R. (Eds.) *Itinera Fiduciae: Trust and Treuhand in Historical Perspective*, Berlin: Duncker & Humblot, 37.

523 A comparison between different national implementations of the trust can be found at: Hansmann, H., Mattei, U. (1998) "The functions of trust law: a comparative legal and economic analysis", *N.Y.U. L. Rev.*, Vol. 73, 434–479. The US has a strong legal tradition on trusts, with the core elements of case law being codified in the American Law Institute's Restatements of the Law. Moreover, a model law – the Uniform Trust Code – forms the basis for the majority of states' local legislation on trusts. An example of a civil law state that has adopted a version of the trust is France: Loi n° 2007-211 du 19 février 2007 instituant la fiducie, *JORF* n°44 of 21 February 2007, 3052 *et seq.* Also Curaçao – part of the Kingdom of the Netherlands – has adopted a trust incarnation. Landsverordening van de 15de december 2011 houdende aanvulling van Boek 3 van het Burgerlijk Wetboek met bepalingen inzake trusts (Landsverordening trust), *Publicatieblad van Curaçao* N° 67; De Boer, J. (2012) "De trust naar Curaçaos recht", *Weekblad voor Privaatrecht, Notariaat en Registratie*, Vol. 143, 287–291. While certain aspects of Belgian law could be used to achieve similar results, Belgium has no concrete trust figure. De Witte, C. (2007) "Kan Trust in België een nuttig instrument zijn voor vermogensplanning?", *Jura Falconis*, Vol. 43, 539–558; Storme, M. E. (1998) "Van trust gespeend? *Trusts* en fiduciaire figuren in het Belgisch privaatrecht", *Tijdschrift voor Privaatrecht*, Vol. 35, 703–814.

524 Note, however, the US Supreme Court's characterization of antitrust law not as a protection of businesses against the workings of the market, but rather as a protection of the public from failure of the market. Spectrum Sports, Inc. *v.* McQuillan, 506 U.S. 447 (1993) at 458.

525 In a landmark case, the US Supreme Court found Standard Oil guilty of monopolizing the oil industry – and thus hindering free competition in this market – and ordered the company to be broken up into smaller companies. Standard Oil Co. of New Jersey *v.* United States, 221 U.S. 1 (1911).

526 In the U.S. Steel case, the US Supreme Court acknowledged that a company formed with the expectation of becoming a monopoly is in itself not sufficient to make a monopoly within the scope of antitrust laws. United States *v.* United States Steel Corp., 251 U.S. 417 (1920).

527 Under the same reasoning as applied in the Standard Oil case – both decisions were even rendered on the same day – the US Supreme Court ordered the dissolution of the American Tobacco Company into smaller business units. United States *v.* American Tobacco Company, 221 U.S. 106 (1911).

528 Sherman Antitrust Act of 1890 (30 February 1890), 15 U.S.C. ch.1.

529 Clayton Antitrust Act of 1914, Pub. L. 63–212.

bears no similarity to the trust notion identified in other scientific disciplines. Over the years, antitrust law has become more well-known as competition law, forming the broader body of laws aiming to preserve market competition by regulating anti-competitive practices.

Investment trust – Somewhat more similar to the trust notion found in trust law is the figure of the investment trust found in the broader field of business law. An investment trust is a company – typically in the form of a public limited liability company – that manages a collective investment scheme.[530] Those schemes are closed-end funds, meaning that only a limited number of shares are issued, which are publicly traded.[531] As an investment company, it is clear that the investment trust entails risks for its shareholders.[532] However, by diversification the investment risk is reduced.[533] Therefore, although there is no direct connection to the concept of trust in the other scientific disciplines discussed here, the investment trust does build upon the idea of a person taking a calculated risk in order to reap benefits from the risk taken.

Legitimate expectations – A different case is where no explicit mention is made of the notion of trust, but where the people's trust in laws and their lawmakers is at stake. An example here is the notion of legitimate expectations, which can be found in administrative law as one of the principles of good governance.[534] Under legitimate expectations, it is understood that if the behavior and acts of a public sector legal entity raise certain expectations with a citizen, then the citizen may rely on the expectation that this public sector legal entity will continue to behave and act as such.[535] Public sector legal entities

[530] J.P. Morgan (2015) "What is an investment trust?", *am.jpmorgan.co.uk*; Bangassaa, K., Sub, C., Joseph, N. L. (2012) "Selectivity and timing performance of UK investment trusts", *Int. Fin. Markets, Inst. and Money*, Vol. 22, 1149.

[531] Britton, N. (2015) "Closed-end Funds Struggle in Flat Market, Outperform Over 10 Years", *Morningstar*, 10 September 2015; Bangassaa, K., Sub, C., Joseph, N. L. (2012) "Selectivity and timing performance of UK investment trusts", *Int. Fin. Markets, Inst. and Money*, Vol. 22, 1149.

[532] Shim, G., Lee, S., Kim, Y. (2008) "How investor behavioral factors influence investment satisfaction, trust in investment company, and reinvestment intention", *Journal of Business Research*, Vol. 61, 47.

[533] This was especially problematic in early investment trusts, as the composition of portfolios was fixed and could not easily be changed to accommodate market trends. However, diversification was already present in the sense that portfolios could not hold significant amounts in a single security. Hutson, E. (2005) "The early managed fund industry: Investment trusts in 19th century Britain", *International Review of Financial Analysis*, Vol. 14, 449–450.

[534] In Belgium and the Netherlands referred to as "*algemene beginselen van behoorlijk bestuur*". The Belgian Council of State considers these as a source of administrative law: RvS 9 September 2008, nr. 186134. In the UK, this has been proposed as a principle of good administration: Abdi v Secretary of State for the Home Department [2005] EWCA Civ 1363, at 68 (22 November 2005).

[535] Vande Lanotte, J., Dujardin, J., Van Damme, M. (2009) *De bronnen van het administratief recht*, Mechelen: Wolters Kluwer, 60–61; De Staercke, J. (2002) "Algemene beginselen van behoorlijk burgerschap: Naar een wederkerig bestuursrecht?", *Jura Falconis*, Vol.

are therefore required to display fairness and reasonableness when a citizen has certain expectations following a promise made by said public sector legal entity or by its long-standing practices. The theory of legitimate expectations was further developed in the UK Wednesbury case.[536] The core of that case – later further developed by the UK's House of Lords – is that if a decision of a public sector legal entity is so unreasonable that no reasonable authority could have made the same decision, then that decision should be subject to judicial review.[537] The theory of legitimate expectations therefore allows for the citizen to 'trust' a public sector legal entity on its acts and behavior. Legitimate expectations are, however, still a different kind of trust than the ones deducted earlier from other scientific disciplines. Legitimate expectations do not necessarily require an active form of risk-taking from the citizen, but rather allows an attitude of reliance.

Pre-contractual statements – A similar concept can be found in private law. If during the negotiation phase of a contractual agreement one of the parties makes certain statements, the opposing party may in all fairness and reasonableness rely on these statements.[538] The reliance theory states that a party relying on statements made by the opposing party, from which he could reasonably conclude that parties' intent, may expect such statements to have led to the conclusion of the agreement.[539] This theory stems from the civil law doctrine of good faith, or *bona fides*, whereby parties to a contract may presume that all parties intend to deal with each other honestly and fairly.

---

38, 505–535. This principle is also referred to as the principle of legal certainty (Dutch: *rechtszekerheidsbeginsel*) or the principle of trust (Dutch: *vertrouwensbeginsel*). Within the UK's legal system, the term 'legitimate expectation' was first coined in: Schmidt & Anor v Secretary of State for Home Affairs [1968] EWCA Civ 1 (19 December 1968).

536 Associated Provincial Picture Houses v Wednesbury Corporation, [1947] 1 KB 223 (10 November 1947). More in particular, this case introduced a three-element test: in order for courts to intervene in a decision, that decision must (1) include factors that should not have been taken into account upon reaching the decision, (2) fail to take into account factors that should have been taken into account, or (3) be so unreasonable that no reasonable authority could have considered it.

537 Lord Diplock formulated this as: "[…] *a decision which is so outrageous in its defiance of logic or of accepted moral standards that no sensible person who had applied his mind to the question to be decided could have arrived at it.*" Council of Civil Service Unions v Minister for the Civil Service, [1984] UKHL 9, at 410 (22 November 1984).

538 Meaning that, even though the pre-contractual phase is open and does not guarantee that a binding agreement will be reached, certain statements made during that phase could already have legal consequences. This is generally referred to as the *culpa in contrahendo*. Geens, H. (2004) "De grondslagen van de culpa in contrahendo", *Jura Falconis*, Vol. 40, 433–460; De Boeck, A. (2009) "De precontractuele aansprakelijkheid anno 2010", In: Stijns, S., Samoy, I., De Boeck, A. (Eds.) *Verbintenissenrecht*, Brugge: die Keure, 10–12.

539 See, for instance on reliance theory in the US: Cohen, M. R. (1933) "The Basis of Contract", *Harvard Law Review*, Vol. 46, 578–580. The Dutch Supreme Court ruled on this in: HR 11 December 1959, Eelman/Hin, *NJ* 1960, 230. For a summary yet critical overview of reliance theory in Belgium (*vertrouwensleer*), see: Cauffman, C. (2005) *De verbindende eenzijdige belofte*, Antwerpen: Intersentia, 284–285.

Trust in evidence – Another incarnation of trust can be found in the laws on evidence. Here the trust notion comes in the guise of a legal fiction in which evidence is considered as valid once it satisfies certain formal requirements.[540] This can be illustrated by an example, as for instance in the case of a written contract between parties. As it is virtually impossible for a court to conduct a full and thorough investigation into the authenticity and integrity of each contract that passes before it, courts will principally award legal validity if certain formal requirements are met. Such requirements may include the issuance of one copy for each party to the contract, the presence of a signature of opposing parties on each party's copy, consecutively numbered pages, etc.[541] Legal validity of evidence can therefore be considered to be based on certain trust in the ability of the established formal criteria to filter out evidence that is to be deemed untrustworthy.[542] The acceptance that a piece of evidence is truly what it purports to be is then only established by a reasonable certainty and not by an absolute certainty.[543] There are, however, limits to how far that trust goes, particularly in the case of electronic evidence. Various legal systems around the world are still having difficulties with fully integrating the notions of electronic documents, electronic transactions, and the resulting electronic evidence.[544] Although the EU has already made laudable efforts in adopting legal instruments on e-commerce[545] and electronic signatures[546], with

---

540 For a more elaborate discusion of this point, see: Vandezande, N. (2015) "Originality in the Belgian Civil Code and the influence of digitalization", *papers.ssrn.com/sol3/papers.cfm?abstract_id=2660222*, 9.

541 These are elements following from article 1325 of the Belgian Civil Code. In general on Belgian evidence law: Storme, M. (2001) "De invoering van de elektronische handtekening in ons bewijsrecht – een inkadering van en commentaar bij de nieuwe wetsbepalingen", *Rechtskundig Weekblad*, 1505–1525. On formal requirements in Belgian civil law: Van den Eynde, S. (2001) "DAVID – Digitale archivering: een stand van zaken vanuit Belgisch perspectief, deel I", *www.edavid.be*, 88p.

542 In other words, the goal of evidence is to convince independent and impartial judges of what is purported, through the means of the evidence presented. Cornelis, L. (2000) *Algemene theorie van de verbintenis*, Antwerpen: Intersentia, 204.

543 *Ibid*, 204–205. The legal truth established in courts is based on a probability bordering to certainty, even when this does not necessarily correspond to the factual truth. Minjauw, H., Vandendriessche, J. (2008) "Titel VI. Het bewijsrecht in burgerlijke zaken", in: Roodhooft, R. (Ed.), *Bestendig Handboek Verbintenissenrecht*, Mechelen: Kluwer, VI.1–4.

544 A concise overview of the issues regarding authentication for e-commerce: Schapper, P. R., Rivolta, M., Veiga Malta, J. (2006) "Risk and law in authentication", *Digital Evidence Journal*, Vol. 3, 10–16.

545 Directive 2000/31/EC of the European Parliament and of the Council of 8 June 2000 on certain legal aspects of information society services, in particular electronic commerce, in the Internal Market ('Directive on electronic commerce'), *OJ* L 178 of 17 July 2000, 1–16.

546 Directive 1999/93/EC of the European Parliament and of the Council of 13 December 1999 on a Community framework for electronic signatures, *OJ* L 13 of 19 January 2000, 12–20. Note that this directive has been repealed by the so-called eIDAS Regulation, as will be discussed in section 3.1 of this chapter. Regulation (EU) No 910/2014 of the European Parliament and of the Council of 23 July 2014 on electronic identification and trust services for electronic transactions in the internal market and repealing Directive 1999/93/EC, *OJ* L 257 of 28 August 2014, 73–114.

supporting provisions found in the tax directive[547] amongst others, a certain lack of trust towards all things "*e*-" can still be discerned in the field of evidence law.[548]

## 2.7 SYNTHESIS

COMMON ELEMENTS – While there are certainly clear divergences between how the different scientific disciplines analyzed here view the concept of trust, there are also a number of common elements to be distinguished. Overall, the abstract notion of trust can be characterized as an attribute to interpersonal relationships that serves as a bet for future possibilities and that constitutes a degree of risk-taking.

INTERPERSONAL RELATIONSHIPS – From the philosophical roots of trust, it already becomes clear that the trust notion is generally considered as an attribute to interpersonal relationships. In conferring trust upon a relationship, the person conferring this trust – the trustor – expresses his expectation that his counterpart in the relationship – the trustee – will act as expected. Scholars of psychology have pointed out that such trust is an important element in human development. Sociologists have considered such trust to be a device for reducing the complexity inherent to interpersonal relationships and to cope with uncertainty.

BET FOR FUTURE POSSIBILITIES – In essence, trust is conferred onto a person – or rather onto the relationship with that person – as a bet for future possibilities. Building forth on sociologists' understanding of trust as a means to cope with uncertainty and unpredictability, the aim of trust can be regarded as to allow the trustor to benefit from the trust relationship. Economic theorists have expanded upon that finding in holding that trust could result in better outcomes to transactions, new business opportunities, or even higher overall market efficiency.

INHERENT RISK – However, despite the potential benefits that can result from conferring trust upon a relationship, trust also inherently constitutes a risk. That risk is manifested as the possibility that the trustee will not act as expected, potentially leaving the trustor off worse than before the now betrayed trust relationship. Therefore, it will be important for the trustor to weigh the potential beneficial outcomes from the trust relationship against its potential negative outcomes. Precisely that analysis has become the main focus of the majority of sociologist and economic literature on trust, and has resulted in the development of risk measurement and management strategies.

---

547 Directive 2006/112/EC of the Council of 28 November 2006 on the common system of value added tax, *OJ* L 347 of 11 December 2006, 1–118.

548 One example is the original-copy dichotomy in Belgian civil law, which has posed particular questions with regard to the sustainability of this matter in light of electronic evidence. Vandezande, N. (2015) "Originality in the Belgian Civil Code and the influence of digitalization", *papers.ssrn.com/sol3/papers.cfm?abstract_id=2660222*, 71p.

TRUST BALANCE – Following from the importance of weighing the potential beneficial and negative outcomes of a trust relationship, economic theory has found that it can therefore be held that a balance must be struck between the level of trust invested into a relationship by a trustor and the level of trustworthiness displayed by the trustee. The latter will depend on the trustor's reasonable level of confidence in the background, the knowledge and the expected behavior of the trustee.

TRUST AND COMPUTATIONAL SYSTEMS – While philosophy, psychology, sociology and economics mainly focus on the interpersonal aspects of trust, the place of computational systems within the trust constellation is becoming increasingly more important. Different fields are at play here. First, Human-Computer Interaction and computer ethics focus on the trust interactions between humans and computational systems. Second, information security focuses on how interactions with and between computational systems can be made trustworthy through cryptographic security. The importance of one particular element developed within the computer science field, the figure of the trusted third party, in operationalizing trust will become clearer in the second part of this chapter.

GAPS IN LEGAL TRUST – As can be concluded from the overview of a number of different incarnations of the trust notion in legal science, there are only a few instances where the legal concept of trust shows certain similarities to the concepts of trust found in the other scientific disciplines discussed here. Overall, the overview of this chapter mainly identified legal concepts of trust that display a significant divergence from the concepts of trust found in other scientific disciplines. In general, it can be concluded that the notion of trust has certainly found its way into legal science, albeit in highly diffuse and divergent forms. In the current legal reality, there is no overarching concept of trust that can be applied to different branches of law.

## 2.8 TRUST IN MODERN SOCIETY

DIVIDED SCHOLARSHIP – Having understood the abstract notion of trust, the next question is what the place of trust is in modern society. Here, scholarship on the issue appears divided. On the one hand, authors like Fukuyama argue that modern society suffers from a decline of trust.[549] On the other hand, other authors argue that modern society relies on institutions without the need for trust.[550]

549 Fukuyama, F. (1995) *Trust: The Social Virtues and the Creation of Prosperity*, New York: Free Press.

550 Cook, K. S., Hardin, R., Levi, M. (2005) *Cooperation Without Trust?* New York: Russell Sage Foundation; Hardin, R. (2004) *Trust and Trustworthiness*, New York City: Russell Sage Foundation.

Trust and community – Fukuyama follows general economic thinking in seeing trust as a necessary factor of growth. Applying that thinking to society, Fukuyama finds that societies with little trust – for instance those who prefer to keep business within the family – achieve less economic growth than societies displaying more trust – such as those with more focus on community building and shared values.[551] The increasing use of legal instruments to govern interpersonal relationships, and the decline of communities, could then result in lesser trust, and thus less economic growth. In that sense, the economic crisis of the past decade could be seen as a crisis of trust.[552]

Trust and institutions – While it can be argued that even ancient societies had to rely at least to some extent on trust, the importance of trust has only grown in modern times.[553] The reason for that is an increasing reliance on institutions – both government and private sector – to manage aspects of our daily lives.[554] While such institutions can take away some insecurity, they do not fully abolish the need for trust.[555] More so, it could even be argued that modern institutions – such as the law, law enforcement, etc. – enhance the possibilities to trust.[556] In that sense, trust has become a part of our emotional language, even serving as a marketing tool to appeal to consumers' emotions.[557]

Trust and virtual currencies – What do these findings mean for virtual currencies? If it is accepted that modern society increasingly relies on institutions to foster trust, then virtual currencies could find themselves confronted with a trust issue. After all, most virtual currencies function outside traditional institutions – such as the classic financial system or even physical-world economies. In some virtual currencies – particularly in the community

551 For instance, high trust societies are more likely to reap the benefits of information technology. Fukuyama, F. (1995) *Trust: The Social Virtues and the Creation of Prosperity*, New York: Free Press, 25–26. High trust societies, according to Fukuyama, are those encouraging free enterprise such as the United States and Japan. More state-centered societies, such as Russia, or family-centered societies, such as Italy, are designated as low-trust societies. *Ibid.*, 49–53.

552 Zerver, A. (2015) "Vertrauen in historischer Perspektive", In: Endreß, M., Lichtblau, K., Moebius, S. (Eds.) *Zyklos 2: Jahrbuch für Theorie und Geschichte der Soziologie*, Wiesbaden: Springer, 407–415.

553 Frevert, U. (2009) "Does Trust Have a History?", *Max Weber Lecture Series MWP-LS 2009/01*, 4–5.

554 *Id.*

555 Möllering, G. (2013) "Trust without knowledge? Comment on Hardin, 'Government without trust'", *Journal of Trust Research*, Vol. 3, 55.

556 Frevert, U. (2009) "Does Trust Have a History?", *Max Weber Lecture Series MWP-LS 2009/01*, 4–5.

557 Frevert, U. (2016) "The History of Emotions", In: Feldman Barrett, L., Lewis, M., Haviland-Jones, J. M. (Eds.) *Handbook of Emotions, Fourth Edition*, New York: Guilford Press, 62; Frevert, U. (2017) "Vertrauen in der moralischen Ökonomie des Teilens und Tauschens", In: Lehmann, K.-D., Ebert, J., Ströhl, A., Blaumer, N. (Eds.) *Teilen und Tauschen*, Frankfurt: Wallstein, 47–57. Frevert further argues that trust replaced fidelity. Fidelity assumed an unbreakable bond, whereas trust is more fluid and can easily be broken. Frevert, U. (2009) "Does Trust Have a History?", *Max Weber Lecture Series MWP-LS 2009/01*, 7.

of cryptocurrencies – those institutions may even be downright rejected. If virtual currencies then want to achieve economic growth, absent trust-fostering institutions, they will have to find other means of allowing the communities developed around them and their stakeholders to trust them.

# 3 TRUST OPERATIONALIZATION THROUGH LAW

TRUST IN LEGAL PRACTICE – The previous section analyzed the notion of trust from an abstract point of view. That analysis has provided valuable insight into how different scientific disciplines interpret the trust notion, and has allowed for the identification of a number of elements common to those at times divergent views. Now, this section will analyze how the concept of trust functions in practice through law. To that end, the analysis will focus on EU legislation regarding trust – or rather trust service providers. In particular, the analysis focuses on legislation adopted at the level of the EU, more precisely on the so-called Electronic Signatures Directive[558] (or e-Signatures Directive) and its successor, the Regulation on electronic identification, electronic signatures and trust services (or eIDAS Regulation).[559] In second order, this section will analyze other forms of trust operationalization through law. This analysis includes the operationalization through law of trusted service providers at the level of the EU Member States[560], the potential creation of other forms of trusted third parties, and the operationalization of trust through adjacent legal domains such as consumer law and financial law. The goal of the analysis is to critically analyze the potential for additional legal measures that could support raising the trustworthiness of virtual currencies, which in turn could support raising the legal certainty on virtual currencies.

## 3.1 TRUST SERVICES IN THE EU

FROM DIRECTIVE TO REGULATION – The first instance in which the EU regulated trusted service providers is in the field of electronic signatures. Here, the EU first adopted a directive, which was subsequently transposed into national law by the

558 Directive 1999/93/EC of the European Parliament and of the Council of 13 December 1999 on a Community framework for electronic signatures, *OJ* L 13 of 19 January 2000, 12–20.

559 Regulation 910/2014 of the European Parliament and of the Council of 23 July 2014 on electronic identification and trust services for electronic transactions in the internal market and repealing Directive 1999/93/EC, *OJ* L 257 of 28 August 2014, 73–114.

560 It is beyond the scope of this research to conduct an in-depth study of how all EU Member States have implemented relevant EU legislation, or of the potential secondary legislation they have adopted in this field. To ensure the feasibility of this analysis, the focus will be put on a select number of notable examples.

Member States. During the review of the directive, it was decided that a more harmonized approach was needed, which in turn resulted in the proposition of a regulation to replace the directive.[561]

### *3.1.1 E-Signatures Directive*

Electronic signatures – As handwritten documents are increasingly becoming a rarity, and more and more transactions are recorded by electronic processes, a challenge is posed to the centerpiece of the rules on evidence, namely the notion of signatures.[562] After all, how should a handwritten signature be affixed to information consisting out of computer bits? An electronic signature is therefore needed to provide a way to satisfy the requirements and goals of a handwritten signature in an electronic manner. One of the earliest examples of such an electronic signature in law can be found in the US state of Utah, in 1995.[563] Here, cryptographic means – more in particular a hashing function and a public key interface (PKI), also known as a digital signature – were used to establish an equivalence between a handwritten and electronic signature. The digital signature model was subsequently adopted in Germany[564] and Italy[565], and became the inspiration for the EU-wide legal framework on electronic signatures in the form of the earlier mentioned e-Signatures Directive. The EU followed a more technology-neutral approach, yet still reserved a specific spot for the technique of the digital signature as its qualified electronic signature.[566] Under the new rules, electronic signatures cannot be denied effectiveness and admissibility as evidence solely on the grounds of them being a signature in electronic form or for not being a qualified electronic signature.[567] National courts, however, retain the competence to accept such an electronic signatures as valid in terms of evidence

---

561 Commission staff working document of 7 June 2012 impact assessment accompanying the document proposal for a regulation of the European Parliament and of the Council on electronic identification and trust services for electronic transactions in the internal market, *SWD(2012) 135 final*, 40.

562 This part is largely taken from earlier research, first published as: Vandezande, N. (2015) "Originality in the Belgian Civil Code and the influence of digitalization", *papers.ssrn.com/sol3/papers.cfm?abstract_id=2660222*, 35–46. In that paper, the challenges of electronic evidence procedures are discussed more elaborately.

563 Utah Digital Signature Act, Utah Code §46-3-101 - 504.

564 Gesetz vom 13. Juni 1997 zur Regelung der Rahmenbedingungen für Informations- und Kommunikationsdienste (Informations- und Kommunikationsdienste-Gesetz - IuKDG), *BGBl. I* 28 July 1997, 1872–6.

565 Legge n. 59 15 marzo 1997 Delega al Governo per il conferimento di funzioni e compiti alle regioni ed enti locali, per la riforma della Pubblica Amministrazione e per la semplificazione amministrativa, *Gazzetta Ufficiale* n. 63 of 17 March 1997.

566 Dumortier, J. (2004) "Legal status of qualified electronic signatures in Europe", In: Paulus, S., Pohlmann, N., Reimer, H. (Eds.) *ISSE 2004-Securing Electronic Business Processes*, Wiesbaden: Vieweg, 281–289.

567 Article 5(2) Directive 1999/93/EC.

or not.[568] Member States can thus decide when to allow electronic signatures, but where they are allowed their effectiveness cannot be denied.[569]

Three types – The e-Signatures Directive established three distinct types of electronic signatures. The most developed type, the qualified electronic signature, is granted automatic equivalence to a handwritten signature.[570] While the directive does establish a non-discrimination principle – prohibiting Member States to deny validity to an electronic signature solely on the basis of it being in electronic form or for not being a qualified electronic signature[571] – the acceptance of the other two types of electronic signatures is mostly left open to the discretion of the Member States. As a result, it is clear that the directive cannot be understood as imposing the use of electronic signatures in all instances where a handwritten signature is required.[572]

Common e-signature – In its most basic form, Directive 1999/93/EC defines an electronic signature as "*data in electronic form which are attached to or logically associated with other electronic data and which serve as a method of authentication*".[573] The directive does not clarify how the different elements of the electronic signature provision should be interpreted. In general, it can be held that the requirement of attachment or logical association should be interpreted as meaning that there should be a clear physical or logical bond between the data serving as a signature and the electronic information intended to be signed.[574] Authentication, in turn, should be considered as establishing the non-reputable origin and the integrity of the signed electronic information.[575] In keeping the

568 This follows from recital 21 to Directive 1999/93/EC, which states that national law must decide upon when to accept electronic signatures and electronic documents and that "*this Directive is without prejudice to the power of a national court to make a ruling regarding conformity with the requirements of this Directive and does not affect national rules regarding the unfettered judicial consideration of evidence*". See: Dumortier, J., Vandezande, N. (2014) "Legal evidence in a digital context: will signatures disappear?", In: Savin, A., Trzaskowski, J. (eds.) *Research Handbook on EU Internet Law*, Cheltenham: Edward Elgar, 435–436.

569 Note that the use of electronic contracts has been strongly enforced by article 9 of Directive 2000/31/EC, thus restricting the freedom of Member States to decide when to allow electronic signatures and electronic contracts.

570 Article 5 (1) Directive 1999/93/EC.

571 See also: Mougenot, D. (2002) *Droit des obligations: la preuve*, Brussel: Larcier, 182.

572 Dumortier, J. (2004) "Legal Status of Qualified Electronic Signatures in Europe", In: Paulus, S., Pohlmann, N., Reimer, H. (Eds.) *ISSE 2004-Securing Electronic Business Processes*, Wiesbaden: Vieweg, 281–289.

573 Art. 2 (1) Directive 1999/93/EC.

574 Van Eecke, P. (2009) "De elektronische handtekening in het recht", *T.B.H.*, 342.

575 *Id.* While it has been argued that the integrity of the electronic information does not necessarily need to follow from the signature technique used and that thus other techniques could be applied to preserve the integrity of the information, this appears to be a minority opinion not generally shared in legal doctrine. Wéry, P., Gobert, D., Kerzmann, L. (2003) "La preuve", In: Coipel, M., Wéry, P., Durant, I., Cruquenaire, A. (Eds.) *Guide juridique de l'entreprise*, Brussel: Kluwer, 53.

definition as broad as possible, it is clear that the EU aimed for its legal framework to apply to all kinds of signatures by electronic means. Following the non-discrimination rule included in the directive, such a common electronic signature cannot be denied legal validity solely on the basis of it being a signature in electronic form or for not being a qualified electronic signature.[576] However, the judge to which evidence signed with an electronic signature is presented remains free to decide whether that signature fulfills all of the requirements – the attachment or logical association and the authentication – in order for it to be accepted as such.[577]

ADVANCED E-SIGNATURE – The second type of electronic signature introduced under Directive 1999/93/EC is the advanced electronic signature. This second type is defined as "*an electronic signature which meets the following requirements: (a) it is uniquely linked to the signatory; (b) it is capable of identifying the signatory; (c) it is created using means that the signatory can maintain under his sole control; and (d) it is linked to the data to which it relates in such a manner that any subsequent change of the data is detectable*".[578] The main difference between the common and the advanced electronic signature is that for the advanced electronic signature the principles of identification, non-repudiation and integrity are clearly defined.[579] While the directive does not explicitly define how those requirements should be met, it is clear that the technique of the digital signature is the preferred method hereto, as well as the only method that is generally accepted.[580] The recognition of the advanced electronic signature is principally the same as that of the common electronic signature: on the basis of the non-discrimination rule, it cannot be denied validity solely on the basis of it being an electronic signature or for it not being a qualified electronic signature, yet it is not granted automatic equivalence to handwritten signatures.[581] However, as the technique of the digital signature is aimed at more clearly and more trustworthily establishing the origin and non-repudiation of the signature, as well as the integrity of the electronic information to which it is transfixed, it can be expected that the advanced electronic signature will be more easily recognized and accepted by a judge.[582]

---

576 Article 5 (2) Directive 1999/93/EC.

577 Van Eecke, P. (2009) "De elektronische handtekening in het recht", *T.B.H.*, 342; Vandenabeele, V. (2002) "De elektronische handtekening: rechten en plichten van de certificatiedienstverlener, de certificaathouder en de vertrouwende derde", *T.B.B.R.*, 611; Mougenot, D. (2002) *Droit des obligations: la preuve*, Brussel: Larcier, 188–189.

578 Article 2 (2) Directive 1999/93/EC.

579 Van Eecke, P. (2009) "De elektronische handtekening in het recht", *T.B.H.*, 343.

580 *Ibid.*, 343; Storme, M. E. (2001) "De invoering van de elektronische handtekening in ons bewijsrecht", *R.W.*, 1516; Dumortier, J., Van Den Eynde, S. (2001) "De juridische erkenning van de elektronische handtekening", *Computerrecht*, 185–194; De Corte, R. (2001) "Elektronische handtekening en identificatie in de virtuele wereld", *P&B*, 225.

581 Van Eecke, P. (2009) "De elektronische handtekening in het recht", *T.B.H.*, 343.

582 *Ibid.*, 344.

Digital signature – The digital signature is not a type of signature in its own right, but rather a cryptographic technique used to create electronic signatures.[583] The technique combines two cryptographic methods, namely asymmetric cryptography using a Public Key Infrastructure (PKI) and a hash function.[584] Before being able to generate signatures, each party operating within such a scheme is issued a key pair, consisting out of a private key and a public key.[585] Those keys correspond with each other in the sense that whatever is encrypted using the private key can only be decrypted using the corresponding public key. Moreover, the relation between the public and private key is so complex that it is impossible to deduct the private key from the public key.[586] When generating a signature to be affixed to certain electronic information, there will first be a hash algorithm used to calculate the unique hash value of the electronic information to which the signature will be affixed.[587] Such a hash value is unique in the sense that if even one single bit of that information is changed, a new hash calculation will result in a different hash value. Next, the PKI is used whereby the signatory's private key is used to encrypt the hash value. The result, the digital signature, is attached to the electronic information. The party receiving that electronic information will then be able to verify the signature by decrypting the encoded

---

583 As a result, the terms 'electronic signature' and 'digital signature' are not interchangeable. All signatures created using the digital signature technique are electronic signatures, but not all electronic signatures are created using the digital signature technique.

584 Dumortier, J. (2010) *ICT-Recht*, Leuven: Acco, 140–143; Storme, M. E. (2001) "De invoering van de elektronische handtekening in ons bewijsrecht", *R.W.*, 1515–1516; Van Eecke, P. (2009) "De elektronische handtekening in het recht", *T.B.H.*, 335–336; Dumortier, J., Van Den Eynde, S. (2001) "De juridische erkenning van de elektronische handtekening", *Computerrecht*, 185–194; De Corte, R. (2001) "Elektronische handtekening en identificatie in de virtuele wereld", *P&B*, 221–224; Vandenabeele, V. (2002) "De elektronische handtekening: rechten en plichten van de certificatiedienstverlener, de certificaathouder en de vertrouwende derde", *T.B.B.R.*, 610; Mougenot, D. (2002) *Droit des obligations: la preuve*, Brussel: Larcier, 174–176.

585 In symmetric cryptography, only one key is used to both encrypt and decrypt information. The obvious weakness of such scheme is that the person encrypting information will have to transfer the key to the recipient, thus exposing it to interception or abuse.

586 Van Eecke, P. (2009) "De elektronische handtekening in het recht", *T.B.H.*, 335; Vandenabeele, V. (2002) "De elektronische handtekening: rechten en plichten van de certificatiedienstverlener, de certificaathouder en de vertrouwende derde", *T.B.B.R.*, 610. The two main weaknesses in asymmetric cryptography are therefore loss of the private key by the owner or cracking of the algorithm. To protect against the latter, keys are generally given a larger bit length, making them harder to crack. In the Belgian electronic identity card, for instance, key lengths of 1024 and 2048 bit are used. De Cock, D., Wolf, C., Preneel, B. (2006) "The Belgian Electronic Identity Card (Overview)", In: Dittmann, J. (Ed.) *Sicherheit 2005, Sicherheit - Schutz und Zuverlässigkeit, Beiträge der 3rd Jahrestagung des Fachbereichs Sicherheit der Gesellschaft für Informatik e.v. (GI), Lecture Notes in Informatics (LNI) LNI P-77*, Bonn: Köllen Verlag, 298–301. As a result, it is recommendable to ensure broad publication of public keys, in order to ensure that recipients of encrypted information can access the public key required to decrypt that information. This can be done, for instance, in public X.500 directories. ITU-T (2008) "Recommendation X.500", *itu.int*.

587 Using, for instance, the Secure Hash Algorithm (SHA), established by the US National Institute for Standards and Technology (NIST). NIST (2012) "Secure Hash Standard (SHS)", *FIPS PUB 180-4*.

hash value using the signatory's public key. He will then calculate the hash value of the electronic information he received and compare it to the decoded hash value. If those values are the same, the information has not been altered between the moment of signing and the moment it is verified. The digital signature is then considered as valid and verified. The process of creating and verifying digital signatures has become easy and user-friendly with the development of several devices and applications capable of performing these tasks.[588] In principle, the digital signature technique – as used in the advanced electronic signature – can provide certain guarantees regarding identification, non-repudiation and integrity. The use of asymmetric cryptography already ensures non-repudiation: what can be decrypted by a certain public key could only have been encrypted using the corresponding private key.[589] The use of the hash function demonstrates whether or not the signed electronic information has been altered since the moment of signing.[590] The only point where the digital signature technique could be argued to fall short is in identifying the signatory, as in principle the technique in itself does not guarantee who a key pair belongs to.[591]

QUALIFIED E-SIGNATURE – To counter the ownership problem of the keys used in the digital signature technique, the use of certificates was introduced. Here, a trusted third party (TTP) – the same figure as discussed earlier – is assigned the role of Certificate Authority (CA), which means that the TTP will certify that a certain key pair belongs to a particular person.[592] Given the importance of that task, the role of CA is often left to public sector bodies. In Belgium, for instance, the Belgian State serves as the root CA that certifies ownership of all the signature certificates included in the Belgium electronic identity card.[593] Also the notion of certification has been included under the scope of Directive 1999/93/EC.[594] Moreover, the directive includes specific requirements for the 'qualified' version of certificates[595], CA's[596] and secure-signature-creation

588 In principle, every computer, tablet or phone could be used for this process. The private key of a PKI key pair is generally stored on a safe token, such as a smart card or a USB-stick.

589 One possible exception is the unauthorized use of that private key by someone else than the owner, for instance when that key has been stolen. Storme, M. E. (2001) "De invoering van de elektronische handtekening in ons bewijsrecht", *R.W.*, 1518; Vandenabeele, V. (2002) "De elektronische handtekening: rechten en plichten van de certificatiedienstverlener, de certificaathouder en de vertrouwende derde", *T.B.B.R.*, 610.

590 Vandenabeele, V. (2002) "De elektronische handtekening: rechten en plichten van de certificatiedienstverlener, de certificaathouder en de vertrouwende derde", *T.B.B.R.*, 610.

591 Van Eecke, P. (2009) "De elektronische handtekening in het recht", *T.B.H.*, 336.

592 *Id.* This CA will keep a list of all valid, expired and revoked certificates, to easily verify their validity. Vandenabeele, V. (2002) "De elektronische handtekening: rechten en plichten van de certificatiedienstverlener, de certificaathouder en de vertrouwende derde", *T.B.B.R.*, 612.

593 *Repository.eid.belgium.be/certificates.php?cert=Root&lang=en.*

594 Article 2 (9) and (11) Directive 1999/93/EC. Note that the CA is addressed here as 'certification service provider'.

595 Annex I Directive 1999/93/EC.

596 Annex II Directive 1999/93/EC.

devices.[597] If an electronic signature is created using a secure-signature-creation device and attested by a qualified certificate – which by definition is issued by a qualified CA – the signature is considered as a qualified electronic signature, the third type of electronic signature proclaimed by the directive.[598] The most important consequence of the qualification of an electronic signature as a qualified electronic signature is that it is automatically considered as equal to a handwritten signature and thus admissible in court proceedings.[599] The reason for this equivalence is that the figure of the qualified electronic signature is considered to completely and reliably fulfill the requirements of identification – by using qualified certificates in the PKI – non-repudiation – by using a certified asymmetric cryptography key pair – and integrity – due to the hash function.

Interoperability – One important element of the automated equivalence between qualified electronic signatures and handwritten signatures is precisely its reference to handwritten signatures. First, it means that the qualified electronic signature fully derives its probative value from that of the handwritten signature.[600] If, for instance, a handwritten signature is not deemed sufficient for something to be accepted as evidence, neither will the qualified electronic signature. Moreover, it is clear that the validity of handwritten signatures is fully determined by national law.[601] As a result, by depending on national provisions concerning handwritten signatures, the precise status of a qualified electronic signature may be rather different between EU Member States, potentially leading to interoperability issues.[602] In 2012, the European Commission acknowledged that the directive – and its national transpositions – had not succeeded in providing electronic signatures with the success originally envisioned and proposed an overhaul of the legal framework.[603]

### *3.1.2 eIDAS Regulation*

Path to the regulation – As any directive, Directive 1999/93/EC was marked for review.[604] While the directive has been slightly amended over the

597 Annex III Directive 1999/93/EC.

598 Article 5 (1) Directive 1999/93/EC.

599 *Id.*

600 Dumortier, J. (2004) "Legal Status of Qualified Electronic Signatures in Europe", In: Paulus, S., Pohlmann, N., Reimer, H. (Eds.), *ISSE 2004-Securing Electronic Business Processes*, Wiesbaden: Vieweg, 281–289.

601 Recital 20 Directive 1999/93/EC.

602 Dumortier, J. (2004) "Legal Status of Qualified Electronic Signatures in Europe", In: Paulus, S., Pohlmann, N., Reimer, H. (Eds.), *ISSE 2004-Securing Electronic Business Processes*, Wiesbaden: Vieweg, 281–289.

603 Commission proposal for a regulation of the European Parliament and of the Council of 4 June 2012 on electronic identification and trust services for electronic transactions in the internal market, *COM(2012) 238 final*.

604 This was to be completed by 19 July 2003 according to article 12 Directive 1999/93/EC.

years[605], no extensive revision was proposed before 2012.[606] In 2010, the Digital Agenda, which establishes a strategic plan for the coming decade, explicitly references the existence of barriers to Europe's digital development and proposed legislation on e-signatures (Key Action 3) and the mutual recognition of e-identification and authentication (Key Action 16).[607] To that end, the European Commission in 2012 proposed a regulation on electronic identification and trust services for electronic transactions in the internal market.[608] Apart from revising the existing framework, it also adds the figure of trust services under the same umbrella. Instead of amending the existing directive, Directive 1999/93/EC was proposed to be revoked and replaced by a regulation. In doing so, the Commission aims to provide for better accessibility of cross-border online services by removing existing barriers.[609] The Commission's proposal was adopted as Regulation 910/2014.[610]

Definitions – The eIDAS Regulation contains a large number of definitions, many of which – those relating to electronic signatures – are taken fairly literally from the original Electronic Signatures Directive.[611] Electronic identification is defined as "*the process of using person identification data in electronic form unambiguously representing a natural or legal person*".[612] Trust services are defined as "*any electronic service normally provided for remuneration which consists of: (a)*

605 Regulation (EC) No 1137/2008 of the European Parliament and of the Council of 22 October 2008 adapting a number of instruments subject to the procedure laid down in Article 251 of the Treaty to Council Decision 1999/468/EC, with regard to the regulatory procedure with scrutiny – Adaptation to the regulatory procedure with scrutiny – Part One, *OJ* L 311 of 21 November 2008, 1–54.

606 In 2006, the European Commission found that "*the objectives of the Directive have been largely fulfilled and that no clear need for its revision has emerged at this stage*". Report from the Commission to the European Parliament and the Council of 15 March 2006 on the operation of Directive 1999/93/EC on a Community framework for electronic signatures", *COM(2006) 120 final*, 10.

607 Communication from the Commission to the European Parliament, the Council, the European Economic and Social Committee and the Committee of the Regions of 26 August 2010, A Digital Agenda for Europe, *COM(2010) 245 final/2.*

608 Commission proposal for a regulation of the European Parliament and of the Council of 4 June 2012 on electronic identification and trust services for electronic transactions in the internal market, *COM(2012) 238 final.*

609 Recital 11, *COM(2012) 238 final.* Amending the existing directive was considered insufficient as "*the freedom given to MS when transposing a Directive (in terms of interpretation and of implementation of the systems) contributed to the current problems of mutual recognition of services and products and of cross-border interoperability*". Commission staff working document of 7 June 2012 impact assessment accompanying the document proposal for a regulation of the European Parliament and of the Council on electronic identification and trust services for electronic transactions in the internal market, *SWD(2012) 135 final*, 40–41.

610 Regulation (EU) No 910/2014 of the European Parliament and of the Council of 23 July 2014 on electronic identification and trust services for electronic transactions in the internal market and repealing Directive 1999/93/EC, *OJ* L 257 of 28 August 2014, 73–114.

611 Article 3 Regulation 910/2014.

612 Article 3(1) Regulation 910/2014.

*the creation, verification, and validation of electronic signatures, electronic seals or electronic time stamps, electronic registered delivery services and certificates related to those services, or (b) the creation, verification and validation of certificates for website authentication; or (c) the preservation of electronic signatures, seals or certificates related to those services;*".[613] As under the e-Signatures Directive, the different services can be offered at three distinct levels: normal, advanced (only for electronic signatures and electronic seals), and qualified. While 'normal' services cannot be denied legal effect solely on the basis of their being offered in electronic form or for not complying with the qualified electronic form, their legal effect is not guaranteed.[614] Where a 'qualified' service is offered, its legal effect is automatically presumed to be equivalent to its non-electronic counterpart.[615] Regarding 'advanced' electronic signatures or electronic seals, it can *a fortiori* be stated that also these electronic signatures or seals cannot be denied legal effect solely for being in electronic form or for not corresponding to the qualified form. Moreover, it is provided that where a Member State requires advanced electronic signatures or seals in the online services of public sector bodies, that Member State must recognize advanced electronic signatures.[616]

Electronic identification – The principles on electronic identification focus on harmonized mutual recognition and acceptance of electronic identification schemes across the EU Member States by holding that one Member State must recognize the electronic identification means issued in another Member State for the purposes of cross-border authentication for online services.[617]

Trust services – Regarding trust services, it should be noted that the eIDAS Regulation does not apply to trust services used within "*closed systems resulting from national law or from agreements between a defined set of participants*".[618] Chapter III of the eIDAS Regulation focuses on the broad range of trust services, with first a number of general and supervisory provisions. For instance, trust service providers are liable for negligent and intentional damages[619], subject to penalties.[620] Supervision is conducted by national supervisory bodies that conduct *ex ante* and *ex post* activities[621], provide mutual assistance[622], and report on security breaches[623] – which trust service providers are to report within 24

613 Article 3(12) Regulation 910/2014.
614 See a.o. article 25, 35, and 41 Regulation 910/2014.
615 Such as the qualified electronic signature's assimilation with the handwritten signature.
616 Articles 27 and 37 Regulation 910/2014.
617 Article 6 Regulation 910/2014.
618 Article 2 (2) Regulation 910/2014.
619 Article 13 Regulation 910/2014.
620 Article 16 Regulation 910/2014.
621 Article 17 Regulation 910/2014.
622 Article 18 Regulation 910/2014.
623 Article 19 Regulation 910/2014.

hours of becoming aware of it. Furthermore, qualified trust service providers must be audited every two years[624] and be verified by a conformity assessment body.[625] Qualified trust service providers are included in trusted lists[626] and can use an EU trust mark.[627] When issuing a qualified certificate, qualified trust service providers need to verify the identity of the person to whom the certificate is issued according to a number of criteria.[628]

Electronic signatures – The specific provisions for electronic signatures mostly follow those known from the e-Signatures Directive. In order to enhance cross-border use, the European Commission may decide on standards for electronic signatures and certificates, and for their creation devices, as standardization is one of the means of this Regulation to enhance trust.[629] There are also specific requirements for validating qualified electronic signatures and for providing qualified validation or preservation services, mainly to be decided by the European Commission by implementing acts.[630]

Types of trust services – The provisions relating to other trust services follow a similar pattern. For electronic seals, for instance, the requirements are almost identical to those for electronic signatures.[631] For electronic time stamps[632] and electronic registered delivery services[633], the provisions regarding legal effect and the requirements for their qualified versions are clearly patterned on those for electronic signatures. Also, the requirements for website authentication are listed in an annex and future standards to be determined by the European Commission.[634] Last, the legal effect of electronic documents is modeled on that of electronic signatures.[635]

A closed category – While the eIDAS Regulation establishes a broad range of trust services – thus significantly expanding the scope of the notion beyond the e-Signature Directive's limitation to CA's as trust services – it does not establish such trust services as an open category. First, the definition of trust services clearly limits the notion to services providing for the creation, validation, verification and preservation of either electronic signatures, electronic seals,

---

624 Article 20 Regulation 910/2014.
625 Article 21 Regulation 910/2014.
626 Article 22 Regulation 910/2014.
627 Article 23 Regulation 910/2014.
628 Article 24 Regulation 910/2014.
629 Articles 27–30 Regulation 910/2014.
630 Articles 32–34 Regulation 910/2014.
631 Articles 35–40 Regulation 910/2014.
632 Articles 41–42 Regulation 910/2014.
633 Articles 43–44 Regulation 910/2014.
634 Article 45 Regulation 910/2014.
635 Article 46 Regulation 910/2014.

electronic time stamps, electronic registered delivery services or website authentication, as well as for the certificates required for such services. Trust services for virtual currencies therefore have to be configured as one of these types, or make use of other service providers providing these services.[636] Second, as the eIDAS Regulation does not apply to purely national schemes or privately established schemes, the applicability to virtual currency services seems difficult. After all, as follows from the analysis of the different types of virtual currencies conducted in chapter I, virtual currency schemes are all privately established as per agreement between their participants.[637] Such does, however, not preclude Member States from adopting additional regulation regarding other types of trust services.[638]

### *3.1.3 Synthesis*

EU TRUST SERVICES – From the previous overview, it becomes clear that the EU does have a clear history of regulating certain trust services, be it particularly in the fields of electronic identification and electronic signatures. That history started in the late 1990's with the inclusion of CA's as TTP's tasked with providing the qualified certificates required for producing qualified electronic signatures under the e-Signatures Directive. Now that the directive has been repealed and replaced by the eIDAS Regulation, the field of trusted service providers has grown significantly, adding a legal framework for the providers of electronic seals, electronic time stamping, website authentication, and electronic registered delivery services.

NEED FOR NATIONAL RULES – However, despite significantly enlarging the field, the eIDAS Regulation does establish a clear *numerus clausus* on its trusted services. Therefore, trusted services aimed particularly at enhancing trust in virtual currencies cannot fall under the scope of the regulation. In other words, the eIDAS Regulation explicitly rules out the regulation of virtual currency trusted services at the level of the EU, at least for the time being. It does, however, allow for the possibility to regulate other trusted services at the level of the Member States. Virtual currency services will therefore either have to make use of the services provided by those trusted service providers regulated at the level of the EU, or seek regulation as their own form of trusted service providers in the Member States.

---

636 For instance, a virtual currency exchange could have its website authenticated by a trust service provider who operates under the eIDAS Regulation.

637 A possible deviation to this point could be found in the sense that these participants must be defined, which is not always the case in virtual currency schemes, of which some were found to be open-ended. Even so, the first point regarding the *numerus clausus* still stands.

638 Such is explicitly addressed in recitals 24 and 25 Regulation 910/2014.

## 3.2 OTHER FORMS OF TRUST OPERATIONALIZATION THROUGH LAW

Three forms – This section will analyze a number of other forms of trust operationalization through law. First, it will put the focus on the rules regarding the adoption of trusted service providers at the level of the EU Member States, a possibility that was already referenced in the previous section. Second, it will look at the development of other forms of trusted third parties, more in particular the trusted custodian. Third, this section will analyze how other existing regulation could assist in augmenting trust. The main focus here will be consumer law, which could prove a valuable tool in enhancing trust in e-commerce, and financial law, in which trust can be considered as a constitutive element.

### *3.2.1 Trusted service providers at the EU Member States' level*

Belgium – On 15 May 2007, the Belgian legislator adopted an Act establishing a legal framework for certain types of trust services.[639] The main reasoning behind that act was that the further development of electronic commerce – or e-commerce – requires a higher level of security and trust.[640] While it was noted that the market of trust services aimed at raising such security and trust in e-commerce was growing, the lack of a clear legal framework on those services was found to result in services that were frequently lacking from a technical and legal point of view.[641] In order to not risk overregulating developing markets, a clear choice was made to regulate only those trust services that were already fairly developed on the Belgian market, namely services regarding electronic archiving, electronic registration, and electronic registered mail delivery.[642] A two-tier approach was proposed: the first section of the act imposes the basic rules common to all types of trust services, and a second section gives a delegation to impose more type-specific technical rules by means of royal

639 Wet 15 mei 2007 tot vaststelling van een juridisch kader voor sommige verleners van vertrouwensdiensten, *Belgian State Gazette* 17 July 2007 (hereinafter: Act of 15 May 2007).

640 Proposal to introduce an Act establishing a legal framework for certain types of trust services, *Parl. St. Kamer* 2006–2007, 2802/1, 5.

641 *Id.*

642 *Ibid.*, 6. Note that electronic signatures were already regulated by the Belgian transposition of the e-Signatures Directive in 2001. Electronic registered delivery was later removed from the act (article 53 Wet 3 december 2010 tot wijziging van de wet van 21 maart 1991 betreffende de hervorming van sommige economische overheidsbedrijven, van de wet van 17 januari 2003 met betrekking tot het statuut van de regulator van de Belgische post- en telecommunicatiesector en tot wijziging van de wet van 9 juli 2001 houdende vaststelling van bepaalde regels in verband met het juridisch kader voor elektronische handtekeningen en certificatiediensten, *Belgian State Gazette* 31 December 2010), but the article removing this form of trust service was later removed itself (article 24 Wet 31 mei 2011 houdende diverse bepalingen inzake telecommunicatie, *Belgian State Gazette* 21 June 2011), thus re-establishing the Act of 15 May 2007 in its original form.

decree.[643] Overall, the act imposes high-level requirements regarding the impartiality of trust service providers, data protection and security, information duties, staff qualifications, and confidentiality.[644] Moreover, the act foresees specific procedures and penalties to counter any violation of its terms.[645] However, as noted, the bulk of the act is not present in the act itself, but in the form of a delegation to the federal government to lay down the specific provisions concerning the different types of trust services by means of a royal decree, which was to be adopted before 1 December 2007.[646] Such a royal decree was never adopted, and can no longer be adopted due to the expiration of the delegation thereto. This lack of executive measures left the Act of 15 May 2007 in a state of legal limbo, since it technically had entered into force, yet had little practical relevance due to its failure to regulate what it intended to regulate. The act was therefore eventually abolished.[647]

Estonia – Another example of an EU Member State that has gone beyond the adoption of the qualified electronic signature service providers required by EU law is Estonia. Its 2000 Digital Signature Act contains a separate chapter on time-stamping services.[648] In order to verify whether an electronic signature was valid at the moment of creation – i.e. whether its certificates were not expired or revoked – the Estonian government has set up a standard Online Certificate Status (OCSP) service that binds the signature, time-stamp and certificates together.[649] The electronic signature and time-stamps are used in a broad range of electronic government – or e-government – services.[650]

Spain, Slovenia, Slovakia, Germany, and Czech Republic[651] – Also Spain has expanded upon the certificates for electronic signatures by also

---

643 Proposal to introduce an Act establishing a legal framework for certain types of trust services, *Parl. St. Kamer* 2006–2007, 2802/1, 7–8.

644 Articles 4–10 Act of 15 Mqy 2007. See also: Dumortier, J., Somers, G. (2007) "De wet van 15 mei 2007 tot vaststelling van een juridisch kader voor sommige verleners van vertrouwensdiensten: een eerste verkenning", *T.B.H.*, 649–659.

645 Articles 11–15 Act of 15 May 2007.

646 Article 16 Act of 15 May 2007.

647 A proposal to this end was already introduced under the 53rd Parliamentary session, yet was at the time not adopted: Article 7 proposal to amend the legislation introducing the law of electronic commerce, *Parl. St. Kamer* 2012–2013, 2745/1, 47. Furthermore, the Act of 15 May 2007 may have to be abolished in view of the eIDAS Regulation, which now regulates some of the trust services originally caught under the act's scope. The act was eventually abolished by article 22 of the Act of 21 July 2016 executing and supplementing Regulation 910/2014 of the European Parliament and the Council of 23 July 2014 concerning electronic identification and trust services for electronic transactions in the internal market, *Belgian State Gazette* 28 September 2016.

648 Chapter 4 Digitaalallkirja seadus, *RT* I 2000, 26, 150.

649 IDABC (2009) "Study on Mutual Recognition of eSignatures: update of Country Profiles – Estonian Country Report", *ec.europa.eu*, 13.

650 *E-estonia.com/components.*

651 See also: Graux, H. (2011) "Rethinking the E-Signatures Directive: On laws, trust services, and the Digital Single Market", *Digital Evidence and Electronic Signature Law Review*, Vol. 8, 20.

including time-stamping services used in all transactions by public sector entities.[652] Moreover, electronic seals have been created as a form of signature for companies.[653] Time-stamping is furthermore regulated in Slovenia[654], Slovakia[655], Germany[656] and the Czech Republic.[657]

OTHER MEMBER STATES – There are several other Member States who until now have limited themselves to regulating electronic signatures as required under the EU's e-Signatures Directive. While the new trust services developed by the EU are in principle regulated by the eIDAS Regulation, the Member States are still required to adopt national legislation to facilitate the interoperability of those trust services.

### *3.2.2 Trusted custodian*

OTHER THAN SIGNATURE – The previously discussed forms of TTP's at the level of the EU and the Member States all revolved to a certain extent around the notion of the electronic signature. That is of course a logical consequence given the origins of the electronic signature notion in cryptography, where the TTP is traditionally used to provide for trustworthy identification and authentication. However, it is perfectly possible apply the notion more broadly. For instance, the figure of the notary – in both its civil law sense as in the common law's notary public – is trusted as an officer with specific powers bestowed onto him by the state.[658] In that sense, the notary can be considered as a TTP.

TRUSTED CUSTODIAN – Another field where a form of TTP can be found is that of archival science. Perhaps one of the most important traits of the archivist – for the purposes of this research – is that he can be regarded as a trusted custodian, being a "*neutral third party who must demonstrate that it has no reason to alter or to allow others to alter the records in its care, and that it has the knowledge*

---

652 While time-stamps are mainly regulated by the Act of 22 June 2007 (see footnote 653), the Royal Decree of 8 January 2010 establishes the Royal Institute and Observatory of the Spanish Navy as time-stamping authority. Real Decreto 4/2010 de 8 de enero por el que se regula el Esquema Nacional de Interoperabilidad en el ámbito de la Administración Electrónica, *BOE* 25 de 29 January 2010; *cert.fnmt.es/catalogo-de-servicios/sellado-de-tiempo/informacion-sobre-sellado-de-tiempo*.

653 Ley 11/2007 de 22 de junio de acceso electrónico de los ciudadanos a los Servicios Públicos, *BOE* 150 of 23 June 2007.

654 Article 2(5) Zakon o elektronskem poslovanju in elektronskem podpisu, *Uradni list RS* 98/2004 of 9 September 2004.

655 §9 Predpis č. 215/2002 Z. z. Zákon o elektronickom podpise a o zmene a doplnení niektorých zákonov, *Zbierka zákonov* Čiastka 91, 2134–2145.

656 §9 Gesetz vom 16. Mai 2001 über Rahmenbedingungen für elektronische Signaturen (Signaturgesetz – SigG), *BGBl.* I S.876.

657 Zákon č. 227/2000 Sb. o elektronickém podpisu a o změně některých dalších zákonů (zákon o elektronickém podpisu).

658 For instance, the civil law notary does not only attest to the parties' identity, he also attests to whether they were in a legal capacity to act as recorded in the deed before him.

*required for attesting to, and ensuring the continuing authenticity of, the records*".[659] In recent years, the introduction of electronic information in archives has given rise to questions regarding the nature of such archival material, as well as regarding the principles and methods for the control and preservation of such material. The evolution toward digital archives has had an undeniable impact on the core ideas of archival science.[660] Archival scientists have therefore gone as far as referring to a paradigm shift, meaning that the advent of electronic information in archives has led to new observations "*that cannot be explained in the terms of the old framework*" and thus "*begin to put into question its validity*" in order to find a new way of thinking about existing concepts.[661] It should, however, be remarked that the custodianship of the archivist has "*always been linked inextricably to the protection and safeguarding of evidence*" and that while electronic information may change the way in which archivists exercise physical ownership over their records, such could also be regarded as just a change in the means by which the archivist exercises his custodial responsibility and not a change in the substance of that task.[662] By ensuring the authenticity[663] of the records under his care, the archivist is of utmost importance in ensuring the enduring trustworthiness of archival records, a task finding its origins in the discipline of diplomatics.[664] That task is especially considered to be important

---

659 Duranti, L. (2009) "From Digital Diplomatics to Digital Records Forensics", *Archivaria*, Vol. 68, 41; Duranti, L. (Ed.) (2002) "The Long-term Preservation of Authentic Electronic Records: Findings of the InterPARES Project – Authenticity Task Force Report", *www.interpares.org/book/interpares_book_d_part1.pdf*, 21.

660 Duranti, L. (2001) "The impact of digital technology on archival science", *Archival Science*, Vol. 1, 39.

661 Taylor, H. A. (1987) "Transformation in the Archives: Technological Adjustment or paradigm Shift?", *Archivaria*, Vol. 25, 12–28; Duranti, L. (2001) "The impact of digital technology on archival science", *Archival Science*, Vol. 1, 41; Macneil, H. (1994) "Archival Theory and Practice: Between Two Paradigms", *Archivaria*, Vol. 37, 6–20.

662 Macneil, H. (1994) "Archival Theory and Practice: Between Two Paradigms", *Archivaria*, Vol. 37, 16.

663 For the purposes of archival science, authenticity must be understood as being "*the quality of being authentic, or entitled to acceptance*", whereby authentic refers to being of "*actual character not counterfeited, imitated, or adulterated [and] connotes definite origin from a source*". Thus, an authentic record is "*a record that is what it purports to be and is free from tampering or corruption*". Duranti, L. (Ed.) (2002) "The Long-term Preservation of Authentic Electronic Records: Findings of the InterPARES Project – Authenticity Task Force Report", *www.interpares.org/book/interpares_book_d_part1.pdf*, 2.

664 Duranti, L. (1998) *Diplomatics: New Uses for an Old Science*, Lanham: Scarecrow Press, 36–45. Diplomatics refers to the study of the intrinsic value of information itself, essentially in order to distinguish authentic information from forgeries, from which archival science is traditionally accepted to have been developed. Ross, S. (2012) "Digital Preservation, Archival Science and Methodological Foundations for Digital Libraries", *New Review of Information Networking*, Vol. 17, 51–53; Cook, T. (1997) "What is past is prologue", Archivaria, Vol. 43, 45. In essence, diplomatics could be considered as providing the tools for "*assessing the trustworthiness of records as evidence after the fact of their creation*". Meehan, J. (2003) *Towards an archival concept of evidence*, Master thesis School of Library, Archival and Information Studies University of British Columbia, 14.

when records are called upon as evidence in a court of law and when their trustworthiness is questioned.[665]

TRUST IN THE CUSTODIAN – What follows from the previous paragraph, is that the position of the archivist as trusted custodian has historically been that of the neutral and independent professional, who possesses the knowledge to ascertain the value of the records under their care.[666] In a notable attempt to reconcile that position with the needs of the current information society, the focus has been put on provenance, namely the understanding and recording of a record's origins and the context of its creation.[667] It is then provenance which allows a decision to be made regarding the trustworthiness of information, which in turn is a task for the custodian.[668]

LEGAL FRAMEWORK – While, as pointed out, trust in archivists as custodians of records has a strong historical dimension, there is also a legal framework at play here. Most states have their own national archival institution, serving as the "*designated custodians of* [the] *national memory*".[669] The legal frameworks supporting such institutions, however, are in principle only aimed at public sector entities. For the private sector within the EU, reference must again be made to the legal framework on electronic signatures and electronic identification. Though archivists are concerned with the authentication of records rather than persons, their expertise regarding durable preservation is needed to ensure that the authenticity and integrity of electronic information can be proven throughout its whole retention period.[670] Therefore, steps have

665 Duranti, L. (2009) "From Digital Diplomatics to Digital Records Forensics", *Archivaria*, Vol. 68, 43.

666 Yeo, G. (2013) "Trust and context in cyberspace", *Archives and Records*, Vol. 34, 217–218.

667 *Ibid.*, 218–219.

668 *Ibid.*, 224–225.

669 E.g. Archives Nationales (France), The National Archives (UK), National Archives and Records Administration (US), Rijksarchief (Belgium), Nationaal Archief (Netherlands). Blouin, F. X., Rosenberg, W. G. (2011) *Processing the past: contesting authority in history and the archives,* New York: Oxford University Press, 98.

670 It is clear that legal documents must be preserved for certain time periods: contracts must be preserved for at least the duration of their execution, fiscal and commercial laws require the retention of certain documents such as invoices, medical law requires the documentation – and retention thereof – of medical examinations and procedures, etc. Electronic information – including electronically signed information – is at a particular risk of becoming inaccessible or unverifiable throughout such retention period. File formats may become obsolete (e.g. WordStar), hardware may become incompatible (e.g. most modern computers will no longer contain a floppy-drive, or even a CD-drive), and certificates may expire (while the expiration of a signature certificate does not render invalid the signatures that were created when the certificate was still valid, it may become difficult to check whether the certificate was really valid at that point in time). This may render it impossible to verify, after a certain time period, whether electronic information was validly signed. Therefore, a strategy is needed to ensure the durable preservation of (signed) electronic information. Fischer-Dieskau, S., Wilke, D.

been undertaken to include trusted archival services under the EU's legal framework on electronic identification, electronic signatures and trust services, as well as under Member States' national laws.[671] For virtual currency service providers, however, it means that also that kind of trusted service provider is currently too narrowly defined by regulation to be applicable to their services. At most, virtual currency service providers will only be able to utilize the services of a trusted archival service provider.

### 3.2.3 *Trust through consumer law*

TRUST THROUGH ADJACENT LEGAL DOMAINS – While the figure of the trusted service provider has in recent years seen significant development in law, the previous sections have made clear that the different forms of that figure as they currently stand show little correspondence to the types of services provided by virtual currency service providers. It does, however, not mean that law cannot provide assistance in raising the trustworthiness of those virtual currency service providers. Solace can be found in adjacent legal domains, whose applicability to virtual currency service providers could raise their trustworthiness.

CONSUMER LAW – One of such legal domains is that of consumer law. Within the EU, e-commerce continues to grow and business-to-consumer e-commerce already represents almost 2% of the entire EU's Gross Domestic Product (GDP).[672] Market research conducted as part of the European Commission's Consumer Conditions Scoreboard indicates that there are still barriers to cross-border purchases.[673] One particular issue that was identified, is that only 9% of consumer respondents was aware of their basic consumer rights.[674] Moreover, the market research found that "*knowledge of consumer rights and trust in institutional and market conditions are crucial to the development of efficient markets*".[675] The existence of effective consumer protection and the consumers' knowledge thereof can therefore be considered as imperative for the growth of consumer trust in e-commerce.[676] That reasoning can also be applied to virtual

---

(2006) "Electronically signed documents: legal requirements and measures for their long-term conservation", *Digital Evidence and Electronic Signature Law Review*, Vol. 3, 40–44.

671 See: articles 34 and 40 Regulation 910/2014; Graux, H. (2011) "Rethinking the E-Signatures Directive: On laws, trust services, and the Digital Single Market", *Digital Evidence and Electronic Signature Law Review*, Vol. 8, 20.

672 European Commission (2015) "Consumer Conditions in the EU Getting up to speed with the digital age", *ec.europa.eu*, 1.

673 *Ibid.*, 2. These barriers exist both *ex ante* (e.g. price discrimination or refusal to sell) and *ex post* (issues with delivery and conformity).

674 European Commission (2015) *Consumer Conditions Scoreboard: Consumers at home in the Single Market (2015 edition)*, Luxembourg: Publications Office of the European Union, 5.

675 *Ibid.*, 17.

676 Yuthayotin, S. (2015) *Access to Justice in Transnational B2C E-Commerce: A Multidimensional Analysis of Consumer Protection Mechanisms*, Berlin: Springer, 23–24.

currencies, given that virtual currencies are generally used as a form of payment and increasingly so in an e-commerce setting. Where consumer law is applicable, it can therefore support the trustworthiness of virtual currency services.

E-commerce Directive – Over the years, EU consumer law has become a well-developed field of law, spread over several texts. At its most basic, reference can be made to the so-called e-Commerce Directive, which contains – amongst others – a number of information requirements, as well as provisions regarding the electronic conclusion of contracts.[677] The e-Commerce Directive applies to services of the information society, which are "*any service normally provided for remuneration, at a distance, by electronic means and at the individual request of a recipient of services*".[678] As noted in chapter I, virtual currency services are principally not provided for free, there will normally be some form of consideration for the provision of the service or of the virtual currency scheme itself be included. Virtual currency services are also increasingly more provided by electronic means, and without the parties involved being present. Last, the services are not provided on a linear basis, but at the request of the user. Therefore, it can be argued that the e-Commerce Directive applies to virtual currency service providers.[679]

Consumer Rights Directive and Distance Marketing of Financial Services Directive – A second directive in the consumer protection field is the Consumer Rights Directive.[680] That directive – which also amends and repeals older directives in the field – focuses on general consumer rights and information rights regarding distance contracts. While it does also apply to digital content, which virtual currencies could be argued to be, it excludes financial services from its scope.[681] The reason for that is that the provision at a distance of financial

677 Directive 2000/31/EC of the European Parliament and of the Council of 8 June 2000 on certain legal aspects of information society services, in particular electronic commerce, in the Internal Market ('Directive on electronic commerce'), *OJ* L 178 of 17 July 2000, 1–16 (hereinafter: e-Commerce Directive).

678 As defined by article 1(2) Directive 98/34/EC of the European Parliament and of the Council of 22 June 1998 laying down a procedure for the provision of information in the field of technical standards and regulations as amended by Directive 98/48/EC of the European Parliament and of the Council of 20 July 1998, *OJ* L 204 of 21 July 1998, 37–48. This directive has now been repealed and replaced by Directive 2015/1535 of the European Parliament and of the Council of 9 September 2015 laying down a procedure for the provision of information in the field of technical regulations and of rules on Information Society services (codification), *OJ* L 241 of 17 September 2015, 1–15. This directive uses the same definition in its article 1(1)(b).

679 Shcherbak, S. (2014) "How should bitcoin be regulated?", *European Journal of Legal Studies*, Vol. 7, 80–81.

680 Directive 2011/83/EU of the European Parliament and of the Council of 25 October 2011 on consumer rights, amending Council Directive 93/13/EEC and Directive 1999/44/EC of the European Parliament and of the Council and repealing Council Directive 85/577/EEC and Directive 97/7/EC of the European Parliament and of the Council, *OJ* L 304 of 22 November 2011, 64–88 (hereinafter: Consumer Rights Directive).

681 Articles 1(11) and 3(3)(d) Directive 2011/83/EC.

services – here defined as "*any service of a banking, credit, insurance, personal pension, investment or payment nature*"[682] – are covered by a separate directive.[683] The latter directive therefore covers the virtual currency services that qualify as financial services provided at a distance, while the Consumer Rights Directive covers those virtual currency services that do not qualify as financial services.

Unfair Commercial Practices Directive – Another consumer rights directive that may apply in business-to-consumer relations regarding virtual currencies is the Unfair Commercial Practices Directive.[684] That legal framework regulates unfair commercial practices – including misleading or aggressive commercial practices – in business-to-consumer relations during and after a commercial transaction in relation to a product.[685] A consumer is for the purposes of the unfair commercial practices legal framework defined as "*any natural person who, in commercial practices covered by this Directive, is acting for purposes which are outside his trade, business, craft or profession*".[686] A product is defined as "*any goods or service including immovable property, rights and obligations*".[687] The commercial practices to which the directive applies are defined as "*any act, omission, course of conduct or representation, commercial communication including advertising and marketing, by a trader, directly connected with the promotion, sale or supply of a product to consumers*".[688] This means that whoever "*for purposes relating to his trade, business, craft or profession*"[689] provides virtual currency services to consumers is bound to refrain from such unfair commercial practices in the provision of those services.

Conclusion – Though delving deeper into the applicability of EU consumer law to virtual currency service providers goes beyond the scope of this research, the preliminary overview of the previous paragraphs already demonstrates that at least parts of the consumer protection legal framework will apply. The result is that consumer law can be held to provide a modicum of legal certainty to virtual

682 Article 1(10) Directive 2011/83/EC.

683 Directive 2002/65/EC of the European Parliament and of the Council of 23 September 2002 concerning the distance marketing of consumer financial services and amending Council Directive 90/619/EEC and Directives 97/7/EC and 98/27/EC, *OJ* L 271 of 9 October 2002, 16–24.

684 Directive 2005/29/EC of the European Parliament and of the Council of 11 May 2005 concerning unfair business-to-consumer commercial practices in the internal market and amending Council Directive 84/450/EEC, Directives 97/7/EC, 98/27/EC and 2002/65/EC of the European Parliament and of the Council and Regulation (EC) No 2006/2004 of the European Parliament and of the Council, *OJ* L 149 of 11 June 2005, 22–39 (hereinafter: Unfair Commercial Practices Directive).

685 Articles 3 & 5 Unfair Commercial Practices Directive.

686 Article 2(a) Unfair Commercial Practices Directive.

687 Article 2(c) Unfair Commercial Practices Directive.

688 Article 2(d) Unfair Commercial Practices Directive.

689 Article 2(b) Unfair Commercial Practices Directive.

currency service users, in the sense that it provides a certain degree of legal protection, even absent a specific legal framework tailored to virtual currencies. In doing so, consumer law could support raising the trustworthiness of virtual currency service providers.

### 3.2.4 *Trust through financial law*

Trust as basis – Another adjacent legal domain in which trust is an important operational element is financial law. As discussed earlier in section 2.4 of this chapter, trust can be considered as a constitutive element of economic conduct, and that also extends to finance. The importance of trust for the financial system was underlined during the global financial crisis of 2007–2008, during which economist Joseph Stiglitz stated that *"financial markets hinge on trust, and that trust has eroded"*.[690] Moreover, research has established a direct correlation between trust and stock market participation.[691] Law, and in this case specifically financial law, can then serve to formalize the trust relations needed for the proper functioning of the financial system.[692]

Financial law – Financial law can be considered as the branch of law regulating the instruments, mechanisms and the institutions, public and private, that operate within monetary and financial markets.[693] From a macro perspective, one of the primary aims of such laws is to preserve the integrity of the financial system, although the micro objectives – such as the protection of the individual investor and his trust – can also contribute to systemic stability.[694] One example where the importance of the trust relationship between actors in financial markets is emphasized, is in the relation between financial institutions and investors. While the rules governing such trust were not always very explicit, or even written, the last decennia have seen major codification efforts resulting in formal laws imposing rules of conduct.[695]

EU financial law and virtual currencies – While for EU consumer law it was fairly clear that a number of provisions could be applied to virtual currency

690 Stiglitz, J. (2008) "The fruit of hypocrisy", *The Guardian*, 16 September 2008.

691 Guiso, L., Sapienza, P., Zingales, L. (2005) "Trusting the stock market", *The Journal of Finance*, Vol. 63, 2558–2559.

692 Tonkiss, F. (2009) "Trust, Confidence and Economic Crisis", *Intereconomics*, 197. Noteworthy here is that finance is littered with emotional terms evoking this trust relationship. Examples are 'securities', 'fiduciary', and 'equity'. Pixley, J. (2002) "Finance organizations, decisions and emotions", *British Journal of Sociology*, Vol. 53, 53–54.

693 Cfr. Lebrun: Lebrun, J. (1992) "La législation financière 1981–1991", In: Horsmans, G. (Ed.) *Le nouveau droit des marchés financiers*, Brussels: Larcier, 12; Colaert, V. (2010) *De meerlagige rechtsverhouding financiële dienstverlener – belegger*, KU Leuven Faculty of Law PhD thesis, 12.

694 Colaert, V. (2010) *De meerlagige rechtsverhouding financiële dienstverlener – belegger*, KU Leuven Faculty of Law PhD thesis, 17 & 95.

695 *Ibid.*, 32–33.

services, it is less clear at this point to what extent EU financial law could be applied to virtual currencies, the services developed around them, and their service providers. One explanation is that consumer law is more directly geared towards the consumer, by protecting his right to economic self-determination.[696] The result is a broad field of rules, applicable when a consumer is involved, often regardless of the type of service or service provider. As discussed in the previous paragraph, the direct aim of financial law is to preserve financial stability, whereby the protection of the individual is more considered as a by-product or indirect goal at most. The resulting regulation is then more aimed at particular service providers and the financial products and services they offer. For virtual currencies this means that it must be assessed to what extent virtual currency developments and the related service providers can fall under the scope of financial regulations. As part of this research, such an analysis will be made for the inclusion of virtual currencies under the EU legal frameworks regarding e-money, payment services, anti-money laundering and markets in financial instruments.

### 3.2.5 *Synthesis*

Limited forms of trust service providers – While the EU's legal framework on electronic signatures does leave room for Member States to adopt additional legislation regulating different forms of trust services than those covered under the EU's current eIDAS Regulation, Member States have only utilized that option in very limited ways. In the cases analyzed here, other forms of trusted service providers regulated at the level of the Member States are only a direct extension of the eIDAS trust services, and do not lay the groundwork for a broader legal framework on trust services. While other forms of trusted service providers can be imagined – such as archival science's recognition of the archivist as a trusted custodian – such forms are only recently becoming the subject of specific regulation, and even then mainly in connection to eIDAS services. The overall finding is therefore that under the current state of the art in law, there is no room for the recognition of virtual currency service providers as trusted service providers. These service providers are, however, free to utilize existing trust services to enhance their own trustworthiness.

Trust augmentation through consumer and financial law – The fact that virtual currency service providers can at the present moment not be considered as trusted service providers does, however, not preclude the augmentation of their overall trustworthiness through the application of other legal principles. Consumer law, for instance, was found to be a major factor contributing to trust in e-commerce, and can therefore be held to support the trustworthiness of virtual currency services where applicable. Likewise, trust is a constitutive element of financial systems. Financial law therefore aims to protect trust of

[696] Terryn, E. (2008) *Bedenktijden in het consumentenrecht*, Antwerp: Intersentia, 26–27.

non-professional users in those systems, in order to contribute to the protection of the integrity and stability of finance.

## 4 INTERIM CONCLUSIONS

Chapter objectives – The first core objective of this chapter was to analyze the notion of trust from an abstract point of view, in order to gain a better understanding of how the trust notion is defined in different scientific disciplines and what the implications thereof are to virtual currencies. In second order, the analysis supported the understanding of how the trustworthiness of virtual currencies could be enhanced through law. To achieve that second objective, a second analysis was conducted of how the notion of trust is currently operationalized through law in practice. The main result to be derived from these analyses is a better understanding of how trust – as operationalized in law – could help raise the overall trustworthiness of virtual currencies and their service providers. If certain trust-enhancing legal measures could be taken, such measures could support a higher degree of legal certainty regarding virtual currencies, even in the absence of a specific legal framework regarding virtual currencies.

Abstract notion of trust – The first analysis, regarding the abstract notion of trust, was conducted from an interdisciplinary point of view. As it was found that different scientific disciplines can have rather divergent definitions of trust, it was assessed how these conceptualizations of trust overlap and differ. The scientific disciplines selected for the interdisciplinary analysis were philosophy, psychology, sociology, economy, computer science and engineering, and law. Here, it became clear that trust is a basic attribute to interpersonal relationships, serving as a bet for future possibilities, yet in doing so also constituting a degree of risk-taking. Despite some divergences between the different scientific disciplines analyzed, it is clear that trust is generally accepted as a basic element in forming interpersonal relationships, and increasingly so also in relation to computational systems. As such relationships can be complex and fraught with uncertainty, the understanding of trust as the expectation of certain behavior can be considered as a device to reduce that complexity. Trust is then considered by both sociologists and economists as serving as a bet for future possibilities, potentially leading to better transaction outcomes, new opportunities, or even higher overall market efficiency. However, another element inherent to such trust relationships is that of risk. Trust can be betrayed, in the sense that the trustee does not act as expected. When such is the case, the trustor could end up worse than before the trust relationship. That unavoidable risk, however, does not mean that trust relationships are discouraged. On the contrary, several scientific disciplines were found to put particular focus on the development of risk measurement and management strategies, thus aiming to level out the potential impact of the risk associated with trust relationships.

Trust balance – Overall, it was found that a balance must be struck between the degree of trust invested into a relationship and the degree of trustworthiness of such a relationship. It is that trust balance that is of particular importance to virtual currencies. As such technological developments require a certain degree of trust from their users – trust in both the underlying technology and the service providers – virtual currencies and their service providers must display an equal degree of trustworthiness. It can therefore be held that in order to raise trust in virtual currencies, it must be assessed how the trustworthiness of virtual currencies can be raised. Here, the analysis on trust operationalization comes into play.

Trust operationalized in law – While legal science was found to not directly have a comparable trust notion as found in the other scientific disciplines analyzed here, the research on trust operationalization found that law is catching up with the notion of trust. A particular figure developed within computer science and engineering – the trusted third party or TTP – has already found its way into law and is currently being further developed. At the level of the EU, it was found that the TTP was already implemented in the legal framework on electronic signatures. Recently, the directive forming the electronic signatures legal framework was replaced by a regulation, which further solidifies the figure of the TTP. Moreover, the eIDAS Regulation adds a couple of new trusted service providers, namely in the fields of electronic seals, electronic timestamps, electronic registered delivery services, and website authentication. However, despite the growing field of trusted service providers, the eIDAS Regulation was found to still maintain a *numerus clausus*, and thus does not leave room for the inclusion of virtual currency service providers as trusted service providers. While some EU Member States were found to have developed a broader range of trusted service providers, also here no room was found for the inclusion of virtual currency service providers. Neither was such an opening found in other developments regarding trusted service providers, such as the trusted custodian.

Virtual currency service providers – The main finding to be derived from the previous analysis is that under the EU's current legal framework there is no room for the designation of virtual currency service providers as a particular form of trusted service providers. Such service providers can of course make use of the services provided by existing trust service providers, for instance regarding website authentication. However, that does not mean that under current EU law there is no possibility at all to raise the trustworthiness of virtual currency service providers. In the final part of the analysis on trust operationalization, it was found that the applicability of adjacent legal domains could be of use here. More in particular, consumer law was identified as a field that – at least to certain extent – could be applicable the services provided by virtual currency service providers. The provisions of the consumer protection legal framework – for instance concerning consumer protection through information duties imposed on the service provider – could provide a minimum of legal certainty regarding the position of the virtual currency service user, and the protection offered thereto. In doing so, consumer law does not take away the risk associated with that form of trust relationship, but serves as a form of risk management. Even absent a legal framework aimed specifically at virtual currencies and their service providers, adjacent domains such as consumer law could therefore support raising the trustworthiness of virtual currency service providers. Also financial law was identified as a field of law in which trust relationships are considered of high importance and are protected. While it is no surprise that virtual currencies – given their nature as instruments that could fulfill certain financial functions, such as payments – could be considered for regulation under financial law, the findings of this chapter show that, even absent a clear legal framework on virtual currencies themselves, other regulatory frameworks under financial law could still be considered for application.

Conclusion – The main conclusion that can be drawn with regard to the abstract notion of trust is that trust is an essential component of interpersonal relationships and transactions. Under the influence of the information society, trust is also becoming more and more of a central aspect in the interactions between people and technology. Despite some differences in their thoughts and definitions, the scientific disciplines analyzed here all agree that trust is needed in order to benefit from relationships that cannot be founded on pure certainty. Trust is therefore needed to put people past the element of risk inherent to such relationships. The same reasoning can also be applied to virtual currencies and their service providers: trust is needed from users in order for them to engage with these technological developments. But how can users be convinced to trust virtual currencies? For that, the analysis conducted here pointed out the concept of the trust balance developed in scientific literature. A certain degree of trust may be needed from users in order to engage with a new technology or service. Such trust may well be granted, if the technology or service can display an equal degree of trustworthiness. Thus, from a practical viewpoint, the question then becomes: how can the trustworthiness of virtual currencies be raised? To that end, the focus was put on trust operationalization in law. One avenue explored in this chapter is the figure of the trusted service provider. While that figure is becoming more developed – not only in computer science and engineering, but also in law – it is clear that the understanding of trusted service providers under current EU law is very different from the services offered by virtual currency service providers. Virtual currency service providers therefore do not seem likely to be able to become one of such trusted service providers. However, there are still other options available under current law to raise the trustworthiness of virtual currency service providers. First, virtual currency service providers could make use of the services offered by existing trusted service providers, e.g. for services regarding website authentication. Second, the applicability of adjacent fields of law – and in particular consumer law and financial law – could support raising the trustworthiness of virtual currency service providers, even in the absence of a legal framework aimed specifically at virtual currencies and their service providers.

# CHAPTER III
# PERSPECTIVES OF MONEY

## 1 INTRODUCTION

VIRTUAL CURRENCIES AS MONEY – Much like the notion of trust analyzed in the previous chapter, money is a concept used in everyday language that can prove hard to define.[697] At its most basic understanding, money could be understood as referring to assets that serve as means to conclude payments. There could, however, also be assets that can be regarded as money, yet which do not serve as means of payment, or means of payment that are not money. But it is the reference to means of payment that raises the question whether virtual currencies can be considered as money. After all, the analysis of different kinds of virtual currencies conducted in chapter I demonstrated that virtual currencies can be used to obtain various goods and services, both in virtual worlds and in the physical world, and thus possess the potential to serve as means to conclude payments. As there are several instances where money can be considered as a legally relevant concept – especially so in financial law – it is important to analyze at this stage of the research whether virtual currencies can be considered as money. Such a qualification then subjects virtual currencies to the rules and regulations to which money is subjected, thus identifying the applicable legal frameworks.

MONEY AS A LEGAL CONCEPT – In legal discourse on money, the focus will often be put on what can be regarded as public money or legal tender, *i.e.* the notes and coins issued by a sovereign state's government. Starting from an analysis of the seminal work on the legal aspect of money by Mann, this chapter will present the core theories underlying the current legal understanding of money.[698] That analysis will include a summary analysis of the credit theory of money, and its importance in the origins of money.[699]

---

697 As already briefly explored in section 2.2.2 of chapter I.

698 Proctor, C. (2012) *Mann on the legal aspect of money*, Oxford: University Press. Though Mann's work is of course heavily influenced by UK law, the theories he presents do have an international outlook.

699 For the sake of feasibility, and in order to avoid a Keynesian 'Babylonian madness', this study will be limited to a more high-level presentation of the most dominant theories regarding the origins of money. It is not within the scope of this research to provide a definite account on the origins of money, or of all the different theories regarding the matter.

Money as an economic concept – While the analysis conducted here will depart from a legal understanding of money, it is clear that the matter of money cannot be approached without taking into account economic scholarship on this subject. Given the division of economic thought in the matter of money, this chapter will consult works of scholars from different schools of thought to present a more balanced view.[700] That economic analysis will serve to ascertain whether certain economic principles applicable to money could apply to the different types of virtual currencies. For instance, in monetary economics discourse, money is generally considered as fulfilling three distinct functions: store of value, medium of exchange and unit of account. Therefore, it is important to analyze whether the different types of virtual currencies discussed here can fulfill those basic functions of money.

Goal of the chapter – The goal of this chapter is to seek whether parallels can be found between the notion of money and the notion of virtual currencies. In doing so, this chapter critically assesses whether the different types of virtual currencies as presented in chapter I can be regarded as money under the theories covered here, or whether they can fulfill the economic functions expected from money. The need for such an analysis rises from the knowledge that money is an important concept under law – even though, as will be seen, it is not always clearly defined – and that the consideration of virtual currencies as money could therefore have clear legal implications. If virtual currencies can be considered as money, an inventory must then be made of which rules will consequently become applicable. If virtual currencies cannot be considered as money, further analysis will be needed of legal frameworks utilizing their own terminology – such as the legal frameworks on e-money, payment services, anti-money laundering, and financial instruments – which may still apply.

## 2 MONEY AS A LEGAL CONCEPT

Definition – In chapter I, reference was already made to a potential legal definition of money. Before anything else, it should be noted that the definition posited there only forms the starting point from which further inquiries into the nature of money can depart. The earlier definition of money is therefore by no means to be understood as the intended endpoint. It is important to acknowledge here that current thinking on money is strongly influenced by modern concepts not in existence at the time money was first developed. Therefore, those concepts are to be used as tools in understanding the historical development of money,

700 The main opposing views of relevance here are Chartalism and Metallism. Furthermore, it will be assessed how these views have been further developed in Keynesian economics, Austrian economics and the more recent school of neo-Chartalism.

and not as a lens through which such a development should be seen.[701] Under the initial definition, money could be understood as a generally accepted medium of exchange, often but not necessarily having the status of legal tender, that represents purchasing power, or assets that can be easily converted into cash.[702] Here, reference can be made to the Uniform Commercial Code (UCC), which considers money as "*a medium of exchange currently authorized or adopted by a domestic or foreign government*", which also extends to units of account established at the level of intergovernmental organizations, such as the euro.[703]

LEGAL TENDER – The first element of the earlier money definition refers to money as being legal tender.[704] Legal tender can be defined as "*the money (bills and coins) approved in a country for the payment of debts, the purchase of goods, and other exchanges for value*".[705] More explicitly, legal tender has been defined in US law as being "*United States coins and currency (including Federal Reserve notes and circulating notes of Federal Reserve banks and national banks)*".[706] Similar provisions exist within EU law.[707] Even where no clear legal definition of legal tender exists, this concept can be held to be generally accepted knowledge.[708] In short, barring a few exceptions, legal tender can be considered as being mandatorily accepted, at face value, for all payment obligations.[709] However,

701 Semenova, A. (2011) *The Origins of Money: Evaluating Chartalist and Metallist theories in the context of ancient Greece and Mesopotamia*, University of Missouri – Kansas City PhD Thesis, 31–44.

702 "money" (2014), *Black's Law Dictionary* (9th ed.), West; "money, n." (2014), *OED Online*, Oxford University Press; "money" (2014), *Merriam-Webster.com*, Merriam-Webster.

703 U.C.C. §1-201(b)(24).

704 This is also found in the money definition employed in the US Code of Federal Regulations: 31 CFR §1010.100(m). More concretely, this definitions refers to "*the coin and paper money of the United States or of any other country that is designated as legal tender and that circulates and is customarily used and accepted as a medium of exchange in the country of issuance*".

705 "legal tender" (2014), *Black's Law Dictionary* (9th ed.), West.

706 31 USC §5103; as provided by: Pub. L. 97–258 of 13 September 1982, 96 *Stat.* 980, and Pub. L. 97–452, §1(19) of 12 January 1983, 96 *Stat.* 2477. Interesting to note is that it is said that legal tender serves "*for all debts, public charges, taxes, and dues*". This includes both public and private debts (Pub. L. 89–81, §102), but does not explicitly address the situation where there is a payment obligation, yet no preexisting debt.

707 For the EU, article 128 of the Treaty on the Functioning of the European Union (TFEU) holds that "*the banknotes issued by the European Central Bank and the national central banks shall be the only such notes to have the status of legal tender within the Union*". For coins, a similar provision is found in article 11 Council Regulation (EC) No 974/98 of 3 May 1998 on the introduction of the euro, *OJ* L 139 of 11 May 1998, 1–5. This view on legal tender was confirmed in: Commission Recommendation of 22 March 2010 on the scope and effects of legal tender of euro banknotes and coins, *OJ* L 83 of 30 March 2010, 70–71.

708 European Commission (2010) "Report of the Euro Legal Tender Expert Group (ELTEG) on the definition, scope and effects of legal tender of euro banknotes and coins", *ec.europa.eu*, 3–4. Although it must be said that there are still some uncertainties surrounding the notion of legal tender, see: Scholten, A. A. (2017) *Juridische aspecten van contant geld*, Zutphen: Paris, 88.

709 European Commission (2010) "Report of the Euro Legal Tender Expert Group (ELTEG) on the definition, scope and effects of legal tender of euro banknotes and coins", *ec.europa.eu*, 4.

it is clear that deviations from accepting legal tender as means of payment are possible, for instance following the principle of contractual freedom and if acting in good faith.[710]

Convertible to cash – Interestingly, the main definition established at the beginning of this section has a second element, namely 'assets that can be easily converted into cash'. That second element deviates from the first element, because as such assets should be convertible to cash, they are not cash themselves and therefore no legal tender. While the first element of the definition seemed to equate money to legal tender, the second element now opens up the possibility of the existence of money that is no legal tender. A clear example of that can be found in practice when central banks report on the money aggregates of their particular states. Money supply can be measured at different levels. At its most narrow, the monetary supply of a state consists purely out of the coins and notes that have been emitted by the state as legal tender and that are currently in circulation.[711] A broader measure takes into account not just the legal tender in and out of circulation, but also assets that can be directly used for payments, such as demand deposits.[712] Looking even broader, a money supply measure can also take into account assets that can be easily converted into legal tender, such as short-term deposits and amounts held in savings accounts or money market accounts.[713] Here, it becomes clear that central banks do take into account assets that are not legal tender themselves, but that are readily convertible into legal tender or directly usable in payment transactions when calculating their state's money supply.[714]

---

710 *Ibid.*, 5–6; Scholten, A. A. (2017) *Juridische aspecten van contant geld*, Zutphen: Paris, 89–90.

711 This constitutes the currency in circulation, which forms part of the monetary base (MB). Note, however, that the definitions of this notion may differ per state. The UK, for instance, includes bank reserves as part of its monetary base. In the US, "*monetary base is defined as the sum of currency in circulation and reserve balances (deposits held by banks and other depository institutions in their accounts at the Federal Reserve)*". *federalreserve.gov/faqs/money_12845.htm*; Geva, B. (2011) *The Payment Order of Antiquity and the Middle Ages: A Legal History*, London: Hart Publishing, 18. By means of example, the US had at the end of 2015 around USD 1.3 trillion in circulation, whereas the Eurozone had slightly over EUR 1 trillion in circulation. Federal Reserve (2015) "Statistical release: H.6 (508) money stock measures", *federalreserve.gov*, table 3; European Central Bank (2015) "Press release: Monetary developments in the euro area: October 2015", *ecb.europa.eu*, s1.

712 This constitutes M1. Within the EU, M1 encompasses legal tender in circulation and overnight deposits. By means of example: the US had at the end of 2015 around USD 3 trillion in M1, the Eurozone around EUR 6.5 trillion. Federal Reserve (2015) "Statistical release: H.6 (508) money stock measures", *federalreserve.gov*, table 1; European Central Bank (2015) "Press release: Monetary developments in the euro area: October 2015", *ecb.europa.eu*, s1.

713 This constitutes M2. For the US, this amounted at the end of 2015 to USD 12.2 trillion, for the EU EUR 10.1 trillion. Federal Reserve (2015) "Statistical release: H.6 (508) money stock measures", *federalreserve.gov*, table 3; European Central Bank (2015) "Press release: Monetary developments in the euro area: October 2015", *ecb.europa.eu*, s1.

714 Note that even broader measures exist. M3, for instance, takes into account the previous measures, as well as longer-term securities. Not all central banks report these larger measures.

# 3 THEORIES ON MONEY

DIFFERENT THEORIES – The two seemingly contradicting elements of the single definition analyzed in the previous section already demonstrate the core difficulty in establishing a legal definition of the concept of money. Essentially, that divergence stems from how different theories view the concept of money. On the one hand, there is the classical state theory of money, which puts monetary policy firmly in the hands of the sovereign state. More recent theories, on the other hand, allow for more flexibility in establishing a more abstract notion of money that transcends state involvement. This section will briefly explore such theories and the origins of money.

## 3.1 THE CREDIT THEORY AND THE ORIGINS OF MONEY

THE BARTERING MYTH – Popular belief has it that money was first created as a solution to the many problems posed by the practice of bartering employed in humanity's earliest societies.[715] After all, bartering requires a buyer not only to find a seller carrying the goods he needs, but also to be able to offer goods the seller would want in exchange.[716] Furthermore, such goods – often in the form of grain and other produce or cattle – are not quite convenient to carry around and are highly perishable.[717] Thus, it is said, merchants replaced that practice by pricing their wares in a certain weight of a – usually precious – metal. Such a use of metals, however, was by no means a perfect solution, as those bars or chunks of metal need to be carefully weighed and checked for their composition.[718] In turn, the latter problem was countered by the creation of institutions that would stamp all sides of a piece of metal, the idea being that those stamps attest to the authenticity and

---

715 This paragraph summarizes the theory on the origins of money popularized by Adam Smith. Smith, A. (1776) *An Inquiry into the Nature and Causes of the Wealth of Nations*, London: W. Strahan and T. Cadell, 27–35. Also Aristotle regarded barter as a natural practice needed to sustain self-sufficiency, with money being a development stemming from trade practices. Also to him, money is regarded as having started as exchanging a certain weight of a commodity metal, with stamps being used to attest to the weight and value of the token. Aristotle (1999) *Politics, translated by Benjamin Jowett*, Kitchener: Batoche Books, 14–15.

716 This problem is addressed as the 'coincidence of wants'. Jevons, W. S. (1876) *Money and the Mechanism of Exchange*, New York: D. Appleton and Co., paragraphs I.5-I.6; Kiyotaki, N., Wright, R. (1989) "On Money as a Medium of Exchange", *Journal of Political* Economy, Vol. 97, 928; Desan, C. (2016) "Money as a Legal Institution", In: Fox, D., Ernst, W. (Eds.) *Money in the Western Legal Tradition: Middle Ages to Bretton Woods*, Oxford: Oxford University Press, 20.

717 This refers to another aspect of the bartering problem, namely what is regarded as the 'saleableness' of goods. Some goods are inherently difficult to divide, which makes their use in barter difficult. A sheep, for instance, may be worth a few chickens, but how can the sheep be divided if its owner only needs one chicken? For Menger, this is a fundamental element leading to the creation of money. He posits that, eventually, people will want to trade their less 'saleable' goods for more 'saleable' goods, with money being the relatively most 'saleable' good. Menger, K. (1892) "On the Origin of Money", *The Economic Journal*, Vol. 2, 242–243 and 248–249.

718 For instance, one could insert lead in a golden bar to seemingly add weight, and thus value.

integrity of that piece, and therefore also to its weight and subsequent value. In doing so, commercial practices and needs gave birth to coin money.[719]

Refuting the myth – The popular theory described in the previous paragraph has in more recent times come under scrutiny. There are two main reasons for such scrutiny. First, there has thus far not been any convincing evidence of such a pure barter economy ever having existed.[720] Second, some of the earliest written texts demonstrate how money as an abstract unit of value – a credit system – already existed before money as a physical medium of exchange – coinage – came into being.

Money before the coin – One of such early written texts is the oldest known code of law, the Code of Ur-Nammu, which denominates debts in weights of silver, or *shekel*.[721] Similar principles were found in the later Code of Hammurabi.[722] Also in the Hebrew Bible evidence can be found for this: units of account for money and units of weight are interchangeable[723], and one single word – '*kessef*' – is used to address both silver and money.[724] However, while debts were denominated in standardized units of silver, those units did not necessarily circulate. They merely served to establish a common unit of account to settle debts.[725] Grierson, in this

719 Desan, C. (2013) "Creation Stories: Myths About the Origins of Money", *Harvard Law School Public Law & Legal Theory Working Paper Series Paper No. 13-20*, 4–8.

720 Graeber, D. (2011) *Debt: The First 5,000 Years*, Brooklyn: Melville House, 29; Desan, C. (2010) "Coin Reconsidered: The Political Alchemy of Commodity Money", *Theoretical Inquiries in Law*, Vol. 11, 365.

721 For instance, a man divorcing his first-ranking wife must pay her 60 shekels of silver, the same price for breaking another man's bones with a club. Roth, M. T. (1995) *Law Collections from Mesopotamia and Asia Minor*, Atlanta: Scholars Press, 18–19. Ur-Nammu was a 21th century B.C. king in the Sumerian Ur III dynasty.

722 For instance, here the price of divorce absent marriage settlement is one mana of silver. Hammurabi was a king in the First Babylonian Dynasty, reigning in the 18th century B.C. Harper, R. F. (1904) *The Code of Hammurabi, King of Babylon*, Chicago: University of Chicago Press, 49. Interestingly, the Code of Hammurabi also refers to payments to be made in grain. This creates a complex monetary system in which several commodities could serve as means of payment. Geva, B. (2011) *The Payment Order of Antiquity and the Middle Ages: A Legal History*, London: Hart Publishing, 20. In ancient Greece, oxen were used as a common unit of account. Semenova, A. (2011) *The Origins of Money: Evaluating Chartalist and Metallist theories in the context of ancient Greece and Mesopotamia*, University of Missouri – Kansas City PhD Thesis, 154–156.

723 This is especially true for the shekel, which was both a unit of account and a unit of weight. Another example is the lira, which is derived from the Roman weight and coin unit *libra*.

724 Geva argues that at some places it is clear that the Hebrew Bible refers to silver to be weighed as means of payment, yet that at other places it is more ambiguous what is meant. Geva, B. (2011) *The Payment Order of Antiquity and the Middle Ages: A Legal History*, London: Hart Publishing, 19–20.

725 Graeber, D. (2011) *Debt: The First 5,000 Years*, Brooklyn: Melville House, 39. Similar findings apply to Anglo-Saxon England: first money was established as a unit of account, only then came coins into circulation. Desan, C. (2010) "Coin Reconsidered: The Political Alchemy of Commodity Money", *Theoretical Inquiries in Law*, Vol. 11, 371; Desan, C. (2013) "Creation Stories: Myths About the Origins of Money", *Harvard Law School Public Law & Legal Theory Working Paper Series Paper No. 13-20*, 46.

sense, put forward the thesis that money as a unit of account developed from the practice of '*wergeld*', which was a fixed compensation for specific personal injuries.[726] It is also evidenced in cases such as Yap's stone money, where such stones served as unit of account without circulation.[727] Coin money, in turn, was only created much later in the western Asia Minor region of Lydia[728], sometime in the 6th or 7th century B.C.[729] Moreover, most of the coins from those times were discovered not far from their point of origin, thus contradicting Aristotle's claim that coin money was invented primarily to facilitate foreign trade.[730]

THE CREDIT THEORY OF MONEY – In refuting the bartering myth, Innes describes a monetary unit as an "*arbitrary denomination, by which commodities are measured in terms of credit, and which serves, therefore, as a more or less accurate measure of the value of all commodities*".[731] Coin money can therefore be argued to be nothing more than an "*obligation to provide a credit by taxation or otherwise for the redemption of the coin and thus enable its possessor to get value for his money*".[732] Innes' idea that money is nothing more than credit became known as the credit theory of money.

## 3.2 STATE THEORY

MONEY AS AN ACT OF STATE AUTHORITY – Even before Innes' work on the credit theory of money, the German economist Georg Friedrich Knapp published his work on the state theory of money.[733] In that work, Knapp posits three general

726 This practice can be found in several ancient cultures. Grierson, P. (1978) "The origins of money", *Research in Economic Anthropology*, Vol. 1, 19.

727 On the Micronesian island of Yap, large circular stone disks – of up to several meters in diameter – with a hole in the middle were traditionally used as currency. As the stones are difficult to move, ownership was transferred orally as part of a transaction. The value of a particular stone depended not just on its size and composition – as would be expected in commodity money – but also on its history. There have been reports of a case where a stone sank to the bottom of the ocean during an attempted transport. While the stone had not been seen for ages, its ownership was still being transferred years thereafter. Friedman, M. (1994) *Money mischief: Episodes in monetary history*, Orlando: Harcourt, 3–7. In his popular science work, Felix Martin provides an interesting account of this practice: Martin, F. (2014) *Money: The unauthorised biography*, London: Vintage Books, 1–6.

728 Present Turkey.

729 Grierson places this during the reign of Croesus. The first coins were not made of gold or silver, but of electrum, a gold and silver alloy. Grierson, P. (1978) "The origins of money", *Research in Economic Anthropology*, Vol. 1, 2.

730 *Ibid.*, 4–5; Von Reden, S. (1995) *Exchange in Ancient Greece*, London: Duckworth, 58–59 & 67; Geva, B. (2011) *The Payment Order of Antiquity and the Middle Ages: A Legal History*, London: Hart Publishing, 80.

731 Innes, M. A. (1913) "What is Money?", *Banking Law Journal*, Vol. 30, 399–400.

732 *Ibid.*, 402.

733 Knapp, G. F. (1905) *Staatliche Theorie des Geldes*, Leipzig: Duncker & Humblot. Here, reference will be made to the English translation published during Knapp's lifetime: Knapp,

principles: *"(1) the choice of the means of payment is a free act of the State's authority; (2) the denomination of the means of payment according to new units of value is a free act of the State's authority; (3) the definition of the new unit is also a free act of the State's authority"*.[734] Knapp denounces what he refers to as 'Metallism', namely the idea that money derives its value from the purchasing power of the commodity used to represent that money.[735] He notes that the purchasing power of money is not directly derived from its minting standards – which are also subject to the state's authority – but is defined by law.[736] He therefore supports a Chartalist view, in which the value of money is determined by the state, rather than by the token's – being a coin or note – inherent value. While that may sound obvious in today's practice of fiat currency, the theory should of course be viewed in light of its era, in which commodity money still existed and the gold standard was very much in vogue.

Broader than legal tender – While it may be easy to deride the state theory as equating money to just legal tender, such was not Knapp's intention. In fact, he specifically addresses forms of money that are not legal tender, yet that are part of the monetary system.[737] The determining factor is therefore not issuance, but

G. F. (1924) *The State Theory of Money*, London: Macmillan & Co. It should be noted that the theory of Knapp is fairly convoluted and makes use of many neologisms coined by the author. In order to avoid having to go into lengthy descriptions of the author's terminology, the explanation of this theory will be achieved by means of paraphrasing.

734 Knapp, G. F. (1924) *The State Theory of Money*, London: Macmillan & Co., 24.

735 For instance, historically precious metals such as gold and silver were used to mint coins. The value of a coin could then be based on the value of that particular amount and purity of the precious metal. The shekel, for instance, was originally a unit of weight. Dilke, O. A. W. (1987) *Reading the Past: Mathematics and measurement*, London: British Museum Publications, 46. It should be noted that 'Metallists' did foresee a reconciliation between their theory and the rise of coins of lesser metals and banknotes: those tokens of lesser value inherit their value from the precious metals backing them. This did, of course, pose some problems when money evolved into pure fiat currency. Bell, S. (2001) "The role of the state and the hierarchy of money", *Cambridge Journal of Economics*, Vol. 25, 153.

736 Knapp, G. F. (1924) *The State Theory of Money*, London: Macmillan & Co., 57–58. For instance, a coin minted in gold may be replaced by a coin minted in a base metal, yet by law still maintain the same purchasing power. Examples of this can be found in the composition of many coins in the late 20th century. The US penny (or one-cent coin) was originally made out of pure copper. At the present moment, copper only represents a small fraction of the coin's composition. And even so, its production cost has risen beyond its actual purchasing power, thus showing that the value of the token and its purchasing power are not necessarily the same. US Mint (2014) "2014 Biennial Report to the Congress", *usmint.gov*, 2. Important to note is that when the state decides to replace one currency with another, it must lay down the rules of conversion. The new currency must in one way or another be linked – by means of conversion – to the currency preceding it. Stern, B. (1998) *Dissolution, Continuation and Succession in Eastern Europe*, The Hague: Kluwer Law International, 36.

737 Knapp, G. F. (1924) *The State Theory of Money*, London: Macmillan & Co., 95. See also: Wray, L. R. (2000) "The Neo-Chartalist Approach to Money", *CFEPS Working Paper 10*, 6. Wray further argues that this means that the state theory is not necessarily limited to physical money. Wray, L. R. (2014) "From the State Theory of Money to Modern Money Theory: An Alternative to Economic Orthodoxy", *Levy Economics Institute Working Paper 792*, 5.

acceptance: only what is accepted as payment by the state, is money.[738] Forms of money that are not legal tender can be considered as convertible, and it is because of the declaration of the state's acceptance thereof that they can subsequently become acceptable to clear private debts.[739] While Knapp is generally considered as the founder of the Chartalist theory, the argument that the value of money derives from the state's acceptance thereof could already be found in Adam Smith's *Wealth of Nations*, though Smith did not fully develop that theory.[740] The acceptance of other forms of money in Knapp's theory is important to note, as it seems to have been misstated in the analyses of later scholars.[741]

Influence on economics – Knapp's theory managed to influence economic thinking on the subjects of money and monetary policy. An early adopter of the Chartalist theory was Keynes, who also understood the state's role in determining what can be regarded as money.[742] Similar views were followed by Minsky.[743] Though it can be remarked that Innes' credit theory shows

---

738 Knapp, G. F. (1924) *The State Theory of Money*, London: Macmillan & Co., 95. Important to note here is that Knapp sees the mere declaration of a state that a certain token has monetary value as insufficient to establish that token as money. Money only receives legitimacy as being such when accepted by that state as a means of payment. See also: Semenova, A. (2011) *The Origins of Money: Evaluating Chartalist and Metallist theories in the context of ancient Greece and Mesopotamia*, University of Missouri – Kansas City PhD Thesis, 49.

739 See also: Wray, L. R. (2014) "From the State Theory of Money to Modern Money Theory: An Alternative to Economic Orthodoxy", *Levy Economics Institute Working Paper 792*, 6; Bell, S. (2001) "The role of the state and the hierarchy of money", *Cambridge Journal of Economics*, Vol. 25, 155. A similar observation was made by Thayer: "*In law, whatever is legal tender is money; but it is not true that whatever is money is legal tender*". Thayer, J. B. (1887) "Legal Tender", *Harvard Law Review*, Vol. 1, 84. There are, however, also authors that do equate money to legal tender. See, for instance: Mill, J. S., Laughlin, J. L. (1885) *Principles of political economy – Abridged, with Critical, Bibliographical, and Explanatory Notes, and a Sketch of the History of Political Economy*, New York City: D. Appleton and Co., 342–343.

740 "*A prince, who should enact that a certain proportion of his taxes should be paid in a paper money of a certain kind, might thereby give a certain value to this paper money; even though the terms of its final discharge and redemption should depend altogether upon the will of the prince.*" Smith, A. (1776) *An Inquiry into the Nature and Causes of the Wealth of Nations*, London: W. Strahan and T. Cadell, 398.

741 It has, for instance been attributed to Schumpeter to have limited Knapp's Chartalism to legal tender laws. Dodd, N. (2014) *The Social Life of Money*, Princeton: University Press, 104; Wray, L. R. (2014) "From the State Theory of Money to Modern Money Theory: An Alternative to Economic Orthodoxy", *Levy Economics Institute Working Paper 792*, 5. It is no secret that Schumpeter was no proponent of certain aspects of Knapp's theory; even in writing an obituary for the latter, he did not spare strong criticism: Schumpeter, J. (1926) "G. F. Knapp", *The Economic Journal*, Vol. 36, 512–514. A potential contributing factor to the confusion surrounding his work may have been Knapp's own opening statement that "*money is a creature of law*". Knapp, G. F. (1924) *The State Theory of Money*, London: Macmillan & Co., 1.

742 Keynes, J. M. (1930) *A Treatise on Money*, New York City: Harcourt, Brace and Co., 3–4; Bell, S. (2001) "The role of the state and the hierarchy of money", *Cambridge Journal of Economics*, Vol. 25, 156; Wray, L. R. (2014) "From the State Theory of Money to Modern Money Theory: An Alternative to Economic Orthodoxy", *Levy Economics Institute Working Paper 792*, 14–15.

743 Minsky, H. P. (2008) *Stabilizing an unstable economy*, New York City: McGraw-Hill, 258.

similarities to Knapp's state theory, there is no clear evidence that Innes was indeed influenced by Knapp's thinking.[744] Further praise was voiced by Weber, even though he found the theory incomplete for substantive money problems.[745] Another economist strongly influenced by Chartalism was Schumpeter. Although he did recognize Knapp as the founder of the Chartalist theory, he was very critical of certain aspects of Knapp's theory, especially his terminology.[746] However, the state theory also had its opponents. Most notably, it was Ludwig von Mises who wrote a lengthy and critical analysis of the theory as an appendix to his *The Theory of Money and Credit*.[747] In more recent years, Knapp's work has found renewed recognition under Wray's Modern Money Theory.[748]

INFLUENCE ON LEGAL SCHOLARSHIP – The state theory also managed to gain traction in legal thinking, perhaps precisely due to its controversial statement that "*money is a creature of law*". It was primarily Frederick Alexander Mann who in his seminal work *The Legal Aspect of Money* fully accepted the state theory.[749] However, Mann's interpretation of the state theory seems to limit money strictly to what has been declared as legal tender by a state.[750] It is precisely that restriction which, as will be argued further on, has resulted in a reconsideration of Mann's theory in recent times.

## 3.3 ROLE OF THE STATE IN MONEY CREATION

METALLISM VS CHARTALISM – Although it is clear that some form of public authority did already play a role in earlier complex monetary systems, it is

---

744 Wray, L. R. (2014) "From the State Theory of Money to Modern Money Theory: An Alternative to Economic Orthodoxy", *Levy Economics Institute Working Paper 792*, 12.

745 Weber, M. (1978) *Economy and Society*, Berkeley: University of California Press, 78 & 184–189; Swedberg, R. (2000) *Max Weber and the Idea of Economic Sociology*, Princeton: University Press, 240.

746 Schumpeter, J. A. (1954) *History of Economic Analysis*, Abingdon: Routledge, 1090–1091; Zazzaro, A. (2003) "How Heterodox is the Heterodoxy of Monetary Circuit Theory? The Nature of Money and the Microeconomics of the Circuit", In: Rochon, L.-P., Rossi, S (Eds.) *The Nature and Role of Money in Capitalist Economies*, Cheltenham: Edward Elgar, 221; Swedberg, R. (2000) *Max Weber and the Idea of Economic Sociology*, Princeton: University Press. 240.

747 Von Mises, L. (1953) *The Theory of Money and Credit*, New Haven: Yale University Press, 463–469. It should be noted that von Mises did accept that monetary debts be paid off by money-substitutes and that the refusal of the law to recognize the validity of such money-substitutes would be undesirable. *Ibid.*, 69–70.

748 Wray, L. R. (2012) *Modern Money Theory: A Primer on Macroeconomics for Sovereign Monetary Systems*, New York City: Palgrave Macmillan, 294p; Wray, L. R. (2014) "From the State Theory of Money to Modern Money Theory: An Alternative to Economic Orthodoxy", *Levy Economics Institute Working Paper 792*, 35p.

749 Proctor, C. (2012) *Mann on the Legal Aspect of Money*, Oxford: University Press, 16. See also: Herrmann, C. (2010) *Währungshoheit, Währungsverfassung und subjektive Rechte*, Frankfurt: Mohr Siebeck, 64.

750 This is particularly evident in the older versions of his work. Mann, F. A. (1992) *The Legal Aspect of Money – Fifth Edition*, Oxford: Clarendon Press, 19–20.

only later that the role of the state became more apparent when the sovereign became the sole issuer of the standard medium of exchange, namely coins.[751] Interestingly, when discussing the precise role of the state in the origins of money, the dispute between the theories of Metallism and Chartalism becomes apparent again. Metallists argue that money as a medium of exchange commodity developed entirely within the context of free trade, whereas Chartalists place the development of money as a unit of account firmly in the hands of a public authority.[752] Going back to the two theories regarding the origins of money put forward in section 3.1, it can then be held that Metallists are more in support of the popular theory that money originated from trade practices in the form of coin.[753] As noted, that popular theory finds little support in historical evidence, which does not help to improve the perception of Metallist theories as "*weak on institutional detail and historical empiricism*" and focusing on models "*whatever the facts may be*".[754] While the Chartalist focus on the role of the state – and thus principally allowing that money preceded coinage – seems more closely founded on historical evidence, it should still be remarked that also Chartalists make the mistake of projecting modern constructs onto ancient societies.[755]

THE STATE IN ANCIENT SOCIETIES – As noted, the Chartalist theory that money did not develop solely out of market practices finds more evidence in history than the Metallist point of view. However, the Chartalist focus on the concept of a state as the driving factor behind the creation of money has also proven to be an overstatement. After all, if money is indeed credit created by private contractual agreements – as put forward by Innes – than the state can only impose the legal

---

751 Geva, B. (2011) *The Payment Order of Antiquity and the Middle Ages: A Legal History*, London: Hart Publishing, 21.

752 Semenova, A. (2011) *The Origins of Money: Evaluating Chartalist and Metallist theories in the context of ancient Greece and Mesopotamia*, University of Missouri – Kansas City PhD Thesis, 4.

753 Menger, who provided much of the groundwork for the Metallist theory, considers money to have evolved naturally from trade practices. Under this theory, state intervention – in recognizing and regulating the issuance of money – came only later when money was already established. While Menger therefore does not categorically rule out any government involvement in the monetary process, he sees such involvement as a tool to expand on what was created spontaneously within the private sector. Menger, K. (1892) "On the Origin of Money", *The Economic Journal*, Vol. 2, 255.

754 Goodhart, C. A. E. (1998) "The two concepts of money: implications for the analysis of optimal currency areas", *European Journal of Political Economy*, Vol. 14, 208–209. Also Innes remarked on the lack of historical proof of the Metallist theory. Innes, M. A. (1913) "What is Money?", *Banking Law Journal*, Vol. 30, 377–378.

755 Semenova refers here to the classic Chartalist position of seeing money as an element of taxation, which is a modern construct not present – at least not in the now known form – in ancient societies. Semenova, A. (2011) *The Origins of Money: Evaluating Chartalist and Metallist theories in the context of ancient Greece and Mesopotamia*, University of Missouri – Kansas City PhD Thesis, 17. Moreover, the practice of '*wergeld*' was not always standardized and often arranged *ad hoc*, thus contradicting the Chartalist idea that the creation of monetary practices always involves a governmental action. Sitta von Reden provides further account of how the application of current economic through to ancient societies leads to circular reasoning: Von Reden, S. (1995) *Exchange in Ancient Greece*, London: Duckworth, 1–4.

terms under which such obligations should be honored.[756] It can, for instance, be argued that coinage mainly originated during the early struggles between the emerging Greek city-states and the existing aristocracy.[757] More particularly, Kurke holds that ancient Greek aristocracy used the practice of giving gifts made of precious metals as a status symbol, and that that gift-giving practice had influence on the emergence of coins minted from precious metals.[758] In doing so, the state – *in casu* the early Greek '*polis*' – broke the monopoly aristocrats held on the float of precious metals and thus asserted itself as the ultimate authority.[759] Coins, therefore, were a merger between precious metals and the civic stamp of the '*polis*'.[760] However, the speed at which fully developed coinage spread throughout the Hellenic world can be argued to provide further evidence that money – as an abstract unit of account – was already well-developed and accepted throughout that realm.[761] In line with the explanation above, specific weights of silver were one example of money existing before – and eventually leading to the development of – coin money, and thus also preceding the origin of the '*polis*'.[762] While the rise of the city-states can therefore be linked to the development of coin money, it does not explain the origins of money as an abstract unit of account. Furthermore, when coin money was in circulation – such as in Ancient Rome – credit remained a widely accepted means of payment.[763] Even when coins subsequently went out of circulation – as in Anglo-

756 Graeber, D. (2011) *Debt: The First 5,000 Years*, Brooklyn: Melville House, 54.

757 Von Reden, S. (1995) *Exchange in Ancient Greece*, London: Duckworth, 175–181; Kurke, L. (1999) *Coins, Bodies, Games, and Gold: The Politics of Meaning in Archaic Greece*, Princeton: University Press, 21–23. While it is true that there were non-Greek coins – such as the earliest examples originating from Lydia – it is clear that the emergence of coin money started in the Hellenic sphere of influence.

758 Kurke, L. (1999) *Coins, Bodies, Games, and Gold: The Politics of Meaning in Archaic Greece*, Princeton: University Press, 12–13.

759 Semenova, A. (2011) *The Origins of Money: Evaluating Chartalist and Metallist theories in the context of ancient Greece and Mesopotamia*, University of Missouri – Kansas City PhD Thesis, 122.

760 Kurke, L. (1999) *Coins, Bodies, Games, and Gold: The Politics of Meaning in Archaic Greece*, Princeton: University Press, 300. However, at the same time the '*polis*' did not take this subversion of the aristocracy too far: while the main precious metal held by the aristocracy was gold, the coins minted in early Greek city-states were made of silver. Note that at the same time it must be reminded that coins and the '*polis*' were both the products of a long development. The city-state did not originate with coins, nor did coins originate with the city-state. Semenova, A., Wray, R. (2015) "The Rise of Money and Class Society: The Contributions of John F. Henry", *Levy Institute Working Paper 832*, 15.

761 Kim, H. (2001) "Archaic Coinage as Evidence for the Use of Money", In: Meadows, A., Shipton, K. (Eds.) *Money and Its Uses in the Ancient Greek World*, Oxford: Oxford University Press, 13; Kurke, L. (1999) *Coins, Bodies, Games, and Gold: The Politics of Meaning in Archaic Greece*, Princeton: University Press, 9–11.

762 Kim, H. (2001) "Archaic Coinage as Evidence for the Use of Money", In: Meadows, A., Shipton, K. (Eds.) *Money and Its Uses in the Ancient Greek World*, Oxford: Oxford University Press, 19.

763 Rüfner, T. (2016) "Money in the Roman Law Texts", In: Fox, D., Ernst, W. (Eds.) *Money in the Western Legal Tradition: Middle Ages to Bretton Woods*, Oxford: Oxford University Press, 94.

Saxon England after the fall of the Romans – the unit of account remained in use.[764]

STATE AND LEGAL TENDER – Despite the conflicts between the different theories regarding the origins of money and the precise role of the state therein, it is clear that the role of the state regarding money has only grown and continues to evolve. As shown, the system of what can be referred to as 'public money' is much younger than the notion of money itself, and legal tender laws are even younger still.[765] An example of the changing role of the state regarding money issuance and legal tender can be found in the US Constitution, which holds that gold and silver coins are designated as the money of the country and that Congress has the power to coin such money and regulate its value.[766] In the meantime, those constitutional commodity coins have been replaced by coins made out of baser metals, as well as by a completely different form of currency, the Federal Reserve notes.[767] While the legality of such bank notes has long been accepted[768], the authors of the Constitution found no firm consensus in this regard.[769]

ABSOLUTE STATE INTERVENTION? – The historic overview presented here can provide certain credence to the Chartalist theory that the involvement of a state has been important to the development of money. It is after all, as Knapp stated, the state's acceptance of a particular form of money that makes that form of money acceptable currency for the people's payment obligations to that state. It is therefore not an intrinsic quality of a particular form of money that renders that form public money or legal tender, but actions by the state. However, it may be questioned how absolute state intervention is in determining acceptable currency. When maintaining a more functionalist approach to the concept of money, it could, for instance, be wondered whether a currency could be established as money without the formal support of a state. Under Innes' credit theory, that question could be answered positively, since credit – and thus money – derives from private transactions. Private money – which today includes the more recent development of virtual currencies – predates public money, and could therefore be considered as the original money. Moreover, alternative currency – i.e. currency

---

764 Desan, C. (2010) "Coin Reconsidered: The Political Alchemy of Commodity Money", *Theoretical Inquiries in Law*, Vol. 11, 377.

765 Oliphant, H. (1920) "The Theory of Money in the Law of Commercial Instruments", *The Yale Law Journal*, Vol. 29, 616.

766 Article I sections 8 and 10 US Constitution.

767 Khan, A. (1999) "The evolution of money: a story of constitutional nullification", *University of Cincinnati Law Review*, Vol. 67, 394–395.

768 It is beyond the scope of this research to discuss in depth the formation process of the US's current monetary order, from the early struggles within the Continental Congress to the current state of affairs. For this, reference can be made to Khan (footnote 767), who provides a thorough account of this process.

769 Thayer, J. B. (1887) "Legal Tender", *Harvard Law Review*, Vol. 1, 79–80.

that is not formally issued or accepted by a state – has been around for many years. Examples include time-based currencies[770], community currencies[771], and corporate scrip.[772] However, such currencies generally operate only within a limited geographic region, or only serve very specific purposes. Thus far, alternative and private currencies have not managed to evolve into widely accepted media of exchange. Such could be said to complicate their qualification as money, even under the more lenient functional theories discussed in the following section. As a result, it can be held that widely accepted media of exchange generally enjoy at least some level of state support, even if they are not legal tender.[773]

## 3.4 FUNCTIONAL THEORIES

Societal theory – A different theory – the Societal theory – looks more to the functional aspects of money within society.[774] More concretely, the Societal theory accepts as money that which is used in commercial life or has the confidence of the people.[775] In other words, according to the Societal theory, it is not the sovereign state that decides what is to be considered as money, but the broader society itself. As this finding leads to the conclusion that money is

---

770 Under a time-based currency system, people invest their skills and experience for a certain amount of time, which earns credits that in turn can be spent on obtaining other people's services. Examples include the Time Dollar and Ithaca Hours. Cahn, E. S. (1999) "Time dollars, work and community: from 'why?' to 'why not?'", *Futures*, Vol. 31, 499–509; Jacob, J., Brinkerhoff, M., Jovic, E., Wheatley, G. (2004) "The Social and Cultural Capital of Community Currency: An Ithaca HOURS Case Study Survey", *International Journal of Community Currency Research*, Vol. 8, 42–56.

771 Examples include Local Exchange Trading Systems (LETS) and Berkshares. Pacione, M. (1997) "Local Exchange Trading Systems as a Response to the Globalisation of Capitalism", *Urban Studies*, Vol. 34, 1179–1199; Williams, C. C. (1996) "The New Barter Economy: An Appraisal of Local Exchange and Trading Systems (LETS)", *Journal of Public Policy*, Vol. 16, 85–101; Shubik, M. (2014) "Simecs, Ithaca Hours, Berkshares, Bitcoins and Walmarts", *Cowley Foundation Discussion Paper 1947*, 13p.

772 Often issued as part of a loyalty program, examples include Disney dollars and Canadian Tire Money. Andolfatto, D., Nosal, E. (2001) "A simple model of money and banking", *Economic Review – Federal Reserve Bank of Cleveland*, Vol. 37, 22; Birch, D. G. W., McEvoy, N. A. (1997) "Electronic cash-technology will denationalise money", In: Hirschfeld, R. (Ed.) *Financial Cryptography, LNCS 1318*, Berlin: Springer, 105.

773 For instance, though a payment using bank transfer is strictly speaking not a payment using legal tender, states have since long accepted this method as a valid means to settle, for instance, tax debts. As stated before, such cases are now by most – if not all – of the theories discussed earlier in this chapter accepted as constituting money.

774 The groundwork for this theory can be found at: Nussbaum, A. (1939) *Money in the Law*, Chicago: Foundation Press, 28. It should be noted that an earlier formulation can already be found at: Von Savigny, F. C. (1851) *Das Obligationenrecht als Theil des heutigen Römischen Rechts I*, Berlin: Veit & Co., 406–407.

775 Proctor, C. (2012) *Mann on the Legal Aspect of Money*, Oxford: University Press, 23–24. See also: Khan, A. (1999) "The evolution of money: a story of constitutional nullification", *University of Cincinnati Law Review*, Vol. 67, 396–397.

that which functions as such, the Societal theory has been regarded in literature as somewhat unsatisfying from a legal point of view, as it fails to provide the concrete elements needed to formulate a legal definition of the money concept.[776]

INSTITUTIONAL THEORY – An attempt to provide a more legalistic approach to the functional consideration of money can be found in the Institutional theory. According to the Institutional theory, money can be regarded as a transferable credit that is accepted as a store of value and as a means of payment, and that is subjected to an institutional legal framework that guarantees its purchasing power.[777] The main quality of the Institutional theory is that – in being a more recently formulated theory – it recognizes that the value of money is determined by the monetary policy of central banks and by market forces.[778] Moreover, the Institutional theory does not put the focus on physical coins and notes that have been appointed as legal tender, but recognizes that money can exist in a non-physical form.[779] Instead, the focus is put on central banks, whose policy determines the value and stability of the money they issue, and who influence the legal framework applicable to commercial banks.[780] In other words, while the state remains an important player, it is no longer the sole authority in determining what constitutes money.[781] However, given its focus on the institutional framework surrounding money, the Institutional theory has been regarded as less a theory on money itself, and more a theory on the order of the monetary system.[782]

IN PRACTICE – Today, it is clear that a theory that limits money strictly to what is regarded as legal tender – as under Mann's variation on the state theory – can no longer be upheld. In everyday practice, examples can be found of money or money-

---

776 In this regard, it has even been remarked that the lawyer *"is constrained to accept Knapp's State Theory of Money, whatever may be its merits from the point of view of economic analysis"*. Renner, K. (2001) *The Institutions of Private Law and their Social Functions,* Abingdon: Routledge, 180–181. Nevertheless, there is evidence of such broad view being supported in case law: Moss *v* Hancock, [1899] 2 Q.B. 111, at 116. At the same time, it may be questioned where the Societal theory truly applies. For instance, when Zimbabwe experienced hyperinflation, citizens started to use foreign currency – such as US dollars – instead of their local legal tender. While this could be interpreted as an application of Societal theory, it must also be said that the state of Zimbabwe condoned this practice and later even endorsed the replacement of its own currency by foreign currency. Proctor, C. (2012) *Mann on the Legal Aspect of Money,* Oxford: University Press, 24–25.

777 Sáinz de Vicuña, A. (2010) "An Institutional Theory of Money", In: Giovanoli, M., Devos, D. (Eds.) *International Monetary and Financial Law: The Global Crisis,* Oxford: University Press, 517.

778 Proctor, C. (2012) *Mann on the Legal Aspect of Money,* Oxford: University Press, 25–26.

779 In this regard, the euro is considered a prime example, as for a few years it did not exist in physical form, yet was already used between banks. Sáinz de Vicuña, A. (2010) "An Institutional Theory of Money", In: Giovanoli, M., Devos, D. (Eds.) *International Monetary and Financial Law: The Global Crisis,* Oxford: University Press, 520–522.

780 *Ibid.*, 523–524. Here, money is described as being *"primarily a credit against a central bank"*.

781 Proctor, C. (2012) *Mann on the Legal Aspect of Money,* Oxford: University Press, 28.

782 Herrmann, C. (2010) *Währungshoheit, Währungsverfassung und subjektive Rechte,* Frankfurt: Mohr Siebeck, 68.

like assets which are not considered legal tender, yet that are widely accepted in payment transactions. It can therefore be posited that a functional approach to the concept of money has closer relevance to what is experienced in practice. A clear example of this can be found in the case law of the Canadian Supreme Court. That Court held that "*money as commonly understood is not necessarily legal tender. Any medium which by practice fulfils the function of money and which everybody will accept in payment of a debt is money in the ordinary sense of the words even although it may not be legal tender*".[783] With regard to virtual currencies – and more in particular the cryptocurrency bitcoin – a Texas district court held that "*it is clear that Bitcoin can be used as money. It can be used to purchase goods or services, and* [...] *used to pay for individual living expenses. The only limitation of Bitcoin is that it is limited to those places that accept it as currency. However, it can also be exchanged for conventional currencies, such as the U.S. dollar, Euro, Yen, and Yuan. Therefore, Bitcoin is a currency or form of money, and investors wishing to invest* [...] *provided an investment of money.*"[784] Even within laws, evidence can be found in support of a more functional approach to the concept of money. The New Dutch Civil Code, for instance, allows that payment of a sum of money can be fulfilled by means of bank transfer, thus foregoing the exchange of physical legal tender.[785] Moreover, the article regulating cash payments in the New Dutch Civil Code[786] refers to 'common money' instead of 'legal tender'.[787] That reference was a deliberate choice made by the Dutch legislator, thereby explicitly deviating from the idea that only legal tender can be money.[788] In Belgium, merchants are obliged to hold a bank account.[789] Moreover, in business-to-business transactions, payments exceeding EUR 250 by means of cheques or money transfer cannot be refused.[790] Those example are clear deviations from the principle that only legal tender must be accepted.

## 3.5 AMENDED STATE THEORY

NEED FOR RECONSIDERATION – The practical value of a more functional approach to the concept of money has shown that it becomes difficult to uphold a

---

783 Reference Re Alberta Statutes [1938] SCR 100, 116. See also: Proctor, C. (2012) *Mann on the Legal Aspect of Money*, Oxford: University Press, 13.

784 Securities and Exchange Commission v. Trendon T. Shavers and Bitcoin Savings and Trust, 4:13-CV-416 (E.D. Tex. 2014), memorandum opinion 6 August 2013, 3. The Court reaffirmed this opinion in its order of 26 August 2014, holding that the relevant notion of 'investment' is not limited to cash (p.11).

785 Article 6:114 New Dutch Civil Code.

786 Article 6:112 New Dutch Civil Code.

787 More concretely: "*money which at the time of payment is common in the country where payment occurs*" (own translation/emphasis).

788 Kamerstukken II 1975–1976, 7729–6, 114.

789 Article 1 Royal Decree nr. 56 of 10 November 1967 promoting the use of scriptural money, *Belgian State Gazette* 14 November 1967.

790 Article 3 Royal Decree nr. 56 of 10 November 1967.

strict view in which only legal tender is accepted as money. However, it was also found that a strictly functional approach to defining the concept of money could prove undesirable. Even though legal tender laws may become less important in the practical use of money, it is clear that they still hold value and that money issuance remains an integral aspect of a state's sovereignty under international law.[791] It has therefore been proposed to not entirely discard Mann's authoritative interpretation of Knapp's state theory of money, but to slightly amend his theory to accommodate the current reality.[792]

Money as legal tender and abstraction – The amended state theory proposed by Proctor recognizes that states can issue money that is designated as legal tender, while at the same time recognizing that money is an abstract concept that is much broader than legal tender alone.[793] More precisely, the amended state theory holds that money must be (1) expressed in reference to the name and denomination of a unit of account that is recognized by a state as legal tender; (2) intended to serve as a generally accepted measure of value and medium of exchange within a state; and (3) must be part of a legal framework that includes institutional authorities – such as central banks – that can regulate monetary policy and oversight on payment systems.[794] In his restatement of this theory, Proctor does not specify the need for a link with the country of origin. A US dollar note – evidently legal tender within the US[795] – can thus be accepted as money in the EU, even if it does not serve as legal tender within that jurisdiction. He does, however, accept that the lack of a link with an issuing state could be problematic, for instance in the case of eurocurrencies.[796]

Extension and limitations – The amended state theory as proposed by Proctor indeed manages to broaden the notion of money compared to Mann's original theory. For instance, by allowing that money is expressed – in name and denomination – in reference to what has been recognized in a jurisdiction as legal tender, it becomes clear that money could go beyond what is strictly regarded as legal tender. An example given here are balances on bank accounts. In the strict sense, those balances represent regular debt obligations of a private institution, the bank, and not legal tender. However, given the rising use of electronic payments, it is clear that those balances can be readily used in payment transactions and therefore should be regarded as money. Any current theory should therefore recognize that money does not anymore exist solely

[791] Proctor, C. (2012) *Mann on the Legal Aspect of Money*, Oxford: University Press, 14 and 30–32.
[792] And, as noted, to possibly correct Mann's interpretation of Knapp's state theory as limiting money to solely legal tender.
[793] Proctor, C. (2012) *Mann on the Legal Aspect of Money*, Oxford: University Press, 41–42.
[794] *Id.*
[795] 31 U.S.C. §5103.
[796] Proctor, C. (2012) *Mann on the Legal Aspect of Money*, Oxford: University Press, 58–63.

in physical form, as the Institutional theory already did. Similarly, payment instruments derived from such balances – such as credit cards and cheques – can readily be accepted to fulfill an obligation for monetary payment, while not being legal tender themselves. At the same time, however, the reformulation of the state theory still maintains a rather limited view on what constitutes money. For instance, the requirement that money is expressed in reference to the name and denomination of a currency that is recognized by a state as legal tender, those payment methods that are expressed in their own denomination are excluded. As will be more elaborately discussed further on – in section 5 of this chapter – such a requirement excludes most, if not all, virtual currencies.

## 4 FUNCTIONS OF MONEY

From four to three core functions – Perhaps the earliest – or at least the most well-known – description of the economic functions of money can be found at Jevons.[797] In his enumeration, four functions were distinguished: medium of exchange, measure of value, standard of value, and store of value.[798] Though Jevons warned that – as a single form of currency could fulfill all four functions – there is a risk of confusing certain functions *"together in thought"*, it appears that precisely this has happened in more recent years.[799] This section will discuss the currently accepted three core functions of money.

### 4.1 MEDIUM OF EXCHANGE

Convenience over barter – As noted before, one of the main drawbacks of an economy based on bartering practices is the problem of coincidence of wants. Not only must a buyer find someone who sells what the buyer wants, this seller must also happen to want what the buyer can provide him. A medium of exchange can serve as an intermediary standard against which the goods or services to be exchanged can be valued. In doing so, a medium of exchange lowers the transaction cost, and thus promotes the economic efficiency of this exchange.[800]

797 Jevons, W. S. (1896) *Money and the mechanisms of exchange*, New York: D. Appleton and Co., 13–18.

798 *Id.*

799 *Ibid.*, 16. See, for instance, Mishkin, F. S. (2004) *The Economics of Money, Banking and Financial Markets – Seventh Edition*, Boston: Pearson, 45–48. Though it can also be turned the other way around: Davies distinguishes up to 10 functions – divided over general and specific, abstract and concrete. Davies, G. (2002) *A History of Money*, Cardiff: University of Wales Press, 27–28.

800 Mishkin, F. S. (2004) *The Economics of Money, Banking and Financial Markets – Seventh Edition*, Boston: Pearson, 45.

PAYMENT – In describing money as a medium of exchange, it is also acknowledged that money can serve as a means of payment. It is, after all, known that "*money buys goods and goods buy money; but goods do not buy goods*".[801] In viewing money as a means of payment, and as solution to the bartering problem, it follows that – in what has earlier been described as the popular theory on the origins of money – the medium of exchange function is considered as the core element of money under Metallist thinking.[802] According to that line of thinking, the reduction of transaction costs – as a medium of exchange can accomplish – is therefore a key aspect of money. Such an argument has mainly been followed within the Austrian school, for instance through von Mises's work.[803]

## 4.2 UNIT OF ACCOUNT

MEASURE OF VALUE – Second, money must serve as a means to measure value. The function of money as unit of account is therefore a logical consequence of economic transactions. After all, in order for parties to conclude a purchase of goods or services, it is more economically efficient if all wares are priced in the same nominal unit. Such pricing allows the parties to compare and interpret prices. While currencies in circulation can generally serve as a unit of account, circulation is not a prerequisite.[804]

HISTORICAL ORIGINS – While the 'Mengerian' ideal of a universal medium of exchange that developed from barter practices holds little ground in historical evidence, the unit of account function does have certain historical origins. As noted in the earlier overview on the origins of money, early units of money, even predating coinage, were derived from units of weight and used to facilitate accounting.[805] Under neo-Chartalist thinking, the potential reduction of transaction costs by a medium of exchange is therefore not the primary

801 Clower, R. W. (1986) *Money and Markets: Essays by Robert W. Clower edited by Donald A. Walker*, Cambridge: University Press, 86.

802 Peacock, M. (2013) *Introducing Money*, Abingdon: Routledge, 17 & 21. In the 'Mengerian' view, serving as medium of exchange is even sufficient to be considered as money.

803 Von Mises, L. (1953) *The Theory of Money and Credit*, New Haven: Yale University Press, 32–34. Rothbard later supported this position: Rothbard, M. N. (2010) *What Has Government Done to Our Money?*, Auburn: Ludwig von Mises Institute, 11. Also Hayek supported the position that other functions of money are derived from the primary function of medium of exchange. Hayek, F. A. (1990) *Denationalisation of Money: The Argument Refined*, Lancing: The Institute of Economic Affairs, 67. See also: Graham, F. D. (1940) "The Primary Functions of Money and their Consummation in Monetary Policy", *The American Economic Review*, Vol. 30, 1.

804 See for instance the European Currency Unit (ECU), which served as a unit of account without ever having coins or banknotes in circulation. Similarly, the euro already served as unit of account between its adoption in 1999 and the launch of coins and notes in 2002.

805 Tymoigne, E., Wray, L. R. (2005) "Money: An Alternative Story", *CFEPS Working Paper 45*, 8. As noted earlier, it were mostly government instances that imposed certain units of account.

consideration, but the establishment of a unit of account is.[806] That view was already apparent in Keynes' earlier work on money, in which he recognized that "*Chartalism begins when the State designates the objective standard which shall correspond to the money-of-account*".[807]

## 4.3 STORE OF VALUE

PURCHASING POWER – Last, money must also be able to hold certain purchasing power. Such purchasing power means that money must be able to hold its value between the moment of receipt and the moment of spending, it must store that value. The store of value function allows money to serve as an asset: it can be amassed to gather wealth.[808] While there are of course other things that can serve as such an asset – for instance jewelry or real estate – money has the highest degree of liquidity.[809] It is precisely that liquidity that makes money an attractive store of value. However, inflation can over time diminish the usefulness of money as a store of value, especially if hyperinflation occurs.[810]

IMPORTANCE IN KEYNESIAN ECONOMICS – Especially in Keynes' later thinking, the emphasis was put on the store of value function of money as its most importance aspect.[811] More particularly, Keynes accepted the practice of hoarding money as a precautionary measure against uncertainty.[812] However, that position was not always accepted, even by followers of Keynes' thought.[813]

---

806 Wray, L. R. (2000) "The Neo-Chartalist Approach to Money", *CFEPS Working Paper 10*, 5.

807 Keynes, J. M. (1930) *A Treatise on Money*, New York City: Harcourt, Brace and Co., 11. See also Ingham, G. (2000) "'Babylonian Madness': On the historical and sociological origins of money", In: Smithin, J. (Ed.) *What is Money?*, London: Routledge, 18.

808 It has, however, been remarked that money's use as store of value – i.e. its ability to retain its value over time – must be viewed separate from its potential use as store of wealth – i.e. its use as an investment asset expected to provide a return. Furthermore, money's use as store of wealth can be criticized, as it generally only yields little return. Sawyer, M. (2003) "Money: Means of Payment or Store of Wealth?", In: Rochon, L.-P., Rossi, S. (Eds.) *Modern Theories of Money: The Nature and Role of Money in Capitalist Economies*, Cheltenham: Edward Elgar, 4.

809 Mishkin, F. S. (2004) *The Economics of Money, Banking and Financial Markets – Seventh Edition*, Boston: Pearson, 47.

810 If, for instance, money is saved up, its amount will nominally remain the same. Inflation. However, will increase prices, thus diminishing the purchasing power of the money that is saved up.

811 Sardoni, C. (2015) "The functions of money and the demand for liquidity", *Università di Roma Sapienza Dipartimento di Scienze Sociali ed Economice Working Paper 3/2015*, 1.

812 Keynes, J. M. (1937) "The General Theory of Employment", *The Quarterly Journal of Economics*, Vol. 51, 210–211.

813 Hicks, for instance, considered the store of value function to be a potential aspect of money, yet not a fundamental one. Sardoni, C. (2015) "The functions of money and the demand for liquidity", *Università di Roma Sapienza Dipartimento di Scienze Sociali ed Economice Working Paper 3/2015*, 5–6.

# 5 VIRTUAL CURRENCIES AS MONEY

ASSESSMENT – Following the theoretical exposition on different theories on money and the functions that money can perform, this section must now assess whether the different types of virtual currencies identified in this research can be considered as money, or whether they can fulfill the functions expected from money.

## 5.1 VIRTUAL CURRENCIES AND THEORIES ON MONEY

LEGAL TENDER – First, reference must be made to the theory that limits the notion of money strictly to what has been statutorily mandated as legal tender. As noted, such a theory can mainly be found in the works of legal scholars such as Mann, and economists such as Schumpeter. Here, it is clear that virtual currencies cannot be considered as money, as at the present moment none of the types identified in chapter I have been proclaimed legal tender. Some consideration was given to the acceptance of virtual currency – or more narrow: e-money – as legal tender in Singapore in the early 2000's, though that plan never materialized.[814]

CREDIT THEORY – Under Innes' credit theory of money, virtual currencies could be accepted as money. Innes considers credit stemming from private transactions as money. As it can be argued that virtual currencies could indeed establish credit, they could be considered as money under this theory.[815]

STATE THEORY – The strict focus of Knapp's state theory on state involvement does not allow virtual currencies to be qualified as money. As noted, an important and sometimes overlooked element of the state theory is that Knapp did allow for other money to exist besides what has been designated as legal tender. Under the state theory, it is not the proclamation of a state that makes money or not, but its acceptance as payment for debts owed to the state. However, as none of the virtual currencies assessed in this research have thus far been accepted by a sovereign state as payment, it must be concluded that also under the state theory virtual currencies cannot be considered as money.

SOCIETAL THEORIES – A more beneficial view on virtual currencies can be found in the Societal theory, as under this theory it are not the actions of the sovereign state that dictate whether something can be considered as money but the actions of society as a whole. As noted in chapter I, the different types of virtual

814 Low, S. K. (2002) "Singapore Electronic Legal Tender (SELT) – A Proposed Concept", In: OECD (Ed.) *The Future of Money*, Paris: OECD, 147–155; Van Hove (2005) "Making electronic money legal tender: pros & cons", *Free University of Brussels Working Paper*, 45p.

815 Bjerg, O. (2016) "How is Bitcoin Money?", *Theory, Culture & Society*, Vol. 33, 67.

currencies identified for the purposes of this research have shown to be accepted as means of payment, at the least within their particular scope of application and often even exceeding that scope. However, also here restraint must be shown. Even though, for instance, some loyalty programs have exceeded their original scope, they can hardly be regarded as generally accepted means of payment. Similarly, even though the growth of acceptance of cryptocurrencies so early in their lifespan is remarkable, it is clear that their use is still a fringe phenomenon at best.[816] On the other end of the spectrum, there are also virtual currencies that expressly are not intended to become societally accepted money.[817] Although it could therefore be said to be premature to proclaim virtual currencies, or some of them, as money under the Societal theory, reference has already been made to case-law where they were accepted as such.[818] As the Societal theory does not provide strong regulatory reference points on which the classification of something as money hinges, it will therefore be further practice that must point out whether virtual currencies can become money under this theory or not.

Institutional theory – Though in the earlier analysis discussed under the functional theories, the Institutional theory demonstrates again a more limited viewpoint on money by putting its focus on the involvement of institutional actors in monetary policy. As discussed in chapter I, the EU's main monetary institution – the European Central Bank – does not consider virtual currencies to be money, nor is it involved with the regulation of their emission. Such would therefore disqualify virtual currencies as money under the Institutional theory.

Amended state theory – Proctor's restatement of Mann's interpretation of the state theory is significantly broader than what Mann envisioned. It also allows for the existence of money that is not legal tender, even of money that does not exist in physical form. However, the core elements to the amended state theory may not be beneficial to virtual currencies. First, the theory requires that money is denominated in a unit of account referencing legal tender. As virtual currencies – as defined for the purposes of this research – have their own unique unit of account – such as bitcoin or Gold in a MMORPG – they cannot be considered as money under the amended state theory. Even if a virtual currency were to be denominated in reference to legal tender, another element may come in the way: Proctor's theory requires that money is intended to serve as a generally accepted measure of value and medium of exchange. As noted under the assessment for

816 For instance, Bitcoin can only process an average of three transactions per second – mainly due to its block size limitation – which is only a fraction of what traditional credit card companies process. This could pose an impediment in Bitcoin's usefulness as societally accepted money.

817 As is the case for most virtual currency schemes with no flow of legal tender into virtual currency and *vice versa*, such as many in-game currencies.

818 See section 3.4.

the Societal theory, such is not the case for all virtual currencies. Last, money must be covered by a legal and institutional framework, governing its issuance and providing oversight. Also this latter element is not fulfilled for several virtual currencies, such as cryptocurrencies. While some of the virtual currencies analyzed in chapter I may comply with one or more of these core requirements, there is at the present moment none that complies with all. Therefore, under the amended state theory, virtual currencies cannot be considered as money.

Money without state? – However, apart from looking at the basic tenets of these theories, a more fundamental issue must be considered. It is clear by now that most of the theories analyzed here assume at least some level of state intervention in designating what constitutes money. While money is, as noted before, much broader than the limited notion of legal tender, the means of payment that are generally considered to be money do still depend on or derive from legal tender. Here, we can again refer to the example of bank account balances. These balances are not legal tender themselves, but are considered as money precisely due to their close relation to legal tender. After all, an important element contributing to the broad acceptance of money on account is the guarantee that banks will exchange those balances into the same amount of legal tender. And states regulate banks in order to safeguard their solvability, and thus their ability to convert money on account into legal tender. Money, therefore, still remains firmly rooted in the belief that the emitting state authority – either itself or by regulating other entities – will respond to the obligations it created by that emission. While Innes' credit theory does allow private currencies to be considered as money in the broadest sense, this does not automatically result in a broad acceptance of such private currencies as money. Indeed, we already noted in section 3.3 that the acceptance of private currencies as money remains very limited. This raises the more conceptual question of whether virtual currencies can ever serve as money without any form of state intervention. The matter can be exemplified by the acceptance of cryptocurrencies such as bitcoin. While a private actor can decide to accept payments in bitcoin, there is no legal framework imploring that party to do so, nor is there any guarantee that this party will be able to spend the received bitcoin payments elsewhere. Can a currency then ever truly be considered as money, if its acceptance is subject solely to the will of those to whom payment in that currency is offered? While answering that question would go beyond the scope of our research, it does remain a matter to be considered when assessing the '*moneyness*' of virtual currencies.

Conclusion – From the assessment of the previous paragraphs, it becomes clear that most of the prevailing theories on money do currently not support the qualification of virtual currencies as money. Such a qualification could only be possible under the credit theory of money. While the Societal theory seems more welcoming to virtual currencies than other theories, it must be noted that also under the Societal theory it is unlikely that virtual currencies can be regarded as money, as they are not sufficiently broadly accepted as means of payment, or are not even intended to become so. However, it also becomes clear from the previous assessment that views on money can evolve over time. After all, some of the theories presented here already have to be interpreted in light of the era in which they were posited, and appear somewhat outdated in light of our current society. It is therefore not unthinkable – and perhaps even desirable – that virtual currencies would at some point be accepted as money under a broadened theory or a new theory on money. Moreover, renewed interest in Innes' work in recent years could result in a broader acceptance of the credit theory. However, aside from the purely theoretical theories on money, it must also be considered whether virtual currencies can conceptually serve as money without any form of state intervention.

## 5.2 VIRTUAL CURRENCIES AND FUNCTIONS OF MONEY

Medium of exchange – At the present moment, there appears to be at least some consensus that virtual currencies can function as a convincing medium of exchange.[819] However, there are also still cases where such is downright rejected.[820] The Dutch National Bank, for instance, argues that the limited range of acceptance of virtual currencies and the often lesser degree of user-friendliness limits their use as a medium of exchange.[821] Going back to the findings under the theories on money, it can be held that some virtual currencies at least do have the propensity to become generally accepted media of exchange – such as cryptocurrencies – whereas others do not – such as most loyalty programs and in-game currencies.

Unit of account – It is still somewhat disputed whether virtual currencies fulfill the unit of account function of money well. In some cases, the fulfillment of the unit of account functionality is accepted.[822] In other cases, it is rejected.[823] Here, it can be held that a unit of account "*must provide a measure of relative*

819 FATF (2014) "Virtual Currencies: Key Definitions and Potential AML/CFT Risks", *fatf-gafi.org*, 4; FinCEN (2013) "Application of FinCEN's Regulations to Persons Administering, Exchanging, or Using Virtual Currencies", *FIN-2013-G001*, 1; Toms, S., Zdrowski, M., Hall, R. (2015) "Virtual currencies: Mining the possibilities", *allenovery.com*, 3; Bal, A. (2014) "Taxation of virtual currency", *PhD Thesis Leiden University*, 61.

820 See, for instance: Krugman, P. (2013) "Bitcoin Is Evil", *New York Times*, 28 December 2013.

821 DNB (2014) "Virtual currencies are not a viable alternative", *dnb.nl*. This point is shared by: Heller, D. (2017) "Do Digital Currencies Pose a Threat to Sovereign Currencies and Central Banks?", *PIIE Policy Brief 17–13*, 8.

822 FATF (2014) "Virtual Currencies: Key Definitions and Potential AML/CFT Risks", *fatf-gafi.org*, 4; Toms, S., Zdrowski, M., Hall, R. (2015) "Virtual currencies: Mining the possibilities", *allenovery.com*, 3; Münzer, J. (2013) "Bitcoins: Aufsichtliche Bewertung und Risiken für Nutzer", *www.bafin.de*; Deutscher Bundestag, Schriftliche Fragen, *17/14530*, 41.

823 DNB (2014) "Virtual currencies are not a viable alternative", *dnb.nl*.

*worth that users can understand on a nearly intuitive level*".[824] This means that users must be able to understand the underlying value from the unit of account itself. Particularly for cryptocurrencies it could then be argued that their volatility makes that their value is still mostly assessed in comparison to a more broadly accepted unit of account. However, also legal tender is never perfectly stable, as it is subject to inflation and deflation. While the volatility of cryptocurrencies could therefore indeed make that they are not a very stable unit of account – or at least: not yet – this alone is not sufficient to completely disregard the unit of account functionality of this type of virtual currencies. Moreover, it can be argued that bitcoin is becoming the standard unit of account for cryptocurrencies, as the values of other cryptocurrencies are often measured in bitcoin. Closed scheme virtual currencies, on the other hand, can be said to fulfill this function well, as they serve as the main unit of account within their own virtual realm.[825]

Store of value – Less contentious but not necessarily more positive for virtual currencies is their use as a store of value. Here, it has been argued that virtual currencies do not satisfy the store of value function of money. Cryptocurrencies, for instance, have been known to demonstrate substantial value fluctuations, which may impede their use as a store of value.[826] On the other hand, it can also be said that history has already shown many examples where state-issued currencies experienced similar fluctuations and instabilities, often as a result of hyperinflation.[827] More problematic, however, are cases where virtual currencies experience planned devaluations, or have expiration dates imposed on their value.[828] In such cases, there is a clear and inherent limitation on the use of such a virtual currency as a store of value.

Conclusion – Overall, it must be concluded that, as of yet, virtual currencies do not appear to satisfactorily fulfill all of the functions expected of money. Even though the medium of exchange functionality could be accepted, it is clear that

---

824 Bal, A. (2014) "Taxation of virtual currency", *PhD Thesis Leiden University*, 61; Heller, D. (2017) "Do Digital Currencies Pose a Threat to Sovereign Currencies and Central Banks?", *PIIE Policy Brief 17-13*, 9.

825 There are virtual worlds that only use a single unit of account, but there are also more complex worlds with different unit of accounts. In any case, also in those more complex scenarios the virtual world will be organized in such a way that each virtual currency functions well as a unit of account.

826 Krugman, P. (2013) "Bitcoin Is Evil", *New York Times*, 28 December 2013; Heller, D. (2017) "Do Digital Currencies Pose a Threat to Sovereign Currencies and Central Banks?", *PIIE Policy Brief 17-13*, 9.

827 Take, for instance, the examples of Germany post-WW I, Hungary post-WW II, and Yugoslavia in the early 1990's.

828 Loyalty programs have been known to undergo devaluations in order to encourage consumption, whereas prepaid currencies often have a limited period of validity. Moreover, several virtual worlds have been shut down by their developers, thus evaporating all value of the currency used therein.

there are virtual currencies that are not intended to become a generally accepted medium of exchange. While virtual currencies as defined for the purposes of this research do serve as their own unit of account, it could still be argued that in some cases – such as cryptocurrencies – this functionality is not fulfilled very well yet. Last, objections can be formulated to the fulfillment of the store of value functionality by virtual currencies. However, also here it must be cautioned that evolution is possible. If a virtual currency were to gain broader acceptance, it is possible that it would end up properly fulfilling the functions of money. While such is not yet the case today, it is certainly not categorically ruled out for the future.

# 6 INTERIM CONCLUSIONS

No clear demarcation – The purpose of this chapter was to present from a legal and economic point of view the main theories on what constitutes money and which functions money fulfills, and to assess whether virtual currencies can correspond thereto. After all, it is clear that money – despite, as this chapter has shown, being a difficult concept to define – is a notion of legal relevance. Many branches of law at a certain point refer to money. When discussing the potential regulation of virtual currencies, the assessment of their qualification as money is therefore the logical and necessary starting point. However, as shown, the establishment of a clear definition of the concept of money has plagued many academics, and even now there remain deep and stark divides between scholarly thought on the subject of money. Following the discussion of the most prominent theories on the concept and functions of money, the answer to the question of whether virtual currencies constitute money or whether they can fulfill the functions of money really depends on the respondent to that question. Perhaps Hayek was right in saying that there is no sharp demarcation line between what constitutes money and what does not, even if the law tries to establish such a line.[829] As a result, this chapter does not purport to have provided the final answer to the matter, but merely serves as an attempt to present and view a number of leading theories in light of the developments regarding virtual currencies.

Money or payment? – Another scholar who understood that the question of what constitutes money would never be fully settled is F. A. Mann. In the opening chapter of his seminal work he expresses clear reluctance in tackling the question of money, yet recognizes that a work entirely devoted to money could hardly afford not to do so.[830] And it is in Mann's attempt to define money that he recognized that the more interesting concept to define is that of payment, and

[829] Hayek, F. A. (1990) *Denationalisation of Money: The Argument Refined*, Lancing: The Institute of Economic Affairs, 56.

[830] Proctor, C. (2012) *Mann on the legal aspect of money*, Oxford: University Press, 5–9.

that therefore the real question at hand asks for what is accepted as payment.[831] Mann's finding also becomes apparent in law, where payments are regulated, yet – apart from the obvious legal tender laws – clear and precise definitions of money are few and far between.[832] And as shown in chapter I, virtual currencies have already proven their capacity for success, with several cases greatly exceeding their original purpose. Even though the question regarding the *'moneyness'* of virtual currencies may remain unsettled, their usability as means of payment is without question.

Assessment – In general, it is clear that virtual currencies at this moment do not correspond to what can be regarded as public money, as found in theories that limit money strictly to legal tender. Also the acceptance of virtual currencies as money under Knapp's original theory is out of the question, given that thus far no government has accepted them as payment. More welcoming to virtual currencies is Innes' credit theory of money. Under a more functional approach, at least some types of virtual currencies could be argued to be money or to have the propensity to become so, if their acceptance were to become broad enough. Finally, under Proctor's restatement of Mann's theory, virtual currencies do not constitute money, as they are not denominated in reference to a unit of account established by a state or lack the required institutional framework. With regard to the functions of money it can be held that there are several elements that limit the ability of virtual currencies to fully fulfill those functions at least at the present moment.

Other legal frameworks – Even though the question of whether virtual currencies can be considered as money, or whether they can fulfill the functions expected from money, must in light of these findings be tentatively answered in the negative sense – with a possible reservation for the credit theory of money – such an answer does not deliver the final judgment on the matter. First, it must be noted that this chapter has made clear that there are several highly different theories on money, and that those theories remain in flux to this day. It can therefore not be ruled out that one day opinions may shift in favor of considering virtual currencies as money. However, that still leaves the conceptual question of whether virtual currencies can serve as money without any form of state intervention. Second, while the current conclusion precludes the qualification

831 *Ibid.*, 9. See also how Inness defined money as a balance sheet operation between credit and debt: Innes, M. A. (1913) "What is Money?", *Banking Law Journal*, Vol. 30, 392.

832 In this sense, it has even been remarked that legal scholars tend to focus solely on payment when discussing money, whereas economists see a broader issue. Von Mises, L. (1953) *The Theory of Money and Credit*, New Haven: Yale University Press, 36–37; Vardi, N. (2011) *The Integration of European Financial Markets: The regulation of monetary obligations*, Abingdon: Routledge, 2; Mishkin, F. S. (2004) *The Economics of Money, Banking and Financial Markets – Seventh Edition*, Boston: Pearson, 44–45.

of virtual currencies as money, it cannot be denied that there are significant similarities between money and virtual currencies – both in terms of benefits and in terms of risks – to the extent that arguments can be made for virtual currencies to be subjected to similar rules. Therefore, if virtual currencies are to be regulated from the point of view of financial and economic law, the focus must be turned to the few distinct legal frameworks in place under which virtual currencies could maybe reside, or be made to reside through legislative action. In the following chapters, it will be analyzed whether virtual currencies can fit under the scope of each of such legal frameworks, or whether – if needed – there is room for amendment of those frameworks. Important to note at this stage of the research is that the financial law legal frameworks selected here generally work from their own set of definitions, and that the qualification of virtual currencies as money or not must therefore be viewed separately from their potential inclusion under those frameworks.

# PART II

# LEGAL ANALYSIS

# CHAPTER IV

# E-MONEY AND PAYMENT SERVICES IN THE EU

## 1 INTRODUCTION

### 1.1 VIRTUAL CURRENCIES, E-MONEY, AND PAYMENT SERVICES

NON-PHYSICAL CURRENCY – As already remarked in the first chapter of this research, virtual currencies and e-money – as regulated in the EU – show a distinct similarity in that they have no physical counterpart. Consequently, it is logical to question whether virtual currencies could be considered to fall under the scope of the current legal framework on e-money in the EU. When such proves not to be the case, it could additionally be questioned whether the e-money legal framework should be amended to apply to virtual currencies. Moreover, given that the services developed around virtual currencies generally support the use of virtual currencies as means of payment, it must also be questioned whether such services constitute payment services as regulated in the EU.

DEMARCATION BETWEEN E-MONEY AND VIRTUAL CURRENCIES – To that end, this chapter will analyze the regulatory process underlying the legal frameworks regarding e-money and payment services in order to gain a better understanding of the *ratio* behind the process that resulted in the regulation of the notions of e-money and payment services within the EU. Moreover, this chapter will analyze the definitions underlying the demarcation between e-money and virtual currencies. The goal of that analysis is to ascertain whether the demarcation of e-money is sound and whether it can be upheld in light of recent developments concerning virtual currencies.

PAYMENT SERVICES – Given the close relation between the legal frameworks on e-money and payment services, and in view of a potential future merger of those frameworks[833], this chapter analyzes both legal frameworks. The findings of this chapter will serve the functional comparison conducted in chapter VII.

[833] See section 4.

As noted, only the EU seems to have chosen to specifically regulate the notion of e-money. Therefore, the analysis of how other countries such as the US regulate the same services and developments without needing to refer to such a notion may provide valuable insight in the value of regulating that particular notion.[834]

Chapter approach and goals – Before going into the main analysis of this chapter, this section will provide a brief overview of the regulatory setting of e-money and payment services in the EU (section 1.2), in order to facilitate a better understanding of the background against which those legal frameworks operate.

The first major part of the analysis conducted here concerns e-money (section 2). Here, this section will present the regulatory process behind the First E-money Directive (EMD1) and the review process leading up to the Second E-money Directive (EMD2). The goal of this analysis is to gain a complete understanding of the involved stakeholders' thought process behind their eventual formulation of the e-money concept, as well as of the evolution of that concept throughout the legislative procedures. Such will allow to establish the precise scope of the e-money concept, which will be further analyzed in section 2.2. Having gained a full understanding of the e-money concept and the regulatory goals behind it, the next section will then assess whether that concept as it currently stands can apply to the different types of virtual currencies identified in chapter I (section 2.3).

This analysis is repeated for the legal framework on payment services (section 3). First, this section will explore the regulatory background regarding the concept of payment services in order to understand how the payment services concept came into being (section 3.1). Then, applying that knowledge, the following section further defines the concept of payment services and its scope (section 3.2). Last, this section applies that concept to the types of virtual currencies identified in chapter I (section 3.3).

In keeping with the normative question of whether the legal frameworks on e-money and payment services could or should be amended to facilitate virtual currencies, the next section first explores what the regulatory future of those frameworks is, given their close relationship and their potential merger (section 4).

The last (section 5) will bring together all findings of this chapter to provide an answer as to whether the current legal frameworks on e-money and payment services can apply to the different types of virtual currencies established here (section 5.1). Where such is not the case, the assessment of the regulatory future of these legal frameworks will allow to analyze whether those frameworks hold potential for the inclusion of these virtual currencies. In closing (section 5.2), an – at this stage preliminary – assessment against the normative criteria

[834] For instance, Google Wallet and PayPal are two examples of services that operate both in the EU and in the US. While in the EU these services are considered to be e-money services, they are of course also subject to regulation in the US, be it without the application of the notion of e-money. Chapter VII will analyze how these services are regulated in the US.

established for the purposes of this research will determine whether there is, according to the findings of this chapter, a need to regulate virtual currencies under the legal frameworks of e-money and payment services.

## 1.2 E-MONEY AND PAYMENT SERVICES IN THE EU

Regulatory background – In order to place the notions of e-money and payment services within the EU's wide body of regulation, reference can be made to the efforts of the last decades to further develop the European single market for payments and payment services. Already in 1997, a directive was adopted to facilitate cross-border credit transfers within the internal market.[835] The introduction of the euro in 1999[836] greatly simplified cash payments across the euro area – as foreign currency exchange would now no longer be needed – but did little to facilitate electronic payments. Therefore, in 2002, "*42 banks, the three European Credit Sector Associations ('ECSA's) and the Euro Banking Association ('EBA') came together*" to create the European Payments Council (EPC) and agreed to work toward the establishment of a Single Payments Area.[837] That initiative, later known as the Single Euro Payments Area (SEPA), was supported by the main EU institutions and the European Central Bank. SEPA serves as the umbrella under which legislative initiatives are adopted aimed at further integrating the market for pan-European cross-border payments, in order to make cross-border payment transactions as easy as payment transactions within a single Member State.[838] One of the results of SEPA is that the existing framework on cross-border payments in euro[839] was replaced by a new regulation[840] in order to eliminate the charges for cross-border and national payments in euro. In turn, the SEPA framework was further amended and expanded in 2012 by the SEPA Regulation[841], and again in 2014.[842]

---

835 Directive 97/5/EC of the European Parliament and of the Council of 27 January 1997 on cross-border credit transfers, *OJ* L 043 of 14 February 1997, 25–30. Mavromati, D. (2008) *The law of payment services in the EU*, Alphen aan de Rijn: Kluwer Law International, 66–67.

836 Though banknotes and coins only came into circulation in 2002.

837 EPC (2006) "'Making SEPA a Reality' – Implementing the Single Euro Payments Area", *www.europeanpaymentscouncil.eu*, EPC066-06, 8.

838 Commission Consultative paper on SEPA Incentives, *ec.europa.eu*, 13 February 2006.

839 Regulation (EC) No 2560/2001 of the European Parliament and of the Council of 19 December 2001 on cross-border payments in euro, *OJ* L 344 of 28 December 2001, 13–16.

840 Regulation (EC) No 924/2009 of the European Parliament and of the Council of 16 September 2009 on cross-border payments in the Community and repealing Regulation (EC) No 2560/2001, *OJ* L 266 of 9 October 2009, 11–18.

841 Regulation (EU) No 260/2012 of the European Parliament and of the Council of 14 March 2012 establishing technical and business requirements for credit transfers and direct debits in euro and amending Regulation (EC) No 924/2009, *OJ* L 94 of 30 March 2012, 22–37 (hereinafter: SEPA Regulation).

842 Regulation (EU) No 248/2014 of the European Parliament and of the Council of 26 February 2014 amending Regulation (EU) No 260/2012 as regards the migration to Union-wide credit transfers and direct debits, *OJ* L 84 of 20 March 2014, 1–3.

Payment services – Another important result of the SEPA initiatives is the European legal framework on payment services. Already in 2003, the European Commission called for a new legal framework in the payments market, specifically targeted at so-called payment service providers.[843] That initiative resulted in a directive to provide a clear legal framework for payment services.[844] For customers, it means that – amongst others – their debit cards will be accepted throughout the whole euro area and that cross-border bank transfers are now executed within one business day. The initiative replaced the existing legal framework on cross-border credit transfers.[845] According to its article 87, the First Payment Services Directive (PSD1) was up for review late 2012, with a proposal for a new directive launched by the European Commission in 2013[846], together with a proposal for a regulation aimed at tackling interchange fees in payment card schemes.[847] Those new legal frameworks were adopted in 2015.[848]

Origins of e-money – While legislative action to regulate a specific type of non-physical means of payment – such as e-money – may seem like a logical next step against this SEPA background, it should be noted that the regulatory interest in e-money, however, significantly predates the more recent developments of SEPA and the rise and growth of electronic and mobile payments or services involving virtual currencies. A first proposal for a clear regulatory framework regarding e-money was published in 1998.[849] Lengthy consultations between the stakeholders involved

---

843 European Commission (2003) "Communication to the Council and the European Parliament concerning a New Legal Framework for Payments in the Internal Market (Consultative Document)", *ec.europa.eu*, COM/2003/0718 final.

844 Directive 2007/64/EC of the European Parliament and of the Council of 13 November 2007 on payment services in the internal market amending Directives 97/7/EC, 2002/65/EC, 2005/60/EC and 2006/48/EC and repealing Directive 97/5/EC, *OJ* L 319 of 5 December 2007, 1–36 (hereinafter: First Payment Services Directive or PSD1).

845 See footnote 835.

846 European Commission (2013) "Proposal for a directive of the European Parliament and of the Council on payment services in the internal market and amending Directives 2002/65/EC, 2013/36/EU and 2009/110/EC and repealing Directive 2007/64/EC", *ec.europa.eu*, COM(2013) 0547.

847 European Commission (2013) "Proposal for a regulation of the European Parliament and of the Council on interchange fees for card-based payment transactions", *ec.europa.eu*, COM(2013) 0550.

848 Regulation (EU) 2015/751 of the European Parliament and of the Council of 29 April 2015 on interchange fees for card-based payment transactions, *OJ* L 123 of 19 May 2015, 1–15; Directive (EU) 2015/2366 of the European Parliament and of the Council of 25 November 2015 on payment services in the internal market, amending Directives 2002/65/EC, 2009/110/EC and 2013/36/EU and Regulation (EU) No 1093/2010, and repealing Directive 2007/64/EC, *OJ* L 337 of 23 December 2015, 35–127 (hereinafter: Second Payment Services Directive or PSD2).

849 *Europa.eu/rapid/press-release_IP-98-727_en.htm*. European Commission (1998) "Proposal for a European Parliament and Council Directive on the taking up, the pursuit and the prudential supervision of the business of electronic money institutions (COM(1998) 0461)", *OJ* C 317 of 15 October 1998, 7–11.

in the legislative process resulted in the first directive in this field in 2000.[850] That directive was a compromise between the more liberal approach proposed by those pursuing market protection and the more strict approach proposed by those pursuing market development.[851] Its scope focused mainly on regulating multi-purpose prepaid cards, for which already in 1994 a report was made to the Council of the European Monetary Institute.[852] It will be shown further on in this chapter that the compromise text, however, was marred with a number of significant shortcomings, which resulted in the directive actually becoming one of the impediments to technological progress in the e-money field and thus not achieving the goal of supporting the growth of e-money.[853] Moreover, the European legislator proved to be more optimistic about the evolution of the market for e-money than turned out to be the case, which is why during the review of the directive steps were proposed to adopt amendments to the e-money legal framework.[854] To remedy those shortcomings, the European Commission proposed[855] a new directive during its review of the EMD1, which was adopted in 2009.[856]

# 2 E-MONEY

## 2.1 REGULATORY BACKGROUND

Compromise – As already hinted at, the legislative procedure leading up to the adoption of the EMD1 in 2000 was the result of discussions between the European Commission and the European Central Bank – and its predecessor the

---

850 Directive 2000/46/EC of the European Parliament and of the Council of 18 September 2000 on the taking up, pursuit of and prudential supervision of the business of electronic money institutions, *OJ* L 275 of 27 December 2000, 39–43 (hereinafter: First E-money Directive or EMD1).

851 The European Commission, for instance, wanted to avoid that the legal framework would end up hampering technological innovation. European Commission (1998) "Proposal for a European Parliament and Council Directive on the taking up, the pursuit and the prudential supervision of the business of electronic money institutions (COM(1998) 0461)", *OJ* C 317, 7. The ECB, however, focused on the potential dangers of e-money and called for broad protection for customers and merchants, and for protection against criminal abuse and market failure. European Central Bank (1998) "Report on Electronic Money", *ecb.europa.eu*, 13–17.

852 European Central Bank (1998) "Report on Electronic Money", *ecb.europa.eu*, 5.

853 DLA Piper (2009) "EU study on the Legal analysis of a Single Market for the Information Society – New rules for a new age?", *ec.europa.eu*, 7–8.

854 European Commission (2006) "Staff Working Document on the Review of the E-Money Directive (2000/46/EC)", *ec.europa.eu*, SEC(2006) 1049.

855 European Commission (2008) "proposal for a Directive of the European Parliament and of the Council of on the taking up, pursuit and prudential supervision of the business of electronic money institutions, amending Directives 2005/60/EC and 2006/48/EC and repealing Directive 2000/46/EC ", *ec.europa.eu*, COM/2008/0627.

856 Directive 2009/110/EC of the European Parliament and of the Council of 16 September 2009 on the taking up, pursuit and prudential supervision of the business of electronic money institutions amending Directives 2005/60/EC and 2006/48/EC and repealing Directive 2000/46/EC, *OJ* L 267 of 10 October 2009, 7–17 (hereinafter: Second E-money Directive or EMD2).

European Monetary Institute (EMI) – which mainly concerned a disagreement regarding the scope of access of market players to e-money services. This section will trace the development of e-money regulation within the EU, from the first discussions regarding the e-money notion in the early 1990's leading up to the adoption of the EMD1, through the review of that directive and up to the adoption of the EMD2. The goal of this overview is to uncover the precise *ratio legis* behind the decision to regulate the e-money concept, and whether it can be held that those underlying goals are achieved.

### *2.1.1 E-money before 2000*

ORIGINS – This section traces the origins of the notion of e-money within the EU's regulatory framework. It begins with an initial report of the European Monetary Institute's Working Group on EU Payment Systems of 1994 and ends with the legislative procedure resulting in the EMD1 in 2000.

#### 2.1.1.1 Working Group on EU Payment Systems 1994

ELECTRONIC PURSE – In May 1994, the Working Group on EU Payment Systems presented its report on prepaid cards to the Council of the European Monetary Institute.[857] In the early 1990's, the use of debit cards was rising steadily, with merchants starting to implement surcharges to cover the cost of accepting that new means of payment.[858] At the same time, the electronic purse – or e-purse – was developed, which represents monetary value in a digital format embedded in an information carrier.[859] Such an information carrier was at that point mainly presented in the format of a chip card. While the development of e-purses was mainly facilitated by the evolution of the information society and presented a very new method of conducting payment transactions, central banks reacted swiftly to assert that such developments did not change the underlying value and importance of money and should therefore be subjected to the same regulatory supervision as the activities of credit institutions.[860] In order to support the development of a legal framework that could subject e-purse service providers to such supervision, the central bank of the Netherlands took the initiative to start a task force on prepaid cards, together with representatives of other European

857 Working Group on EU Payment Systems (1994) "Report to the Council of The European Monetary Institute on Prepaid Cards", *ecb.europa.eu*.

858 Duisenberg, W.F. (1995) "Toespraak ter gelegenheid van de introductie van de chipknip in Arnhem", 26 October 1995, *www.simonl.org/docs/readeremdnb.pdf*, 4. The main issue here was that the supervision of payment products as such had not been explicitly defined. Lelieveldt, S. (1997) "How to regulate electronic cash: an overview of regulatory issues and strategies", *The American University Law Review*, vol. 46, 1173–1174.

859 Duisenberg, W.F. (1995) "Toespraak ter gelegenheid van de introductie van de chipknip in Arnhem", 26 October 1995, *www.simonl.org/docs/readeremdnb.pdf*, 5.

860 *Id.*

national banks.[861] The discussions held in that task force resulted in the EMI's Working Group on EU Payment Systems 1994 report.

Prepaid – The report focuses mainly on the developments regarding multi-purpose prepaid cards, the so-called e-purses.[862] Those physical cards are held to "*contain real purchasing power, for which the customer has paid in advance*".[863] If the use of such multi-purpose prepaid cards were to become commonplace, the report finds that they could become direct competitors to physical banknotes and coins and the existing cashless payment instruments – such as the debit and credit card. During the initial discussions of the aforementioned task force in 1993, the multi-purpose prepaid cards were still under development. That was considered as the ideal moment to introduce legislation to regulate the nascent market, as it was feared that redressing undesired situations once the market was developed would be more difficult.[864]

Multi-purpose – The reason why multi-purpose prepaid cards drew the attention of national banks lies mainly in their broad potential. Earlier, single-purpose prepaid cards had already been developed – such as telephone cards – whereby the issuer of the card and the provider of goods or services to be obtained using such a card were the same entity. Therefore, the report found that such cards did not possess the potential for broad use and constituted little concern to central banks.[865] Multi-purpose prepaid cards on the other hand would have a theoretically unlimited use potential. That concerned central banks for three reasons.[866] First, unregulated payment instruments

---

861 *Id.* Note that the report does not directly call for the adoption of a new European legal framework to this end, but rather leaves it to the different national banks to analyze how they aim to handle this development. For instance, in the Netherlands it was decided that the existing legal framework regarding the supervision of credit institutions – Wet Toezicht Kredietwezen – could already in its current form be applied to e-purse service providers. Van der Wielen, H. (1996) "Elektronisch geld in Nederland", 10 October 1996, *www.simonl.org/docs/readeremdnb.pdf*, 13.

862 Working Group on EU Payment Systems (1994) "Report to the Council of The European Monetary Institute on Prepaid Cards", *ecb.europa.eu*, 1. Also referred to as stored-value cards. Lee, B.C., Longe-Akindemowo, O. (1998) "Regulatory Issues in Electronic Money: A Legal-Economics Analysis", Department of Economics, University of Wollongong, Working Paper 98–2, *ro.uow.edu.au*, 2.

863 Working Group on EU Payment Systems (1994) "Report to the Council of The European Monetary Institute on Prepaid Cards", *ecb.europa.eu*, 1.

864 *Id.*

865 *Id.* It must be noted here that the report only looks at the situation from the perspective of central banks. For the users, for instance, loss or theft of a single-purpose prepaid card could have consequences. While these cards are generally regarded as being intended for low-value payments only, there is theoretically nothing preventing a single-purpose prepaid card to be loaded with a larger sum. As a result, the risks posed to the user are more closely tied to the amount of money placed on a prepaid card, rather than solely to how widespread that card can be used.

866 *Ibid.*, 2.

could affect consumer confidence in all payment systems and institutions.[867] Second, the control of central banks over the general money supply should not be hindered.[868] Third, direct competition could have consequences to central bank's activities and revenues.[869] To counter such concerns, the general finding of the report is that the right to issue e-purses should be limited to credit institutions, being the traditional banks.[870] Such would protect the integrity of retail payment systems, consumer confidence and the monetary policy, and ensure fair competition.[871] That finding is supported by the Working Group's reasoning that the issuer of a multi-purpose prepaid card receives bank deposits in return for its issuing of the instrument.[872] Therefore, such issuers should be subjected to the same regulations as credit institutions, as deposit-taking is an activity reserved for such institutions.[873] While the central banks did not want to hinder the development of the e-purses market, they did see it as their task to remain closely appraised of its development and to timely intervene.[874] It is clear by now that the concerns voiced by the central banks regarding risks to monetary policy and stability were fairly overblown. E-purses would have to gain quite a dominant market position in the payments landscape before such risks could ever materialize. However, it is the reasoning used by central banks

867 The report especially references security concerns. Working Group on EU Payment Systems (1994) "Report to the Council of The European Monetary Institute on Prepaid Cards", *ecb.europa.eu*, 8–9.

868 *Ibid.*, 9.

869 *Ibid.*, 9–10.

870 In effect, this means that every service provider aiming to issue e-purses would have to register as a credit institution or set up a joint venture with such institution. Dutch telecom operator KPN, for instance, worked together with credit institution Postbank to launch the Chipper e-purse. Lelieveldt, S. (2006) "Impact of the E-Money Directive – Its application to 'hybrid' operators issuing e-money", presented at the E-Money Directive (2000/46/EC) – Round Table Meeting, Brussels, 8 March 2006, *simonl.org*, 5. This policy was also confirmed by the deputy director of the central bank of the Netherlands: Van der Wielen, H. (1997) "Electronic Money: a European Perspective", presented at the Seminar on Electronic Money, hosted by the Bank of England, London 4 February 1997, *www.simonl.org/docs/readeremdnb.pdf*, 20.

871 Working Group on EU Payment Systems (1994) "Report to the Council of The European Monetary Institute on Prepaid Cards", *ecb.europa.eu*, 2; Lee, B.C., Longe-Akindemowo, O. (1998) "Regulatory Issues in Electronic Money: A Legal-Economics Analysis", Department of Economics, University of Wollongong, Working Paper 98–2, *ro.uow.edu.au*, 20.

872 Working Group on EU Payment Systems (1994) "Report to the Council of The European Monetary Institute on Prepaid Cards", *ecb.europa.eu*, 7–8. Note that later it would be disputed that e-money institutions can take deposits. This demonstrates how the early regulatory discussions in this field fully embraced the idea that e-money issuance should be limited to credit institutions.

873 *Id.* Note that the report also provides an exception to the requirement of e-purse issuers to become full credit institutions if: *"(i) they provide only domestic payment services; (ii) they are subject to appropriate regulations, in particular, with respect to liquidity requirements; (iii) they are supervised by the institution which supervises credit institutions"*.

874 Working Group on EU Payment Systems (1994) "Report to the Council of The European Monetary Institute on Prepaid Cards", *ecb.europa.eu*, 7.

at the time, and even today monetary policy and stability are still often used as reason to consider regulatory action for emerging technologies.[875]

INTERNATIONAL – Also, while the report is a clear European effort, there is also a call for the development of an international common position, given the potential cross-border scope of e-purses.[876] If, for instance, every country were to develop its own e-purse system, it is clear that compatibility issues would rise in the context of cross-border payments.[877] An industry effort to counter the compatibility problem was made, resulting in the Common Electronic Purse Specifications (CEPS) in 1999.[878] Essentially, it required a migration of existing e-purse systems to the new standard. While there was initial interest in adopting that standard, the practical implementation has not seemed to materialize.

BENEFITS – The main benefit expected from e-purses is that consumers need to carry less cash for low-value transactions.[879] Moreover, e-purses can incorporate security features, such as PIN codes, which according to the report might diminish the risk of robbery.[880] While prepaid cards do need to be charged in advance, they allow for payments to be conducted without a direct link to the user's bank account.[881] For merchants, the main benefit would also be the limitation of cash money they need to handle, as well the fact that funds are transferred instantly, lowering the risk of refused transactions.[882] Another important benefit, at least at the time, was that the terminals used by e-purses could mostly operate offline, only requiring a network connection at regular intervals. That greatly diminished the associated telecommunications costs, which in those days were still fairly prohibitive for many merchants.

TERMINOLOGY – Some of the most important observances to the report concern its terminology.

---

875 See, for instance, the European Central Bank's opinion on virtual currencies: European Central Bank (2012) "Virtual Currency Schemes", *ecb.europa.eu*, 37–42.

876 *Ibid.*, 12.

877 It has been argued that cross-border incompatibility between e-purse systems only present a real issue for payments on the Internet, and not so much for transactions in the physical realm: Van Hove, L. (1999) "Electronic purses, interoperability and the Internet", *First Monday*, Vol. 4.

878 EUROSMART (2000) "A White Paper: The Euro in the Electronic Purse – Interoperability issues of smartcard based e-payments in Europe", *it.uc3m.es/~celeste/docencia/emaster/e-cash.pdf*, 26–36.

879 *Ibid.*, 5–6. As noted in footnote 865, the report only notes that e-purses might be used for low-value payments, yet does not provide argumentation as to why they would not be used for payments of larger value as well.

880 EUROSMART (2000) "A White Paper: The Euro in the Electronic Purse – Interoperability issues of smartcard based e-payments in Europe", *it.uc3m.es/~celeste/docencia/emaster/e-cash.pdf*, 5–6.

881 *Id.*

882 *Id.*

First, the report makes no reference at all to the notion of e-money, but uses the term e-purse. While the report does make it clear that the purchasing power embedded[883] on the multi-purpose prepaid cards has real monetary value – and could even influence monetary policy – it does not directly address the cards as money. The cards are the e-purses, which contain money, rather than being money in their own right.[884] However, the money embedded in such e-purses does not have the status of legal tender.[885] Important to note here is that the report does not propose a legal framework based on a narrowly defined concept, but rather aims to put the service providers that issue e-purses under the regulation and supervision imposed on credit institutions.

Second, the report makes it clear that it focuses on multi-purpose prepaid cards. This means that single-purpose prepaid cards are excluded from its scope. It also excludes prepaid cards of limited purpose, where the use is limited to particular points of sale or a location – such as a university campus.[886] However, as it is often not immediately clear whether a prepaid card's use is single-purpose, limited-purpose or multi-purpose, the report proposes to have central banks judge this on a case-by-case basis – pending the adoption of a clear legal framework that would determine this matter.[887] Moreover, it must be remarked that no demarcation is made based on the amount of money embedded on a card. The demarcation is made solely on the basis of the range of acceptance of the card. This shows that the report already *a priori* established that such cards should only be used for low-value transactions, yet without really arguing why such would be the case. In practice, limitations on the technology and the reloading of the e-purses resulted in a *de facto* use of e-purses for low value payments only. Another reason for limiting e-purses to low value payments is the risk of loss or theft, though such a risk is of course equally present for cash or debit and credit cards.

Third, by focusing on the notion of prepaid cards, the report makes it clear that it does not reference existing debit and credit cards. Such cards merely function as an access token to an account or credit line and do not have their purchasing power embedded.

---

883 Note that, in practice, the value was not always really embedded on the card. Some systems, for instance, relied more on shadow-accounts operated in the issuer's back-offices.

884 Some authors defend using the term 'e-purse' to address multi-purpose prepaid cards, reasoning that the cards are merely the storage device for a value and not the value itself. Moreover, unlike money, storage cards are retained by their holder and are not circulated. Fullenkamp, C., Nsouli, S.M. (2004) "Six Puzzles in Electronic Money and Banking", *IMF Working* Paper, WP/04/19, 7–8.

885 *Ibid.*, 10. Such is noted to be potentially problematic if e-purses surpass the use of physical money and thus influence monetary policy to the extent that their values replace what is currently regarded as legal tender. This necessitates re-evaluation of what is considered as legal tender or measures to preserve the possibility to pay with banknotes and coins.

886 Working Group on EU Payment Systems (1994) "Report to the Council of The European Monetary Institute on Prepaid Cards", *ecb.europa.eu*, 4.

887 *Id.*

### 2.1.1.2 EMI Council opinion 1997

EMI IMPACT STUDY – After the 1994 report, discussions in the EMI continued. In its annual report for 1997, the EMI reported having conducted a new study *"of the impact on EU economies of the emergence of electronic money"*.[888] The EMI Council opinion following from that study has been included in the annual report. From a terminological point of view, it is important to note that in the years between the focus has shifted away from the notion of e-purses toward the notion of e-money.[889] The reason for this shift is that the notion of e-purses was by then linked to the physical multi-purpose prepaid cards discussed in the 1994 report. However, in the meantime, developments had occurred concerning network-based non-physical money, which raised similar questions to central banks as the physical e-purses did.[890] E-purses and network money were thus both to be addressed under the broader term 'e-money'.[891]

ECASH – Between the development of e-purses and server-based e-money, there was another development called eCash.[892] eCash stored non-physical money that was cryptographically signed by a bank on the user's local computer. Security and privacy of transactions was ensured by blind signature technology, based on existing principles of public key technology. The technology was marketed through the US-based company DigiCash and became available in some EU Member States as well. However, as the use of credit cards in e-commerce transactions rose, DigiCash went bankrupt in 1998.[893] Interestingly, some of the basic principles of that system would later be applied in the blockchain technology underlying cryptocurrencies such as Bitcoin.

---

888 EMI (1998) "Annual Report 1997", *ecb.europa.eu*, 10–11.

889 For instance, already in a 1995 speech director of the central bank of the Netherlands Wim Duisenberg clearly refers to the 1994 report as concerning e-money, used within e-purses. Duisenberg, W.F. (1995) "Toespraak ter gelegenheid van de introductie van de chipknip in Arnhem", 26 October 1995, *www.simonl.org/docs/readeremdnb.pdf*, 5. Also his deputy-director, Henny van der Wielen, consistently uses the term e-money in 1996 and 1997 communications. Van der Wielen, H. (1996) "Elektronisch geld in Nederland", 10 October 1996, *www.simonl.org/docs/readeremdnb.pdf*, 8–13; Van der Wielen, H. (1997) "Electronic Money: a European Perspective", presented at the Seminar on Electronic Money, hosted by the Bank of England, London 4 February 1997, *www.simonl.org/docs/readeremdnb.pdf*, 14–21.

890 Van der Wielen, H. (1997) "Electronic Money: a European Perspective", presented at the Seminar on Electronic Money, hosted by the Bank of England, London 4 February 1997, *www.simonl.org/docs/readeremdnb.pdf*, 16. In the same presentation, reference is made to *"electronic cash (on cards or networks)"*, further evidencing that e-money could be used as the broader term, applying to both card-based and network-based systems.

891 As will still be noted further on, this evolution is not without controversy.

892 Chaum, D. (1983) "Blind signatures for untraceable payments", *Advances in Cryptology Proceedings*, Vol. 82, 199–203.

893 Pitta, J. (1999) "Requiem for a Bright Idea", *Forbes*, 1 November.

E-MONEY REQUIREMENTS – The 1997 opinion largely follows the 1994 report. It is held that even though e-money is not widespread yet, it could develop into a phenomenon with significant implications for monetary policy.[894] Referring back to the 1994 report, it is found that the recommendation to apply the national legislations regarding credit institutions to the issuers of multi-purpose prepaid cards has not been followed by all Member States and that – because of this – the European Commission has started work on a proposal for an EU-wide framework on the matter.[895] Given the importance of the matter, the opinion provides a number of minimal requirements which must be fulfilled[896]:

- The term 'e-money' should be defined and distinguished from single-purpose and limited-purpose prepaid cards;
- E-money issuers should be subjected to regulatory supervision;
- E-money issuing should be subjected to "*solid and transparent legal arrangements*";
- E-money must be redeemable at par value, meaning that the user must be able to have his e-money converted into central bank money;
- It should be possible to impose reserve requirements on e-money issuers;
- Insurance schemes could be used to protect the public.

In order to avoid changes to the institutional settings involved here, the opinion re-iterates the 1994 position that issuing of e-money should be reserved to credit institutions.[897] As the EMI Council does agree that some e-money issuers may not wish to take up the whole scope of credit institution activities, it is proposed to amend the definition of credit institutions. Such would create a 'light' credit institution, for parties wishing to only issue e-money. Pending legislative action to that end, the EMI Council proposes an interim approach and also re-iterates the call for international coordination in the field.[898]

FINDINGS AND EVOLUTIONS – The opinion leads to a number of interesting findings.

First, there is of course the terminological shift toward the notion of 'e-money'. As already noted, it does not indicate a major shift in terms of content, but rather is the result of a scope enlargement. E-money is now considered as a fully dematerialized matter, independent of its carrier. Such a carrier can be

894 EMI (1998) "Annual Report 1997", *ecb.europa.eu*, 74.
895 *Id.*
896 *Ibid.*, 74–75.
897 *Ibid.*, 75. Reference is made to the definition of credit institutions in article 1 of the First Banking Coordination Directive. First Council Directive 77/780/EEC of 12 December 1977 on the coordination of the laws, regulations and administrative provisions relating to the taking up and pursuit of the business of credit institutions, *OJ* L 322 of 17 December 1977, 30–37.
898 EMI (1998) "Annual Report 1997", *ecb.europa.eu*, 75.

a physical prepaid card – the e-purse – or a computer network storing non-physical network money. Outside of the opinion, the annual report also provides a list of definitions. It defines e-money as "*an electronic store of monetary value on a technical device that is used for making payments to undertakings other than the issuing institution without necessarily involving bank accounts in the transaction, but as a prepaid bearer instrument*".[899] That technology-neutral definition indeed demonstrates the EMI Council's aim to cover both physical e-purses and non-physical network money.[900] Also, it confirms that there is monetary value used for making payments. Moreover, the definition distinguishes e-money from regular bank accounts[901] and from single- or limited-purpose prepaid instruments.[902] It can, however, be questioned whether it is the right terminology to refer to that particular development. As found in chapter I, 'money' could be understood as a more strict term that often refers to legal tender. As it is clear that e-money was not intended to become legal tender[903], perhaps the term 'currency' would have been more suitable. Moreover, the new term introduced here somewhat foregoes the earlier nuance that the e-purses are the devices – mostly cards – that hold a certain monetary purchase power, but are not money in itself.

Second, while the position that e-money issuing should be reserved for credit institutions is maintained, the opinion provides the foundations for a more tailored approach. Such would allow potential market players to register as a specific type of credit institution, thus not having to offer the whole breadth of credit institution services and being subject to less stringent requirements.

Third, while the opinion does still primarily call for clear regulation of the service provider – by considering them as credit institutions – it now also emphasizes the requirement that e-money should be convertible, meaning that users of e-money should be able to convert their e-money back into central bank money – here meaning either bank deposits or physical coins and banknotes.

#### 2.1.1.3 ECB report 1998

From EMI to ECB – By August 1998, the EMI had been replaced by the ECB as part of the further development of the Economic and Monetary Union (EMU).

---

899 *Ibid.*, 115.

900 For reference, the report also defines e-purses or multi-purpose prepaid cards as "*a prepaid card which can be used at the outlets of several service providers for a wide range of purposes, which has the potential to be used on a national or international scale but may sometimes be restricted to a certain area. Also known as an electronic purse*". EMI (1998) "Annual Report 1997", *ecb.europa.eu*, 118. This definition fully follows the description of e-purses in the 1994 report.

901 By not requiring the presence of a bank account in an e-money transaction. This part of the definition is further enforced by the reference to e-money acting as a prepaid bearer instrument.

902 By requiring that e-money must be accepted by "*undertakings other than the issuing institution*".

903 At least not in the EU. Singapore did consider making e-money legal tender, as noted in chapter III.

While the European Commission was working on a legislative proposal to regulate e-money and its issuers[904], the ECB released another report, further developing earlier findings of the EMI.[905]

Confirmation of earlier work – The report confirms the definition found in the 1997 opinion, affirming the terminological development of focusing on the monetary value – the e-money – rather than the specific carrier used – such as the e-purse in the 1994 report.[906] Moreover, the report also confirms the difference between e-money and money held in traditional bank accounts.[907] In terms of the potential future value of e-money, the report specifically addresses the rising number of multi-purpose prepaid card schemes in development all over the EU at that time, as well as the then pending introduction of the euro in 1999 with coins and banknotes only becoming available in 2002.[908] While it is noted that some Member States had not yet adapted their national legislation to require e-money issuers to register as credit institutions, such was found to not pose any practical problems as *de facto* all e-money was effectively issued by institutions already registered as credit institutions.[909]

Call for regulation – Despite the finding that in practice e-money issuing was already left to existing credit institutions, the report does re-affirm the earlier call for clear regulation in the field. Such would be needed to preserve price stability and the unit of account function of money.[910] The ECB report proposes to mitigate such risks by taking measures to limit the over-issuing of e-money, for instance by requiring e-money issuers to maintain a certain amount of central

904 The intention hereto had been stated in a 1997 communication regarding electronic commerce: European Commission (1997) "Communication on a European Initiative in Electronic Commerce", *ec.europa.eu*, COM(1997) 0157, 17.

905 ECB (1998) "Report on electronic money", *ecb.europa.eu*.

906 ECB (1998) "Report on electronic money", *ecb.europa.eu*, 7.

907 *Id.* The report refers to 'access devices' – such as computers and telephones – that can be used to access traditional deposit accounts in order to transfer those deposits. With e-money, the value is intrinsically included in the carrier – be it a physical card or non-physical software.

908 ECB (1998) "Report on electronic money", *ecb.europa.eu*, 9. The report also addresses the potential of e-money for low-value transactions.

909 The technical development of e-money schemes could be done by private parties, but the actual e-money issuing was effectively always left to credit institutions. Such was, for instance, the case in the Dutch Chipper scheme, developed by telecom operator KPN with the e-money being issued by Postbank. ECB (1998) "Report on electronic money", *ecb.europa.eu*, 10–11.

910 ECB (1998) "Report on electronic money", *ecb.europa.eu*, 13–14. Here, the report argues that if "*certain electronic money products were to spread at a rapid rate, market views about the creditworthiness of issuers could be affected and electronic money products from different issuers could start to be traded at varying exchange rates*". As a result, it is argued, a redeemability requirement is needed to preserve the unit of account function of money.

bank money for redeemability of e-money.[911] Moreover, supervision is held to protect consumers and merchants against the potential unsound investment policies of the issuer.[912] Also, the report confirms the intention to aim for early regulation of this emerging market, which could help raise consumer confidence in such a market and prevent undesired developments within that market.[913]

Regulatory needs – In terms of minimum requirements, the report confirms most of the requirements found in the 1997 EMI Council's opinion. For instance, it is held that issuers of e-money should be subjected to regulatory supervision, that the rights and obligations of all actors within an e-money scheme must be clearly defined and disclosed, that adequate measures must be taken to ensure technical security[914], that e-money schemes must be protected against criminal abuse such as money laundering, and that statistics relevant to monetary policy must be reported.[915] More important for the purposes of the present analysis, is the requirement that e-money must be redeemable, meaning that holders of e-money must be able to exchange their e-money at par value back to central bank money at the issuer of the e-money.[916] Here, it is clarified that such would prevent a situation where a merchant only accepts e-money below par value – for instance if the issuer's trustworthiness is compromised – which hinders the basic functions of money.[917] By requiring e-money issuers to be able to exchange the e-money they issued back at par with central bank money, the redeemability requirement aims to preserve the unit of account role of money. The redeemability requirement is closely linked to another requirement concerning the imposition of reserve requirements.[918] Less relevant yet desirable objectives stated in the report concern the interoperability of different schemes, and the inclusion of guarantees and insurances.[919] Regarding the status of e-money issuers, it is

---

911 *"Such a requirement would guarantee that the role of money in providing a common financial denominator for the whole economy will be maintained."* ECB (1998) "Report on electronic money", *ecb.europa.eu*, 14.

912 After all, the issuing of e-money to a consumer against the receipt of funds thereto creates a liability on the issuer, payable to the merchant. As with all deposits, investments could be made with the assets received, which in turn could lead to the liabilities becoming of higher value than the assets. ECB (1998) "Report on electronic money", *ecb.europa.eu*, 15.

913 ECB (1998) "Report on electronic money", *ecb.europa.eu*, 20–21.

914 Referencing a specific report hereto, drafted by the G-10's Committee on Payment and Settlement Systems at the Bank for International Settlements (BIS): Bank for International Settlements (1996) "Security of electronic money", *www.bis.org*. This report focuses on the organizational and technical measures that should be implemented within e-money schemes, with strong attention to the use of cryptography.

915 ECB (1998) "Report on electronic money", *ecb.europa.eu*, 23–26.

916 *Ibid.*, 26–27.

917 *Id.* Also here, a link is made to the concern of over-issuing.

918 ECB (1998) "Report on electronic money", *ecb.europa.eu*, 27.

919 *Ibid.*, 27–28. Though the need for interoperability was regularly mentioned at this stage of the legislative procedure, the final directive would make no mention of it. This has resulted in the development of many smaller incompatible schemes, which only raises costs for

repeated that such entities should be credit institutions.[920] However, the earlier statement that e-money issuers in the strict sense could become a special type of credit institutions is reiterated.[921] An important deviation from earlier discussions is that the 1998 report proposes to also include limited-purpose schemes – whereas such schemes were explicitly excluded in the 1994 report. However, given the lesser degree of concerns applicable to such limited-purpose schemes, the ECB proposed a less stringent regulatory framework for them.[922]

Findings – While valuable in further developing the findings of the 1997 opinion, the 1998 ECB report adds only few new insights.

First, terminology-wise the report maintains the definition set out in the 1997 opinion. E-money is considered as a dematerialized monetary value, independent of a particular carrier. The distinction between the e-money notion and others – such as regular bank accounts and single-purpose prepaid instruments – is maintained.

Second, the report confirms again the intention to regulate the issuers of e-money as credit institutions. While the 1997 opinion already provided the option to have e-money issuers recognized as a specific type of credit institutions – rather than requiring them to become full-fledged credit institutions – the 1998 report adds a further option to have limited-purpose e-money issuers put under a lighter regulatory regime.

Third, the main addition of the report is the further explanation of the redeemability requirement. The ECB makes it clear that such a requirement is needed to prevent over-issuing of e-money, which in turn can help protecting price stability and the unit of account function of money. While the ECB leaves open how such a requirement should be implemented, it is clear that in practice it requires e-money issuers to hold certain reserves.

### 2.1.1.4 EC proposal and explanatory memorandum 1998

Regulatory initiative – On 21 September 1998, the European Commission submitted its proposal for an e-money directive to the European Parliament and the European Council.[923] In its recitals, the Commission recognizes the

---

retailers. Newman, S., Sutter, G. (2002) "Electronic Payments – the smart card: Smart cards, e-payments, & law – Part II", *Computer Law & Security Report,* Vol. 18, 312. An example here is the Dutch market, where two incompatible systems, Chipper and Chipknip, both aimed to gain wide adoption.

920 This was also the position of several players in the European banking market. Simon, P. (1999) "La position de la profession sur la monnaie électronique", *Revue d'économie financière*, nr. 53, 37–38.

921 *Ibid.*, 29.

922 *Ibid.*, 31. Note that the report does call for clear criteria to distinguish limited- and multi-purpose schemes. For instance, for limited-purpose schemes a maximum of monetary value could be imposed.

923 This includes a proposal for a directive regarding e-money, as well as a proposal for a directive amending the definition of credit institutions: European Commission (1998) "Proposal

importance of this developing market and therefore proposes a "*technology-neutral legal framework that harmonises the prudential supervision of electronic money institutions to the extent necessary for ensuring their sound and prudent operation and their financial integrity in particular*".[924] Moreover, it proposes the introduction of a single license for e-money institutions, with home Member State supervision.[925] While the proposal fully supports the need for a separate legal framework on the matter, it does deviate from the earlier discussions at the EMI – and later the ECB – in stating that the issuance of e-money cannot be regarded as a deposit-taking activity.[926] Instead, the reason for the adoption of such a legal framework is based on the specific risks posed by e-money issuance and the need for supervision on the conduct of those activities.[927] In terms of scope, article 1 of the proposal states its application to e-money institutions, which are undertakings other than credit institutions that issue e-money or invest the proceeds of such activities.[928]

E-MONEY DEFINITION – E-money itself is defined as:

> monetary value which is;
> (i) stored electronically on an electronic device such as a chip card or a computer memory;
> (ii) accepted as means of payment by undertakings other than the issuing institution;
> (iii) generated in order to be put at the disposal of users to serve as an electronic surrogate for coins and banknotes; and

---

for a European Parliament and Council Directive on the taking up, the pursuit and the prudential supervision of the business of electronic money institutions (COM(1998) 461)", *OJ* C 317 of 15 October 1998, 7–11; European Commission (1998) "Proposal for a European Parliament and Council Directive amending Directive 77/780/EEC on the coordination of laws, regulations and administrative provisions relating to the taking up and pursuit of the business of credit institutions (COM(1998) 461)", *OJ* C 317 of 15 October 1998, 12.

924 European Commission (1998) "Proposal for a European Parliament and Council Directive on the taking up, the pursuit and the prudential supervision of the business of electronic money institutions (COM(1998) 461)", *OJ* C 317 of 15 October 1998, 7.

925 *Id.*

926 *Ibid.*, 7–8. Here, reference is made to the general prohibition of deposit-taking activities for other persons or entities than credit institutions, as found in article 3 of the Second Banking Coordination Directive. Second Council Directive 89/646/EEC of 15 December 1989 on the coordination of laws, regulations and administrative provisions relating to the taking up and pursuit of the business of credit institutions and amending Directive 77/780/EEC, *OJ* L 386 of 30 December 1989, 1–13. In the explanatory memorandum, the Commission further explains its reasoning. Here, it is held that deposits are generally considered for safe keeping and handling, which is not the aim of the consumer wishing to obtain e-money. The consumer only aims to receive goods or services from the merchants that accept the e-money he obtained. European Commission (1998) "Explanatory memorandum – what is electronic money?", *ec.europa.eu*, COM(1998) 461.

927 European Commission (1998) "Proposal for a European Parliament and Council Directive on the taking up, the pursuit and the prudential supervision of the business of electronic money institutions (COM(1998) 461)", *OJ* C 317 of 15 October 1998, 8.

928 *Id.*

(iv) generated for the purpose of effecting electronic transfers of limited value payments.[929]

The definition deviates from the definitions employed earlier by the EMI and ECB on a number of points. First, the reference to chip cards and computer memory could be understood as making the definition less technology-neutral than aimed for. The third point – referencing e-money as a surrogate for coins and banknotes – seems superfluous and does not add any relevance to the definition. The final point confirms the course first established by the 1994 Working Group report that most e-money transactions are likely to be low-value transactions. However, as noted before, it is never explained why e-money would be limited to only extend to low-value payments by definition, and it can be questioned whether such is even desirable.

E-MONEY INSTITUTIONS – Furthermore, the proposal restricts the activities of e-money institutions, further implementing the creation of e-money as a specific type of credit institutions.[930] As expected from the earlier reports and opinions, e-money institutions are subjected to specific requirements regarding initial capital and own funds, as well as being limited in their investments.[931] They must implement measures ensuring their sound and prudent operation and their compliance with the requirements set out by the proposed directive will be checked at least twice a year by competent authorities.[932] However, the proposal does allow that for small-scale e-money institutions a number of waivers be granted, and that existing e-money schemes can be 'grandfathered'.[933] The second proposal submitted by the Commission amends the definition of credit institutions found in the First Banking Coordination Directive. Essentially, it adds to the existing definition that credit institutions can also be e-money institutions.[934]

REASONING – In an explanatory memorandum to the proposal, the Commission mainly refers to e-money as a form of digital cash – and as opposite to credit and debit cards.[935] The memorandum also states that e-money can be used for low value transactions, also referred to as micro-payments, yet again neglects

929 *Id.* Article 1 (3) (b).

930 *Ibid.*, 8–9. Article 1 (4). This also becomes clear in article 2, where the application of rules applicable to credit institutions is limited for e-money institutions.

931 *Ibid.*, 9–10. Articles 3 and 4.

932 *Ibid.*, 10. Articles 5 and 6.

933 *Ibid.*, 10–11. Articles 7 and 8.

934 Article 1 European Commission (1998) "Proposal for a European Parliament and Council Directive amending Directive 77/780/EEC on the coordination of laws, regulations and administrative provisions relating to the taking up and pursuit of the business of credit institutions (COM(1998) 461)", *OJ* C 317 of 15 October 1998, 12.

935 European Commission (1998) "Explanatory memorandum – what is electronic money?", *ec.europa.eu*, COM(1998) 461.

to consider its usability for higher value transactions.[936] In terms of risk, the memorandum argues that "*it is evident that a substantial amount of electronic money could be in circulation exposing consumers, but especially traders and retailers, to failure and, in this event, the possibility of systemic risk*".[937] With the proposal for a legal framework on the matter, the Commission expresses its hope to secure the financial integrity and the operations of e-money institutions, as well as to raise consumer confidence.[938] While it was not the intention to impose strict harmonization in the e-money field – the proposal clearly indicates its goal as an instrument of minimal necessary harmonization – the Commission is concerned that the divergent national approaches implemented at that time could hinder the development of the market.[939] Regarding the application of the regulatory supervision, the Commission finds that a less burdensome regime should be imposed on e-money institutions in order to not discourage potential new market players.[940]

FINDINGS – While the proposal and the explanatory memorandum make it clear that the European Commission did not always agree with the reasoning behind the EMI and ECB's earlier opinion and reports, the proposal does seem to implement most of the suggestions made by the central banks. In terms of definition, the proposal does not seem to succeed strongly in its goal to maintain a technology-neutral approach. In terms of regulation of e-money institutions, the proposal provides a lighter regime for such actors – while still placing them under the definition of credit institutions – and also provides for further waivers for smaller market players. An important deviation from the texts discussed before is that the proposal does not consider the issuance of e-money as a deposit-taking activity. As a result, the proposal also does not consider redeemability as a constitutive requirement.[941]

936 *Id.*

937 *Id.*

938 *Id.*

939 *Id.* The adoption of a legal framework in this field is also considered important in light of the introduction of the euro. This would allow consumers and businesses to already conduct transactions in 'virtual' euros, pending the introduction of the coins and banknotes in 2002.

940 *Id.* This position seems to be the result of a compromise between the ECB and the European Commission. While agreeing to consider e-money institutions as credit institutions – as asked by the central banks – the European Commission pressed to create a lighter regime, in order to leave the market open to a broader array of potential players.

941 Article 2 holds that "*the contract between the issuer and the user shall define if the stored electronic money is redeemable or not, and, if appropriate, the conditions, the formalities and the time period of redeemability*". European Commission (1998) "Proposal for a European Parliament and Council Directive on the taking up, the pursuit and the prudential supervision of the business of electronic money institutions (COM(1998) 461)", *OJ* C 317 of 15 October 1998, 9.

### 2.1.1.5 ECB opinion 1999

Request for opinion – At the request of the Council of the European Union, the ECB provided its opinion on the European Commission's proposed directives on 18 January 2014.[942] In its opinion, the ECB makes a reference to the 1998 report, re-stating the minimum requirements formulated there.[943]

Scope – In terms of scope, the ECB remarks that the proposed directive only applies to a specific type of credit institutions – namely the e-money institutions created by the second proposal – but not to regular credit institutions. In order to ensure a level playing field, the proposed measures should apply to both.[944] The ECB also finds the other activities of the proposed e-money institutions to be too broadly formulated. Such a broad formulation could, for instance, lead to the less strictly regulated e-money institutions to take up tasks normally reserved for full-fledged credit institutions[945], or to engage in risky non-financial activities.[946] Moreover, to further strengthen the confidence of e-money users and to protect them against losses, the ECB welcomes the introduction of measures such as guarantee, loss-sharing or insurance schemes.[947] Such also applies to the limitation of investments, where the ECB wants to prohibit e-money institutions from offering credit to their users.[948] In order to support harmonization for the passporting system, the ECB also proposes to impose risk limitations at the level of the EU instead of leaving the matter to the Member States.[949] It also extends to the waiver proposed for small size e-money institutions, where the ECB welcomes a certain minimum level of regulation.[950]

---

942 ECB (1999) "Opinion of the European Central Bank of 18 January 1999 at the request of the Council of the European Union under Article 105(4) of the Treaty establishing the European Community and Article 4(a) of the Statute of the European System of Central Banks and of the European Central Bank on 1. a Commission proposal for a European Parliament and Council Directive on the taking up, the pursuit and the prudential supervision of the business of electronic money institutions, and 2. a Commission proposal for a European Parliament and Council Directive amending Directive 77/780/EEC on the coordination of laws, regulations and administrative provisions relating to the taking up and pursuit of the business of credit institutions", *OJ* C 189 of 6 July 1999, 7–10.

943 *Ibid.*, paragraphs 7–8.

944 *Ibid.*, paragraph 10.

945 *Ibid.*, paragraph 13.

946 *Ibid.*, paragraph 14.

947 *Ibid.*, paragraph 18.

948 Which can be argued to be somewhat at odds with their status as credit institution. Kohlbach, M. (2004) "Making Sense of Electronic Money", *Journal of Information, Law and Technology*, 4.

949 ECB (1999) "Opinion of the European Central Bank of 18 January 1999 at the request of the Council of the European Union under Article 105(4) of the Treaty establishing the European Community and Article 4(a) of the Statute of the European System of Central Banks and of the European Central Bank on 1. a Commission proposal for a European Parliament and Council Directive on the taking up, the pursuit and the prudential supervision of the business of electronic money institutions, and 2. a Commission proposal for a European Parliament and Council Directive amending Directive 77/780/EEC on the coordination of laws, regulations and administrative provisions relating to the taking up and pursuit of the business of credit institutions", *OJ* C 189 of 6 July 1999, paragraph 21.

950 *Ibid.*, paragraph 24.

E-MONEY DEFINITION – For the definition of e-money, the ECB finds the proposed definition too focused on the technical aspects.[951] Moreover, the reference to the limited value of e-money transactions is found to be unnecessary and to potentially lead to the impression that large value transactions are not covered by the directive.[952] It is therefore suggested to amend the proposed definition, stating that "*electronic money represents a claim on the issuer of electronic money, which claim is redeemable in either legal tender or scriptural money, that is incorporated in an electronic medium, and accepted as an instrument of payment by (non-affiliated) undertakings other than the issuing institution*".[953]

REDEEMABILITY – The ECB also strongly urges to include a redeemability requirement, as proposed by the ECB in its 1998 report.[954] Such also allows e-money users to leave a particular e-money scheme at all times, thus preventing user lock-in. While the 1998 report did not go into the specific workings of such redeemability, the ECB now proposes a number of concrete elements. First, the user should be able to choose between redemption in legal tender or by transfer to a bank account of his choosing. Moreover, redemption should be made on the local business day following the day of the request thereto and should principally be free of charge, except for the charge of acceptable costs related to such an action communicated in advance. Also, for a determined period after the expiration of the e-money, redemption should still be allowed. Redeemability should also apply equally for all e-money institutions, irrespective of their size. Furthermore, "*redemption payments should be denominated in the same currency as the currency in which the relevant electronic money liability is denominated*".[955] The sentence in the proposed article 2 (4) that could be construed as disregarding the need for redeemability, is interpreted by the ECB as meaning that redeemability should not be addressed by the Member States.[956]

FINDINGS – Overall, the ECB welcomes the initiative and seems to agree with most of its provisions. It is, however, clear that the ECB is a strong proponent of stricter regulation of e-money institutions than envisioned by the European Commission. In terms of definition, the ECB's proposal seems to be more technology-neutral and also omits the unnecessary elements found in the third and fourth paragraphs of the Commission's proposal. However, the ECB deviates from the definitions it maintained earlier by dropping the reference to e-money as having monetary value, instead referring to a redeemable claim on

---

951 *Ibid.*, paragraph 12.

952 *Id.*

953 *Id.*

954 *Ibid.*, paragraph 19. The ECB explains its earlier reasoning that such requirement is needed to preserve the unit of account function of money, to maintain price stability and to safeguard the controllability of liquidity conditions and the short-term interest rates.

955 *Id.*

956 As it would already be addressed at the level of the EU by the inclusion of the requirement proposed by the ECB.

the issuer. While some reference to redeemability was thus already included in the definition, the ECB proposes a number of elements that should make up a clear and substantive redeemability requirement.

#### 2.1.1.6 Economic and Social Committee opinion 1999

CALL FOR STRONGER ACTION – The Council of the European Union also requested the opinion of the Economic and Social Committee, which was delivered on 27 January 1999.[957] Also that Committee recognizes the need for legislative initiative in the e-money field, given the potential impact of e-money and its importance for the development of e-commerce within the EU.[958] As a general remark, the Committee warns that the minimal harmonization pursued by the European Commission may have harmed the strength of the proposal. For instance, it is found that the mild supervision does not take into account the full scope of supervision required in the financial sector.[959] Moreover, it is feared that the definitions used in the proposal do not fully take into account the potential scope of e-money.[960] Reference is also made to the lack of provisions regarding the international framework in the matter, or regarding consumer protection.[961]

E-MONEY DEFINITION – Regarding the definition of e-money, the Committee points out the difficulty in managing different products under the same term.[962] As did the ECB, the Committee finds the inclusion of the reference to low value transactions out of place in such a definition.[963] Regarding

957 Economic and Social Committee (1999) "Opinion of the Economic and Social Committee on the 'Proposal for a European Parliament and Council Directive on the taking up, the pursuit and the prudential supervision of the business of electronic money institutions', and the 'Proposal for a European Parliament and Council Directive amending Directive 77/780/EEC on the coordination of laws, regulations and administrative provisions relating to the taking up and pursuit of the business of credit institutions'", *OJ* C 101 of 12 April 1999, 64–70.

958 *Ibid.*, paragraphs 1.1–1.5. Note that also here, e-money is principally understood as being a broader term, covering both physical prepaid cards and non-physical network money.

959 *Ibid.*, paragraph 2.2.

960 *Ibid.*, paragraphs 2.6–2.9. The Committee refers back to the initial purpose of regulating multi-purpose prepaid cards, which was later expanded to include network money. While prepaid cards are generally considered to be low value transactions, network money has a much larger potential which the Committee fears is not sufficiently covered. Therefore, the Committee would welcome a more differentiated approach that would better take into account the inherent differences between these two developments.

961 *Ibid.*, paragraph 2.12–2.13.

962 See footnote 960.

963 Paragraph 3.1.2, Economic and Social Committee (1999) "Opinion of the Economic and Social Committee on the 'Proposal for a European Parliament and Council Directive on the taking up, the pursuit and the prudential supervision of the business of electronic money institutions', and the 'Proposal for a European Parliament and Council Directive amending Directive 77/780/EEC on the coordination of laws, regulations and administrative provisions relating to the taking up and pursuit of the business of credit institutions'", *OJ* C 101 of 12 April 1999, 64–70.

redeemability, the Committee is of the opinion that unused funds should always be reimbursed.[964]

E-MONEY INSTITUTIONS – Regarding the activities of e-money institutions, the Committee proposes stronger capital requirements, a stricter limitation of investments, and stronger controls on par with those for other financial institutions.[965] While the Committee does take a positive stance regarding the reasoning behind the proposed waiver regime to support development of the market, it also questions whether the encouragement of small schemes would be beneficial to the market, for instance in terms of interoperability.[966] Therefore, it opposes the waiver for storage amounts below ECU 150.[967]

FINDINGS – While the Committee seems to agree with the overall intentions of the Commission's proposal, it points out a number of shortcomings. First, the Committee welcomes a much stricter regime, far surpassing what the Commission proposed or what the ECB discussed earlier. Second, the Committee points out that it sees a high potential for risks in the use of network money. To handle such risks, the Committee welcomes a differentiation within the proposal between prepaid cards and network money. Here, it is pointed out that the current proposal clearly builds forth on the earlier discussions regarding multi-purpose prepaid cards, to which network money was later added. In doing so, the Committee feels that the intrinsic properties of network money are not sufficiently taken into account.

#### 2.1.1.7 European Parliament first reading 1999

COMMITTEE REPORT – Within the European Parliament, the European Commission's proposal was referred to the Committee on Legal Affairs and Citizens' Rights as the responsible committee. Its report was tabled on 25 March 1999.[968] In the explanatory statement to the report, e-money is considered

---

964 *Ibid.*, paragraph 3.2.2. Furthermore, the Committee is not convinced of the reasoning employed by the European Commission in not considering the issuing of e-money involving a collection of deposits.

965 *Ibid.*, paragraphs 3.3–3.5.

966 *Ibid.*, paragraph 3.7.

967 As the waiver is for storage amounts of maximum ECU 150, it can be concluded that e-money can be stored for higher values, without limit. By its anonymous nature – as pointed out by the Commission – high value e-money storage bears significant risks for loss. Therefore, the Committee refers to payment cards, where the Commission had earlier defined a tolerable loss at ECU 150. Applying the same logics, the Committee proposes to limit all multi-purpose prepaid cards to a maximum value of that same amount.

968 European Parliament (1999) "Report on the proposal for a European Parliament and Council Directive on the taking up, the pursuit and the prudential supervision of the business of electronic money institutions (COM(98)0461 – C4-0531/98 – 98/0252(COD)) and on the proposal for a European Parliament and Council Directive amending Directive 77/780/

as a "*unit of account acknowledged by the purchaser and by the vendor*".[969] The general consensus that regulation is needed to ensure consumer trust in e-money developments is also present here, with reference to the bankruptcy of an e-money institution which at the time caused a stir in the enthusiasm for e-money.[970]

CORE PRINCIPLES – The assessment of the report shows three main principles in the proposed directive: (1) EU passporting to allow for the free movement of financial services; (2) the understanding that funds advanced by bearers are not deposits; and (3) the creation of non-bank institutions that can issue e-money.[971] Like the Economic and Social Committee, the report calls for more measures regarding consumer protection.[972] In relation to the discussion of consumer protection, the report also refers to the need for a redeemability option, as the proposal does not introduce a cap on the maximum amount of e-money that can be stored.[973] Also reference to the need for interoperability is made, be it that it is expected here that the banking sector will sort out that issue through self-regulation.[974]

E-MONEY DEFINITION – Regarding the definition of e-money, the report welcomes the broad definition, but agrees with the opinions discussed earlier that the reference to low value transactions should be removed[975], which was accomplished through the proposed amendments.[976] Apart from some minor terminological changes[977], it also introduces the notion that e-money "*does not give rise to the levying of charges on the user at the time of payment*".[978] Another

EEC on the coordination of laws, regulations and administrative provisions relating to the taking up and pursuit of the business of credit institutions (COM(98)0461 – C4-0532/98 – 98/0253(COD))", *europarl.europa.eu*, A4-0156/99.

969 *Ibid.*, 18. Also here, e-money is found to include multi-lateral prepaid cards and network money. The Committee on Economic and Monetary Affairs and Industrial Policy also provided a report, in which it considers e-money as a "*means of payment which transfers funds from one person to another in a manner equivalent to the use cash, but without a physical medium*". Here, the emphasis is put on e-money being a non-physical equivalent to cash. *Ibid.*, 26.

970 *Ibid.*, 19. The case referenced is that of DigiCash, which went bankrupt in 1998.

971 *Ibid.*, 20.

972 *Ibid.*, 21. Here, the report proposes to adopt another directive aimed at regulating the relationship between issuers and bearers of e-money. Amendment 3.

973 *Ibid.*, 21. Note that the report also proposes flexibility by introducing a EUR 10 minimum threshold on redemption.

974 *Ibid.*, 22. The interoperability concern was also expressed by the Committee on Economic and Monetary Affairs and Industrial Policy. *Ibid.*, 27.

975 *Ibid.*, 23.

976 *Ibid.*, amendment 15. Moreover, the notion "*stored electronically on an electronic device*", is shortened to "*stored on an electronic device*".

977 It changes 'users' for 'bearers' and 'undertakings' for 'natural and legal persons'.

978 European Parliament (1999) "Report on the proposal for a European Parliament and Council Directive on the taking up, the pursuit and the prudential supervision of the business of electronic money institutions (COM(98)0461 – C4-0531/98 – 98/0252(COD)) and on the proposal for a European Parliament and Council Directive amending Directive 77/780/EEC on the coordination of laws, regulations and administrative provisions relating to the

committee, the Committee on Economic and Monetary Affairs and Industrial Policy, also introduced changes to the definition, for instance holding that e-money serves as a surrogate for coins and banknotes "*wherever these are legal tender*"[979] and that e-money should be accepted as means of payment "*for a wide variety of goods and services*".[980] Those two amendments, however, were not taken over in the text adopted by the European Parliament in plenary session.[981] Regarding redeemability, the report follows the ECB's finding that redemption should always be possible, without charges "*other than those strictly necessary to carry out that operation*".[982] It also proposes the inclusion of a separate article dedicated to the issue of redeemability.[983]

Findings – The general conclusion of the report is in agreement with the more liberal approach proposed by the European Commission. While the need for prudential supervision is recognized, the report also expresses the need to allow for vigorous and sound competition in the market.[984] The report agrees with the Commission that there is little use in limiting the e-money market to traditional banks, as non-bank institutions could then still acquire a bank or set up a joint venture with a bank.[985] Apart from that and the acceptance of the Commission's position that funds advanced by bearers are not deposits, the report does not go into further detail on the discussion regarding the precise nature and status of e-money institutions. Instead, at this point most of the discussion seems to have shifted toward the concept of e-money itself. The report does not seem to follow the Economic and Social Committee's opinion that the proposed provisions are too focused on the original concept of multi-purpose prepaid cards, and thus insufficiently take into account the other aspect of e-money that is network money. Generally, the European Parliament's first reading – where

taking up and pursuit of the business of credit institutions (COM(98)0461 – C4-0532/98 – 98/0253(COD))", *europarl.europa.eu*, A4-0156/99, amendment 15.

979 *Ibid.*, 30.

980 *Ibid.*, 31.

981 European Parliament (1999) "Legislative resolution embodying Parliament's opinion on the proposal for a European Parliament and Council Directive on the taking up, the pursuit and the prudential supervision of the business of electronic money institutions (COM(98)0461 C4-0531/98 98/0252(COD))", *OJ* C 219 of 30 July 1999.

982 European Parliament (1999) "Report on the proposal for a European Parliament and Council Directive on the taking up, the pursuit and the prudential supervision of the business of electronic money institutions (COM(98)0461 – C4-0531/98 – 98/0252(COD)) and on the proposal for a European Parliament and Council Directive amending Directive 77/780/EEC on the coordination of laws, regulations and administrative provisions relating to the taking up and pursuit of the business of credit institutions (COM(98)0461 – C4-0532/98 – 98/0253(COD))", *europarl.europa.eu*, A4-0156/99, amendment 18. This opinion is shared by the Committee on Economic and Monetary Affairs and Industrial Policy. *Ibid.*, 27.

983 *Ibid.*, amendment 19.

984 *Ibid.*, 24.

985 *Ibid.*, 20.

the Committee on Legal Affairs and Citizens' Rights' report was accepted – introduced very few significant changes to the e-money definition apart from the removal of the reference to low value transactions and the introduction of the requirement to not give rise to the levying of charges at the time of payment.

#### 2.1.1.8 Council common position 1999

FINDING THE BALANCE – On 29 November 1999, the Council of the European Union adopted a common position, expressing its own findings and its views on the amendments proposed by the European Parliament.[986] In general, the Council agrees with the need to strike a balance between the need to allow for market development and the need to preserve financial integrity and to protect consumers.[987]

E-MONEY DEFINITION – Regarding definitions, the Council aimed to formulate the concept of e-money in a more precise way.[988] For instance, it removes the references to the specific forms e-money can be presented in, as well as the references to e-money being a substitute for cash and of low value, and adds that e-money presents a claim on the issuer. Moreover, it is added that e-money must be paid for fully, meaning that no more e-money can be issued than what was paid for. The Council does mostly agree with the amendments proposed by the European Parliament, but chose to formulate them differently or include them elsewhere in the text.[989]

E-MONEY INSTITUTIONS – Regarding other provisions, the Council agrees with the European Commission that e-money issuing in itself does not involve deposit-taking. In agreement with other opinions, the Council adds a specific provision regarding redeemability.[990] Also, the Council retains the waiver proposed, but broadens up its scope, leaving the Member States with more flexibility in implementing this.[991] In other provisions, the Council seems to mainly take over the amendments proposed by the European Parliament, be it in reworded form.

FINDINGS – In general, the Council's common position does not provide substantial deviations from what was already found in the amendments adopted by the European Parliament in its first reading. The most important additions concern the definition of e-money, from which a few provisions of dubious

986 Council of the European Union (1999) "Common Position (EC) No 8/2000 adopted by the Council on 29 November 1999 with a view to adopting a Directive 2000/.../EC of the European Parliament and of the Council of ... on the taking-up, pursuit of and prudential supervision of the business of electronic money institutions", *OJ* C 26 of 28 January 2000, 1–11.

987 *Ibid.*, 7.

988 *Ibid.*, 7–8.

989 *Ibid.*, 8.

990 *Ibid.*, new article 3.

991 *Ibid.*, 9–10.

value were removed. Notably, it is here that the notions 'claim on the issuer' and 'issued on receipt of funds of an amount not less in value than the monetary value issued' find their origin. The reasons for adding the former notion have, however, not been explained by the Council, apart from finding that it made the definition more precise. Regarding the latter notion, the Council explains this as a measure to prevent over-issuing of e-money. While the ECB did indeed call for such a measure, it also already considered redeemability to provide a solution.

#### 2.1.1.9 Further procedure 2000

COMMISSION'S REACTION – After the Council's common position, the European Commission published a reaction stating that it finds the common position fully acceptable.[992] Regarding the definition of e-money, the Commission finds that the new additions by the Council provide consistency with the redeemability clause and "*ensure parity between cash and electronic money*".[993]

PARLIAMENT'S SECOND READING – Following the Commission's statement, the European Parliament conducted a second reading. In the report from the Committee on Economic and Monetary Affairs, it is held that the Council's common position was the result of a compromise after long negotiations.[994] Generally, it is found that the Council "*managed to reach a balanced and constructive position which will serve the interests of all the parties concerned*".[995] It is therefore decided to accept the changes proposed by the Council, with the introduction of a few minor amendments holding that redeemability must be 'at par value'.[996] While the reporting Committee also proposed to reduce the number of provisions regarding the waiver procedure,

---

992 European Commission (2000) "Communication to the European Parliament pursuant to the second subparagraph of Article 251 (2) of the EC-Treaty concerning the Common Position adopted by the Council with a view to the adoption of a European Parliament and Council Directive on the taking up, the pursuit and the prudential supervision of the business of electronic money institutions and a European Parliament and Council Directive amending Directive 77/780/EEC on the co-ordination of laws, regulations and administrative provisions relating to the taking up and pursuit of the business of credit institutions", *ec.europa.eu*, SEC(2000) 0069.

993 *Id.*

994 European Parliament (2000) "Committee on Economic and Monetary Affairs Recommendation for second reading on the Council common position for adopting a European Parliament and Council directive on the taking up, the pursuit and the prudential supervision of the business of electronic money institutions (12004/2/1999 – C5-0306/1999 – 1998/0252(COD)) and on the Council common position for adopting a European Parliament and Council directive amending Directive 77/780/EEC on the co-ordination of laws, regulations and administrative provisions relating to the taking up and pursuit of the business of credit institutions (12005/1/1999 – C5-0307/1999 – 1998/0253(COD))", *europarl.europa.eu*, A5-0080/2000, 9.

995 *Id.*

996 *Ibid.*, amendments 1 and 2.

in order to not undermine the ECB's pursuit of monetary stability, that amendment was not included in the European Parliament's final position.[997]

Adoption – The two amendments proposed in the European Parliament's second reading were accepted by the European Commission, as they "*involve no change of substance but merely clarify a point which was already included in the common position*".[998] On 16 June 2000, the Council also accepted the amendments proposed by the European Parliament, leading to the adoption of the EMD1 on 18 September 2000.[999]

### 2.1.1.10 Findings

A compromise between different objectives – The legislative procedure preceding the adoption of the EMD1 demonstrates how the institutions involved held rather divergent opinions on how the developments regarded as e-money should be regulated. On the one side, the ECB – and the EMI before it – proposed a strong regulatory framework, expressing the need for prudential supervision on the issuers of e-money. That position was largely shared by the Economic and Social Committee. On the other side, the European Commission proposed a more liberal approach, fearing that too strict regulation would hinder the development of the nascent market. That opinion was mainly shared by the European Parliament and – to lesser extent – by the Council of the European Union.

A special type of credit institutions – The disagreement between different institutions and the resulting compromise becomes clearly visible when tracing the different steps of the legislative procedure. At first, the focus of discussions was put on the e-money issuers and what their specific status should be. The initial position proposed in the 1994 report was to limit the issuance of e-money to credit institutions. Eventually, a compromise was reached, which allowed the creation of e-money institutions that serve as a specific type of credit institutions subject to lighter supervision than traditional credit institutions. Following that

---

997 *Ibid.*, amendment 3. European Parliament (2000) "Position adopted at second reading on 11 April 2000 with a view to the adoption of European Parliament and Council Directive 2000/.../EC on the taking up, pursuit of and prudential supervision of the business of electronic money institutions (1998/0252(COD) – PE2)", *OJ* C 40 of 7 February 2001, 35–36.

998 European Commission (2000) "Opinion of the Commission pursuant to Article 251 (2) (c) of the EC Treaty, on the European Parliament's amendments to the Council's common position regarding the proposal for a Directive of the European Parliament and of the Council on the taking up, the pursuit and the prudential supervision of the business of electronic money institutions and for a Directive of the European Parliament and of the Council amending Directive 77/780/EEC on the co-ordination of laws, regulations and administrative provisions relating to the taking up and pursuit of the business of credit institutions", *ec.europa.eu*, COM(2000) 0333, 3.

999 Council of the European Union (2000) "2273rd Council meeting Fisheries at Luxembourg, 16 June 2000", *consilium.europa.eu*, ST 9407 2000 ADD 1, 3.

compromise, the discussions seem to have moved on to other aspects of the text, such as the definition of e-money.

From e-purse to e-money – From the evolution of this topic, it becomes clear that the main focus has always been e-purses, or multi-purpose prepaid cards.[1000] The notion of e-money was only coined to also include network money, a later development. However, as held by the Economic and Social Committee, it could be remarked that the inherent differences between physical cards and non-physical systems were never fully explored in the discussions between institutions. While originally the notion of e-money was defined in very broad terms – in order to fully capture all of its potential forms and new developments in this field – later evolution in the legislative process seems to have significantly restricted its definition. From the EMI Council's 1997 opinion[1001], over the European Commission's original proposal[1002], to the final text[1003], the scope of what constitutes e-money has changed rather substantially. For instance, while it is agreed by all parties that e-money is a non-physical phenomenon and is therefore not intrinsically linked to a specific carrier[1004], the move toward the notion of 'stored on an electronic device' could prevent the application of the definition to network money, or server-based e-money.[1005] Also, the focus of the Commission's proposal on low value transactions could further limit the scope of e-money and demonstrates how discussions on e-money were still very much tied to the concept of multi-purpose prepaid cards – which were indeed found to mainly serve low value transactions in practice – and does not take into account the potential scope of network money. But perhaps the most important limitation of the scope of e-money has been imposed by the introduction of an issuance requirement in the definition of the e-money concept. In order to

---

1000 With specific attention to demarcating these cards from single- or limited-purpose prepaid cards and regular debit and credit cards.

1001 "*An electronic store of monetary value on a technical device that is used for making payments to undertakings other than the issuing institution without necessarily involving bank accounts in the transaction, but as a prepaid bearer instrument*". EMI (1998) "Annual Report 1997", *ecb.europa.eu*, 115.

1002 "*Monetary value which is; (i) stored electronically on an electronic device such as a chip card or a computer memory; (ii) accepted as means of payment by undertakings other than the issuing institution; (iii) generated in order to be put at the disposal of users to serve as an electronic surrogate for coins and banknotes; and (iv) generated for the purpose of effecting electronic transfers of limited value payments.*" Article 1 (3) (b) European Commission (1998) "Proposal for a European Parliament and Council Directive on the taking up, the pursuit and the prudential supervision of the business of electronic money institutions (COM(1998) 461)", *OJ* C 317 of 15 October 1998.

1003 "*Monetary value as represented by a claim on the issuer which is: (i) stored on an electronic device; (ii) issued on receipt of funds of an amount not less in value than the monetary value issued; (iii) accepted as means of payment by undertakings other than the issuer.*" Article 1 (3) (b) EMD1.

1004 Thus differing from the notion of 'e-purses' as these refer to a specific carrier in the form of a multi-purpose prepaid card.

1005 As will be discussed in section 2.1.2, this did in fact pose practical problems during the implementation of the directive.

protect financial stability against the over-issuing of e-money, the ECB proposed to introduce a redeemability requirement. As all other parties agreed that such redeemability requirement was needed, the requirement was added to the proposed directive in a fairly early stage of the legislative procedure. However, at a later stage the Council of the European Union implemented another requirement aimed at preventing the over-issuing of e-money, namely that e-money could not be issued for a higher value than was paid for. Thus, while financial stability was supposed to be protected by a redeemability requirement in the directive, it now also received protection through an issuance requirement that became a constitutive element of the notion of e-money.[1006, 1007]

Product versus service providers – While it was originally the intention to only regulate the behavior of market players offering services regarding e-money – which could initially be interpreted broadly – the final product could be argued to place a disproportionate burden on the notion of e-money itself. As a result, the directive could give the impression of being more aimed at regulating the phenomenon of e-money, rather than the service providers.

### 2.1.2 *First E-money Directive*

Implementation and review – Having explored the legislative discussions preceding the adoption of the EMD1 in 2000, this section will discuss the following phase in the regulation of e-money in the EU, covering the implementation of that directive and its later review leading up to the 2009 EMD2. First, it will present the principles of the EMD1. Next, this section will discuss a consultation procedure held by the European Commission in order to clarify the scope of the directive. This is followed by an analysis of the positions of Member States and market players, in order to understand how the directive was received in practice. That analysis will lead into the review process.

#### 2.1.2.1 Directive

Overview – The general principles of the EMD1 were already largely explored in the previous section. This section only provides a brief overview of the different principles.

---

1006 Also here, this element of the definition did lead to issues during the implementation of the directive by Member States. See section 2.1.2.

1007 Lelieveldt, for instance, finds it strange that this notion has been included in the definition. While the ECB wanted a requirement specifically to prevent the creation of inflated e-money schemes, the final e-money definition in fact allows such schemes as they do not fall within the scope of the definition of e-money. As a result, such schemes are not covered by the directive. Lelieveldt, S. (2001) "Why is the Electronic Money-Directive Significant?", *EPSO Newsletter*, 7, May 2001. The same argument is made by: Vereecken, M. (2001) "A Harmonised EU Legal Framework for Electronic Money", *EPSO Newsletter*, 7, May 2001.

DEFINITIONS – Article 1 of the directive holds that the directive applies to e-money institutions[1008], with the definition of e-money being "*monetary value as represented by a claim on the issuer which is (i) stored on an electronic device; (ii) issued on receipt of funds of an amount not less in value than the monetary value issued; (iii) accepted as means of payment by undertakings other than the issuer*". Those e-money institutions are the only institutions allowed to issue e-money, and are restricted in their other activities.

NO DEPOSIT-TAKING – Article 2 lays out the regulatory framework for the e-money institutions, but confirms that their receipt of funds does not constitute deposit-taking.

REDEEMABILITY – Article 3 introduces the redeemability requirement, holding that e-money can be redeemed at par value during its period of validity. Conditions hereto should be stated in the contract between issuer and bearer, and no other fees than necessary for the redemption can be charged. Redemption can be in cash or by bank transfer, with a minimum threshold of EUR 10 maximum.

CAPITAL, FUNDS AND INVESTMENTS – Article 4 lays down the initial capital and ongoing funds requirements. E-money institutions are, for instance, required to hold at least EUR 1 million in initial capital. Article 5 concerns the limitation of investments by e-money institutions. For instance, it lists a number of assets in which those institutions can invest, such as zero credit risk weighted assets and Zone A credit institution sight deposits.

VERIFICATION AND SOUND OPERATION – Article 6 ensures that competent authorities can regularly verify whether the capital, fund and investment requirements are complied with. Article 7 follows up on that, holding that e-money institutions must adopt measures and procedures ensuring their sound and prudent operation.

---

[1008] As discussed before, the second proposal by the European Commission introduced e-money institutions as a specific type of credit institutions. Directive 2000/28/EC of the European Parliament and of the Council of 18 September 2000 amending Directive 2000/12/EC relating to the taking up and pursuit of the business of credit institutions, *OJ* L 275 of 27 October 2000, 37–38. Directive 2000/12/EC of the European Parliament and of the Council of 20 March 2000 relating to the taking up and pursuit of the business of credit institutions (*OJ* L 126 of 26 May 2000, 1–59) was later repealed by Directive 2006/48/EC of the European Parliament and of the Council of 14 June 2006 relating to the taking up and pursuit of the business of credit institutions (recast) (*OJ* L 177 of 30 June 2006, 1–200). Directive 2006/48/EC took over e-money institutions in its article 4 (1) (b). The result of this legislative compromise, in which a special form of credit institutions is created who cannot actually provide credit, has been referred to as awkward. Kohlbach, M. (2004) "Making Sense of Electronic Money", *Journal of Information, Law and Technology*, 4.

WAIVER – Article 8 provides that smaller e-money institutions – whose total amount of liabilities regarding outstanding e-money normally does not exceed EUR 5 million and never exceeds EUR 6 million – or those operating in a limited or local scheme can be waived from compliance with some of the aforementioned requirements.[1009] In such cases, the maximum e-money storage amount is limited to EUR 150.

OTHER PROVISIONS – The directive also provides a grandfathering scheme (article 9), to allow already active e-money institutions to be recognized and continue their operations while they adjust to the new regulatory requirements. The directive was to be implemented by 27 April 2002 (article 10), with a review planned by 27 April 2005 (article 11).

#### 2.1.2.2 DG Internal Market Consultation Paper

DIFFERENT INTERPRETATIONS – As already hinted at in the discussion of the legislative procedure leading up to the adoption of the EMD1, the final definition of e-money can be considered to contain a number of flaws. One of those flaws became visible during the implementation phase of the directive, when it became clear that Member States used different interpretations of the directive, thus resulting in a different treatment of identical cases around the EU.

MOBILE OPERATORS – More particularly, the most notable case concerned the services of mobile operators. When such operators issue prepaid cards that could only be used for making calls using a mobile phone, it can be held that they operate a single-purpose scheme, thus falling outside of the scope of the directive. However, already shortly after the adoption of the directive, the market had evolved. Mobile operators now issued prepaid cards that could be used for a variety of services. For instance, mobile phone users could use the balance on their prepaid cards to purchase goods and services such as ringtones, weather forecasts or concert tickets. That led to the conclusion that Member States could very well consider those mobile operators as running a multi-purpose prepaid card scheme, and thus being an e-money institution.

E-MONEY ISSUANCE – In an initial assessment, the European Commission came to the conclusion that in the cases where the monetary value represented by the prepaid card can be used to obtain goods and services other than call

---

[1009] Note, however, that when a Member State grants a waiver, such waiver only applies within that Member State. A waived institution therefore cannot benefit from the passporting scheme. Weber, R. (2001) "The European E-Money Directive: Background, Problems, and Prospects", *Yearbook of International Financial & Economic Law*, Vol. 5, 301.

minutes, from a wider range of service providers than the mobile operator, the mobile operator issuing such prepaid cards does indeed issue e-money.[1010] The European Commission therefore consulted market players to hear about their precise business models, in order to assess how the situation works in practice and what an appropriate response should entail.

Difficulties for mobile operators – From the stakeholder consultation, it became clear that the legal uncertainty regarding the issue was damaging the market.[1011] As could be expected, the telecom sector did not react positively to the idea that they might become subject to the requirements and supervision imposed by the EMD1, holding that such could have "*potential negative impact on the development of new market segments*", and that the "*costs of regulation would in any case be disproportionate to the expected benefits*".[1012] Other stakeholders – mainly e-money associations, payment service providers and banking associations – on the other hand argued to cover all e-money institutions under the same regulatory framework.[1013] Mobile operators argued that their services constitute little risk to financial stability or consumer protection, and that their financial solidity is already checked by authorities before being granted a license to operate.[1014] Moreover, it was found that mobile operators generally act as an intermediary between the consumer/mobile phone user and the merchant of services or goods that can be purchased by the consumer, which contradicts the spirit of the directive – which considers e-money as a substitute for cash, thus not necessitating an intermediary.[1015] Also the redeemability requirement was found by mobile operators to be highly difficult to implement in practice.[1016] Generally, the mobile operators that participated in the consultation process refer to "*the Lisbon process and the Commission commitments made in the Information Society policy context to stress that this sector needs a different treatment and needs more than other a certain regulatory flexibility*".[1017]

---

1010 European Commission (2004) "Consultation paper of DG Internal Market – Application of the E-money Directive to mobile operators", *ec.europa.eu*, 7–8.

1011 European Commission (2005) "Application of the E-money Directive to mobile operators – Summary of replies to the Consultation paper of DG Internal Market", *ec.europa.eu*, 2.

1012 *Ibid.*, 2.

1013 *Ibid.*, 4.

1014 *Ibid.*, 5.

1015 *Ibid.*, 8.

1016 *Ibid.*, 11. For instance, it was argued that the funds received in exchange for the prepaid cards are used by mobile operators to cover their operating costs. Having to hold parts of these funds for redeemability purposes would necessitate the development of a new financial operational model.

1017 European Commission (2005) "Application of the E-money Directive to mobile operators – Summary of replies to the Consultation paper of DG Internal Market", *ec.europa.eu*, 15.

Hybrid issuers – The European Commission – in its initial assessment and in a later guidance document[1018] – considered mobile operators as 'hybrid' e-money issuers, in the sense that the e-money issuance is a side effect of their business and not a core element of their general activities. While e-money associations stressed the need to preserve the level playing field for all market players, the telecom sector mainly called upon its special status to receive an exclusion of the sector from the scope of the EMD1.[1019] The European Commission focused mainly on the status of mobile operators acting as an intermediary, transferring the payment between consumer and third-party merchant.[1020] In such cases, it is argued, there is no e-money relationship as such requires a direct debtor-creditor relation between consumer and merchant.[1021] The Commission therefore supported the application of waivers to mobile operators and aimed to look for a better long-term solution during its review of the directive.[1022]

Other sectors? – As will become clear in the next sub-section, this skirmish between the European Commission and the telecom sector proved to be only the first in a long list of issues underlying the application of the EMD1. While for now the application of the directive to the telecom sector could be waived, questions remained regarding what this means for other sectors and for how long such a waiver could be applied.[1023]

#### 2.1.2.3 Implementation in Member States

Transposition period – According to its article 10, the EMD1 had to be transposed into national law by the Member States by 27 April 2002. Article 11 required the European Commission to report to the European Parliament and the Council on particular aspects regarding the application of the directive by 27 April 2005. To fulfill that obligation, the Commission launched a consultation on 14 July 2005.[1024]

---

1018 European Commission (2005) "Application of the E-money Directive to mobile operators – Guidance Note from the Commission Services", *ec.europa.eu*.

1019 European Commission (2005) "Application of the E-money Directive to mobile operators – Summary of replies to the Consultation paper of DG Internal Market", *ec.europa.eu*, 17–18.

1020 European Commission (2005) "Application of the E-money Directive to mobile operators – Guidance Note from the Commission Services", *ec.europa.eu*, 4.

1021 *Id.*

1022 *Ibid.*, 4–5.

1023 Lelieveldt, for instance, questions the reasoning of the European Commission – namely that this nascent market needed a lighter regulatory approach to support innovation and development – since shortly after the consultation process it already became clear that this sector was already developing very well. It is therefore questioned whether the European Commission would impose a threshold from where the service providers concerned here would be considered as regular e-money institutions. Lelieveldt, S. (2006) "Impact of the E-Money Directive – Its application to 'hybrid' operators issuing e-money", presented at the E-Money Directive (2000/46/EC) – Round Table Meeting, Brussels, 8 March 2006, *simonl.org*.

1024 European Commission (2005) "Questionnaire on the Electronic Money Directive (2000/46/EC)", *ec.europa.eu*, 13p.

Consultation outcome – The responses to the Commission's questionnaire and the results of further analyses were presented on 17 February 2006.[1025] In the report, it is remarked that the e-money market had changed significantly since the legislative procedure leading up to the adoption of the directive, and that the directive may have ended up constraining the development of this market rather than supporting it.[1026] That became clear in the market analysis conducted as part of the report, where it is found that multi-purpose prepaid cards in 2003 only represented 0,7% of all cashless payment transactions in the EU-15.[1027] A new development in the market at the time were smartcards for transportation, often using contactless technology.[1028] Also pre-funded online payment schemes – such as PayPal – were noted as growing rapidly and becoming e-money's new paradigm.[1029] The report also addressed a number of developments of which it at that time was still unclear whether they constituted e-money or not. Such developments include e-vouchers and prepaid services of mobile operators.[1030] In terms of market size, it was reported that only a handful of market players had been registered as e-money institutions, most of them in the UK.[1031]

Differences between Member States – Regarding the implementation of the directive by the Member States, it was found that national rules on the subject vary significantly.[1032] Many Member States only transposed the directive after the deadline, and only two Member States held an extensive consultation of industry representatives.[1033] While the definition of e-money was generally found appropriate, the results from the Commission's questionnaire revealed a clear call for clarification of certain principles, as they have allowed for a broad range of different interpretations.[1034] The main issue with the definition was the criterion that e-money must be "*issued on receipt of funds of an amount not less in value than the monetary value issued*". Here, several Member States were found to have limited that criterion to "*issued on receipt of funds*", or to have added a

1025 The Evaluation Partnership ltd. (2006) "Evaluation of the E-money Directive (2000/46/EC) – final report", *ec.europa.eu*, 168p.

1026 *Ibid.*, 11.

1027 *Ibid.*, 22. Even the Belgian Proton system – the most widely used card-based e-money scheme in the EU – failed to reach its projected goals. Moreover, use of this system peaked in 2002 and has been decreasing ever since, before being completely phased out in 2015.

1028 *Ibid.*, 27–28. Here, some discussion remains on the precise qualification of such schemes. Transport for London, for instance, argues that it acts as an intermediary – using the same reasoning as mobile operators – and that their scheme therefore does not constitute e-money.

1029 *Ibid.*, 30.

1030 *Ibid.*, 33.

1031 *Ibid.*, 35. As reason for operating within the UK, the report cites the risk-weighted approach maintained by the Financial Services Authority (FSA, since then this responsibility has been shifted to the new Financial Conduct Authority (FCA)).

1032 *Ibid.*, 44.

1033 *Id.*

1034 *Ibid.*, 46–47.

prohibition on the issuance of e-money at a discount, or to have even completely omitted this criterion.[1035] Regarding e-money institutions, most Member States seem to agree that those are a particular type of credit institutions, or that at least similar rules apply to them.[1036] In practice, however, some Member States were found to apply the same strict rules of credit institutions to e-money institutions – thus imposing heavy requirements to a developing market – while others had a more differentiated approach.[1037] Other principles – such as capital requirements, redeemability, restriction of other activities, and limitation of investments – were clearer to lawmakers, but were generally found to be too onerous by industry stakeholders.[1038] Verification was found to vary greatly, with some Member States demanding monthly reports and others only demanding a report two times a year.[1039] Similarly, the application of the waiver system varies greatly, potentially leading market players to opt for settlement in a more lenient Member State.[1040] Regarding hybrid e-money issuers – mainly mobile network operators – most Member States were found to have exempted such issuers, based on the absence of a direct consumer-merchant relationship in the schemes they operate.[1041] It is noted that such uncertainty also applies to the aforementioned account-based schemes, e-vouchers and transport smartcards.[1042]

Meeting the regulatory objectives? – In terms of achieving the regulatory objectives of the directive, it was found that the EMD1 did create more legal certainty regarding the status of e-money institutions, but left open questions regarding scope and applicability and allowed for diverse interpretations.[1043] Such was argued to hinder the development of this market. While another goal of the directive was to not hamper technological innovation, many stakeholders now seemed to subscribe to the Economic and Social Committee's earlier opinion that the text was too focused on card-based schemes.[1044] While the directive did open the playing field for more institutions than the classic credit institutions, especially industry players seem to question whether the playing field is truly level.[1045] On the other hand, due to certain requirements being received as excessive, most stakeholders do agree that the directive managed to

1035 *Ibid.*, 48.
1036 *Ibid.*, 51.
1037 *Ibid.*, 52.
1038 *Ibid.*, 54.
1039 *Ibid.*, 58.
1040 *Ibid.*, 63–64.
1041 *Ibid.*, 65.
1042 For PayPal, for instance, some Member States at the time considered this service as e-money issuance, while others considered the account-scheme not to be different from regular deposit-taking business. *Ibid.*, 66.
1043 *Ibid.*, 71.
1044 *Ibid.*, 77–78.
1045 *Ibid.*, 82.

ensure stability and soundness of e-money institutions.[1046] Last, the passporting scheme was found to be adequate, but more limited than the passporting rights of banks.[1047] However, it should be noted that similarly disappointing growth was recorded outside of the EU as well, where the directive of course did not apply. It is, therefore, not just the EMD1 that limited the growth of e-money, but perhaps rather the lack of a convincing use-case. One notable success story is Hong Kong's Octopus Card, which started out from a clear use-case with a significant demand – namely to serve as a means for paying public transport fare – and gradually expanded its use. That is in clear contrast with most European e-money schemes – such as the Belgian Proton – which just started as general means of payment without being built around a particular use-case or corresponding demand.

Findings – The problems encountered during the transposition of the directive by the Member States and the application of these provisions to all relevant stakeholders confirm a few earlier concerns. As noted by the Economic and Social Committee during the legislative procedure, the text of the proposed E-money Directive was too much focused on multi-purpose prepaid cards. While network money was principally already included in the notion e-money, the consultation showed that in practice this was not so clear or straightforward. As card-based schemes were found to not have reached their projected success, a reorientation of the directive seems in order. Second, certain elements of the e-money definition were found to be unclear or problematic. Such was mainly found to be the case for the inclusion of the redeemability requirement in the definition, introduced by the Council of the European Union. Overall, the definition allowed for too broad a range of interpretations, leading to uncertainty regarding the application of the directive to several services, such as transport smartcards, account-based online schemes, and services by mobile network operators. Third, many stakeholders within the e-money industry found the requirements imposed on e-money institutions too onerous. That may have been reflected in the market, as only very few e-money institutions were registered at the time of the consultation – though, as noted, e-money growth proved disappointing worldwide.

#### 2.1.2.4 Review

New approach – Following the final report on the consultation, the European Commission presented a working document regarding the review of the EMD1 on 19 July 2006.[1048] In that document, the Commission acknowledged that the

---

1046 *Ibid.*, 86. As a result, most industry stakeholders did call for a more differentiated risk-based approach. Some e-money institutions were even found to prefer the regular banking regime, as it would allow more flexibility in managing and investing their float.

1047 *Ibid.*, 89.

1048 European Commission (2006) "Commission Staff working document on the Review of the E-Money Directive (2000/46/EC)", *ec.europa.eu*, SEC(2006) 1049.

EMD1 did not succeed at achieving its projected goals and that a new approach may be needed.[1049] Reference was also made to the legislative procedure underlying the PSD1, which was ongoing at that point.[1050] To eliminate overlaps between those directives, it was already then proposed to investigate the possibilities for integrating their texts.[1051]

Clarifications – Generally, the working document confirmed and summarized the findings of the consultation report. It also proposed a number of specific aspects that should be improved. First, in terms of scope the definition of e-money must be clarified.[1052] For instance, it must be clarified that the definition also covers server-based e-money. The issuance requirement added by the Council of the European Union was proposed to be removed from the definition.[1053] It must also be clarified which services can or cannot be understood as falling under the scope of the directive, to prevent uncertainties as was the case for mobile network operators. Second, while the core requirements regarding redeemability, initial capital, own funds, limitation of investments and restriction of activities would be retained, they should be made less onerous and more proportionate.[1054] Third, more uniform waiver and passporting regimes should be implemented.[1055]

Impact assessment – Before proposing amendments to the EMD1, the Commission conducted an impact assessment in 2008.[1056] Here, the Commission identifies two aspects of the problem, namely that (1) the definition of e-money and the scope of the directive were unclear, and (2) that the legal framework – mainly the prudential requirements and the waivers – was inadequate.[1057] Also here, it was acknowledged that the e-money market failed to develop as expected, with only a handful of e-money institutions registered and the most valuable market player –

---

1049 *Ibid.*, 3; Wilusz, D. (2011) "Legal determinants of electronic money systems development in European Union", *Prawny i ekonomiczny przegląd prawa gospodarczego*, vol. 2, 129.

1050 European Commission (2006) "Commission Staff working document on the Review of the E-Money Directive (2000/46/EC)", *ec.europa.eu*, SEC(2006) 1049, 3.

1051 However, it was also noted that such integration would delay the Payment Services Directive, which still needed to be adopted in time for the SEPA deadline. The 'middle ground' proposed was to first correct the faults in the EMD1 and to later integrate those provisions into the Payment Services Directive. *Ibid.*, 11.

1052 *Ibid.*, 11. See also: Athanassiou, P. (2006) "When is e-money not e-money? Reflections on the revision of the E-money Directive", *Euredia*, nr. 2006/3-4, 334–335.

1053 European Commission (2006) "Commission Staff working document on the Review of the E-Money Directive (2000/46/EC)", *ec.europa.eu*, SEC(2006) 1049, 11.

1054 *Ibid.*, 12–13.

1055 *Ibid.*, 13–14.

1056 European Commission (2008) "Draft Commission Staff working document – Accompanying document to the proposal for a Directive of the European Parliament and of the Council amending Directive 2000/46/EC on the taking up, pursuit of and prudential supervision of the business of electronic money institutions – Impact Assessment", *ec.europa.eu*, SEC(2008)2573.

1057 *Ibid.*, 6.

PayPal – eventually registering as a traditional credit institution.[1058] Moreover, a significant incompatibility with the by then adopted PSD1 was identified, in that the activities that can be exercised by payment service providers are broader than those that can be exercised by e-money institutions, thus prohibiting a service provider from holding both types of licenses.[1059] In order to remedy the problems of the EMD1, the impact assessment proposed five packages of options: (1) do nothing, (2) release a guidance note, (3) align e-money with the PSD1 using the regulatory regime proposed there, (4) align e-money with the PSD1 while retaining a separate prudential regime, or (5) repeal the EMD1.[1060] It was clear that options 1 and 5 would do nothing to improve the legal uncertainty regarding e-money. Option 2 would be insufficient, as a non-binding note would not change the regulatory regime, leaving only options 3 and 4 as feasible. Option 3's proposal to merge e-money institutions into the payment service providers under the PSD1 was considered feasible given the limited impact of e-money on the market.[1061] Option 4 would be stricter, integrating e-money to some extent into the framework set by the PSD1, but keeping a separate prudential regime that allows for specific requirements for e-money institutions.[1062]

Proposal for a new directive – On 9 October 2008, the European Commission presented its proposal for the review of the EMD1.[1063] Given the rather fundamental changes made, the Commission proposed to repeal the existing directive and implement a new framework.[1064] Generally, the proposal aimed to provide a simpler and more neutral definition, together with the use of the fourth policy option proposed in the impact assessment whereby certain aspects of the regulatory regime for payment service providers are combined with some requirements specific to e-money institutions.[1065] Overall, the Commission seemed to have moved away from the stricter regime that was implemented as part of its earlier compromise with the ECB. In terms of scope, the proposed new directive applies to payment service providers that issue e-money.[1066] Limited-purpose instruments – such as store cards, transport cards, membership cards and meal vouchers – are explicitly excluded from the scope, as are the services to which the operator added intrinsic value "*e.g. in the form of access, search or distribution*

1058 *Ibid.*, 7.
1059 *Ibid.*, 11.
1060 *Ibid.*, 22–24.
1061 *Ibid.*, 27.
1062 *Ibid.*, 30.
1063 European Commission (2008) "Proposal for a Directive of the European Parliament and of the Council on the taking up, pursuit and prudential supervision of the business of electronic money institutions, amending Directives 2005/60/EC and 2006/48/EC and repealing Directive 2000/46/EC", *ec.europa.eu*, COM(2008) 0627.
1064 *Ibid.*, 6.
1065 *Ibid.*, 6–7.
1066 *Ibid.*, recital 5.

*facilities*".[1067] In terms of definition, e-money is considered as "*a monetary value as represented by a claim on the issuer which is stored electronically and issued on receipt of funds, for the purpose of making payment transactions as defined in Article 4(5) of Directive 2007/64/EC, and is accepted by natural or legal persons other than the issuer*".[1068] The main deviations from the definition under the EMD1 were the removal of the notion 'stored on an electronic device' in favor of 'stored electronically', the reduction of the second element to 'issued on receipt of funds' – as it was already interpreted by a number of Member States – and the addition of the notion that e-money must be used for making payment transactions as defined under the PSD1. The issuing of e-money is reserved for e-money institutions, credit institutions and payment service providers (article 4).[1069] Redeemability at par value is maintained, be it that fees can only be charged if redemption is asked before the date of the termination of the contract (article 5). While a number of prudential rules are shared between the PSD1 and the proposed EMD2 (article 3), the proposal included separate rules regarding initial capital (article 6) and own funds (article 7) for e-money institutions. The limitation of activities had been loosened, allowing e-money institutions to also offer payment services and granting certain credit (article 8).[1070] Furthermore, the proposal introduced a more straightforward waiver regime (article 10). Regarding the precise status of e-money institutions, the proposal amends the Capital Requirements Directive to reflect e-money institutions as financial institutions that issue e-money, and thus no longer as a specific type of credit institution (article 17).

ECB OPINION – In its opinion, the ECB expressed concern over the requalification of e-money institutions as financial institutions and over the lighter supervisory regime proposed by the European Commission.[1071] More in particular, the ECB did not agree with the statement that e-money institutions do not take deposits.[1072] The ECB reasoned that, under the definition of credit institutions as "*undertaking*

1067 *Ibid.*, recital 5 and article 1. The latter are essentially the services offered by mobile operators that were the subject of the earlier discussion.

1068 *Ibid.*, article 2 (2).

1069 Important to note here is that the concepts of 'e-money issuer' and 'e-money institution' must be clearly separated here. All e-money institutions under the directive are also e-money issuers. However, not all e-money issuers are e-money institutions. This distinction is important since some of the provisions – such as the requirements regarding initial capital, own funds, and other activities are only applicable to e-money institutions, and thus not to other e-money issuers.

1070 Note that article 9 adds additional safeguarding requirements.

1071 ECB (2008) "Opinion of the European Central Bank of 5 December 2008 on a proposal for a Directive on the taking up, pursuit and prudential supervision of the business of electronic money institutions", *OJ* C 30 of 9 February 2009, 1–9.

1072 While the EMD1 indeed stated that e-money issuing does not constitute deposit-taking, recital 8 did also state that "*receipt of funds from the public in exchange for electronic money, which results in a credit balance left on account with the issuing institution, constitutes the receipt of deposits or other repayable funds*". Following this, "*the ECB considers that receiving funds in this manner amounts to deposit-taking*" as every receipt of money could amount to deposit-taking if repayment of the money received is involved.

*the business of which is to take deposits or other repayable funds from the public and to grant credits for its own account*"[1073], an undertaking must be allowed to conduct both deposit-taking and credit-granting activities by its statutes in order to be considered as a credit institution.[1074] While credit-granting was an activity prohibited to e-money institutions under the EMD1, the Commission's proposal for a new directive allows this activity. Thus, the ECB argued, e-money institutions would become even more aligned with the definition of credit institutions than they were before, while suddenly becoming requalified as financial institutions.[1075] Such a requalification could lead to difficulties, for instance regarding reserve requirements.[1076] The ECB was also fairly critical regarding the proposed new supervisory framework, fearing that the closer integration of e-money into the legal framework for payment services weakens consumer protection.[1077] Regarding the proposed e-money definition, the ECB found that the definition is broadly formulated and could even include regular bank accounts.[1078]

EcoSoc opinion – While the European Economic and Social Committee originally also took a stricter stance in its opinion on the proposal for the EMD1, it now seemed to have relaxed that position. Referring to the 2008 credit crisis, the Committee found an adequate and proportionate proposal, not applying to the banks that caused that crisis.[1079] While calling for the inclusion of more consumer protection measures and a better alignment with anti-money laundering principles, the Committee generally found the proposal to give the e-money market a second chance.[1080] It was found that the definition had been clarified and that server-based e-money was now fully included in the scope.[1081] Regarding the prohibition on deposit-taking activities, the Committee proposed to have e-money institutions convert their received funds immediately into e-money.[1082]

1073 Article 4(1)(1) Regulation (EU) No 575/2013 of the European Parliament and of the Council of 26 June 2013 on prudential requirements for credit institutions and investment firms and amending Regulation (EU) No 648/2012, *OJ* L 176 of 27 June 2013, 1–337.

1074 ECB (2008) "Opinion of the European Central Bank of 5 December 2008 on a proposal for a Directive on the taking up, pursuit and prudential supervision of the business of electronic money institutions", *OJ* C 30 of 9 February 2009, 2.

1075 *Ibid.*, 4–5.

1076 *Ibid.*, 5–6.

1077 *Ibid.*, 6–7.

1078 *Ibid.*, 8.

1079 European Economic and Social Committee (2009) "Opinion of the European Economic and Social Committee on the Proposal for a directive of the European Parliament and of the Council on the taking up, pursuit and prudential supervision of the business of electronic money institutions, amending Directives 2005/60/EC and 2006/48/EC and repealing Directive 2000/46/EC", *OJ* C 218 of 11 September 2009, paragraph 1.8.

1080 *Ibid.*, paragraphs 1.9, 1.13 and 1.15.

1081 *Ibid.*, paragraph 3.3.

1082 *Ibid.*, paragraph 4.3.2.

European Parliament committee – On 16 February 2009, the European Parliament's Committee on Economic and Monetary Affairs reported on the proposal.[1083] Also here, the consensus was that the strict regime imposed by the EMD1 prevented the development of the e-money market rather than supporting it and that a new approach was needed.[1084] Generally, the reporting committee was very positive about the proposal, hoping that the alignment of e-money institutions with payment institutions would bring the boost needed by the market.[1085] Most of the amendments proposed by the reporting committee were aimed at clarifying terms and provisions or at ensuring correct alignment between the proposed EMD2 and the PSD1 to which it refers extensively. Regarding the e-money definition, the committee added that e-money could also be stored magnetically, and not just electronically.[1086] It also proposed a higher minimum for the initial capital requirement[1087] and stricter own funds requirements.[1088]

Council compromise package – While the proposal was being discussed in the European Parliament's Committee on Economic and Monetary Affairs, the Committee of Permanent Representatives (COREPER II) on 25 March 2009 also proposed a number of amendments in the form of a draft overall compromise package.[1089] That package was submitted to the European Parliament as a single amendment, with the understanding that if the European Parliament were to adopt the amendment, an agreement between all institutions was reached at the stage of first reading.[1090] One of the notable changes introduced was the notion that if a limited-purpose instrument were to develop into a general-purpose instrument, the exemption should no longer apply.[1091] The viewpoints that e-money issuance does not constitute a deposit-taking activity and that e-money institutions should not be considered as credit institutions had been maintained.[1092] In terms of scope, the amended proposal added a few other institutions that can issue e-money as well.[1093] Regarding definition, the

1083 European Parliament (2009) "Report on the proposal for a directive of the European Parliament and of the Council on the taking up, pursuit and prudential supervision of the business of electronic money institutions, amending Directives 2005/60/EC and 2006/48/EC and repealing Directive 2000/46/EC", *europarl.europa.eu*, A6–0056/2009.

1084 *Ibid.*, 28.

1085 *Ibid.*, 29.

1086 *Ibid.*, amendment 9.

1087 Set at EUR 200.000 instead of EUR 125.000. *Ibid.*, amendment 14.

1088 *Ibid.*, amendments 15 and 16.

1089 Council of the European Union (2009) "Proposal for a Directive of the European Parliament and of the Council of on the taking up, pursuit and prudential supervision of the business of electronic money institutions, amending Directives 2005/60/EC and 2006/48/EC and repealing Directive 2000/46/EC – Letter to European Parliament", *consilium.europa*.eu, 7760/09.

1090 *Ibid.*, 3.

1091 *Ibid.*, recital 5.

1092 *Ibid.*, recitals 13 and 25.

1093 *Ibid.*, article 1 (1). More in particular, this concerns credit institutions, post office giro institutions, national central banks and the ECB when not acting in their capacities as authority

COREPER II amendment also included the reference to magnetic storage, as found in the European Parliament's reporting Committee's amendments.[1094] It also included broader prudential rules and a higher initial capital requirement of EUR 350.000.[1095] Regarding other activities, the amendment maintained that e-money institutions can grant credit - but no interest - be it that such credit cannot be granted from the funds covered by the safeguarding requirement and that funds received should be exchanged for e-money without delay.[1096]

Adoption – In order to allow the legislative matter to be resolved before the 2009 European elections, the European Parliament swiftly adopted the COREPER II amendment.[1097] The text adopted by the European Parliament on 24 April 2009[1098] received the endorsement of the European Commission[1099] and of the Council and was thus approved.[1100] The EMD2 was adopted on 16 September 2009.[1101]

### 2.1.3 *Second E-money Directive*

#### 2.1.3.1 Directive

EMD2 – As noted, the EMD2 is the second major attempt by the EU to regulate the matter of e-money. Its first attempt, the 2000 directive, had attained some of its original objectives but never managed to result in absolute legal certainty for the user in this field, due to its unclear scope of application.[1102] Even more

---

and Member State authorities when acting in their capacities as public authorities. Note that the payment service providers included in the original proposal are no longer included.

1094 *Ibid.*, article 2 (2).

1095 *Ibid.*, articles 3, 6 and 10c. Though this initial capital requirement is still significantly lower than the EMD1's EUR 1 million requirement.

1096 *Ibid.*, article 8.

1097 However, the rapporteur of the Committee on Economic and Monetary Affairs explicitly stated being "*rushed through the legislative process for a first-reading agreement in order to get this measure enacted before the European elections*" and even held that the compromise text still has the prospect of an uneven playing field. European Parliament (2009) "Debates Friday 24 April 2009 - CRE 24/04/2009 - 3", *europarl.europa.eu*, A6-0056/2009.

1098 European Parliament (2009) "Position of the European Parliament adopted at first reading on 24 April 2009 with a view to the adoption of Directive 2009/.../EC of the European Parliament and of the Council on the taking up, pursuit and prudential supervision of the business of electronic money institutions amending Directives 2005/60/EC and 2006/48/EC and repealing Directive 2000/46/EC", *europarl.europa.eu*, EP-PE_TC1-COD(2008)0190.

1099 European Commission (2009) "Commission Communication on the action taken on opinions and resolutions adopted by Parliament at the April 2009 I and II part-sessions", *ec.europa.eu*, SP(2009)3507.

1100 Council of the European Union (2009) "Directive of the European Parliament and of the Council on the taking up, pursuit and prudential supervision of the business of electronic money institutions amending Directives 2005/60/EC and 2006/48/EC and repealing Directive 2000/46/EC", *consilium.europa.eu*, PE-CONS 3666/09.

1101 See footnote 856.

1102 For instance, "*questions about if and how the legal framework should apply to certain schemes (certain account-based schemes, electronic vouchers) and issuers (mobile network operators,*

so, "*some of its provisions were considered to have hindered the emergence of a true single market for electronic money services and the development of such user-friendly services*".[1103] Noting the legal framework set by the PSD1, the 2009 revision of the E-money Directive aims to create a level playing field. Interesting to note is that the directive also – in part – calls for full harmonization in this matter, aiming at equal implementation throughout the EU.[1104] Also, in order to allow for a more elaborate market to flourish in this field, the 2009 directive considers electronic money institutions as financial institutions instead of the more heavily regulated credit institutions.

Scope – Important to note in terms of scope, is that the EMD2 clearly wants to maintain a limited focus.[1105] Therefore, the directive does not apply to monetary value stored on specific prepaid instruments with a limited scope, such as "*store cards, petrol cards, membership cards, public transport cards, meal vouchers or vouchers for services*".[1106] That limitation of scope seems to include loyalty reward programs, which can offer a certain value to their users, but are generally limited to a specific purpose. However, the directive also states that these programs are only exempt from its scope because of their use limitations. If a scheme expands beyond its original platform and becomes a general-purpose instrument, it can and should fall within the scope of the directive.[1107] For other scope limitations, the EMD2 directly references the two main scope limitations of the Payment Services Directive.[1108]

E-money definition – The EMD2 is mainly aimed at the providers of e-money services, being the e-money institutions.[1109] A major departure from the EMD1 is that such e-money institutions are no longer regarded as a specific form of credit institutions. Only the properly registered e-money institutions, as well as credit institutions, post office giro institutions, the ECB and national central banks, and Member States or their regional or local authorities are allowed to issue e-money.[1110] E-money is defined as "*electronically, including magnetically, stored monetary value as represented by a claim on the issuer which is issued on receipt of funds for the purpose of making payment transactions as defined in*

*transport providers) have led to a considerable degree of legal uncertainty*". The Evaluation Partnership Limited, "Evaluation of the E-money Directive (2000/46/EC) – Final Report", *ec.europa.eu*, 2006, 7–8.

1103 Recital 2 EMD2.

1104 Article 16 EMD2.

1105 Recital 5 EMD2.

1106 *Id.*

1107 Recital 5 EMD2.

1108 Article 1 (4) and (5) EMD2. These two scope limitations will be further discussed in the analysis of the Payment Services Directives in section 3.2.2.

1109 Article 1 EMD2.

1110 Article 10 EMD2.

*point 5 of Article 4 of Directive 2007/64/EC, and which is accepted by a natural or legal person other than the electronic money issuer".*[1111]

RULES FOR SERVICE PROVIDERS – As noted in the discussion of the legislative procedure leading up to this directive, the EMD2 contains specific rules on how e-money institutions can conduct their business, including procedural rules in case of a corporate merger or takeover, clearly referencing the framework set by the PSD1.[1112] The rules set on initial capital and own funds that need to be held by electronic money institutions have been loosened, with the initial capital requirement down to EUR 350.000.[1113] While e-money institutions can also provide additional services – such as the payment services defined in the annex of the PSD1 – they must also adopt safeguards for the funds they have acquired in exchange for the e-money that has been issued.[1114] If the e-money institution has not generated an average outstanding e-money of more than EUR 5.000.000 – or less, as defined by the Member States – the Member States can exempt that institution from certain of the requirements for registration.[1115] E-money must still be issued and redeemed at par value with received funds.[1116] The directive clearly states which transactions may become subject to fees, but prohibits granting interest or other benefits relating to the duration of the user's holding of the electronic money funds.[1117] As under the PSD1, the EMD2 provides for an out-of-court complaint and redress procedure for the settlement of disputes.[1118]

#### 2.1.3.2 Implementation in the Member States

TRANSPOSITION – The EMD2 should have been transposed by the Member States by 30 April 2011.[1119] A first review was envisioned together with that of the PSD1, by November 2012.[1120] The transposition of the EMD2 has proven to be a difficult process. By May 2012, a year after the deadline set by the directive, there were still six Member States – Belgium, Spain, France, Cyprus, Poland and Portugal – that needed to implement these provisions.[1121] By November 2012, only Belgium still had not transposed the directive, with the European Commission referring the case to the European Court of Justice and asking for a

1111 Article 2 (2) EMD2.
1112 Article 3 EMD2.
1113 Article 4 – 5 EMD2.
1114 Article 6 – 7 EMD2.
1115 Article 9 EMD2.
1116 Article 11 EMD2.
1117 Article 11 – 12 EMD2.
1118 Article 13 EMD2.
1119 Article 22 EMD2.
1120 Article 17 EMD2.
1121 *Europa.eu/rapid/press-release_IP-12-418_en.htm.*

daily fine of almost EUR 60.000.[1122] The Belgian act implementing the directive was adopted within days of this notice.[1123]

IMPACT ASSESSMENT DELAYED – Because of the delays in the transposition, the European Commission postponed its planned impact assessment. In 2012, only a conformity assessment was conducted.[1124] Overall, it was found that most Member States had transposed the directive in a conform manner, with a few exceptions.[1125]

#### 2.1.3.3 Review

RELATIONSHIP TO PSD1 – From the moment the legislative work on the PSD1 began, several members of the advisory groups set up by the European Commission have proposed to merge the legal frameworks on payment services and e-money, especially when it became clear that the EMD2 would to substantial extent lean on the principles set by the PSD1.[1126]

PSD1 REVIEW – On 24 July 2013, the European Commission presented its strategy for the review of the PSD1.[1127] Due to the late implementation of the EMD2 by a large number of Member States, it was found that there has not been enough time to fully judge the practical experiences with the framework. The review for the EMD2 was therefore pushed back to 2014, thus ruling out a merger between both frameworks at least for the time being.[1128] In 2013, the European Commission confirmed that a study evaluating the impact of the EMD2 had been contracted, due to be delivered in September 2014.[1129] While the PSD1 was repealed and replaced by a Second Payment Services Directive (PSD2) in 2015,

---

1122 *Europa.eu/rapid/press-release_IP-12-1248_en.htm.*

1123 Act of 27 November 2012 amending the act of 21 December 2009 concerning the statute of payment institutions, access to the profession of payment service provider and access to payment systems and of other acts relating to the statute of payment institutions and institutions for electronic money and of the credit institutions of the professional credit, *Belgian State Gazette* 30 November 2012.

1124 Payments Committee (2012) "Sixth meeting of the Payments Committee, Wednesday, 21 March 2012", *ec.europa.eu*, PC/005/12, 7.

1125 The results of this study are available at: *ec.europa.eu/internal_market/payments/emoney/transposition/by-country_en.htm.*

1126 See, for instance: Payments Council (2012) "Minutes of the Seventh meeting of the Payments Committee, Monday, 9 July 2012", *ec.europa.eu*, PC/010/12, 2; Payment Systems Market Expert Group (2012) "Minutes of the meeting of 27 March 2012, Brussels", *ec.europa.eu*, 3–4.

1127 RAPID Press Release (2013) "New rules on Payment Services for the benefit of consumers and retailers", *IP/13/730* of 24 July 2013.

1128 European Commission (2013) "Proposal for a Directive of the European Parliament and of the Council on payment services in the internal market and amending Directives 2002/65/EC, 2013/36/EU and 2009/110/EC and repealing Directive 2007/64/EC", *COM(2013) 547*, 2–3.

1129 Payment Systems Market Expert Group (2013) "Minutes of the meeting of 24 October 2013, Brussels", *ec.europa*.eu, 5.

the European Commission has yet to announce its plans regarding the review of the EMD2.

### *2.1.4 Evaluation*

Systemic protection – From the earliest discussions on e-money – or e-purses at the time – it becomes clear that the main regulatory goal here was to protect the role of central banks and their monetary policy, as it was feared that e-money issuing by other actors than (central) banks would destabilize those institutions and their policies. Consumer or market protection were only secondary goals, in the sense that consumer trust could be breached by unstable or insecure payment systems. The intention to protect the position and policies of central banks becomes apparent in the push to restrict the issuing of e-money to credit institutions. Also further documents evidence the primary goal of protecting financial integrity. Here, it may be questioned whether that risk was as pertinent as perceived. Moreover, the stringent requirements of the EMD1 were found to, at least in part, have hindered the development of the e-money market.

Specific type of credit institutions – After much debate, e-money institutions were eventually classified as a special type of credit institutions, subject to less stringent requirements. That fulfills the initial regulatory goal of protecting central banks' interests and policies, while still allowing market entry by new participants. However, it did require the consideration that receipt of funds against which e-money is issued cannot constitute deposit-taking, as such is reserved for regular credit institutions. In the second iteration of the e-money legal framework, e-money institutions were reclassified as financial actors other than credit institutions.

E-money – While first the focus was put on e-purses, or multi-purpose prepaid cards, a terminological shift was made to the notion of e-money in order to also capture server-based money. In doing so, the European legislator pursued technological neutrality. Practice, however, proved that the initial definition failed in achieving this goal. The EMD2 has a more neutral definition, but still seems to fail to provide sufficient certainty regarding the precise scope of the notion.

Redeemability – One of the biggest concerns of stakeholders was that e-money issuers would over-issue e-money, and that such would threaten monetary stability. Such an over-issuing was countered by the introduction of the redeemability requirement. However, as will be discussed further on, the redeemability requirement was mistakenly introduced into the definition. Though the matter was remedied during the review, redeemability remains one of the core requirements of e-money.

## 2.2 E-MONEY SCOPE

Goal of analysis – Having analyzed the origins of the current EU-wide legal framework regarding e-money, this section will critically analyze the precise scope of the e-money legal framework. The goal of such an analysis is to assess whether the EMD2 can apply to virtual currencies in its current form in order to provide certainty regarding the legal qualification of such virtual currencies.

### *2.2.1 Definition*

Four elements – Electronic money is defined in the EMD2 as 'electronically, including magnetically, stored monetary value as represented by a claim on the issuer which is issued on receipt of funds for the purpose of making payment transactions as defined in point 5 of Article 4 of Directive 2007/64/EC, and which is accepted by a natural or legal person other than the electronic money issuer'.[1130] The definition includes four constitutive elements that require further analysis: (1) an electronically, including magnetically, stored value (2) that is represented by a claim on the issuer, (3) that is issued on the receipt of funds for making payment transactions, and (4) that is accepted by institutions other than their issuer.

#### 2.2.1.1 Electronically, including magnetically, stored value

Broadened by EMD2 – The first part of the definition includes one of the most important changes brought by the 2009 revision of the E-money Directive. The EMD1 required e-money to be stored on an electronic device.[1131] While it was the aim of the European Commission to introduce technology-neutral terminology, the text of the 2000 directive missed that goal as it was unclear whether the e-money notion could apply to new business models – which include, for instance, loyalty cards, mobile prepaid cards, etc.[1132] Moreover, while the 1997 EMI Council opinion already found[1133] that e-money should include both card-based services – the e-purses that were the subject of the original 1994 Working Group on EU Payment Systems' report – and computer-based services – so-called network money that was developing in the late 1990's – it was unclear whether the reference to 'electronic device' could be interpreted

---

1130 Article 2 (2) EMD2.

1131 Article 1 (3) (b) (i) EMD1.

1132 DLA Piper (2009) "EU study on the Legal analysis of a Single Market for the Information Society – New rules for a new age?", *ec.europa.eu*, 8; Athanassiou, P. (2006) "When is e-money not e-money? Reflections on the revision of the E-money Directive", *Euredia*, nr. 2006/3–4, 335–336; Halpin, R., Moore, R. (2009) "Developments in electronic money regulation – the Electronic Money Directive: A better deal for e-money issuers?", *Computer Law & Security Review*, vol. 25, 565.

1133 EMI (1998) "Annual Report 1997", *ecb.europa.eu*, 74.

as also applying to software-based services.[1134] As a result, under the EMD2 this element was broadened to 'electronically, including magnetically, stored value'.

Exclusion of debit cards – The first part of the definition can be considered as excluding traditional debit cards from the scope of the directive.[1135] After all, such cards are not considered to hold their underlying value on the card itself, and while the e-money definition was expanded to also include e-money not stored directly on a card, traditional debit cards merely function as a means to identify the cardholder and to access the associated account.

Available to bearer – The main criterion to be employed here is that the e-money funds must be available and accessible to the bearer. It is not required for the bearer to physically hold the funds – remote access schemes are therefore allowed as well[1136] – as long as he can use them without the intervention of a third party.[1137] Important to note is that it is not required by the definition that the recipient of an e-money payment can immediately dispose of the funds himself. For instance, in the case of the Belgian multi-purpose prepaid card Proton, funds are transferred from the user's card to the merchant's terminal. The funds remain on that terminal until they are transferred to the merchant's account – which generally only happened every two weeks – only after which they become available to that merchant.[1138, 1139]Such is, however, mainly an issue with card-based e-money as other forms of e-money – such as PayPal – put the funds at the immediate disposal of the recipient.

---

1134 As noted by the European Social and Economic Committee, see section 2.1.1.6 of this chapter. See also: DLA Piper (2009) "EU study on the Legal analysis of a Single Market for the Information Society – New rules for a new age?", *ec.europa.eu*, 8; European Commission (2006) "Commission Staff Working Document on the Review of the E-Money Directive (2000/46/EC)", *SEC(2006) 1049*, 11.

1135 Vereecken, M. (2000) "Electronic Money: EU Legislative Framework", *European Business Law Review*, Vol. 11, 418.

1136 See recital 8 EMD2.

1137 European Commission (2004) "Consultation paper of DG Internal Market – Application of the E-money Directive to mobile operators", *ec.europa.eu*, 7.

1138 Which of course raises the question of when the payment has occurred: when the terminal is credited or when the merchant's account is credited. For more on this: Steennot, R. (2012) "Betaling", In: Dirix, E., Van Oevelen, A. (Eds.) *Bijzondere Overeenkomsten: Artikelsgewijze commentaren*, Mechelen: Kluwer, 40–41.

1139 Note that there are also authors finding the availability of the funds to the recipient to be an essential requirement for e-money. According to this theory, a system such as Proton could not be considered as constituting e-money. Schrans, G., Steennot, R. (2003) *Algemeen deel van het financieel recht*, Antwerpen: Intersentia, 64–65. However, it must be acknowledged that the Belgian legislator does consider a system such as Proton to be e-money. Steennot, R. (2011) "Betalingsdiensten", In: Steennot, R., Stuyck, J., Vanhees, H., Wymeersch, E. (Eds.) *Overzicht Financieel Recht: Artikelsgewijze commentaren*, Mechelen: Kluwer, 19.

No legal tender – Despite the reference to monetary value, it must be stressed that according to the current state of the law, e-money is no legal tender. As analyzed in chapter III, legal tender within the euro area constitutes only the bank notes and coins emitted under the supervision of the European Central Bank.[1140] Consequently, no party to a payment transaction is held to pay or to accept payment in e-money, unless those parties have agreed to do so.[1141] At the same time, however, it must be reminded that traditional debit and credit cards are legal tender neither, yet are widely accepted as means of payment. The legal tender status of a particular means of payment, or lack thereof, therefore has fairly little consequence with regards to its acceptance.

### 2.2.1.2 Represented by a claim on the issuer

Added in legislative proceedings – The requirement that e-money must represent a claim on the issuer was not part of the European Commission's proposal for the EMD1. That requirement was suggested in the ECB's opinion on the Commission's proposal, and formally added to the definition of e-money through the Council's common position. This second part of the definition remained unchanged in the EMD2.

Ownership – The monetary value held electronically must represent a claim on the issuer. That can be interpreted as meaning that the person holding the e-money does not directly own it, but only possesses such a claim.[1142] On the other hand, the presence of such a claim does imply that the holder of e-money can demand reimbursement, which is further evidenced by the redeemability requirement.[1143] In that sense, e-money can be considered as fiduciary money.[1144] Like other forms of fiduciary money, e-money does not derive its

---

1140 For the EU, article 128 of the Treaty on the Functioning of the European Union (TFEU) holds that "*the banknotes issued by the European Central Bank and the national central banks shall be the only such notes to have the status of legal tender within the Union*". For coins, a similar provision is found in article 11 Council Regulation (EC) No 974/98 of 3 May 1998 on the introduction of the euro, *OJ* L 139 of 11 May 1998, 1–5. This view on legal tender was confirmed in: Commission Recommendation of 22 March 2010 on the scope and effects of legal tender of euro banknotes and coins, *OJ* L 83 of 30 March 2010, 70–71.

1141 De Prez, P., Timmermans, V. (2013) "Een doorstart voor het elektronisch geld? Analyse van de nieuwe regelgeving", *Bank en Financieel Recht*, nr. 2013/I, paragraph 12.

1142 Steennot, R. (2011) *Giraal en elektronisch betalingsverkeer*, Mechelen: Kluwer, 51. It also signifies that this issuer holds the ultimate financial responsibility towards the e-money holder. European Central Bank (2000) "Issues arising from the emergence of electronic money", *ECB Monthly Bulletin*, November 2000, 50; De Prez, P., Timmermans, V. (2013) "Een doorstart voor het elektronisch geld? Analyse van de nieuwe regelgeving", *Bank en Financieel Recht*, nr. 2013/I, paragraph 12.

1143 This was also discussed during the legislative procedure concerning the Belgian implementation of the EMD2: *Parl. St.* Kamer, 53-2431/001, 10.

1144 Vereecken, M. (2000) "Electronic Money: EU Legislative Framework", *European Business Law Review*, Vol. 11, 417–418; Weber, R. (2001) "The European E-Money Directive:

value from its intrinsic qualities – such as the value of the metal used in physical coins – but from the understanding that it can be used to conduct payments for their underlying value.[1145]

2.2.1.3 Issued on receipt of funds for making payment transactions

LEGISLATIVE COMPROMISE – The requirement of e-money being issued on receipt of funds was not present in the original discussions regarding e-purses and e-money at the EMI in the 1990's, nor in the European Commission's original proposal for the directive. This third element of the definition was only introduced in one of the later stages of the legislative process leading up to the EMD1, namely in the Council of the European Union's common position. More in particular, the Council introduced the element of "*issued on receipt of funds of an amount not less in value than the monetary value issued*" into the definition of e-money, stating that "*the bearer must always pay in full for the electronic money received*" and that it will "*thus not be possible to issue electronic money for a higher amount than that paid in exchange*".[1146] With that reasoning, the Council seems to have wanted to seek a compromise with the ECB's concern for the over-issuing of e-money, or inflationary schemes.[1147] As noted before[1148], that concern was already addressed by the inclusion of a redeemability requirement. The introduction of the issuance requirement in the definition can therefore be considered as somewhat superfluous, as the redeemability requirement already deals with the ECB's concerns regarding the potential dangers of unrestricted e-money creation.[1149] Moreover, its inclusion in the definition of e-money can be argued to even have adverse results, as it does not prohibit over-issuing of e-money, but simply excludes over-issuing schemes from the scope of the

Background, Problems, and Prospects", *Yearbook of International Financial & Economic Law,* Vol. 5, 302.

1145 *Id.*

1146 Council of the European Union (1999) "Common Position (EC) No 8/2000 adopted by the Council on 29 November 1999 with a view to adopting a Directive 2000/.../EC of the European Parliament and of the Council of ... on the taking-up, pursuit of and prudential supervision of the business of electronic money institutions", *OJ* C 26 of 28 January 2000, 7.

1147 As expressed, for instance, in ECB (1998) "Report on electronic money", *ecb.europa.eu*, 13–14. See also: Kohlbach, M. (2004) "Making Sense of Electronic Money", *Journal of Information, Law and Technology,* 4; Athanassiou, P. (2006) "When is e-money not e-money? Reflections on the revision of the E-money Directive", *Euredia,* nr. 2006/3–4, 337–339.

1148 In the conclusion to section 2.1.1.8.

1149 While one author has argued that this element is integral to the definition of e-money – and proposed to go even further by fully including the redeemability requirement into the definition as well – this reasoning does not appear to fully respond to the criticism voiced by other authors, as well as the problems encountered by the Member States during the implementation of this element. Athanassiou, P., Mas-Guix, N. (2008) "Electronic money institutions", ECB Legal Working Paper Series nr.7, *ssrn.com/abstract_id=1000855*, 20–22.

directive.[1150] In doing so, the schemes feared most by the ECB were not subjected to regulation, but placed outside the e-money legal framework.

Amended by EMD2 – As noted in section 2.1.2.3, it was found that several Member States had issues implementing this particular element of the e-money definition.[1151] As a result, it was changed to "*issued on receipt of funds for the purpose of making payment transactions as defined in point 5 of Article 4 of Directive 2007/64/EC*".[1152] The latter part of this third element brings the EMD2 in line with the PSD1.[1153] A payment transaction according to the PSD1 is an "*act, initiated by the payer or by the payee, of placing, transferring or withdrawing funds, irrespective of any underlying obligations between the payer and the payee*".[1154] That definition is very broad and neutral and aims to cover a whole range of possible transactions whereby a monetary value is transferred between two parties, regardless of the existence of an obligation hereto between them.

Prepaid good – From the requirement that e-money is to be issued on receipt of funds it follows that the issuer of e-money cannot simply create new e-money units at will.[1155] Consequently, the monopoly on money creation remains in the hands of central banks.[1156] Because e-money can only be issued when funds are received thereto[1157], e-money can be considered as a prepaid good.[1158, 1159] The

1150 Lelieveldt, S. (2001) "Why is the Electronic Money-Directive Significant?", *EPSO Newsletter*, 7, May 2001; Vereecken, M. (2001) "A Harmonised EU Legal Framework for Electronic Money", *EPSO Newsletter*, 7, May 2001; Kohlbach, M. (2004) "Making Sense of Electronic Money", *Journal of Information, Law and Technology*, 7–8; DLA Piper (2009) "EU study on the Legal analysis of a Single Market for the Information Society – New rules for a new age?", *ec.europa.eu*, 8; Schudelaro, A. (2003) "To Be or Not to Be Electronic Money, That's the Question", *Information & Communications Technology Law*, Vol. 12, 50; Athanassiou, P. (2006) "When is e-money not e-money? Reflections on the revision of the E-money Directive", *Euredia*, nr. 2006/3–4, 338.

1151 The Evaluation Partnership ltd. (2006) "Evaluation of the E-money Directive (2000/46/EC) – final report", *ec.europa.eu*, 48.

1152 Article 2(2) EMD2.

1153 De Prez, P., Timmermans, V. (2013) "Een doorstart voor het elektronisch geld? Analyse van de nieuwe regelgeving", *Bank en Financieel Recht*, nr. 2013/I, paragraph 12.

1154 Article 4(5) PSD1.

1155 Weber, R., Darbellay, A. (2010) "Legal issues in mobile banking", *Journal of Banking Regulation*, Vol. 11, 135.

1156 Verhaeghe, L. (2013) "PingPing en PayPal: Juridisch kader, rechten en plichten", *Thesis UGent Faculty of Law*, 41–42. Godschalk and Krueger argue that central banks insisted on the inclusion of this criterion precisely to preserve their monopoly. Godschalk, H., Krueger, M. (2000) "Why e-money still fails – chances of e-money within a competitive payment instrument market", presented at the *Third Berlin Internet Economics Workshop*, Berlin, May 26–27, 5.

1157 Though it is reminded that this receipt of funds cannot be considered as deposit-taking. Recitals 13 and 18 and article 6 (2) and (3) EMD2.

1158 *Id.* This of course relates back to the original conception of e-money as being multi-purpose prepaid cards. A clear consequence of this is that traditional credit card schemes are thus excluded from the field of e-money, as these schemes involve a credit line and not access to a prepaid value.

1159 Though the use of the term 'prepaid' has been criticized: it could be argued that the e-money user does not pay on beforehand for the services to be delivered – as is the case for the classic

finding that e-money is a prepaid good may prove to be the main element preventing virtual currency schemes from falling within the scope of the EMD2, as will be discussed in section 2.3.

PAID BY WHOMEVER – The definition does not state by whom the funds upon which e-money is issued must be paid. That is important for the inclusion of certain loyalty schemes – as analyzed in chapter I – under the scope of e-money. If a broad loyalty scheme were to be set up – with an acceptance beyond the issuer and exceeding the limited use scope exemption that will be discussed in section 3.2.2 – in which the scheme operator issues a virtual currency to participating merchants upon payment thereto, the merchants can transfer that virtual currency to their customers, who subsequently become the e-money bearers without being the party having directly provided the funds for their issuing.[1160] However, given the limited scope of most loyalty schemes, that finding may remain mostly theoretical.

#### 2.2.1.4 Accepted by institutions other than their issuer

LIMITATION TO MULTI-PURPOSE INSTRUMENTS – The main goal of the fourth element of the definition is to distinguish multi-purpose instruments from single- or limited-purpose instruments.[1161] The latter are only accepted by their issuer, or within a limited network around the issuer, and are not covered by the scope of the directive. The former are much more broadly accepted, and therefore become subject to the legal framework on e-money. However, the main difficulty with this fourth element of the definition is that there is no guidance regarding the demarcation between limited-purpose and multi-purpose. Such can result in a broad range of different interpretations between Member States.[1162]

REFERENCE TO PSD1 – It should be reminded that the EMD2 refers to exemptions under the PSD1, which also apply to e-money.[1163] Therefore, providers of e-money services could, for instance, be exempt from the scope of application of the EMD2 if they do not act as a mere intermediary. Also, if their services are aimed

single-purpose telephone card – as those services are yet to be determined. E-money in this sense constitutes nothing more than the exchange of traditional money into e-money, and not an advance payment. Fransens, D., Dedryvere, M. (2003) "De juridische draagwijdte van het begrip elektronisch geld: is de lading groter dan de vlag (Deel II)", *Tijdschrift Financieel Recht*, nr. 2003/4, 555–556.

1160 Vereecken, M. (2000) "Electronic Money: EU Legislative Framework", *European Business Law Review*, Vol. 11, 418.

1161 Kohlbach, M. (2004) "Making Sense of Electronic Money", *Journal of Information, Law and Technology*, 4.

1162 DLA Piper (2009) "EU study on the Legal analysis of a Single Market for the Information Society – New rules for a new age?", *ec.europa.eu*, 8; Athanassiou, P., Mas-Guix, N. (2008) "Electronic money institutions", ECB Legal Working Paper Series nr.7, *ssrn.com/abstract_id=1000855*, 22.

1163 Which, as noted, will be further discussed in section 3.2.2 of this chapter.

at a 'limited network' of providers or a 'limited range' of goods and services, they will also be exempt from the e-money legal framework. Those exemptions clearly refer to the fourth element of the e-money definition, indicating that a limited range of acceptance of a virtual currency can be considered as impeding its qualification as e-money under the scope of the EMD2.[1164] The idea that e-money must be broadly accepted can be said to stem from the intention of e-money to serve as "*surrogate for coins and banknotes*".[1165] The exemptions to the PSD1 and PSD2 will be more elaborately discussed below, in section 3.2.2.

### *2.2.2 Redeemability*

Issued at par value – Another element that must be taken into account – while since the EMD2 no longer being explicitly part of the definition itself – is that e-money must be issued at par value.[1166] That means that the user must be allowed to have the monetary value of his e-money redeemed.[1167] In order to facilitate such redemption, it can thus be found that the EMD2 preserves a clear link between e-money and its physical world counterpart.[1168] Though neither directive explicitly states that e-money must be redeemed in the same denomination as that of the funds against which it was issued, it is clear that such was at least the ECB's intention behind the redeemability requirement.[1169]

---

1164 And it has been argued that these exceptions at least to some extent clarify that element of the EMD2. DLA Piper (2009) "EU study on the Legal analysis of a Single Market for the Information Society – New rules for a new age?", *ec.europa.eu*, 11.

1165 Recital 13 EMD2; Verhaeghe, L. (2013) "PingPing en PayPal: Juridisch kader, rechten en plichten", *Thesis UGent Faculty of Law*, 43.

1166 Article 11 EMD2.

1167 Though conditions, such as fees, hereto can be agreed upon between e-money institution and user.

1168 European Central Bank (2012) "Virtual Currency Schemes", *ecb.europa.eu*, 16.

1169 The ECB's 1999 opinion, for instance, states that "*redemption payments should be denominated in the same currency as the currency in which the relevant electronic money liability is denominated*". ECB (1999) "Opinion of the European Central Bank of 18 January 1999 at the request of the Council of the European Union under Article 105(4) of the Treaty establishing the European Community and Article 4(a) of the Statute of the European System of Central Banks and of the European Central Bank on 1. a Commission proposal for a European Parliament and Council Directive on the taking up, the pursuit and the prudential supervision of the business of electronic money institutions, and 2. a Commission proposal for a European Parliament and Council Directive amending Directive 77/780/EEC on the coordination of laws, regulations and administrative provisions relating to the taking up and pursuit of the business of credit institutions", *OJ* C 189 of 6 July 1999, paragraph 19. This position was confirmed in the ECB's 2009 opinion on the proposal for a new directive: ECB (2008) "Opinion of the European Central Bank of 5 December 2008 on a proposal for a Directive on the taking up, pursuit and prudential supervision of the business of electronic money institutions", *OJ* C 30 of 9 February 2009, 6. Moreover, e-money institutions can stipulate such requirement in their user agreement. PayPal, for instance, stipulates that balances must be withdrawn in the user's home currency. Conversion fees apply to withdrawals in other denominations. *paypal.com/be/webapps/mpp/ua/useragreement-full?locale.x=en_BE#6*.

Such essentially prevents e-money users from using e-money to speculate on potential gains to be made out of foreign currency exchange.[1170]

Other units? – Such redeemability at par value will generally not form a problem to e-money expressed in the same units as those against which it was exchanged, such as euros or US dollars. That is, however, not the case for virtual currencies as defined for the purposes of this research, which are expressed in their own unit of account. However, it can be argued that the redeemability requirement does not mean that e-money must necessarily be expressed in legal tender denominations, only that the exchange rate between both must be fixed.[1171] It can then be questioned where the added value lies in creating a different denomination, given the requirement of redeemability at par value. Such essentially constitutes a legal tender denomination 'by any other name'[1172], purely for the sake of using a different denomination.[1173] Regardless, there are also cases where the exchange value between the physical world currency and the virtual currency fluctuates – as evidenced in the example of cryptocurrencies – which may make it more difficult for users to retrieve their funds, if those funds can be redeemed at all.[1174]

Exchangeability – The final point made here leads to another issue, namely that the redeemability requirement can cause difficulties with regard to virtual currencies that do not allow for bidirectional exchange and thus cannot be redeemed. However, in such a case it must first be assessed to what extent virtual currencies could even

---

1170 Though the OECD in 2002 warned that e-money could end up being used as a "*transmission mechanism for currency substitution on an extensive scale for a global financial elite*", such does not seem to have materialized in practice. OECD (2002) *The Future of Money,* Paris: OECD Publications Service, 133.

1171 Godschalk, for instance, argues that this requirement is satisfied as long as the user can redeem the same amount of funds as with which he obtained the e-money. Godschalk, H. (2013) "Can an overseer overlook some basics? – The ECB on e-money and virtual currencies", *DGC Magazine,* 11 August 2013; Godschalk, H. (2001) "Genesis of the EU-Directive on Electronic Money Institutions", *EPSO Newsletter,* 7, May 2001; Godschalk, H., Krueger, M., Strauch, C. (2013) "The ECB on e-money and virtual currencies: Does the regulator know the regulations?", *PaySys SEPA Newsletter,* July 2013, 4–5. This point is followed by the ECB in acknowledging that e-money could result in the development of several units of account, and that the redeemability requirement can help to preserve the link between e-money and central bank money: European Central Bank (2000) "Issues arising from the emergence of electronic money", *ECB Monthly Bulletin,* November 2000, 55. On community currencies which, despite a different denomination, may also trade at par with legal tender: Warner, J. (2014) "The future of Community Currencies: physical cash or solely electronic?", In: Deutsche Bundesbank (Ed.) *International Cash Conference 2014: The usage, costs and benefits of cash – revisited,* Frankfurt am Main: Deutsche Bundesbank, 482.

1172 In reference to Shakespeare's *Romeo and Juliet,* Act II, Scene II.

1173 Nor does this matter seem to have gained hold in practice. The research conducted here has found no examples of currently existing e-money schemes utilizing such fictitious denomination.

1174 Though it has been warned that in such case the positive network externalities of the existing network cannot be benefitted from. Krueger, M. (2001) "Offshore E-money Issuers and Monetary Policy", *First Monday,* Vol. 6, nr. 10.

be considered as e-money under the present e-money definition. After all, if virtual currencies cannot be considered as e-money under the present state of the law, the redeemability requirement will be of no importance to them.

## 2.3 E-MONEY AND VIRTUAL CURRENCIES

Demarcation – Having analyzed the constitutive elements of the EU's legal framework on e-money, what is then the demarcation between what the ECB considers as unregulated virtual currencies and e-money as regulated by the EMD2?[1175] As a general remark, it must be noted that such a demarcation has to significant extent been left to the Member States, as neither directive provides a definite answer hereto.[1176] While the EMD2 does manage to provide more clarity than its predecessor, there are still several elements open to different interpretations by the Member States.

### 2.3.1 *Closed scheme virtual currencies*

Closed schemes – For what has been identified in chapter I as closed scheme virtual currencies, the answer is very straightforward. As noted, those virtual currencies cannot be obtained with legal tender or similar means of payment, nor can they be exchanged into legal tender or similar means of payment. The consequence is that those virtual currencies cannot fulfill the criterion of being issued upon receipt of funds, and therefore cannot be considered as e-money under the current EMD2's framework.

### 2.3.2 *Unidirectional scheme virtual currencies*

Unidirectional schemes – As noted in chapter I, unidirectional virtual currencies can be obtained with legal tender or similar means of payment. They can, however, not be exchanged back into legal tender or similar means of payment, thus limiting their convertibility. From a high-level view, that means that those virtual currencies could indeed be issued upon receipt of funds and could therefore – if the other criteria are fulfilled as well – qualify as e-money. Such would, however, pose a problem, as the redeemability requirement demands e-money to be fully convertible.

Loyalty programs – In four-party loyalty schemes, for instance, it can be held that there can be a form of exchange of legal tender or similar means of payment

1175 European Central Bank (2012) "Virtual Currency Schemes", *ecb.europa.eu*, 13.
1176 Kohlbach, M. (2004) "Making Sense of Electronic Money", *Journal of Information, Law and Technology*, 13.

for virtual currency, be it that it will often not be the consumer receiving the loyalty points who makes such an exchange.[1177] As already analyzed in section 2.2.1.3, it would therefore be theoretically possible to set up an e-loyalty scheme that corresponds to most elements of the e-money definition, including the requirement that e-money must be issued upon receipt of funds.[1178] However, as loyalty points are principally no general-purpose payment instrument, and thus only accepted at the issuing merchant or a small group of merchants participating in the loyalty scheme, there is a high probability of such a scheme either not meeting the final element of the e-money definition, or falling under one of the broad scope exemptions of the EMD2.[1179] Moreover, such a scenario relies on the assumption of a scheme in which there is indeed an exchange of legal tender or similar means of payment for virtual currency. Smaller loyalty schemes, for instance those in which a single merchant issues loyalty points to its customers without payment thereto, may well lack such an exchange and thus also not fulfill the 'issued upon receipt of funds' criterion.

Differentiation – Looking more closely then, it becomes clear that more differentiation is needed. Going back to the example given in the previous paragraph, there are several variables in the given scenario that in a slightly different configuration would result in a virtual currency that does not correspond to the current e-money definition. The same applies to other forms of unidirectional currencies. Prepaid value currencies, for instance, could utilize a "*transfer of centrally stored anonymous claims that have been purchased in advance*".[1180] However, the examples of such virtual currency discussed in section 3.3 of chapter I are issued at the sole discretion of their scheme operator, and thus not necessarily only upon receipt of funds.[1181] For instance, such prepaid currencies could be issued to reward certain behavior or activities, in which case there is no corresponding transfer of funds and thus the e-money definition not being fulfilled.[1182] Similar uncertainty exists regarding virtual currencies used

---

1177 See chapter I, section 3.1.

1178 Krueger, M. (2002) "E-money regulation in the EU", In: Pringle, R., Robinson, M. (Eds.), *E-Money and Payment Systems Review*, London: Centralbanking, 4.

1179 And by way of reference also the PSD2, see section 3.2.2.

1180 European Central Bank (2004) "E-payments without frontiers", *Issues paper for the ECB Conference on 10 November 2004*, 48; DLA Piper (2009) "EU study on the Legal analysis of a Single Market for the Information Society – New rules for a new age?", *ec.europa.eu*, 17. Note that when the value is not stored on the card, such products can be regarded as server-based e-money. The mere fact that the card itself does not hold the prepaid value does not disqualify it from being e-money.

1181 Vandezande, N. (2014) "Between Bitcoins and mobile payments: will the European Commission's new proposal provide more legal certainty?", *International Journal of Law and Information Technology*, vol. 22, 301. Also the ECB does not appear to consider schemes such as the Facebook Credits discussed in chapter I as e-money. European Central Bank (2012) "Virtual Currency Schemes", *ec.b.europa.eu*, 14.

1182 DLA Piper (2009) "EU study on the Legal analysis of a Single Market for the Information Society – New rules for a new age?", *ec.europa.eu*, 18.

in vouchers and gift cards, though it must be noted that those can – given their limited usability – most likely benefit from one of the scope exemptions to the EMD2.[1183] Another example noted in section 3.1.3 of chapter I are the schemes which are evolving away from earning-based to spending-based schemes. Also there, the result may be a mixed account of which some virtual currencies were issued upon receipt of funds and others were not. Last, also for the in-game currencies that can be regarded as unidirectional virtual currencies, there is often a mix between earned currency and purchased currency. Again, given the limited usability of such currencies, there is a high probability of not meeting the final element of the e-money definition or of a scope exemption being applicable, thus still putting the virtual currency outside of the e-money legal framework.

### 2.3.3 *Bidirectional scheme virtual currencies*

Bidirectional schemes – As noted in chapter I, bidirectional virtual currencies enjoy full interchangeability, meaning that they can be obtained using legal tender or similar means of payment and can be exchanged back into legal tender or similar means of payment. While at first glance that seems to satisfy the redeemability requirement, it must be cautioned that interchangeability is not necessarily at par value. Cryptocurrencies, for instance, are known to have a fairly volatile exchange rate. Such would of course fail to comply with the redeemability requirement. As for the definition of e-money itself, similar conclusions can be drawn as for unidirectional virtual currencies. While a bidirectional virtual currency could certainly be issued upon receipt of funds, consist of electronically stored value, represent a claim on the issuer, and be accepted by institutions other than the issuer, it is not the case for all of them. Again, reference can be made to cryptocurrencies, where the issuing is controlled by the underlying algorithm and serves as a reward for mining activities. That implies that also cryptocurrency exchanges should not be considered as e-money institutions – if it is accepted that they do not issue cryptocurrency themselves – since, in principle, they must also obtain cryptocurrencies either by mining or by purchase, and cannot just create new units at will.[1184] In the case of cryptocurrencies, there is thus no direct correlation

1183 *Ibid.*, 21.

1184 *Contra:* Jacobs, E. (2011) "Bitcoin: A Bit Too Far?", *Journal of Internet Banking and Commerce*, vol. 16, 3. Jacobs' argument hinges on the consideration that providing cryptocurrency in exchange for money constitutes issuance upon receipt of funds. However, as it is clear that also cryptocurrency exchanges must procure their cryptocurrency units by buying them from customers willing to sell their cryptocurrency units, by buying them from another exchange, or by being rewarded new units for their mining activities, there is no doubt that they cannot issue new units at will. From the historic legislative overview presented in this chapter, it can be understood that the legislator intended to address the creation of e-money – and particularly the over-issuing thereof whereby more e-money is created than funds received thereto. Since the procurement of cryptocurrency units by exchanges does not constitute the creation of new units at will, it could then be argued that in this sense such procurement may not be considered

between funds received and the creation of new units, thus disqualifying that form of bidirectional virtual currencies from being considered as e-money.[1185] Another example of a bidirectional virtual currency not fitting the e-money definition is Second Life's Linden dollar. While Linden dollar is fully interchangeable, it can only be used within the realm of Second Life. Therefore, it does not fulfill the requirement that e-money must be accepted by institutions other than the issuer.[1186]

### *2.3.4 Evaluation*

EVALUATION – In evaluating the application of the EU's legal framework on e-money to the different types of virtual currencies identified in chapter I, it must be held that only limited generalizing conclusions can be drawn. Only for closed scheme virtual currencies there is a consensus that virtual currencies of this type cannot be considered as e-money, due to the principal impossibility to obtain such virtual currencies with legal tender or similar means of payment. For unidirectional and bidirectional virtual currencies, however, more granularity is needed. It has been found that within each of the types identified in chapter I very divergent examples can be distinguished, some of which could theoretically correspond to the e-money definition, though most would not. Here, a case-by-case assessment can therefore be recommended.[1187] While the

---

as issuance. Godschalk in this sense finds that the legal framework on e-money only concerns issuing, and not trading. Godschalk, H. (2013) "Can an overseer overlook some basics? – The ECB on e-money and virtual currencies", *DGC Magazine,* 11 August 2013. See also: Weber, R. (2010) "Legal issues in mobile banking", *Journal of Banking Regulation,* Vol. 11, 135.

1185 Stokes, R. (2012) "Virtual money laundering: the case of Bitcoin and the Linden dollar", *Information & Communications Technology Law,* Vol. 21, 227–228; European Banking Authority (2014) "EBA Opinion on 'virtual currencies'", *eba.europa.eu,* EBA/Op/2014/08, 11; Jacobs, E. (2011) "Bitcoin: A Bit Too Far?", *Journal of Internet Banking and Commerce,* vol. 16, 3; Bal, A. (2014) "Taxation of virtual currency", *PhD Thesis Leiden University,* 66; De Filippi, P. (2014) "Bitcoin: a regulatory nightmare to a libertarian dream", *Internet Policy Review,* Vol. 3, 7; Houben, R. (2015) "Bitcoin: there are two sides to every coin", *Tijdschrift voor Belgisch Handelsrecht,* nr. 2, 156–157; Kubát, M. (2015) "Virtual currency bitcoin in the scope of money definition and store of value", *Procedia Economics and Finance,* Vol. 30, 411–412, Vardi, N. (2016) "Bit by Bit: Assessing the Legal Nature of Virtual Currencies", in: Gimigliano, G. (Ed.) *Bitcoin and Mobile Payments: Constructing a European Union Framework,* London: Macmillan Publishers, 61; Trzaskowski, J., Savin, A., Lundqvist, B., Lindskoug, P. (2015) Introduction to *EU Internet Law,* Copenhagen, Ex Tuto, 303. Boedts further argues that cryptocurrencies cannot be considered as representing a claim on their issuer, since strictly speaking there is no issuer. Boedts, T. (2014) "Kunnen crowdfunding en virtuele munten innoveren zonder bijkomende regulering?" in: IBJ (Ed.) *L'innovation, source de droit. Le droit, source d'innovation / Innovatie, bron van recht. Recht, bron van innovatie,* Brussels: Bruylant, 159; Shcherbak, S. (2014) "How should Bitcoin be regulated?", *European Journal of Legal Studies,* Vol. 7, 56; Künnapas, K. (2016) "From Bitcoin to Smart Contracts: Legal Revolution or Evolution from the Perspective of de lege ferenda?", In: Kerikmäe, T., Rull, A. (Eds.), *The Future of Law and eTechnologies,* Cham: Springer, 116.

1186 European Central Bank (2012) "Virtual Currency Schemes", *ecb.europa.eu,* 29.

1187 While it would be possible to determine sub-types of virtual currencies – as to some extent has been done when providing the practical examples discussed in chapter I – it is clear that significant differences remain even within those sub-types.

EMD2 does provide more clarity than its predecessor, there are a number of cases in which its application is still not fully clear.[1188] However, even when a fairly broad view of e-money is adopted, there are still other concerns at play.[1189] In the examples of such cases discussed here, for instance, the virtual currency could only be used at a particular issuer, or in a small network of merchants around that issuer. As a result, the broad scope exemptions to the directive could become applicable. While that does not provide a definitive answer as to whether such virtual currencies are e-money, the end-result of not being e-money or of being e-money yet benefitting from a scope exemption turns out to be the same in practice.[1190]

Normative assessment – As noted in the introduction to this chapter, the question that must then be posed is whether the e-money legal framework could or should be amended to facilitate virtual currencies. Given the close relationship between both frameworks, that analysis will be conducted for the legal frameworks on e-money and payment services together in section 5.

# 3 PAYMENT SERVICES

## 3.1 REGULATORY BACKGROUND

Legislative overview – This section will explore the regulatory background to the EU's legal framework on payment services by means of a legislative overview. First, it will trace the steps leading up to the PSD1. Next, after a summary discussion of that directive, it will present the review process conducted between 2012 and 2015. That process resulted in the PSD2, discussed at the end of this section. As noted in the introduction to this chapter, a historic overview mainly serves to gain a better understanding of the *ratio legis* behind the regulation of payment services, as well as of the precise scope of that legal framework. The overview presented in this section will therefore support the next steps in the process, namely further demarcating the scope of the payment services legal framework and assessing whether virtual currencies and their service providers are currently caught under that scope.

---

1188 For instance in the case of vouchers and gift cards.

1189 Godschalk, for instance, argues that in principle every form of prepaid virtual currency could correspond to what the European legislator initially had in mind for e-money. Godschalk, H. (2013) "Can an overseer overlook some basics? – The ECB on e-money and virtual currencies", *DGC Magazine*, 11 August 2013. However, even in this broad view, there are still cases – such as cryptocurrencies – that would fall outside of the e-money scope.

1190 Though in the case of application of a scope exemption, it may have to be reviewed whether this exemption can remain applicable as the scheme develops, as evidenced in the limited networks exemption.

### *3.1.1 Before 2007*

#### 3.1.1.1 Early stages

SINGLE PAYMENTS AREA – The origins of the PSD1 date back to 2000, when the European Commission presented its plan to establish a Single Payments Area.[1191] In that plan, the Commission specifically addressed concerns of legislators to keep up with the developments in the field of electronic payments. One noted development was that of electronic purses. While the legal framework on e-money was expected[1192] to provide more clarity on the rules regarding institutions that provide e-money services, a broader framework for all kinds of payments was found to be necessary.[1193] As noted in the introduction to this chapter, the support of the financial sector following the Commission's plan has enabled the creation of the SEPA framework, within which the legislative developments discussed here can be placed.

WORKING DOCUMENT – In 2002, the Commission presented a working document outlining its objectives and approach to the Single Payments Area.[1194] Regarding payments, it was remarked that at the time of writing such transactions were still mainly subjected to national law, where better economies of scale could be achieved from a transnational approach, which would require a more coherent legal framework.[1195] Furthermore, the Commission recognized that regulation was needed for non-bank institutions that want to enter the payments market.[1196]

CONSULTATIVE DOCUMENT – The working document was followed by a consultative document in 2003.[1197] Also in that document, the fragmentation of the payments landscape within the Internal Market was pointed out.[1198] While the introduction of the euro and Regulation 2560/2001/EC on cross-border payments in euro had already improved the payments situation, further action was deemed necessary to fully realize a Single Euro Payment Area where there exists a domestic payment market within the Internal Market.[1199]

---

1191 European Commission (2000) "Payment systems: Commission pledges to use full powers to create a Single Payment Area", press release *IP/00/1283*.

1192 At this time, the EMD1 was still in its legislative procedure.

1193 European Commission (2000) "Communication from the Commission to the Council and the European Parliament on Retail Payments in the Internal Market", *COM(2000)36*, 9–10.

1194 European Commission (2002) "Working document on a possible legal framework for the Single Payment Area in the Internal Market", *MARKT/208/2001 – Rev. 1.*

1195 *Ibid.*, 5–6.

1196 *Ibid.*, 13–14.

1197 European Commission (2003) "Communication from the Commission to the Council and the European Parliament concerning a New Legal Framework for Payments in the Internal Market", *COM(2003) 718 final.*

1198 *Ibid.*, 5.

1199 *Ibid.*, 5–6.

The remaining divergences between Member States were found to cause legal uncertainty, which hindered the development of payment services and the uptake thereof by users.[1200] Also regarding technological developments in the payments landscape, the Commission remarked that there was need for more "*security, information and legal certainty requirements*".[1201] A potential new legal framework in the payments field would therefore have to focus on efficiency, security, ensuring market access and a level playing field, ensuring a high level of customer protection, all while preserving technological neutrality.[1202] The Commission also remarked that there were significant similarities between payment services and e-money services, thus giving rise to the need to ensure that the right framework is applied at the right time.[1203] The proposal would be to create institutions licensed to provide payment services, much like the existing licensing of credit institutions and e-money institutions.

#### 3.1.1.2 Proposal PSD1

A DISTINCT FRAMEWORK – The European Commission formally presented its proposal for a Payment Services Directive on 1 December 2005.[1204] In that proposal, the Commission restated its findings outlined in the earlier documents discussed in the previous subsection, explaining the need for a new legal framework in the payments market. The Commission also explained the need for a separate framework for particular payment services, distinct from existing rules applying to, for instance, credit institutions and e-money institutions, thus establishing a new category of licensed service providers.[1205] While a clear legal framework was needed, derogations should also be possible to ensure that service providers who cannot comply with the whole breadth of requirements can still be registered.[1206] The proposed directive focused on transparency and information duties.[1207] It limited the liability of payment service users to cases where they acted fraudulently or with gross negligence.[1208]

SCOPE – One important limitation of the scope of the proposed directive was that it does not apply to cash or cheques payments, nor to payments exceeding

1200 *Ibid.*, 7.
1201 *Ibid.*, 9–10.
1202 *Ibid.*, 11–15.
1203 *Ibid.*, 22–25.
1204 European Commission (2005) "Implementing the Community Lisbon programme: Proposal for a directive of the European Parliament and of the Council on payment services in the internal market and amending Directives 97/7/EC, 2000/12/EC and 2002/65/EC", *COM(2005) 603 final* (hereinafter: Proposal PSD1).
1205 Recitals 7 – 8 Proposal PSD1.
1206 Recital 11 Proposal PSD1.
1207 Recitals 17 – 18 Proposal PSD1.
1208 Recital 21 Proposal PSD1.

the value of EUR 50.000.[1209] The proposed directive establishes four types of payment service providers: credit institutions, e-money institutions, post-office giro institutions, and payment institutions.[1210] It applies only to payment services, as defined in its annex, made in any currency.[1211] Those include cash deposits on and withdrawals from a payment account, execution of payment transactions held on a deposit account of from a credit line, issuing of payment cards, payment transactions involving the issuing of e-money, money remittance services, and payment transactions executed by IT devices where the service provider does not provide the goods or services through that device or where the service provider arranges a transfer of funds without intervention in the service provided. The directive has a broad range of scope exemptions, ranging between different forms of cash operations, technical services, limited network services, and added value services.[1212] One of the core elements of payment services would be funds, defined as "*cash, scriptural money and electronic money*".[1213]

Payment Institutions – The payment institutions governed by the proposed directive would have to apply for authorization, and can only engage in a limited set of activities, which excludes deposit-taking or e-money issuing.[1214] They are subjected to specific rules of conduct and supervision by competent authorities, though derogations are possible.[1215]

Transparency rules – All payment service providers would have to ensure transparency of the services they offer, for instance by providing prior general information on those services and their conditions, both for single payment transactions and for framework contracts.[1216] In the latter case, specific provisions are foreseen for information regarding the communication of single transactions.

Rights and obligations – Title IV of the proposed directive established general rights and obligations. Those concern, for instance, the provision of the payer's consent to the transaction, the use of payment verification instruments, liability for losses in the case of unauthorized payments, and refunds.[1217] It also provided the rules regarding the execution of transactions, for instance when

1209 Recitals 14 – 15 Proposal PSD1.
1210 Article 1 Proposal PSD1.
1211 Article 2 Proposal PSD1.
1212 Article 3 Proposal PSD1.
1213 Article 4 (8) Proposal PSD1.
1214 Articles 5 – 10 Proposal PSD1.
1215 Articles 11 – 22 Proposal PSD1.
1216 Articles 24 – 38 Proposal PSD1.
1217 Articles 41 – 53 Proposal PSD1.

payment orders must be accepted or when they can be refused, the timing for execution, and the availability of funds.[1218]

Other provisions – Last, the proposed directive also foresaw provisions regarding data protection, penalties, and procedures for the settlement of disputes.[1219] The proposal foresaw full harmonization.[1220]

#### 3.1.1.3 European Central Bank Opinion

Positive initiative – The ECB delivered its opinion on the Commission's proposal on 26 April 2006.[1221] Overall, the ECB welcomed the initiative to harmonize the European payments market, yet cautioned that such payment services must be clearly distinguished from e-money services.[1222]

Demarcation of activities – However, the ECB found that the activities of the payment institutions were not sufficiently demarcated.[1223] For instance, while it was clear that payment institutions would not be able to hold deposits or to issue e-money, it was found unclear how to treat funds with similar economic and legal characteristics. As deposit-taking, as broadly interpreted by European case law, is in principle reserved for credit institutions, and as the receipt of funds by payment institutions could also be considered as such deposit-taking, the ECB cautioned that a more stringent supervisory regime – akin closer to that for credit institutions – would be warranted.[1224] The ECB therefore proposed the introduction of capital requirements and other safeguards in the supervisory regime for payment institutions, and to clarify the responsibilities and powers of the home and host Member State's competent authorities.[1225] Given the nature of the risks of payment institutions holding customers' funds, the ECB proposed to limit certain activities to credit or e-money institutions, and to limit payment institutions' activities as well as the duration during which they can holds the funds received and what can be done with those funds.[1226]

Other issues – The ECB further drew attention to the fact that the transition to SEPA would begin in 2008, and that delays in the adoption of the proposal could

---

1218 Articles 54 – 70 Proposal PSD1.
1219 Articles 71 – 75 Proposal PSD1.
1220 Article 78 Proposal PSD1.
1221 European Central Bank (2006) "Opinion of the European Central Bank of 26 April 2006 on a proposal for a directive on payment services in the internal market (ECB/2006/21)", *OJ* C 109 of 9 May 2006, 10–30.
1222 *Ibid.*, 10.
1223 *Ibid.*, 11.
1224 *Ibid.*, 11–12.
1225 *Ibid.*, 12–13.
1226 *Ibid.*, 13–14.

also delay SEPA.[1227] Regarding the scope exemptions, the ECB warned that the proposed directive discriminates between physical and electronic payments, and that some of the proposed exemptions could be subject to different interpretations.[1228] Also, some of the definitions were found to be unclear.[1229]

Amendments – The ECB's opinion was accompanied by 31 amendments that reflected the ECB's concerns. One notable amendment limited the definition of funds to "*banknotes and coins and scriptural money*".[1230]

#### 3.1.1.4 European Economic and Social Committee Opinion

A lighter approach – The European Economic and Social Committee delivered its opinion on 13 September 2006.[1231] Much like the ECB, the Committee welcomed the proposal as an integral part of the ongoing SEPA efforts.[1232] However, the Committee differed from the ECB in finding that the proposed provisions should be kept to a minimum and that "*more consideration be given to self-regulation and co-regulation tools*".[1233] Moreover, the Committee favored limiting the geographic scope to transactions purely conducted within the EU.[1234]

Requirements and supervision – The Committee's preference for a lighter regulatory approach also showed in its other comments. For instance, it feared that access to payment systems would be limited to institutions operating under a banking license, and thus proposed to ensure access for payment institutions.[1235] Regarding the transparency requirements, the Committee found that existing consumer protection rules could well offer better protection then what the Commission proposed to offer.[1236] At the same time, however, the Committee also cautioned for too much protection, finding that in terms of liability a more fair burden-sharing is needed.[1237] Furthermore, the Committee proposed

1227 *Ibid.*, 14–15.
1228 *Ibid.*, 16.
1229 *Ibid.*, 17.
1230 *Ibid.*, amendment 8. Furthermore, amendment 14 specified that scriptural money refers to deposit balances or e-money.
1231 European Economic and Social Committee (2006) "Opinion of the European Economic and Social Committee on Implementing the Community Lisbon programme: Proposal for a Directive of the European Parliament and of the Council on payment services in the internal market and amending Directives 97/7/EC, 2000/12/EC and 2002/65/EC COM(2005) 603 final - 2005/0245 (COD)", *INT/301*.
1232 *Ibid.*, 1.
1233 *Ibid.*, 3.
1234 *Ibid.*, 4.
1235 *Ibid.*, 5.
1236 *Ibid.* 5–6.
1237 *Ibid.*, 6–7.

dividing the obligations of the different payment service providers involved in executing payments, and to establish more practicable execution periods.[1238]

### 3.1.1.5 Council negotiations

Presidency – Early 2006, the Council of the European Union's Presidency started work on discussing and amending the Commission's proposal. By the end of June 2006, those negotiations resulted in a first tentative text.[1239] In terms of scope, the upper limit of EUR 50.000 was removed, but more discretion was given to micro-enterprises. The wording of the negative scope had been polished, but more alignment with the EMD1 was needed. In terms of the prudential regime, delegations agreed to follow the ECB's suggestion to draft initial capital requirements. Moreover, it was agreed to require the separation of customers' funds, and to clarify that payment institutions cannot engage in deposit-taking.[1240] The changes to titles III and IV mainly concerned more harmonized consumer protection.[1241]

Compromise negotiations – Further iterations of a possible compromise text were reached in August, September, and November.[1242] On 20 November 2006, it was reported that the relevant Committee in the European Parliament had already voted, but that a plenary vote was being held off until an interinstitutional compromise could result in adoption in first reading.[1243] In March 2007, it was reported that main outstanding discussion points concerned capital requirements, ring-fencing, granting of credit by payment institutions, and derogations for low-value payments.[1244] It is in that period that, next to capital requirements, the own funds requirements were introduced.[1245] The

1238 *Ibid.*, 8–9.

1239 Council of the European Union (2006) "Proposal for a Directive of the European Parliament and of the Council on payment services in the internal market", *11146/06*.

1240 *Ibid.*, 2.

1241 *Ibid.*, 3–4.

1242 Council of the European Union (2006) "Proposal for a Directive of the European Parliament and of the Council on payment services in the internal market", *12285/06*; Council of the European Union (2006) "Proposal for a Directive of the European Parliament and of the Council on payment services in the internal market", *13061/06*; Council of the European Union (2006) "Proposal for a Directive of the European Parliament and of the Council on payment services in the internal market", *14765/06*; Council of the European Union (2006) "Proposal for a Directive of the European Parliament and of the Council on payment services in the internal market", *15384/06*.

1243 Council of the European Union (2006) "Proposal for a Directive of the European Parliament and of the Council on payment services in the internal market", *15064/06*, 2.

1244 Council of the European Union (2007) "Proposal for a Directive of the European Parliament and of the Council on payment services in the internal market", *7546/06*, 2.

1245 See for instance: Council of the European Union (2007) "Proposal for a Directive of the European Parliament and of the Council on payment services in the internal market", *6634/07*, 31–34.

broad lines of the scope of the payment services legal framework, however, were fairly close to their final iteration by this point. During the Trilogue discussions, the European Parliament indicated that it prefers that payment institutions could only grant short-term credit, although it could agree with the Council's position if the term for such credit-granting could be shortened.[1246] The three major institutions reached an agreement on a compromise text on 27 March 2007.[1247]

#### 3.1.1.6 European Parliament adoption

COMMITTEE OPINIONS – Already in September 2006, the responsible Committee within the European Parliament – the Committee on Economic and Monetary Affairs – adopted its opinion on the Commission's proposal. Two other committees delivered an opinion: the Committee on the Internal Market and Consumer Protection and the Committee on Legal Affairs.

COMMITTEE ON ECONOMIC AND MONETARY AFFAIRS – The main reporting Committee was the Committee on Economic and Monetary Affairs. Regarding scope, this Committee proposed to limit the scope to payments within the Internal Market, thus only covering Euro payments, or payments in other currencies used within the EU.[1248] It further proposed to tighten a number of provisions regarding payment institutions, to foster greater consumer trust. That included minimum capital requirements, and the limitation of activities that can be conducted by those service providers.[1249]

COMMITTEE ON INTERNAL MARKET AND CONSUMER PROTECTION – The second Committee delivering an opinion concurred in limiting the scope to payments conducted within the Internal Market.[1250] Moreover, it was proposed to remove the upper applicability threshold of EUR 50.000, and to bring mobile operators under the scope of the directive.[1251] Also here it was proposed to tighten the regulatory framework on payment institutions, also imposing capital requirements and limiting activities.[1252] The notion of micro-payments was limited to EUR 10.[1253]

---

1246 Council of the European Union (2007) "Proposal for a Directive of the European Parliament and of the Council on payment services in the internal market", *7666/07*, 3.

1247 Council of the European Union (2007) "Proposal for a Directive of the European Parliament and of the Council on payment services in the internal market", *7665/1/07 REV 1*.

1248 *Ibid.*, for instance amendments 16 and 34.

1249 *Ibid.*, for instance amendments 6, 75 – 87, 101 – 104, and 129.

1250 *Ibid.*, amendment 3.

1251 *Ibid.*, for instance amendments 2, 5, and 6.

1252 *Ibid.*, amendments 14 – 24.

1253 *Ibid.*, amendment 12.

Committee on Legal Affairs – The final Committee reporting proposed to repeal Directive 97/5/EC and Regulation 2560/2001.[1254] Also in that report, it was proposed to limit the scope of the directive to payments within the EU alone.[1255]

Compromise adoption – Although the Committee opinions were available, the vote in the plenary meeting's first reading was, as noted in the previous subsection, held off while interinstitutional negotiations were under way. The matter only came to a vote in April 2007, when the amendments proposed by the Committees were suppressed and the compromise text was proposed as a single amendment. That amendment was adopted on 24 April 2007.[1256] The text adopted by the European Parliament was approved by the Council on 15 October 2007, thus concluding the legislative procedure and adopting the directive.[1257]

### 3.1.2 *First Payment Services Directive*

Payment Service Providers – The PSD1 provided a legal framework for Payment Service providers (PSP) as well as the "*rules concerning transparency of conditions and information requirements for payment services, and the respective rights and obligations of payment service users and payment service providers in relation to the provision of payment services as a regular occupation or business activity*".[1258] The PSPs addressed by the directive were all regulated institutions.[1259] A service provider aspiring to provide payment services was therefore subjected to specific regulation under the directive, be it that certain provisions were only applicable to the payment institutions regulated under the directive.[1260]

Negative scope – The directive also defined a negative scope, indicating a list of situations to which it was not applicable. Such situations ranged from cash transfers between parties without intermediary intervention[1261], to services that allow the user to withdraw cash from automated teller machines (ATM).[1262] The negative scope, or the scope exemptions, will be discussed more elaborately in section 3.2.2.

---

1254 *Ibid.*, amendment 1.

1255 *Ibid.*, amendments 11 and 12.

1256 European Parliament (2007) "Minutes of the sitting of Tuesday 24 April 2007", *PE 387.045*, 17.

1257 Council of the European Union (2007) "2823$^{rd}$ meeting of the Council of the European Union (General Affairs and External Relations)", 13911/07.

1258 Article 1 PSD1.

1259 Article 1 PSD1 specified six categories of payment service providers, similar to the EMD2.

1260 The initial capital and own funds requirements, for instance, were only applicable to payment institutions, and thus not to other payment service providers such as credit institutions.

1261 Article 3 (a) PSD1.

1262 Article 3 (o) PSD1.

Positive scope – Within its definitions, the directive further clarified its scope.[1263] Payment services, as explicated in the annex to the directive, were defined as services that enable cash deposits and withdrawals on payment accounts and all operations required for operating a payment account.[1264] It also covered the "*execution of payment transactions, including transfers of funds on a payment account with the user's payment service provider or with another payment service provider,* [including the] *execution of payment transactions through a payment card or a similar device*".[1265] This also included the issuance of payment instruments and money remittance, as well as payment transactions executed and consented to by telecommunication, digital or IT devices to the provider of such a device or network and acting as an intermediary between the user and the supplier of the goods and services.[1266]

Operational requirements – The PSD1 required payment institutions – and thus not the other types of payment service providers – to be granted authorization in order to perform their tasks and duties.[1267] As part of their application to obtain such an authorization[1268], candidate payment institutions had to prove that they hold sufficient capital, which could range from EUR 20.000 for money remittance services or EUR 50.000 for the intermediaries for electronic transactions to EUR 120.000 for the other payment services defined in the directive's annex.[1269] Those institutions also had to hold their own funds, calculated according to one of the methods proposed by the directive.[1270] The funds received from the payment service users or through another payment service provider for the execution of payment transactions had to be safeguarded by keeping the funds of different users separate and protecting them from other creditors, or by obtaining suitable insurance for their value.[1271] The directive provided the general framework – to be transposed by the Member States – that governed the authorization procedure, the withdrawal thereof and the registration of authorized payment institutions.[1272] Apart from the payment services identified in the directive's annex, the authorized payment institutions could perform a number of ancillary services.[1273] Apart from that, the PSD1 contained provisions relating to the use of agents, the liability and recordkeeping duties of payment institutions, the supervision by

1263 Article 4 PSD1.
1264 Article 4 (3) PSD1 and annex.
1265 Annex to PSD1.
1266 *Id.* This provision could be understood as requiring the payments to be made directly to the intermediary provider, although this is not directly clear from the text of the directive.
1267 Article 4 (4) PSD1.
1268 Article 5 PSD1.
1269 Article 6 PSD1.
1270 Article 7 and 8 PSD1.
1271 Article 9 PSD1.
1272 Article 10 – 15 PSD1.
1273 Article 16 PSD1.

competent authorities and the exercise of the right to establishment and freedom to provide services.[1274] For smaller payment institutions – executing transactions not exceeding EUR 3 million per month – the competent authorities could waive the full or partial authorization procedure.[1275]

Common provisions – Apart from the specific rules and requirements for payment institutions, the directive also listed a number of common provisions, applicable to all payment service providers. As a detailed discussion of those provisions would go beyond the scope of this brief analysis of the directive for the purposes of this research, it can be summarized that the directive provided the framework ensuring access to payment systems, that the conditions set by payment institutions are transparent, and that they provide their users with adequate information.[1276]

Provision of payment services – Regarding the provision and use of payment services, the directive provided a number of general principles with which payment transactions had to comply, with possible derogations for low value payments – also referred to as micropayments.[1277] For instance, transactions could only be executed when the payer had given consent thereto.[1278] Apart from imposing duties on the payment service provider, the directive also required the user of such services to display certain behavior, such as keeping the personalized security measures secret.[1279] The onus of proof of proper authorization when executing a payment transaction, however, was kept on the PSP.[1280] In case of unauthorized payment transactions, the directive provided clear rules on the division of liability between PSP and user, as well as on potential refunds.[1281] Payment orders had to be received and – principally – executed within one business day.[1282] Users were responsible for payments made to the wrong payee, if they provided the wrong unique identifier for the intended payee.[1283] To settle differences, the directive provided an out-of-court settlement and redress procedure.[1284]

Transposition – The PSD1 needed to be transposed into national law by the Member States by 1 November 2009. The transposition was, however, only accomplished in 2011 when Poland adopted its transposing measures.[1285] As

---

1274 Article 17 – 25 PSD1.
1275 Article 26 PSD1.
1276 Article 30 – 50 PSD1.
1277 Article 53 PSD1.
1278 Article 54 PSD1.
1279 Article 56 PSD1.
1280 Article 59 PSD1.
1281 Article 60 – 63 PSD1.
1282 Article 68 – 73 PSD1.
1283 Article 74 PSD1.
1284 Article 80 – 83 PSD1.
1285 TIPIK (2012) "Conformity Assessment of Directive 2007/64/EC, Poland", *ec.europa.eu*.

a result, the late 2012 review required by article 87 of the directive would only be conducted throughout 2013 at the earliest, as it was in 2012 found to be too early to already make a full assessment of the impact of the directive.[1286] In the meantime, a number of non-conformities regarding the implementation of the payment services legal framework in the national legal order of the Member States were identified, further impeding the full benefit from the directive's provisions.[1287] However, a 2012 regulation explicitly referenced the PSD1 and its planned 2012 revision, thus putting more time pressure on the review process.[1288]

### *3.1.3 Review*

Review – As any EU directive, the PSD1 was marked for review. In 2013, the European Commission proposed a major overhaul of the payment services legal framework, by means of a new directive. The PSD2, repealing the first directive, was adopted late 2015.

#### 3.1.3.1 Implementation, green paper, and consultation

Implementation – Throughout the implementation phase of the PSD1, it already became clear that the transposition of certain provisions proved problematic for some Member States, leading to divergent interpretations and thus not fully reaching the goal of full harmonization of the directive.[1289] Especially the 'limited networks' and added value scope exemptions were found difficult to implement, leaving "*room for conflicting interpretation and abuse*".[1290] It was noted by Member States that such broad exceptions allowed market players to adapt their business models in order for them to fall into the negative scope of the directive, thus being exempt from having to comply with the payment services legal framework.[1291] It was also noted that many service providers did not consult with authorities, thus creating an unsupervised sector much larger than the supervised one.[1292]

---

1286 Wandhöfer, R. (2012) "The 2012 Payment Services Directive Review: Too Much too Soon?", *EPC Newsletter*.

1287 TIPIK (2011) "Directive 2007/64/EC – General report on the transposition by the Member States", *ec.europa.eu*.

1288 Recital 32 Regulation (EU) No 260/2012 of the European Parliament and of the Council of 14 March 2012 establishing technical and business requirements for credit transfers and direct debits in euro and amending Regulation (EC) No 924/2009, *OJ* L 94 of 30 March 2012, 22–37.

1289 European Commission (2013) "Report on the application of Directive 2007/64/EC on payment services in the internal market and on Regulation 924/2009 on cross-border payments in the Community", *COM(2013) 549 final*, 2–3.

1290 Payment Committee (2012) "Summary Record of the Sixth meeting of the Payments Committee of 21 March 2012", *ec.europa.eu*, PC/005/12, 3.

1291 *Id.*

1292 *Id.*

Green paper – In 2012, the Commission published a green paper on card, Internet, and mobile payments.[1293] The paper details a number of changes in the payments landscape, and the influence of SEPA on this evolution. More in particular, it highlights the importance of e- and m-payments, and the barriers posed by the fragmented European payments landscape to those developments.[1294] The paper mainly served to pose a number of questions to stakeholders that help the Commission to identify where gaps in the regulatory landscape remain.

Consultation process – From the feedback acquired from research and consultation processes, it became clear that the PSD1 certainly did have a positive impact, yet had not fully reached its intended goals, mainly due to its broadly phrased scope exemptions. Therefore, competent supervisory authorities and industry experts proposed to abandon the model of describing the 'limited network' and replacing that scope exemption by all transactions lower than a certain value, for instance EUR 5, as such would reach the desired level of legal certainty by leaving no room for continuing discussions on the scope for eligibility of a limited network/range.[1295] That idea could be expanded to the full scope of the directive, which could be constituted to protect consumer payment transactions of a certain value, regardless of their type or other attributes.[1296] Similarly, while the 'added value' exemption was found to be more clear on its scope than the 'limited networks' exemption, also there it was found that the provision leaves sufficient room for service providers to adapt their services in such a way that they would not be covered by the legal framework set by the directive.[1297]

Other forms of payment services – Additionally, the consultation process made it clear that there are also uncertainties regarding the precise scope of the payment services covered by the directive, which was found to leave several forms of payment services, as well as entirely new forms, not covered by the PSD1.[1298] Concerns were voiced regarding the applicability of the legal framework to mobile payments, as well as regarding the inclusion of e-money, prepaid instruments, and virtual currencies.[1299] Regarding e-money, a

---

1293 European Commission (2012) "Towards an integrated European market for card, internet and mobile payments", *COM(2011) 941 final.*

1294 *Ibid.*, 6.

1295 London Economics (2013) "Study on the impact of directive 2007/64/EC on payment services in the internal market and on the application of regulation (EC) No. 924/2009 on cross-border payments in the Community", *MARKT/2011/120/H3/ST/OP*, 121–122.

1296 Payment Committee (2012) "Summary Record of the Eighth meeting of the Payments Committee of 17 October 2012", *ec.europa.eu*, PC/013/12, 3. See also: Digital Policy Alliance (2013) "Position Paper on the proposed review of the Payment Services Directive", *dpalliance.org.uk*, 5.

1297 London Economics (2013) "Study on the impact of directive 2007/64/EC on payment services in the internal market and on the application of regulation (EC) No. 924/2009 on cross-border payments in the Community", *MARKT/2011/120/H3/ST/OP*, 123.

1298 Such as payment initiation services. *Ibid.*, 105–112.

1299 *Ibid.*, 112–114.

divergence between both legal frameworks was noted, as payment services that incorporate e-money are subjected to both legal frameworks, which complicates the matter of choosing the right regime regarding the customer.[1300] However, the distinction between funds under payment services and e-money was found to be increasingly irrelevant.[1301] The consultation process thus revealed a clear preference from all stakeholders to merge both legal frameworks, or at least to provide more clarity on the applicability of either framework.[1302] It was also remarked that the PSD1 provided a disadvantage to low-value payments, as those service providers would still need to be authorized before being subjected to lighter conduct of business rules.[1303]

#### 3.1.3.2 Proposal PSD2

No EMD2 merger – On 24 July 2013, the European Commission presented its strategy for the review of the PSD1.[1304] Due to the late implementation of the EMD2 by a large number of Member States, it was found that there has not been enough time to fully judge the practical experiences with the new e-money framework. The review for the EMD2 was therefore pushed back to 2014, thus ruling out a merger between both frameworks at least for the time being.[1305] In its press release, the Commission addressed two issues: interchange fees and payment services.

Interchange fees – First, there is the matter of interchange fees for card-based payment transactions, where the Commission aimed to make Internet payments cheaper and safer for retailers and consumers.[1306] To that end, the Commission proposed a regulation that caps so-called Multilateral Interchange Fees (MIFs) in 'four party' card schemes, such as the well-known Visa and MasterCard.[1307] Such fees are generally agreed between the acquiring and issuing payment service provider in a card scheme and are passed on to consumers, thus raising

---

1300 *Ibid.*, 156–158.

1301 *Id.*

1302 *Ibid.*, 162.

1303 *Ibid.*, 154–155.

1304 RAPID Press Release (2013) "New rules on Payment Services for the benefit of consumers and retailers", *IP/13/730.*

1305 European Commission (2013) "Proposal for a Directive of the European Parliament and of the Council on payment services in the internal market and amending Directives 2002/65/EC, 2013/36/EU and 2009/110/EC and repealing Directive 2007/64/EC, *COM(2013) 547/Final*, 2–3 (hereinafter: Proposal PSD2).

1306 RAPID Press Release (2013) "New rules on Payment Services for the benefit of consumers and retailers", *IP/13/730.*

1307 European Commission (2013) "Proposal for a Regulation of the European Parliament and of the Council on interchange fees for card-based payment transactions", *COM(2013) 550/Final* (hereinafter: Proposal Regulation).

the overall price of goods and services.[1308] Moreover, those fees were found to limit the possibilities of market entrance for new and innovative payment service providers.[1309] More in particular, the proposed regulation would apply to consumer transactions using payment instruments, where both the payer's payment service provider and the payee's payment service provider are established within the EU.[1310] The regulation would exclude, for instance, three party payment card schemes and cash withdrawals at automated teller machines, as well as transactions initiated as part of a business activity instead out of purely consumer ends. In essence, the proposed regulation would limit the interchange fees to 0,2% in the case of debit card transactions or 0,3% in the case of credit card transactions.[1311] The proposal aimed to lift restrictions on, for instance, territorial issuing of cards and co-badging, while also imposing information duties on the payment service providers.[1312] The regulation was adopted on 29 April 2015.[1313]

Proposal PSD2 – Second, the Commission decided to repeal the PSD1 and to replace it with a new framework, also in the form of a directive.[1314] The proposed directive aimed to facilitate and render more secure the use of low cost internet payment services by including so-called payment initiation services, to raise fraud protection, and to promote the emergence of new players and the development of innovative mobile and internet payments in Europe.[1315] The proposed directive would still be aimed at payment service providers, with a broader definition of its negative scope than of its positive scope.[1316] The payment services covered by the directive would still be defined in an annex, where the main change of the proposal was that the service where the telecommunication, IT system or network operator acts only as an intermediary had been replaced by services '*based on access to payment accounts provided by a payment service provider who is not the account servicing payment service provider, in the form of: (a) payment initiation services; (b) account information services*'.[1317] As many services are aimed at providing access to a user's payment account at another service and thus could not dispose of the funds moved on said account at any time, such services were excluded from the scope of the PSD1. By now regulating

1308 *Ibid.*, 2.
1309 *Ibid.*, 3.
1310 Article 1 Proposal Regulation.
1311 First for cross-border transactions, later for all transactions: Article 3 – 4 Proposal Regulation.
1312 Chapter 3 Proposal Regulation.
1313 Regulation (EU) 2015/751 of the European Parliament and of the Council of 29 April 2015 on interchange fees for card-based payment transactions, *OJ* L 123 of 19 May 2015, 1–15.
1314 Proposal PSD2.
1315 RAPID Press Release (2013) "New rules on Payment Services for the benefit of consumers and retailers", *IP/13/730*.
1316 Article 1 – 3 Proposal PSD2.
1317 Annex to the Proposal PSD2.

these services, so-called third party services, the Commission aimed to '*enhance new low cost e-payment solutions on the internet while ensuring appropriate security, data protection and liability standards'*.[1318]

Positive scope – Regarding definitions, the most remarkable addition was that of 'payment initiation service', being a payment service that gives access to a payment account at a third party payment service provider, "*where the payer can be actively involved in the payment initiation or the third party payment service provider's software, or where payment instruments can be used by the payer or the payee to transmit the payer's credentials to the account servicing payment service provider*".[1319] In essence, such payment initiation services operate between the merchant and the consumer's bank, providing cheap and efficient electronic payment services that do not require the use of a credit card.[1320] The Commission aimed to subject these service providers to the same standards of regulation, also requiring banks to heighten online transaction security.

Scope exemptions – The European Commission's proposal for a PSD2 still included a broad range of scope exceptions.[1321] The added value, limited network, and exchange services exemptions have been retained, albeit that the former two have been slightly reformulated as they were found to leave "*room for conflicting interpretation and abuse*".[1322] Those exemptions will be further discussed in section 3.2.2.

Other provisions – For payment service providers, there would still be requirements for being granted authorization[1323], capital, funds and safeguard requirements[1324] and registration.[1325] Also rules regarding liability[1326] and supervision[1327] remained mostly the same, as did most transparency and information requirements.[1328] Some new information duties had been added to cover payment initiation services.[1329] Provisions had been formulated to

1318 Proposal PSD2, 12.
1319 Article 4 (32) Proposal PSD2.
1320 RAPID Press Release (2013) "New rules on Payment Services for the benefit of consumers and retailers", *IP/13/730*. More in particular, examples such as Sofort in Germany, IDeal in the Netherlands and Trustly in Scandinavia are named.
1321 Article 3 Proposal PSD2.
1322 Payment Committee (2012) "Summary Record of the Sixth meeting of the Payments Committee of 21 March 2012", *ec.europa.eu*, PC/005/12, 3.
1323 Article 5 Proposal PSD2, now including more security control and mitigation measures.
1324 Article 7 – 9 Proposal PSD2.
1325 Article 13 – 14 Proposal PSD2, including a web portal.
1326 Article 19 Proposal PSD2.
1327 Article 22 Proposal PSD2.
1328 Title III Proposal PSD2.
1329 Article 39 – 40 Proposal PSD2.

regulate the access to and use of payment account information by third party payment service provider and instrument issuers.[1330] One notable change in that part of the directive concerned the payer's liability for unauthorized payment transactions, which was limited to EUR 50, down from EUR 150.[1331] Moreover, in the case of direct debits where the exact amount of the transaction was not specified when the authorization was made or if the amount of the payment transaction exceeded the amount the payer could reasonably have expected, the consumer would be granted an unconditional right for refund, to be exercised within a period of eight weeks from the date on which the funds were debited.[1332] Also, a new chapter was added, dedicated to 'operational and security and authentication'.[1333] In that chapter, payment service providers would have to make a yearly "*assessment of the operational and security risks associated with the payment services they provide and on the adequacy of the mitigation measures and control mechanisms implemented in response to these risks*".[1334] Incidents needed to be reported and security measures had to comply with regularly updated guidelines. Strong customer authentication would be required.[1335] A final significant addition was the inclusion of a provision governing internal dispute resolution.[1336]

#### 3.1.3.3 European Economic and Social Committee Opinion

Focus on interchange fees – The European Economic and Social Committee delivered its opinion on the Commission's proposal on 11 December 2013.[1337] The Committee welcomes both legislative initiatives, but focuses mainly on the proposed regulation on interchange fees. Regarding the Proposal PSD2, the Committee mainly addresses the potential charges from banks to third party payment service providers, and the need for interoperable standards for payments across the EU.[1338]

---

1330 Article 58 – 59 Proposal PSD2.

1331 Article 66 Proposal PSD2. Note that in their national implementation, some Member States already applied a lower limit, such as GBP 50. Section 62 of the Payment Services Regulations 2009, *S.I.* 2009 No. 209.

1332 Article 67 Proposal PSD2.

1333 Title IV, Chapter 5 Proposal PSD2.

1334 Article 86 Proposal PSD2.

1335 Article 87 Proposal PSD2.

1336 Article 90 Proposal PSD2.

1337 European Economic and Social Committee (2013) "Opinion of the European Economic and Social Committee on the Proposal for a Regulation of the European Parliament and of the Council on interchange fees for card-based payment transactions COM(2013) 550 final – 2013/0265 (COD) and the Proposal for a Directive of the European Parliament and of the Council on payment services in the internal market and amending Directives 2002/65/EC, 2013/36/EU and 2009/110/EC and repealing Directive 2007/64/EC COM(2013) 547 final – 2013/0264 (COD)", *INT/711*.

1338 *Ibid.*, 2.

#### 3.1.3.4 European Central Bank Opinion

General agreement – The European Central Bank delivered its opinion on the Commission's proposal on 5 February 2014.[1339] In its opinion, the ECB is especially positive about the harmonization of operational and security requirements, the strengthening of competent authorities' enforcement powers, and the tightening of certain provisions that left too much discretion to the Member States.[1340] Generally, the ECB agrees with the proposed definitions, but finds that some could be further clarified.

Remarks and amendments – In terms of scope, the ECB finds that title IV should apply equally in respect of all currencies.[1341] Most of the other remarks in the opinion mainly consider security matters, generally in relation to the introduction of third party payment service providers. The amendments formulated by the ECB reflect the same concerns.

#### 3.1.3.5 European Parliament Committee Stage – First attempt

Committee report – On 2 April 2014, the Committee on Economic and Monetary Affairs presented its report to the plenary meeting of the European Parliament.[1342] The Committee proposed a total of 201 amendments to the Commission's original proposal, with a further 19 amendments by the Committee on Legal Affairs. Most of those amendments, however, concerned the introduction of third party payment service providers (TPPs), and not the general scope of the directive. For the added value exemption, it was proposed to lower the monetary threshold introduced by the Commission's proposal to EUR 20 for single transactions, with a total monthly limit of EUR 100.[1343] Furthermore, it was proposed to extend the technical service providers exemption to mobile wallet providers, granted that they do not enter into possession of the funds processed through those wallets.[1344]

---

1339 European Central Bank (2014) "Opinion of 5 February 2014 on a proposal for a directive of the European Parliament and of the Council on payment services in the internal market and amending Directives 2002/65/EC, 2013/36/EU and 2009/110/EC and repealing Directive 2007/64/EC (CON/2014/9)", *OJ* C 224 of 15 July 2014, 1–25.

1340 *Ibid.*, 2.

1341 *Ibid.*, 3.

1342 European Parliament Committee on Economic and Monetary Affairs (2014) "Report on the proposal for a directive of the European Parliament and of the Council on payment services in the internal market and amending Directives 2002/65/EC, 2013/36/EU and 2009/110/EC and repealing Directive 2007/64/EC (COM(2013)0547 – C7-0230/2013 – 2013/0264(COD))", *A7-0169/2014*.

1343 *Ibid.*, amendment 47.

1344 *Ibid.*, amendment 14.

Referred back – While the Commission's proposal was principally adopted as amended, the vote on the European Parliament's draft legislative resolution was postponed according to rule 57 (2) of the European Parliament's rules of procedure.[1345] According to that rule, the matter was deemed to be referred back to the committee responsible for reconsideration.

#### 3.1.3.6 Council General Approach

Elections and negotiations – Due to the referral back to the Committee responsible, the procedure could no longer be completed before the 2014 European Parliamentary elections. Moreover, before a new Committee report was tabled, interinstitutional negotiations had already begun with the report amended in the plenary meeting.

General approach – A first Council Presidency compromise text was presented on 27 June 2014.[1346] One change to the original proposed introduced there follows the ECB's opinion in that title IV would get a broader field of application.[1347] Furthermore, e-commerce platforms that enter into possession of payment service users' funds are excluded from the scope exemptions.[1348] The added value and limited networks scope exemptions were clarified, as will be further discussed in section 3.2.2. A later text, of 23 July 2014, added that the limited networks exemption cannot be cumulated, meaning that one instrument should only be usable within a single limited network.[1349] Another text, dated 12 September 2014, somewhat clarified the language of that addition.[1350] The text went through a number of further revisions, focusing mainly on polishing the language of the changes introduced in previous versions. On 1 December 2014, the Council's Presidency reached a broad agreement on the text and approved a negotiations mandate.[1351] Following Trilogue discussions in December, the

---

1345 European Parliament (2014) "Minutes of the sitting of Thursday 3 April 2014", *PE 533.119*, 13–14.

1346 Council of the European Union (2014) "Proposal for a directive of the European Parliament and of the Council on payment services in the internal market and amending Directives 2002/65/EC, 2013/36/EU and 2009/110/EC and repealing Directive 2007/64/EC – Presidency compromise", *11148/14*.

1347 *Ibid.*, 35.

1348 *Ibid.*, 36.

1349 Council of the European Union (2014) "Proposal for a directive of the European Parliament and of the Council on payment services in the internal market and amending Directives 2002/65/EC, 2013/36/EU and 2009/110/EC and repealing Directive 2007/64/EC – Presidency compromise", *12134/14*, 7 and 43.

1350 Council of the European Union (2014) "Proposal for a directive of the European Parliament and of the Council on payment services in the internal market and amending Directives 2002/65/EC, 2013/36/EU and 2009/110/EC and repealing Directive 2007/64/EC – Presidency compromise", *13149/14*, 8 and 47..

1351 Council of the European Union (2014) "Proposal for a directive of the European Parliament and of the Council on payment services in the internal market and amending Directives

general approach was confirmed by the Council early 2015.[1352] A reservation was made by Luxembourg, as it feared the general approach would weaken the existing passporting system.[1353] After more negotiations, a final compromise was reached between the three major EU institutions.[1354]

#### 3.1.3.7 European Parliament Committee Stage – Second attempt and adoption

ADOPTING THE COMPROMISE – Following the compromise text reached during the Trilogue discussions, it was indicated that if the European Parliament adopted that text during its first reading, the Council would approve of it, thus adopting the directive and concluding the legislative procedure. The Committee on Economic and Monetary Affairs did indeed propose the compromise text as a single amendment without further changes.[1355] That text was adopted by the European Parliament on 8 October 2015, followed by the Council on 16 November.[1356]

### *3.1.4 Second Payment Services Directive*

PSD2 – The PSD2 was officially adopted on 25 November 2015.[1357] Its recitals detail how certain services remained outside the scope of the PSD1, and how new services have developed, thus sparking the need for a revised legal framework. In terms of its interaction with the EMD2, it is indicated that the latter regulates the

2002/65/EC, 2013/36/EU and 2009/110/EC and repealing Directive 2007/64/EC – Presidency compromise", *16154/14*; Council of the European Union (2014) "Proposal for a directive of the European Parliament and of the Council on payment services in the internal market and amending Directives 2002/65/EC, 2013/36/EU and 2009/110/EC and repealing Directive 2007/64/EC – Approval of a negotiating mandate", *16155/14*.

1352 Council of the European Union (2015) "3356th meeting of the Council of the European Union (Economic and Financial Affairs)", *16699/14 ADD 1*.

1353 *Ibid.*, 5.

1354 Council of the European Union (2015) "Proposal for a directive of the European Parliament and of the Council on payment services in the internal market and amending Directives 2002/65/EC, 2013/36/EU and 2009/110/EC and repealing Directive 2007/64/EC – Confirmation of the final compromise text with a view to agreement", *9337/15*.

1355 European Parliament Committee on Economic and Monetary Affairs (2015) "Supplementary report on the proposal for a directive of the European Parliament and of the Council on payment services in the internal market and amending Directives 2002/65/EC, 2013/36/EU and 2009/110/EC and repealing Directive 2007/64/EC (COM(2013)0547 – C7-0230/2013 – 2013/0264(COD))", *A8-0266/2015*.

1356 *Europarl.europa.eu/oeil/popups/sda.do?id=26167&l=en;* Council of the European Union (2015) "3425th meeting of the Council of the European Union (Agriculture and Fisheries)", *14167/15*.

1357 Directive 2015/2366 of the European Parliament and of the Council of 25 November 2015 on payment services in the internal market, amending Directives 2002/65/EC, 2009/110/EC and 2013/36/EU and Regulation (EU) No 1093/2010, and repealing Directive 2007/64/EC, *OJ* L 337 of 23 December 2015, 35–127 (hereinafter: PSD2).

issuing of e-money, whereas the former only regulates the execution of payment transactions, even if the funds constitute e-money.[1358]

Scope – As became clear from the review process, the geographical scope of the PSD2 has been enlarged in that parts of titles III and IV can also apply to transactions where one party involved is not located within the EU.[1359] In terms of institutions that can offer payment services, the list of the PSD1 was maintained.[1360] As far as the negative scope – also referred to as exclusions or exemptions – is concerned, the main principles have been maintained, with more substantial revisions applied to the limited networks and added value exemptions.[1361] The types of payment services covered by the payment services legal framework are still listed in an annex, the most notable changes here being the removal of the payment transactions through telecommunications, digital or IT devices whereby the operator only acts as an intermediary, and the addition of payment initiation services and account information services.[1362]

Definitions – The main changes to the definitions are the additions of new forms of payment service providers, the so-called third party payment service providers. These are: (1) payment initiation service, "*a service to initiate a payment order at the request of the payment service user with respect to a payment account held at another payment service provider*"; (2) account information service, "*an online service to provide consolidated information on one or more payment accounts held by the payment service user with either another payment service provider or with more than one payment service provider*"; (3) account servicing payment service provider, "*a payment service provider providing and maintaining a payment account for a payer*".[1363] Furthermore, the definitions for a number of security features are included, such as strong customer authentication and personalized security credentials.[1364]

Payment institutions – Payment institutions, one of the forms of payment service providers covered by the scope of the directive, are still subjected to a number of requirements, such as prior authorization – with added attention to compliance with security requirements to be proposed by the European Banking Authority – initial capital and own funds requirements, registration, and limitation of their activities.[1365] They are still subjected to supervision by the competent national

1358 Recital 25 PSD2.
1359 Article 2 PSD2. This is often referred to as the extension to one-leg transactions, as opposed to the two-legs principle under the PSD1 where all parties had to be located within the EU.
1360 Article 1 PSD2.
1361 Article 3 PSD2. See also section 3.2.2.
1362 Annex PSD2.
1363 Article 4 (15) – (17) PSD2.
1364 Article 4 (30) and (31) PSD2.
1365 Articles 5 – 18 PSD2.

authorities.[1366] Smaller enterprises can still be exempted from certain provisions, as can account information service providers.[1367] Access rules have been maintained, with addition of access to accounts maintained with credit institutions.[1368]

Transparency, information, rights and obligations – The provisions of title III have been mostly maintained, with a number of additions to facilitate the third party payment service providers.[1369] Similar conclusions can be drawn for title IV, with most changes reflecting the addition of third party payment service providers.[1370] Furthermore, the payer's liability for unauthorized payment transactions has been lowered from EUR 150 to EUR 50.[1371] Also, a new chapter addresses operational and security risks, for instance by requiring payment service providers to follow guidelines and regulatory technical standards to be drafted by the EBA, to report incidents, and to use strong authentication.[1372]

Other provisions – The European Commission will produce a leaflet to inform consumers of their rights under this new legal framework.[1373] The PSD2 maintains the principle of full harmonization and is to be reviewed by January 2021.[1374] The new legal framework is to be transposed by the Member States by 13 January 2018, at which point the PSD1 is repealed.[1375] Transitional provisions are foreseen for existing payment service providers and new actors entering the market before 2018.[1376]

EMD2 – Given these significant changes, a number of other texts referencing the PSD1 are amended. That includes the EMD2, where a few provisions are amended to refer to the PSD2.[1377] However, those amendments do not affect all references in the EMD2 to the legal framework on payment services. The application of the limited networks and added value exemptions of the payment services framework to e-money, for instance, keep their reference to the PSD1. Here, the general principle of article 114 of the PSD2 applies, meaning that such references must be construed as referencing the PSD2 from the moment of repeal of the PSD1 onwards. However, given that the scope of those exemptions has been tightened, it must be cautioned that there is a possibility that e-money issuers who in the

---

1366 Articles 22 – 31 PSD2.
1367 Articles 31 – 34 PSD2.
1368 Articles 35 – 37 PSD2.
1369 Articles 38 – 60 PSD2.
1370 Articles 61 – 103 PSD2.
1371 Article 74 PSD2.
1372 Articles 95 – 98 PSD2.
1373 Article 106 PSD2.
1374 Articles 107 – 108 PSD2.
1375 Articles 114 – 115 PSD2.
1376 Article 109 PSD2.
1377 Article 111 PSD2.

past benefitted from a broader interpretation of these scope exemptions, could now find themselves no longer benefitting from the stricter interpretation of those scope exemptions, and thus become subjected to the legal framework on e-money after all. In other words, the PSD2 could be construed as having altered, to certain extent, the scope of the legal framework on e-money as well.

### *3.1.5 Evaluation*

Framing within SEPA – As noted, SEPA forms the background against which the legislative initiative regarding payment services can be framed. While the – at the time new – framework on e-money regulated the particular development of e-money, further initiative was deemed necessary to facilitate cross-border electronic payments across the EU. Such an initiative needed to remedy the divergent approaches of Member States regarding payments, create a level playing field for market entrants, and raise legal certainty for consumers.

Non-financial actors – While during the drafting of the legal framework on e-money difficult discussions arose regarding whether the issuing of e-money should be reserved for credit institutions or not, for payment services it was accepted from the beginning that the payments market would be opened up to other service providers than traditional financial actors. Unlike e-money institutions – which were under the initial EMD1 a specific type of credit institutions – payment institutions were established as a new type of service provider. To satisfy concerns voiced by more conservative stakeholders – such as the ECB – strict requirements were imposed on payment service providers, similar but somewhat less stringent to those imposed on e-money institutions.

Payment services – While some points in the payment services legal framework elicited long discussions before a compromise could be reached, the designation of the payment services covered under the directive was only changed very limitedly between the original proposal and the eventual PSD1. Also the adoption of the PSD2 provided only limited change here, mainly the introduction of third party payment service providers.

Negative scope – Though the provisions forming the negative scope of the payment services legal framework did go through a number of revisions throughout the initial legislative process, they also elicited fairly little discussion. While practice pointed out a number of implementation issues for certain scope exemptions, their review brought some rephrasing but little discussion.

Result – It are the operational requirements for payment institutions that were debated the most during the legislative procedure. The positive and negative scope received only fairly little discussion, thus unfortunately providing little further insight on the European Commission's intentions with those provisions.

## 3.2 PAYMENT SERVICES SCOPE

DEFINITION AND SCOPE EXEMPTIONS – Having analyzed the legislative procedures leading up to both Payment Services Directives and the main provisions of each directive, this section will delve deeper into the scope of the payment services legal framework. On the one hand, the focus will be put on the positive scope, by analyzing what constitutes payment services under the payment services legal framework. On the other hand, the focus is put on the negative scope, by analyzing a number of the scope exemptions to the payment services legal framework.

### *3.2.1 Positive scope*

PAYMENT SERVICES – Both the PSD1 and the PSD2 apply to the provision of payment services by payment service providers. That approach is similar to the E-money Directives, where a particular service is identified – the issuing of e-money – and where subsequently the service providers that can provide such a service are listed and regulated. In both Payment Services Directives, payment services are listed in an annex. The difference between both directives is that the PSD1 listed the "*execution of payment transactions where the consent of the payer to execute a payment transaction is given by means of any telecommunication, digital or IT device and the payment is made to the telecommunication, IT system or network operator, acting only as an intermediary between the payment service user and the supplier of the goods and services*"[1378], whereas the PSD2 removes that provision and adds payment initiation services and account information services.

USERS – A payment service is provided to a payment service user, which is "*a natural or legal person making use of a payment service in the capacity of payer, payee, or both*".[1379] The fact that such a user can be either a natural person or a legal person indicates that in principle no differentiation is made between consumers and non-consumers.[1380] It is, however, important to ascertain whether a payment service user is a consumer or not, as certain principles –

1378 Annex, point 7. PSD1.

1379 Article 4 (10) PSD1; article 4 (10) PSD2.

1380 A consumer is, for the purposes of the directives, defined as "*a natural person who, in payment service contracts covered by this Directive, is acting for purposes other than his or her trade, business or profession*" (emphasis added). Article 4 (11) PSD1; article 4 (20) PSD2.

such as the information duties and the division of liability – are different for consumer payment service users.[1381]

Main activity – Moreover, both directives state that they should only be applied to those service providers that provide payment services as part of their main or regular occupation or business activity.[1382] The incidental provision of a payment service should therefore not be subjected to the scope of the payment services legal framework.[1383] That point can be criticized, as it essentially creates a duality between different service providers offering the same service, whereby one does so occasionally, and the other does it primarily.[1384]

Funds – As a core principle, the payment services covered by the directives revolve around the notion of 'funds', which is defined as "*banknotes and coins, scriptural money or electronic money as defined in point (2) of Article 2 of Directive 2009/110/EC*".[1385] A couple of remarks must be made regarding that definition.

First, it is clear that virtual currencies are not banknotes or coins, at the very least due to them being non-physical. Earlier in this chapter, it was also held that the virtual currencies analyzed here will not constitute e-money. In the definition of 'funds', virtual currencies would then have to classify as 'scriptural money'. The European Commission has attempted to define the latter notion, holding that it is the opposite of coins and banknotes, constituting funds "*on any kind of accounts*".[1386] It is said that those accounts must be held by banks or

1381 Berger, P. E., Landuyt, S. (2012) "Toepassingsgebied van de wet betalingsdiensten en de wet betalingsinstellingen", In: Instituut Financieel Recht (Ed.), *Financiële regulering in de kering*, Antwerpen: Intersentia, 130–131; Steennot, R. (2010) "Girale en elektronische betalingen: nieuwe wettelijke regeling", *Nieuw Juridisch Weekblad*, nr. 226, 519; Byttebier, K., Wera, T. (2011) "Het toepassingsgebied van de wet van 10 december 2009 betreffende de betalingsdiensten (samen) ge(s)teld", In: Feron, B. (Ed.) *Betalingsdiensten: de nieuwe regeling onder de loep genomen / Services de paiement: la nouvelle réglementation passée au crible*, Antwerpen: Intersentia, 95–96.

1382 Recital 6 PSD1; recital 24 PSD2. Both recitals are to be read jointly with article 1 (2) of their respective directives. However, these payment services are not necessarily the provider's only services offered. Mavromati, D. (2008) *The law of payment services in the EU*, Alphen aan de Rijn: Kluwer Law International, 150.

1383 Houben, R. (2015) "Bitcoin: there are two sides to every coin", *Tijdschrift voor Belgisch Handelsrecht*, nr. 2015/2, 156; Berger, P. E., Landuyt, S. (2012) "Toepassingsgebied van de wet betalingsdiensten en de wet betalingsinstellingen", In: Instituut Financieel Recht (Ed.), *Financiële regulering in de kering*, Antwerpen: Intersentia, 101 & 136–138. This was confirmed by the European Commission in its Q&A on payment services: European Commission (2011) "Your questions on PSD", *ec.europa.eu/internal_market/payments/docs/framework/transposition/faq_en.pdf*, question 125.

1384 Digital Policy Alliance (2013) "Position paper on the proposed review of the Payment Services Directive", *dpalliance.org.uk*, 5–6.

1385 Article 4 (25) PSD2. Article 4(15) PSD1 uses the same definition, albeit that this 2007 directive referred to the EMD1. Note also that, while payment services may involve the use of e-money, payment institutions cannot issue e-money. Mavromati, D. (2008) *The law of payment services in the EU*, Alphen aan de Rijn: Kluwer Law International, 168.

1386 *Ec.europa.eu/internal_market/payments/docs/framework/transposition/faq_en.pdf*, question 255.

other payment service providers. Such means that virtual currencies would in any case only be able to constitute 'funds' in the sense of the payment services legal framework when held on accounts at banks or payment service providers.

Second, the European Commission has at one point also remarked that privately issued currencies could fall under the scope of the 'funds' definition, regardless of their denomination.[1387] Here, it must be noted that such a broad interpretation – not embedded within the directives themselves – has not been followed in the national transpositions.[1388] It therefore does not immediately follow from the Commission's statement that virtual currencies – despite essentially being privately issued currencies – could fall under the scope of the 'funds' notion as employed in the payment services legal framework. Moreover, it must be remarked that the European Commission, at the time of its statement, did not specifically address virtual currencies. Additionally, that statement was also made at a time where cryptocurrencies were not widely known yet, or at least had not yet come to the attention of legislators. It therefore seems unlikely that the European Commission had the particular development of virtual currencies in mind.

Last, where funds are not denominated in euro or a currency of an EU Member State outside of the Euro Area the PSD1 provided that titles III and IV of the directive do not apply.[1389] The PSD2 is broader in this regard: titles III and IV can still apply – barring a few exceptions – if all payment service providers are – or if the sole payment service provider involved is – located within the EU, for the aspects of the transaction conducted within the EU.[1390] When one of the payment service providers involved is located within the EU, titles III and IV will apply as well, but with more exceptions.[1391]

Relation to Directive 2013/36/EU – The approach of listing the activities covered by the legal framework in an annex is not entirely new. It closely follows the approach of Directive 2013/36/EU on access to the activity of credit institutions.[1392] The main difference is that the legal framework on payment services focuses on 'payment accounts', which are accounts held in the name of one or more payment service users, and used for the execution of payment

---

1387 *Ibid.*, question 164.

1388 In Belgium, for instance, such broader interpretation does not appear to find support. Boedts, T. (2014) "Kunnen crowdfunding en virtuele munten innoveren zonder bijkomende regulering?" in: IBJ (Ed.) *L'innovation, source de droit. Le droit, source d'innovation / Innovatie, bron van recht. Recht, bron van innovatie*, Brussels: Bruylant, 162.

1389 As follows from Article 2(2) PSD1.

1390 Article 2 (3) PSD2.

1391 Article 2 (4) PSD2.

1392 Directive 2013/36/EU of the European Parliament and of the Council of 26 June 2013 on access to the activity of credit institutions and the prudential supervision of credit institutions and investment firms, amending Directive 2002/87/EC and repealing Directives 2006/48/EC and 2006/49/EC, *OJ* L 176 of 27 June 2013, 338–436.

transactions.[1393] In doing so, the European legislator has attempted to steer payment services clear from the more traditional banking activities.[1394]

Cash placement and withdrawal – The first two types of payment services relate to services enabling the placement of cash on and the withdrawal of cash from a payment account as well as all the operations required for operating a payment account. Those types are fairly straightforward: since most payment services will require the user to have a payment account, the user must be given the possibility to place cash on that account, or to withdraw cash from it. Such a placement of cash on an account includes deposits performed in person at a credit institution, electronic deposits, as well as the deposit of funds on an e-money account.[1395] Operations required for operating a payment account can include the remote access to such an account.[1396]

Transactions funded by payment account or credit line – The following two types of payment services relate to the execution of payment transactions, including transfers of funds on a payment account with the user's payment service provider or with another payment service provider, or where the funds are covered by a credit line[1397] for a payment service user. Neither directive

---

1393 Article 4 (14) PSD1; article 4 (12) PSD2.

1394 Malaguti, M. C. (2009) "The Payment Services Directive: Pitfalls between the Acquis Communautaire and National Implementation", *CEPS-ECRI Research Report No. 9*, 5–7. Malaguti argues here that this distinction is not fully clear-cut, and is "*rather a matter of nuances and personal interpretation*". Steennot argues that savings accounts and term deposits are not covered by this scope, as they either do not offer the possibility to conduct deposits or withdrawals, or are not intended for regular deposits and withdrawals. Steennot, R. (2015) "Betalingsdiensten", In: Steennot, R., Stuyck, J., Vanhees, H., Wymeersch, E., Straetmans G. (Eds.) *Overzicht Financieel Recht Artikelsgewijze commentaren,* Mechelen: Kluwer, 66. See also: Byttebier, K., Wera, T. (2011) "Het toepassingsgebied van de wet van 10 december 2009 betreffende de betalingsdiensten (samen)ge(s)teld", In: Feron, B. (Ed.) *Betalingsdiensten: de nieuwe regelgeving onder de loep genomen / Services de paiement: la nouvelle réglementation passée au crible,* Antwerpen: Intersentia, 82–83; Lauwers, Y., Vanweddingen, I. (2008) "Toepassingsgebied Richtlijn betreffende betalingsdiensten in de interne markt", *Bank en Financieel Recht,* nr. 2008/VI, 372–386.

1395 Steennot, R. (2015) "Betalingsdiensten", In: Steennot, R., Stuyck, J., Vanhees, H., Wymeersch, E., Straetmans G. (Eds.) *Overzicht Financieel Recht Artikelsgewijze commentaren,* Mechelen: Kluwer, 48; Berger, P. E., Landuyt, S. (2012) "Toepassingsgebied van de wet betalingsdiensten en de wet betalingsinstellingen", In: Instituut Financieel Recht (Ed.), *Financiële regulering in de kering,* Antwerpen: Intersentia, 104–105; De Poorter, I. (2011) "De wet betreffende de betalingsdiensten leidt tot een betere bescherming van de consument", *Rechtskundig Weekblad,* nr. 32, 1332.

1396 Vandoolaeghe, A. (2010) "De Wet Betalingsdiensten op de korrel genomen", *Droit de la Consommation - Consumentenrecht,* nr. 89, 64.

1397 Such credit line can be extended within the framework of a traditional credit card agreement, but can also include so-called overdraft facilities. Berger, P. E., Landuyt, S. (2012) "Toepassingsgebied van de wet betalingsdiensten en de wet betalingsinstellingen", In: Instituut Financieel Recht (Ed.), *Financiële regulering in de kering,* Antwerpen: Intersentia,

distinguishes whether those services are conducted by paper or electronically.[1398] Such transactions must relate to: (a) the execution of direct debits, including one-off direct debits; (b) the execution of payment transactions through a payment card or a similar device; or (c) the execution of credit transfers, including standing orders. Also those types are relatively simple: payment services will to large extent involve the execution of payment transactions. Such payment transactions are defined as "*an act, initiated by the payer or on his behalf or by the payee, of placing, transferring or withdrawing funds, irrespective of any underlying obligations between the payer and the payee*".[1399] The funds that are being transferred can come from either a payment account, or from a credit line.[1400] Direct debit is defined as "*a payment service for debiting a payer's payment account, where a payment transaction is initiated by the payee on the basis of the consent given by the payer to the payee, to the payee's payment service provider or to the payer's own payment service provider*".[1401] Direct debit is often used to automatically pay utility bills, such as for telecom services, gas, or electricity. While the directives do not define what a "*payment card or a similar device*" is, it can be gathered that it includes credit, debit, and e-money cards.[1402] Last, credit transfers are defined

---

108; Mavromati, D. (2008) *The law of payment services in the EU*, Alphen aan de Rijn: Kluwer Law International, 162–163.

1398 De Poorter, I. (2011) "De wet betreffende de betalingsdiensten leidt tot een betere bescherming van de consument", *Rechtskundig Weekblad*, nr. 32, 1333; Steennot, R. (2015) "Betalingsdiensten", In: Steennot, R., Stuyck, J., Vanhees, H., Wymeersch, E., Straetmans G. (Eds.) *Overzicht Financieel Recht Artikelsgewijze commentaren*, Mechelen: Kluwer, 49; Vandevoorde, W. (2011) "De Belgische omzetting van Richtlijn 2007/64/EG betreffende betalingsdiensten in de interne markt. Een overzicht.", *Tijdschrift Financieel Recht*, nr. 2011/3, 11. Though it is noted that special provisions can be made for paper-based transactions, such as the extension of the execution time (article 83 PSD2).

1399 Article 4 (5) PSD1; article 4 (5) PSD2. This definition was made sufficiently broad in order to cover both actions initiated by the payee – such as direct debits – and actions initiated by the payer – such as credit transfers. The result of this broad definition is that the list of transactions included here should not be considered as exhaustive. Berger, P. E., Landuyt, S. (2012) "Toepassingsgebied van de wet betalingsdiensten en de wet betalingsinstellingen", In: Instituut Financieel Recht (Ed.), *Financiële regulering in de kering*, Antwerpen: Intersentia, 105–106; Steennot, R. (2015) "Betalingsdiensten", In: Steennot, R., Stuyck, J., Vanhees, H., Wymeersch, E., Straetmans G. (Eds.) *Overzicht Financieel Recht Artikelsgewijze commentaren*, Mechelen: Kluwer, 50–51, Proctor, C. (2010) *The law and practice of international banking*, Oxford: University Press, 78. Steennot argues that also meal vouchers and service cheques could be considered under the scope of this notion, as can payments using e-money, albeit that some of these could still be subject to one of the scope exemptions of articles 3 of both directives.

1400 The difference being that the funds are already available on a payment account, whereas with a credit line the funds are made available on that credit.

1401 Article 4 (28) PSD1; article 4 (23) PSD2.

1402 Baker & McKenzie (2015) "Research project regarding payment services, bank group regulations and others, for Japan Financial Services Agency – Final report – Europe", *fsa.go.jp*, 2; Byttebier, K., Wera, T. (2011) "Het toepassingsgebied van de wet van 10 december 2009 betreffende de betalingsdiensten (samen)ge(s)teld", In: Feron, B. (Ed.) *Betalingsdiensten: de nieuwe regeling onder de loep genomen / Services de paiement: la nouvelle réglementation passée au crible*, Antwerpen: Intersentia, 85; Berger, P. E., Landuyt, S. (2012) "Toepassingsgebied van de wet betalingsdiensten en de wet betalingsinstellingen", In:

as "*a payment service for crediting a payee's payment account with a payment transaction or a series of payment transactions from a payer's payment account by the payment service provider which holds the payer's payment account, based on an instruction given by the payer*".[1403] Such credit transfers can be used for recurrent payments of a fixed amount, such as the payment of rent.[1404]

Issuing or acquiring of instruments – The next type of payment services concerns the issuing of payment instruments and/or acquiring of payment transactions. A payment instrument is defined as a "*personalised device(s) and/or set of procedures agreed between the payment service user and the payment service provider and used in order to initiate a payment order*".[1405] That is a very broad definition, which could encompass traditional payment cards[1406], vouchers, or even technical instruments such as mobile phones, but also procedures – such as a login and password, or PIN codes.[1407] The PSD2 also adds a definition for the issuing of payment instruments, considering it as "*a payment service by a payment service provider contracting to provide a payer with a payment instrument to initiate and process the payer's payment transactions*".[1408] The traditional example here is the credit institution issuing a debit card to its customer. The PSD2 also defines acquiring, considering it as "*a payment service provided by a payment service provider contracting with a payee to accept and process payment transactions, which results in a transfer of funds to the payee*".[1409] Typically, the acquirer provides the merchant with the terminals needed to receive payments.[1410]

---

Instituut Financieel Recht (Ed.), *Financiële regulering in de kering*, Antwerpen: Intersentia, 107; De Poorter, I. (2011) "De wet betreffende de betalingsdiensten leidt tot een betere bescherming van de consument", *Rechtskundig Weekblad*, nr. 32, 1333.

1403 Article 4 (24) PSD2. Note that the PSD1 did not include a definition for this notion.

1404 Berger, P. E., Landuyt, S. (2012) "Toepassingsgebied van de wet betalingsdiensten en de wet betalingsinstellingen", In: Instituut Financieel Recht (Ed.), *Financiële regulering in de kering*, Antwerpen: Intersentia, 108.

1405 Article 4 (23) PSD1; article 4 (14) PSD2.

1406 Both credit and debit cards. Mavromati, D. (2008) *The law of payment services in the EU*, Alphen aan de Rijn: Kluwer Law International, 165.

1407 Baker & McKenzie (2015) "Research project regarding payment services, bank group regulations and others, for Japan Financial Services Agency – Final report – Europe", *fsa.go.jp*, 3; European Commission (2011) "Your questions on PSD", *ec.europa.eu/internal_market/payments/docs/framework/transposition/faq_en.pdf*, question 34; Vandevoorde, W. (2011) "De Belgische omzetting van Richtlijn 2007/64/EG betreffende betalingsdiensten in de interne markt. Een overzicht.", *Tijdschrift Financieel Recht*, nr. 2011/3, 11–12; Alter, C. (2010) *Droit bancaire général*, Brussels: Larcier, 249–250. Also, the Court of Justice of the European Union found that procedures "*for ordering transfers through online banking constitute payment instruments within the meaning of that provision*". CJEU, T-Mobile Austria GmbH *v.* Verein für Konsumenteninformation, *C-616/11*, paragraph 44.

1408 Article 4 (45) PSD2.

1409 Article 4 (44) PSD2.

1410 Steennot, R. (2015) "Betalingsdiensten", In: Steennot, R., Stuyck, J., Vanhees, H., Wymeersch, E., Straetmans G. (Eds.) *Overzicht Financieel Recht Artikelsgewijze commentaren*, Mechelen: Kluwer, 51–52.

Money remittance – The following type of payment services is money remittance. That notion is defined under both Payment Services Directives as "*a payment service where funds are received from a payer, without any payment accounts being created in the name of the payer or the payee, for the sole purpose of transferring a corresponding amount to a payee or to another payment service provider acting on behalf of the payee, and/or where such funds are received on behalf of and made available to the payee*".[1411] In other words, such services allow users to transfer money without requiring an account.[1412] It is a simple payment service, usually cash-based, that is provided by non-financial actors such as supermarkets, merchants and other retailers in the form of bill-paying services.[1413]

Third parties – As noted, the PSD2 adds two new types of payment services, namely regarding the so-called third party payment service providers. Those concern payment initiation services and account information services. Payment initiation services operate as a bridge between, typically, the merchant's website and the payer's bank account.[1414] Account information services aggregate users' financial information across different accounts and service providers, thus helping to centralize financial management and spending.[1415] In both cases, such service providers will not come into possession of users' funds and therefore they are not subjected to the full scope of the payment services legal framework.[1416]

Intermediary operator – The PSD2 also removes a type of payment services, namely regarding the execution of payment transactions where the consent of the payer to execute a payment transaction is given by means of any telecommunication, digital or IT device and the payment is made to the telecommunication, IT system or network operator, acting only as an intermediary between the payment service user and the supplier of the goods and services. The main goal of that element was to ensure that developments in mobile payments could also be brought under the scope of the payment services legal framework.[1417] Essentially, it required the operator to act

1411 Article 4 (13) PSD1; article 4 (22) PSD2.

1412 A typical example here is Western Union. Vandevoorde, W. (2011) "De Belgische omzetting van Richtlijn 2007/64/EG betreffende betalingsdiensten in de interne markt. Een overzicht.", *Tijdschrift Financieel Recht*, nr. 2011/3, 13–14.

1413 Recital 7 PSD1; recital 9 PSD2.

1414 Essentially, payers are redirected from the merchant's website to the payment initiation service, where they can enter their banking details before being presented with a pre-filled payment form. Donnelly, M. (2016) "Payments in the digital market: Evaluating the contribution of Payment Services Directive II", *Computer Law & Security Review*, Vol. 32, 4.

1415 *Ibid.*, 5.

1416 *Id.* Though it must be noted there is still an initial capital requirement imposed on payment initiation services providers, even higher than that of those only providing money remittance: article 7 (b) PSD2.

1417 Baker & McKenzie (2015) "Research project regarding payment services, bank group regulations and others, for Japan Financial Services Agency – Final report – Europe",

only as a mere intermediary, thus not providing added value to the services provided.[1418]

### 3.2.2 *Scope exemptions*

Negative scope – As already referred to earlier, both Payment Services Directives list a rather significant number of cases that fall outside their scope of application. Each directive lists 15 scope exemptions, concerning services that are principally payment services according to the annex to the directives, but which were then excluded from the scope by means of those exemptions. A number of those exemptions concern services involving the use of physical cash money or paper instruments such as cheques. Here, the focus will be put only on three exemptions relevant for the purposes of this research. Note that the first two exemptions discussed here also apply to the legal framework on e-money.

#### 3.2.2.1 Added value exemption

Added value exemption – The first of scope exception relevant for the purposes of this research is the added value exception. The PSD1 considered payment services as, amongst others, payment transactions executed and consented to by telecommunication, digital or IT devices to the provider of such a device or network and acting as an intermediary between the user and the supplier of the goods and services.[1419] For those purposes, the position of the payment service provider as an intermediary is important, as a more elaborate role could be considered to fall under a scope exemption.[1420] If a payment service provider were therefore to add value to his role by offering a broader range of services, it could thus exceed the role of a mere intermediary.[1421] A mobile

---

*fsa.go.jp*, 3; Vandoolaeghe, A. (2010) "De Wet Betalingsdiensten op de korrel genomen", *Droit de la Consommation – Consumentenrecht*, nr. 89, 65.

1418 Steennot, R. (2015) "Betalingsdiensten", In: Steennot, R., Stuyck, J., Vanhees, H., Wymeersch, E., Straetmans G. (Eds.) *Overzicht Financieel Recht Artikelsgewijze commentaren*, Mechelen: Kluwer, 52–53. Steennot provides the example of the SMS parking ticket, whereby the payment is made through the network operator, but where that network operator provides no additional service. Mavromati, D. (2008) *The law of payment services in the EU*, Alphen aan de Rijn: Kluwer Law International, 169–171; Byttebier, K., Wera, T. (2011) "Het toepassingsgebied van de wet van 10 december 2009 betreffende de betalingsdiensten (samen) ge(s)teld", In: Feron, B. (Ed.) *Betalingsdiensten: de nieuwe regeling onder de loep genomen / Services de paiement: la nouvelle réglementation passée au crible*, Antwerpen: Intersentia, 86–87; Jacquemin, H. (2010) "Les paiements électroniques dans les contrats à distance depuis la loi du 10 décembre 2009", *Revue du Droit des Technologies de l'Information*, nr. 41, 7–8.

1419 Annex to the PSD1.

1420 Article 3 (l) PSD1; DLA Piper (2009) "EU study on the Legal analysis of a Single Market for the Information Society – New rules for a new age?", *ec.europa.eu*, 12–13.

1421 DLA Piper (2009) "EU study on the Legal analysis of a Single Market for the Information Society – New rules for a new age?", *ec.europa.eu*, 12–13. See also recital 6 to the PSD1, providing that it is appropriate for the '*legal framework to apply to cases where the operator*

operator, for instance, who does not just act as the intermediary between user and service provider, but who provides that very service itself – for instance selling ringtones – can fall under the added value scope exemption.[1422] The exemption, however, only applies to goods or services delivered to and used by telecommunication, digital or IT devices.[1423] It therefore does not apply when physical goods are purchased.

Proposal PSD2 – The proposal for a revised Payment Services Directive stated with regard to the added value exemption that the payment transaction must be conducted by a "*provider of electronic communication networks or services*" to a subscriber to those networks or services for the purchase or consumption of the received content, regardless of what device is used, or performed from or via an electronic device and charged to the related bill within the framework of a charitable activity or for the purchase of tickets. That means that the provision of digital content must be seen as an ancillary service to the electronic communications services provided by the network or service provider. Moreover, the European Commission proposed a clear value limit, limiting the scope of the exemption to single transactions of maximum EUR 50 and cumulative transactions of maximum EUR 200 per billing month. All transactions exceeding that value will automatically fall under the scope of the payment services legal framework, meaning that the providers of such transactions will need to comply with the duties and responsibilities imposed upon them. The clarification that the added value exemption should only apply to providers of electronic communications services means that the exemption is unlikely to apply to the providers of, for instance, cryptocurrency services.[1424] The inclusion of a value limit can, however, be welcomed as an important element in raising legal

---

*acts only as an intermediary who simply arranges for payment to be made to a third-party supplier*' (emphasis added).

1422 Steennot, R. (2015) "Betalingsdiensten", In: Steennot, R., Stuyck, J., Vanhees, H., Wymeersch, E., Straetmans G. (Eds.) *Overzicht Financieel Recht Artikelsgewijze commentaren*, Mechelen: Kluwer, 129–130; Donnelly, M. (2016) "Payments in the digital market: Evaluating the contribution of Payment Services Directive II", *Computer Law & Security Review*, Vol. 32, 6. This exemption thus aims to correct the issue regarding mobile operators falling under the scope of the EMD1. It applies to both the legal framework on payment services and that of e-money. Mansour, Y. (2014) "Regulating payments for M-Content: The positive impact of the deregulation", *International Review of Law*, Vol. 9, 10. De Prez and Timmermans further remind that in the case of mobile operators, this exemption can with regard to e-money only apply in prepaid schemes, not in post-paid schemes. De Prez, P., Timmermans, V. (2013) "Een doorstart voor het elektronisch geld? Analyse van de nieuwe regelgeving", *Bank en Financieel Recht*, nr. 2013/I, paragraph 29.

1423 Note also that in such case, the provider could be viewed as not directly receiving payments, although this is unclear from the text of the directive and may be difficult if not impossible for the user to discern. According to the PSD1, only the technical service provider (Article 3 (j)) is prohibited from entering into possession of funds in order to benefit from the scope exemption.

1424 Unless such service provider would indeed be a provider of electronic communication networks or services.

certainty regarding the applicability of the payment services legal framework to a certain payment transaction or not.[1425] It eliminates the need to analyze and interpret the description of the exemption and allows the user to evaluate for himself whether or not a particular transaction will be covered by the payment services framework or not just by looking at the value thereof. Beyond the value limit, however, there is still an important part of the provision defined by its description, albeit a more clearly defined description than was the case under the PSD1. The focus has been put not on the device, but on the provider of electronic communication networks or services. Also, moving away from the much debated concept of an intermediary in favor of the use of 'services ancillary to electronic communications services' can be considered as a clear attempt at restricting the originally rather broad scope of the added value scope exemption.

PSD2 – The final text of the PSD2 follows the Commission's proposal fairly closely, with a few added elements.[1426] First, it is specified that the payment transactions must be performed *in addition* to electronic communications services for a subscriber to the network or service.[1427] Second, apart from digital content, the text adds voice-based services, as well as that the transaction can also relate to consumption of the digital content, charged to the related bill. Also transactions performed from or via an electronic device and charged to the related bill within the framework of a charitable activity or for the purchase of tickets are included. Third, the cumulative monthly value has been raised to EUR 300, and also applies to prepaid accounts.

#### 3.2.2.2 Limited network exemption

LIMITED NETWORKS EXEMPTION – The second scope exemption relevant to this research is the limited networks exemption, which held that the PSD1 did not apply to services used for the acquisition of goods or services '*within a limited network of service providers or for a limited range of goods or services*'.[1428] Here could, for instance, closed and curated online store platforms – also referred to as 'walled gardens' – be argued to pass as limiting the range of services offered, as well as the range of service providers offering their services. As the application of the limited networks scope exemption has proven problematic in practice, arguments could be made either way.[1429]

---

1425 Vandezande, N. (2014) "Between Bitcoins and mobile payments: will the European Commission's new proposal provide more legal certainty?", *International Journal of Law and Information Technology*, Vol. 22, 306.

1426 Article 3 (l) PSD2.

1427 Recital 15 PSD2 gives a number of examples such as ringtones and premium SMS services, or voting and contest participation in TV and radio shows.

1428 Article 3 (k) PSD1.

1429 DLA Piper (2009) "EU study on the Legal analysis of a Single Market for the Information Society – New rules for a new age?", *ec.europa.eu*, 18.

Proposal PSD2 – For the limited network exemption, the proposal referred to examples such as "*store cards, fuel cards, membership cards, public transport cards, meal vouchers or vouchers for specific services*", as also found in the EMD2.[1430] Moreover, the Proposal PSD2 added phrases such as 'specific instruments' and 'used in a limited way'. From that description, it already is clear that the Commission has not followed a proposal to replace the limited networks scope exemption description by a value of transactions that would be exempt from the applicability of the payment services legal framework. While the proposed clarifications could be understood as an effort to demarcate and narrow down the exemption's scope, such vague and undefined terminology leaves the same potential for broad and divergent interpretations as the original wording did. It could therefore be expected that the limited networks scope exemption – if it were been adopted in its original form – would still result in divergent application practices between Member States. What can be considered as a 'specific instrument'? Which are the 'precise needs' that should be addressed by the services covered by the scope exemption? What is the qualification of a 'professional issuer'? Without such a proper definition, the additions to the 'limited networks' scope exemption did not seem to provide for the more objective, adequate or transparent criteria required to define the exemption.[1431]

PSD2 – The final text of the PSD2 maintains the examples given in its recitals, and tones down some of the unspecified language of the proposal.[1432], [1433] The focus of the exemption has been put on three cases. First, there are the instruments allowing the holder to acquire goods or services only in the

1430 Recital 12 Proposal PSD2.

1431 Bond Pearce (2013) "Review of payment services (and e-money) requirements – a development to watch...", *bondpearce.com*, 2; Digital Policy Alliance (2013) "Position Paper on the proposed review of the Payment Services Directive", *dpalliance.org.uk*, 6.

1432 Article 3 (k) PSD2.

1433 Recital 14 PSD2. It must be noted that the degree of limitation of certain of these instruments can be debated. The meal vouchers used in Belgium, for instance, can be used not just to buy meals at a very wide range of restaurants, but can also be used to buy food-products in supermarkets. They are therefore a payment instrument that can be used for a wide range of products, at a wide range of service providers. However, the Belgian legislator has expressed its clear intention to keep these instruments under the scope exemption. Steennot, R. (2015) "Betalingsdiensten", In: Steennot, R., Stuyck, J., Vanhees, H., Wymeersch, E., Straetmans G. (Eds.) *Overzicht Financieel Recht Artikelsgewijze commentaren*, Mechelen: Kluwer, 126; Berger, P. E., Landuyt, S. (2012) "Toepassingsgebied van de wet betalingsdiensten en de wet betalingsinstellingen", In: Instituut Financieel Recht (Ed.), *Financiële regulering in de kering*, Antwerpen: Intersentia, 127–128; De Prez, P., Timmermans, V. (2013) "Een doorstart voor het elektronisch geld? Analyse van de nieuwe regelgeving", *Bank en Financieel Recht*, nr. 2013/I, paragraph 21. The recital to the Second Services Directive, however, allows that the exemption should no longer apply when one of these instruments evolves into a general-purpose payment instrument, which is arguably the case for the Belgian meal voucher. See also: Gürkaynak, G., Yilmaz, I. (2015) "Regulating payment services and electronic money: A comparative regulatory approach with a specific focus on Turkish legislation", *Computer Law & Security Review*, Vol. 31, 403–404.

premises of the issuer or within a limited network of service providers under direct commercial agreement with a professional issuer. Second, there are the instruments which can be used only to acquire a very limited range of goods or services. Third, there are the instruments valid only in a single Member State provided at the request of an undertaking or a public sector entity and regulated by a national or regional public authority for specific social or tax purposes to acquire specific goods or services from suppliers having a commercial agreement with the issuer. Moreover, some more clarification is offered in the recitals to the directive, where it is held that a limited network concerns a specific retailer or chain of retailers, a limited range of goods or services, or when it concerns a payment instrument locally regulated for specific tax or social purposes.[1434]

### 3.2.2.3 Money exchange exemption

MONEY EXCHANGE SERVICES – Finally, it must be noted that the PSD1 did not include money exchange services under its scope of application.[1435] As many cryptocurrency services are aimed at providing precisely exchange services, that could at first regard also put those service providers outside of the scope of the directive. However, the scope exemption clarifies that it concerns cash-to-cash operations, where the funds are not held on a payment account, which seems difficult to apply to the non-physical virtual currencies.[1436] During the review process of the directive, it was remarked that the exemption created a system where physical exchange services would be exempt, yet where exchange services where an account comes into play – and the directive does not specify whether it concerns the exchanger's or the user's account – are covered by the directive.[1437]

PSD2 – Apart from some minor changes in word order, the money exchange exemption was not modified in the PSD2.

---

1434 Recital 13 PSD2. Furthermore, recital 14 lists a number of examples, as was already done in the EMD2.

1435 Article 3 (f) PSD1.

1436 Indeed, while coins and banknotes are included under the scope of 'funds', cash transactions are generally excluded from the scope of application. Smits, R. (2008) "The Changing Payments Landscape of Europe: Issues of Regulation and Competition", *Yearbook of European Law*, Vol. 27, 428. Steennot notes that this exemption is primarily aimed at physical exchange bureaus. Steennot, R. (2015) "Betalingsdiensten", In: Steennot, R., Stuyck, J., Vanhees, H., Wymeersch, E., Straetmans G. (Eds.) *Overzicht Financieel Recht Artikelsgewijze commentaren,* Mechelen: Kluwer, 115; Proctor, C. (2010) *The law and practice of international banking,* Oxford: University Press, 80. Berger and Landuyt, however, argue for a broader application whereby payment for foreign funds received in cash at an exchange bureau can be conducted electronically. Berger, P. E., Landuyt, S. (2012) "Toepassingsgebied van de wet betalingsdiensten en de wet betalingsinstellingen", In: Instituut Financieel Recht (Ed.), *Financiële regulering in de kering,* Antwerpen: Intersentia, 122.

1437 London Economics (2013) "Study on the impact of directive 2007/64/EC on payment services in the internal market and on the application of regulation (EC) No. 924/2009 on cross-border payments in the Community", *MARKT/2011/120/H3/ST/OP,* 128.

## 3.3 PAYMENT SERVICES AND VIRTUAL CURRENCIES

Application of legal framework – Having analyzed the positive and negative scope of the EU's legal framework on payment services, this section will now analyze whether or not services developed around the types of virtual currencies identified in chapter I can be considered as payment services.

### 3.3.1 *Closed scheme virtual currencies*

Closed schemes – Transactions can generally be regarded as involving a transfer of funds by one party, and the delivery of goods or services by another party.[1438] A payment system is then "*a funds transfer system with formal and standardised arrangements and common rules for the processing, clearing and/or settlement of payment transactions*".[1439] Virtual currencies have been compared to retail payment systems without financial intermediaries, in the sense that payment instruments – authorizing and submitting the payment – are used in the process of processing and clearing transactions – meaning the exchange of a payment instruction between creditor and debtor – resulting in the settlement of debits and credits in the user's account.[1440] While closed scheme virtual currencies operate in an isolated virtual world, they could be regarded as facilitating transactions within that world. However, for the purposes of the EU legal framework on payment services, it is clear that services regarding closed scheme virtual currencies are not considered under its scope. Moreover, the services regarding closed scheme virtual currencies are in any case be able to benefit from the limited networks exemption, as they can only be used within a limited network – *in casu* a virtual world.

### 3.3.2 *Unidirectional scheme virtual currencies*

Unidirectional schemes – For what has been identified in chapter I as unidirectional virtual currencies, it can be said that related services typically benefit from the limited networks exemption, insofar as they could be considered as payment services, as they can mostly only be redeemed at the issuer or in a limited network around that issuer. However, attention must be drawn to the fact that those instruments could theoretically develop into more general-purpose payment instruments, in which case the limited networks exemptions should no longer apply. One example where the initial purpose of a virtual currency has been exceeded are frequent-flyer programs, where the virtual currencies used here can often already be used for much broader purposes than simply booking

1438 European Central Bank (2012) "Virtual Currency Schemes", *ecb.europa.eu*, 17.

1439 Article 4 (6) PSD1; article 4 (7) PSD2.

1440 European Central Bank (2012) "Virtual Currency Schemes", *ecb.europa.eu*, 17; Kokkola, T. (2009) *The payment system: payments, securities and derivates, and the roles of the Eurosystem*, Frankfurt: European Central Bank, 25.

flights – such as car rentals or hotel bookings. While such does not necessarily constitute an excess of the limited networks exemption yet – as such services are still clearly linked to a limited network around the issuer – further enlargement of the use of that virtual currency could have such an effect.

### 3.3.3 *Bidirectional scheme virtual currencies*

#### 3.3.3.1 General remarks

Bidirectional schemes – For services developed around bidirectional virtual currencies, the answer is less straightforward. In chapter I, there were bidirectional virtual currencies identified – such as cryptocurrencies – that are, at least theoretically, general-purpose payment instruments. There are, however, also bidirectional virtual currencies – such as Second Life's Linden dollars – that can principally only be used in a limited realm around their issuer. It is clear that in the latter case, the limited networks exemption could apply.[1441] In the case of the former, a closer look is needed.[1442]

Application to cryptocurrency service providers – From their scope of application, it can be derived that the PSD1 and PSD2 aim to regulate only the service providers themselves and not the issuers of the funds used in such payments. As a result, neither directive can regulate the emission of cryptocurrency.[1443] Moreover, the formulation of payment services to which the directives apply does not appear to leave much room for the inclusion of cryptocurrencies.[1444] Therefore, the focus will have to be put on the application of the directives to third-party cryptocurrency service providers, such as cryptocurrency exchanges and virtual

1441 Also the narrowed scope of this exemption under the PSD2 would be applicable.

1442 The focus will be on cryptocurrencies. For M-Pesa, it was noted earlier that this service is within the EU registered as an e-money institution.

1443 European Central Bank (2012) "Virtual Currency Schemes", *ecb.europa.eu*, 43. The ECB mainly states that the PSD1 does not regulate e-money issuance, and therefore cannot apply to bitcoin. However, the ECB did earlier in the same opinion already state that bitcoin cannot be considered as e-money. Moreover, it is clear that the goal of the Payment Services Directives is to regulate certain service providers, not the emission of (e-)money. It is therefore unfortunate that the ECB neglected to delve deeper into the matter by analyzing whether third party cryptocurrency service providers could still be covered by the payment services legal framework.

1444 Stokes, for instance, argues that none of the payment services described here fit the workings of bitcoin. Stokes, R. (2012) "Virtual money laundering: the case of Bitcoin and the Linden dollar", *Information & Communications Technology Law*, Vol. 21, 228–229. This view is shared by Shcherbak: Shcherbak, S. (2014) "How should Bitcoin be regulated?", *European Journal of Legal Studies*, Vol. 7, 56–61. Moreover, both authors find several problems with the applicability of the relevant definitions to cryptocurrency ecosystems. For instance, since cryptocurrencies are principally at least pseudonymous, the element of "*held in the name of one or more payment service users*" of the definition of 'payment account' does not seem fulfilled. This, in turn, contributes to issues regarding the applicability of other definitions, such as that of 'payer'.

wallet service providers.[1445] Here, it is reminded that it was already established in section 3.2.1 that privately issued currencies could, at least according to the European Commission's interpretation, be considered as 'funds' for the purposes of the legal framework on payment services, be it that there are in such case limitations to the applicability of titles III and IV of the Payment Services Directives. Following that interpretation, it is theoretically possible for certain third-party cryptocurrency service providers to fall under the scope of the Payment Services Directives, be it with a limited field of application, insofar as they provide payment services.[1446] However, it must also be reminded that such a broad interpretation has not gained widespread following, and that it is unlikely to extend to virtual currencies.

#### 3.3.3.2 Member States' opinions

France – It has been argued in France that in the case of cryptocurrency exchanges, there is a receipt of funds – in the strict sense of banknotes, coins, scriptural money or e-money – in exchange for cryptocurrency, which could then be argued to constitute a payment service.[1447] That reasoning, however, flows from an interpretation of the payment services legal framework by mainly French authorities and courts, and does not appear to have gained widespread following.[1448]

---

1445 Regarding wallet service providers, a distinction must be made between those providing only the technical platform and those that enter into custody of their users' keys and/or funds. The former could be argued to fall under the scope of the technical service providers exemption (article 3 (j) of both Payment Services Directives), while the latter provides services closely related to those of exchange platforms, or even provided jointly with such services. European Commission (2016) "Impact assessment accompanying the document Proposal for a Directive of the European Parliament and the Council amending Directive (EU) 2015/849 on the prevention of the use of the financial system for the purposes of money laundering or terrorist financing and amending Directive 2009/101/EC", *SWD(2016) 223 final*, 31–32.

1446 Shcherbak, S. (2014) "How should Bitcoin be regulated?", *European Journal of Legal Studies*, Vol. 7, 57.

1447 Such is at least the position of the French banking supervisor Autorité de contrôle prudentiel et de resolution (ACPR). ACPR (2014) "Position de l'ACPR relative aux opérations sur Bitcoins en France Position", *2014-P-01*. This position was earlier hinted at by the French national bank: Banque de France (2013) "Les dangers liés au développement des monnaies virtuelles: l'exemple du bitcoin", *Focus*, nr. 10, 5–6; De Vauplane, H. (2015) "La fascination autour du Bitcoin et des "monnaies virtuelles": comment les définir?", *Alternatives Economiques*, 7 November 2015; Boedts, T. (2014) "Kunnen crowdfunding en virtuele munten innoveren zonder bijkomende regulering?" in: IBJ (Ed.) *L'innovation, source de droit. Le droit, source d'innovation / Innovatie, bron van recht. Recht, bron van innovatie*, Brussels: Bruylant, 162–163; Shcherbak, S. (2014) "How should Bitcoin be regulated?", *European Journal of Legal Studies*, Vol. 7, 64–66.

1448 While in one decision the Parisian Court of Appeals did not follow in one party's reasoning that a cryptocurrency exchange service constitutes a payment service, it did in a later decision – on the same case – rule that such service constitutes a payment service, thus requiring the service provider to comply with the requirements imposed on payment institutions under the payment services legal framework. The commercial court in Créteil came to the same conclusion in that case. It should be noted, however, that the facts of this particular case related more to the finding that the service provider had opened an account for its

GERMANY – In Germany, for instance, the financial supervisor BaFin considers cryptocurrencies to be *"financial instruments in the form of units of account pursuant to section 1 (11) sentence 1 of the German Banking Act (Kreditwesengesetz – KWG)"*.[1449] That means they are not considered under the scope of the German Payment Services Supervision Act (Zahlungsdiensteaufsichtsgesetz – ZAG). Normal use, mining or even the sale of cryptocurrencies would then not be put under supervision or authorization requirements. Only when a sale incorporates an element of contribution to create or preserve such a market, authorization requirements would be triggered. Important to note here is that the German KWG transposes MiFID1[1450] into German law. Therefore, that example will be examined more closely in chapter VI.[1451] In April 2017, BaFin acted against several companies involved in the OneCoin scheme, holding that they operated as unauthorized money remittance businesses.[1452] That is because they allowed payments to be made *"to various accounts held by IMS International Marketing Services GmbH with different credit institutions in Germany and forwarded this money on behalf of OneCoin Ltd to third parties"*.[1453]

---

main software retail business activities, and that the use of such account was incompatible with its side activities regarding a payment service providing bitcoin exchange. The courts declined to rule on the precise classification of bitcoin, finding it irrelevant in light of the company in question conducting all of its transactions in euro. The conclusion of the case is not generally accepted. Bonneau, for instance, argues that the particular activities in that case makes the company in question a payment service *user*, rather than a payment service *provider*. He further argues that none of the payment services listed by the directive would be applicable here. Court of Appeals Paris, 26 August 2011, nr. 11/15269; Court of Appeals Paris, 26 September 2013, nr. 12/00161; Commercial Court Créteil, 6 December 2011, nr. RG 2011F00771; De Vauplane, H. (2015) "Bitcoin et monnaies virtuelles: entre réglementation et essai de définition juridique", In. Daems, H., De Meuleneere, I., Houssa, C., Ragheno, N. (Eds.) *Digital Finance / La finance numérique*, Antwerpen: Intersentia, 37; Chaaben, M. (2016) *Le Financement participatif*, Saint-Denis: Connaissances et Savoirs, 166; Laverdet, C. (2014) "Bitcoin: par ici la cryptomonnaie!", *Revue Lamy Droit de l'Immatériel*, nr. 100, 91–92; Bonneau, T. (2014) "Une société qui utilise un compte bancaire sur lequel transitent des bitcoins est-elle un prestataire de service de paiement?", *La Semaine Juridique Entreprise et Affaires*, nr. 8, 1091; Crédot, F., Samin, T. (2012) "Clôture du compte en raison des activités exercées par le titulaire", *Revue de Droit bancaire et financier*, nr. 1–2012, comm. 2.

1449 Münzer, J. (2014) "Bitcoins: Supervisory assessment and risks to users", *bafin.de*.

1450 Directive 2004/39/EC of the European Parliament and of the Council of 21 April 2004 on markets in financial instruments amending Council Directives 85/611/EEC and 93/6/EEC and Directive 2000/12/EC of the European Parliament and of the Council and repealing Council Directive 93/22/EEC, *OJ* L 145 of 30 April 2004, 1–44.

1451 See also: Boehm, F., Pesch, P. (2014) "Bitcoin: A First Legal Analysis With Reference to German and US-American Law", In: Böhme, R., Brenner, M., Moore, T., Smith, M. (Eds.) *Financial Cryptography and Data Security, FC 2014 Workshops, LNCS 8438*, Berlin: Springer, 44–45.

1452 BaFin (2017) "IMS International Marketing Services GmbH: account freezing and winding-down of unauthorised money remittance business", *bafin.de*, 10 April; BaFin (2017) "Onecoin Ltd, Dubai: Prohibition of involvement in unauthorised money remittance business", *bafin.de*, 18 April.

1453 BaFin (2017) "Onecoin Ltd, Dubai: Prohibition of involvement in unauthorised money remittance business", *bafin.de*, 18 April.

LUXEMBOURG – Luxembourg, on the other hand, does appear to take a similar position as France, arguing that everyone planning to conduct activities within the financial sector – which includes virtual currency services – must notify the local regulator in order to have their need for prior authorization assessed. As in France, that position hinges on a very liberal interpretation of certain notions, including those of 'funds' and 'e-money'.[1454] The Commission de Surveillance du Secteur Financier (CSSF) has by now indeed licensed a number of service providers. One example is Snapswap, which operates a mobile messenger allowing instant cross-currency transactions via blockchain technology, which is licensed – as of August 2016 – as an e-money institution.[1455] Bitcoin exchange Bitstamp, on the other hand, is licensed as a payment service provider, allowing it to provide payment account transactions, money remittances, and operating as intermediary.[1456]

UK – The UK, by contrast, does not currently consider virtual currencies to fall under the scope of its existing legislation in the payment services field, though that may change in the future.[1457] However, Circle – a payments application provider that also utilizes virtual currencies – has been registered as an e-money institution.[1458]

### 3.3.3.3 European Commission's opinion

NO CLARITY IN THE TEXT – What is clear, is that the PSD1 does not provide a definitive answer as to whether third party services developed around cryptocurrencies can be considered as one of the payment services covered in its annex. The PSD2 does not provide any substantial changes in that regard, which would therefore ostensibly leave the final answer dependent on how Member States interpret the relevant provisions of the directive and their national implementation thereof.[1459]

INDICATION IN NEW PROPOSAL – However, in its proposal for amendments to the AMLD4[1460], the European Commission explicitly states that it did not want to

1454 Commission de Surveillance du Secteur Financier (2014) "Virtual Currencies", *Press release* 14 February.

1455 CSSF nr. W00000007.

1456 CSSF nr. Z00000012.

1457 HM Treasury, Baldwin, H. (2015) "UK to lead on big data research, says Harriett Baldwin", *gov.uk*, speech 14 October.

1458 FCA nr. 900480.

1459 For now, certain cryptocurrency exchanges have taken steps to ensure that their businesses are in order. The French exchange Paymium, for instance, relies on HiPay (registered as HPME), an e-money institution authorized in Belgium.

1460 Directive (EU) 2015/849 of the European Parliament and of the Council of 20 May 2015 on the prevention of the use of the financial system for the purposes of money laundering or terrorist financing, amending Regulation (EU) No 648/2012 of the European Parliament and of the Council, and repealing Directive 2005/60/EC of the European Parliament and of the

bring virtual currency exchange platforms under the scope of the PSD2, as such would "*submit them to broader consumer protection rules, licensing requirements and safeguarding requirements*".[1461] The Commission mainly feared that such would legitimize virtual currencies and "*drive consumers to believe VCs are safe and sound products*".[1462] The result is that third party cryptocurrency service providers are, as of yet and according to the European legislator, not covered by the EU legal framework on payment services.

#### 3.3.3.4 Exemptions

Limited networks exemption – Since cryptocurrencies are not very broadly accepted yet, they could have benefited from the limited networks scope exemption under the PSD1's wider range of possible interpretations.[1463] However, the application of that scope exemption as more narrowly redefined under the PSD2 to cryptocurrencies appears less plausible.

Money exchange exemption – Also the money exchange exemption would, as discussed in section 3.2.2, be difficult to apply given that it targets physical exchanges and cryptocurrency exchanges that by nature operate online, thus requiring the use of an account.[1464]

Added value exemption – Finally, the added value exemption would – due to the PSD2's narrowing down of its scope to electronic communications providers – not be applicable to those service providers.

#### 3.3.3.5 Additional remark

Case-by-case approach – It must be added that the analysis conducted here assumes the presence of all the typical elements of a virtual currency exchange service – such as the use of a payment account where funds are held. Given the variety of service providers active in the virtual currency field, it is possible that

Council and Commission Directive 2006/70/EC, *OJ* L 141 of 5 June 2015, 73–117. The anti-money laundering legal framework will be discussed in chapter V.

1461 European Commission (2016) "Impact assessment accompanying the document Proposal for a Directive of the European Parliament and the Council amending Directive (EU) 2015/849 on the prevention of the use of the financial system for the purposes of money laundering or terrorist financing and amending Directive 2009/101/EC", *SWD(2016) 223 final*, 30–31.

1462 *Ibid.*, 31.

1463 Houben, R. (2015) "Bitcoin: there are two sides to every coin", *Tijdschrift voor Belgisch Handelsrecht*, nr. 2, 156; Jacobs, E. (2011) "Bitcoin: A Bit Too Far?", *Journal of Internet Banking and Commerce*, vol. 16, 3.

1464 One example where this exemption could prove useful are the bitcoin ATM's. Essentially, these operate much like a physical exchange bureau – rather than like a traditional ATM – thus not requiring the use of a payment account in the sense of the payment services legal framework.

different conclusions can be reached for a particular service provider. As in the assessment of the applicability of the EMD2 earlier in this chapter, a case-by-case approach must therefore be prescribed.

### *3.3.4 Evaluation*

Evaluation – Unlike the findings regarding the applicability of the legal framework on e-money to virtual currencies, somewhat more generalizing conclusions can be drawn here. For closed scheme virtual currencies, it is clear that they should not be considered under what the European legislator intended to regulate with the legal framework on payment services. For unidirectional scheme virtual currencies, it can be held that – insofar as they can be considered as payment services – those virtual currency service providers most likely benefit from the limited networks exemption. Only for bidirectional scheme virtual currencies, the answer is less straightforward. Here, the usability of the virtual currency can become determinative. For limited-purpose instruments, the limited networks exemption could apply. For more general-purpose instruments, further assessment is needed. In the case of cryptocurrencies, it was found that cryptocurrency service providers should, principally, not be considered as payment service providers, despite interpretations to the contrary by certain Member States. However, given the broad range of business models and practices present in the virtual currency field, it is wise to also prescribe a case-by-case approach for bidirectional scheme virtual currencies as different operational configurations could lead to a different outcome.

Normative assessment – Also here, it must then be questioned whether the payment services legal framework could or should be amended to facilitate virtual currencies. Again, such an analysis is referred to section 5 of this chapter, as the legal frameworks on e-money and payment services should be assessed together.

## 4 TOWARD A UNIFIED FRAMEWORK?

Revision of EMD2[1465] – Article 17 of the EMD2 holds that the European Commission was to present a report on the implementation and impact of that directive by 1 November 2012. Such was intended to coincide with the review of the PSD1, suggesting a possible merger between both legal frameworks. However, due to the late implementation of the EMD2 by the Member States, such a report

1465 This section was first developed at: Valcke, P., Vandezande, N., Van de Velde, N. (2015) "The Evolution of Third Party Payment Providers and Cryptocurrencies Under the EU's Upcoming PSD2 and AMLD4", *SWIFT Institute Working Paper No. 2015-001*, 56–59.

has, as of the time of writing, not been presented yet.[1466] The result – together with the PSD2 being adopted already – is that the European Commission may propose amendments to the EMD2, adopt a Third E-money Directive (EMD3), or immediately integrate the e-money legal framework with that set by the PSD2.

Wide scope exceptions – When considering the possibility of a revision of the legal framework on e-money, a number of observations regarding the EMD2 can be made. While the EMD2 did correct some of the problems experienced with the EMD1[1467], its scope exemptions are still too wide and have caused differences in treatment between Member States.[1468] The result is that e-money institutions are still found to be concentrated in those Member States that employ a favorable interpretation.[1469]

Evolution away from prepaid cards – Moreover, a more fundamental observation regarding the EMD2's objectives can be made. Originally, it were multi-purpose prepaid cards that sparked the discussions that would lead up to the EMD1.[1470] By now, however, connected point-of-sale (POS) terminals that accept debit and credit cards have become ubiquitous in stores all over the world, transaction and telecom costs have been lowered, and transaction processing time has been shortened significantly. The result is that multi-purpose prepaid cards have outlived their general usefulness, and their most prominent examples are being discontinued.[1471] Luckily, the European legislator already foresaw an

---

1466 The European Commission has ordered a study on the impact of the EMD2. The results of this study were presented before the Payment Systems Market Expert Group on 28 April 2015, but the final report is yet to be released.

1467 Such as the definition of e-money, which stated that e-money must be *"issued on receipt of funds of an amount not less in value than the monetary value issued"*. This criterion was not adopted in full or at all by all Member States. The Evaluation Partnership ltd. (2006) "Evaluation of the E-money Directive (2000/46/EC) – final report", *ec.europa.eu*, 48. Another issue concerned mobile operators: as the prepaid credit they issue can be used for other purposes than making phone calls – such as buying ringtones or paying parking tickets – the practice of issuing such prepaid credit essentially made mobile operators e-money institutions. Mobile operators, of course, did not agree with being subjected to the e-money legal framework. European Commission (2005) "Application of the E-money Directive to mobile operators – Summary of replies to the Consultation paper of DG Internal Market", *ec.europa.eu*, 2. The result of this controversy was that the European Commission issued a guidance document, in which it pleads for a differentiated treatment of mobile operators. European Commission (2005) "Application of the E-money Directive to mobile operators – Guidance Note from the Commission Services", *ec.europa.eu*, 4.

1468 Janowski, P. (2015) "Study on the impact of Directive 2009/110/EC on the taking up, pursuit and prudential supervision of the business of electronic money institutions", *circabc.europa.eu/sd/a/16b51176-38ec-40f8-9dce-1d46e1c35ad9/4%20-%20Presentation%20EMD%20-%20April%2028th%20Meeting.ppt*, slide 8.

1469 *Ibid.*, slide 14.

1470 Such as Proton in Belgium, Chipknip in the Netherlands, and Geldkarte in Germany.

1471 Proton was terminated in 2014, as was Chipknip. Geldkarte is currently being phased out and will be discontinued in 2018.

extension of the scope of the e-money framework. Rather than focusing solely on the notion of electronic purses, as such multi-purpose prepaid cards are often called, the focus was specifically put on the broader notion of e-money. That notion is to be understood as also including network-based non-physical money, although the precise scope of the e-money notion has not always been very clear.[1472] Over the years, it has become evident that such has allowed pre-funded online payment schemes – such as PayPal – to become the foremost example of e-money.[1473]

Then what is e-money? – The application of the e-money legal framework to service providers such as PayPal or Google Pay has, however, never been very straightforward. Services such as those essentially allow their users to transfer money from their regular bank accounts to accounts held at the service provider, in order to allow for easy further transfers to other account holders.[1474] Here, some authors have argued that such account-based transfers do not fall under the scope of what was intended for the EU's legal framework on e-money.[1475] Nevertheless, PayPal did successfully register as an e-money institution in the UK.[1476] A few years later, however, it decided to register as a bank in

1472 Van der Wielen, H. (1997) "Electronic Money: a European Perspective", presented at the Seminar on Electronic Money, hosted by the Bank of England, London 4 February 1997, *www.simonl.org/docs/readeremdnb.pdf*, 16. In the same presentation, reference is made to "*electronic cash (on cards or networks)*", further evidencing that e-money could be used as the broader term, applying to both card-based and network-based systems. In its proposal for an Electronic Money Directive, the European Commission proposes a "*technology-neutral legal framework that harmonises the prudential supervision of electronic money institutions to the extent necessary for ensuring their sound and prudent operation and their financial integrity in particular*". European Commission (1998) "Proposal for a European Parliament and Council Directive on the taking up, the pursuit and the prudential supervision of the business of electronic money institutions (COM(1998) 461)", *OJ* C 317 of 15 October 1998, 7. Despite this clear desire to use broad terminology, a number of elements – such as the technical references in the EMD's e-money definition and the focus on low-value transactions – did maintain the impression that e-money mostly revolves around multi-purpose prepaid cards.

1473 The Evaluation Partnership ltd. (2006) "Evaluation of the E-money Directive (2000/46/EC) – final report", *ec.europa.eu*, 30.

1474 For instance, when a PayPal account is linked to a debit card, money is transferred from the bank account to which the debit card acts as access instrument to the PayPal account. The user can use this PayPal balance to conduct subsequent transfers to other PayPal accountholders.

1475 González, A.G. (2004) "PayPal: The legal status of C2C payment systems", *Computer Law & Security Review*, Vol. 20, 297–298. González further argues that PayPal does essentially engage in deposit-taking activities as defined under EU law, despite its terms of use stating otherwise. Fullenkamp and Nsouli argue that PayPal uses a digitalized version of public government-issued money, as traditional e-banking services provided by credit institutions do. Their argument is that e-money in the true sense should use a privately issued currency. Fullenkamp, C., Nsouli, S.M. (2004) "Six Puzzles in Electronic Money and Banking", *IMF Working Paper WP/04/19*, 8–9. Also Kohlbach finds that there is no way to explain why a service that works the same way all around the world would somehow need to involve a transfer to and from e-money in the EU. Kohlbach, M. (2004) "Making Sense of Electronic Money", *Journal of Information, Law and Technology*, 11–12.

1476 As the UK Financial Services Authority's firm reference number 226056.

Luxembourg.[1477] Google Pay, formerly Google Wallet and Android Pay, which provides services similar to those of PayPal, is currently registered in the UK as an e-money institution.[1478] The UK's Financial Services Authority – the predecessor of the current Financial Conduct Authority – has drawn the line between deposits and e-money as follows: "*a deposit involves the creation of a debtor-creditor relationship under which the person who accepts the deposit stores value for eventual return. E-money, in contrast, involves the purchase of a means of payment.*"[1479] The European Commission, however, does not seem to share the reasoning that e-money instruments are mainly means of payment as it created a separate legal framework precisely for payment services.[1480] Moreover, the members of the Payment Systems Market Expert Group have already remarked that the differences between payment services and e-money services are disappearing, explicitly mentioning the example of PayPal.[1481]

Consequences for virtual currencies – The uncertainty of what precisely constitutes e-money has a direct impact on virtual currencies. For instance, many types of virtual currencies are not prepaid instruments, thus disqualifying them as e-money.[1482] The result is that at the present moment those virtual currencies can by definition be considered as payment instruments that do not fall under the scope of the EMD2's legal framework.[1483] Also in the virtual currencies that do utilize prepaid value – such as store gift

[1477] More in particular, PayPal is a partnership limited by shares under Luxembourg law authorized to operate as a bank under article 2 of the Law of 5 April 1993 on the financial sector, supervised by the "Commission de surveillance du secteur financier" (CSSF).

[1478] As the UK Financial Conduct Authority's firm reference number 900008.

[1479] Financial Services Authority (2011) "Implementation of the second Electronic Money Directive: supplement to HM Treasury's consultation – Feedback on CP10/25 and part of CP10/24, and final rules", *Policy Statement PS11/2*, 73.

[1480] González, A.G. (2004) "PayPal: The legal status of C2C payment systems", *Computer Law & Security Review*, Vol. 20, 297–298. The author also references a direct statement from the European Commission that services such as PayPal are closer to credit transfers, thus indicating that they fit better under the scope of the PSD than under the EMD. European Commission (2003) "Communication concerning a New Legal Framework for Payments in the Internal Market", *COM(2003) 718 final*, 23.

[1481] Payment Systems Market Expert Group (2012) "Minutes of the meeting of 27 March 2012, Brussels", *ec.europa.eu*, 4. Contra: Trzaskowski, J., Savin, A., Lundqvist, B., Lindskoug, P. (2015) Introduction to *EU Internet Law*, Copenhagen, Ex Tuto, 304. These authors argue that the status of PayPal as e-money issuer is clearer under the EMD2, as its services concern the storing of funds on its servers against the receipt of funds.

[1482] Cryptocurrencies, for one, are issued per their underlying algorithm, not on receipt of funds. Other forms of virtual currencies – such as the now discontinued Microsoft Points and Facebook Credits – can be obtained through store-bought cards carrying a code that relates to a certain balance of that virtual currency. These balances are therefore issued before the funds from users buying those cards are received.

[1483] This is the reasoning followed by the European Central Bank, which explicitly considers all virtual currencies as the unregulated opposite of regulated e-money: European Central Bank (2012) "Virtual Currency Schemes", *ecb.europa.eu*, 11.

cards – the applicability of the e-money definition is uncertain.[1484] Moreover, the scope exemptions applicable to the legal framework on e-money could still place those virtual currencies outside of the scope of the e-money legal framework.[1485]

New objectives for e-money – Which conclusions can then be drawn from that with regard to a potential new legal framework on e-money, possibly merged into the legal framework for payment services? First, it is clear that the original objectives for the EU's legal framework on e-money are becoming increasingly irrelevant. On the one hand, multi-purpose prepaid cards are largely being phased out. On the other hand, the general feeling toward network-based e-money is that such services are so closely related to payment services that it may be questioned whether the duality between the frameworks set by the PSD2 and the EMD2 can still be upheld. Second, from the early results of consultations on the impact of the EMD2, it becomes clear that the directive has only provided marginal improvement over the EMD1 in clarifying what constitutes e-money. At the present moment, there is an ever increasing number of novel payment methods and instruments that is excluded from the EMD2's narrow scope. That group, in part what constitutes virtual currencies at large, is already becoming larger than what still constitutes e-money and will likely continue to grow in the coming years. If there were a future for e-money, it would prove unwise to bar those virtual currencies from its scope.

## 5 INTERIM CONCLUSIONS

Chapter goals – The main goal of this chapter was to analyze to what extent virtual currencies are regulated by the existing EU legal frameworks on e-money and payment services. If it were found that those legal frameworks already apply to virtual currencies, it needs to be assessed whether such a situation is be sufficient – according to the normative criteria of legal certainty, proportionality, trust and regulatory coherence – or whether gaps remain. If it were found that those legal frameworks can, in their current form, not be applied to virtual currencies, it needs to be assessed whether it is necessary – again according to the normative criteria established for the purposes of this research – to propose that future legislative initiative bring virtual currencies under their scope, and whether such an action would not be hindered by fundamental incompatibilities.

---

[1484] Also due to their limited usability outside of the premises of the issuer.

[1485] For instance, store gift cards can generally only be redeemed at the issuing store, thus allowing for the application of the limited networks exemption.

## 5.1 FINDINGS

E-MONEY – CURRENT FRAMEWORK – Regarding the current EU legal framework on e-money, it was found that the application of the e-money legal framework to virtual currencies is problematic. Most of the different forms of virtual currencies identified in chapter I cannot fulfill the criterion of being issued upon receipt of funds, thus disqualifying them as e-money. Moreover, several types of virtual currencies are only accepted by their issuer, or in a limited network around that issuer. Such further hinders the application of the e-money definition, or allow for the application of a scope exemption. Given the substantial differences between different forms of virtual currencies – even within the same type – a case-by-case assessment remains needed.

E-MONEY – REGULATORY POTENTIAL – Would it then be possible to amend the current legal framework on e-money to include virtual currencies? For that, reference must be made to the original policy goals that resulted in the EMD1. Here, it was found that the EMD1 was meant to provide the legal framework for – mainly – multi-purpose prepaid cards, as well as to facilitate the introduction of the euro. It is clear that the latter goal is no longer relevant, following the 2002 introduction of physical euro banknotes and coins. Also the first objective seems to be losing its relevance, given that the prime examples of multi-purpose prepaid cards have by now all been abolished. While the scope of e-money was indeed broadened to also cover server-based initiatives, it is clear that the application of the e-money legal framework to new technological developments in the broader payments landscape has proven difficult. Overall, the European e-money market has never managed to realize its originally projected potential[1486], something for which the ambiguity of the e-money legal framework and its complex relationship with the legal framework on payment services can be held at least partially responsible. It can therefore be argued that the e-money legal framework is in need of a fundamental revision, which could indeed include bringing virtual currencies under its scope.

PAYMENT SERVICES – CURRENT FRAMEWORK – The EU legal framework on payment services cannot regulate the emission of virtual currencies. At most, it can regulate the (third party) providers of services developed around virtual currencies, insofar such services constitute payment services. Here, it was found that most of such services – principally with regard to closed scheme virtual currencies and unidirectional scheme virtual currencies – do certainly not constitute payment services. And even if some could be argued to constitute payment services, one of the scope exemptions would likely be applicable. Only

[1486] One of the reasons why the e-money legal framework has been called out as an example of 'bad law': Reed, C. (2010) "How to Make Bad Law: Lessons from Cyberspace", *The Modern Law Review*, Vol. 73, 918–919.

with regard to cryptocurrency services – mainly the cryptocurrency exchanges – a few arguments could be made in favor of considering such services to be payment services. However, those arguments are not widely accepted and do not represent the view of the European legislator, according to whom these services are currently not regulated by the legal framework on payment services.

Payment Services – regulatory potential – The scope of the payment services legal framework – the regulation of payment service providers – is clear. That scope was expanded with the adoption of the PSD2 to include third party service providers. For that extension, the scope of the payment services covered by the legal framework was explicitly expanded to include payment initiation services and account information services. In the same vein, it is then possible to further expand the scope to also cover certain virtual currency services. The possibility of such an action was confirmed in the European Commission's proposal to amend the AMDL4, but was not retained because such was feared to provide legitimacy to virtual currency services.

Regulatory action – The legal framework on e-money would arguably benefit the most of a renewed direction, but also requires a more substantial overhaul to bring virtual currencies under its scope. At the moment, the main element of the e-money definition demarcating e-money from virtual currencies appears to be the "issued upon receipt of funds" requirement. That element expresses the desire of the legislator to capture prepaid instruments, and while it could still be broadened to cover certain forms of virtual currencies, a prepaid requirement always excludes other forms, such as cryptocurrencies. In order to capture all forms of virtual currencies, the e-money definition essentially would have to be broadened to also cover the definition of virtual currencies adopted for the purposes of this research, namely "*digital representations of value, which are not legal tender, which serve as a unit of account, separate from existing state- or central bank-issued currencies, and which can serve as a means to conclude payments*". The result of covering every form of virtual currency under the e-money legal framework would of course impose stringent requirements on every virtual currency issuer, including for instance game developers issuing virtual currencies within their virtual game world. That effect could be offset by scope exemptions or waivers. The legal framework on payment services in comparison makes it more difficult to include every form of virtual currency service under its scope, but does allow for easier differentiation in deciding which type of services – such as for instance cryptocurrency exchange services – should be regulated. The decision whether to include virtual currencies under the legal framework of e-money or payment services will therefore in part rely on the policy decision to regulate all virtual currencies or to limit regulation to specific services – for instance those posing particular risks.

## 5.2 NORMATIVE ASSESSMENT

Regulatory need – Having found that both the current legal framework on e-money and that on payment services can in their current form not be applied to virtual currencies, as well as that there are arguments to be made for the potential inclusion of virtual currencies under either framework, the question remains whether those frameworks should be considered for the regulation of virtual currencies. As the following chapters will analyze more candidate frameworks for the regulation of virtual currencies, the definitive answer to that question can only be provided when bringing together all results of this research. At this stage, however, a preliminary analysis can be made, based on the elements uncovered in this chapter.

Legal certainty – First, from the viewpoint of legal certainty, it is clear that a continuation of the current situation is unwanted. There are many conflicting views on whether the legal frameworks on e-money and payment services can be applied to virtual currencies, which results – as shown by the example of France – in divergent approaches across Member States in a field of supposed maximum harmonization.[1487] At the very least, more clarity is needed on whether virtual currencies are regulated by those legal frameworks or not. The current uncertainty has resulted in a situation where virtual currency service providers are submitting to be licensed under legal frameworks that are principally not applicable to the services they provide.[1488] This is undesirable for several reasons. It may, for instance, raise the perception of trustworthiness of virtual currency service providers at a time where most of those service providers are still unregulated, and where not all of them have good intentions. Such could negate the efforts made by regulators in Member States to warn consumers and businesses of the risks involved with certain virtual currency schemes. It could also prove to be negative for the development of the virtual currency market. The currently licensed virtual currency service providers could use such legitimacy as a competitive advantage over unlicensed rivals. Such could impose a particular burden on potential market entrants, for whom the licensing requirements could be prohibitive. Last, it could be questioned what the consequences can be of the broad interpretations provided by certain national supervisors – as in France and Luxembourg – for the passporting system set up by the legal frameworks on e-money and payment services.

1487 While both directives do foresee several occasions for diversions by the Member States, these do not extend to the basic scope of the payment services legal framework.

1488 Though, of course, also here a case-by-case analysis is needed. It may, for instance, be found that a particular service provider also provides additional services that may constitute the issuance of e-money or the provision of payment services. In such case, the service provider needs to be licensed, but on the basis of those activities and not its virtual currency activities.

Proportionality – Second, the need for regulation must be weighed against the principle of proportionality. A legislative measure should not only achieve its desired outcome, and do so using the least restrictive means, it must also avoid excessive effect on the interests at stake. In analyzing the background of the legal framework on e-money, it became clear how a, in hindsight disproportionate, concern for a particular interest – *in casu* the protection of monetary stability – could have a detrimental effect on the development of a nascent market. It further underscores the need for this research to adopt a neutral stance, avoiding a policy decision by which a particular interest would be accorded more weight than others. That said, bringing every form of virtual currencies under either of the legal frameworks analyzed here institutes a burden on their service providers disproportionate to the risks posed by certain virtual currencies on the stakeholders involved. For instance, the regulation of closed scheme virtual currencies under the legal frameworks on e-money and payment services is disproportionate to the risks posed by that type of virtual currencies. If it is decided to regulate virtual currencies under the legal frameworks of e-money or payment services, a differentiated approach – by excluding certain forms of virtual currencies or by instituting a waiver regime – can be recommended from the viewpoint of proportionality.

Trust – Third, attention must be paid to the importance of user trust in virtual currencies. As those currencies are not legal tender, nor were they found to be offered specific protection through the legal frameworks on e-money and payment services, their users must put their trust in the issuers of virtual currencies and the providers of services developed around them. The matter of trust was also brought up when regulation of e-money was first discussed. There, it was said that e-money is only able to develop into a widely usable means of payment if there would be complete trust in the issuer, which, at the time, was said to require the involvement of (central) banks.[1489] While at the present moment there is, as noted by the European Central Bank itself, no direct need to require the involvement of central banks, it is clear that the current uncertain legal status of virtual currencies does not help in augmenting user trust.

Regulatory coherence – Last, also from the viewpoint of regulatory coherence it is clear that the current uncertainty regarding the regulation of virtual currencies under the legal frameworks on e-money and payment services can only provide undesirable results. Practice has indeed shown that certain Member States do consider at least one of those frameworks applicable to virtual currencies and their service providers, while others do not. As it concerns a field

[1489] Van der Wielen, H. (1997) "Electronic Money: a European Perspective", presented at the Seminar on Electronic Money, hosted by the Bank of England, London 4 February 1997, *www.simonl.org/docs/readeremdnb.pdf*, 15–16.

of maximum harmonization, a more unified position across the Member States would be recommendable. Chapter VII will analyze how such a position relates to the international regulatory plane.

Conclusion – Concluding, while it is at this stage of the research too early to draw definitive conclusions regarding the need to regulate virtual currencies, it is clear that at the very least the current uncertainties regarding the application of the legal frameworks on e-money and payment services should be remedied. While the conclusion of this chapter is that those frameworks can, in their current forms, not be applied, it has also been shown that current practice within the EU demonstrates different interpretations. One possible action, in the case of non-regulation under the legal frameworks on e-money and payment services, is then to explicitly exclude virtual currencies from their scope. Such would establish a clear and unified EU-wide stance, thus ending the current uncertainty caused by the different approaches followed by the Member States.

# CHAPTER V
# ANTI-MONEY LAUNDERING IN THE EU

## 1 INTRODUCTION

AML – Having analyzed in chapter IV whether the EU's legal frameworks on e-money and payment services can be applied to virtual currencies, this chapter will conduct the same analysis from the viewpoint of EU anti-money laundering legislation (AML). Anti-money laundering legislation was developed worldwide from the late 1980's onwards. While originally aimed particularly at the proceeds from criminal activities, anti-money laundering legislation now also targets the destination of the funds – such as the use of funds for terrorist financing. This is important for virtual currencies, as they could both be gained from criminal activities[1490], and used for such activities.[1491]

Goals – First, this chapter aims to analyze whether virtual currencies and the services developed around them can fall under the scope of the EU's legal framework regarding anti-money laundering rules as it stands with the 2015 Fourth Anti-Money Laundering Directive. Second, this chapter will analyze the 2018 amendments to the 2015 legal framework to explicitly bring certain virtual currency services under the scope of anti-money laundering rules. This will serve to assess the impact of regulatory evolution on virtual currencies and their service providers.

Reasoning – There are two reasons for selecting the anti-money laundering framework for further analysis under the scope of this research. First, in the risk assessment conducted in section 5 of chapter I, it was found that anonymity is regarded as one of the primary risks posed by virtual currencies. By requiring the subjects of the anti-money laundering legal framework to identify their

1490 See, for instance, the notorious Silk Road case. Silk Road operated as a dark web marketplace, where users could buy all kinds of illicit goods, mainly narcotics. Payments on Silk Road were conducted using the cryptocurrency bitcoin. When the FBI arrested the operator of this website, it seized around USD 28,5 million worth of bitcoins. Greenberg, A. (2013) "FBI Says It's Seized $28.5 Million In Bitcoins From Ross Ulbricht, Alleged Owner Of Silk Road", *Forbes*, 25 October.

1491 In the wake of the 2015 Paris and the 2016 Brussels terrorist attacks, it is feared that the perpetrators may have been funded using virtual currencies. Barnato, K. (2016) "Will terror attacks end bitcoin free-for-all in Europe?", *CNBC*, 2 May.

customers – also known as know-your-customer (KYC) rules – and by requiring them to assess the risk posed by these customers – a process known as customer due diligence (CDD) – anti-money laundering rules generally aim to counter precisely such anonymity. Second, as already noted in the previous paragraph, the European legislator has taken steps to expand the Fourth Anti-Money Laundering Directive to explicitly include particular virtual currency service providers. This marks the first legislative initiative taken at the level of the EU that is aimed particularly at virtual currencies. As a result, such a regulatory initiative must be assessed against the normative criteria established for the purposes of this research, in order to ascertain whether additional regulatory steps are needed.

# 2 MONEY LAUNDERING AND THE EU DIRECTIVES

## 2.1 THE CONCEPT OF MONEY LAUNDERING

MONEY LAUNDERING – The notion of money laundering can best be described as a process intended to make the proceeds from criminal activities appear legitimate by bringing them into the regular economy.[1492] In money laundering, it is therefore the origin of the money – being derived from criminal activity – that catches the attention of lawmakers and law enforcement. As already noted in the introduction, the notion of money laundering is more and more being supplemented with that of terrorist financing. In terrorist financing, the origins of the money may be legitimate, but the destination – to finance terrorist activities – is not.

THE MONEY LAUNDERING PROCESS – Generally, the money laundering process consists of three stages: placement, layering, and integration.[1493] First, money obtained from criminal activity is introduced into the financial system. Second, transactions are carried out with that money with the aim to conceal its criminal origins. Third, the money is invested in legitimate ventures in order to make it seem as if it originated from entirely legitimate business practices.

MONEY LAUNDERING AND VIRTUAL CURRENCIES – Traditionally, money laundering has favored cash-based processes, as cash transactions leave little to no traces. The relative anonymity of virtual currencies thus makes them of potential interest for money laundering practices. However, some of the types of virtual currencies identified for the purposes of this research hold little value for money

1492 Unger, B. (2013) "Money Laundering Regulation: from Al Capone to Al Qaeda", In: Unger, B., Van Der Linde, D. (Eds.) *Research Handbook on Money Laundering*, Cheltenham: Edward Elgar, 19; Royer, S. (2016) "Bitcoins in het Belgische strafrecht en strafprocesrecht", *Rechtskundig Weekblad*, 491.

1493 Royer, S. (2016) "Bitcoins in het Belgische strafrecht en strafprocesrecht", *Rechtskundig Weekblad*, 491; FinCEN (2017) "History of Anti-Money Laundering Laws", *fincen.gov*.

laundering. Closed scheme virtual currencies, for instance, have no interaction with the physical world economy, thus making them inherently unsuited for money laundering purposes. Unidirectional scheme virtual currencies have no flow from virtual currency to legal tender or similar means of payment, thus not allowing money to flow out of the system. While 'dirty money' could still be invested in a unidirectional scheme virtual currency, with that virtual currency then being used as a legitimate means of payment, it is clear that such a method is fairly unsuited for larger scale money laundering operations. It are, then, particularly bidirectional scheme virtual currencies that hold significant potential for money laundering. For instance, even though in the case of cryptocurrencies all transactions are recorded in a public ledger, the lack of a clear link between a wallet and the identity of the person behind that wallet, as well as the existence of services to further obfuscate the precise origins of transactions[1494], make cryptocurrencies a useful money laundering tool.[1495] Also online games offering a bidirectional virtual currency could be targeted by money launderers.[1496]

Anti-money laundering – It is difficult to assess the full scale of global money laundering activities, but estimates range from billions to trillions of US dollars.[1497] In order to combat this massive and global crime, the main goal of anti-money laundering rules is to oblige certain actors within the financial system to identify their customers and to report certain suspicious transactions to financial intelligence units (FIU).[1498] FIU's are government agencies that process and analyze the information they receive from obliged entities under anti-money laundering rules.[1499] National FIU's can share relevant information with each other through initiatives for international cooperation such as the Egmont Group of Financial Intelligence Units. When evidence of money laundering is found, FIU's will report this to appropriate law enforcement authorities.

## 2.2 ROAD TO ANTI-MONEY LAUNDERING DIRECTIVE 4

Rise of financial crime – Money laundering and financial crime came to the public awareness in the late 1970's and early 1980's. It was the boom in narco-

1494 Also called mixing or tumbling services. *en.bitcoin.it/wiki/Mixing_service.*

1495 Royer, S. (2016) "Bitcoins in het Belgische strafrecht en strafprocesrecht", *Rechtskundig Weekblad*, 492.

1496 Richet, J.-L. (2013) "Laundering Money Online: a review of cybercriminals' methods", presented at Tools and Resources for Anti-Corruption Knowledge, United Nations Office on Drugs and Crime (UNODC), 1 June.

1497 Unger, B. (2013) "Money Laundering Regulation: from Al Capone to Al Qaeda", In: Unger, B., Van Der Linde, D. (Eds.) *Research Handbook on Money Laundering*, Cheltenham: Edward Elgar, 21.

1498 Royer, S. (2016) "Bitcoins in het Belgische strafrecht en strafprocesrecht", *Rechtskundig Weekblad*, 492.

1499 For instance, in Belgium this is the Belgian Financial Intelligence Processing Unit CTIF-CFI.

trafficking in the 1980's that resulted in the first international efforts against this sort of crime.[1500] More so, it was the 1988 UN convention on narco-trafficking that first called for the global consideration of money laundering in narco-trafficking as a crime.[1501] At the same time, the Basel Committee on Banking Supervision stated ethical principles calling for the identification of customers, followed by a Council of Europe convention.[1502]

FATF – In 1989, the G-7 established the Financial Action Task Force on Money Laundering (FATF) in Paris. The main responsibilities of this task force are "*examining money laundering techniques and trends, reviewing the action which had already been taken at a national or international level, and setting out the measures that still needed to be taken to combat money laundering*".[1503] The most well-known output of the FATF is a set of regularly updated recommendations, aimed at providing a plan for its members in the fight against money laundering.[1504] These recommendations provide the basis to the EU directives.

AMLD1 – The First Anti-Money Laundering Directive (AMLD1) was adopted in 1991.[1505] Importantly, the directive broadens up the scope of money laundering, from narcotics-related offenses to all criminal activities.[1506] It calls for cooperation from credit and financial institutions, for whom banking secrecy must be lifted in such cases.[1507]

AMLD2 – In 1995 and 1998, the European Commission reported on the implementation of the AMLD1.[1508] Also, in 1996, the FATF updated its recommendations.[1509] In light of these developments, the European Commission

1500 Ernoult, J., Hemetsberger, W., Schoppmann, H., Wengler, C. (2008) *European Banking and Financial Services Law (3rd edition)*, Brussels: Larcier, 205.

1501 United Nations Convention against Illicit Traffic in Narcotic Drugs and Psychotropic Substances, Vienna, 20 December 1988.

1502 Basel Committee on Banking Supervision (1998) "Prevention of criminal use of the banking system for the purpose of money-laundering", *bis.org;* Convention Nr. 141 on Laundering, Search, Seizure and Confiscation of the Proceeds from Crime, Strasbourg, 08 November 1990.

1503 *Www.fatf-gafi.org/about/historyofthefatf.*

1504 The most recent version of these recommendations was adopted in 2012: FATF (2012) *Recommendations – International Standards on Combatting Money Laundering and the Financing of Terrorism & Proliferation,* Paris: FATF.

1505 Council Directive 91/308/EEC of 10 June 1991 on prevention of the use of the financial system for the purpose of money laundering, *OJ* L 166 of 28 June 1991, 77–82 (hereinafter: First Anti-Money Laundering Directive or AMLD1).

1506 Recital 9 First Anti-Money Laundering Directive.

1507 Recital 15 First Anti-Money Laundering Directive.

1508 European Commission (1995) "First Commission's report on the implementation of the Money Laundering Directive (91/308/EEC) to be submitted to the European Parliament and to the Council", *COM(95) 54 final*; European Commission (1998) "Second Commission report to the European Parliament and the Council on the implementation of the Money Laundering Directive", *COM(1998) 401 final.*

1509 European Commission (1998) "Second Commission report to the European Parliament and the Council on the implementation of the Money Laundering Directive", *COM(1998) 401 final*, 4.

proposed a directive that significantly amended the AMLD1.[1510] The resulting Second Anti-Money Laundering Directive (AMLD2) was adopted in 2001.[1511] The new directive adds obliged entities such as casinos, dealers in high-value goods, real estate agents, and legal professionals.[1512] It also significantly expands what is considered as criminal activities under the anti-money laundering legal framework.[1513]

AMLD3 – By 2004, the money laundering landscape had changed again, with an update of the FATF Recommendations, and with more attention being paid to the problem of terrorist financing. As a result, the European Commission proposed an entirely new directive, which replaced the existing legal framework.[1514] That proposal also introduces a risk-based approach, whereby simplified due diligence is proposed for cases with lower risk, as well as enhanced due diligence for high risk cases.[1515] The Third Anti-Money Laundering Directive (AMLD3) was adopted in 2005.[1516]

## 3 FOURTH ANTI-MONEY LAUNDERING DIRECTIVE

### 3.1 PROPOSAL FOURTH ANTI-MONEY LAUNDERING DIRECTIVE

Review – In 2012, the European Commission found that a periodic revision of the legal framework would be required in order to be able to respond

---

1510 European Commission (1999) "Proposal for a European Parliament and Council Directive amending Council Directive 91/308/EEC of 10 June 1991 on prevention of the use of the financial system for the purpose of money laundering", *COM(1999) 352 final.*

1511 Directive 2001/97/EC of the European Parliament and of the Council of 4 December 2001 amending Council Directive 91/308/EEC on prevention of the use of the financial system for the purpose of money laundering, *OJ* L 344 of 28 December 2001, 76–82 (hereinafter: Second Anti-Money Laundering Directive or AMLD2).

1512 Article 1.2 Second Anti-Money Laundering Directive; Ernoult, J., Hemetsberger, W., Schoppmann, H., Wengler, C. (2008) *European Banking and Financial Services Law (3rd edition),* Brussels: Larcier, 206.

1513 Article 1.1 Second Anti-Money Laundering Directive.

1514 European Commission (2004) "Proposal for a Directive of the European Parliament and of the Council on the prevention of the use of the financial system for the purpose of money laundering, including terrorist financing", *COM/2004/0448 final.*

1515 *Ibid.*, 5.

1516 Directive 2005/60/EC of the European Parliament and of the Council of 26 October 2005 on the prevention of the use of the financial system for the purpose of money laundering and terrorist financing, *OJ* L 309 of 25 November 2005, 15–36 (hereinafter: Third Anti-Money Laundering Directive or AMLD3). The amendments adopted during the European Parliament's first reading mainly focused on separating money laundering and terrorist financing as two different offenses, both caught under the anti-money laundering legal framework.

to newfound threats.[1517] Even though no fundamental shortcomings were identified under the existing legal framework, the Commission did find a number of minor modifications required to bringing the legal framework in line with the newly-revised FATF Recommendations, publishing a formal proposal for what became the Fourth Anti-Money Laundering Directive (AMLD4) in 2013.[1518]

Proposal and virtual currencies – Much like its predecessors, the initial proposal for the AMLD4 makes no mention of virtual currencies. During the legislative procedure leading up to the directive, none of the opinions issued by the European Central Bank, the European Economic and Social Committee, or of the European Data Protection Supervisor reference developments in virtual currencies, which by then had already attracted the attention of regulators and law enforcement.[1519] Only the report tabled by the Committee assigned by the European Parliament in its first reading included an amendment that refers to anonymous e-money products.[1520]

EBA opinion – In 2014, as the legislative procedure was ongoing, the EBA published its opinion on virtual currencies.[1521] In that opinion, the EBA urges regulators to bring virtual currencies – including cryptocurrencies – under an existing legal framework. More particularly, the EBA proposed that virtual currencies could be included under the scope of the EU's legal framework regarding anti-money

---

1517 European Commission (2013) "Frequently Asked Questions: Anti-Money Laundering", *MEMO 13/64*.

1518 European Commission (2013) "Proposal for a Directive of the European Parliament and of the Council on the prevention of the use of the financial system for the purpose of money laundering and terrorist financing", *COM(2013) 45 final*.

1519 European Central Bank (2013) "Opinion of 17 May 2013 on a proposal for a directive on the prevention of the use of the financial system for the purpose of money laundering and terrorist financing and on a proposal for a regulation on information accompanying transfers of funds", *CON/2013/32*; European Economic and Social Committee (2013) "Opinion of 23 May 2013 on the Proposal for a Regulation of the European Parliament and of the Council on information accompanying transfers of funds COM(2013) 44 final – 2013/0024 (COD) and the Proposal for a Directive of the European Parliament and of the Council on the prevention of the use of the financial system for the purpose of money laundering and terrorist financing COM(2013) 45 final – 2013/0025 (COD)", *ECO/344*; European Data Protection Supervisor (2013) "Executive summary of the Opinion on a proposal for a Directive of the European Parliament and of the Council on the prevention of the use of the financial system for the purpose of money laundering and terrorist financing, and a proposal for a Regulation of the European Parliament and of the Council on information on the payer accompanying transfers of funds", *OJ* C 32 of 4 February 2014, 9–12.

1520 European Parliament (2014) "Committee on Economic and Monetary Affairs and Committee on Civil Liberties, Justice and Home Affairs: Report on the proposal for a directive of the European Parliament and of the Council on the prevention of the use of the financial system for the purpose of money laundering and terrorist financing (COM(2013)0045) – C7–0032/2013 – 2013/0025(COD))", *A7–0150/2014*, amendment 10.

1521 European Banking Authority (2014) "Opinion on 'virtual currencies'", *EBA/Op/2014/08*.

laundering.[1522] Though more comprehensive action would be favored in the long run, the inclusion of virtual currencies under an existing legal framework such as that regarding anti-money laundering rules could provide a short-term solution to "*'shield' regulated financial services from V*[irtual ]*C*[urrency] *schemes*".[1523] The EBA's call to action was well-received by the European Commission, where it was said that the possibility to include virtual currencies under the scope of the AMLD4 would be discussed during the trilogue proceedings.[1524]

Further procedure – Those trilogue discussions were held early 2015, shortly after the January 2015 terrorist attack on the magazine *Charlie Hebdo.* In response to that terrorist attack, France voiced its clear support to strengthen the efficiency of the legal framework regarding anti-money laundering in the fight against terrorist financing. More specifically, the need to assess the risks posed by virtual currencies was addressed.[1525] This call for action was echoed in a joint declaration of the Commission and the Council in the context of the endorsement of the Anti-Money Laundering (AML) package, but with the indication that such regulation of virtual currencies would be subject to further efforts, to be taken after the adoption of the AMLD4.[1526] As a result, the Council's common position adopted in April 2015 did not explicitly include virtual currencies.[1527] The Council's text did include a new recital, nr. 19, that referred to new technologies and held that "*competent authorities and obliged entities should be proactive in combating new and innovative ways of money laundering*", be it without specifying whether such a statement was made in reference to virtual currencies.

Adoption – After the adoption of the Council's position, a number of Committees within the European Parliament issued a draft report in which they supported the Council's position and recommended the plenary meeting to adopt that text without further amendment in its second reading.[1528] Also the

---

1522 *Ibid.*, 6.

1523 *Id.*

1524 Payment Systems Market Expert Group (2014) "Minutes of the meeting of 22 October 2014, Brussels", *PSMEG 008/14*, 2–3.

1525 Council of the European Union (2015) "Proposal for a regulation of the European Parliament and of the Council on information accompanying transfers of funds Proposal for a directive of the European Parliament and of the Council on the prevention of the use of the financial system for the purpose of money laundering and terrorist financing – Declarations by Member States", *5116/15 ADD 3 REV 4*, 4–5.

1526 *Id.*

1527 Council of the European Union (2015) "Position of the Council at first reading with a view to the adoption of a Directive of the European Parliament and of the Council on the prevention of the use of the financial system for the purposes of money laundering or terrorist financing, amending Regulation (EU) No 648/2012 of the European Parliament and of the Council, and repealing Directive 2005/60/EC of the European Parliament and of the Council and Commission Directive 2006/70/EC – Adopted by the Council on 20 April 2015", *5933/4/15 REV 4*.

1528 European Parliament (2015) "Committee on Economic and Monetary Affairs and Committee on Civil Liberties, Justice and Home Affairs: Draft Recommendation for second reading

European Commission expressed its agreement with the Council's position, thus paving the way for the adoption of the final text.[1529] The AMLD4 was adopted on 20 May 2015.[1530]

## 3.2 FOURTH ANTI-MONEY LAUNDERING DIRECTIVE

E-money – As noted in the previous subsection, the AMLD4 is the first directive in the matter of anti-money laundering to specifically address e-money. More concretely, a recital to the directive finds that this substitute for bank accounts should also be subjected to anti-money laundering rules.[1531] However, exemptions and simplified due diligence are possible for low-risk circumstances and under strict risk-mitigating conditions.[1532] And as also noted in the previous subsection, "*competent authorities and obliged entities should be proactive in combating new and innovative ways of money laundering*".[1533]

Tax crimes and gambling sector – In an effort to address tax evasion, the AMLD4 explicitly includes tax crimes within its consideration of criminal activities.[1534] This addition also explains the added attention to the identification and verification of beneficial owners, and the establishment of a central database holding such information.[1535] While casinos were already covered in previous directives, the AMLD4 expands the scope to the entire gambling sector, when single transactions exceed EUR 2.000.[1536]

on the Council position at first reading with a view to the adoption of a directive of the European Parliament and of the Council on the prevention of the use of the financial system for the purposes of money laundering or terrorist financing, amending Regulation (EU) No 648/2012 of the European Parliament and of the Council, and repealing Directive 2005/60/EC of the European Parliament and of the Council and Commission Directive 2006/70/EC (05933/3/2015 – C8–0109/2015 – 2013/0025(COD))", *PE554.948*.

1529 European Commission (2015) "Communication pursuant to Article 294(6) of the Treaty on the Functioning of the European Union concerning the position of the Council on the adoption of a Directive of the European Parliament and of the Council on the prevention of the use of the financial system for the purpose of money laundering and terrorist financing", *COM(2015) 188 final*.

1530 Directive (EU) 2015/849 of the European Parliament and of the Council of 20 May 2015 on the prevention of the use of the financial system for the purposes of money laundering or terrorist financing, amending Regulation (EU) No 648/2012 of the European Parliament and of the Council, and repealing Directive 2005/60/EC of the European Parliament and of the Council and Commission Directive 2006/70/EC, *OJ* L 141 of 5 June 2015, 73–117 (hereinafter: Fourth Anti-Money Laundering Directive or AMLD4).

1531 Recital 7 AMLD4.

1532 As defined in article 12 AMLD4.

1533 Recital 19 AMLD4.

1534 Recital 11, article 3(4)(f) AMLD4.

1535 Recitals 12 – 14, articles 30 – 31 AMLD4.

1536 Recital 21 AMLD4.

Risk-based approach – The AMLD4 acknowledges that the risk of money laundering or terrorist financing is not the same in every case. The severity of rules should therefore be commensurate to the risk posed by a particular situation.[1537] As a result, the AMLD4 allows for simplified[1538] or enhanced[1539] due diligence, to ensure an approach tailored to any particular situation. The Commission will report on the risks of money laundering and terrorist financing affecting the internal market and relating to cross-border activities, with the aim to formulate recommendations to Member States on how to address such risks.[1540] Also Member States and obliged entities will carry out risk assessments, with national mechanisms to be defined to coordinate responses.[1541] For the due diligence analysis, annex I to the directive lists a number of risk variables to be taken into account.

Money laundering and obliged entities – The AMLD4 maintains the description of money laundering used in the AMLD3.[1542] The main changes to the obliged entities include the lowering of the threshold for other persons trading in goods to EUR 10.000, and an expansion to the entire gambling sector.[1543] The directive does foresee in more derogations depending on the risk posed by particular transactions. A number of new definitions further narrow down the scope.[1544]

Enforcement – The directive includes stronger enforcement measures.[1545] This includes measures for greater cooperation at the national level, between European Supervisory Authorities and between Financial Intelligence Units and the Commission.[1546] More unified sanctions are proposed.[1547]

1537 Recital 22 AMLD4.
1538 Articles 15 – 17 AMLD4. Annex II details a number of low-risk situations.
1539 Article 18 *et seq.* AMLD4. Annex III details a number of high-risk situations.
1540 Article 6 AMLD4. Also new provisions on FIUs are added: article 32 AMLD4.
1541 Articles 7 – 8 AMLD4.
1542 Article 1 AMLD4.
1543 Article 2 AMLD4. The result is that there are now several thresholds in article 11: EUR 1.000 for a transfer of funds as under Regulation (EU) 2015/847, EUR 2.000 for gambling transactions, EUR 10.000 for persons trading in goods, and EUR 15.000 for regular single or interlinked transactions.
1544 Article 3 AMLD4.
1545 Chapter VI AMLD4.
1546 Article 48 *et seq.* AMLD4.
1547 Article 59 AMLD4.

# 4 AMENDMENTS TO FOURTH ANTI-MONEY LAUNDERING DIRECTIVE

## 4.1 COMMISSION PROPOSAL AND LEGISLATIVE PROCEDURE

Commission Action Plan – Though the text of the AMLD4 may not provide an explicit answer regarding the applicability of the directive to virtual currencies and their service providers, the European legislator has made its position on the subject clear. In February 2016, the European Commission presented its Action Plan to strengthen the fight against terrorist financing.[1548] In that document, the Commission explicitly acknowledged that virtual currencies were not regulated at the level of the EU, which includes the legal framework regarding anti-money laundering. In doing so, the Commission implicitly acknowledged that the reference to anonymous e-money products in the AMLD4 cannot be understood as applying to virtual currencies.[1549] However, the Commission also expressed its clear intent to bring certain virtual currency service providers under the scope of the anti-money laundering legal framework.[1550] While at the level of the European Supervisory Authorities a few consultations have been held that included matters related to virtual currencies[1551], no stakeholder consultation specifically addressed the inclusion of virtual currencies under the EU anti-money laundering framework.

AMLD4 amendments – The European Commission's proposal to amend the AMLD4 was published in July 2016.[1552] With this proposal, the Commission clearly aimed to address anonymous transactions, explicitly calling out the lack of oversight on cash or virtual currency transactions and anonymous prepaid cards.[1553] Regarding cash transactions, several Member States already limit the amounts that can be paid in cash.[1554] If at some point in the future the notion of

---

1548 European Commission (2016) "Commission presents Action Plan to strengthen the fight against terrorist financing", *IP/16/202*.

1549 Which should not come as a surprise, since – as found in chapter IV of this research – most forms of virtual currencies cannot be considered as e-money under the EU's Second E-money Directive.

1550 European Commission (2016) "Communication from the Commission to the European Parliament and the Council on an Action Plan for strengthening the fight against terrorist financing", *COM(2016) 50 final*, 5.

1551 Such as the EBA's Discussion Paper on its approach to fintech (*eba.europa.eu/regulation-and-policy/other-topics/approach-to-financial-technology-fintech-)* or the ESMA's consultation on distributed ledger technology applied to securities markets (*esma.europa.eu/press-news/consultations/consultation-distributed-ledger-technology-applied-securities-markets*).

1552 European Commission (2016) "Proposal for a Directive of the European Parliament and of the Council amending Directive (EU) 2015/849 on the prevention of the use of the financial system for the purposes of money laundering or terrorist financing and amending Directive 2009/101/EC", *COM(2016) 450 final* (hereinafter: Proposal AMLD4 amendments).

1553 *Ibid.*, 2.

1554 European Commission (2010) "Report of the Euro Legal Tender Expert Group (ELTEG) on the definition, scope and effects of legal tender of euro banknotes and coins", *ec.europa.eu*, 44–54.

'cash' were expanded to include virtual currencies, they would become subject to such limitations as well. Also, in response to the controversy surrounding the Panama Papers, the Commission addressed the lack of transparency regarding offshore-constructions allowing for concealment of funds and ownership.[1555] The Commission aimed to subject trusts and companies such as those mentioned in the Panama Papers to greater scrutiny and tighter rules. The result of the Commission's amendments would be that the possibilities to conduct (semi-)anonymous electronic transactions will become scarce. It could, then, be argued that reducing the possibilities for conducting anonymous transactions would infringe upon the right to privacy, as enshrined in fundamental rights texts. Here, the argument of the European legislator is that the right to privacy is not absolute and that it can be limited if such were necessary in the general interests of the Union and its citizens, and if such a limitation were proportionate.[1556] And, of course, the European legislator does consider the planned limitations on cash and anonymous transactions as being necessary and proportionate.[1557] Time will tell whether the measures planned by the legislator will indeed pass the test of proportionality.

Regulating service providers – Regarding virtual currencies, the Commission proposed to include virtual currency exchange platforms and custodian wallet providers under the list of obliged entities under the AMLD4.[1558] Such also includes defining the notion of 'virtual currency'. The inclusion of certain virtual currency service providers needs to address the main risk emanating from virtual currency transactions, namely their higher degree of anonymity.[1559] The Commission found that such anonymity could allow terrorist organizations to use virtual currencies to conceal financial transfers.[1560] By including the service providers targeted here under the scope of the AMLD4, these service providers become obliged to monitor virtual currency transactions, and to prevent and report suspicious activities. Moreover, the Commission investigates the possibility to set up a "*central database registering users' identities and wallet addresses accessible to FIUs, as well as self-declaration forms for the use of virtual currency users*".[1561]

Reasoning – The Commission did recognize the potential benefits of virtual currencies, and particularly the possibilities emanating from the blockchain technology underlying cryptocurrencies.[1562] Though the subjection of virtual

1555 Proposal AMLD4 amendments, 2.
1556 European Commission (2017) "Proposal for an EU initiative on restrictions on payments in cash", *ec.europa.eu*, 5.
1557 *Id.*
1558 *Ibid.*, 12.
1559 *Ibid.*, 12.
1560 *Ibid.*, 8–9.
1561 Article 1(22) Proposal AMLD4 amendments.
1562 *Ibid.*, 13.

currencies to anti-money laundering rules indeed impose strict requirements on the virtual currency service providers addressed by the Commission's proposal, the Commission did not find that the imposition of such requirements would have negative effects to the benefits and technological advances of virtual currencies. On the contrary, the Commission argued that the use of virtual currencies for criminal purposes could diminish their credibility and that their "*anonymity will become more a hindrance than an asset for virtual currencies taking up and their potential benefits to spread*".[1563] In an attempt to limit the anonymity surrounding virtual currency transactions, the Commission found that "*national Financial Intelligence Units (FIUs) should be able to associate virtual currency addresses to the identity of the owner of virtual currencies*".[1564]

ECB OPINION – In October 2016, the ECB adopted its opinion on the proposed amendments.[1565] Generally, the ECB recognized that virtual currencies may hold benefits, but warned that the Commission's proposal could be viewed as promoting their use.[1566] The ECB found this concerning, as the proposal did not fully address all of the potential risks associated with virtual currencies.[1567] As a result, the ECB wanted the final text to make it clear that it should not be construed as an endorsement of virtual currencies.

COUNCIL PRESIDENCY – Late 2016, the Council of the European Union began working on a compromise proposal, resulting in five texts before the end of the Slovak Presidency.[1568] Those compromise texts clearly took into account the ECB's opinion by making a stronger distinction between virtual currencies and legal tender, by stressing the limitations of the legislative proposal to money laundering and terrorist financing concerns, and by toning down the language on the potential benefits of virtual currencies.[1569]

EUROPEAN PARLIAMENT COMMITTEES – The main committees responsible within the European Parliament were the committees on Economic and Monetary

1563 Recital 7 Proposal AMLD4 amendments.

1564 *Id.*

1565 European Central Bank (2016) "Opinion of 12 October 2016 on a proposal for a directive of the European Parliament and of the Council amending Directive (EU) 2015/849 on the prevention of the use of the financial system for the purposes of money laundering or terrorist financing and amending Directive 2009/101/EC", *ecb.europa.eu*.

1566 *Ibid.*, 2–3.

1567 *Id.* These risks were analyzed in chapter I.

1568 Council of the European Union (2016), document numbers *13872/16*; *14433/16*; *14884/16*; *15468/16* and *15605/16*.

1569 Introduced already in the first compromise text: Council of the European Union (2016) "Proposal for a directive of the European Parliament and of the Council amending Directive (EU) 2015/849 on the prevention of the use of the financial system for the purposes of money laundering or terrorist financing and amending Directive 2009/101/EC = Presidency compromise text", *13872/16*, 4.

Affairs (ECON) and on Civil Liberties, Justice and Home Affairs (LIBE). Also the committees on Development (DEVE), International Trade (INTA) and Legal Affairs (JURI) provided opinions, though only the latter committee proposed amendments to the provisions relating to virtual currencies, most of which in line with the ECB's opinion.[1570] In accordance to rule 69c of the Rules of Procedure of the European Parliament, interinstitutional negotiations were opened on the basis of this report, with a view on adopting the final directive during the Parliament's first reading. Those interinstitutional negotiations were concluded with a final compromise text at the end of 2017, with a view to adoption early 2018.[1571]

## 4.2 VIRTUAL CURRENCIES

Terminology – In terms of terminology, the ECB objected to the use of the notion of 'currency', fearing that this notion may imply a reference to legal tender.[1572] While it is true that the notion of 'currency' has indeed been used in reference to legal tender[1573], it was found in chapter I of this research that such seems to be even more the case for the notion of 'money', and that 'currency' could be understood as referring to a circulating medium of exchange. In that

---

1570 European Parliament (2016) "Opinion of the Committee on Development for the Committee on Economic and Monetary Affairs and the Committee on Civil Liberties, Justice and Home Affairs on the proposal for a directive of the European Parliament and of the Council amending Directive (EU) 2015/849 on the prevention of the use of the financial system for the purposes of money laundering or terrorist financing and amending Directive 2009/101/EC (COM(2016)0450 – C8-0265/2016 – 2016/0208(COD))", *PE594.116*; European Parliament (2016) "Opinion of the Committee on International Trade for the Committee on Economic and Monetary Affairs and the Committee on Civil Liberties, Justice and Home Affairs on the proposal for a directive of the European Parliament and of the Council amending Directive (EU) 2015/849 on the prevention of the use of the financial system for the purposes of money laundering or terrorist financing and amending Directive 2009/101/EC (COM(2016)0450 – C8-0265/2016 – 2016/0208(COD))", *PE594.132*; European Parliament (2016) "Opinion of the Committee on Legal Affairs for the Committee on Economic and Monetary Affairs and the Committee on Civil Liberties, Justice and Home Affairs on the proposal for a directive of the European Parliament and of the Council amending Directive (EU) 2015/849 on the prevention of the use of the financial system for the purposes of money laundering or terrorist financing and amending Directive 2009/101/EC (COM(2016)0450 – C8-0265/2016 – 2016/0208(COD))", *PE594.003*.

1571 Council of the European Union (2017) "Proposal for a Directive of the European Parliament and of the Council
amending Directive (EU) 2015/849 on the prevention of the use of the financial system for the purposes of money laundering or terrorist financing and amending Directive 2009/101/EC – Analysis of the final compromise text with a view to agreement", *15849/17*.

1572 European Central Bank (2016) "Opinion of 12 October 2016 on a proposal for a directive of the European Parliament and of the Council amending Directive (EU) 2015/849 on the prevention of the use of the financial system for the purposes of money laundering or terrorist financing and amending Directive 2009/101/EC", *ecb.europa.eu*, 3.

1573 For instance in article 2(a) Directive 2014/62/EU of the European Parliament and of the Council of 15 May 2014 on the protection of the euro and other currencies against counterfeiting by criminal law, and replacing Council Framework Decision 2000/383/JHA, *OJ* L 151 of 21 May 2014, 1–8.

latter sense, the ECB's desire to see virtual currencies clearly distinguished from legal tender could be more easily included in the definition of the virtual currency notion, as the ECB also proposed itself in an amendment.[1574] That solution can be preferred over the alternative of making up entirely new terminology, which would only deviate from the by now well-established use of the notion of 'virtual currencies', thus creating unnecessary confusion. Finally, the ECB recommended to more clearly define virtual currencies as not being legal tender, and to refer to them as "*means of exchange and possibly also for other purposes*", rather than just means of payment.[1575]

Commission proposal – Virtual currencies themselves were in the Commission's proposal defined as "*digital representation of value that is neither issued by a central bank or a public authority, nor necessarily attached to a fiat currency, but is accepted by natural or legal persons as a means of payment and can be transferred, stored or traded electronically*".[1576] This is a very broad definition, which could potentially bring a wide range of service providers currently not regulated by the anti-money laundering legal framework under the scope thereof. Recital 8 to the proposal did clarify that "*local currencies (also known as complementary currencies) that are used in very limited networks such as a city or a region and among a small number of users should not be considered as virtual currencies*".[1577] The wording of that recital is reminiscent of the so-called limited networks exemption found in the legal framework regarding payment services.[1578] Unfortunately, such a recital carries little weight by its own. It would, therefore, be better to insert such an exemption into the definition itself. The European Parliament's draft resolution maintained most of the wording of the virtual currencies definition of the Commission's proposal.[1579]

Council compromise text – The definition of 'virtual currencies' was in one of the earlier compromise texts changed into "*digital representation of value that can be digitally transferred, stored or traded and is accepted by natural or legal persons as a medium of exchange, but does not have legal tender status and which is not funds as defined in point (25) of Article 4 of the Directive*

---

1574 European Central Bank (2016) "Opinion of 12 October 2016 on a proposal for a directive of the European Parliament and of the Council amending Directive (EU) 2015/849 on the prevention of the use of the financial system for the purposes of money laundering or terrorist financing and amending Directive 2009/101/EC", *ecb.europa.eu*, 7.

1575 *Ibid.*, 6–7.

1576 Article 1(2)(c) Proposal AMLD4 amendments.

1577 Recital 8 Proposal AMLD4 amendments.

1578 Article 3(k) of both the First and Second Payment Services Directives. This exemption also applies to the Second E-money Directive.

1579 European Parliament (2017) "Report on the proposal for a directive of the European Parliament and of the Council amending Directive (EU) 2015/849 on the prevention of the use of the financial system for the purposes of money laundering or terrorist financing and amending Directive 2009/101/EC (COM(2016)0450 – C8-0265/2016 – 2016/0208(COD))", *PE593.836*, 22.

*2015/2366/EC nor monetary value stored on instruments exempted as specified in Article 3(k) and 3(l) of that Directive*".[1580] This new definition followed the ECB's recommendations, by clearly setting apart virtual currencies from 'funds' as defined under the PSD2 – banknotes and coins, scriptural money, and e-money – and from monetary value stored on instruments caught under the payment services framework's limited networks and added value exemptions.[1581] In essence, the Council thus moved the clarification of the Commission's recital 8 to the definition, which is indeed a more suitable place for such a scope demarcation. The final compromise text, however, moved back to the wordings of the Commission's original definition.[1582] A new recital 7a does state that virtual currencies should be distinguished from e-money, from funds as defined in the payment services framework, from monetary value as exempted in the payment services framework's added value and limited networks exemptions, and from closed scheme in-game currencies.[1583] Moreover, the same recital adds that the amendments aim to cover all uses of virtual currencies, be it payment uses, investment uses, or others.[1584] However, as noted before, the value of such a recital is very limited. If the European legislator wanted to exclude certain matters – such as closed scheme in-game currencies – from the scope of application, it should have done so through the definition, and not through a mere recital.

Evaluation – The virtual currency definition originally proposed by the Commission fairly closely follows the definition established for the purposes of this research, namely "*digital representations of value, which are not legal tender, which serve as a unit of account, separate from existing state- or central bank-issued currencies, and which can serve as a means to conclude payments*". The amended definition from the early Council compromise texts maintained the focus on the transferability of virtual currencies. Additionally, the early compromise texts added the language of the limited networks exemption to its virtual currency definition. In doing so, it created a much more narrow definition. While the definition established for the purposes of this research spans all types of virtual currencies, the early compromise texts' definition essentially limited the scope to bidirectional scheme virtual currencies only.

1580 Council of the European Union (2016) "Proposal for a directive of the European Parliament and of the Council amending Directive (EU) 2015/849 on the prevention of the use of the financial system for the purposes of money laundering or terrorist financing and amending Directive 2009/101/EC = Negotiating mandate", *15605/16*, 21.

1581 These elements relating to the legal framework on payment services were discussed more elaborately in chapter IV.

1582 Council of the European Union (2017) "Proposal for a Directive of the European Parliament and of the Council amending Directive (EU) 2015/849 on the prevention of the use of the financial system for the purposes of money laundering or terrorist financing and amending Directive 2009/101/EC – Analysis of the final compromise text with a view to agreement", *15849/17*, 28.

1583 *Ibid.*, 6.

1584 *Id.*

More so, the combination of that definition with the particular service providers targeted here makes that the amendments, despite the use of the broader term 'virtual currency', really only target cryptocurrencies. This of course raises the question whether these amendments can truly handle the money laundering concerns raised by virtual currencies at large, if only one particular example of a virtual currency is targeted. The final compromise text corrected the matter by returning to the original broader definition. It is, however, regrettable that the European legislator expressed its intentions to exclude certain matters through a recital, yet did not include such exclusion in the definition itself.

## 4.3 VIRTUAL CURRENCY SERVICE PROVIDERS

EXCHANGE PLATFORMS – The Commission's proposal defined[1585] virtual currency exchange platforms as "*providers engaged primarily and professionally in exchange services between virtual currencies and fiat currencies*".[1586] However, the Council's compromise text removed the qualifier of "*primarily and professionally*", meaning that also those providing these services occasionally would be caught under the scope.[1587] This raises the question of whether a virtual currency user, who on a non-commercial basis – for instance as a gesture to a friend – exchanges some units of virtual currency for legal tender or similar instruments, could become an obliged entity under the anti-money laundering framework. Such would be a significant scope increase, going beyond what seems to be the Commission's intent with its amendments to the anti-money laundering framework.

CUSTODIAN WALLET PROVIDERS – Custodian wallet providers, in turn, were defined as "*wallet providers offering custodial services of credentials necessary to access virtual currencies*".[1588] This provision appears to exclude wallets that do not hold keys for their customers, though the precise wording does leave uncertainty regarding so-called multisig wallets. Multisig wallets essentially require several keys, one or more of which may be held by the wallet service provider. If the provider holds some but not all keys, will it still fall under the scope of this provision? The Commission's proposal cannot provide a clear answer to this, even though it has substantial impact on the precise scope of

---

1585 Oddly, rather than defining these service providers in the definitions (article 3 AMLD4) and including them under the scope (article 2 AMLD4), the proposal defined them under the scope. The later Council compromise text moves the definition of 'custodian wallet provider' to the definitions, but not that of 'virtual currency exchange'.

1586 Article 1(1) Proposal AMLD4 amendments.

1587 Council of the European Union (2016) "Proposal for a directive of the European Parliament and of the Council amending Directive (EU) 2015/849 on the prevention of the use of the financial system for the purposes of money laundering or terrorist financing and amending Directive 2009/101/EC = Negotiating mandate", *15605/16*, 20–21.

1588 Article 1(1) Proposal AMLD4 amendments.

the proposed changes. The Council's compromise text amended the definition of 'custodian wallet provider' into "*an entity that provides services to safeguard private cryptographic keys on behalf of their customers, to holding, store and transfer virtual currencies*".[1589] Also this amendment clarified little on the question of multisig wallets.

Other service providers? – One notable amendment by the European Parliament would have drastically increased the scope of the proposed amendments, by considering "*issuers, administrators, intermediaries and distributors of virtual currencies*" as obliged entities.[1590] Such essentially puts all virtual currency service providers – or at least those servicing what is considered as virtual currencies under the scope of the proposed amendments – under the scope of the legal framework regarding anti-money laundering rules. It can be questioned to what extent such is needed given that certain participants in virtual currency ecosystems – such as miners in cryptocurrencies – are in principle purely technical service providers, or whether such is even feasible when there is no central issuer – as is the case for cryptocurrencies. This scope extension, however, was not inserted into the final European Parliament legislative resolution.[1591]

Consequences – The virtual currency service providers targeted here need to be licensed or registered, though the later compromise text held that they only need to be registered.[1592] Moreover, those holding a management function in such virtual currency service providers, and those being the beneficial owners must be fit and proper persons.[1593]

1589 Council of the European Union (2016) "Proposal for a directive of the European Parliament and of the Council amending Directive (EU) 2015/849 on the prevention of the use of the financial system for the purposes of money laundering or terrorist financing and amending Directive 2009/101/EC = Negotiating mandate", *15605/16*, 20–21.

1590 European Parliament (2016) "Opinion of the Committee on Legal Affairs for the Committee on Economic and Monetary Affairs and the Committee on Civil Liberties, Justice and Home Affairs on the proposal for a directive of the European Parliament and of the Council amending Directive (EU) 2015/849 on the prevention of the use of the financial system for the purposes of money laundering or terrorist financing and amending Directive 2009/101/EC (COM(2016)0450 – C8-0265/2016 – 2016/0208(COD))", *PE594.003*, amendment 21.

1591 European Parliament (2017) "Report on the proposal for a directive of the European Parliament and of the Council amending Directive (EU) 2015/849 on the prevention of the use of the financial system for the purposes of money laundering or terrorist financing and amending Directive 2009/101/EC (COM(2016)0450 – C8-0265/2016 – 2016/0208(COD))", *PE593.836*, 20.

1592 Article 1(16) Proposal AMLD4 amendments; Council of the European Union (2016) "Proposal for a directive of the European Parliament and of the Council amending Directive (EU) 2015/849 on the prevention of the use of the financial system for the purposes of money laundering or terrorist financing and amending Directive 2009/101/EC = Presidency compromise text", *13872/16*, 34.

1593 Article 1(16) Proposal AMLD4 amendments.

# 5 VIRTUAL CURRENCIES UNDER ANTI-MONEY LAUNDERING RULES

## 5.1 VIRTUAL CURRENCIES AS MONEY LAUNDERING TOOL

No reference to virtual currencies – The first three Anti-Money Laundering Directives make no mention of virtual currencies. From the legislative procedure leading up to the AMLD4, it becomes clear that it was at the time not the intention to explicitly include virtual currencies under the scope of the anti-money laundering legal framework. The final text therefore does not take up the matter of virtual currencies, and, as noted before, nor should the reference to anonymous e-money instruments be understood as referring to virtual currencies.

Member States' discretion – However, the absence of virtual currencies in the EU's anti-money laundering legal framework does not preclude Member States from taking action on their own. Member States could, for instance, still decide to bring virtual currencies under the scope of their national implementations of the anti-money laundering framework, something the UK, for one, at one point proposed to do.[1594] Therefore, despite the initial lack of a clear formulation concerning the inclusion of virtual currencies under the scope of the EU anti-money laundering legal framework, the matter could have still become subject to national regulation by the Member States next to their implementation of the directive.[1595] Such a regulatory action could very well coexist with the harmonized domain of the anti-money laundering framework.

Property under AMLD – The main focus of the EU legal framework regarding anti-money laundering is on property derived from criminal activity.[1596] Property is defined as "*assets of any kind, whether corporeal or incorporeal, movable or*

1594 HM Treasury (2015) "Digital currencies: response to the call for information", *gov.uk/government/uploads/system/uploads/attachment_data/file/414040/digital_currencies_response_to_call_for_information_final_changes.pdf*, 19. At the same time, however, the UK government seems to have adopted a cautious regulatory path in order to not deter investments in the growing fintech industry. HM Treasury and Baldwin, H. (2015), "UK to lead on big data research, says Harriett Baldwin", speech delivered to the Alan Turing Institute for Data Science, 14 October, London, *www.gov.uk/government/speeches/uk-to-lead-on-big-data-research-says-harriett-baldwin*. Also the UK's financial regulator, the Financial Conduct Authority (FCA), has expressed the need to not disturb the development of the technologies underlying virtual currencies, and the markets that are being developed out of those technologies. Woolard, C. (2016), "UK FinTech: Regulating for innovation", speech delivered at the FinTech: Regulating for innovation event, 22 February, London, *www.fca.org.uk/news/uk-fintech-regulating-for-innovation*.

1595 While the European Commission did acknowledge that virtual currency exchange platforms were not included under the directive, it did propose "*to look again into virtual currencies*". Payment Systems Market Expert Group (2015) "Minutes of the meeting of 28 April 2015", *PSMEG/005/15*, 3. Its first initiative in this regard was the amendment of the AMLD4 (section 4 of this chapter).

1596 Article 1(3) AMLD4.

*immovable, tangible or intangible, and legal documents or instruments in any form including electronic or digital, evidencing title to or an interest in such assets"*.[1597] This broad definition makes it clear that the anti-money laundering legal framework does not focus solely on money in the strictest sense of the word, being the traditional banknotes and coins. Already since the AMLD1, the property definition has also included incorporeal and intangible assets. Interestingly, for terrorist financing the focus is not put on 'property', but on 'funds'.[1598] While the anti-money laundering directive itself does not define such 'funds', the FATF Recommendations provide a definition that is identical to the notion of 'property' under the directive.[1599] It can therefore be assumed that both notions must be interpreted in the same way, as there is no evidence that the European legislator wanted to distinguish between them. It could then be argued that virtual currencies could be considered as such incorporeal and intangible assets.[1600] If such an interpretation is followed, the legal framework on anti-money laundering rules could be held to apply to virtual currencies gained from criminal activity, or used for terrorist financing, even before the amendments to the AMLD4.

Property under national law – Franco-Belgian tradition – However, it must be remarked that the notion of incorporeal assets is not always an easy matter to place under existing principles of national private law. Property law, for instance, is often linked to corporeal assets. While it should be remarked that a distinction between corporeal and incorporeal assets was already present in Roman law, this does not mean that property rights could always be vested on incorporeal assets.[1601] Over time, a number of incorporeal assets did become explicitly recognized under property law, for instance through the legal framework on intellectual property rights. Another example is article 529 of the Belgian Civil Code, which recognizes as incorporeal moveable goods obligations and claims, shares, and interests. Also electricity and gas are traditionally recognized as moveable goods.[1602] However, even if an incorporeal asset is recognized under property law, there are still questions remaining regarding the particular nature of

1597 Article 3(3) AMLD4.

1598 Article 1(5) AMLD4.

1599 FATF (2016) *FATF Recommendations 2012 – International Standards on Combating Money Laundering and the Financing of Terrorism & Proliferation (2016 update)*, Paris: FATF, 121.

1600 Kaiser, C. (2016) "The Classification of Virtual Currencies and Mobile Payments in Terms of the Old and New European Anti-Money Laundering Frameworks", In: Gimigliano, G. (Ed.) *Bitcoin and Mobile Payments: Constructing a European Union Framework*, London: Palgrave – Macmillan, 213.

1601 See: Gaius, *Institutiones*, II, §11–14.

1602 Sagaert, V. (2005) "Het goederenrecht als open systeem van verbintenissen? Poging tot een nieuwe kwalificatie van de vermogensrechten", *Tijdschrift voor Privaatrecht*, Vol. 42, 991; Catala, P. (1966) "La transformation du patrimoine dans le droit civil moderne", *Revue trimestrielle du droit civil*, Vol. 64, 200–201; Lecocq, P. (2012) *Manuel de droit des biens – Tome 1*, Brussels: Larcier, 33–34; Loiseau, G. (2011) "Biens meubles par détermination de la loi ou meubles incorporels", *JurisClasseur Code Civil – art. 527–532*, Fasc. 20, paragraph 2.

such asset. Rights regarding property are traditionally classified as either personal rights, rights *in rem*, or intellectual rights.[1603] A growing number of incorporeal assets is not easy to place within those three categories.[1604] But, while the notion of property is certainly evolving over the years, it should also be cautioned not to hollow out the meaning of property by overstretching the notion through an overcreation of new rights under the 'property' umbrella.[1605]

Property under national law – German tradition – One example where the legal position of incorporeal assets could prove problematic can be found in Germany. The relevant notion regarding the anti-money laundering provision in the German Criminal Code, namely '*Gegenstand'*, does not seem fit to address virtual currencies.[1606] While it is accepted in literature that the notion of '*Gegenstand*' covers all kinds of financial assets – such as securities and jewelry – the notion principally only extends to property and rights.[1607] Under German private law, such property can only take the form of material goods, thus principally excluding virtual currencies as they are not material.[1608] Rights, in turn, traditionally mean transferable rights, thus making it difficult to classify – at least

[1603] Vanuxem S. (2010) "Les choses saisies par la propriété. De la chose-objet aux choses-milieux", *Revue interdisciplinaire d'études juridiques*, Vol. 64, 128; Lecocq, P. (2012) *Manuel de droit des biens - Tome 1*, Brussels: Larcier, 31–34; Malekzadem, J. (2010) "Beslag op domeinnamen. Een eerste verkenning", *Rechtskundig Weekblad*, Vol. 73, 1498; Tilleman, B., Verbeke, A.-L., Sagaert, V. (2007) *Vermogensrecht in kort bestek*, Antwerpen: Intersentia, 3; Ginossar, S. (1960) *Droit réel, propriété et créance: élaboration d'un système rationnel des droits patrimoniaux*, Paris: Librairie Générale de Droit et de Jurisprudence, 86.

[1604] Périnet-Marquet, H. (2010) "Regard sur les nouveaux biens", *La Semaine Juridique Edition Générale*, nr. 44, paragraph 21–22; Tilleman, B., Verbeke, A.-L., Sagaert, V. (2007) *Vermogensrecht in kort bestek*, Antwerpen: Intersentia, 4–5; Loiseau, G. (2011) "Biens meubles par détermination de la loi ou meubles incorporels", *JurisClasseur Code Civil - art. 527–532*, Fasc. 20, paragraph 2–3.

[1605] Storme, M. E., Helsen, F. (forthcoming) "The function of private property and its future", In: Lauroba, E., Tarabal, J. (Eds.) *El derecho de la propiedad en la construcción del Derecho privado europeo: índices, sistemas adquisitivos y objetos / El dret de la proprietat en la construccio del dret privat europeu / The right of ownership in the construction of European private law*, Barcelona: Tirant lo Blanch, 135–138.

[1606] §261 Strafgesetzbuch (StGB); Boehm, F., Pesch, P. (2014) "Bitcoin: A First Legal Analysis With Reference to German and US-American Law", In: Böhme, R., Brenner, M., Moore, T., Smith, M. (Eds.) *Financial Cryptography and Data Security, FC 2014 Workshops, LNCS 8438*, Berlin: Springer, 47–48.

[1607] Ruhmannseder, F. (2016) "StGB §261 Geldwäsche; Verschleierung unrechtmäßig erlangter Vermögenswerte", In: von Heintschel-Heinegg, B. (Ed.) *Beck'scher Online Kommentar StGB (32. Edition)*, München: Verlag C.H. Beck, Rn. 8; Kühl, K. (2016) "StGB §261 Geldwäsche; Verschleierung unrechtmäßig erlangter Vermögenswerte", In: Kühl, K, Heger, M. (Eds.) *Strafgesetzbuch Kommentar (28. Auflage)*, München: Verlag C.H. Beck, Rn. 3; Schmidt, W., Krause, J. (2010) "§261", In: Laufhütte, H. W., Rissing-van Saan, R., Tiedemann, K. (Eds.) *Strafgesetzbuch Leipziger Kommentar (12. Auflage)*, Berlin: Walter de Gruyter, 669; Glaser, R. (2009) *Geldwäsche (§261 StGB) durch Rechtsanwälte und Steuerberater bei der Honorarannahme*, München: Herbert Utz Verlag, 8.

[1608] §903 Bundesgesetzbuch (BGB) defines property ('*Eigentum*') in relation to '*Sache*'. The latter notion is defined under §90 BGB as being only material goods.

certain – virtual currencies as such rights given their limited transferability.[1609] However, as it has been accepted that scriptural money falls under the scope of the '*Gegenstand*' provision, some authors argue that the application of the anti-money laundering legal framework to virtual currencies could be acceptable, given that scriptural money is not material either.[1610] Given the aim of the anti-money laundering legal framework to cover anything that holds economic value, such would – as noted earlier here – indeed seem in line with the European legislator's intentions. However, a possible counterargument against that line of thought is that scriptural money can be considered as a claim, thus constituting a transferable right.[1611] And, as noted, transferable rights are indeed covered by the '*Gegenstand*' provision. If this counterargument is followed, virtual currencies could only be covered by the AMLD4 if they constitute transferable rights. In this regard, it is reminded that it was already found in chapter IV that it is for several virtual currencies disputed whether they could indeed constitute a claim, and thus a transferable right.[1612] While there is merit to the counterargument referenced here, it cannot be denied that it goes against at least the spirit of the European legislator's intentions with the anti-money laundering framework.

RESEARCH DEMARCATION – The German example demonstrates how the reluctance of private law to provide a full-fledged legal qualification for incorporeal assets could affect the rules on money laundering, typically considered as part of financial or, broader, economic law. However, it is beyond the scope of this research to delve further into the matter of incorporeal assets under private law. For the purposes of this research, it can suffice to conclude that the European legislator has at least partially solved this problem by amending the AMLD4. As a result of those amendments, there is no longer any doubt that virtual currencies are covered by the anti-money laundering framework, and that they can thus serve

---

1609 Glaser, R. (2009) *Geldwäsche (§261 StGB) durch Rechtsanwälte und Steuerberater bei der Honorarannahme*, München: Herbert Utz Verlag, 9; Schröder, M. (2014) "Bitcoin: Virtuelle Währung – reelle Problemstellungen", *JurPC Web-Dok. 104/2014*, Abs. 24–32.

1610 Boehm, F., Pesch, P. (2014) "Bitcoin: A First Legal Analysis With Reference to German and US-American Law", In: Böhme, R., Brenner, M., Moore, T., Smith, M. (Eds.) *Financial Cryptography and Data Security, FC 2014 Workshops, LNCS 8438*, Berlin: Springer, 47–48. Schröder argues that in keeping with the *ratio legis* it must be accepted that all financial assets be covered by the scope of the anti-money laundering legal framework, even if those assets are not (yet) recognized by law. Schröder, M. (2014) "Bitcoin: Virtuelle Währung – reelle Problemstellungen", *JurPC Web-Dok. 104/2014*, Abs. 119.

1611 Glaser, R. (2009) *Geldwäsche (§261 StGB) durch Rechtsanwälte und Steuerberater bei der Honorarannahme*, München: Herbert Utz Verlag, 8–9. Note furthermore that in Belgium it has already been accepted that property rights can be vested on debt claims. Sagaert, V. (2005) "Het goederenrecht als open systeem van verbintenissen? Poging tot een nieuwe kwalificatie van de vermogensrechten", *Tijdschrift voor Privaatrecht*, Vol. 42, 991; Boddaert, C. (2009) "Pand op een levende bankrekening", In: Cattaruzza, J., Kupers, W., Peeters, I. (Eds.) *Liber Amicorum Achilles Cuypers*, Brussel: Larcier, 12–13.

1612 Schröder, M. (2014) "Bitcoin: Virtuelle Währung – reelle Problemstellungen", *JurPC Web-Dok. 104/2014*, Abs. 24–32.

as the property targeted by that legal framework. It is now up to the Member States to reconcile the inclusion of virtual currencies under the anti-money laundering framework with potential issues under their national private law.

## 5.2 VIRTUAL CURRENCY SERVICE PROVIDERS UNTIL AMLD4

Obliged entities – The bigger question is then whether the entities providing virtual currency services – such as cryptocurrency exchanges – could be considered as obliged entities under the scope of the anti-money laundering legal framework. It are, after all, the obliged entities that need to report on activities that are potentially related to money laundering or terrorist financing activities. If virtual currency service providers were not covered under the scope of the anti-money laundering framework, there is a real possibility that money laundering activities utilizing virtual currencies would not be reported.[1613] In other words, the qualification of virtual currencies gained from criminal activities or used to finance such activities as money laundering under the anti-money laundering legal framework loses a significant part of its value if there are no obliged entities involved that need to report on suspicious virtual currency activities. Note also that, even now that certain virtual currency service providers are regulated under the amended AMLD4, the question remains whether other virtual currency service providers could be caught under the scope of other obliged entities.

Obliged entities under original AMLD4 – Obliged entities under the initial AMLD4 are firstly credit institutions and financial institutions.[1614] In second order, it are legal and natural persons acting in the exercise of their professional activities, particularly auditors, external accountants and tax advisors; notaries and other independent legal professionals; other trust or company service providers; estate agents; other persons trading in goods to the extent that payments are made or received in cash in an amount of EUR 10 000 or more; and providers of gambling services.[1615]

Other means of payment – Financial institutions are defined as undertakings other than a credit institution performing one or more of the activities listed in Annex I to Directive 2013/36/EU; insurance undertakings; investment firms; collective investment undertakings; insurance intermediaries; and branches.[1616]

1613 The main reason here is that virtual currencies generally operate outside of the scope of the traditional financial system. In-game currencies, for instance, will only be used within the virtual world they operate in. Virtual currencies in loyalty programs are only used in relation to other actors within that loyalty scheme. These actors are unlikely to be obliged entities under the anti-money laundering framework.

1614 Article 2(1) (1) and (2) AMLD4.

1615 Article 2(1) (3) AMLD4.

1616 Article 3(2) AMLD4.

Interestingly, one of the services under Directive 2013/36/EU referenced here concerns "*issuing and administering other means of payment (e.g. travellers' cheques and bankers' drafts)*" insofar such is not a payment service.[1617] Here, an Estonian court found that the virtual currency services provided in the case at hand constituted alternative means of payment, under Estonia's implementation of Directive 2013/36/EU.[1618] This case demonstrates how Member States could deviate from the intentions of the European legislator in their national interpretations and implementations. Such a deviation could even be argued to be mandatory to certain extent, as the directive requires Member States to extend the scope of their legal frameworks to professions and categories of undertakings – other than the obliged entities covered under the anti-money laundering framework – that engage in activities that are likely to be used for money laundering purposes.[1619] However, no evidence was found to indicate support of the Estonian interpretation in other Member States.[1620] It is therefore unlikely that such an interpretation will gain a broad adoption.

Exchange offices – Another entity covered under the definition of financial institutions under the anti-money laundering legal framework are currency exchange offices.[1621] In the case of cryptocurrencies, most users will at one point use an exchange service to obtain cryptocurrencies, or to exchange them against legal tender or similar instruments.[1622] The question is then whether the providers of such cryptocurrency exchange services fall under the scope of the currency exchange offices meant here. Alternatively, it can be questioned whether Member States have expanded the notion of financial institutions in a way that could encompass virtual currency exchange services.

With regard to the applicability of currency exchange offices to virtual currency exchanges, some authors have argued in favor of such applicability.[1623] However,

1617 Point 5 Annex I Directive 2013/36/EC. Payment services are covered in a separate point.

1618 Künnapas, K. (2016) "From Bitcoin to Smart Contracts: Legal Revolution or Evolution from the Perspective of de lege ferenda?", In: Kerikmäe, T., Rull, A. (Eds.), *The Future of Law and eTechnologies*, Cham: Springer, 119–120.

1619 Article 4 AMLD4. However, such extension is subject to requirements, such as a risk assessment and notification of the European Commission.

1620 Moreover, the case is currently being challenged at the EU level. De Voogd, O. (2016) "Estonia vs Bitcoin saga: Requesting EC Start Infringement Proceedings Against Estonia", *steemit.com*, 16 September.

1621 Article 3(2)(a) AMLD4.

1622 Given the significant increase in mining difficulty, it is unlikely that the average private user will still gain cryptocurrencies from mining. Cryptocurrencies must therefore be obtained by receiving cryptocurrencies – as consideration for goods or services delivered or as a donation – or by exchanging legal tender for cryptocurrencies. While it is possible to hold cryptocurrencies, many users will likely want to convert them into legal tender, or similar instruments, at some point, given the relatively limited acceptance of this form of virtual currency.

1623 Kaiser, C. (2016) "The Classification of Virtual Currencies and Mobile Payments in Terms of the Old and New European Anti-Money Laundering Frameworks", In: Gimigliano, G. (Ed.)

reference can be made to the legal framework on payment services, where – as discussed in chapter IV – the notion of exchange bureaus is meant to apply only to physical cash-to-cash operations. As a result, a virtual currency exchange service could not be considered as a money exchange service under the legal framework on payment services. The AMLD4 does not state whether or not its notion of currency exchange offices refers only to physical exchange bureaus or whether it also includes online services. However, there is a notion of gambling services – which is clearly meant to extend to online services – next to that of physical casinos. If the same pattern were applied to exchange services, this could be interpreted as indicating that the notion of exchange bureaus itself should be limited to physical establishments, and that online exchanges should become subject of a separate notion. This interpretation is demonstrated in practice by, for instance, the implementation of the anti-money laundering framework into Belgian law: currency exchange offices are defined as conducting manual operations.[1624] Moreover, the European Commission's initiative to add virtual currency service providers as a separate type of obliged entities under the anti-money laundering legal framework further evidences that virtual currency exchanges were not already covered under the existing notion of currency exchange offices.

With regard to potential Member States' deviations, reference can be made to the UK, where the definition of financial institutions includes a reference to 'money service businesses'. Such a money service business, in turn, is defined as an "*undertaking which by way of business operates a currency exchange office, transmits money (or any representations of monetary value) by any means or cashes cheques which are made payable to customers*".[1625] The broad inclusion of 'any representations of monetary value' could possibly leave room for application to virtual currencies.[1626] However, two remarks must be made here. First, the definition of money services business attaches the 'any representations of monetary value' to the element of money transmission. Such a money transmission is listed as a different business operation than that of currency exchange. Thus, the addition of 'any representations of monetary value' does not apply to the business operations of a currency exchange office, and therefore cannot be held to state whether or not cryptocurrency exchanges were covered under the notion of money services business. Second, money services businesses still need to supply one of the services listed under Annex I to Directive 2013/36/

*Bitcoin and Mobile Payments: Constructing a European Union Framework*, London: Palgrave – Macmillan, 214–215.

1624 Royal Decree of 27 December 1994 concerning the currency exchange offices and the currency trade, *Belgian State Gazette* 18 January 1995.

1625 Article 3(3)(a) Money Laundering Regulations 2007, 2007 No. 2157, references the banking consolidation directive (2006/48/EC), which was replaced by Directive 2013/36/EU.

1626 Stokes, R. (2012) "Virtual money laundering: the case of Bitcoin and the Linden dollar", *Information & Communications Technology Law*, Vol. 21, 228.

EU[1627], which was in the previous paragraph found not to be a clear-cut case either. As a result, it seems unlikely that the UK's notion of 'money service business' is able to be applied to virtual currency exchanges.

Payment Services and e-money – Other services listed in Annex I to Directive 2013/36/EU that are provided by financial institutions as understood under the anti-money laundering framework include payment services and e-money issuing.[1628] While in chapter IV it was noted that the provision of virtual currency services would not lead to a qualification as payment institution or e-money institution under the respective legal frameworks in this regard, it was also found that in practice several virtual currency service providers are being authorized as payment institutions and e-money institutions. When such an authorization is granted, these services providers are subjected to anti-money laundering rules, by virtue of the application of the legal framework on payment services or e-money.

Other persons trading in goods – A final element under the anti-money laundering framework where virtual currency service providers could be included as obliged entities concerns "*other persons trading in goods to the extent that payments are made or received in cash in an amount of EUR 10 000 or more, whether the transaction is carried out in a single operation or in several operations which appear to be linked*".[1629] Following the analysis of chapter III, it can be held that virtual currencies are currently unlikely to be considered as cash. It must then be questioned whether they constitute 'goods' under the 'persons trading in goods' provision. Certain virtual currencies – mainly cryptocurrencies – have in literature been argued to be commodities.[1630] However, at the same time it should be remarked that commodities are meant to be tangible and have inherent value.[1631] Virtual currencies are most certainly not tangible, and their inherent value can be disputed. The result is that a qualification of virtual currencies as commodities is discussable yet not that straightforward, and thus far does not appear to be generally accepted.[1632] Additionally, reference can be made to a decision by the Court of Justice of the European Union, where the Court

1627 Article 3(3) with reference to article 2(1) Money Laundering Regulations 2007, 2007 No. 2157.

1628 Points 4 and 15 Annex I to Directive 2013/36/EU.

1629 Article 2(1)(3)(e) AMLD4.

1630 Grinberg, R. (2013) "Bitcoin: An Innovative Alternative Digital Currency", *Hastings Science & Technology Law Journal*, Vol. 4, 199–200; Kaplanov, N. (2012) "Nerdy Money: Bitcoin, the Private Digital Currency, and the Case Against its Regulation", *Loyola Consumer Law Review*, Vol. 25, 113; Springael, B. (2014) "Bitcoins: het virtuele goud?", *Tijdschrift voor Financieel Recht*, nr. 468, 759–763.

1631 Grinberg, R. (2013) "Bitcoin: An Innovative Alternative Digital Currency", *Hastings Science & Technology Law Journal*, Vol. 4, 199–200; Bonneau, T. (2016) "Analyse critique de la contribution de la CJUE à l'ascension juridique du bitcoin", In: De Loustal, J. (Ed.) *Liber Amicorum Blanche Sousi: L'Europe bancaire, financière et monétaire*, Paris: Revue Banque Edition, 298.

1632 Houben, R. (2015) "Bitcoin: there are two sides to every coin", *Tijdschrift voor Belgisch Handelsrecht*, nr. 2, 144.

held that the exchange of traditional currencies for units of virtual currency constitutes a supply of services for consideration within the meaning of the VAT Directive.[1633, 1634] The supply of such services are transactions exempt from VAT, within the meaning of article 135(1)(e) of the VAT Directive, which exempts "*transactions, including negotiation, concerning currency, bank notes and coins used as legal tender, with the exception of collectors' items, that is to say, gold, silver or other metal coins or bank notes which are not normally used as legal tender or coins of numismatic interest*".[1635] The Court argued in favor of the application of the VAT exemption to virtual currencies, holding that "*to interpret that provision as including only transactions involving traditional currencies would deprive it of part of its effect*".[1636] Important in this decision is that the Court recognizes virtual currencies as means of payment, which are not 'tangible property' within the meaning of article 14 of the VAT Directive.[1637] As a result, the Court finds that obtaining virtual currencies through exchange against traditional currency does not constitute a supply of goods for the purposes of EU VAT law.[1638] While this case could then provide an indication that virtual currencies should not be considered as goods under the 'other persons trading in goods' provision of the anti-money laundering framework discussed here, it should also be remarked that this particular case and the specificity of VAT law do not allow for such generalizing conclusions to be drawn from the Court's findings. Two other thoughts can then be put forward. First, given their virtual nature, virtual currencies will not often be involved in cash transactions.[1639] Second, given the often limited range of acceptance of most types of virtual currencies, they will not often be part of a transaction – or several linked transactions for that matter – exceeding EUR 10.000.[1640] The result of these two thoughts taken together is that – at least at the moment – it is difficult to imagine a scenario where a cash transaction exceeding EUR 10.000 involving virtual currencies is warranted.[1641]

---

1633 Council Directive 2006/112/EC of 28 November 2006 on the common system of value added tax, *OJ* L 347 of 11 December 2006, 1–118 (hereinafter: VAT Directive).

1634 CJEU, Skatteverket *v* David Hedqvist, C-264/14, paragraph 31.

1635 *Ibid.*, paragraph 57.

1636 *Ibid.*, paragraph 51.

1637 *Ibid.*, paragraph 24.

1638 *Ibid.*, paragraph 26. See also: Bonneau, T. (2016) "Analyse critique de la contribution de la CJUE à l'ascension juridique du bitcoin", In: De Loustal, J. (Ed.) *Liber Amicorum Blanche Sousi: L'Europe bancaire, financière et monétaire*, Paris: Revue Banque Edition, 296–297.

1639 For instance, cryptocurrency exchanges operate solely online. While physical tokens do exist – such as those issued through cryptocurrency ATMs – this is a fringe phenomenon, and such tokens only serve to hold the keys needed to access the cryptocurrency wallet online.

1640 Such seems only feasible for bidirectional scheme virtual currencies, and more particularly for cryptocurrencies. Given their propensity for broader use, they could more easily be used in larger transactions.

1641 Whereas it is of course possible that such transaction would be carried out precisely for the purposes of money laundering, this also means that the entities conducting these transactions are unlikely to voluntarily fulfill the obligations they could have as obliged entities under the anti-money laundering legal framework.

In other words, the usability of the 'other persons trading in goods' provision in identifying instances of money laundering or terrorist financing using virtual currencies appears to be severely limited, even if virtual currencies were to be considered as the 'goods' required here.

## 5.3 VIRTUAL CURRENCY SERVICE PROVIDERS AFTER AMLD4 AMENDMENTS

Scope – In terms of scope, it must be questioned to what extent the European Commission aims to regulate virtual currency service providers with its amendments to the AMLD4. The notion of 'virtual currencies' itself is defined broadly enough in the Commission's initial proposal and the final interinstitutional compromise text. However, the obliged entities show that the extent of the anti-money laundering regulation of virtual currencies is limited to certain bidirectional scheme virtual currencies only, and more in particular cryptocurrency service providers. After all, the virtual currency exchanges and custodian wallet providers found in practice are aimed toward cryptocurrencies, and not toward other types of virtual currencies.[1642] This would, of course, limit the extent of the practical application of the Commission's amendments. Moreover, as correctly remarked by the ECB in its opinion on the matter, virtual currencies could be used to attain goods and services without requiring exchange into legal tender or similar instruments, or the use of a custodian wallet provider.[1643] Neither made the Commission's proposal mention of virtual currency to virtual currency exchanges. Such activities could still result in money laundering or terrorist financing activities, yet are not caught by the scope of the amended AMLD4. The amendments also do not address other use cases of particularly cryptocurrencies, such as in investment products, despite a reference in a recital to such use cases.[1644]

Exchange platforms and wallet providers – The result of the seemingly minor modifications to the AMLD4 for virtual currency service providers is clear: virtual currency exchange platforms and custodian wallet providers will have to be registered or licensed, though later texts only speak of

---

1642 Another example of a bidirectional virtual currency, Second Life's Linden dollars, would be exempted from the definition of virtual currencies used here, by virtue of the applicability of the Second Payment Services Directive's limited networks exemption included in that definition. As a result, Linden dollars are not virtual currencies under the scope of this framework, and their service provider is not an exchange provider.

1643 European Central Bank (2016) "Opinion of 12 October 2016 on a proposal for a directive of the European Parliament and of the Council amending Directive (EU) 2015/849 on the prevention of the use of the financial system for the purposes of money laundering or terrorist financing and amending Directive 2009/101/EC", *ecb.europa.eu*, 2.

1644 *Ibid.*, 3–4.

registration.[1645] They will have to adopt measures to comply with customer due diligence obligations, not just in relation to new customers but also to existing customers.[1646] As a result, their customers' identities must be verified even before establishing a business relationship or carrying out a transaction. Such is expected to allow competent authorities to effectively monitor the use of virtual currencies. It must also be noted that such a registration will be dependent on national implementation, and that in principle no passporting rules stemming from a different legal framework apply here, due to the virtual currency service providers targeted here not being considered as financial institutions.[1647] Furthermore, since the proposed changes do not specify how such a registration is to occur, the precise rules could end up being very different across Member States.[1648] Last, the behavior of managers and beneficial owners must be assessed as fit and proper, even though there is at the moment no directive or guideline that provides for how such an assessment must be conducted for these particular service providers.[1649]

Virtual currency users – This proposal also has clear consequences for the users of virtual currencies. More precisely, these amendments touch upon the core of what is considered by many users to be one of the main benefits from virtual currencies, especially cryptocurrencies, namely anonymity. Certain activities regarding virtual currencies – such as cryptocurrency mining – would principally not be affected by the amendments. However, since many – if not most – users will acquire their virtual currencies from exchange platforms, or use the services of custodian wallet providers in their payments, these users will now be required to verify their identity towards service providers. Though such potentially limits the risk posed to users by anonymity, the EBA has remarked that the proposal does little to address other risks to users – or other stakeholders and the market for that matter.[1650] Moreover, as noted earlier, the Commission wants to investigate the possibilities of assembling a central database linking virtual currency wallet addresses to their users' identities. Such fully abolishes whatever anonymity or pseudonymity virtual currencies can offer their users. Virtual currency service

---

1645 Council of the European Union (2016) "Proposal for a directive of the European Parliament and of the Council amending Directive (EU) 2015/849 on the prevention of the use of the financial system for the purposes of money laundering or terrorist financing and amending Directive 2009/101/EC = Negotiating mandate", *15605/16*, 37.

1646 Article 1(5) Proposal AMLD4 amendments.

1647 European Banking Authority (2016) "Opinion of the European Banking Authority on the EU Commission's proposal to bring Virtual Currencies into the scope of Directive (EU) 2015/849 (4AMLD)", *EBA-Op-2016-07*, 6–7.

1648 *Ibid.*, 8.

1649 *Ibid.*, 7–8.

1650 European Banking Authority (2016) "Opinion of the European Banking Authority on the EU Commission's proposal to bring Virtual Currencies into the scope of Directive (EU) 2015/849 (4AMLD)", *EBA-Op-2016-07*, 5.

providers will be obliged to process the personal data of their clients, and they will have to share that data with competent authorities. While of course such personal data processing must comply with the EU's legal framework in this regard, the move toward full and mandatory identification will undoubtedly repel certain users, and not just those using virtual currencies for illegitimate purposes.

Market impact – The virtual currency service providers now targeted by the anti-money laundering framework, up to now operating without regulatory oversight, will be subjected to the full scope of anti-money laundering rules. While the Commission clearly expressed that it is not its intention to limit access to the virtual currency market, the new legal framework will of course have an impact on existing service providers and new market entrants. After all, financial service providers are well-known to consider the implementation of anti-money laundering rules as costly, and have questioned their efficiency in stopping money laundering practices.[1651] At the same time, it must be acknowledged that, at least certain, virtual currencies can indeed serve money laundering and terrorist financing purposes. From that perspective, it was of course only a matter of time before regulatory action would be taken. Virtual currencies are currently not regulated under the main legal frameworks in this field of law – namely those on e-money and payment services – and the oft-perceived lawlessness of virtual currencies can only increase their desirability for criminal intent. Examples such as the Silk Road case demonstrate that virtual currencies are indeed used in criminal schemes. Virtual currencies are not issued by state actors, which means their usability fully depends on users' trust in the virtual currency schemes themselves. It is therefore hard to argue with an initiative that aims to "*contribute to increasing trust of their good-faith users*".[1652]

Perceived legitimacy? – However, the ECB warns that the amendments could be perceived as lending legitimacy to virtual currencies, though they does not address all of the associated risks – such as price volatility and the potential to disrupt price stability.[1653] Also the EBA has in this regard remarked that the inclusion of certain virtual currency service providers under the legal framework of anti-money laundering does not include the imposition of consumer protection or prudential safeguards.[1654] As a result, the EBA finds that the appearance that

1651 Though a study conducted at the level of the EU found it impossible to assess the real costs and benefits of this policy. ECOLEF (2013) "The Economic and Legal Effectiveness of Anti-Money Laundering and Combating Terrorist Financing Policy", *www2.econ.uu.nl/users/unger.*

1652 Proposal AMLD4 amendments, 11.

1653 European Central Bank (2016) "Opinion of 12 October 2016 on a proposal for a directive of the European Parliament and of the Council amending Directive (EU) 2015/849 on the prevention of the use of the financial system for the purposes of money laundering or terrorist financing and amending Directive 2009/101/EC", *ecb.europa.eu*, 2–3.

1654 European Banking Authority (2016) "Opinion of the European Banking Authority on the EU Commission's proposal to bring Virtual Currencies into the scope of Directive (EU) 2015/849 (4AMLD)", *EBA-Op-2016-07*, 5.

virtual currency service providers are now regulated or authorized may give the false impression that such safeguards are in place, where in fact they are not.[1655] In the opinion of the EBA, there is therefore a need for more comprehensive regulation of virtual currencies, corresponding to the risks not mitigated by the original proposal, as well as for better communication to stakeholders on the precise legal status of virtual currencies.[1656] The later compromise texts somewhat address this matter by removing the statements on the benefits of virtual currencies, only focusing on the fact that the proposed amendments aim to – partially – address the risk posed by anonymity.[1657] It should, however, be remarked that the comments of the ECB and EBA in this regard may be somewhat overblown. It is true that the anti-money laundering framework is a one-issue legal framework, and that measures of consumer protection and prudential safeguards need to be sought elsewhere, but this of course applies to all of the obliged entities under the anti-money laundering framework and not just to virtual currency service providers. The limitations of the anti-money laundering framework should therefore not be a reason not to expand this framework to new areas of money laundering, such as virtual currencies. On the contrary, in order to effectively combat money laundering, the reach of obliged entities under the anti-money laundering framework must be as broad as possible.

International framing – Also from an international perspective, the inclusion of certain virtual currency service providers under the EU's anti-money laundering framework should come as no surprise.[1658] The US state of New York, for instance, already adopted a legal framework governing virtual currency services in 2015, which chapter VII will discuss more elaborately.[1659] Under that legal framework, virtual currency service providers need to be licensed, which also requires them to adopt an anti-money laundering program.[1660] At the federal level, the US Financial Crimes Enforcement Network

1655 *Id.*

1656 *Ibid.*, 5–6.

1657 Council of the European Union (2016) "Proposal for a directive of the European Parliament and of the Council amending Directive (EU) 2015/849 on the prevention of the use of the financial system for the purposes of money laundering or terrorist financing and amending Directive 2009/101/EC = Negotiating mandate", *15605/16*, 4.

1658 Another example is Japan, which in 2016 amended it Payment Services Act (Act No. 59 of 24 June 2009) to consider virtual currencies as a store of value that is not legal tender, requiring service providers such as exchange platforms to register and to comply with a number of requirements, which includes anti-money laundering rules. Okano, Y. (2016) "Virtual currencies: issues remain after Payment Services Act amended", *Iakyara*, Vol. 243, 2–3; Vandezande, N. (2017) "Virtual currency law is Zen for Yen", *Policy Forum*, 20 April.

1659 It should also be noted that the definition of 'virtual currency business activity' used in that legal framework is much broader than the two forms of service providers captured by the European Commission's proposal. 23 CRR-NY 200.2(q).

1660 23 CRR-NY 200.15.

(FinCEN), a bureau of the United States Department of the Treasury, considers virtual currencies as media of exchange that can operate like a currency, but that do not possess the attributes of real currency, such as being legal tender.[1661] The result is that, according to FinCEN, virtual currency service providers – such as exchange platforms – can operate as money service businesses, which requires them to register and to maintain an anti-money laundering program.[1662]

# 6 INTERIM CONCLUSIONS

## 6.1 FINDINGS

Chapter goals – The aim of this chapter was to assess whether virtual currencies and their service providers fall under the scope of the EU's anti-money laundering framework. Where such is the case, further assessment against the normative criteria established for the purposes of this research is needed to ascertain whether such regulation is satisfactory. Where virtual currencies and their service providers do not fall under the scope of the anti-money laundering legal framework, it must be assessed against the same normative criteria whether such regulation is be possible and desirable.

Until AMLD4 – Although up to and including the original AMLD4 no explicit mention was made of virtual currencies, it has been shown that they could principally be considered as the 'property' derived from criminal activity – or the 'funds' used in terrorist financing – covered by the anti-money laundering legal framework. However, such needs to be determined by the Member States' national transposition of the anti-money laundering legal framework, where it was found that the qualification of virtual currencies under national private law could prove difficult. For virtual currency service providers, it was found that they cannot be considered as obliged entities under the first four Anti-Money Laundering Directives. Only a single deviating opinion to that effect was found, which gained no further following.

After AMLD4 amendments – Though the amendments to the AMLD4 include a definition of virtual currencies, they are still not explicitly included under the scope of the 'property' or 'funds' meant in the anti-money laundering legal framework. However, the definition of virtual currencies taken together with the inclusion of certain virtual currency service providers makes it clear that virtual currencies should be considered as possible money laundering

1661 FinCEN (2013) "Guidance Document – Application of FinCEN's Regulations to Persons Administering, Exchanging, or Using Virtual Currencies", *FIN-2013-G001*, 1.

1662 *Ibid.*, 3–5.

or terrorist financing tools under the amended anti-money laundering legal framework. In terms of service providers, the amendments bring two particular virtual currency service providers under the scope of the anti-money laundering framework. However, it was found that these service providers are mainly focused on particular bidirectional scheme virtual currencies – namely cryptocurrencies – meaning that other bidirectional virtual currency service providers and service providers for other types of virtual currencies are still not caught under the scope of the anti-money laundering legal framework.

## 6.2 NORMATIVE ASSESSMENT

Normative assessment – It is clear that the anti-money laundering legal framework could still be expanded for a broader inclusion of virtual currencies and service providers. For instance, the list of obliged entities could be expanded with other virtual currency service providers. It must, however, be assessed whether such an expansion is desirable. For those service providers now included under the anti-money laundering legal framework, it must be assessed whether their inclusion can be justified in light of the risks posed in the provision of their services. As in chapter IV, only a preliminary assessment can be made at this stage of the research, given that other candidate legal frameworks are assessed in separate chapters.

Legal certainty – In terms of legal certainty, there was little doubt that virtual currency service providers were not to be considered as obliged entities before the amendments to the AMLD4. While the inclusion of certain virtual currency service providers can indeed provide more legal certainty regarding their status under the anti-money laundering legal framework, it is reminded that the anti-money laundering legal framework can only address one particular risk – anonymity – and that consumer and prudential safeguards still have to be sought elsewhere. Purely from the point of view of legal certainty, there thus seems to be little incentive to include virtual currencies or their service providers under the anti-money laundering legal framework, or to extend such an inclusion to other virtual currency service providers.

Proportionality – There is no doubt that the anti-money laundering rules can be burdensome on the obliged entities, but this of course applies to all obliged entities and not just to virtual currency service providers. It is also true that the anti-money laundering legal framework only addresses one particular risk posed by virtual currencies, namely anonymity. Purely in terms of risks, the two previous points mean that the anti-money laundering framework imposes heavy burdens, yet addresses only one of the risks that were identified in chapter I of this research. Additional legislative initiative to address other risks would then still be necessary. Such an initiative – such as regulation of virtual currency service providers under the payment services framework – can also result in the applicability of anti-money laundering rules, which renders the 2018 amendments to the AMLD4 superfluous. However, when assessing the situation as it stands today, it can be concluded that – while the anti-money laundering rules are indeed burdensome – there is no clear justification for a different treatment of virtual currency service providers under the anti-money laundering framework than the other obliged entities. Regulating one entity using money under the anti-money laundering framework, while not regulating a similar entity using virtual currencies under the same framework, can be argued to foster unfair competition. In terms of the differences in risks between the types of virtual currencies, the anti-money laundering framework's risk-based approach does provide for a differentiated approach according to the precise risks posed by each type of virtual currency.

Trust – As noted, the ECB has remarked that the regulation of virtual currencies and certain of their service providers under the anti-money laundering legal framework could have the effect of creating the illusion that such regulation covers all of the particular risks posed by virtual currencies, whereas only the risk of anonymity is truly addressed here. This perception could, according to the ECB, result in unwarranted augmented trust in virtual currencies and their service providers. However, this is of course the same for all obliged entities and not just for virtual currency service providers. More reasonable, then, is the point made by the EBA, in stating that consumer protection and prudential safeguards would be needed to truly raise the trustworthiness of virtual currencies and their service providers for many of the involved stakeholders.

Regulatory coherence – Regarding the position of virtual currency service providers before the 2018 amendments, there is a consensus – with only a single deviating case identified – against the applicability of the anti-money laundering legal framework. Such indicates that there was not a great need to improve regulatory coherence through a legislative initiative in the field of anti-money laundering rules. Nevertheless, the 2018 amendments cannot be denied to have improved regulatory coherence across the EU. Moreover, the same amendments are in line with international developments in the field of anti-money laundering laws, such as in the US – as chapter VII will discuss.

Conclusion – Following the assessment against the normative criteria, it can be held that from the points of view of legal certainty and regulatory coherence, there was a lesser need for the inclusion of virtual currencies and their service providers under the anti-money laundering legal framework than what was found for the e-money and payment services frameworks. There are two main reasons for this. First, there was little uncertainty regarding the non-applicability of the anti-money laundering legal framework before the amendments to the AMLD4, as well as no clear divergence between Member States' national approaches. Second, the anti-money laundering legal framework can essentially only serve to address one of the risks posed by virtual currencies, namely anonymity. As a result, it can be argued that the application of a legal framework that addresses more of those risks, as well as the anti-money laundering risk – which, for instance, the application of the payment services framework would accomplish – is preferable over regulation of virtual currency service providers under the anti-money laundering framework alone. Also from the points of view of proportionality and trust, such a more comprehensive regulatory initiative is preferable.

# CHAPTER VI
# FINANCIAL INSTRUMENTS IN THE EU

## 1 INTRODUCTION

MiFID – Another legal framework that could be considered for the regulation of virtual currencies is the EU framework regulating investment services. That legal framework is mainly set by the First Markets in Financial Instruments Directive (MiFID1)[1663], which in 2018 will be replaced by the Second Markets in Financial Instruments Directive (MiFID2)[1664] and the Markets in Financial Instruments Regulation (MiFiR).[1665] As chapter IV has shown that virtual currencies will not be considered as e-money or payment services under the corresponding legal frameworks, it must be questioned whether they could instead be considered as financial instruments under the MiFID framework. If such is the case, then virtual currencies are already regulated under that framework. It must then be further questioned whether MiFID is the correct framework to regulate virtual currencies, or whether a different regulatory initiative is desirable. As noted in the risk assessment conducted in chapter I, virtual currencies can to a certain extent be used as investment tools, posing particular risks to such investors. This last risk makes the MiFID legal framework a possible candidate for the regulation of virtual currencies. Moreover, as briefly hinted at in chapter IV, there are indications that at least one EU Member State – Germany – may already be considering its implementation of MiFID for the regulation of virtual currencies, further indicating the need for a closer analysis of the MiFID legal framework.

---

1663 Directive 2004/39/EC of the European Parliament and of the Council of 21 April 2004 on markets in financial instruments amending Council Directives 85/611/EEC and 93/6/EEC and Directive 2000/12/EC of the European Parliament and of the Council and repealing Council Directive 93/22/EEC, *OJ* L 145 of 30 April 2004, 1–44 (hereinafter: MiFID1 or First Markets in Financial Instruments Directive).

1664 Directive 2014/65/EU of the European Parliament and of the Council of 15 May 2014 on markets in financial instruments and amending Directive 2002/92/EC and Directive 2011/61/EU, *OJ* L 173 of 12 June 2014, 349–496 (hereinafter: MiFID2 or Second Markets in Financial Instruments Directive).

1665 Regulation (EU) No 600/2014 of the European Parliament and of the Council of 15 May 2014 on markets in financial instruments and amending Regulation (EU) No 648/2012, *OJ* L 173 of 12 June 2014, 84–148 (hereinafter: MiFiR or Markets in Financial Instruments Regulation).

Goal – First, this chapter analyzes whether the EU legal framework on investment services – as set originally by MiFID1 and later by MiFID2 and MiFiR – can be applied to virtual currencies. More precisely, it assesses whether virtual currencies can be considered as the financial instruments covered by the MiFID legal framework, particularly transferable securities or derivative products. Second, if such is found to be the case, it assesses – against the normative criteria established for the purposes of this research – whether inclusion under the MiFID framework is sufficient in regulating virtual currencies, or whether more initiative is desired. If it is found that the MiFID legal framework can in its current form not apply to virtual currencies, this chapter must establish whether such an inclusion is necessary, again via assessment against the normative criteria.

Approach – In keeping with the approach of the previous chapters, this chapter will first provide a brief overview of the regulatory background to the EU's legal framework on investment services (section 2). This will allow to trace how the MiFID legal framework was formed and what the European legislator's intents were regarding the scope thereof. Then, this chapter will further analyze the notion of financial instruments itself (section 3), in order to gain a full understanding of the scope of that notion. After all, it is important to pay attention to the underlying nature of the instrument in question, and the intent with which it is propagated. By means of example, works of art are generally accepted as a potential investment, given the expectation that their value will appreciate. However, such is of course not the primary purpose of these goods, nor does their nature make them suitable to be considered as financial instruments under the scope of the MiFID framework. Similarly, concert tickets are often purchased with the intent to resell them at a higher price on secondary markets. Also here there is a clear suitability of the goods to serve as means of investment, although such does not necessarily make them subject to the MiFID framework. The real question that must then be answered, is whether goods serving means of investment can be considered as the financial instruments targeted by the MiFID framework. This question therefore forms the central theme of this chapter. Next, the knowledge gained from the previous sections will be applied to virtual currencies, assessing whether they can be considered as financial instruments under the MiFID legal framework (section 4). Last, the results of the previous analyses will allow to conclude whether or not the MiFID legal framework can in its current form apply to virtual currencies (section 5). As in the previous chapters, the normative criteria established for the purposes of this research will allow to conclude whether – if MiFID legal framework is applicable – such an application is sufficient or whether more regulatory action is needed, or – if the legal framework is not applicable – whether an extension of this framework is desirable. When citing stakeholders, the focus is put on available opinions by legislators and regulators. While at the level of the European

Supervisory Authorities a few consultations have been held that included matters related to virtual currencies, no stakeholder consultation specifically addressed the inclusion of virtual currencies under the MiFID framework.[1666]

# 2 REGULATORY BACKGROUND

## 2.1 BEFORE 2004

Origins and connection to consumer law – The origins of securities law can be traced back very far in history, possibly even to ancient Rome.[1667] However, it is only from the financial crisis of the 1930's onwards that this branch of law gradually started to focus more on protecting the investor-consumer.[1668] At the European level, the very first steps towards consumer law already established the importance of a consumer protection and information policy.[1669] Although it was held by the Council of the European Union that such consumer protection and information policy should extend to financial services, investment services and financial instruments were often excluded from the scope of consumer law.[1670] Only in the 1990's, the European legislator started to really consider the consumer aspects of financial services.[1671] While financial services were not included in the 1997 Distance Contracts Directive[1672], they received their own 2002 Distance Marketing of Consumer Financial Services Directive.[1673] These initiatives resulted in the establishment of a securities law, or broader financial law, which clearly took into account consumer protection needs.

---

1666 Such as the EBA's Discussion Paper on its approach to fintech (*eba.europa.eu/regulation-and-policy/other-topics/approach-to-financial-technology-fintech-)* or the ESMA's consultation on distributed ledger technology applied to securities markets (*esma.europa.eu/press-news/consultations/consultation-distributed-ledger-technology-applied-securities-markets*). While in this last consultation also a number of MiFID-related questions were raised, the main focus was on the use of blockchain technology, rather than on virtual currencies *in se*.

1667 Colaert, V. (2011) *De rechtsverhouding financiële dienstverlener-belegger*, Brugge: die Keure, 51.

1668 *Id.*

1669 Council Resolution of 14 April 1975 on a preliminary programme of the European Economic Community for a consumer protection and information policy, *OJ* C 092 of 25 April 1975, 1–16.

1670 *Ibid.*, 6; Colaert, V. (2011) *De rechtsverhouding financiële dienstverlener-belegger*, Brugge: die Keure, 70.

1671 European Commission (1995) "Communication on Priorities for Consumer Policy 1996–1998", *COM(95) 519 final*, 3–4 & 6–7.

1672 Directive 97/7/EC of the European Parliament and of the Council of 20 May 1997 on the protection of consumers in respect of distance contracts, *OJ* L 144 of 4 June 1997, 19–27 (hereinafter: Distance Contracts Directive).

1673 Directive 2002/65/EC of the European Parliament and of the Council of 23 September 2002 concerning the distance marketing of consumer financial services and amending Council Directive 90/619/EEC and Directives 97/7/EC and 98/27/EC, *OJ* L 271 of 09 October 2002 16–24 (hereinafter: Distance Marketing of Consumer Financial Services Directive).

Internal market – This gradual move towards more protection for the investor-consumer is evident in EU policy throughout the years.[1674] In the 1980's, a plan to complete the internal market provided the basis of the first generation of directives regarding financial services.[1675] This eventually resulted in the Investment Services Directive (ISD).[1676] Originally, the goal of this directive was to subject investment firms to prudential rules, allowing local supervision and passporting across the EU. Conduct of business rules ensuring investor protection were only added in a later phase, even though the difficult discussions during the legislative procedure have been argued in literature to have resulted in vague rules.[1677] The instruments to which the investment services covered by the ISD apply, listed in an annex, are "*transferable securities, units in collective investment undertakings, money-market instruments, financial-futures contracts, including equivalent cash-settled instruments, forward interest-rate agreements (FRAs), interest-rate, currency and equity swaps, and options to acquire or dispose of any such instruments*".[1678]

Road to MiFID – It became clear that the ISD did not capture the fast-changing financial landscape of the late 1990's.[1679] In 1999, the European Commission proposed its Financial Services Action Plan, in which it stressed the need for a high level of consumer protection in financial services.[1680] Moreover, in 2001, the Lamfalussy Report proposed a new regulatory approach for financial services.[1681]

1674 Colaert, V. (2011) *De rechtsverhouding financiële dienstverlener-belegger*, Brugge: die Keure, 87–88.

1675 *Ibid.*, 89–90; European Commission (1985) "White Paper on Completing the Internal Market", *COM(85) 310 final*, 27–29. More particularly, this paper proposes measures of minimum harmonization, with supervision in the home Member State and mutual recognition, the basis of the later passporting system.

1676 Council Directive 93/22/EEC of 10 May 1993 on investment services in the securities field, *OJ* L 141 of 11 June 1993, 27–46 (hereinafter: Investment Services Directive or ISD).

1677 Colaert, V. (2011) *De rechtsverhouding financiële dienstverlener-belegger*, Brugge: die Keure, 90–91; Cruickshank, C. (1998) "Is there a Need to Harmonise Conduct of Business Rules?", In Ferrarini, G. (Ed.) *European Securities Markets: The Investment Services Directive and Beyond*, London: Kluwer Law International, 131–134.

1678 Annex B ISD.

1679 European Commission (2002) "Proposal for a Directive of the European Parliament and of the Council on investment services and regulated markets, and amending Council Directives 85/611/EEC, Council Directive 93/6/EEC and European Parliament and Council Directive 2000/12/EC", *COM(2002) 625 final*, 3.

1680 European Commission (2009) "Communication on Implementing the framework for financial markets: action plan", *COM(1999) 232 final*, 1.

1681 The Lamfalussy process operates on four levels: Level 1: adoption of directive or regulation, Level 2: adoption of technical implementing measures, Level 3: national supervisors provide guidelines for implementation, Level 4: Commission ensures enforcement by Member States. Next to MiFID1, this process would result in the Market Abuse Directive, the Prospectus Directive, and the Transparency Directive: Directive 2003/6/EC of the European Parliament and of the Council of 28 January 2003 on insider dealing and market manipulation (market

## 2.2 FIRST MARKETS IN FINANCIAL INSTRUMENTS DIRECTIVE

MiFID1 – The proposal for a new directive, replacing the ISD, published in 2002 was heavily influenced by the Lamfalussy Report.[1682] After a fairly fast legislative procedure, the First Markets in Financial Instruments Directive (MiFID1) was adopted on 21 April 2004. Level 2 measures under the Lamfalussy process were adopted in 2006.[1683]

Scope – Like the ISD, MiFID1 applies to investment firms, with an added reference to regulated markets.[1684] The scope of 'financial instruments' as contained in the annex has been significantly extended, with several provisions referring to options, futures, swaps, forwards and any other derivative contracts relating to securities or commodities and their different means of settlement.[1685] Also derivative instruments for the transfer of credit risk have been included.[1686]

---

abuse), *OJ* L 96 of 12 April 2003, 16–25; Directive 2003/71/EC of the European Parliament and of the Council of 4 November 2003 on the prospectus to be published when securities are offered to the public or admitted to trading and amending Directive 2001/34/EC, *OJ* L 345 of 31 December 2003, 64–89; Directive 2004/109/EC of the European Parliament and of the Council of 15 December 2004 on the harmonisation of transparency requirements in relation to information about issuers whose securities are admitted to trading on a regulated market and amending Directive 2001/34/EC, *OJ* L 390 of 31 December 2004, 38–57. The process was supported by three committees: the Committee of European Securities Regulators (CESR), the Committee of European Banking Supervisors (CEBS) and the Committee of European Insurance and Occupational Pensions Supervisors (CEIOPS). In 2011, these committees were replaced by the European Supervisory Authorities (ESAs): European Banking Authority (EBA), European Securities and Markets Authority (ESMA), and European Insurance and Occupational Pensions Authority (EIOPA). *ec.europa.eu/info/node/11713*. See also: Moloney, N. (2015) "Financial Markets Regulation", In: Chalmers D., Arnull A. (Eds.) *The Oxford Handbook of European Union Law*, Oxford: University Press, 773–774.

1682 European Commission (2002) "Proposal for a Directive of the European Parliament and of the Council on investment services and regulated markets, and amending Council Directives 85/611/EEC, Council Directive 93/6/EEC and European Parliament and Council Directive 2000/12/EC", *COM(2002) 625 final*, 5.

1683 Commission Directive 2006/73/EC of 10 August 2006 implementing Directive 2004/39/EC of the European Parliament and of the Council as regards organisational requirements and operating conditions for investment firms and defined terms for the purposes of that Directive, *OJ* L 241 of 2 September 2006, 26–58; Commission Regulation (EC) No 1287/2006 of 10 August 2006 implementing Directive 2004/39/EC of the European Parliament and of the Council as regards record-keeping obligations for investment firms, transaction reporting, market transparency, admission of financial instruments to trading, and defined terms for the purposes of that Directive, *OJ* L 241 of 2 September 2006, 1–25.

1684 Article 1(1) MiFID1.

1685 Annex 1 Section C MiFID1.

1686 *Id.*

Changing landscape – While MiFID1 was deemed a significant improvement over the ISD, a number of shortcomings arose.[1687] As a result, it was found that a more tightened set of rules was needed. This resulted in two proposals: a regulation to provide a number of common rules for all Member States (MiFiR), and a directive to amend the requirements set by the existing directive (MiFID2).[1688] Both proposals were published by the European Commission in November 2011[1689], with the final texts adopted on 15 April 2014.[1690]

## 2.3 MARKETS IN FINANCIAL INSTRUMENTS REGULATION AND SECOND DIRECTIVE

Demarcation – MiFID2 and MiFiR each clarify their respective goals. MiFID2, on the one hand, establishes requirements regarding the authorization and operating conditions for investment firms, the provision of investment services or activities by third-country firms through the establishment of a branch, the authorization and operation of regulated markets, the authorization and operation of data reporting services providers, and the supervision, cooperation and enforcement by competent authorities.[1691] MiFiR, on the other hand, provides uniform requirements for disclosure of trade data to the public, reporting of transactions to the competent authorities, trading of derivatives on organized venues, non-discriminatory access to clearing and non-discriminatory access to trading in benchmarks, product intervention powers of competent authorities, ESMA and EBA and powers of ESMA on position management controls and position limits, and the provision of investment services or activities by third-country firms following an applicable equivalence decision by the Commission with or without a branch.[1692]

Scope – MiFID2 applies to investment firms, as well as market operators, data reporting services providers, and third-country firms providing investment services or performing investment activities through the establishment of a

1687 European Commission (2011) "Proposal for a directive of the European Parliament and of the Council on markets in financial instruments repealing Directive 2004/39/EC of the European Parliament and of the Council", *COM(2011) 656 final*, 2.

1688 *Ibid.*, 2–3.

1689 European Commission (2011) "Proposal for a directive of the European Parliament and of the Council on markets in financial instruments repealing Directive 2004/39/EC of the European Parliament and of the Council", *COM(2011) 656 final* (hereinafter: Proposal MiFID2); European Commission (2011) "Proposal for a regulation of the European Parliament and of the Council on markets in financial instruments and amending Regulation [EMIR] on OTC derivatives, central counterparties and trade repositories", *COM(2011) 652 final* (hereinafter: Proposal MiFiR).

1690 European Parliament (2012) "Results of Votes of 15 April 2014", *PV 15/04/2014 – 17.7 & 17.8*, 39–40.

1691 Article 1(2) MiFID2.

1692 Article 1(1) Markets in Financial Instruments Regulation.

branch in the Union.[1693] MiFIR mainly applies to investment firms, and credit institutions when providing investment services.[1694] Exemptions are still present in MiFID2, with a number of provisions being reformulated.[1695] In terms of definitions, the notion of 'investment firm' remains the same as under MiFID1.[1696] For the investment services listed in Annex I Section A, MiFID2 adds Organized Trading Facilities.[1697] For the financial instruments, references to Organized Trading Facilities are included, as well as the trading of emissions allowances.[1698]

# 3 FINANCIAL INSTRUMENTS SCOPE

## 3.1 PERSONAL SCOPE OF MIFID1 AND 2

INVESTMENT FIRMS AND REGULATED MARKETS – As noted, the MiFID legal framework primarily applies to investment firms and regulated markets.[1699] MiFID2 adds data reporting services providers and third-country firms providing investment services.[1700] Investment firms are the firms that regularly provide investment services or professionally perform investment activities.[1701] Regulated markets are authorized multilateral systems operated by a market operator, that in respect of the financial instruments admitted to trading under their rules and/or systems facilitate multiple third-party buying and selling interests in financial instruments – in the system and in accordance with their non-discretionary rules – resulting in a contract.[1702] Also credit institutions, where providing investment services or performing investment activities, are caught under the scope of the MiFID framework.[1703] However, not all entities

1693 Article 1(1) MiFID2. As before, credit institutions providing investment services are subjected to only a few of the directive's provisions (article 1(3)).

1694 Article 1(2) Markets in Financial Instruments Regulation. Note that some titles can also apply to other service providers.

1695 Articles 2 and 3 MiFID2. Note that, following the discussions in the European Parliament, optional exemptions are foreseen for commodities, emission allowances and/or derivatives thereof (article 3(1)(d)).

1696 Article 4(1)(1) MiFID2.

1697 Annex 1 Section A MiFID2.

1698 Annex 1 Section C MiFID2.

1699 Article 1(1) MiFID1.

1700 Article 1(1) MiFID2.

1701 Article 4(1)(1) MiFID1 and MiFID2. Note that the directives also allow Member States to consider natural persons as investment firms, be it that such natural persons should then be subjected to certain operational requirements and safeguards. Note also that the directives provide exemptions for those not acting in their professional capacity, but subject to conditions. This means that incidental provision of investment services could be outside of the scope of the MiFID legal framework, but not necessarily. Lieverse, K. (2017) "The Scope of MiFID II", In: Busch, D., Ferrarini, G. (Eds.) *Regulation of the EU Financial Markets: MiFID II and MiFIR*, Oxford: University Press, para. 2.13.

1702 Article 4(1)(14) MiFID1; article 4(1)(21) MiFID2.

1703 Article 1(2) MiFID1; article 1(3) MiFID2.

under the scope of this framework are subjected to both the operational requirements and the conduct of business requirements.[1704]

Exemptions – The directives also include a list of exemptions, some of which are optional and up to the Member States to implement.[1705] The exemptions only apply for the specific services they cover. If, for instance, an insurance undertaking also offered investment services, it would still fall under the scope of the MiFID framework for those investment services.[1706]

## 3.2 MATERIAL SCOPE OF MIFID1 AND 2 – INVESTMENT SERVICES

Investment services and activities – The investment services and activities of investment firms are defined as a list of services relating to financial instruments.[1707] Important to note here is that the provision of only ancillary services – which is a separate list – does not make a firm an investment firm.[1708] Such firms are therefore not bound by these provisions.[1709] While the directives tell only little about the difference between investment services and investment activities, literature on this matter clarifies that the existence of a client relationship is the defining element of an investment service, whereas such a relationship is absent in investment activities.[1710]

## 3.3 MATERIAL SCOPE OF MIFID1 AND 2 – FINANCIAL INSTRUMENTS

Core notion – The aforementioned investment services must relate to at least one financial instrument. If such a service is provided in relation to only instruments that cannot be considered as financial instruments, the service cannot be considered as an investment service for the purposes of the

1704 For instance, as credit institutions are already licensed, they do not need to undergo additional licensing under the MiFID legal framework.

1705 In both directives, article 2 contains the general exemptions, with article 3 containing the optional exemptions.

1706 European Commission (2008) "Your questions on MiFID", *ec.europa.eu*, 16.

1707 Article 4(1)(2) MiFID1 and MiFID2.

1708 Colaert, V. (2011) *De rechtsverhouding financiële dienstverlener-belegger*, Brugge: die Keure, 114.

1709 However, an investment firm is also for the exercise of ancillary services bound by these rules. Article 19(1) MiFID1; article 24(1) MiFID2; Colaert, V. (2011) *De rechtsverhouding financiële dienstverlener-belegger*, Brugge: die Keure, 114.

1710 Lieverse, K. (2017) "The Scope of MiFID II", In: Busch, D., Ferrarini, G. (Eds.) *Regulation of the EU Financial Markets: MiFID II and MiFIR*, Oxford: University Press, para. 2.10; Colaert, V., Van Dyck, T. (2008) "MiFID en de gedragsregels: Een nieuw juridisch kader voor beleggingsdiensten", *Tijdschrift voor Belgisch Handelsrecht*, nr. 3, 236–237.

MiFID legal framework.[1711] However, when mixed services are provided – with at least one relating to a financial instrument, but others not – then the framework will apply. As a result, the notion of financial instruments forms the core of the scope of the MiFID legal framework. The notion of financial instruments is defined by way of reference to the list of such instruments under the directives' annex.[1712] It is irrelevant for the scope of this notion whether or not the instrument in question has been admitted to trading on a regulated market.[1713]

TRANSFERABLE SECURITIES – Transferable securities are defined as "*those classes of securities which are negotiable on the capital market, with the exception of instruments of payment, such as: (a) shares in companies and other securities equivalent to shares in companies, partnerships or other entities, and depositary receipts in respect of shares; (b) bonds or other forms of securitised debt, including depositary receipts in respect of such securities; (c) any other securities giving the right to acquire or sell any such transferable securities or giving rise to a cash settlement determined by reference to transferable securities, currencies, interest rates or yields, commodities or other indices or measures*".[1714] Securities generally facilitate the collection of monetary means in the form of capital or debt financing.[1715] The notion of securities must be interpreted in its broadest form as encompassing any form of negotiable instrument generally used for means of investment and conferring certain rights.[1716] This interpretation references the theory that "*a transferable security is defined by an inherent link between the rights incorporated in it and the carrier of such rights*".[1717] The primacy, for

1711 Lieverse, K. (2017) "The Scope of MiFID II", In: Busch, D., Ferrarini, G. (Eds.) *Regulation of the EU Financial Markets: MiFID II and MiFIR*, Oxford: University Press, para. 2.43.

1712 Article 4(1)(17) MiFID1; article 4(1)(15) MiFID2.

1713 Colaert, V. (2011) *De rechtsverhouding financiële dienstverlener-belegger*, Brugge: die Keure, 115; Steennot, R., Schrans, G. (2003) *Algemeen deel van het financieel recht*, Antwerpen: Intersentia, 121. See also: European Commission (2008) "Your questions on MiFID", *ec.europa.eu*, 9.

1714 Article 4(1)(18) MiFID1; article 4(1)(44) MiFID2.

1715 Vermaere, K. (2016) "Artikel 2, 1° 'financieel instrument'", In: Berger, P., Cerfontaine, J., Colaert, V., Lannoy, H. (Eds.) *Economisch recht Deel 8: Financiële Markten en Diensten*, Brussel: Larcier, 239.

1716 Steennot, R., Schrans, G. (2003) *Algemeen deel van het financieel recht*, Antwerpen: Intersentia, 102–103; Della Faille D'huysse, P. (2008) *La modernisation des marchés financiers*, Limal: Anthemis, 17–18. Important here is that the right is incorporated in the security. Vermaere, K. (2016) "Artikel 2, 1° 'financieel instrument'", In: Berger, P., Cerfontaine, J., Colaert, V., Lannoy, H. (Eds.) *Economisch recht Deel 8: Financiële Markten en Diensten*, Brussel: Larcier, 239; Van Dyck, T. (2009) "De geharmoniseerde prospectusplicht: Kritische analyse van de geharmoniseerde prospectusplicht in de Prospectusrichtlijn 2003/71/EG en haar omzettingswetten in België, Nederland, Frankrijk, het Verenigd Koninkrijk en Duitsland", *Thesis KU Leuven Faculty of Law*, 382.

1717 Gorzelak, K. (2008) "The legal nature of emission allowances following the creation of a Union Registry and adoption of MiFID II – are they transferable securities now?", *Capital Markets Law Journal*, Vol. 9, 381.

the purposes of the MiFID framework, of securities as means of investment is underlined by the exclusion of instruments of payment.[1718] The latter are securities that primarily serve payment needs, rather than investment needs, such as cheques and bills of exchange.[1719] That securities are negotiable means that they must be tradable.[1720] The capital market on which such instruments can be traded must also be interpreted in the broadest sense, meaning any context where "*buying and selling interest in securities meet*".[1721] As a result, it was the intention of the European legislator to ensure that only under very limited circumstances a negotiated share would not fall under the definition of financial instruments.[1722]

Money-market instruments – Money-market instruments are defined as "*those classes of instruments which are normally dealt in on the money market, such as treasury bills, certificates of deposit and commercial papers and excluding instruments of payment*".[1723] Treasury bills are short-term debt certificates issued by a government.[1724] Certificates of deposit are debt certificates encompassing a particular debt claim, also generally issued as short-term instruments.[1725] This allows to satisfy short-term credit needs through the money-market, rather than through longer-term credit.[1726] Typically, these money-market instruments mature in less than one year.[1727]

Units in collective investment undertakings – Collective investment undertakings aim to attract funds from the public.[1728] Such funds are managed

1718 Vermaere, K. (2016) "Artikel 2, 1° 'financieel instrument'", In: Berger, P., Cerfontaine, J., Colaert, V., Lannoy, H. (Eds.) *Economisch recht Deel 8: Financiële Markten en Diensten*, Brussel: Larcier, 241.

1719 European Commission (2008) "Your questions on MiFID", *ec.europa.eu*, question 2.

1720 *Ibid.*, question 115; Steennot, R., Schrans, G. (2003) *Algemeen deel van het financieel recht*, Antwerpen: Intersentia, 119–121; Van Dyck, T. (2009) "De geharmoniseerde prospectusplicht: Kritische analyse van de geharmoniseerde prospectusplicht in de Prospectusrichtlijn 2003/71/EG en haar omzettingswetten in België, Nederland, Frankrijk, het Verenigd Koninkrijk en Duitsland", *Thesis KU Leuven Faculty of Law*, 384.

1721 European Commission (2008) "Your questions on MiFID", *ec.europa.eu*, question 2; Steennot, R., Schrans, G. (2003) *Algemeen deel van het financieel recht*, Antwerpen: Intersentia, 119.

1722 European Commission (2008) "Your questions on MiFID", *ec.europa.eu*, question 61.

1723 Article 4(1)(19) MiFID1; article 4(1)(17) MiFID2.

1724 Steennot, R., Schrans, G. (2003) *Algemeen deel van het financieel recht*, Antwerpen: Intersentia, 191.

1725 *Ibid.*, 192.

1726 *Id.;* Van Dyck, T. (2009) "De geharmoniseerde prospectusplicht: Kritische analyse van de geharmoniseerde prospectusplicht in de Prospectusrichtlijn 2003/71/EG en haar omzettingswetten in België, Nederland, Frankrijk, het Verenigd Koninkrijk en Duitsland", *Thesis KU Leuven Faculty of Law*, 383.

1727 European Commission (2008) "Your questions on MiFID", *ec.europa.eu*, question 167; Vermaere, K. (2016) "Artikel 2, 1° 'financieel instrument'", In: Berger, P., Cerfontaine, J., Colaert, V., Lannoy, H. (Eds.) *Economisch recht Deel 8: Financiële Markten en Diensten*, Brussel: Larcier, 241.

1728 *Ibid.*, 187.

collectively by an undertaking, meaning that the individual investors cannot intervene directly in management decision and thus do not enjoy personal wealth management.[1729] Such undertakings can either be open-ended – meaning they have dynamic participation rights – or closed-ended – having fixed participation rights.[1730] Those participation rights are the units envisioned here, to the extent that such participation rights are the subject of investment services.[1731]

Derivatives – The MiFID framework lists a very broad range of derivatives.[1732] These can be derivative contracts or commodity derivatives, settled physically or in cash. Derivative instruments can also serve to transfer credit risk, or for financial differences.[1733] Moreover, derivatives can rely on other indicators such as climatic variables, freight rates, inflation rates or other official economic statistics.[1734] Trading in emission allowances is, under MiFID2, added as a separate instrument.[1735]

# 4 MARKETS IN FINANCIAL INSTRUMENTS AND VIRTUAL CURRENCIES

## 4.1 CLOSED SCHEME VIRTUAL CURRENCIES

No financial instrument – Given their nature, closed scheme virtual currencies can, principally, not be obtained with legal tender or similar instruments, nor can they be exchanged for legal tender or similar instruments. Moreover, their

1729 FSMA (2012) "Reglementair kader voor crowdfunding", *fsma.be*, 6; Decoster, S., Lewalle, C. (2014) "Le Crowdfunding: réglementation applicable, enjeux et perspectives", *Forum Financier, Revue Bancaire et Financière*, nr. 6, 463; Boedts, T. (2014) "Kunnen crowdfunding en virtuele munten innoveren zonder bijkomende regulering?", In: IBJ (Ed.) *L'innovation, source de droit. Le droit, source d'innovation / Innovatie, bron van recht. Recht, bron van innovatie*, Brussel: Bruylant, 140.

1730 Vandezande, N., Van de Velde, N. (2017) "Juridische aspecten van crowdfunding in België", In: Storme, M.E., Helsen, F. (Eds.) *Innovatie en disruptie in het economisch recht*, Antwerpen: Intersentia, 194–196; Steennot, R., Schrans, G. (2003) *Algemeen deel van het financieel recht*, Antwerpen: Intersentia, 189–191.

1731 Della Faille D'huysse, P. (2008) *La modernisation des marchés financiers*, Limal: Anthemis, 18–19.

1732 For a more elaborate discussion, see, *inter alea*: Lieverse, K. (2017) "The Scope of MiFID II", In: Busch, D., Ferrarini, G. (Eds.) *Regulation of the EU Financial Markets: MiFID II and MiFIR*, Oxford: University Press, para. 2.47 *et seq.*; Steennot, R., Schrans, G. (2003) *Algemeen deel van het financieel recht*, Antwerpen: Intersentia, 125 *et seq.*

1733 Steennot, R., Schrans, G. (2003) *Algemeen deel van het financieel recht*, Antwerpen: Intersentia, 156; Vermaere, K. (2016) "Artikel 2, 1° 'financieel instrument'", In: Berger, P., Cerfontaine, J., Colaert, V., Lannoy, H. (Eds.) *Economisch recht Deel 8: Financiële Markten en Diensten*, Brussel: Larcier, 238.

1734 Della Faille D'huysse, P. (2008) *La modernisation des marchés financiers*, Limal: Anthemis, 19.

1735 Recital 11 MiFID2.

transferability is limited at best.[1736] This makes these virtual currencies inherently unsuitable to serve as instruments for investment purposes. Indeed, the closed scheme virtual currencies identified for the purposes of this research do not demonstrate any use for investment purposes. The result of these particular properties is that it is difficult to consider this type of virtual currencies as the financial instruments envisioned by the MiFID framework. It is also unlikely that derivative products would be based on this type of virtual currencies.

No investment service – Even if these virtual currencies were considered as financial instruments, it would still need to be assessed whether their service providers provide investment services or activities as listed under the MiFID framework. Also here, it can be found that the services generally provided by closed scheme virtual currency service providers do not correspond to such investment services and activities.[1737]

## 4.2 UNIDIRECTIONAL SCHEME VIRTUAL CURRENCIES

No financial instrument – Unidirectional virtual currencies can be obtained with legal tender or similar instruments. From the examples analyzed in chapter I, it follows that they generally have limited transferability, and little to no negotiability. Moreover, they are often subjected to expiration.[1738] Again, these properties make unidirectional virtual currencies fairly unsuited for investment purposes, and none of the examples analyzed in chapter I displayed such use. For all of the investigated examples of unidirectional virtual currencies, it is clear that these virtual currencies serve as means of payment. As with closed scheme virtual currencies, this makes it difficult to classify these virtual currencies as the financial instruments intended by the MiFID framework. Also here, derivative products based on this type of virtual currencies seem unlikely.

No investment service – As for closed scheme virtual currencies, it can – hypothesizing that these virtual currencies constitute financial instruments – be questioned whether the services provided by unidirectional scheme virtual currency service providers correspond to any of the investment services or activities listed under the MiFID framework. Also here, it can be concluded that

1736 While some virtual worlds allow users to transfer in-game virtual currency to another user, this is not possible in all virtual worlds. Even where such is possible, they can only be transferred within that virtual world.

1737 Only in the case of Diablo III's short-lived Real Money Auction House some comparisons could be drawn with the operation of a multilateral trading facility. However, in this case the virtual currency would start to function as a bidirectional virtual currency, and no longer as a closed scheme virtual currency.

1738 As is the case for most loyalty scheme virtual currencies.

the services provided in the examples analyzed for the purposes of this research do not correspond to the investment services or activities intended by the MiFID framework.

## 4.3 BIDIRECTIONAL SCHEME VIRTUAL CURRENCIES

SUITABILITY – Also for bidirectional scheme virtual currencies, it must be assessed whether the virtual currency in question is suited as a means of investment. One of the examples of bidirectional scheme virtual currencies identified in chapter I, namely Second Life's Linden dollar, does not appear suited to serve as a means of investment, given that the central issuer keeps the exchange rate between this virtual currency and legal tender at a stable level. Of the bidirectional virtual currencies identified for the purposes of this research, only cryptocurrencies appear to have a certain disposition to serve as means of investment.

PURPOSE DISTINCTION – The cryptocurrency landscape has changed significantly over the last few years. While originally it was clear that cryptocurrencies primarily served as means of payment, such is no longer a clear-cut matter. Even in cryptocurrencies primarily serving payment purposes, such as bitcoin, the investment use has risen sharply. Moreover, new forms of cryptocurrencies are put on the market, which only serve investment purposes. For this reason, a distinction will be made between cryptocurrencies primarily serving as means of payment – such as bitcoin – and those primarily intended to serve as means of investment – such as DAO tokens.

### *4.3.1 Cryptocurrencies intended as means of payment*

#### 4.3.1.1 EU perspective

FOCUS ON SERVICE PROVIDERS – Given the focus of the MiFID framework on the service providers that provide investment services, it cannot apply to the virtual currency as a system in itself. The Bitcoin system, for instance, is not a legal person, neither does it provide investment services. The MiFID framework can therefore not apply to the Bitcoin system. As a result, it must be analyzed whether particular stakeholders utilizing a virtual currency use it in the provision of investment services. For instance, in the case of a user that wants to pay using virtual currencies, or a merchant accepting payments in virtual currencies, it is clear that such use does not constitute an investment service, and is therefore not covered by the scope of the MiFID framework.[1739] For virtual currency exchange

---

[1739] Shcherbak, S. (2014) "How should Bitcoin be regulated?", *European Journal of Legal Studies*, Vol. 7, 61.

service providers, on the other hand, it is less clear whether or not their services could constitute investment services.

Virtual currencies as securities – As noted earlier, transferable securities in the sense of the MiFID framework must be interpreted in the broadest sense. Here, it has been argued in literature that where the value of a virtual currency is determined by the market – as is the case for cryptocurrencies – that virtual currency can be considered as a negotiable instrument.[1740] Moreover, this virtual currency can considered as tradable, since ownership over the virtual currency can be transferred as part of a transaction.[1741] According to this line of reasoning, such virtual currencies would then be considered as transferable securities in the sense of the MiFID legal framework.[1742] However, that line of thought has not gained widespread following, with a clear majority of authors that have analyzed this matter arguing against the consideration of virtual currencies as transferable securities.[1743] This latter opinion is shared by the European Central Bank.[1744] Moreover, the fact that transferable securities assume a right on their issuer is problematic to apply to the case of payment cryptocurrencies, where

1740 *Ibid.*, 66–67.

1741 *Ibid.*, 67.

1742 *Id.* While Shcherbak's analysis certainly contains valuable arguments, there are also a few points that require further scrutiny. One is that he supports his conclusion by reference to the German financial supervisor's opinion on the matter. Important to note here is that this supervisor does actually not consider virtual currencies as transferable securities, as will be further discussed in section 4.3.1.2. Another point is that the author considers virtual currency exchanges to be both investment firms and payment institutions. However, this does not take into account that the Payment Services Directives exempt transactions regarding securities asset servicing (article 3(i) of both directives). This means that if the account held by a user at an investment firm is used to conduct investment related transactions, it cannot simultaneously be caught under the scope of the payment services framework. Last, the author does not analyze whether virtual currencies are indeed securities, but merely focuses on their negotiability and tradability. While the European legislator did indeed intend for the notion of 'transferable securities' to be interpreted broadly here, it does still require the presence of a security. The fact that a certain instrument is negotiable does not automatically make it a security.

1743 De Vauplane, H. (2015) "Bitcoin et monnaies virtuelles: entre réglementation et essai de définition juridique", In. Daems, H., De Meuleneere, I., Houssa, C., Ragheno, N. (Eds.) *Digital Finance / La finance numérique*, Antwerpen: Intersentia, 38; Houben, R. (2015) "Bitcoin: there are two sides to every coin", *Tijdschrift voor Belgisch Handelsrecht*, nr. 2, 149; Frew, L., Folsom, R., van Wingerden, S. (2015) "Legal and regulatory issues relating to virtual currencies", *Butterworths Journal of International Banking and Financial Law*, Vol. 7, 4; Cassar, C. (2015) "Virtual Currencies: Risks and regulations in Malta and Other Jurisdictions", *elsa.org*, 14; Vardi, N. (2016) "Bit by Bit: Assessing the Legal Nature of Virtual Currencies", in: Gimigliano, G. (Ed.) *Bitcoin and Mobile Payments: Constructing a European Union Framework*, London: Macmillan Publishers, 66–67; Kubát, M. (2015) "Virtual currency bitcoin in the scope of money definition and store of value", *Procedia Economics and Finance*, Vol. 30, 412; Baukema, J. (2014) "Virtuele valuta: (toezichtrechtelijke) stand van zaken", *Tijdschrift voor Financieel Recht*, nr. 9, 377; Navas Navarro, S. (2015) "Un mercado financiero floreciente: el del dinero virtual no regulado (Especial atención a los BITCOINS)", *Revista CESCO de Derecho de Consumo*, Nr. 13/2015, 102–105.

1744 European Central Bank (2015) "Virtual Currency Schemes – a further analysis", *ecb.europa.eu*, 30.

there generally is no identifiable issuer, nor does a payment cryptocurrency seem to confer any particular right.[1745] It should also be reminded that payment instruments are excluded from the scope of transferable securities. At this moment, virtual currencies are not considered as such payment instruments. However, a Court of Justice of the European Union judgment regarding the VAT treatment of virtual currencies may indicate a possible intention towards that very direction. While the specificity of that case does not allow generalizing conclusions to be derived from it, the reasoning used in the case does indicate a possible evolution in thinking on this matter.[1746] The MiFID framework does include foreign exchange services as ancillary services, though only when such services are provided in connection to investment services.[1747] Foreign exchange services, insofar as this notion is applicable to virtual currency exchanges, are therefore not an investment service in itself.[1748]

Virtual currencies as money-market instruments – As noted in section 3.3, money-market instruments can be considered as short-term debt instruments. This makes this instrument unsuitable for application to virtual currencies, as virtual currencies do not serve to transfer debts, nor do they have a predefined maturity date.

Virtual currency derivatives – A potential inclusion of virtual currencies under the MiFID framework can be found in the broad group of derivatives. The focus is therefore not put on the virtual currencies themselves, but on derivative products that may constitute financial instruments in their own right and that have virtual currencies as underlying asset. Here, it can be argued that derivatives relating to virtual currencies are caught under the scope of the MiFID framework.[1749] Moreover, if a broader application were given to the aforementioned Court of Justice of the European Union's judgment[1750], this would further solidify the conclusion that virtual currency derivatives are indeed covered under the cash derivatives provision.[1751,1752] Furthermore, the ESMA

1745 Spaas, T., Van Roey, M. (2015) "Quo vadis Bitcoin?", *Computerrecht*, nr. 84, 118.

1746 See further section 4.3.2.2 and Houben, R. (2016) "The CJEU's view of whether Bitcoins are a currency: a Belgian perspective", *International Company and Commercial Law Review*, Vol. 27, 62–63.

1747 Annex I Section B(4) MiFID1 and MiFID2.

1748 CJEU, Banif Plus Bank Zrt. *v.* Márton Lantos, Mártonné Lantos, *C-312/14*, paragraph 66.

1749 Houben, R. (2015) "Bitcoin: there are two sides to every coin", *Tijdschrift voor Belgisch Handelsrecht*, nr. 2, 149; Baukema, J. (2014) "Virtuele valuta: (toezichtrechtelijke) stand van zaken", *Tijdschrift voor Financieel Recht*, nr. 9, 377; Frew, L., Folsom, R., van Wingerden, S. (2015) "Legal and regulatory issues relating to virtual currencies", *Butterworths Journal of International Banking and Financial Law*, Vol. 7, 4.

1750 However, it must be reminded that such broad application may not be possible, see further section 4.3.2.2.

1751 In this case: annex I Section C(4) MiFID1 and MiFID2.

1752 Houben, R. (2016) "The CJEU's view of whether Bitcoins are a currency: a Belgian perspective", *International Company and Commercial Law Review*, Vol. 27, 62–63.

has identified several firms offering contracts for differences relating to virtual currencies.[1753] In the same analysis, the ESMA also identified several virtual currency collective investment schemes, though it was unclear whether any of these operate from within the EU.[1754] The competent Belgian financial supervisor – the Financial Services and Markets Authority (FSMA) – has already moved to prohibit the commercialization of certain financial instruments, including those relating to virtual currencies, to non-professional investors.[1755] Such a prohibition has been criticized by opponents of regulation, as derivatives could be used by investors to hedge their risks, which in the case of cryptocurrencies is said to possibly help counter their volatility.[1756] However, this opposition does not take into account that cryptocurrency volatility persists to this day, even though virtual currency derivatives are already present on markets worldwide.

#### 4.3.1.2 Member State deviation: Germany

BaFin opinion – The German financial supervisor Bundesamt für Finanzdienstleistungen (BaFin) has stated that it considers virtual currencies[1757] to

[1753] ESMA (2015) "Call for evidence: Investment using virtual currency or distributed ledger technology", *ESMA/2015/532*, 18.

[1754] *Ibid.*, 19. This raises the question whether virtual currencies could be caught under the scope of the UCITS Directive (Directive 2009/65/EC of the European Parliament and of the Council on the coordination of laws, regulations and administrative provisions relating to undertakings for collective investment in transferable securities (UCITS), *OJ* L 302 of 17 November 2009, 32–96 (hereinafter: UCITS Directive)) or the AIFMD (Directive 2011/61/EU of the European Parliament and of the Council on Alternative Investment Fund Managers and amending Directives 2003/41/EC and 2009/65/EC and Regulations (EC) No 1060/2009 and (EU) No 1095/2010, *OJ* L 174 of 1 July 2011, 1–73 (hereinafter: AIFMD)). Given the focus of the UCITS Directive on transferable securities, it would seem that virtual currencies cannot fall under its scope (article 1(2)). However, derivatives regarding virtual currencies could also here be included (article 50(1)(g)). The AIFMD, on the other hand, is less focused on the underlying instruments (article 4(1)(a)). As a result, virtual currency collective investment funds could fall under its scope. Depending on the precise product, a qualification as packaged retail and insurance-based investment product (PRIIP) could also be in order: Article 4(1)-(4) Regulation (EU) No 1286/2014 of the European Parliament and of the Council of 26 November 2014 on key information documents for packaged retail and insurance-based investment products (PRIIPs), *OJ* L 352 of 9 December 2014, 1–23.

[1755] Royal Decree of 24 April 2014 approving the regulation of the Financial Services and Markets Authority concerning the prohibition of commercialization of certain financial products to non-professional clients, *Belgian State Gazette* 20 May 2014.

[1756] Brito, J., Shadab, H., Castillo, A. (2014) "Bitcoin financial regulation: securities, derivatives, prediction markets, and gambling", *Columbia Science & Technology Law Review*, Vol. 16, 158; Houben, R. (2015) "Bitcoin: there are two sides to every coin", *Tijdschrift voor Belgisch Handelsrecht*, nr. 2, 154.

[1757] Although the term 'virtual currencies' is used here, it is clear from the description used in the text that BaFin focuses primarily on cryptocurrencies. For instance, it is stated that virtual currencies can only be created through mining, which is of course only true for cryptocurrencies and not for the other virtual currencies considered in this research. BaFin (2016) "Virtual Currency (VC)", *bafin.de*. In another opinion, BaFin focuses solely on bitcoin and other cryptocurrencies. Münzer, J. (2014) "Bitcoins: Supervisory assessment and risks to users", *bafin.de*.

be units of account in the sense of section 1 (11) sentence 1 of the German Banking Act.[1758, 1759] That particular provision lists the instruments that are to be considered as financial instruments under German law. More particularly, BaFin points out that virtual currencies – or rather: cryptocurrencies – are similar to foreign exchange or units of account.[1760] As a result, they are "*units similar to foreign currencies and not of legal tender*", which can function as private means of payment as a private substitute currency.[1761] A few observations can be made regarding BaFin's opinion.

FINANCIAL INSTRUMENTS – First, it is clear that the German supervisor considers virtual currencies to be financial instruments, by referring to the corresponding article in the German Banking Act. Moreover, by particularly singling out the reference to foreign currencies[1762], it follows that BaFin does not consider virtual currencies to fall under the scope of other financial instruments, such as transferable securities, money-market instruments, or derivatives.

GERMAN MARKET ONLY – Second, it must be noted that BaFin's interpretation is possible due to a unique deviation in the German transposition of the MiFID framework. Neither directive includes foreign exchange units of account as financial instruments *in se*. Only derivative contracts regarding currencies are included.[1763] The German legislator has therefore gone beyond the requirements of the directives by adding a financial instrument to the list provided by the European legislator.[1764] This means that no generalizing conclusions can

---

1758 Gesetz über das Kreditwesen (Kreditwesengesetz – KWG), *BGBl.* I of 9 September 1998, 2776 *et seq* (hereinafter: German Banking Act).

1759 Münzer, J. (2014) "Bitcoins: Supervisory assessment and risks to users", *bafin.de*. This position was confirmed by parliamentary secretary of state Hartmut Koschyk. Deutscher Bundestag, Schriftliche Fragen, *17/14530*, 41; Boehm, F., Pesch, P. (2014) "Bitcoin: A First Legal Analysis With Reference to German and US-American Law", In: Böhme, R., Brenner, M., Moore, T., Smith, M. (Eds.) *Financial Cryptography and Data Security, FC 2014 Workshops, LNCS 8438*, Berlin: Springer, 44.

1760 *Id.;* The Law Library of Congress (2014) "Regulation of Bitcoin in Selected Jurisdictions", *loc.gov*, 10.

1761 Münzer, J. (2014) "Bitcoins: Supervisory assessment and risks to users", *bafin.de;* De Filippi, P. (2014) "Bitcoin: a regulatory nightmare to a libertarian dream", *Internet Policy Review*, Vol. 3, 6; Sonderegger, D. (2015) "Regulatory and Economic Perplexity: Bitcoin Needs Just a Bit of Regulation", *Washington University Journal of Law & Policy*, Vol. 47, 202.

1762 Section 1(11), first sentence, nr. 7 German Banking Act.

1763 Annex I Section C (4) MiFID1 and MiFID2.

1764 "*Der Gesetzgeber ging bei der Umsetzung der MiFID – wie bereits bei der Adaption der* [Wertpapierdienstleistungsrichtlinie] – [...] *mit der Berücksichtigung von Devisen und Rechnungseinheiten als Finanzinstrumente im Sinne des KWG über die Vorgaben der Richtlinie hinaus.*" The deviation was thus already present in Germany's transposition of the ISD, and was maintained when transposing MiFID1. BaFin (2013) "Merkblatt Finanzinstrumente (Aktien, Vermögensanlagen, Schuldtitel, sonstige Rechte, Anteile an Investmentvermögen, Geldmarktinstrumente, Devisen und Rechnungseinheiten)", *bafin.de;* Auffenberg, L. (2015) "Bitcoins als Rechnungseinheiten – Eine kritische Auseinandersetzung mit der aktuellen Verwaltungspraxis der BaFin", *Neue Zeitschrift für Verwaltungsrecht*, Vol. 17, 1185.

be drawn from BaFin's interpretation, as such a deviation goes beyond the harmonization intended by the MiFID framework.[1765] The deviation also raises issues when cross-border services are provided. As Germany is, thus far, the only Member State regulating certain virtual currency service providers under the MiFID framework, service providers located outside of Germany cannot obtain suitable authorization in their home Member State. Then there is the question of how far German law reaches. It is clear that service providers incorporated in Germany are subjected to the laws of that country. Less clear is the situation where services are aimed at German citizens, but where the service provider has no physical presence in Germany. Here, the German supervisor, albeit controversially, appears to support the view that such cases also fall under German law.[1766]

Authorization for investment services – Third, the obvious result of the qualification of virtual currencies as financial instruments is that certain service providers – those providing investment services and activities relating to virtual currencies – will have to be properly authorized under German law. This is important to note because it means that not all services are necessarily covered. General use of virtual currencies as a means of payment between two private parties, for instance, or even mining cryptocurrencies are in themselves not investment services.[1767] The particular virtual currency services that would become subject to authorization include operating a multilateral trading system relating to virtual currencies, virtual currency investment and contract broking, as well as proprietary trading.[1768] Such includes virtual currency exchange services, regardless of whether the platform handles the transactions itself (broking), or whether the platform brings together the parties to a transaction (multilateral trading). Such activities correspond, according to BaFin's interpretation, to execution of orders on behalf of clients, or to dealing on own account as provided under the MiFID framework.[1769] Similar conclusions can be

1765 For instance, article 2, 1° of the Belgian Act of 2 August 2002 concerning the supervision on the financial sector and financial services (*Belgian State Gazette* of 4 September 2002) does not include foreign exchange units of account as a separate type of financial instruments. Only derivatives are mentioned, as provided by the directives.

1766 Boehm, F., Pesch, P. (2014) "Bitcoin: A First Legal Analysis With Reference to German and US-American Law", In: Böhme, R., Brenner, M., Moore, T., Smith, M. (Eds.) *Financial Cryptography and Data Security, FC 2014 Workshops, LNCS 8438*, Berlin: Springer, 45; Fischer, R., Müller, C. (2016) "§32 Erlaubnis", In: Boos, K.-H., Fischer, R., Schulte-Mattler, H. (Eds.) *Kommentar zu Kreditwesengesetz, VO (EU) Nr. 575/2013 (CRR) und Ausführungsvorschriften - Band I (5. Auflage)*, München: Verlag C. H. Beck, para. 19–24.

1767 Münzer, J. (2014) "Bitcoins: Supervisory assessment and risks to users", *bafin.de*.

1768 *Id.*; section 1(1a), second sentence, nrs. 1–4 German Banking Act.

1769 While the German Banking Act inpart transposes MiFID1 into German law, its references to broking are closely related to what under the MiFID2 would become known as 'matched principal trading'. Article 4(1)(38) MiFID2.

drawn for mining pools that commercially share profits, and for cryptocurrency ATMs.[1770]

Own funds trading – In April 2017, BaFin issued a notice that it had ordered companies involved in the OneCoin scheme to cease their activities in Germany.[1771] According to BaFin, the way in which these companies operated constituted *"Eigenhandel (own funds trading) of financial instruments in the meaning of §1 (1a) sentence 2 no. 4 of the German Federal Banking Act ("KWG")"*.[1772] This notice is a clear implementation of BaFin's earlier view, considering that the OneCoin virtual currency acted as the financial instrument that was traded in this case.

### *4.3.2 Cryptocurrencies intended as means of investment*

#### 4.3.2.1 EU perspective

From money-substitute… – While the first cryptocurrencies – such as bitcoin – were indeed conceived first and foremost as means of payment, new forms have been created that greatly expand the possibilities of these virtual currencies. Most of such developments are related to Ethereum[1773], which uses the blockchain technology underlying cryptocurrencies to implement smart contracts.[1774] A simple use case here is to record a certain transaction on the blockchain, thus providing cryptographic proof of said transaction – similar to how a notary provides proof of a deed.[1775] However, much more complex use cases are arising. One example is the creation of an entity which is fully enforced by smart contracts, referred to as a decentralized autonomous organization.

… to autonomous investment vehicle – The main goal of a decentralized autonomous organization is to create an entity that fully operates by means of smart contracts on the blockchain. The underlying reasoning is that – at its most basic

1770 Münzer, J. (2014) "Bitcoins: Supervisory assessment and risks to users", *bafin.de*; Rolland, A.-S. (2016) "Virtual currencies: how will the EU face this challenge?", *Thesis KU Leuven Faculty of Law*, 37–39.

1771 BaFin (2017) "Onecoin Ltd (Dubai), OneLife Network Ltd (Belize) und One Network Services Ltd (Sofia/Bulgaria): BaFin issues cease and desist orders holding the companies to stop own funds trading in "OneCoins" in Germany", *bafin.de*, 27 April.

1772 *Id.*

1773 *Ethereum.org.*

1774 Popper, N. (2016) "Ethereum, a Virtual Currency, Enables Transactions That Rival Bitcoin's", *New York Times*, 27 March.

1775 One example of where this has been implemented can be found at the Luxembourg Stock Exchange. Here, documents that must be made available to the public via the exchange's public website are given a digital signature using blockchain technology. This provides cryptographically irrefutable proof of existence. Luxembourg Stock Exchange (2016) "Luxembourg Stock Exchange introduces blockchain into reporting service", *bourse.lu.*

level – any organization or company could be reduced to a bundle of agreements – between employees, shareholders, customers, etc. – that are enforced by the law and the judiciary system.[1776] The idea is then to replace those agreements with smart contracts running on a blockchain, thus creating what is supposed to be an autonomous entity. This entity then essentially becomes a company existing purely out of code, without the need of intervention by employees, a board of directors, or others.[1777] The primary example of a decentralized autonomous organization – aptly named The DAO – was created to serve as an investment vehicle.

THE DAO – The workings of The DAO were similar to those of venture capital funds.[1778] First, The DAO began by issuing units – DAO tokens – that could be purchased with ether – Ethereum's main unit of account. Contractors could propose projects for which they wanted to obtain funding to The DAO.[1779] DAO token holders could then vote on the proposals they like to see funded.[1780] Once approved, a proposal receives the requested funding from The DAO's ether holdings. If a funded project turns out successful, profits flow back to DAO token holders. The launch of The DAO proved to be a success. Soon enough, its ether holdings amassed from the sale of DAO tokens were valued at over USD 150 million.[1781] However, things went very much south after that. Due to an unforeseen bug in the underlying code, a third of The DAO's ether holdings was siphoned away to a separate smart contract by an unknown party, where they were temporarily frozen.[1782] A fierce debate within the community followed, which eventually resulted in an operation to restore the stolen funds to their original owners, requiring a so-called hard fork.[1783] While the funds were

---

1776 Buterin, V. (2013) "Bootstrapping A Decentralized Autonomous Corporation: Part I", *Bitcoin Magazine*, 19 September.

1777 Lee, T. B. (2016) "Ethereum, explained: why Bitcoin's stranger cousin is now worth $1 billion", *Vox*, 24 May.

1778 X (2016) "The DAO of accrue", *The Economist*, 19 May.

1779 Though The DAO would not have employees, a team of volunteers called 'curators' was foreseen to scrutinize project proposals before submitting them to the public. Waters, R. (2016) "Automated company raises equivalent of $120M in digital currency", *Financial Times*, 17 May.

1780 Rather than relying on its managing team to make such decisions – as a traditional venture capital fund would do – The DAO relies on the wisdom of its crowd, deciding by majority. Lee, T. B. (2016) "Ethereum, explained: why Bitcoin's stranger cousin is now worth $1 billion", *Vox*, 24 May.

1781 Macheel, T. (2016) "The DAO Might Be Groundbreaking, But Is It Legal?", *American Banker*, 19 May; Lee, T. B. (2016) "Ethereum, explained: why Bitcoin's stranger cousin is now worth $1 billion", *Vox*, 24 May; X (2016) "The DAO of accrue", *The Economist*, 19 May; Popper, N. (2016) "Ethereum, a Virtual Currency, Enables Transactions That Rival Bitcoin's", *New York Times*, 27 March.

1782 Popper, N. (2016) "A Hacking of More Than $50 Million Dashes Hopes in the World of Virtual Currency", *New York Times*, 17 June; Finley, K. (2016) "A $50 Million Hack Just Showed That the DAO Was All Too Human", *Wired*, 18 June.

1783 In principle, a blockchain follows a linear path, with one block following the other. A fork can create two alternatives, with *in casu* one path accepting that the stolen funds could not be recuperated, and the second path implementing what was essentially a roll-back of the contested transaction. With the majority of users accepting the hard fork into the second path,

eventually recuperated, The DAO was effectively shut down. Despite this failure, the concept of decentralized autonomous organizations is still being further developed.[1784] Moreover, a related phenomenon – the initial coin offering (ICO) – is swiftly gaining ground.[1785] In an ICO, a company can offer units of its own cryptocurrency to the public with the goal of attracting funding through that sale. An ICO therefore primarily serves as a crowdfunding tool. The usability of the cryptocurrency units sold in an ICO can differ greatly between projects. In some cases, these units can confer voting rights, in other they do not confer any rights. If a project is successful, the value of those units is expected to rise, which is how investors aim to gain profits.

Investment cryptocurrencies as financial instruments – The nature of cryptocurrencies issued for the sole purposes of serving as means of investment makes them more naturally suited to be considered as financial instruments in the sense of the MiFID framework than cryptocurrencies issued primarily to serve as means of payment. However, it must still be analyzed whether these investment cryptocurrencies can indeed constitute financial instruments in the sense of the MiFID framework. The creators of The DAO point out that The DAO did not directly hold investors funds – because the DAO tokens could only be purchased using ether – and that the token holders are not called shareholders.[1786] Moreover, since The DAO was not an incorporated entity, the tokens in principle do not constitute equity in a traditional company. However, these properties could just as well be disregarded as an attempt to avoid the application of the MiFID legal framework. It can indeed be held that such cryptocurrencies can be considered as securities, at least under US law – as will be further discussed in chapter VII.[1787] Also under EU law, a classification of these investment

---

the expectation was that the first path would naturally die out. However, the possibility of such operation brings into question the immutability of transactions touted as one of the core tenets of blockchain technology. Del Castillo, M. (2016) "Bitcoin Developers Warn Ethereum Fork Sets Unsettling Precedent", *CoinDesk*, 22 July. The result of this debate is that the original path is still maintained as Ethereum Classic, meaning that the two alternative paths now uneasily co-exist. Hertig, A. (2016) "Ethereum's Two Ethereums Explained", *CoinDesk*, 28 July.

1784 Hertig, A. (2017) "Rebranding The DAO: The Contentious Blockchain Concept is Back", *CoinDesk*, 20 February.

1785 *Cointelegraph.com/explained/ico-explained.*

1786 Macheel, T. (2016) "The DAO Might Be Groundbreaking, But Is It Legal?", *American Banker*, 19 May.

1787 Santori, M. (2016) "Appcoin Law: ICOs the Right Way", *CoinDesk*, 15 October; Macheel, T. (2016) "The DAO Might Be Groundbreaking, But Is It Legal?", *American Banker*, 19 May; Torpey, K. (2017) "Are crypto 'tokens' securities by another name?", *American Banker*, 9 March; Agrawal, N. (2016) "Is your crypto-crowdsale a security?", *CoinCenter*, 18 July; Byrne, P. (2016) "#THEDAO: Broken, but worth fixing", *prestonbyrne.com*, 17 May; Padovano, C. (2016) "Yes, Crypto-token Crowdsales Can Be Classified As Securities. Here's Why:", *decentralizedlegal.com*, 15 August, Hinkes, A. (2016) "The Law of The DAO", *CoinDesk*, 19 May. Earlier, the US Securities and Exchange Commission (SEC) already charged an enterprise

cryptocurrencies as securities is most suited.[1788] Here, the MiFID framework does not limit securities to shares or bonds in a company, but allows all securities *"equivalent to shares in companies, partnerships or other entities"*.[1789] Moreover, the tokens in question are negotiable because they can be traded in what can be understood as the capital market under the MiFID framework, thus making them transferable. As a result, it can be argued that these investment virtual currencies do indeed constitute financial instruments in the sense of the MiFID framework. However, even if the MiFID legal framework does apply to this case, it can still be questioned how such an application needs to work in practice, given that there is no direct legal entity upon whom the resulting obligations can be imposed. At the same time, it is also clear from the The DAO use case that certain operational elements, such as the absence of a legal person, are at least in part designed to skirt legal obligations. The difficulty to apply the legal framework should therefore in itself not be considered as sufficient reason to result in non-application.

### 4.3.2.2 Member State case: Belgium

#### A. Investment instruments

Investment instruments – A legal framework related to that of MiFID concerns the prospectus duty that applies when certain instruments are offered to the public or traded on the market. At the EU level, the framework on the prospectus duty is set by the Prospectus Directive.[1790] In Belgium, that directive has been transposed through the Prospectus Act of 16 June 2006.[1791] While the directive focuses on securities, the Belgian Prospectus Act has a broader

offering shares against virtual currencies for offering unregistered securities. Securities and Exchange Commission (2014) "SEC Charges Bitcoin Entrepreneur With Offering Unregistered Securities", *sec.gov*. Thus far, at least one fund has gone as far as recognizing its token sale as an offering of securities, going through the necessary legal procedure to do so: Stanley, A. (2017) "Investment Firm Blockchain Capital is Launching a $10 Million ICO", *CoinDesk*, 16 March.

1788 Given that these investment virtual currencies are not short-term debt instruments, a classification as money-market instruments seems unlikely. Since the token holders discussed here can intervene in the decision-making process by voting, it would seem that a classification as units in collective investment undertakings is also unsuited.

1789 See section 3.3.

1790 Directive 2003/71/EC of the European Parliament and of the Council of 4 November 2003 on the prospectus to be published when securities are offered to the public or admitted to trading and amending Directive 2001/34/EC, *OJ* L 345 of 31 December 2003, 64–89 (hereinafter: Prospectus Directive).

1791 Act of 16 June 2006 on the public offering of investment instruments and the admission of investment instruments on a regulated market, *Belgian State Gazette* 21 June 2006 (hereinafter: Prospectus Act). It should be noted that the Prospectus Act is not solely the transposition of the Prospectus Directive. As a result, there is a harmonized part of the Act – following the Prospectus Directive – and a non-harmonized part – going beyond the Prospectus Directive.

scope by focusing on investment instruments.[1792] Moreover, these investment instruments contain a provision referring to *"all other instruments enabling the execution of a financial investment, regardless of the underlying asset"*.[1793] This latter provision must be interpreted as a non-limitative open category, allowing for the inclusion of any means of investment.[1794] The result is that, given the use of certain types of virtual currencies for investment purposes, such investment virtual currencies could fall under the scope of the prospectus legislation.[1795] In that case, the service providers offering investment virtual currencies to the market are bound to a prospectus duty.[1796] Moreover, reference can be made to the Belgian legal framework on information duties regarding the commercialization of financial products.[1797] Such financial products include investment products, which in turn include the investment instruments of the Prospectus Act.[1798] Therefore, the same conclusion can apply.

DERIVATIVES – Also derivatives can be covered by the prospectus duty. Therefore, investment virtual currency derivatives also fall under the prospectus legal framework.[1799]

CURRENCIES – An important exemption to the prospectus legal framework is foreign exchange currency (Dutch: 'deviezen').[1800] If virtual currencies were considered as foreign exchange currencies, they would therefore be exempted from the prospectus legal framework.[1801] One possible indication under Belgian law of what could be understood as foreign exchange currencies refers to legal tender only.[1802] While the scope of the provision referring to legal tender is limited,

---

1792 Articles 1 and 2(1)(a) Prospectus Directive; article 4 Prospectus Act; Houben, R. (2016) "The CJEU's view of whether Bitcoins are a currency: a Belgian perspective", *International Company and Commercial Law Review*, Vol. 27, 63–64.

1793 Article 4, §1, 10° Prospectus Act.

1794 Houben, R. (2015) "Bitcoin: there are two sides to every coin", *Tijdschrift voor Belgisch Handelsrecht*, nr. 2, 149–150; Peeters, J., Van Dyck, T. (2006) "De prospectusplicht in de prospectuswet van 16 juni 2006", *Bank- en Financieel Recht*, nr. 2006/IV, para. 37.

1795 Houben, R. (2015) "Bitcoin: there are two sides to every coin", *Tijdschrift voor Belgisch Handelsrecht*, nr. 2, 149–150.

1796 Houben, R. (2016) "The CJEU's view of whether Bitcoins are a currency: a Belgian perspective", *International Company and Commercial Law Review*, Vol. 27, 64.

1797 Royal Decree of 25 April 2014 regarding certain information duties for the commercialization of financial products to non-professional clients, *Belgian State Gazette* 12 June 2014 (hereinafter: Royal Decree of 25 April 2014).

1798 Articles 2, 3° and 2, 5° Royal Decree of 25 April 2014; article 2, 39° Act of 2 August 2002 concerning the supervision on the financial sector and financial services, *Belgian State Gazette* 4 September 2002.

1799 *Id.*

1800 Article 4, §2, 2° Prospectus Act.

1801 However, as under the MiFID framework, derivative contracts regarding currencies are included under the scope.

1802 Article 212 Act of 4 December 1990 on financial transactions and the financial market, *Belgian State Gazette* 22 December 1990.

it provides an indication of how the legislator perceives the notion of foreign exchange.[1803] Here, reference can also be made to the decision of the Court of Justice of the European Union – discussed previously in chapter V – regarding the VAT treatment of virtual currency exchange transactions. By allowing the application of an exemption intended for currencies to virtual currencies, this case could be interpreted as having the Court considering virtual currencies as currencies. If such were to be the case, payment virtual currencies could be exempted from the scope of the prospectus legal framework, as it does not apply to currencies. However, given the specificity of the case referenced here, and of the domain of VAT law, it seems far-fetched to derive such a generalization from that case.[1804] At most, it indicates that the concept of 'currencies' can evolve over time, and that therefore a future recognition of payment virtual currencies as currencies is possible.

### B. Crowdfunding

Crowdfunding – Late 2016, the Belgian legislator adopted a new framework on crowdfunding.[1805] More particularly, the Belgian Crowdfunding Act provides the licensing and operational requirements for alternative financing platforms, as well as the conduct of business rules for the provision of alternative financing services.[1806] Such services are defined as "*the service consisting of commercializing investment instruments, through a website or any other electronic means, issued by entrepreneur-issuers, starter funds or financing vehicles in the framework of an offering, public or otherwise, without the provision of an investment service regarding these investment instruments, with the exception of, where applicable, the following services: provision of investment advice, receiving and transmitting orders*".[1807]

Investment instruments – The fact that investment instruments must be present indicates that the crowdfunding legal framework does not intend to address crowdfunding based on donations, or against rewards in kind.[1808] More concretely, such investment instruments are defined by reference to the aforementioned Prospectus Act, indicating a broad and non-limitative interpretation.[1809]

1803 Houben, R. (2015) "Bitcoin: there are two sides to every coin", *Tijdschrift voor Belgisch Handelsrecht*, nr. 2, 150.

1804 Houben, R. (2016) "The CJEU's view of whether Bitcoins are a currency: a Belgian perspective", *International Company and Commercial Law Review*, Vol. 27, 63.

1805 Belgian Act of 18 December 2016 regulating the recognition and demarcation of crowdfunding and holding diverse provisions regarding finances, *Belgian State Gazette* 20 December 2016 (hereinafter: Belgian Crowdfunding Act).

1806 Article 2 Belgian Crowdfunding Act. Note that also a prospectus duty may apply.

1807 Article 4, 1° Belgian Crowdfunding Act (own translation).

1808 On the diverse types of crowdfunding: Vandezande, N., Van de Velde, N. (2017) "Juridische aspecten van crowdfunding in België", In: Storme, M.E., Helsen, F. (Eds.) *Innovatie en disruptie in het economisch recht*, Antwerpen: Intersentia, 180–185.

1809 Article 4, 4° Belgian Crowdfunding Act.

PLATFORMS AND ISSUERS – The alternative financing platforms addressed by the crowdfunding framework, then, are natural and legal persons professionally providing alternative financing services within Belgium.[1810] Regulated entities, such as credit institutions and investment firms, do not need an additional license to provide such services, but they are bound to the conduct of business rules of the crowdfunding framework in the provision of those services. The investment instruments targeted here can be issued by an entrepreneur-issuer – being an issuer whose core activity is a commercial, artisanal, liberal, industrial or real estate activity – a starter fund – as defined under Belgian law – or a financing vehicle. This last entity is defined as "*an issuer of investment instruments that is not a collective investment fund, whose activity consists of taking part in or granting loans to one or more entrepreneur-issuers and that are financed by investors who themselves choose the entrepreneur-issuer they want to finance through their investment in the vehicle, understanding that the return on their investment is solely determined by the return offered by the entrepreneur-issuer for the participation taken or loan granted by the vehicle*".[1811]

CRYPTOCURRENCIES AS ALTERNATIVE FINANCING? – The definition of a financing vehicle under the crowdfunding legal framework closely resembles the case of The DAO.[1812] Such indicates that a qualification of such a cryptocurrency investment vehicle as alternative financing platform under the crowdfunding legal framework can be considered, insofar such a cryptocurrency investment vehicle is not already considered as an investment firm under the MiFID framework. However, the practical concern of the technical absence of a particular legal entity associated with such a cryptocurrency investment vehicle may complicate the application of the crowdfunding legal framework. At the same time, such an absence should not prohibit the application of the crowdfunding legal framework. For instance, if it is found that there is a financing vehicle as determined under the crowdfunding legal framework, then such a vehicle is obliged to take on a corporate form that limits the liability of its investors to their investment.[1813]

TERRITORIAL SCOPE – The crowdfunding legal framework, however, only applies to the provision of alternative financing services to Belgian investors. This means that the platform must be incorporated in Belgium, and the service must be aimed at Belgian investors, for instance by using a Belgian website, advertising in

1810 Note that this also applies when the services are just provided as a complementary or side activity. Article 4, 2° Belgian Crowdfunding Act.

1811 Article 4, 7¨ Belgian Crowdfunding Act.

1812 While an ICO also serves as a crowdfunding effort, the applicability of the MiFID legal framework will depend on the precise organization of such ICO. A company could, for instance, hold an ICO for its own shares without the use of a crowdfunding platform, thus falling outside the scope of this framework. However, there are platforms designed to market ICO's to the public – such as TokenMarket – which could possibly be argued to fall under the scope of this framework.

1813 Article 28, §1, 4° Belgian Crowdfunding Act.

Belgium, or featuring a large number of Belgian entrepreneur-issuers. Given the international nature of the developments regarding investment cryptocurrencies, the application of the Belgian Crowdfunding Act will therefore only have a limited scope in practice.[1814]

# 5 INTERIM CONCLUSIONS

## 5.1 FINDINGS

Chapter goals – The aim of this chapter was to assess whether virtual currencies and their service providers fall under the scope of the EU's MiFID framework. Where such is the case, further assessment against the normative criteria established for the purposes of this research is needed to ascertain whether such regulation under the MiFID framework is satisfactory. Where virtual currencies and their service providers do not fall under the scope of the MiFID legal framework, it must be assessed against the same normative criteria whether such regulation is possible and desirable.

Closed and unidirectional scheme virtual currencies as means of payment – Closed scheme and unidirectional scheme virtual currencies were found only to serve as means of payment. Furthermore, their limited transferability and negotiability make these types of virtual currencies inherently unsuitable to serve as means of investment. It can therefore be concluded that these virtual currencies do not fall within what the European legislator had in mind as financial instruments under the MiFID framework. Moreover, the services developed around these types of virtual currencies do not correspond to the investment services and activities covered by the MiFID legal framework.

Bidirectional scheme virtual currencies as means of payment – The assessment of bidirectional scheme virtual currencies, however, is less straightforward. While most bidirectional scheme virtual currencies do primarily serve as means of payment, there are examples – particularly cryptocurrencies – that have displayed clear use for investment purposes in practice. Despite this, it was found that considering payment bidirectional scheme virtual currencies as financial instruments under the MiFID framework remains problematic. Although these virtual currencies are indeed transferable, the absence of a right on their issuer makes it difficult to consider them as the securities – or other financial instruments – envisioned by the European legislator. Moreover, although it is not certain that these payment bidirectional scheme virtual

1814 Thus far there is no European framework on crowdfunding, meaning that this Belgian framework cannot provide passporting rights.

currencies can be considered as the payment instruments excluded from the scope of the MiFID framework, their primary use as means of payment does make the applicability of such an exclusion more plausible. One particular Member State deviation was found in Germany, where units of account similar to foreign exchange are also considered as financial instruments. The German regulator BaFin considers virtual currencies as such units of account. Additionally, practice has demonstrated the existence of derivative instruments that rely on virtual currencies as underlying assets. Such derivatives can then indeed be considered as financial instruments under the MiFID framework in their own right.

Virtual currencies as means of investment – There were also virtual currencies identified which primarily serve as means of investment. These could take the form of an investment vehicle operated through smart blockchain contracts, or the form of a crowdfunding campaign. Given that these investment bidirectional scheme virtual currencies do generally confer certain rights on their holders, they can be argued to constitute financial instruments under the MiFID framework. Also here, potential derivative products can be considered as financial instruments.

Future inclusion – The question is then whether the MiFID framework could be extended to include a broader range of virtual currencies. Here, reference can be made to the German implementation of the legal framework, which adds units of account similar to foreign exchange to the list of financial instruments. As noted, the German regulator BaFin considers virtual currencies to fall under the scope of such units of account similar to foreign exchange. A similar extension could therefore be considered at the EU level. Such an extension could capture all types of virtual currencies, regardless of their use as means of payment or means of investment. What remains, then, is to assess whether such an extension is desirable according to the normative criteria established for the purposes of this research. As in the previous chapters, only a preliminary analysis can be conducted at this stage, given that a final assessment can only be made by taking into account all of the different frameworks analyzed in this research.

## 5.2 NORMATIVE ASSESSMENT

Legal certainty – At the moment, there is still some uncertainty regarding the inclusion of virtual currencies under the scope of the MiFID framework. While it has been argued in this chapter that virtual currencies primarily serving as means of payment are not covered by the MiFID framework – though adding that derivatives relying on such virtual currencies can be considered as financial instruments in their own right – and that virtual currencies primarily serving as means of investment could be covered by that framework, there are opinions to the contrary. However, most of the uncertainty in literature appears to find its origin in relying on the German consideration of virtual currencies, where it must be remarked that this consideration is due to a unique deviation of German law from which no generalizing conclusions can be drawn. From the point of view of legal certainty, it can therefore be remarked that a clarification of the situation – be it by clearly excluding virtual currencies from the scope of the MiFID framework or by clearly including them – is desirable.

Proportionality – The MiFID framework imposes broad operational and conduct of business rules on the entities covered by its scope. While these requirements can be fairly burdensome, they could manage to cover a broad range of the risks associated with virtual currencies that were identified in chapter I. It could, for instance, address several of the risks posed to virtual currency users, it could help addressing certain market risks, it addresses most of the identified investor risks, and it could address some of the service provider risks. As a result, inclusion of virtual currencies under the MiFID framework can be defended for at least the types of virtual currencies posing higher risks. However, as noted, closed scheme and unidirectional scheme virtual currencies pose lesser risks, and do not have the propensity to serve as means of investment. The inclusion of these latter virtual currencies under the MiFID framework therefore seems disproportionate to their use and respective risks. Clear differentiation is needed according to the precise risks posed by a virtual currency, and according to the precise use of that virtual currency.

Trust – Particularly for virtual currencies used as means of investment, inclusion of such virtual currencies under the MiFID framework could help increasing user and investor trust. While any investment includes an element of risk – even more so when dealing with high volatility as with cryptocurrencies – the current absence of clear regulation contributes to the lack of trustworthy service providers and thus increases the risks of using virtual currencies as means of investment. Regulation of virtual currency service providers under the MiFID framework could then indeed raise the trustworthiness of those service providers, given that they become subjected to strict operational, licensing, and conduct of business rules.

Regulatory coherence – Thus far, little disparity has been noted regarding the approaches of Member States concerning the treatment of virtual currencies under the MiFID framework. The notable exception here is Germany, where a deviation in its national implementation of this framework results in the consideration of virtual currencies as financial instruments. However, taken together with the findings of chapter IV – indicating that certain Member States would like to consider particular virtual currency services under the legal framework of payment services – incompatibilities could rise when the same service is considered under different legal frameworks across Member States.

From the point of view of regulatory coherence, one service should therefore be considered under the same legal framework in all Member States.

Conclusion – As noted, it can be argued that bidirectional scheme virtual currencies primarily serving as means of investment, as well as all virtual currency derivative products, can already fall under the scope of the MiFID framework. Thus far, no disparity on this matter has been noted between Member States, indicating little to no legal uncertainty or regulatory incoherence on this part. Moreover, such an inclusion can be defended from the point of view of proportionality – given the higher degree of risks presented in these particular virtual currencies – and from the point of view of trust – as regulation could help raise the trustworthiness of service providers. The question whether virtual currencies primarily serving as means of payment – which includes closed scheme and unidirectional scheme virtual currencies – should also be covered by the MiFID legal framework, is more debatable. Given the little use of closed scheme and unidirectional scheme virtual currencies as means of investment, and given the fewer associated risks, inclusion of these virtual currencies under the MiFID framework seems to go beyond the intentions of the European legislator, as well as being disproportionate to the associated risks. Inclusion of bidirectional scheme virtual currencies primarily serving as means of payment can be considered – insofar they would demonstrate significant use as means of investment and are not already considered as a payment service – given that such an inclusion can be argued to be proportionate to the associated risks when these virtual currencies are used for investment purposes and given that it could help raise the trustworthiness of their service providers. From the viewpoints of legal certainty and regulatory coherence, to avoid future disparity between Member States, clearer inclusion or exclusion of these payment virtual currencies under the MiFID framework can be considered. In doing so, attention must be paid to the potential desirability of inclusion of these payment virtual currencies – and their service providers – under other legal frameworks, such as that on payment services.

# CHAPTER VII

# VIRTUAL CURRENCIES AND SERVICE PROVIDERS IN THE US

## 1 INTRODUCTION

US PERSPECTIVE – In the previous chapters, some of the core EU legal frameworks in the field of financial law were analyzed in order to assess their applicability to virtual currencies and virtual currency service providers. Given that virtual currencies are a global phenomenon, inspiration regarding the regulation – or even the need for regulation – of virtual currencies can be sought in other jurisdictions. As noted in the introduction to this research, the US was selected as the main candidate for such comparative research. This is, first of all, because many developments regarding virtual currencies originated, or are still being developed, in the US market. Second, US legislators and regulators – at both federal and state levels – have already taken regulatory steps regarding virtual currencies. Such can demonstrate how virtual currencies and their services can be embedded in existing legal frameworks, or whether entirely new frameworks are needed. Last, US law provides a high practical and linguistic accessibility of its primary and secondary sources. While Japan has recently taken interesting regulatory steps as well, the linguistic barrier and the lack of trustworthy translations of the relevant primary and secondary sources would complicate a more in-depth comparison.[1815]

GOAL – The goal of this chapter is to assess whether – and if so: how – the types of virtual currencies identified for the purposes of this research are regulated under US federal and state law. The focus on the treatment of particular cases – rather than on the legal frameworks governing them as a whole – will allow to draw more direct comparisons to the situation within the EU, as uncovered in the previous chapters. Following this analysis, the situation in the US can be compared to that in the EU, taking into account the normative criteria established for the purposes of this research. Such may provide inspiration for the need for regulation of virtual currencies within the EU, and – if such regulatory need is found – for what form such regulation could take.

---

1815 Vandezande, N. (2017) "Virtual currency law is Zen for Yen", *Policy Forum*, 20 April.

Approach – First (section 2), this chapter will elaborate upon the methodology for such comparative research. Such will allow to clearly delineate the scope and the limitations of this comparison. Then (section 3), this chapter will analyze the application of the relevant legal frameworks under US federal and state law to virtual currencies. As this analysis will mainly focus on the *lex lata*, the following section (section 4) will focus on a number of developments *de lege ferenda* currently being debated at both the US federal and state levels. Last (section 5), this chapter will synthesize the findings into interim conclusions.

## 2 METHODOLOGY

Functional comparison – For the comparison intended here, this chapter will employ the functional method of comparative law. As noted in the general introduction to this research, the functional method allows to focus on the effects of law as responses to actual situations, rather than strictly focusing on doctrine.[1816] Such is necessary, given the at times significant differences between US and EU financial law. For instance, the US has no direct equivalent to the EU's e-money notion analyzed in chapter IV, thus complicating a direct comparison of e-money regulation between the EU and the US. Instead, the focus will be put on the regulation of virtual currencies within the US on four levels: the regulation of money, the regulation of payment transactions, anti-money laundering rules, and the regulation of investment instruments. At each of these four levels, this chapter will analyze whether the relevant legal frameworks can apply to the three types of virtual currencies established for the purposes of this research.

Goals and limitations – The main objective of the functional comparison is not to analyze the full extent of potentially applicable legal frameworks, but to verify whether or not such frameworks can apply to virtual currencies on the four levels selected here. Given the significant differences between US and EU financial law, a comparison of the different effects of these legal frameworks goes beyond the scope of this research, in which the focus is put mainly on the (in) applicability of those frameworks to virtual currencies. The goal of this chapter is rather to seek similarities and differences in the treatment of virtual currencies under legal frameworks in the EU and the US that largely serve the same purposes. If, for instance, certain virtual currencies are considered as securities under US law, such could provide an argument – given the international reach of certain virtual currencies – to also consider them as securities under EU law, even if these two legal frameworks may have different consequences for the service providers involved with such securities – unless, of course, the notion

[1816] Michaels, R. (2006) "The Functional Method of Comparative Law", In: Reimann, M., Zimmermann, R. (eds.) *The Oxford Handbook of Comparative Law*, Oxford: University Press, 342.

of securities under US law are found to be completely incompatible with this notion under EU law. As in the previous chapters, the normative criteria of legal certainty, proportionality, trust, and regulatory coherence will serve as a means to provide an interim evaluation of the desirability of such an outcome.

Scope – In terms of scope, this comparison will span both federal and state law. With regard to state law, the goal is not to systematically analyze all states, but to focus on prominent examples providing insight in how virtual currencies are regulated under US law at the four levels selected here. The main focus will be put on the laws as currently applicable. Section 4 of this chapter will separately discuss legislative developments – both ongoing initiatives and recently adopted frameworks that have not yet yielded significant practical experiences.

Sources – The primary source material for this comparison is legal scholarly literature focusing on both US federal and state levels. These sources will lead to the consultation of the relevant primary sources, and case law – with preference for federal cases – where available.

# 3 US REGULATORY FRAMEWORKS

## 3.1 MONEY

Legitimacy of virtual currencies – As noted in chapter III, US law only recognizes US dollar coins and notes as legal tender. Virtual currencies can therefore not be considered as legal tender in the US. While this in itself of course does not prohibit the issuing and use of virtual currencies as alternative private currency, there are a few provisions in US law that need to be taken into account.

### *3.1.1 Constitution*

Coins and bills of credit – The US Constitution determines that "*no state shall* [...] *coin money* [or] *emit bills of credit*".[1817] Since to 'coin money' must be understood in its most literal sense – namely the production of physical metallic coins – it is clear that this notion does not apply to non-physical means of payment such as virtual currencies.[1818] Similarly, the bills of credit referenced in the Constitution should be understood as meaning circulating physical

1817 US Constitution, art. I, section 10. Section 8 of the same article reserves the authority to coin money to the federal government.

1818 Legal Tender Cases, 110 U.S. 421, at 462 (1884). Kaplanov, N. M. (2012) "Nerdy Money: Bitcoin, the Private Digital Currency, and the Case Against its Regulation", *Loyola Consumer Law Review*, Vol. 25, 142; Brito, J., Castillo, A. (2013) *Bitcoin: A Primer for Policymakers*, Arlington: George Mason University Mercatus Center, 42.

paper.[1819] Moreover, this provision of the Constitution applies only to states and local municipalities.[1820] Private non-governmental actors are therefore not bound by the prohibition found in the US Constitution.[1821]

State laws – However, the US Constitution does leave states free to adopt legislation that limits the use of alternative currencies.[1822] Such legislation is mostly aimed to protect employees from being paid in company scrip, rather than in US dollars.[1823] As a result, also in such state legislation the focus appears to be on physical currency only.[1824]

### *3.1.2 Stamp Payments Act 1862*

Historic setting – At the time of the Civil War, the US was experiencing inflation, which caused the metal of which the coins in circulation at that time were minted to become more valuable than the coins' face value.[1825] As a result, people starting hoarding these coins – thus taking them out of circulation – and started trading in notes backed by the coins, or fractions thereof, in their possession.[1826] These notes could be regarded as a form of private currency. To counter this practice, the federal government followed the example of a number of states to step in.[1827] The resulting act, the Stamp Payments Act, was adopted on 17 July 1862.[1828] On the one hand, this act allowed for dues

---

1819 Craig *v.* State of Missouri, 29 U.S. 410, at 415 (1830).

1820 *Ibid.*, at 432; Kaplanov, N. M. (2012) "Nerdy Money: Bitcoin, the Private Digital Currency, and the Case Against its Regulation", *Loyola Consumer Law Review*, Vol. 25, 143; Grinberg, R. (2012) "Bitcoin: An Innovative Alternative Digital Currency", *Hastings Science & Technology Law Journal*, Vol. 4, 182; Turpin, J. B. (2014) "Bitcoin: The Economic Case for a Global, Virtual Currency Operating in an Unexplored Legal Framework", *Indiana Journal of Global Legal Studies*, Vol. 21, 353.

1821 Briscoe *v.* Bank of Commonwealth of Kentucky, 36 U.S. 257, at 348 (1837) ("*It does not prohibit private persons or private partnerships or private corporations (strictly so called) from issuing bills of credit.*"); Bryans, D. (2014) "Bitcoin and Money Laundering: Mining for an Effective Solution", *Indiana Law Journal*, Vol. 89, 448.

1822 Kaplanov, N. M. (2012) "Nerdy Money: Bitcoin, the Private Digital Currency, and the Case Against its Regulation", *Loyola Consumer Law Review*, Vol. 25, 143–144.

1823 Solomon, L. D. (1996) *Rethinking Our Centralized Money System: The Case for a System of Local Currencies*, Westport: Praeger Publishers, 104–105.

1824 Kaplanov, N. M. (2012) "Nerdy Money: Bitcoin, the Private Digital Currency, and the Case Against its Regulation", *Loyola Consumer Law Review*, Vol. 25, 166.

1825 Smith, D. (2012) "More Money, More Problems: The Bitcoin Virtual Currency and the Legal Problems that Face It", *Case Western Reserve Journal of Law, Technology & the Internet*, Vol. 3, 437–438; Tu, K. V., Meredith, M. W. (2015) "Rethinking Virtual Currency Regulation in the Bitcoin Age", *Washington Law Review*, Vol. 90, 316–317.

1826 Dion, D. (2013) "I'll Gladly Trade You Two Bits on Tuesday for a Byte Today: Bitcoin, Regulating Fraud in the E-conomy of Hacker-Cash", *Journal of Law, Technology & Policy*, Vol. 2013, 174–175.

1827 Grinberg, R. (2012) "Bitcoin: An Innovative Alternative Digital Currency", *Hastings Science & Technology Law Journal*, Vol. 4, 183.

1828 Stamp Payments Act 1862, 12 Stat. 592, ch. 196.

to the US of less than five[1829] US dollars to be paid in postage stamps.[1830] It thus aimed to promote the use of postage stamps as means of payment for low-value sums. On the other hand, the Stamp Payments Act prohibited anyone to "*make, issue, circulate, or pay any note, check, memorandum, token, or other obligation, for a less sum than one dollar, intended to circulate as money or to be received or used in lieu of lawful money of the United States*".[1831] This second part of the act was intended to prevent the aforementioned form of private currency from competing with legal tender.[1832] While the context in which virtual currencies are developed or developing is of course very different from the situation giving cause to the Stamp Payments Act, the second section of the 1862 act is still in force today. It must therefore be assessed whether or not it can be applied.

INTENTION – A first element is that there must be circulation and the intention to be used instead of legal tender. Here, it is reminded that many virtual currencies have a limited scope – for instance in that they can only be used within a closed realm or at certain service providers – and are not redeemable for money. As a result, it can be argued that such virtual currencies do not appear to violate the circulation and intention requirement. Case law confirms that tickets with a particular purpose – *in casu* to serve a toll bridge – could not be considered to be in circulation or to be intended to circulate as money, and similar conclusions were drawn with regard to store gift certificates, given their limited usability and given that their obligations are not payable in money.[1833]

ONE US DOLLAR – Second, the provision only applies to notes of values lower than one US dollar – lowered from five US dollar in the original text. As a result, many private currencies simply do not issue notes lower than this threshold, even though the limited circulation of most private currencies already place them outside the reach of this provision of the Stamp Payments Act.[1834]

---

1829 This was later lowered to one US dollar: Grinberg, R. (2012) "Bitcoin: An Innovative Alternative Digital Currency", *Hastings Science & Technology Law Journal,* Vol. 4, 183.

1830 Section 1, Stamp Payments Act 1862.

1831 Section 2, Stamp Payments Act 1862.

1832 Congressional Research Service (2014) "Bitcoin: Questions, Answers, and Analysis of Legal Issues", *crs.gov,* 12.

1833 United States *v.* Monongahela Bridge Co., 26 F. Cas. 1292, at 1293 (W.D. Pa. 1863); United States *v.* Van Auken, 96 U.S 366, at 368 (1878); Grinberg, R. (2012) "Bitcoin: An Innovative Alternative Digital Currency", *Hastings Science & Technology Law Journal,* Vol. 4, 184; Congressional Research Service (2014) "Bitcoin: Questions, Answers, and Analysis of Legal Issues", *crs.gov,* 12; Tu, K. V., Meredith, M. W. (2015) "Rethinking Virtual Currency Regulation in the Bitcoin Age", *Washington Law Review,* Vol. 90, 317; Smith, D. (2012) "More Money, More Problems: The Bitcoin Virtual Currency and the Legal Problems that Face It", *Case Western Reserve Journal of Law, Technology & the Internet,* Vol. 3, 440.

1834 Grinberg, R. (2012) "Bitcoin: An Innovative Alternative Digital Currency", *Hastings Science & Technology Law Journal,* Vol. 4, 186.

Form – While the second provision of the Stamp Payments Act only explicitly refers to physical items, this does not necessarily mean that non-physical items are excluded. Even if it could be argued that non-physical currencies are not "*intended to circulate as money*" due to their lack of physical properties, courts could also "*focus on similarities arising from non-physical properties, such as the rights and obligations of the holders*".[1835] The element of "*intended to circulate as money*" alone should therefore not be taken as sufficient argument to exclude non-physical currencies from the act's scope.

Obligation – A last element is that all of the examples in the Stamp Payments Act are obligations in the sense that they require one party – generally the issuer – to pay the holder. Moreover, following from the earlier paragraphs, such an obligation must include payment in money, given that US Supreme Court case law clearly indicates that payments in goods or services are not considered payments "*for a less sum than one US dollar*".[1836]

### *3.1.3 Counterfeiting statutes*

Liberty Dollar – While private currencies can be considered legal – barring state limitations hereto – it must of course be ensured that such private currencies remain distinct from the US dollar.[1837] Apart from the Stamp Payments Act, there are also more particular anti-counterfeiting rules to be found in federal US law. In the Liberty Dollar case, the issuer of this example of a private currency was found to have specifically designed its coins to resemble and compete with US dollar coins.[1838] Such was found in violation of anti-counterfeiting rules.[1839] Important to note here is that the Liberty Dollar case should be interpreted as being strictly aimed at counterfeiting and fraud, and not as an assault on the capacity of private entities to issue private currencies.[1840]

Physical coins – As a result of anti-counterfeiting rules, virtual currencies may not resemble the US dollar, although this should – given the non-physical nature of

1835 Smith, B. W., Wilson, R. J. (1997) "How Best to Guide the Evolution of Electronic Currency Law", *American University Law Review*, Vol. 46, 1110; Grinberg, R. (2012) "Bitcoin: An Innovative Alternative Digital Currency", *Hastings Science & Technology Law Journal*, Vol. 4, 188–189. *Contra:* Congressional Research Service (2014) "Bitcoin: Questions, Answers, and Analysis of Legal Issues", *crs.gov*, 12.

1836 United States *v.* Van Auken, 96 U.S 366, at 368–369 (1878).

1837 Bryans, D. (2014) "Bitcoin and Money Laundering: Mining for an Effective Solution", *Indiana Law Journal*, Vol. 89, 448; Kaplanov, N. M. (2012) "Nerdy Money: Bitcoin, the Private Digital Currency, and the Case Against its Regulation", *Loyola Consumer Law Review*, Vol. 25, 144.

1838 Federal Bureau of Investigation (2011) "Defendant Convicted of Minting His Own Currency", *Press release* 18 March.

1839 As provided by 18 U.S.C. §485.

1840 Grinberg, R. (2012) "Bitcoin: An Innovative Alternative Digital Currency", *Hastings Science & Technology Law Journal*, Vol. 4, 192.

virtual currencies – not be a hard requirement to fulfill. Moreover, it can be argued that the no-resemblance requirement, also applied in the Liberty Dollar case, only extends to physical coins and bars.[1841] As a result, the no-resemblance requirement of the federal anti-counterfeiting rule does not apply to virtual currencies.

Confusion and fraud – Moreover, in the Liberty Dollar case it was clear that this form of private currency was brought on the market with the intention to confuse and even defraud unsuspecting users.[1842] Such was in violation of the second element of the federal anti-counterfeiting rule, namely that "*false, forged, or counterfeit*" coins and bars should not be brought into circulation "*with intent to defraud*".[1843] A virtual currency that does not have such an intent to confuse and defraud should therefore not be considered as a violation of the 'intention to defraud' element of the anti-counterfeiting rules.

### *3.1.4 Application to virtual currencies*

Constitution and anti-counterfeiting – It is clear that the US Constitution does not prohibit the circulation of virtual currencies. Even if the current thinking of bills of credit as paper bills were expanded to include non-physical currencies, the scope of the money issuance provision in the US Constitution is limited to states and local governments only. As a result, the money issuance provision does not affect privately issued virtual currencies.[1844] The only *caveat* here is to stay clear from anti-counterfeiting rules, meaning that virtual currencies should not resemble the US dollar, nor attempt to confuse or defraud their users.

Stamp Payments Act – It is clear that closed scheme and unidirectional scheme virtual currencies should not be considered to fall under the scope of the Stamp Payments Act. They only have limited circulation, are not intended to compete with legal tender, and cannot be redeemed for money. Moreover, when not denominated below one US dollar, they would certainly fall outside of the scope of the act. The answer is, however, less

1841 Turpin, J. B. (2014) "Bitcoin: The Economic Case for a Global, Virtual Currency Operating in an Unexplored Legal Framework", *Indiana Journal of Global Legal Studies*, Vol. 21, 354; Grinberg, R. (2012) "Bitcoin: An Innovative Alternative Digital Currency", *Hastings Science & Technology Law Journal*, Vol. 4, 192.

1842 The fraud was alleged on the basis that the face value of the coins was much higher than their actual value. Grinberg, R. (2012) "Bitcoin: An Innovative Alternative Digital Currency", *Hastings Science & Technology Law Journal*, Vol. 4, 193; Brito, J., Castillo, A. (2013) *Bitcoin: A Primer for Policymakers*, Arlington: George Mason University Mercatus Center, 42–43; Dion, D. (2013) "I'll Gladly Trade You Two Bits on Tuesday for a Byte Today: Bitcoin, Regulating Fraud in the E-conomy of Hacker-Cash", *Journal of Law, Technology & Policy*, Vol. 2013, 172–174.

1843 18 U.S.C. §485.

1844 Kaplanov, N. M. (2012) "Nerdy Money: Bitcoin, the Private Digital Currency, and the Case Against its Regulation", *Loyola Consumer Law Review*, Vol. 25, 166.

straightforward for bidirectional scheme virtual currencies, and particularly for cryptocurrencies.[1845] These virtual currencies do enjoy a wider circulation and can be used to obtain all kinds of goods and services.[1846] They are fully interchangeable and could be issued below the one US dollar threshold of the Stamp Payments Act.[1847] One argument against the application of the Stamp Payments Act is that the act intended to curb competition with legal tender coins. Given that virtual currencies are not often used in face-to-face transactions, they will rarely directly compete with such coins.[1848] Moreover, it is established that criminal statutes must be interpreted strictly, and that therefore caution must be paid in applying them to technological developments unforeseen at the time of their adoption.[1849] While such could, then, lead to the argument that the Stamp Payments Act did not foresee non-physical currency, it has been shown that this is not a particularly strong argument. The better argument therefore appears to be that cryptocurrencies are not obligations. Cryptocurrencies are issued by their underlying algorithm, and thus do not create an obligation on their issuer – insofar as there even is an identifiable issuer. Such puts these virtual currencies outside the aims of the Stamp Payments Act.[1850] Additionally, it can be said that the limited amount of cryptocurrency transactions complicates the argument that they are 'intended to compete' with the US dollar.[1851] While such could of course still happen in the future, if the use of cryptocurrencies were to expand drastically, it is more likely that US legislators would at that point intervene with new rules, rather than relying on this outdated statute.

---

1845 Note, however, that bidirectional scheme virtual currencies with limited usability – such as Second Life's Linden dollar – could follow the same argumentation as for closed scheme and unidirectional scheme virtual currencies.

1846 Tu, K. V., Meredith, M. W. (2015) "Rethinking Virtual Currency Regulation in the Bitcoin Age", *Washington Law Review*, Vol. 90, 319.

1847 Farmer, P. H. Jr. (2014) "Speculative Tech: The Bitcoin Legal Quagmire & the Need for Legal Innovation", *Journal of Business & Technology Law*, Vol. 9, 95.

1848 Grinberg, R. (2012) "Bitcoin: An Innovative Alternative Digital Currency", *Hastings Science & Technology Law Journal*, Vol. 4, 187; Tu, K. V., Meredith, M. W. (2015) "Rethinking Virtual Currency Regulation in the Bitcoin Age", *Washington Law Review*, Vol. 90, 319; Kien-Meng Ly, M. (2014) "Coining Bitcoin's "legal-bits": Examining the regulatory framework for Bitcoin and virtual currencies", *Harvard Journal of Law & Technology*, Vol. 27, 599.

1849 United States *v.* Gellman, 44 F. Supp. 360, at 365–66 (D. Minn. 1942).

1850 Smith, D. (2012) "More Money, More Problems: The Bitcoin Virtual Currency and the Legal Problems that Face It", *Case Western Reserve Journal of Law, Technology & the Internet*, Vol. 3, 438–439; Congressional Research Service (2014) "Bitcoin: Questions, Answers, and Analysis of Legal Issues", *crs.gov*, 12; Grinberg, R. (2012) "Bitcoin: An Innovative Alternative Digital Currency", *Hastings Science & Technology Law Journal*, Vol. 4, 188–189; Dion, D. (2013) "I'll Gladly Trade You Two Bits on Tuesday for a Byte Today: Bitcoin, Regulating Fraud in the E-conomy of Hacker-Cash", *Journal of Law, Technology & Policy*, Vol. 2013, 191–192.

1851 Kien-Meng Ly, M. (2014) "Coining Bitcoin's "legal-bits": Examining the regulatory framework for Bitcoin and virtual currencies", *Harvard Journal of Law & Technology*, Vol. 27, 598–599; Tu, K. V., Meredith, M. W. (2015) "Rethinking virtual currency regulation in the Bitcoin age", *Washington Law Review*, Vol. 90, 319.

## 3.2 PAYMENTS

VIRTUAL CURRENCY TRANSFERS – The second legal framework analyzed here concerns electronic fund transfers. At the federal level, the matter of electronic fund transfers is mainly regulated through the 1978 Electronic Fund Transfer Act. At the state level, this matter is part of the Uniform Commercial Code, which has been widely adopted by all US states, Washington, D.C. and US territories. The main difference between the federal and state level regulation is that the Uniform Commercial Code goes much further in providing for a "*comprehensive scheme governing rights and obligations in connection with carrying out payment transactions*".[1852] Such consumer protection measures under the Uniform Commercial Code are comparable to the EU's payment services framework.

### *3.2.1 Electronic Fund Transfer Act 1978*

ACT AND REGULATIONS – The Electronic Fund Transfer Act was adopted on 10 November 1978 as Title XX of the Financial Institutions Regulatory and Interest Rate Institutions Control Act of 1978.[1853] The legislator found that "*due to the unique characteristics of such systems, the application of existing consumer protection legislation is unclear, leaving the rights and liabilities of consumers, financial institutions, and intermediaries in electronic fund transfers undefined*"[1854] and that therefore a basic framework had to be provided "*establishing the rights, liabilities, and responsibilities of participants in electronic fund and remittance transfer systems*".[1855] Further regulations were later adopted by the Federal Reserve, better known as Regulation E.[1856]

ELECTRONIC FUND TRANSFER – Electronic fund transfers are defined as "*any transfer of funds, other than a transaction originated by check, draft, or similar paper instrument, which is initiated through an electronic terminal, telephonic instrument, or computer or magnetic tape so as to order, instruct, or authorize a financial institution to debit or credit an account*".[1857] The Electronic Fund Transfer Act provides a number of examples of what is included under its scope, namely point-of-sale transfers, automated teller machine transactions, direct deposits or withdrawals of funds, and transfers initiated by telephone. The act

---

1852 Geva, B. (2009) "The harmonization of payment services law in Europe and uniform and federal funds transfer legislation in the USA: which is a better model for reform?", *Euredia*, 2009/4, 706.

1853 *Pub. L.* 95-630. Codified under 15 U.S.C. §1693.

1854 15 U.S.C. §1693(a).

1855 15 U.S.C. §1693(b).

1856 12 C.F.R. Part 205.

1857 15 U.S.C. §1693a(7).

also lists a number of exclusions.[1858] The definition of electronic fund transfer in Regulation E closely follows this definition, but provides more guidance.[1859]

Financial institution – For the purposes of the Electronic Fund Transfer Act, a financial institution should be understood as "*a State or National bank, a State or Federal savings and loan association, a mutual savings bank, a State or Federal credit union, or any other person who, directly or indirectly, holds an account belonging to a consumer*".[1860] Regulation E adds services providers issuing access devices and agreeing with a consumer to provide electronic fund transfer services.[1861] An account, as mentioned here, should be interpreted as being a personal, family, or household "*demand deposit (checking), savings, or other consumer asset account (other than an occasional or incidental credit balance in a credit plan)*", or a payroll card account.[1862] However, such an account must be held by a financial institution, thus leading to the somewhat circular reasoning that an entity is a financial institution when it holds an account, but said account can only be held if the entity is a financial institution.[1863]

Prepaid rules – Applicability – Other, closely related provisions of the Electronic Fund Transfer Act affect prepaid instruments. Under these provisions, a general-use prepaid card is defined as "*a card, code, or other device that is: (i) Issued on a prepaid basis primarily for personal, family, or household purposes to a consumer in a specified amount, whether or not that amount may be increased or reloaded, in exchange for payment; and (ii) Redeemable upon presentation at multiple, unaffiliated merchants for goods or services, or usable at automated teller machines.*"[1864] Given the last element of that definition, only more widely accepted bidirectional virtual currencies could possibly be caught

1858 Namely: "*(A) any check guarantee or authorization service which does not directly result in a debit or credit to a consumer's account; (B) any transfer of funds, other than those processed by automated clearinghouse, made by a financial institution on behalf of a consumer by means of a service that transfers funds held at either Federal Reserve banks or other depository institutions and which is not designed primarily to transfer funds on behalf of a consumer; (C) any transaction the primary purpose of which is the purchase or sale of securities or commodities through a broker-dealer registered with or regulated by the Securities and Exchange Commission; (D) any automatic transfer from a savings account to a demand deposit account pursuant to an agreement between a consumer and a financial institution for the purpose of covering an overdraft or maintaining an agreed upon minimum balance in the consumer's demand deposit account; or (E) any transfer of funds which is initiated by a telephone conversation between a consumer and an officer or employee of a financial institution which is not pursuant to a prearranged plan and under which periodic or recurring transfers are not contemplated*".

1859 12 C.F.R. §205.3.

1860 15 U.S.C. §1693a(9).

1861 12 C.F.R. §205.2(i).

1862 12 C.F.R. §205.2(b).

1863 Pacifici, E. (2015) "Making PayPal pay: Regulation E and its application to alternative payment services", *Duke Law & Technology Review*, Vol. 13, 105.

1864 12 C.F.R. §1005.20(a)(3).

under the scope of prepaid instruments under the Electronic Fund Transfer Act. It has been argued in literature that Bitcoin credentials used to purchase units of bitcoin could fall under the scope of such prepaid instruments.[1865] However, that reasoning assumes that virtual currencies can indeed constitute prepaid value for the purposes of the Electronic Fund Transfer Act.[1866] Moreover, it assumes that virtual currencies can only be obtained through purchase.[1867]

PREPAID RULES – EXPANSION – While traditionally prepaid products fell outside of the scope of the Electronic Fund Transfer Act or Regulation E, they were included here by the Credit Card Accountability Responsibility and Disclosure (CARD) Act of 2009.[1868] Moreover, the Consumer Financial Protection Bureau (CFPB) in 2012 expressed its intention to expand the framework set by the Electronic Fund Transfer Act.[1869] Initially, such an expansion would have included bringing virtual currencies under the scope of the Electronic Fund Transfer Act. However, the final text of the expansion does not explicitly put virtual currencies under the scope of prepaid products, thus leaving the application of the Electronic Fund Transfer Act to virtual currencies up for further debate.[1870]

### *3.2.2 Uniform Commercial Code*

UCC – The Uniform Law Commission and the American Law Institute adopted the first version of the Uniform Commercial Code (UCC) in 1952. The goal of such a uniform law was to harmonize state laws in the field of commercial transactions, in order to facilitate transactions across state borders. Since then, the UCC has been – in one form or the other – implemented in all US states, Washington, D.C., US territories, as well as by most Native American tribes.[1871] Over time, several amendments and additions to the UCC have passed. One of such additions is article 4A, added in 1989, covering funds transfers. This article 4A – in the form implemented by the states – governs funds transfer transactions at the state level. Note that the UCC explicitly does not apply to

---

1865 The Clearing House, Independent Community Bankers of America (2014) "Virtual currency: risks and regulation", *theclearinghouse.org*, 12–13.

1866 Though the rules do not mention anything specific on this themselves, FinCEN interprets prepaid access as being denominated in real currency, and not in virtual currencies. FinCEN (2013) "Guidance Document – Application of FinCEN's Regulations to Persons Administering, Exchanging, or Using Virtual Currencies", *FIN-2013-G001*, 5.

1867 For instance, when a virtual currency is given or mined, there is no prior consideration, thus negating the prepaid element.

1868 *Pub. L.* 111–24.

1869 The Clearing House, Independent Community Bankers of America (2014) "Virtual currency: risks and regulation", *theclearinghouse.org*, 13.

1870 Bureau of Consumer Financial Protection (2016) "Prepaid Accounts under the Electronic Fund Transfer Act (Regulation E) and the Truth In Lending Act (Regulation Z)", *4810-AM-P*, 164.

1871 For a complete overview with references to relevant state laws, see: *en.wikipedia.org/wiki/Uniform_Commercial_Code_adoption*.

funds transfer transactions governed at the federal level by the Electronic Fund Transfer Act.[1872]

Funds transfers – For the purposes of the UCC, funds transfers are defined as a "*series of transactions, beginning with the originator's payment order, made for the purpose of making payment to the beneficiary of the order*", including payment orders "*issued by the originator's bank or an intermediary bank intended to carry out the originator's payment order*".[1873] Such a funds transfer requires acceptance of the payment order by the beneficiary's bank in order to complete the transaction. It encompasses both credit and debit transactions, but does not apply to transactions governed by the Electronic Fund Transfer Act.[1874]

Payment order – A payment order is defined as "*an instruction of a sender to a receiving bank, transmitted orally, electronically, or in writing, to pay, or to cause another bank to pay, a fixed or determinable amount of money to a beneficiary*".[1875] Such an instruction may not state any other condition to the payment other than its time.[1876] The sender of the instruction will have to reimburse the receiving bank, for instance by debiting his account.[1877] The sender has to transmit the instruction directly to "*the receiving bank or to an agent, funds-transfer system, or communication system for transmittal to the receiving bank*".[1878]

Money and contracts – As seen in the definitions of the UCC, a payment order requires an instruction to pay money. While article 4A does not explicitly state what is to be understood as 'money' here, the general definitions of article 1 apply.[1879] In article 1, money is defined as "*a medium of exchange currently authorized or adopted by a domestic or foreign government*".[1880] Such would limit the notion of 'money' to legal tender, thus in principle excluding virtual currencies.[1881] However, virtual currency transactions can still be valid under

1872 UCC §4A-108. Although it could apply to a remittance transfer as defined in the Electronic Fund Transfer Act, unless such transfer would constitute an electronic fund transfer. In case of inconsistencies, federal law takes precedence.

1873 UCC §4A-104(a).

1874 Kiss, J. (2009) "International Payments Law Reform: Introduction of Global Code of Payments", *Banking and Finance Law Review*, Vol. 25, 408–410; Hughes, S. J., Middlebrook, S. T. (2015) "Advancing a Framework for Regulating Cryptocurrency Payments Intermediaries", *Yale Journal on Regulation*, Vol. 32, 551.

1875 UCC §4A-103(a)(1). If more than one payments are ordered, the instruction can be considered as a separate payment order for each of those payments. UCC §4A-103(b). The order is issued when sent to the receiving bank. UCC §4A-103(c).

1876 UCC §4A-103(a)(1)(i).

1877 UCC §4A-103(a)(1)(ii).

1878 UCC §4A-103(a)(1)(iii).

1879 UCC §4A-105(d).

1880 UCC §1–201(b)(24).

1881 Geva, B. (2016) "Disintermediating electronic payments: digital cash and virtual currencies", *Journal of International Banking Law and Regulation*, Vol. 31, 665.

the UCC. If virtual currencies were considered as equal to foreign currency, the UCC provides that the medium of payment can be determined by the contract itself.[1882] Even if virtual currencies were considered as goods, the UCC would still cover its transactions as barter.[1883]

BANKS – However, in order for article 4A to apply, it is clear that there must be involvement of a bank in such a transaction. A bank is for the purposes of article 4A defined as "*a person engaged in the business of banking and includes a savings bank, savings and loan association, credit union, and trust company*".[1884] This definition means that the scope of article 4A remains strictly limited to transactions going through the traditional banking system.[1885]

### *3.2.3 Application to virtual currencies*

ELECTRONIC FUND TRANSFER – The precise scope of application of the Electronic Fund Transfer Act with regard to new means of payment has always been the object of dispute. For instance, despite several cases on precisely the matter of scope, there is still no definitive interpretation that finds whether PayPal is subjected to the Electronic Fund Transfer Act's legal framework.[1886] The main question, with regard to virtual currencies, is whether a virtual currency account could be considered as a consumer asset account – given the seeming inapplicability of the other types of account mentioned – though neither the Electronic Fund Transfer Act nor Regulation E define the notion of consumer asset account. Alternatively, it can be questioned whether there is an access device, meaning "*card, code, or other means of access to a consumer's account, or any combination thereof*" used to provide electronic fund transfers.[1887] Here, it has been argued in literature that the

---

1882 UCC §3-107 ("*Unless the instrument otherwise provides, an instrument that states the amount payable in foreign money may be paid in the foreign money or in an equivalent amount in dollars calculated by using the current bank-offered spot rate at the place of payment for the purchase of dollars on the day on which the instrument is paid.*"); Kaplanov, N. M. (2012) "Nerdy Money: Bitcoin, the Private Digital Currency, and the Case Against its Regulation", *Loyola Consumer Law Review*, Vol. 25, 163–164.

1883 UCC §2-304(1) ("*The price can be made payable in money or otherwise.*"); Kien-Meng Ly, M. (2014) "Coining Bitcoin's "legal-bits": Examining the regulatory framework for Bitcoin and virtual currencies", *Harvard Journal of Law & Technology*, Vol. 27, 600; Kaplanov, N. M. (2012) "Nerdy Money: Bitcoin, the Private Digital Currency, and the Case Against its Regulation", *Loyola Consumer Law Review*, Vol. 25, 164.

1884 UCC §4-105(a)(2).

1885 Bollen, R. (2013) "The Legal Status of Online Currencies – Are Bitcoins the Future?", *ssrn.com/abstract=2736021*, 23.

1886 Pacifici, E. (2015) "Making PayPal pay: Regulation E and its application to alternative payment services", *Duke Law & Technology Review*, Vol. 13, 103–104. In all of the cases mentioned, PayPal obtained a settlement without admitting to be subjected to these rules. However, PayPal does offer protection to its customers that even exceeds the requirements of the electronic fund transfers legal framework.

1887 12 C.F.R. §205.2(a).

provision of cryptographic keys in a cryptocurrency scheme could be argued to constitute such an access device.[1888] However, even in such a scenario there would still need to be a third party – the financial institution – providing electronic fund transfers for a consumer. Since most virtual currency transactions can be initiated directly by the user – without the need for such an intermediary – it seems that there are only limited scenarios imaginable where virtual currency service providers fall under the scope of the Electronic Fund Transfer Act.[1889] Only certain intermediaries, particularly operating in the field of cryptocurrencies, could then be said to fall under the scope of the electronic fund transfer legal framework.[1890]

UCC – As noted, certain provisions of the UCC could apply to virtual currency transactions. If, for instance, a contract for the sale of goods or services were concluded, and if such a contract demanded payment in virtual currencies, that contract could be covered by the general contract provisions of the UCC – or rather: the states' implementation thereof. However, the application of article 4A – concerning funds transfers – appears less likely. Article 4A mainly requires the involvement of a bank, to which a payment order is made. Since, at least at the present moment, no traditional bank conducts payments in virtual currencies, article 4A cannot be applied to virtual currency transactions, even if virtual currencies could constitute the money that is the subject of a payment order. It has, however, been suggested by authors that article 4A could be amended or that it could provide the basis for a new framework regulating consumer protection aspects of virtual currency payments.[1891]

## 3.3 ANTI-MONEY LAUNDERING

Anti-money laundering – As chapter V did for EU law, this subsection will analyze whether the legal framework holding anti-money laundering rules in the

1888 Kaplanov, N. M. (2012) "Nerdy Money: Bitcoin, the Private Digital Currency, and the Case Against its Regulation", *Loyola Consumer Law Review*, Vol. 25, 157–158.

1889 *Id.*; Congressional Research Service (2014) "Bitcoin: Questions, Answers, and Analysis of Legal Issues", *crs.gov*, 19; Kien-Meng Ly, M. (2014) "Coining Bitcoin's "legal-bits": Examining the regulatory framework for Bitcoin and virtual currencies", *Harvard Journal of Law & Technology*, Vol. 27, 599.

1890 Marshall, R. (2015) "Bitcoin: Where Two Worlds Collide", *Bond Law Review*, Vol. 27, 108–109. However, also here caution needs to be paid whether or not the user initiated the transfer. Such may exempt most wallet providers, as they do not initiate transactions themselves. Brito, J., Castillo, A. (2013) *Bitcoin: A Primer for Policymakers*, Arlington: George Mason University Mercatus Center, 32–33. Tunstall notes that "*currently, consumer protections contained in financial regulations such as the Electronic Funds Transfer Act and its implementing regulation, Regulation E, do not apply to virtual currencies*". US Senate Banking Committee (2013) "The Present and Future Impact of Virtual Currency – Testimony of Mercedes Kelley Tunstall", *banking.senate.gov*, 6.

1891 Hughes, S. J., Middlebrook, S. T. (2015) "Advancing a Framework for Regulating Cryptocurrency Payments Intermediaries", *Yale Journal on Regulation*, Vol. 32, 549–556.

US can apply to virtual currencies. At the federal level, this section discusses two main acts. First, there is the 1970 Bank Secrecy Act, which imposes the rule that certain transactions must be reported to the US Department of the Treasury. As a result, the Bank Secrecy Act mainly aims to *"prevent dirty money from entering the U.S. financial system in the first place"*.[1892] Second, the 1986 Money Laundering Control Act provides for the criminalization and sanctioning of money laundering.[1893] Therefore, the Money Laundering Control Act is more punitive in nature, whereas the Bank Secrecy Act serves more as a preventive measure.

### *3.3.1 Bank Secrecy Act 1970*

FEDERAL LAW – The first legal instrument regarding anti-money laundering rules at the US federal level is the Bank Secrecy Act – also referred to as the Currency and Foreign Transactions Reporting Act, though the latter only constitutes Title II of the broader act – adopted on 26 October 1970.[1894] Over time, the act has been amended several times.[1895] In 1990 – and later confirmed in 2002 – the US Department of the Treasury delegated its powers under the act to an internal bureau, the Financial Crimes Enforcement Network (FinCEN).[1896] Such a delegation also allows FinCEN to adopt the regulations necessary to perform its duties, codified under Title 31 of the Code of Federal Regulations. The Money Laundering Suppression Act of 1994, Title IV of the Riegle Community Development and Regulatory Improvement Act of 1994, added a number of relevant sections to Title 31 of the US Code.

MONEY TRANSMITTING BUSINESS AND CASH RECEIPT – The US Code determines that anyone who owns or controls a money transmitting business must register with the Secretary of the Treasury – as delegated to FinCEN.[1897] Also, whoever is engaged in trade or business and receives USD 10.000 in coins or currency in one transaction or several related transactions, must report such an event to FinCEN.[1898] These money transmitting businesses must maintain anti-money laundering programs, which includes know-your-customer obligations[1899], and are bound to reporting and recordkeeping duties.[1900]

---

1892 Bryans, D. (2014) "Bitcoin and Money Laundering: Mining for an Effective Solution", *Indiana Law Journal*, Vol. 89, 455–456; Brito, J., Castillo, A. (2013) *Bitcoin: A Primer for Policymakers*, Arlington: George Mason University Mercatus Center, 43.

1893 Grinberg, R. (2012) "Bitcoin: An Innovative Alternative Digital Currency", *Hastings Science & Technology Law Journal*, Vol. 4, 205.

1894 *Pub. L.* 91–508.

1895 Some important changes were implemented through the infamous USA PATRIOT Act, *Pub. L.* 107–56.

1896 Treasury Order 105–08; Treasury Order 180–01.

1897 31 U.S.C. §5330(a)(1).

1898 31 U.S.C. §5331(a).

1899 31 C.F.R. §1022.210.

1900 31 C.F.R. §1022 subparts C and D.

PROHIBITION OF UNREGISTERED AND UNLICENSED BUSINESS – Whoever knowingly[1901] operates a money transmitting business affecting interstate or foreign commerce without complying with the federal registration requirement set out in the previous paragraph, or with state laws requiring a license for money transmitting businesses, can be fined or imprisoned.[1902] The applicability of the federal registration requirement will be discussed in the following paragraphs, while state licensing laws will be the focus of section 3.3.3. While here it can already be stated that most states do require money transmitter businesses to be licensed, the main problem in applying the licensing provision may be the requirement of knowing to be operating a money transmitting business. However, here case law provides that no exemption should be given for willful blindness.[1903] If, therefore, the service provider should have known that it was acting as a money transmitting business, it can be held to be caught under the scope of the licensing provision.

FROM MONEY TRANSMITTING BUSINESS... – The US Code only provides that money transmitting businesses are "*any business other than the United States Postal Service which (A) provides check cashing, currency exchange, or money transmitting or remittance services, or issues or redeems money orders, travelers' checks, and other similar instruments or any other person who engages as a business in the transmission of funds, including any person who engages as a business in an informal money transfer system or any network of people who engage as a business in facilitating the transfer of money domestically or internationally outside of the conventional financial institutions system; (B) is required to file reports under section 5313; and (C) is not a depository institution (as defined in section 5313(g))*".[1904]

... TO MONEY SERVICES BUSINESS – FinCEN has made use of its delegated powers to further define what is to be understood as a 'money transmitting business'. First of all, FinCEN found the term 'money transmitting business' to be potentially confusing, and proposed a change to the term 'money services business'.[1905] The following subparagraphs will discuss the constituting elements of the 'money services business' definition.

---

1901 Knowledge is required of the fact that a money transmitting business is being operated and that it is unlicensed. Knowledge of federal or state licensing laws is not required. United States *v.* Elfgeeh, 515 F.3d 100, at 133 (2d Cir. 2008).

1902 18 U.S.C. §1960; Bryans, D. (2014) "Bitcoin and Money Laundering: Mining for an Effective Solution", *Indiana Law Journal*, Vol. 89, 461.

1903 United States *v.* Schnabel, 939 F.2d 197, at 203 (4th Cir. 1991); Bryans, D. (2014) "Bitcoin and Money Laundering: Mining for an Effective Solution", *Indiana Law Journal*, Vol. 89, 463; Dion, D. (2013) "I'll Gladly Trade You Two Bits on Tuesday for a Byte Today: Bitcoin, Regulating Fraud in the E-conomy of Hacker-Cash", *Journal of Law, Technology & Policy*, Vol. 2013, 178.

1904 31 U.S.C. §5330(d)(1).

1905 64 F.R. 45438.

A *money services business* must do business in one of the seven capacities listed.[1906] Whether or not such business is conducted on a regular basis or as an organized or licensed business concern does not matter. The business must be conducted wholly or in substantial part within the United States, including but not limited to maintenance of any agent, agency, branch, or office within the United States. Banks – domestic or foreign – persons already registered with the SEC, the CFTC or a similar foreign financial agency, and natural persons who infrequently and not for gain or profit conduct such business activities are exempt.[1907] Each of the seven capacities in which these money services businesses act contains thresholds, designed to exempt "*those businesses, such as grocery stores and hotels, that cash checks or exchange currency as an accommodation to customers who are otherwise purchasing goods, services, or lodging from the businesses involved.*"[1908]

The first capacity listed concerns *dealers in foreign exchange*.[1909] These businesses accept currency or other instruments in exchange for currency or other monetary instruments. The threshold here is USD 1.000 per person per day in one or more transactions, whether or not for same-day delivery.

The second capacity concerns *check cashers*.[1910] These businesses accept checks or other monetary instruments in return for currency or other monetary instruments. Also here, a threshold of USD 1.000 per person per day for one or more transactions applies. There are, however, also a number of exceptions: (A) selling prepaid access in exchange for checks; (B) solely accepting monetary instruments as payment for goods or services other than check cashing services; (C) engaging in check cashing for the customer buying goods or services who made the check; (D) redeeming own checks; or (E) only holding a customer's check as collateral for repayment by the customer of a loan.

Third, there are the *issuers or sellers of traveler's checks or money orders*.[1911] These businesses either issue or sell traveler's checks or money orders for an amount greater than USD 1.000 per person per day in one or more transactions.

Fourth, the rules list *providers of prepaid access*.[1912] These businesses participate in a prepaid program and agree to serve as principal conduits for access to information from fellow program participants. A prepaid program is an arrangement under

---

1906 31 C.F.R. §1010.100(ff); Bryans, D. (2014) "Bitcoin and Money Laundering: Mining for an Effective Solution", *Indiana Law Journal*, Vol. 89, 456–457.

1907 31 C.F.R. §1010.100(ff)(8).

1908 64 F.R. 45446.

1909 31 C.F.R. §1010.100(ff)(1).

1910 31 C.F.R. §1010.100(ff)(2).

1911 31 C.F.R. §1010.100(ff)(3).

1912 31 C.F.R. §1010.100(ff)(4).

which people acting together provide prepaid access. A number of exclusions apply here: (A) when closed loop prepaid access to funds below USD 2.000 per day are provided; (B) when prepaid access is provided solely to funds provided by "*a Federal, State, local, Territory and Insular Possession, or Tribal government agency*"; (C) when prepaid access is provided only to funds from "*pre-tax flexible spending arrangements for health care and dependent care expenses, or from Health Reimbursement Arrangements for health care expenses*"; or (D) when prepaid access is provided only to employment benefits, incentives, wages or salaries; or to funds not exceeding USD 1.000 maximum value and from which no more than USD 1.000 can be initially or subsequently loaded, used, or withdrawn per day through a device or vehicle. In the latter case, it is not permitted to transmit funds or value internationally; to transfer between or among users of prepaid access within a prepaid program; or to load additional funds or the value of funds from non-depository sources. Each prepaid access program must determine a single provider of prepaid access. When no such a provider is registered, it should be the participant with principal oversight and control over the prepaid program. Some indications are provided as to what constitutes "*principal oversight and control*": (A) organizing the prepaid program; (B) setting the terms and conditions of the prepaid program; (C) determining the other businesses that will participate in the prepaid program; (D) controlling or directing the appropriate party to initiate, freeze, or terminate prepaid access; and (E) engaging in activity that demonstrates oversight and control of the prepaid program.

The fifth capacity listed here concerns *money transmitters*.[1913] On the one hand, these businesses are persons providing money transmission services. Such services include the acceptance of currency, funds, or other value substituting for currency from one person and the transmission thereof to another location or person by any means.[1914] On the other hand, these businesses are any persons engaged in the transfer of funds. A number of exclusions are provided to: (A) those that provide delivery, communication, or network access services used by money transmitters to support money transmission services; (B) those that act as payment processors and are authorized by the creditor or seller to facilitate the purchase of goods or services through clearance and settlement systems; (C) those that operate clearance and settlement systems or otherwise act as intermediaries between regulated institutions; (D) those that primarily provide physical transport of currency or other monetary value substituting for currency from one person to another location or to an account belonging to the same person at a financial institution and having no more than a custodial interest in the transport; (E) those that

1913 31 C.F.R. §1010.100(ff)(5).

1914 "Any means" is meant to be interpreted in the broadest sense. A number of examples are provided: the use of "*a financial agency or institution; a Federal Reserve Bank or other facility of one or more Federal Reserve Banks, the Board of Governors of the Federal Reserve System, or both; an electronic funds transfer network; or an informal value transfer system*".

provide prepaid access; or (F) those that accept and transmit funds only integral to the sale of goods or the provision of services, other than money transmission services, by whom is accepting and transmitting the funds. The scope of the money transmitter notion was notably expanded under the USA PATRIOT Act.[1915]

The sixth capacity concerns the *US Postal Service*.[1916] Their services, excluding the sale of postage or philatelic products, can be covered by the money services business provision. Prior regulation considered the US Postal Service as a financial institution only with regard to its sale of money orders. FinCEN then changed this to treating the Postal Service as a financial institution with respect to its provision of any money services products.[1917]

The seventh and final capacity listed here concerns *sellers of prepaid access*.[1918] These businesses receive funds in exchange for initial or subsequent loading of prepaid access. Important is that such prepaid access should either be offered under a prepaid program that can be used to verify customers' identities; or involve the sale of prepaid access for more than USD 10.000 per person per day, and where the seller has not implemented policies and procedures reasonably adapted to prevent such a sale. The difference with the fourth capacity is that a provider of prepaid access exercises oversight and control over a prepaid scheme, whereas a seller only sells prepaid access to its clients, and thus does not necessarily have such an oversight and control over the prepaid scheme.

FinCEN guidance[1919] – In 2013, FinCEN issued an interpretative guidance regarding the applicability of the money services business provisions of the Bank Secrecy Act to virtual currencies, virtual currency users and virtual currency service providers. Generally, FinCEN considers virtual currencies as media of exchange that can operate like currencies, but that do not possess the attributes of real currencies[1920], such as being legal tender.[1921] Despite virtual currencies

---

1915 Bryans, D. (2014) "Bitcoin and Money Laundering: Mining for an Effective Solution", *Indiana Law Journal*, Vol. 89, 457; Claxton. N. (2011) "Progress, Privacy, and Preemption: A study of the regulatory history of stored-value cards in the United States and the European Union", *Arizona Journal of International & Comparative Law*, Vol. 28, 514–515.

1916 31 C.F.R. §1010.100(ff)(6).

1917 64 F.R. 45447.

1918 31 C.F.R. §1010.100(ff)(7).

1919 The following paragraphs were first developed at: Valcke, P., Vandezande, N., Van de Velde, N. (2015) "The Evolution of Third Party Payment Providers and Cryptocurrencies Under the EU's Upcoming PSD2 and AMLD4", *SWIFT Institute Working Paper No. 2015-001*, 61–62.

1920 According to 31 C.F.R. §1010.100(m), currencies are "*coin and paper money of the United States or of any other country that is designated as legal tender and that circulates and is customarily used and accepted as a medium of exchange in the country of issuance*". Bryans, D. (2014) "Bitcoin and Money Laundering: Mining for an Effective Solution", *Indiana Law Journal*, Vol. 89, 457.

1921 FinCEN (2013) "Guidance Document – Application of FinCEN's Regulations to Persons Administering, Exchanging, or Using Virtual Currencies", *FIN-2013-G001*, 1.

not being considered real currencies, FinCEN does consider virtual currency exchangers – those that exchange virtual currency for real currency, funds, or other virtual currency – and administrators – those that issue or redeem virtual currency[1922] – as money services businesses within the meaning of the Bank Secrecy Act when they (1) accept and transmit convertible virtual currencies; or (2) buy or sell convertible virtual currencies for any reason.[1923] More precisely, such entities act as money transmitters.[1924] Users who only obtain convertible virtual currency and use it to purchase real or virtual goods or services are not considered to conduct money services businesses.[1925] However, when users do sell their virtual currencies for money, they could theoretically become money transmitters.[1926] Theoretically, because reference must be made to one of the aforementioned exemptions applicable here, namely when the activity is conducted on an "*infrequent basis and not for gain or profit*". While that exemption does provide some leeway for the occasional transaction that could be conducted, for instance between friends, it still does not fully settle the threshold between applicability and non-applicability of the money services business provisions.[1927] In the meantime, FinCEN did adopt a number of rulings on the

---

1922 This part only seems to apply to centralized virtual currencies, as decentralized virtual currencies – such as cryptocurrencies – do not have a central issuer. Van Valkenburgh, P. (2017) "The Bank Secrecy Act, Cryptocurrencies, and New Tokens: What is Known and What Remains Ambiguous", *Coin Center Report*, 7–8.

1923 *Ibid.*, 3.

1924 *Id.* The reasoning used here is that the "*definition of a money transmitter does not differentiate between real currencies and convertible virtual currencies*". Bryans, D. (2014) "Bitcoin and Money Laundering: Mining for an Effective Solution", *Indiana Law Journal*, Vol. 89, 457; Hughes, S. J., Middlebrook, S. T. (2015) "Advancing a Framework for Regulating Cryptocurrency Payments Intermediaries", *Yale Journal on Regulation*, Vol. 32, 507; Middlebrook, S. T., Hughes, S. J. (2014) "Regulating Cryptocurrencies in the United States: Current Issues and Future Directions", *William Mitchell Law Review*, Vol. 40, 829–830; Marshall, R. (2015) "Bitcoin: Where Two Worlds Collide", *Bond Law Review*, Vol. 27, 101; Brito, J., Castillo, A. (2013) *Bitcoin: A Primer for Policymakers*, Arlington: George Mason University Mercatus Center, 45; Kien-Meng Ly, M. (2014) "Coining Bitcoin's "legal-bits": Examining the regulatory framework for Bitcoin and virtual currencies", *Harvard Journal of Law & Technology*, Vol. 27, 601; Farmer, P. H. Jr. (2014) "Speculative Tech: The Bitcoin Legal Quagmire & the Need for Legal Innovation", *Journal of Business & Technology Law*, Vol. 9, 96.

1925 As their activities do not fall under the scope of the definition of "money transmission services". Bryans, D. (2014) "Bitcoin and Money Laundering: Mining for an Effective Solution", *Indiana Law Journal*, Vol. 89, 458; Comizio, V. G. (2016) "Virtual Currencies: Growing Regulatory Framework and Challenges in the Emerging Fintech Ecosystem", *Fried Frank*, 7; Middlebrook, S. T., Hughes, S. J. (2014) "Regulating Cryptocurrencies in the United States: Current Issues and Future Directions", *William Mitchell Law Review*, Vol. 40, 830; Marshall, R. (2015) "Bitcoin: Where Two Worlds Collide", *Bond Law Review*, Vol. 27, 101; Pflaum, I., Hateley, E. (2014) "A bit of a problem: National and extraterritorial regulation of virtual currency in the age of financial disintermediation", *Georgetown Journal of International Law*, Vol. 45, 1197.

1926 Bryans, D. (2014) "Bitcoin and Money Laundering: Mining for an Effective Solution", *Indiana Law Journal*, Vol. 89, 458–459.

1927 *Id.* Bryans provides the example of a person selling a large amount of virtual currencies for an expensive good, such as a car, which would fall outside of the scope of regulation since it is an exchange for goods and not for money. When the same person sells a small amount of virtual

matter, which further demarcate the scope of application, and which clarify that the occasional exchange of virtual currency for real currency for personal purposes does not automatically make a user a money transmitter.[1928]

Reasoning – This classification of virtual currency service providers as being subject to regulation under the Bank Secrecy Act's framework was made possible due to FinCEN's earlier efforts, in 2011, to update the aforementioned definitions in order to provide the "*needed flexibility to accommodate innovation in the payment systems space under our preexisting regulatory framework*".[1929] The core element of importance to virtual currencies is that money transmission can include the transmission of "*other value that substitutes for currency*", rather than limiting it to the transmission of legal tender.[1930] Moreover, FinCEN has explicated that virtual currency exchangers and administrators cannot be considered as providers or sellers of prepaid access, given that FinCEN limits prepaid access to real currencies.[1931] Likewise, neither are virtual currency exchangers and administrators dealers in foreign exchange, given that virtual currencies are not real currencies according to FinCEN's interpretation of the Bank Secrecy Act.[1932] The result of FinCEN's guidance is that virtual currency exchangers and administrators must register as money services businesses, and adhere to recordkeeping and anti-money laundering control measures.[1933]

---

currencies for some change, he could face regulation because there is an exchange for money. However, Bryans neglects to take into account the exemption mentioned here, for which the one-time and not-for-profit transaction he describes would certainly qualify. See also: Van Valkenburgh, P. (2017) "The Bank Secrecy Act, Cryptocurrencies, and New Tokens: What is Known and What Remains Ambiguous", *Coin Center Report*, 7.

1928 For instance, it was ruled that a virtual currency trading platform is covered by the scope of money services business (FIN-2014-R011), yet not a rental system for cryptocurrency mining hardware (FIN-2014-R007). Also cryptocurrency users that perform mining activities for private use are not considered a money services business, nor does their occasional conversion of cryptocurrency into real currency make them a money transmitter (FIN-2014-R001). Moreover, a company's purchasing and selling of convertible virtual currency as an investment exclusively for the company's benefit is not acting as a money transmitter (FIN-2014-R002). See also: Hughes, S. J., Middlebrook, S. T. (2015) "Advancing a Framework for Regulating Cryptocurrency Payments Intermediaries", *Yale Journal on Regulation*, Vol. 32, 509–510; Brito, J., Castillo, A. (2013) *Bitcoin: A Primer for Policymakers*, Arlington: George Mason University Mercatus Center, 45–46; Van Valkenburgh, P. (2017) "The Bank Secrecy Act, Cryptocurrencies, and New Tokens: What is Known and What Remains Ambiguous", *Coin Center Report*, 17.

1929 US Senate Committee on Homeland Security and Governmental Affairs (2013) "Beyond Silk Road: Potential Risks, Threats and Promises of Virtual Currencies – Testimony of Jennifer Shasky Calvery", *hsgac.senate.gov*, 8.

1930 31 C.F.R. 1010.100(ff)(5)(i)(A).

1931 FinCEN (2013) "Guidance Document – Application of FinCEN's Regulations to Persons Administering, Exchanging, or Using Virtual Currencies", *FIN-2013-G001*, 5.

1932 *Id;* Comizio, V. G. (2016) "Virtual Currencies: Growing Regulatory Framework and Challenges in the Emerging Fintech Ecosystem", *Fried Frank*, 7–8.

1933 US Senate Committee on Homeland Security and Governmental Affairs (2013) "Beyond Silk Road: Potential Risks, Threats and Promises of Virtual Currencies – Testimony of Jennifer Shasky Calvery", *hsgac.senate.gov*, 9; FinCEN (2013) "Guidance Document – Application of

ENFORCEMENT BY FINCEN – FinCEN has also been active in enforcing the money services business framework with regards to virtual currency service providers. After the release of the guidance document, the US Department of Homeland Security seized accounts belonging to a US-based subsidiary of then-largest bitcoin-exchange Mt.Gox on the basis of that company not being registered as a money services business.[1934] FinCEN also took action against Liberty Reserve, basing its action on provisions added by the USA PATRIOT Act.[1935] In 2015, FinCEN pursued action against Ripple, a payment system and currency exchange supporting various legal tender currencies, virtual currencies, as well as its own native currency XRP. The Ripple system is operated by Ripple Labs, which wholly owns a subsidiary – XRP II – that engages in selling the XRP virtual currency. Thus, under FinCEN's rules, XRP II engages in money transmission, requiring it to register as a money services business. While XRP II did eventually register as a money services business in 2013, it was later found to not have implemented an anti-money laundering program nor having conducted reporting duties. As a result, XRP II was fined USD 700.000.[1936]

### 3.3.2 *Money Laundering Control Act 1986*

TWO SECTIONS – The Money Laundering Control Act was adopted on 27 October 1986.[1937] Its first section prohibits engaging with proceeds from criminal activities, while its second section aims to punish those that spend value over USD 10.000 derived from specified unlawful activities. The main difference between both sections is that the first section requires a certain intent to conceal the criminal activity, whereas such an intent is not required in the second section.

---

FinCEN's Regulations to Persons Administering, Exchanging, or Using Virtual Currencies", *FIN-2013-G001*, 3–5.

1934 Mt.Gox did later receive the necessary license. Buterin, V. (2013) "MtGox Gets FinCEN MSB License", *Bitcoin Magazine*, 29 June 2013.

1935 More in particular, the action was based on section 311, finding Liberty Reserve's transactions of primary money laundering concern. US Department of the Treasury (2013) "Treasury Identifies Virtual Currency Provider Liberty Reserve as a Financial Institution of Primary Money Laundering Concern under USA Patriot Act Section 311", *Press release,* 28 May 2013. One of the people involved in the scheme was given the maximum sentence for conspiring to operate an unlicensed money transmitting business. US Department of Justice (2014) "Chief Technology Officer of Liberty Reserve Sentenced to Five Years in Prison", *Press release 14-1393*, 12 December 2014; Middlebrook, S. T., Hughes, S. J. (2014) "Regulating Cryptocurrencies in the United States: Current Issues and Future Directions", *William Mitchell Law Review*, Vol. 40, 836–838.

1936 FinCEN (2015) "FinCEN Fines Ripple Labs Inc. in First Civil Enforcement Action Against a Virtual Currency Exchanger", *Press release*, 5 May 2015; Comizio, V. G. (2016) "Virtual Currencies: Growing Regulatory Framework and Challenges in the Emerging Fintech Ecosystem", *Fried Frank,* 8–9; Van Valkenburgh, P. (2017) "The Bank Secrecy Act, Cryptocurrencies, and New Tokens: What is Known and What Remains Ambiguous", *Coin Center Report*, 10.

1937 *Pub. L.* 99–570. Its main provisions were codified at 18 U.S.C. §1956 and §1957.

First section – The first section of the Money Laundering Control Act requires knowledge that the property in a financial transaction – or several linked transactions – was derived from criminal activities.[1938] It also requires knowledge that the transaction in question was designed to either "*conceal or disguise the nature, the location, the source, the ownership, or the control of the proceeds of specified unlawful activity*" or "*to avoid a transaction reporting requirement under State or Federal law*".[1939] Furthermore, it requires intent to "*promote the carrying on of specified unlawful activity*" or to violate tax laws.[1940] Once these knowledge criteria are fulfilled, a fine and/or prison sentence can be imposed. Similar requirements apply for transporting such property to or from the US, and for conducting or attempting to conduct such a transaction.[1941] The definitions of the Money Laundering Control Act provide a list of specified unlawful activities, which include *inter alea*: racketeering, narco-trafficking, fraud, criminal enterprises, as well as environmental crimes.[1942]

Second section – The second section of the Money Laundering Control Act requires knowledge that the monetary transaction of a value over USD 10.000 derived from criminal activity.[1943] However, it is not required to know that such an activity constituted specified unlawful activity.[1944] Such a particular lack of knowledge can therefore not be used as a defense.[1945] Also here, a fine and/or prison sentence can be imposed.[1946] For the purposes of section two of the Money Laundering Control Act, specified unlawful activity follows the definition of the first section of that act.[1947] Monetary transaction is defined as "*deposit, withdrawal, transfer, or exchange, in or affecting interstate or foreign commerce, of funds or a monetary instrument* [...] *by, through, or to a financial institution*".[1948]

E-gold – One scheme tried under the Money Laundering Control Act was e-gold. In the case of e-gold, non-physical tokens were issued – thus establishing a virtual currency – denominated in grams of gold held by the scheme operators. The e-gold currency was fully interchangeable and was accepted by a wide

---

1938 18 U.S.C. §1956(a)(1); Bryans, D. (2014) "Bitcoin and Money Laundering: Mining for an Effective Solution", *Indiana Law Journal*, Vol. 89, 459–460.

1939 18 U.S.C. §1956(a)(1)(B).

1940 18 U.S.C. §1956(a)(1)(A).

1941 18 U.S.C. §1956(a)(2) and (3).

1942 18 U.S.C. §1956(c)(7).

1943 18 U.S.C. §1957(a).

1944 18 U.S.C. §1957(c).

1945 Bryans, D. (2014) "Bitcoin and Money Laundering: Mining for an Effective Solution", *Indiana Law Journal*, Vol. 89, 460; United States *v.* Flores, 454 F.3d 149, at 155 (3d Cir. 2006).

1946 18 U.S.C. §1957(b).

1947 18 U.S.C. §1957(f)(3).

1948 18 U.S.C. §1957(f)(1).

range of service providers. For many years, the operators of the e-gold scheme believed not to be caught under the Bank Secrecy Act's scope, which allowed the scheme to operate without anti-money laundering controls such as customer identification.[1949] This regulatory freedom made the scheme – offering relative anonymity – attractive for criminal intent, much like today is the case for cryptocurrencies.[1950] Eventually, the suspicions of the use of e-gold by criminals resulted in criminal proceedings against the e-gold scheme operators. Apart from charges for operating an unregistered money services business, the scheme operators were also alleged to conspire to engage in money laundering.[1951]

### *3.3.3 State regulation*

#### 3.3.3.1 Uniform Money Services Act

UMSA – In 2000, the Uniform Law Commission adopted the Uniform Money Services Act.[1952] Like any uniform act, it proposes law to be implemented by the states, with a view on harmonizing the money services field across states. Thus far, laws based on this uniform act have been adopted in Alaska, Arkansas, Iowa, New Mexico, Puerto Rico, Texas, US Virgin Islands, Vermont, and Washington.

Services – For the purposes of the Uniform Money Services Act, money services include money transmission, check cashing, and currency exchange.[1953] Money transmission is defined as "*selling or issuing payment instruments, stored value*[1954], *or receiving money or monetary value for transmission*".[1955] This definition excludes delivery, online or telecommunications services, as well as network access. Check cashing entails the receipt of compensation for taking payment instruments or stored value – other than traveler's checks – in exchange

1949 Twomey, P. (2013) "Halting a shift in the paradigm: the need for bitcoin regulation", *Trinity College Law Review*, Vol. 16, 80.

1950 US Department of Justice (2008) "Digital Currency Business E-Gold Pleads Guilty to Money Laundering and Illegal Money Transmitting Charges", *Press release* 21 July.

1951 One of the allegations was that the operators of the scheme knew that the funds involved were derived from unlawful activity. Middlebrook, S. T., Hughes, S. J. (2014) "Regulating Cryptocurrencies in the United States: Current Issues and Future Directions", *William Mitchell Law Review*, Vol. 40, 822–828; Grinberg, R. (2012) "Bitcoin: An Innovative Alternative Digital Currency", *Hastings Science & Technology Law Journal*, Vol. 4, 205; Dion, D. (2013) "I'll Gladly Trade You Two Bits on Tuesday for a Byte Today: Bitcoin, Regulating Fraud in the E-conomy of Hacker-Cash", *Journal of Law, Technology & Policy*, Vol. 2013, 179.

1952 Uniform Money Services Act (amended 2004) (hereinafter: UMSA).

1953 UMSA §102(13); Bryans, D. (2014) "Bitcoin and Money Laundering: Mining for an Effective Solution", *Indiana Law Journal*, Vol. 89, 464.

1954 Stored value means "*monetary value that is evidenced by an electronic record*". UMSA §102(21). Note that in order to be considered as monetary value, the stored value would have to be considered as a medium of exchange.

1955 UMSA §102(14).

for money, payment instruments, or stored value.[1956] Currency exchange means the "*receipt of revenues from the exchange of money of one government for money of another government*".[1957]

MONETARY VALUE – While the Uniform Money Services Act equates 'money' to 'legal tender', the act does also provide a broader definition of 'monetary value', which includes any medium of exchange regardless of whether or not it is redeemable in money.[1958] The reference to medium of exchange is meant to connote that the value must be somewhat widely accepted.[1959] Barter and value that is only accepted by a single issuer or in a small geographic region are therefore excluded.[1960] A university payment card only valid on-campus would thus be excluded. According to the commentary on the Uniform Money Services Act, its drafters found inspiration for this geographic exemption in the EU's EMD1. The geographic exemption also extends to virtual currencies, where regulators will have to determine when a form of monetary value has reached sufficient circulation to become a medium of exchange.[1961]

INTERNET PAYMENTS – The 'monetary value' definition of the Uniform Money Services Act was purposely broadened in order to include Internet payments and stored value, since it was clear that such evolutions could not fall under the traditional narrow definition of 'money' used here. More particularly, a number of specific cases are covered.

First, there is *stored value* in itself. This includes stored-value cards, which are the multi-purpose prepaid cards that gave cause to the EU's e-money framework. Server-based products can be caught under this as well.[1962]

Second, there are e-money and Internet payment mechanisms. E-money should be taken to refer to "*money or a money substitute that is transformed into information stored on a computer chip or a personal computer so that it can be transferred over information systems such as the Internet*".[1963] On the one hand, it includes traditional mechanisms such as credit cards and automated clearing houses, where the internet only serves as a means of communication. On the other hand, it includes Internet-based tokens or notational systems that serve as cash substitutes, as well as account-based systems whereby existing debit or credit accounts are used to obtain value that is stored by the e-money issuer to be withdrawn.

---

1956 UMSA §102(4).

1957 UMSA §102(6).

1958 UMSA §102(11) and (12).

1959 UMSA §102 comment 10.

1960 Though states can, of course, provide certain deviations in their implementation of this act.

1961 UMSA §102 comment 10; Bryans, D. (2014) "Bitcoin and Money Laundering: Mining for an Effective Solution", *Indiana Law Journal*, Vol. 89, 464–465.

1962 UMSA Prefatory Note D.1.

1963 UMSA Prefatory Note D.2.

Third, *Internet scrip* denotes value that may be exchanged over the Internet, but which is not redeemable for money.[1964] This includes reward-based programs and gift cards.

Fourth, *Internet funds transfer* allows users to transfer money over the Internet using an e-mail address.[1965]

Fifth, *gold and precious metals transfer and payment* operates in the same way as Internet funds transfer, but having precious metals as underlying value.[1966]

Last, *Internet bill payment services* provide payments to bills following their users' authorization thereto.

### 3.3.3.2 California

MONEY TRANSMISSION ACT – The California Money Transmission Act regulates the money services matter at the state level. It defines money transmission as (1) selling or issuing payment instruments[1967]; (2) selling or issuing stored value[1968]; or (3) receiving money for transmission.[1969, 1970] Monetary value is defined broadly, meaning "*a medium of exchange, whether or not redeemable in money*".[1971] This definition results in a broad field of application, in which almost anyone who takes funds from another party in order to either store them for later use by that party or in order to pay a third party on the second party's behalf, could fall under the scope of the California Money Transmission Act's provisions.[1972] Virtual currency service providers that enter into possession of funds from their users, could thus be caught under the scope of the California Money Transmission Act[1973], and could therefore become bound to the state's

[1964] UMSA Prefatory Note D.3.

[1965] UMSA Prefatory Note D.4.

[1966] UMSA Prefatory Note D.5. This point is a clear reference to the e-gold scheme.

[1967] Defined as "*check, draft, money order, traveler's check, or other instrument for the transmission or payment of money or monetary value, whether or not negotiable. The term does not include a credit card voucher, letter of credit, or any instrument that is redeemable by the issuer for goods or services provided by the issuer or its affiliate.*" Cal. Fin. Code §2003(s).

[1968] Meaning "*monetary value representing a claim against the issuer that is stored on an electronic or digital medium and evidenced by an electronic or digital record, and that is intended and accepted for use as a means of redemption for money or monetary value or payment for goods or services. The term does not include a credit card voucher, letter of credit, or any stored value that is only redeemable by the issuer for goods or services provided by the issuer or its affiliate, except to the extent required by applicable law to be redeemable in cash for its cash value*". Cal. Fin. Code §2003(x).

[1969] This means "*receiving money or monetary value in the United States for transmission within or outside the United States by electronic or other means. The term does not include sale or issuance of payment instruments and stored value*". Cal. Fin. Code §2003(u).

[1970] Cal. Fin. Code §2003(q).

[1971] Cal. Fin. Code §2003(o).

[1972] Bryans, D. (2014) "Bitcoin and Money Laundering: Mining for an Effective Solution", *Indiana Law Journal*, Vol. 89, 467.

[1973] Closed scheme virtual currencies would thus be exempt. Unidirectional schemes could be exempt, insofar the issuer only sells the non-convertible virtual currency for use within its

licensing requirements.[1974] Thus far, the local regulator has at least once tried to enforce that point with regard to virtual currencies.[1975]

#### 3.3.3.3 Virginia

Money order sellers and money transmitters – Similar provisions are found in Virginia. In the Virginia Code, money transmission is defined as "*receiving money or monetary value for transmission by wire, facsimile, electronic means or other means or selling or issuing stored value*".[1976] Monetary value is defined in the same was as in California, stored value is defined as "*monetary value that is evidenced by an electronic record*".[1977] Also in Virginia, a license is required.[1978] Given the similarities between the California Money Transmission Act and the Virginia Code's provision on the matter of money services – and given the broader definition of stored value in Virginia – the same conclusion can be drawn. Also in Virignia, the local regulator has intervened in virtual currency businesses violating the licensing requirement.[1979]

### *3.3.4 Application to virtual currencies*

Bank Secrecy Act – As made clear by the FinCEN guidance, the Bank Secrecy Act can apply to certain virtual currency service providers, such as cryptocurrency exchanges. However, as was the case for EU law, the scope of such an application remains fairly limited. Regular users paying their transactions with merchants in virtual currencies would, for instance, not fall under the scope of the Bank Secrecy Act. Also, since FinCEN only targets exchanges between virtual currencies and real currencies, closed scheme virtual currencies do not fall under the scope of the Bank Secrecy Act since they do not have such an exchange. Similarly, unidirectional scheme virtual currencies are not targeted by FinCEN's guidance. Those service providers that are caught under the scope of the Bank Secrecy Act are bound to federal registration requirements, as well as to anti-money laundering rules.

---

own network. For instance, if a gift card is only redeemable at the issuer, it is exempted. If the issuer pays a third party for redemption, there is money transmission and thus the legal framework applies. See: *dbo.ca.gov/Laws_&_Regs/dfi_orders_files/2015/Stored_Value_Gift_Cards_and_Digital_Goods.pdf.*

1974 Cal. Fin. Code §2030.

1975 Kien-Meng Ly, M. (2014) "Coining Bitcoin's "legal-bits": Examining the regulatory framework for Bitcoin and virtual currencies", *Harvard Journal of Law & Technology*, Vol. 27, 602–603.

1976 Va. Code §6.2-1900.

1977 *Id.*

1978 Va. Code §6.2-1901.

1979 Summers, J. (2013) "FastCash4Bitcoins Suspends Sales", *Bitcoin Magazine*, 3 June; Bryans, D. (2014) "Bitcoin and Money Laundering: Mining for an Effective Solution", *Indiana Law Journal*, Vol. 89, 468–469; Brito, J., Castillo, A. (2013) *Bitcoin: A Primer for Policymakers*, Arlington: George Mason University Mercatus Center, 48.

Money Laundering Control Act – While theoretically the Money Laundering Control Act could be applied to virtual currency transactions, practice may prove more cumbersome. First, it needs to be proven that a specified unlawful activity has occurred, and second, the parties to the transaction need to be identified.[1980] However, given that – following FinCEN's guidance – the Bank Secrecy Act can be applied to certain virtual currency service providers, identification should no longer be a concern – given the resulting applicability of know-your-customer obligations. As a result, it is possible to also apply the Money Laundering Control Act to virtual currency transactions, insofar such transactions are found to constitute money laundering.

Uniform Money Services Act and state laws – The limitations of the monetary value definition of the Uniform Money Services Act – inspired by those found in the EU's e-money framework – certainly exclude closed scheme virtual currencies and likely most unidirectional scheme virtual currencies from the scope of application of this uniform act. Bidirectional virtual currencies, however, can be caught under the scope of the Uniform Money Services Act, insofar as they constitute a circulating medium of exchange, given the broad interpretations of stored value and e-money used in the act.[1981] In terms of services, certain virtual currency service providers, such as exchanges, can then be caught under the scope of money transmitters.[1982] While not many states have thus far adopted laws based on the Uniform Money Services Act, the examples analyzed here did show that certain virtual currency service providers will be caught under local money transmitter laws.[1983] As a result, both federal registration and state licensing requirements can apply to such service providers.

## 3.4 INVESTMENTS

Securities and derivatives – The final field of regulation to be investigated here concerns the regulation of virtual currencies as means of investment. As noted in chapter VI, certain virtual currencies – particularly cryptocurrencies –

---

1980 Bryans, D. (2014) "Bitcoin and Money Laundering: Mining for an Effective Solution", *Indiana Law Journal*, Vol. 89, 460–461.

1981 Thus exempting Second Life Linden dollars.

1982 Bryans, D. (2014) "Bitcoin and Money Laundering: Mining for an Effective Solution", *Indiana Law Journal*, Vol. 89, 466. As noted by Bryans, while 'currency exchange' would seem like a logical fit, its limitation to exchange of legal tender to legal tender essentially excludes virtual currencies, at least for as long as they are not accepted as legal tender.

1983 See also: Kaplanov, N. M. (2012) "Nerdy Money: Bitcoin, the Private Digital Currency, and the Case Against its Regulation", *Loyola Consumer Law Review*, Vol. 25, 155–156; Tu, K. V., Meredith, M. W. (2015) "Rethinking Virtual Currency Regulation in the Bitcoin Age", *Washington Law Review*, Vol. 90, 307–308; Brito, J., Castillo, A. (2013) *Bitcoin: A Primer for Policymakers*, Arlington: George Mason University Mercatus Center, 47.

can serve as means of investment alongside their main goal of serving as means of payment. Moreover, virtual currencies are being developed that primarily, even solely, serve as means of investment. Additionally, derivative instruments that have virtual currencies as underlying assets are increasingly being used in practice. At the US federal level, the relevant legal framework can be divided between securities regulation on the one hand and derivatives regulation on the other hand. State level regulations in the securities and derivatives field are commonly referred to as 'blue sky laws'.

### *3.4.1 Securities regulation*

#### 3.4.1.1 Overview

Legal history – Securities regulation at the US federal level originated in the Great Depression. Initially, the Securities Act of 27 May 1933 regulated the sale or offering of securities using means and instrumentalities of interstate commerce and imposes registration and prospectus duties.[1984] A year later, the Securities Exchange Act of 6 June 1934 regulated the secondary trading of securities and created the Security and Exchange Commission (SEC).[1985] Debt securities were added to the securities framework by the Trust Indenture Act of 3 August 1939.[1986] Investment companies and investment advisers were added in 1940.[1987] Later significant amendments to the securities framework were made by the Sarbanes–Oxley Act of 30 July 2002[1988], which enforced the position of the SEC, and the Dodd–Frank Wall Street Reform and Consumer Protection Act of 21 July 2010, enhancing investor protection and improving the regulation of securities.[1989] Most of those federal laws have been codified in Title 15 of the U.S. Code. Further regulations by the SEC are codified in Title 17, Chapter II of the Code of Federal Regulations. Furthermore, US securities law is a field of law heavily influenced by case law. The 1947 *Howey* case, for instance, provided the framework – refined through later cases – for interpreting the notion of investment contracts.[1990]

---

1984 *Pub. L.* 73–22; Long, J. C., Kaufman, M. J., Wunderlich, J. M. (2017) *Blue Sky Law*, New York City: Thomson Reuters, §1:4.

1985 *Pub. L.* 73–291. A 1938 amendment allowed for the creation of a self-regulatory body. This resulted in the Financial Industry Regulatory Authority (FINRA), regulating member brokerage firms and exchange markets. Another body, the Municipal Securities Rulemaking Board (MSRB), focuses on the municipal securities market. The Securities Investor Protection Act of 1970 (Pub. L. 91–598) created the Securities Investor Protection Corporation (SIPC). Note that this is not a self-regulatory body, but an insurance fund aimed at protecting investors from losses caused by insolvency of a member.

1986 *Pub. L.* 76–253.

1987 Investment Company Act of 22 August 1940 (*Pub. L.* 76–768); Investment Advisers Act of 22 August 1940 (Title II of *Pub. L.* 76–768).

1988 *Pub. L.* 107–204.

1989 Investor Protection and Securities Reform Act of 2010, Title IX of *Pub. L.* 111–203.

1990 Securities and Exchange Commission *v.* W. J. Howey Co., 328 U.S. 293 (1946).

Registration – The main point of the securities framework is to require any transaction in any kind of security on a national securities exchange to be subject to registration.[1991] This means that both the security itself, and the exchange must be registered with the SEC. This also applies to exchange-traded funds (ETF).[1992] Several other requirements are imposed as well – such as a prospectus duty anti-fraud measures – but will not be further discussed here.[1993]

Security – The result of the frequent amendments to the legal framework on securities is that the definition of securities has become fairly convoluted.[1994] Currently, a security is defined as *"any note, stock, treasury stock, security future, security-based swap, bond, debenture, evidence of indebtedness, certificate of interest or participation in any profit-sharing agreement, collateral-trust certificate, preorganization certificate or subscription, transferable share, investment contract, voting-trust certificate, certificate of deposit for a security, fractional undivided interest in oil, gas, or other mineral rights, any put, call, straddle, option, or privilege on any security, certificate of deposit, or group or index of securities (including any interest therein or based on the value thereof), or any put, call, straddle, option, or privilege entered into on a national securities exchange relating to foreign currency, or, in general, any interest or instrument commonly known as a "security", or any certificate of interest or participation in, temporary or interim certificate for, receipt for, guarantee of, or warrant or right to subscribe to or purchase, any of the foregoing"*.[1995] It is, however, clear that many of those elements are unlikely to apply to virtual currencies themselves. In the following paragraphs, the focus will therefore be put on the elements that require further analysis: notes and stock on the one hand, and investment contracts on the other hand. Note that there are also exempted securities, but these mainly concern government and municipal securities, as well as collective investments not falling under the scope of the Investment Company Act of 1940.[1996]

#### 3.4.1.2 Notes

Note – Notes are not explicitly defined by federal legislation itself. Moreover, it is clear that notes can serve all kinds of purposes, and therefore do not

1991 15 U.S.C. §78l.

1992 Thus far, however, the SEC has not shown itself willing to register an exchange-traded fund tied to cryptocurrencies. Early 2017, the Commission rejected two of such applications. Higgins, S. (2017) "SEC Rejects Winklevoss Bitcoin ETF Bid", *CoinDesk*, 10 March; Higgins, S. (2017) "SEC Denies SolidX Bitcoin ETF Proposal", *CoinDesk*, 28 March.

1993 Alberts, J. E., Fry, B. (2016) "Is Bitcoin a Security?", *Boston University Journal of Science & Technology Law*, Vol. 21.1, 4–6.

1994 *Ibid.*, 8.

1995 15 U.S.C. §77b(a)(1).

1996 15 U.S.C. §78c(a)(12).

necessarily require an investment.[1997] Therefore, the US Supreme Court has created what is referred to as a "family resemblance" test to determine whether a note constitutes a security.[1998] According to that test, a note can be held to be a security unless "*it bears a strong resemblance*" to an instrument that is not considered to be a security.[1999]

GUIDELINES – The US Supreme Court establishes four guidelines.[2000] First, there must be money raised to fund business ventures or investments, with an expectation of profit for the investor. Second, it must be examined whether there is an instrument allowing for "*common trading for speculation or investment*".[2001] Third, the reasonable expectations of the public must be taken into account. Fourth, it is examined whether there is a factor that reduces the risks of the instrument – such as the applicability of another legal framework – which render the application of securities laws unnecessary.

VIRTUAL CURRENCIES AS NOTES – When assessing whether virtual currencies can constitute notes, it must first be said that notes – also referred to as promissory notes – are legal instruments that require the issuer to pay money to the holder.[2002] It is clear that such is not the case for all virtual currencies, at least not for those primarily intended to serve as means of payment.[2003]

PAYMENT VIRTUAL CURRENCIES UNDER THE GUIDELINES – Even if accepting virtual currencies with the primary purpose of serving as means of payment as such notes, they do not seem to satisfy the US Supreme Court's "family resemblance" test. With regard to the first element of the test, the court held that if the "*note is exchanged to facilitate the purchase and sale of a minor asset or*

---

1997 Here, it must be remarked that the securities legal framework only aims to regulate the securities market and does not "*provide a broad federal remedy for all fraud*". Marine Bank *v.* Weaver, 455 U. S. 551, at 556 (1982).

1998 Reves *v.* Ernst & Young, 494 U.S. 56 (1990); Alberts, J. E., Fry, B. (2016) "Is Bitcoin a Security?", *Boston University Journal of Science & Technology Law*, Vol. 21.1, 13–14.

1999 *Id.*

2000 *Ibid.*, at 66–67; Kaplanov, N. M. (2012) "Nerdy Money: Bitcoin, the Private Digital Currency, and the Case Against its Regulation", *Loyola Consumer Law Review*, Vol. 25, 146.

2001 SEC *v.* C.M. Joiner Leasing Corp., 320 U. S. 344, at 351 (1943).

2002 "note" (2014), *Black's Law Dictionary* (10$^{th}$ ed.), West.

2003 Grinberg, R. (2012) "Bitcoin: An Innovative Alternative Digital Currency", *Hastings Science & Technology Law Journal,* Vol. 4, 195–196; Kien-Meng Ly, M. (2014) "Coining Bitcoin's "legal-bits": Examining the regulatory framework for Bitcoin and virtual currencies", *Harvard Journal of Law & Technology,* Vol. 27, 598; Dion, D. (2013) "I'll Gladly Trade You Two Bits on Tuesday for a Byte Today: Bitcoin, Regulating Fraud in the E-conomy of Hacker-Cash", *Journal of Law, Technology & Policy,* Vol. 2013, 177 & 193; Alberts, J. E., Fry, B. (2016) "Is Bitcoin a Security?", *Boston University Journal of Science & Technology Law,* Vol. 21.1, 13; Farmer, P. H. Jr. (2014) "Speculative Tech: The Bitcoin Legal Quagmire & the Need for Legal Innovation", *Journal of Business & Technology Law,* Vol. 9, 100.

*consumer good, to correct for the seller's cash-flow difficulties, or to advance some other commercial or consumer purpose, on the other hand, the note is less sensibly described as a "security"*".[2004] Since payment virtual currencies serve precisely such purposes, they do not seem to constitute securities under this element of the test. Moreover, given that payment virtual currencies are known to serve primarily as means of payment, it is difficult to establish reasonable expectations of the public that such instruments would constitute securities.[2005] While it could be argued that the other two elements of the test could be fulfilled, the final result is that payment virtual currencies do not pass the test of being regarded as notes.[2006]

Investment virtual currencies under the guidelines – With regard to virtual currencies primarily serving as means of investment, it could be argued that such investment virtual currencies could correspond to all elements of the *Reves* test. Moreover, given the wide range of ways in which such investment currencies could be operationalized, it is possible that investment virtual currencies could constitute promissory notes. In that case, they would be considered as securities.

### 3.4.1.3 Stock

Stock – A stock can be regarded as "*proportional part of a corporation's capital represented by the number of equal units (or shares) owned, and granting the holder the right to participate in the company's general management and to share in its net profits or earnings*".[2007]

Characteristics – In order to determine whether an instrument constitutes a stock, it must be analyzed whether it displays "*some of the significant characteristics typically associated with*" stock.[2008] The US Supreme Court has determined what those characteristics are: "*(i) the right to receive dividends contingent upon an apportionment of profits; (ii) negotiability; (iii) the ability to be pledged or hypothecated; (iv) the conferring of voting rights in proportion to the number of shares owned; and (v) the capacity to appreciate in value*".[2009]

---

2004 Reves *v.* Ernst & Young, 494 U.S. 56, at 66 (1990); United Housing Foundation, Inc. *v.* Forman, 421 U.S. 837, at 851 (1975).

2005 Kaplanov, N. M. (2012) "Nerdy Money: Bitcoin, the Private Digital Currency, and the Case Against its Regulation", *Loyola Consumer Law Review*, Vol. 25, 160.

2006 *Id.*

2007 "stock" (2014), *Black's Law Dictionary* (10th ed.), West.

2008 United Housing Foundation, Inc. *v.* Forman, 421 U.S. 837, at 851 (1975).

2009 Landreth Timber Co. *v.* Landreth, 471 U.S. 681, at 686 (1985); Alberts, J. E., Fry, B. (2016) "Is Bitcoin a Security?", *Boston University Journal of Science & Technology Law*, Vol. 21.1, 10.

Payment virtual currencies – It is clear that virtual currencies primarily serving as means of payment do not possess such characteristics, and can therefore not be considered as stock in the sense of the securities legal framework.[2010]

Investment virtual currencies – However, for virtual currencies primarily serving as means of investment, it must again be concluded that they could be operationalized in a way that satisfied such characteristics. In that case, such investment virtual currencies would indeed constitute stock and thus become securities.

#### 3.4.1.4 Investment contracts

Investment contracts – Another important type of security is an investment contract. Also the notion of investment contract is not clearly defined within the securities legal framework itself, thus relying on case law to provide guidance on the scope of that notion. The landmark case in this regard was decided by the US Supreme Court in 1946.[2011] That case resulted in what is referred to as the *Howey* test, which only applies to investment contracts.[2012] According to the court, in interpreting what constitutes a security, form must be "*disregarded for substance, and emphasis* [...] *placed on economic reality*".[2013] In doing so, the court follows the reasoning that US Congress intended to regulate investments by enacting securities laws, regardless of the form in which such investments are made and how they are called.[2014] It therefore "*embodies a flexible, rather than a static, principle, one that is capable of adaptation to meet the countless and variable schemes devised by those who seek the use of the money of others on the promise of profits*".[2015]

Howey test – According to the court, the Howey test aims to determine "*whether the scheme involves an investment of money in a common enterprise with profits to come solely from the efforts of others.*"[2016] From this, four elements can be derived: (1) there must be an investment of money, (2) in a common

[2010] Grinberg, R. (2012) "Bitcoin: An Innovative Alternative Digital Currency", *Hastings Science & Technology Law Journal,* Vol. 4, 195; Kien-Meng Ly, M. (2014) "Coining Bitcoin's "legal-bits": Examining the regulatory framework for Bitcoin and virtual currencies", *Harvard Journal of Law & Technology*, Vol. 27, 598; Alberts, J. E., Fry, B. (2016) "Is Bitcoin a Security?", *Boston University Journal of Science & Technology Law*, Vol. 21.1, 10.

[2011] Securities and Exchange Commission *v.* W. J. Howey Co., 328 U.S. 293 (1946).

[2012] Reves *v.* Ernst & Young, 494 U.S. 56, at 64 (1990).

[2013] Securities and Exchange Commission *v.* W. J. Howey Co., 328 U.S. 293, at 298 (1946); Tcherepnin *v.* Knight, 389 U. S. 332, at 336 (1967).

[2014] A recent example: Traffic Monsoon was a pay-per-click scheme offering its investors 'AdPacks' that promised significant return on investment. The Securities and Exchange Commission found these 'AdPacks' to constitute securities. Securities and Exchange Commission *v.* Traffic Monsoon et al., 2:16-cv-00832-JNP (D. Utah, filed 26 July 2016).

[2015] Securities and Exchange Commission *v.* W. J. Howey Co., 328 U.S. 293, at 299 (1946).

[2016] *Ibid.*, at 301.

enterprise, (3) which leads to an expectation of profits, (4) in which such profits are solely derived from the efforts of the promotor of the scheme or a third party related thereto.[2017] All of these elements must be present in order to pass the test.[2018] Over the years, the Howey test has been refined through several more cases. The following paragraphs will further discuss each element.

Money investment – First, there must be an investment of money. Here, it is clear that unidirectional and bidirectional scheme virtual currencies – for both payment and investment purposes – can be obtained with money.[2019] More contentious is the matter where the investment is made with virtual currencies themselves. As discussed in chapter VI, DAO tokens could only be obtained with ether, the cryptocurrency of the Ethereum network. If such virtual currencies are not considered to be money, does this mean they can also not serve to satisfy the money investment element of the *Howey* test? No, case law has established that such an investment does not require the presence of money in the strictest sense of the word, but also allows for the presence of any form of capital or assets, even goods and services, as well as promissory notes.[2020] In that sense, there is a money investment whenever the investor potentially subjects himself to financial loss.[2021] Important here is that such implies that there must still be a risk factor.[2022] Once that risk has subsided, there is a lesser likelihood of there being an investment in the sense of the securities framework.[2023] For the cases where the investment is made in virtual currencies themselves, including the investment virtual currencies discussed in chapter VI[2024], it can

2017 *Ibid.*, at 298; Grinberg, R. (2012) "Bitcoin: An Innovative Alternative Digital Currency", *Hastings Science & Technology Law Journal,* Vol. 4, 196.

2018 Coin Center (2016) "A Securities Law Framework for Blockchain Tokens", *coincenter.org*, 12; Long, J. C., Kaufman, M. J., Wunderlich, J. M. (2017) *Blue Sky Law*, New York City: Thomson Reuters, §2:48.

2019 Grinberg, R. (2012) "Bitcoin: An Innovative Alternative Digital Currency", *Hastings Science & Technology Law Journal,* Vol. 4, 196–197.

2020 Teamsters *v.* Daniel, 439 U.S. 551, at 559–561 (1979); Hector *v.* Wiens, 533 F.2d 429, at 432–433 (9th Cir. 1976); Sandusky Land, Ltd. V. Uniplan Groups, Inc., 400 F. Supp. 440, at 445 (N.D. Ohio 1975); Coin Center (2016) "A Securities Law Framework for Blockchain Tokens", *coincenter.org*, 12.

2021 Hector *v.* Wiens, 533 F.2d 429, at 432–433 (9th Cir. 1976); El Khadem *v.* Equity Sec. Corp., 494 F.2d 1224, at 1228–1229 (9th Cir. 1974); Santori, M. (2016) "Appcoin Law: ICOs the Right Way", *CoinDesk*, 15 October.

2022 Long, J. C., Kaufman, M. J., Wunderlich, J. M. (2017) *Blue Sky Law*, New York City: Thomson Reuters, §1:24.

2023 For instance, case law has determined that memberships of projects yet to be realized can constitute an investment. Memberships of projects already realized, however, did not. All Seasons Resorts *v.* Abrams, 68 NY 2d 81, at 92–95 (CA New York 1986); Silver Hills Country Club *v.* Sobieski, 155 Cal.2d 811, at 814–815 (SC California 1961); Van Valkenburgh, P. (2016) "Framework for Securities Regulation of Cryptocurrencies v1", *Coin Center Report*, 43.

2024 For the different examples discussed there – DAO tokens and ICO's – it can be held that there is an investment that exposes the investor to a risk of financial loss. In both cases, the risk factor is still present, as they constitute investments in projects that still need to materialize.

thus be concluded that these virtual currencies can indeed constitute a money investment under the *Howey* test.[2025]

COMMON ENTERPRISE – The second element requires the investment to be made to a common enterprise, implying multiple investors.[2026] Here, there appears to be some disagreement between lower courts on whether such a commonality should be established horizontally or vertically.[2027] Horizontal commonality implies the funds of all investors to be pooled together, so that their profits or losses are correlated.[2028] If the investments and subsequent profits were not pooled, there would then not be a common enterprise under the *Howey* test.[2029] Other courts, however, require there to be ties between the investors and the promotor. Either their fortunes are tied – in which case both investors and the promotor gain profits or losses depending on those fortunes, also referred to as narrow verticality – or the investors rely on the expertise and efficacy of the promotor for their profits – also referred to as broad verticality.[2030] For

---

2025 A Texas District Court also ruled that an investment made in bitcoin can be considered as a money investment. Securities and Exchange Commission *v.* Shavers, Case No. 4:13-CV-416 (DC Texas 2013); Alberts, J. E., Fry, B. (2016) "Is Bitcoin a Security?", *Boston University Journal of Science & Technology Law*, Vol. 21.1, 15; Brito, J., Shadab, H., Castillo, A. (2014) "Bitcoin Financial Regulations: Securities, Derivatives, Prediction Markets, and Gambling", *Columbia Science & Technology Law Review*, Vol. 16, 189; Twomey, P. (2013) "Halting a shift in the paradigm: the need for bitcoin regulation", *Trinity College Law Review*, Vol. 16, 81; Tu, K. V., Meredith, M. W. (2015) "Rethinking Virtual Currency Regulation in the Bitcoin Age", *Washington Law Review*, Vol. 90, 309–310; Thompson, S. L. (2009) "Securities Regulation in a Virtual World", *UCLA Entertainment Law Review*, Vol. 16, 103; Congressional Research Service (2014) "Bitcoin: Questions, Answers, and Analysis of Legal Issues", *crs.gov*, 14–15.

2026 Gordon, J. D. (2011) "Defining a Common Enterprise in Investment Contracts", *Ohio State Law Journal*, Vol. 72, 71.

2027 *Ibid.*, 66–68 ("*The Third, Sixth, and Seventh Circuits require horizontal commonality. By contrast, the Fifth and Eleventh Circuits use broad vertical commonality. The First, Fourth, and D.C. Circuits accept horizontal commonality but have not ruled on vertical commonality. The Second Circuit accepts horizontal commonality, rejects broad vertical commonality, and has not ruled on narrow vertical commonality. The Ninth Circuit recognizes both horizontal commonality and narrow vertical commonality. The Tenth Circuit has rejected a requirement of horizontal commonality in favor of an "economic reality" approach.*"). Note that *Howey* only determined that there has to be a common enterprise, not how such commonality has to be established. Here, it could even be argued that no horizontal commonality was present in *Howey* itself. *Ibid.*, 73–75.

2028 Curran *v.* Merrill, Lynch, 622 F.2d 216, at 222–224 (6th Cir. 1980); Alberts, J. E., Fry, B. (2016) "Is Bitcoin a Security?", *Boston University Journal of Science & Technology Law*, Vol. 21.1, 15; Van Valkenburgh, P. (2016) "Framework for Securities Regulation of Cryptocurrencies v1", *Coin Center Report*, 45; Gordon, J. D. (2011) "Defining a Common Enterprise in Investment Contracts", *Ohio State Law Journal*, Vol. 72, 66–67; Long, J. C., Kaufman, M. J., Wunderlich, J. M. (2017) *Blue Sky Law*, New York City: Thomson Reuters, §2:58.

2029 Coin Center (2016) "A Securities Law Framework for Blockchain Tokens", *coincenter.org*, 13, referring to: Hirk *v.* Agri-Research Council, Inc., 561 F.2d 96, at 101 (7th Cir. 1977); Wals *v.* Fox Hills Dev. Corp., 24 F.3d 1016, at 1018 (7th Cir. 1994).

2030 Coin Center (2016) "A Securities Law Framework for Blockchain Tokens", *coincenter.org*, 13; referencing: SEC *v.* Eurobond, Exchange Ltd., 13 F.3d 1334, at 1339 (9th Cir. 1994); SEC *v.* Continental Commodities Corp., 497 F.2d 516, at 522–523 (5th Cir. 1974). Alberts, J. E., Fry,

investment virtual currencies, it could then be possible to establish a horizontal commonality. In the case of The DAO, funds were pooled together and all participants would benefit or lose equally.[2031] Alternatively, as in the case of most ICO's, there is a central seller developing those virtual currencies, who generally aims to profit together with the investors – thus establishing narrow vertical commonality.[2032] It is, however, also possible that the central developer invests its own gains in further development, and thus not share in the profits. In that case, there would be no narrow vertical commonality, though it must be noted that there could still be broad vertical commonality, or even horizontal commonality. Indeed, horizontal commonality seems almost impossible to avoid in the cases of investment virtual currencies discussed here and in chapter VI.[2033] For payment virtual currencies, commonality is harder to establish. First, in most cases there may not be an expectation of profit – as will be discussed in the following paragraph – and in the case of cryptocurrencies – where gains can be made out of value fluctuations – there is no central party to rely on for vertical commonality.[2034] While a decentralized system – as found in cryptocurrencies – could give the impression of being a common enterprise, there is no pooling of all participants' assets towards a single endeavor.[2035]

Expectation of profit – Third, there must be an expectation of profit. This means that the investor must be expecting a certain return on his investment,

B. (2016) "Is Bitcoin a Security?", *Boston University Journal of Science & Technology Law*, Vol. 21.1, 18–19; Gordon, J. D. (2011) "Defining a Common Enterprise in Investment Contracts", *Ohio State Law Journal*, Vol. 72, 67; Long, J. C., Kaufman, M. J., Wunderlich, J. M. (2017) *Blue Sky Law*, New York City: Thomson Reuters, §2:56-§2:57.

2031 Coin Center (2016) "A Securities Law Framework for Blockchain Tokens", *coincenter.org*, 14.

2032 Santori, M. (2016) "Appcoin Law: ICOs the Right Way", *CoinDesk*, 15 October.

2033 *Id*; Coin Center (2016) "A Securities Law Framework for Blockchain Tokens", *coincenter.org*, 14–15; Van Valkenburgh, P. (2016) "Framework for Securities Regulation of Cryptocurrencies v1", *Coin Center Report*, 46. One important exception, referenced by Van Valkenburgh, concerns the Paycoin scheme. This scheme involved units that were not perfectly fungible, resulting in a higher profitability for some participants in the scheme than for others. Such would be an argument against horizontal commonality.

2034 Kaplanov, N. M. (2012) "Nerdy Money: Bitcoin, the Private Digital Currency, and the Case Against its Regulation", *Loyola Consumer Law Review*, Vol. 25, 160–161; Alberts, J. E., Fry, B. (2016) "Is Bitcoin a Security?", *Boston University Journal of Science & Technology Law*, Vol. 21.1, 19; Grinberg, R. (2012) "Bitcoin: An Innovative Alternative Digital Currency", *Hastings Science & Technology Law Journal*, Vol. 4, 197–198.

2035 Alberts, J. E., Fry, B. (2016) "Is Bitcoin a Security?", *Boston University Journal of Science & Technology Law*, Vol. 21.1, 16–17; Grinberg, R. (2012) "Bitcoin: An Innovative Alternative Digital Currency", *Hastings Science & Technology Law Journal*, Vol. 4, 197–198; Kien-Meng Ly, M. (2014) "Coining Bitcoin's "legal-bits": Examining the regulatory framework for Bitcoin and virtual currencies", *Harvard Journal of Law & Technology*, Vol. 27, 598. This is the main difference between a payment cryptocurrency and an investment cryptocurrency: payment cryptocurrencies can be used for a wide variety of purposes, whereas investment cryptocurrencies clearly serve just one single purpose. *Contra:* Twomey, P. (2013) "Halting a shift in the paradigm: the need for bitcoin regulation", *Trinity College Law Review*, Vol. 16, 82. Note, however, that Twomey does not take into account the need to pool investments.

which can take any form.[2036] Furthermore, the expectation of profit must be the predominant reason for the investment.[2037] Moreover, such an expectation must follow from "*the promoter's sales presentation*".[2038] It is clear that some virtual currencies – particularly closed scheme and unidirectional scheme virtual currencies – cannot satisfy this element of the *Howey* test. The value of those virtual currencies will not appreciate, and may even depreciate, thus making them inherently unprofitable.[2039] In principle, those who invest in a bidirectional payment virtual currency should not expect a profit – as the virtual currency remains primarily a means of payment – but the strong value fluctuations of this type of virtual currency have resulted in a practice where many – if not most – market participants acquire this type of virtual currency with the intent to profit from those value fluctuations, rather than to use it as means of payment.[2040] In the case of investment virtual currencies, it is clear that such a virtual currency is usually acquired with the predominant intention to profit.[2041]

Effort from others – An important qualifier for the expectation of profit is the final element of the *Howey* test, namely that such a profit must be derived from the efforts of others, namely the promotor of the scheme or a third party related to this promotor. This means that the investor must be a passive player in the equation, and not be responsible for the creation of profit himself. For instance, if the investor gains profits on a secondary market, this element of the *Howey* test is not fulfilled.[2042] As a result, not any type of profit can satisfy the test, but only those profits gained passively – which is why the last two elements of the test are often considered together. While the original text of the *Howey* case states that profits must be derived *solely* from the efforts of others, later case

2036 SEC *v.* Edwards, 540 U.S. 389, at 390 (2004).

2037 For instance, while shares in cooperative housing may be acquired with the hopes of reselling them at a profit, the predominant reason for their acquisition will normally be to live in that housing. Santori, M. (2016) "Appcoin Law: ICOs the Right Way", *CoinDesk*, 15 October.

2038 Aldrich *v.* McCulloch Prop. Inc., 627 F.2d 1036, at 1039–1040 (10th Cir. 1980); Long, J. C., Kaufman, M. J., Wunderlich, J. M. (2017) *Blue Sky Law*, New York City: Thomson Reuters, §2:59.

2039 For instance, there might be an expiration date on the virtual currency.

2040 Grinberg, R. (2012) "Bitcoin: An Innovative Alternative Digital Currency", *Hastings Science & Technology Law Journal*, Vol. 4, 198.

2041 Another development in this area are so-called *appcoins*, which are cryptocurrencies issued on platforms such as Ethereum. These cryptocurrencies serve as tokens necessary to access the platform and develop applications, for instance relating to smart contracts. These tokens therefore do not serve as means of payment, neither do they necessarily serve investment purposes. For these *appcoins* it must therefore be concluded that it is possible that they do not create an expectation of profit, though there could of course be cases where such expectation is created. It will therefore have to be assessed for each case what the predominant goal of the token is. Van Valkenburgh, P. (2016) "Framework for Securities Regulation of Cryptocurrencies v1", *Coin Center Report*, 48–49.

2042 Unless, of course, the promotor of the scheme created such second market himself in order to provide profitability. Santori, M. (2016) "Appcoin Law: ICOs the Right Way", *CoinDesk*, 15 October.

law has demonstrated some flexibility in this regard. For instance, it has been held that it must be determined "*whether the efforts made by those other than the investor are the undeniably significant ones, those essential managerial efforts which affect the failure or success of the enterprise.*"[2043] Consequently, the efforts of the promotor and related persons must be predominant, but not necessarily exclusive.[2044] When, for instance, the investor invests in a company, it must be determined whether he has an active role in that company – meaning that the company is member-managed – or whether he is a passive actor that lets the promotor take the lead – meaning a manager-managed company.[2045] So what does this mean for virtual currencies? For closed scheme and unidirectional scheme virtual currencies, this element of the *Howey* test seems moot since those virtual currencies in principle do not provide an expectation of profit to begin with. Bidirectional payment virtual currencies – particularly cryptocurrencies – could, in turn, appreciate in value and thus create profits for those that invested in them. However, it seems that such profits are more the result of market forces at work, rather than resulting from the efforts of a single promotor or related entities.[2046] Such does not satisfy this element of the *Howey* test.[2047] Investment virtual currencies, finally, could be argued to satisfy this element of the test. In the case of most ICO's, it is clear that there is a central issuer upon whom investors depend to generate profit. The matter could be somewhat more contentious in the case of a platform, such as The DAO, where investors do have a certain active participation through their votes, and where there is in principle

[2043] SEC *v.* Glenn W. Turner Enterprises, Inc., 474 F.2d 476, at 482 (9th Cir. 1973); Coin Center (2016) "A Securities Law Framework for Blockchain Tokens", *coincenter.org*, 17; Long, J. C., Kaufman, M. J., Wunderlich, J. M. (2017) *Blue Sky Law*, New York City: Thomson Reuters, §2:74.

[2044] Long, J. C., Kaufman, M. J., Wunderlich, J. M. (2017) *Blue Sky Law*, New York City: Thomson Reuters, §1:31.

[2045] Sync Labs LLC *v.* Fusion Mfg., 2013 WL 4776018, at 9 (DC New Jersey 2013).

[2046] Grinberg, R. (2012) "Bitcoin: An Innovative Alternative Digital Currency", *Hastings Science & Technology Law Journal*, Vol. 4, 198–199. Twomey, however, argues that certain exchanges could use their power to influence the market value of a cryptocurrency, as evidenced in the drop in bitcoin value after early exchanges such as Mt.Gox went bankrupt. While such events could indeed influence the cryptocurrency's market value, it seems somewhat overblown to take this as meaning that these actors predominantly provide the efforts that result in profit. Twomey, P. (2013) "Halting a shift in the paradigm: the need for bitcoin regulation", *Trinity College Law Review*, Vol. 16, 83. A similar argument is put forward by Farmer, relying on the perception that a single promotor, or a limited group around that promotor, would be responsible for the profitability of cryptocurrencies. While it can be accepted that a certain group – for instance: core developers – do indeed have particular power or authority within that cryptocurrency's community, the actual market value of said currency is still determined by supply-and-demand of the market participants, and not predominantly by that group. Farmer, P. H. Jr. (2014) "Speculative Tech: The Bitcoin Legal Quagmire & the Need for Legal Innovation", *Journal of Business & Technology Law*, Vol. 9, 102.

[2047] Noa *v.* Key Futures, Inc., 638 F.2d. 77, at 79–80 (9th Cir. 1980); Alberts, J. E., Fry, B. (2016) "Is Bitcoin a Security?", *Boston University Journal of Science & Technology Law*, Vol. 21.1, 20.

no central promotor.[2048] However, the eventual profitability of investments depends on the efforts of the promotors of the projects funded through the platform. Moreover, The DAO relied heavily on so-called Curators, who possessed the sole authority to decide which proposals would be put forward to investors.[2049] Such could be argued to satisfy this element of the test: while there is some effort of the investors, it is still predominantly the effort of others that determines profitability.[2050] Moreover, it is reminded that traditional security holders also often have voting rights, which does not preclude the qualification of their securities.[2051]

#### 3.4.1.5 Currency

Currency – The 1934 Securities Exchange Act explicitly excludes currencies from being considered as securities.[2052] That exclusion has been confirmed by case law, and is regarded as generally accepted knowledge.[2053] Important to note is that certain foreign currency transactions can be regarded as commodity futures contracts.[2054] That brings such foreign currency transactions under the ambit of derivatives regulation, and the supervision of the Commodity Futures

2048 Although it must be said that the developers of The DAO were heavily involved in promoting the platform, propagating themselves as experts on the matter. Such *de facto* authority could result in investors possibly relying on their expertise to make the platform successful.

2049 This reasoning would later be confirmed by the SEC: SEC (2017) "Report of Investigation Pursuant to Section 21(a) of the Securities Exchange Act of 1934: The DAO", *SEC release 81207*, 12–13.

2050 Hinkes, A. (2016) "The Law of The DAO", *CoinDesk*, 19 May; Padovano, C. (2016) "Yes, Crypto-token Crowdsales Can Be Classified As Securities. Here's Why:", *decentralizedlegal.com*, 15 August.

2051 Coin Center (2016) "A Securities Law Framework for Blockchain Tokens", *coincenter.org*, 18–19. Although the authors note a number of cases where the voting rights of investors did preclude the qualification as security, it would appear that the courts based their reasoning on the actual level of involvement and the expertise of the investors. In the case of The DAO, no active involvement was required – any token holder could choose to exercise their rights or not – nor was there any requirement of prior expertise. Moreover, while The DAO could be argued to be more akin to a general partnership, it has already been held that their interests could also constitute securities, as in a limited partnership. SEC *v.* Merchant Capital, L.L.C., 483 F.3d 747 (11th Cir. 2007). The Securities and Exchange Commission would later remark on this case that the voting rights of the DAO token holders were limited, meaning that those votes were not the predominant effort towards profitability. SEC (2017) "Report of Investigation Pursuant to Section 21(a) of the Securities Exchange Act of 1934: The DAO", *SEC release 81207*, 13–15.

2052 15 U.S.C. §78c(a)(10). While the definition of securities used in the 1933 Securities Act does not explicitly mention currency, these definitions are accepted as being equivalent: Reves *v.* Ernst & Young, 494 U.S. 56, at 76 (1990).

2053 Reves *v.* Ernst & Young, 494 U.S. 56, at 73–74 (1990); Kaplanov, N. M. (2012) "Nerdy Money: Bitcoin, the Private Digital Currency, and the Case Against its Regulation", *Loyola Consumer Law Review*, Vol. 25, 149.

2054 Lauzon, E. D. (2002) "Annotation: What are "Contracts of Sale of a Commodity for Future Delivery" Within Meaning of Commodity Exchange Act (7 U.S.CA. §§1 et seq.)", *182 A.L.R. Fed. 559*, §3–4.

Trading Commission (CFTC). The derivatives regulatory framework will be discussed in section 3.4.2.

Virtual currencies as currencies – The question is then whether virtual currencies can be regarded as the currencies exempted under federal US securities law. On the one hand, it could be argued that virtual currencies function in the same way foreign currency does, and therefore should be regarded as currencies as well.[2055] On the other hand, it could be argued that US Congress maybe did not want to exclude just any medium of exchange, but only those that are "*generally accepted in some geographic or political area*", which excludes most – if not all – virtual currencies from being considered as currencies.[2056] Of course, it must be reminded here that even if the currency exemption does not apply to virtual currencies, such does not necessarily make virtual currencies subject to federal US securities law. And as became clear in the previous subsections, it would be difficult to qualify payment virtual currencies as securities under the securities framework.

### *3.4.2 Derivatives regulation*

Legal history – Already in 1864, US Congress attempted to regulate derivatives, more particularly gold futures.[2057] At the time, fiat currency was trading at a low value compared to gold. Derivatives regulation thus aimed to prohibit the trading of gold futures. However, the Anti-Gold Futures Act, adopted on 17 June 1864, resulted in an even sharper drop in value for fiat currency, thus resulting in the act being repealed in a matter of weeks.[2058] A second attempt, the Future Trading Act of 24 August 1921, was aimed at grain futures contracts.[2059] That act was found to be unconstitutional by the US Supreme Court.[2060] Shortly thereafter, it was replaced by the Grain Futures Act of 21 September 1922, which was held up by the US Supreme Court.[2061] The legal framework set by the Grain Futures Act was later expanded to encompass all commodities futures trading through the Commodity Exchange Act of

---

2055 Kaplanov, N. M. (2012) "Nerdy Money: Bitcoin, the Private Digital Currency, and the Case Against its Regulation", *Loyola Consumer Law Review*, Vol. 25, 161–162.

2056 Grinberg, R. (2012) "Bitcoin: An Innovative Alternative Digital Currency", *Hastings Science & Technology Law Journal*, Vol. 4, 203–204. Grinberg argues that "*Congress did not mean to exempt a currency that is also a security.*" While this argument is correct, it must be noted that Grinberg concluded that – *in casu* – bitcoin is not a security. As a result, exempting a virtual currency that is not a security would not violate Congress' intentions.

2057 13 Stat. 132.

2058 Federal Reserve Board (1997) "Remarks by Chairman Alan Greenspan: Government regulation and derivative contracts", presented at the *Financial Markets Conference of the Federal Reserve Bank of Atlanta*, Coral Gables, Florida, 21 February.

2059 *Pub. L.* 67–66.

2060 Hill *v.* Wallace, 259 U.S. 44 (1922).

2061 *Pub. L.* 67–331; Board of Trade of City of Chicago *v.* Olsen, 262 U.S. 1 (1923).

15 June 1936.[2062] The Commodity Exchange Act was first administered by the Commodity Exchange Authority, part of the US Department of Agriculture. That agency was later replaced by the CFTC, through the Commodity Futures Trading Commission Act of 23 October 1974.[2063] Later updates to the derivatives legal framework are the Commodity Futures Modernization Act of 21 December 2000[2064] – subjecting certain over-the-counter derivatives only to general safety and soundness standards and thus not more strictly regulating such products as futures or securities – and the Dodd–Frank Wall Street Reform and Consumer Protection Act of 21 July 2010 – expanding the scope of the derivatives legal framework over the swaps market.[2065] Furthermore, the CFTC can also adopt additional regulations.[2066]

Commodity – The main focus of the derivatives legal framework is put on commodities. Commodities are defined by a list of agricultural products, with the additional catch-all phrasing "*and all other goods and articles,* [...] *and all services, rights, and interests* [...] *in which contracts for future delivery are presently or in the future dealt in*".[2067] If commodities were then to be understood in the broadest possible way – meaning: everything not captured by securities laws – it could be argued that virtual currencies could constitute commodities, if they are indeed not securities. However, if commodities are understood as having inherent and tangible value, such a qualification may become more complicated.[2068] Fortunately, the matter of interpretation has been settled by the CFTC. In 2015, the CFTC issued an order against a company found to connect buyers and sellers of standardized bitcoin options and futures contracts without complying with the derivatives legal framework. In said order, the CFTC confirms the very broad scope of the commodity notion.[2069] Indeed, case law has established that "*literally anything* [...] *could become a "commodity" and thereby subject to CFTC regulation simply by its futures being traded on some exchange*".[2070] Because of this, the CFTC concluded that bitcoins – and by extension all virtual currencies – are commodities.[2071] In 2017, the CFTC

2062 *Pub. L.* 74–675.

2063 *Pub. L.* 93–463. The act also authorized the futures industry to create a national self-regulatory body. This body, the National Futures Association (NFA), was founded in 1982.

2064 Appendix E to the Consolidated Appropriations Act, 2001, *Pub. L.* 106–554.

2065 *Pub. L.* 111–203.

2066 Codified under 17 C.F.R. Chapter I.

2067 7 U.S.C. §1a(9).

2068 Grinberg, R. (2012) "Bitcoin: An Innovative Alternative Digital Currency", *Hastings Science & Technology Law Journal,* Vol. 4, 200.

2069 In re Coinflip, Inc., d/b/a/ Derivabit, et al., *CFTC Docket No. 15-29* (2015), 3; Hughes, S. J., Middlebrook, S. T. (2015) "Advancing a Framework for Regulating Cryptocurrency Payments Intermediaries", *Yale Journal on Regulation*, Vol. 32, 510–511.

2070 Board of Trade of City of Chicago *v.* SEC, 677 F. 2d 1137, at 1142–1143 (7th Cir. 1982).

2071 In re Coinflip, Inc., d/b/a/ Derivabit, et al., *CFTC Docket No. 15-29* (2015), 3.

confirmed that its earlier view could also extend to investment tokens issued as part of an ICO or DAO, depending on the precise circumstances.[2072]

Exempt commodity – Apart from listing what is regarded as a commodity, the derivatives legal framework also maintains an overview of excluded commodities.[2073] Additionally, commodities that are not excluded or agricultural commodities can still be exempted as well.[2074] Although it has been argued that virtual currencies could be considered as such exempted commodities, this does not appear to be the position followed by the CFTC.[2075]

Future delivery – Under the derivatives legal framework, the CFTC has jurisdiction over all "*transactions involving swaps or contracts of sale of a commodity for future delivery*".[2076] This "*does not include any sale of any cash commodity for deferred shipment or delivery*".[2077] In other words, if a sales transaction were conducted instantaneously or near instantaneous, the derivatives legal framework would not apply.[2078] However, such a limitation resulted in a significant weakness of the derivatives legal framework against so-called spot exchanges, whereby foreign exchange and commodities are traded 'on the spot'. The 2010 Dodd-Frank Act provided some relief here, giving the CFTC competence over that kind of financed retail transactions.[2079] An important exception to the expanded competence applies when there is a contract of sale establishing an enforceable obligation to deliver, or actual delivery within 28 days.[2080] The latter notion must be interpreted as meaning that the customer must receive the traded commodities in full, although initially some uncertainty on the precise scope of the delivery notion remained.[2081] In

2072 CFTC (2017) "LabCFTC: A CFTC Primer on Virtual Currencies", *cftc.gov*, 14.

2073 7 U.S.C. §1a(19)(1).

2074 7 U.S.C. §1a(20).

2075 Shadab, H. B. (2014) "Regulating Bitcoin and Block Chain Derivatives", *Written statement to the Commodity Futures Trading Commission Global Markets Advisory Committee 'Digital Currency Introduction – Bitcoin'*, 9 October, 5; Brito, J., Shadab, H., Castillo, A. (2014) "Bitcoin Financial Regulations: Securities, Derivatives, Prediction Markets, and Gambling", *Columbia Science & Technology Law Review*, Vol. 16, 162.

2076 7 U.S.C. §2(a)(1)(A).

2077 7 U.S.C. §1a(27).

2078 Kaplanov, N. M. (2012) "Nerdy Money: Bitcoin, the Private Digital Currency, and the Case Against its Regulation", *Loyola Consumer Law Review*, Vol. 25, 162.

2079 This was, in part, a reaction to the *Zelener* case. CFTC *v.* Zelener, 373 F.3d 861 (7th Cir. 2004). This case highlighted a blind spot in federal regulations, although it has been argued that the type of transactions used in this case could still have been covered under certain state laws. Feigin, P. A. (2011) "The Model State Commodity Code in 2011 and new CFTC jurisdiction – Whither the states? Can "new dogs" learn "old tricks"?", *Banking & Financial Services Policy Report*, Vol. 31, 2.

2080 7 U.S.C. §2(c)(2)(D)(ii)(III)(aa); Felsenthal, D., Old, G., Kalbag, M. (2016) "CFTC Bitfinex Enforcement Action", *Clifford Chance*, 2.

2081 Batteh, K. (2016) "Why the CFTC Bitfinex Enforcement Actually Benefits Bitcoin Exchanges", *CoinDesk*, 6 June; Rizzo, P. (2016) "Petition Pushes CFTC to Clarify Rules on Blockchain

December 2017, the CFTC proposed an interpretation of this rule with regard to virtual currencies.[2082] Concretely, there would be actual delivery of a retail commodity transaction in virtual currency if the customer attains the ability to "*(i) take possession and control of the entire quantity of the commodity, whether it was purchased on margin, or using leverage, or any other financing arrangement, and (ii) use it freely in commerce (both within and away from any particular platform) no later than 28 days from the date of the transaction*", without the offeror and counterparty seller retaining "*any interest in or control over any of the commodity purchased on margin, leverage, or other financing arrangement at the expiration of 28 days from the date of the transaction*".[2083] If there is indeed such an actual delivery, the expanded legal framework does not apply. As a result, a regular virtual currency exchange transaction – in which legal tender or equivalent is instantaneously exchanged for virtual currency or vice versa and where there is an actual delivery – would in principle not be covered by the derivatives legal framework. Only when instruments such as futures, options, or swaps are used for future delivery, the derivatives legal framework comes into play. Additionally, when there is no actual delivery of the exchange, the derivatives legal framework can apply.[2084]

Foreign currency – Transactions merely denominated in foreign currency are principally not regulated under the derivatives legal framework.[2085] Moreover, (domestic) currency itself falls under the scope of excluded commodities.[2086] It are therefore only transactions in foreign currency derivatives that are regulated under the derivatives legal framework, such as foreign exchange forwards and swaps.[2087] Such derivatives must be traded on a registered exchange, by registered entities.[2088]

'Delivery'", *CoinDesk*, 20 July; Feigin, P. A. (2011) "The Model State Commodity Code in 2011 and new CFTC jurisdiction – Whither the states? Can "new dogs" learn "old tricks"?", *Banking & Financial Services Policy Report*, Vol. 31, 4–7; Lauzon, E. D. (2002) "Annotation: What are "Contracts of Sale of a Commodity for Future Delivery" Within Meaning of Commodity Exchange Act (7 U.S.CA. §§1 et seq.)", *182 A.L.R. Fed. 559*, §2[a].

2082 CFTC (2017) "CFTC Issues Proposed Interpretation on Virtual Currency "Actual Delivery" in Retail Transactions", *pr7664-17.*

2083 CFTC (2017) "Retail Commodity Transactions Involving Virtual Currency", *RIN 3038-AE62*, 14–15.

2084 In the case of cryptocurrency exchange Bitfinex, the Commodity Futures Trading Commission found that the exchange did not actually deliver bitcoins to customers, but held them under its own custody. As a result, the Commission found that there was no actual delivery. Consequently, the legal framework applies, and Bitfinex was found to conduct illegal off-exchange transactions. In re BFXNA, Inc. d/b/a BITFINEX, *CFTC Docket No. 16-19* (2016), 6.

2085 7 U.S.C. §2(c)(1)(A); Lauzon, E. D. (2002) "Annotation: What are "Contracts of Sale of a Commodity for Future Delivery" Within Meaning of Commodity Exchange Act (7 U.S.CA. §§1 et seq.)", *182 A.L.R. Fed. 559*, §11.

2086 7 U.S.C. §1a(19)(1).

2087 7 U.S.C. §1a(24) and (25).

2088 The Clearing House, Independent Community Bankers of America (2014) "Virtual currency: risks and regulation", *theclearinghouse.org*, 20.

Registration – Those aiming to operate a foreign exchange or commodity derivative trading facility must be registered with the CFTC. Thus far, at least two facilities trading in bitcoin derivatives have been fully registered as swap execution facilities (SEF), with more pending approval.[2089]

### *3.4.3 State regulation*

#### 3.4.3.1 Blue sky laws and federal preemption

Blue sky laws – State laws have historically complemented or even duplicated federal law.[2090] Such laws are often referred to as 'blue sky laws', referring to fraudulent investment schemes backed by nothing more than blue skies. The term is attributed to the Kansas banking commissioner who advocated the first of such laws – adopted in 1911 and thus predating federal laws in the securities field – and popularized through a 1917 US Supreme Court opinion.[2091]

Federal preemption – In 1996, the competence of states to regulate what is regarded as 'covered securities' was significantly restricted.[2092] The main consequence of the restriction of state competence in the securities field is that states cannot adopt laws that require registration of securities or securities transactions with regard to covered securities.[2093] This restriction also means that states may not "*directly or indirectly prohibit, limit, or impose any conditions upon the use of*" an offering document, such as a prospectus, with regard to those securities.[2094] Moreover, it also extends to the application of merit requirements.[2095] While such may appear to be a significant restriction of states'

---

2089 Higgins, S. (2016) "CFTC Grants Full Registration to Bitcoin Swaps Trading Platform", *CoinDesk*, 26 May; CFTC (2017) "CFTC Grants SEF Registration to LedgerX LLC", *Press release pr7584-17*, 6 July; Del Castillo, M. (2017) "Bitcoin Options Firm LedgerX Crosses Key Launch Hurdle", *CoinDesk*, 23 January; Brito, J., Shadab, H., Castillo, A. (2014) "Bitcoin Financial Regulations: Securities, Derivatives, Prediction Markets, and Gambling", *Columbia Science & Technology Law Review*, Vol. 16, 170–171; Hughes, S. J., Middlebrook, S. T. (2015) "Advancing a Framework for Regulating Cryptocurrency Payments Intermediaries", *Yale Journal on Regulation*, Vol. 32, 529–530; Brito, J., Castillo, A. (2013) *Bitcoin: A Primer for Policymakers*, Arlington: George Mason University Mercatus Center, 58.

2090 However, this does not mean that federal and state laws have the same scope or intent. State laws, for instance, traditionally imposed a more merit-based regulation. Federal law, on the other hand, focuses on disclosure only. Long, J. C., Kaufman, M. J., Wunderlich, J. M. (2017) *Blue Sky Law*, New York City: Thomson Reuters, 5:1.

2091 Hall *v.* Geiger-Jones Co., 242 U.S. 539, at 550 (1917); Long, J. C., Kaufman, M. J., Wunderlich, J. M. (2017) *Blue Sky Law*, New York City: Thomson Reuters, §1:1.

2092 National Securities Markets Improvement Act of 11 October 1996, *Pub. L.* 104–290.

2093 15 U.S.C. §77r(a) and (b).

2094 15 U.S.C. §77r(a)(2); Long, J. C., Kaufman, M. J., Wunderlich, J. M. (2017) *Blue Sky Law*, New York City: Thomson Reuters, §5:3.

2095 Long, J. C., Kaufman, M. J., Wunderlich, J. M. (2017) *Blue Sky Law*, New York City: Thomson Reuters, §5:10.

competence in the securities field, it was already accepted practice in most states to exempt such transactions from local registration requirements.[2096] In this regard, the restriction merely codified existing practice.

State competence – Even so, blue sky regulation remains a necessity for other aspects of the securities field. For instance, states do retain competence to investigate and enforce actions regarding fraud, deceit, or unlawful behavior of a broker or dealer.[2097] Moreover, states can still require registration for securities not considered as covered securities. These include securities traded on smaller or second tier exchanges, etc.[2098] Especially the registration element may prove important to virtual currencies that qualify as securities: if virtual currencies can be considered as covered securities, they will only be subjected to federal registration requirements, if not, they become subject to the full scope of state laws. Generally, covered securities are those listed on national securities exchanges – such as the New York Stock Exchange or NASDAQ.[2099] It is clear that such is – at least at the present moment – not the case for the virtual currencies that can be considered as securities. Moreover, exemptions[2100] do not seem to apply here.[2101]

#### 3.4.3.2 Uniform Securities Act

Uniform Securities Act – Already in 1956, the Uniform Law Commission adopted a Uniform Securities Act.[2102] That uniform act underwent major revisions in 1988 and 2002, as well as minor revisions in 2005.[2103] As of today, most states, US territories and Washington, D.C. have adopted laws based on one of the versions of this uniform act.[2104]

---

2096 Bloomenthal, H. S., Wolff, S. (2017) *Securities Law Handbook*, New York City: Thomson Reuters, §24:6.

2097 15 U.S.C. §77r(c); Long, J. C., Kaufman, M. J., Wunderlich, J. M. (2017) *Blue Sky Law*, New York City: Thomson Reuters, §5:14-§5:17.

2098 Bloomenthal, H. S., Wolff, S. (2017) *Securities Law Handbook*, New York City: Thomson Reuters, §24:8.

2099 15 U.S.C. §77r(b)(1).

2100 Certain exempted securities are also considered as covered securities.

2101 One example is the so-called crowdfunding exemption, which allows an entity to raise up to USD 1 million per year through crowdfunding without having to comply with federal registration requirements. However, this exemption does require the sale to be conducted through a registered broker or funding portal (15 U.S.C. §77d(a)(6)(C)). This intermediary requirement does not appear to be fulfilled in the case of developments such as The DAO or ICOs, thus not allowing the application of this exemption. See also: Long, J. C., Kaufman, M. J., Wunderlich, J. M. (2017) *Blue Sky Law*, New York City: Thomson Reuters, §5:31.

2102 This act was even preceded by the Uniform Sales of Securities Act of 1930. This uniform act was only adopted in a few states, before being scrapped by the Uniform Law Commission. Some state laws are still based on this uniform act, albeit with substantial amendments over time.

2103 *Uniformlaws.org/Act.aspx?title=Securities%20Act.*

2104 Long, J. C., Kaufman, M. J., Wunderlich, J. M. (2017) *Blue Sky Law*, New York City: Thomson Reuters, §12:1.

SECURITIES – The uniform act defines securities in quasi identical wordings as federal law.[2105] For investment contracts, the uniform act specifies the need for the four elements of the *Howey* test to be fulfilled. With regard to the common enterprise, the uniform act provides that the fortunes of the investors must be interwoven with those of the promotor, a third party, or each other.[2106] That phrasing thus allows for both horizontal and narrow vertical commonality.

REGISTRATION – The 2002 version of the uniform act acknowledges federal preemption by listing exempt covered securities and exempt covered securities transactions. Other exemptions include securities issued by domestic and foreign authorities – including banking institutions – and securities in non-profit organizations or cooperatives.[2107] Other exempted transactions include, *inter alea*, certain non-issuer transactions, transactions between issuers and underwriters, certain transactions involving mortgage-backed securities, and different offers to sell.[2108] Selling securities under the uniform act is only lawful if the security is a federal covered security, a security exempted under the act, or a security registered under the act.[2109] Similar registration requirements apply for broker-dealers transacting business in the state, agents, and (federal covered) investment advisors and their representatives.[2110]

FRAUD – Since the federal preemption of registration requirements, much of the focus of state legislators has been put on anti-fraud measures. Any fraudulent scheme, statement, or behavior regarding the offer, sale, or purchase of securities is considered unlawful under the uniform act.[2111] This applies to all cases, even to federal covered or exempt securities, as well as to investment advisors.[2112] Violation may result in criminal penalties, as well as civil liability.[2113] State administrators have the authority to investigate and enforce this uniform act.[2114]

### 3.4.3.3 State commodity laws

STATE COMPETENCE – States can adopt laws regarding off-exchange commodities and derivative transactions. While at first there was some uncertainty regarding

---

2105 Section 102(28) Uniform Securities Act 2002.
2106 Section 102(28)(D) Uniform Securities Act 2002.
2107 Section 201 Uniform Securities Act 2002.
2108 Section 202 Uniform Securities Act 2002.
2109 Section 301 Uniform Securities Act 2002. The other sections of article 3 provide the various registration procedures.
2110 Article 4 Uniform Securities Act 2002. Note that section 411 imposes a number of post-registration requirements regarding finances, recordkeeping, audits, and continuing education.
2111 Section 501 Uniform Securities Act 2002.
2112 Section 502 Uniform Securities Act 2002.
2113 Sections 508 and 509 Uniform Securities Act 2002.
2114 Article 6 Uniform Securities Act 2002.

the precise scope of states' competence to enact laws in the derivatives field, the Futures Trading Act of 1982 provided more clarity on the matter.[2115] States can now enact rules regarding any transaction involving commodities not subjected to the rules of a contract market, a foreign exchange or market, or the CFTC.[2116] Moreover, states are allowed to bring their own enforcement actions against those not obtaining the necessary registration.[2117]

Model code – In 1985 the North American Securities Administrators Association (NASAA) adopted the Model State Commodity Code. That model code has been implemented by approximately half of the states, with some incorporating its provisions in their securities laws.[2118] The model code particularly regulates certain off-exchange commodity contracts, as their exchange-traded counterparts are regulated by federal law.[2119]

Current state – However, as off-exchange commodity scams dwindled during the 1990's, interest in the model code and the adoption thereof decreased significantly.[2120] Today, states seem hesitant in bringing forth cases, even when it fits within their competence.[2121] Nevertheless, they do remain competent to prosecute cases that manage to evade the CFTC's expanded powers.[2122]

### 3.4.4 *Application to virtual currencies*

Securities regulation – The main legislative framework regarding federal US securities law is set by the 1933 Securities Act, and subsequent amendments thereto. Securities covered by the securities framework must be registered at the

---

2115 Section 229, *Pub. L.* 97–444.

2116 *Id.*

2117 *Id.*; Allen, J. M. (1985) "Kicking the Bucket Shop: The Model State Commodity Code as the Latest Weapon in the State Administrator's Anti-Fraud Arsenal", *Washington & Lee Law Review*, Vol. 42, 891.

2118 Todd, M. (2010) "The Murky Waters of State Commodity Laws", *Securities and Investment Blog – Cosgrove Law Group*, 27 July; Feigin, P. A. (2011) "The Model State Commodity Code in 2011 and new CFTC jurisdiction – Whither the states? Can "new dogs" learn "old tricks"?", *Banking & Financial Services Policy Report*, Vol. 31, 2.

2119 Allen, J. M. (1985) "Kicking the Bucket Shop: The Model State Commodity Code as the Latest Weapon in the State Administrator's Anti-Fraud Arsenal", *Washington & Lee Law Review*, Vol. 42, 890.

2120 Feigin, P. A. (2011) "The Model State Commodity Code in 2011 and new CFTC jurisdiction – Whither the states? Can "new dogs" learn "old tricks"?", *Banking & Financial Services Policy Report*, Vol. 31, 2.

2121 The aforementioned (footnote 2079) *Zelener* case was a clear example where states could have prosecuted this matter, even in the absence of federal competence in this regard. However, no state cases were brought forth. Feigin, P. A. (2011) "The Model State Commodity Code in 2011 and new CFTC jurisdiction – Whither the states? Can "new dogs" learn "old tricks"?", *Banking & Financial Services Policy Report*, Vol. 31, 3.

2122 *Ibid.*, 7.

SEC. The notion of securities itself is defined very broadly, listing a whole range of instruments. For the purposes of this research, some of those instruments were further analyzed.

Regarding notes, the US Supreme Court has developed a "family resemblance" test in the *Reves* case. According to that test, there must be money raised with an expectation of profit. The instrument must allow for common trading for speculation or investment. Reasonable expectations of the public must be taken into account, as well as other risk-reducing factors. Furthermore, it is clear that notes constitute a promise to pay the holder. Therefore, payment virtual currencies cannot be considered as notes, as they do not provide such a promise. Moreover, since payment virtual currencies mainly serve to purchase assets or goods, they do not satisfy the test. Investment virtual currencies, on the other hand, could – depending on the precise operational factors – satisfy all elements of the *Reves* test, and thus be regarded as notes.

Regarding stock, the US Supreme Court established a number of characteristics in the *Landreth* case that are typically associated with stock. Also here, the conclusion is that payment virtual currencies do not correspond to those characteristics, while investment virtual currencies could – again depending on operational factors.

Regarding investment contracts, the US Supreme Court has adopted a flexible test that takes into account economic reality in the *Howey* case. That test requires an investment of money in a common enterprise, leading to the expectation of profits generated predominantly by the efforts of the promotor or others. The first element of the test excludes closed scheme virtual currencies – as there is no money investment – and unidirectional scheme virtual currencies – as there is little to no risk involved. Bidirectional virtual currencies – for both payment and investment purposes – do satisfy this element of the test. The second element excludes closed scheme and unidirectional scheme virtual currencies – as there is no commonality. Also for bidirectional scheme virtual currencies such a commonality is difficult to establish. Investment virtual currencies, on the other hand, could have vertical commonality, and will almost always have horizontal commonality. However, it must be noted that case law is split amongst courts, meaning that the final assessment will depend on jurisdiction. The third element of the test is not satisfied by closed scheme and unidirectional scheme virtual currencies, as they do not provide an expectation of profit. Bidirectional virtual currencies could provide such an expectation, and investment virtual currencies will certainly do so. However, when combined with the last element of the test, it can be concluded that the potential profits for bidirectional scheme virtual currencies are the result of market forces, thus not relying on the efforts of others. Only investment virtual currencies can then be held to satisfy all elements of the *Howey* test, and thus be regarded as investment contracts. Late July 2017, the SEC presented a report confirming that such token sales, including those by The

DAO, can satisfy the *Howey* test, and thus constitute securities.[2123] The platforms offering such tokens then has to register as a national securities exchange – unless an exemption applies.[2124] One possible derogation from the full scope of securities law would be to limit the sale to accredited investors only.[2125]

The conclusion of this analysis is that payment virtual currencies – be it closed scheme, unidirectional scheme, or bidirectional scheme virtual currencies – do not correspond to the different types of securities found under US federal law. Only investment virtual currencies can fall under the scope of securities law, either as note, stock, or investment contract. Given the wide range of operational factors here, case-by-case analysis remains needed to provide a final assessment on the applicability of each type.[2126]

Derivatives regulation – Commodity derivatives transactions – such as futures and options – are regulated at the federal level as well. The notion of commodities has been defined very broadly, and it has been confirmed by the CFTC that the commodities definition encompasses virtual currencies. Important here is that the derivatives legal framework regulates transactions for future delivery. If actual delivery takes place within 28 days, the legal framework would, in principle, not apply. This is an important element for certain virtual currency service providers, such as exchanges. If such exchanges merely exchange money for virtual currency, and if they actually deliver the virtual currency to the user, an exchange transaction does not qualify as a commodity derivatives transaction. On the other hand, if there is no actual delivery – for instance due to the exchange keeping the virtual currency under its own custody – or if the transaction concerns the purchase of derivative instruments that do not give rise to actual delivery, the derivatives legal framework will become applicable.[2127]

State laws – With regard to state laws, it must first be noted that federal law has preempted the field of securities law to certain extent. As a result, state laws are more limited in scope, and can only regulate those aspects or those securities or commodity transactions not subjected to federal law. Nevertheless,

---

2123 SEC (2017) "Report of Investigation Pursuant to Section 21(a) of the Securities Exchange Act of 1934: The DAO", *SEC release 81207*, 11–15.

2124 *Ibid.*, 16–17.

2125 Batiz-Benet, J., Clayburgh, J., Santori, M. (2017) "The SAFT Project: Toward a Compliant Token Sale Framework", *saftproject.com*, 15–17.

2126 For an assessment of some of the elements that could lead to a qualification or disqualification of virtual currencies as securities, see: Coin Center (2016) "A Securities Law Framework for Blockchain Tokens", *coincenter.org*, 10–11. Also the Securities and Exchange Commission confirms that any qualification will depend on the precise facts and circumstances of a given case. SEC (2017) "Report of Investigation Pursuant to Section 21(a) of the Securities Exchange Act of 1934: The DAO", *SEC release 81207*, 17–18.

2127 Felsenthal, D., Old, G., Kalbag, M. (2016) "CFTC Bitfinex Enforcement Action", *Clifford Chance*, 2–3.

state laws remain important to this field, and can be applicable to certain transactions involving the virtual currencies that are considered as securities, or as commodity futures. For instance, if a certain virtual currency could be considered as a security, it is at the present moment unlikely to pass as a federal covered security. In that case, state registration requirements will apply, as well as general state anti-fraud measures. Similar conclusions can be drawn with regard to state commodity laws, which may apply where the federal framework is inapplicable.

## 4 LEGISLATIVE DEVELOPMENTS

Overview – This section provides an overview of legislative developments regarding virtual currencies at the US federal and state levels. As before, the goal here is not to provide an exhaustive overview of all such developments, but rather to focus on a number of noteworthy initiatives that may help shape the regulation of virtual currencies in the future. Some of these developments are still ongoing, and therefore may not be adopted in their current form, if at all. Other developments have been formally adopted, yet their implementation has thus far not yielded significant practical experience.

### 4.1 FEDERAL LEVEL

SB1241 – At the federal level, the most significant legislative initiative regarding virtual currencies comes in the form of a Senate bill, submitted in May 2017.[2128] That bill, introducing the 'Combating Money Laundering, Terrorist Financing, and Counterfeiting Act of 2017', primarily aims to tighten the federal anti-money laundering framework.[2129] With regard to virtual currencies, the bill expands current reporting duties regarding financial transactions to issuers, redeemers, or cashiers of digital currency, as well as to "*any digital exchanger or tumbler of digital currency*".[2130] Moreover, the bill requires the Secretary of Homeland Security to consult with the Commissioner of U.S. Customs and Border Protection in order to develop a strategy to "*interdict and detect prepaid access devices, digital currencies, or other similar instruments, at border crossings and other ports of entry for the United States*".[2131]

---

2128 Although it must be stated that several of the provisions of this bill are a re-introduction of an earlier bill: A bill to improve the prohibitions on money laundering, and for other purposes, *S. 1731*, 112th Cong. (2011).

2129 A bill to improve the prohibitions on money laundering, and for other purposes, *S. 1241*, 115th Cong. (2017).

2130 *Ibid.*, section 13.

2131 *Id.*

Consequences – The first elements of the bill relating to virtual currencies simply aim to bring them under the scope of the Bank Secrecy Act. The last element of the bill appears to aim to prevent individuals from bringing undeclared virtual currency assets into the US.[2132] However, that element of the bill in principle only requires the addressed authorities to report to Congress, it does not directly mandate policy in itself.[2133] Nevertheless, the fear that the bill will result in such a policy where all virtual currency holdings must be declared at the border is gaining hold rapidly.[2134] While the broader aim of the bill – to target and disrupt the cash flow of criminals – is in line with international sentiment under the current political and social climate, the broad strokes with which virtual currencies have been put under the bill's framework could be seen as regulatory overreach. However, it could also be held that such an overreach in an initial bill is deliberate, in order to allow for "*negotiation and compromise*" during the legislative proceedings.[2135] Given their non-physical nature, virtual currencies are not likely to be physically brought within the US. A policy requiring persons entering the US to declare whether they own over USD 10.000 worth of virtual currencies would then seem to go beyond mere anti-money laundering goals. More importantly, given the 2013 FinCEN guidance[2136], the bill could be considered as redundant since it has already been established clearly by now that certain virtual currency service providers are covered by the current anti-money laundering framework.[2137] Furthermore, the bill does not provide any explanation on what is to be considered as a digital currency, or who the different actors targeted here are, unlike FinCEN's guidance.[2138] The bill's unclear language, deviating from by now established terminology, could thus end up being counterproductive.

HR 2433 – Another bill was introduced in the House of Representatives in May 2017. That bill, providing for the Homeland Security Assessment of Terrorists Use of Virtual Currencies Act, would direct the Under Secretary of Homeland Security for Intelligence and Analysis to develop a "*threat assessment regarding the actual and potential threat posed by individuals using virtual currency to*

---

2132 Such undeclared assets may be seized and forfeited, as provided by the Bank Secrecy Act.

2133 Brito, J. (2017) "Congress's new anti-money laundering bill likely duplicates existing law on digital currency", *Coin Center*, 23 June.

2134 Higgins, S. (2017) "Forfeit Your Bitcoin? Congressional Bill Draws Fire Over Border Check Rules", *CoinDesk*, 19 June; McElroy, W. (2017) "Prepare For SB1241's Pit Bull Assault on Bitcoin Freedom", *Bitcoin.com*, 7 June; Cuen, L. (2017) "Bitcoin News: US Lawmakers Want Travelers To Declare Cryptocurrency Assets At Border", *International Business Times*, 19 June.

2135 McElroy, W. (2017) "Prepare For SB1241's Pit Bull Assault on Bitcoin Freedom", *Bitcoin.com*, 7 June.

2136 See section 3.3.1 of this chapter.

2137 Brito, J. (2017) "Congress's new anti-money laundering bill likely duplicates existing law on digital currency", *Coin Center*, 23 June.

2138 *Id.*

*carry out activities in furtherance of an act of terrorism, including the provision of material support or resources to a foreign terrorist organization*".[2139] A virtual currency is defined as "*a digital representation of value that functions as a medium of exchange, a unit of account, or a store of value*".[2140] That definition supposes that all virtual currencies can fulfill the core functions of money. However, as noted in chapter III, such is not necessarily the case. Essentially, the bill aims to investigate how the risk of virtual currencies used in terrorist financing should be handled. However, thus far there are no indications that such a risk is actually materializing.[2141] A focus on, as the bill suggests, "*the actual and potential threat*" is therefore imperative in order for such an endeavor to succeed. In this sense, the bill is more laudable than the aforementioned Senate bill, which appears to depart from the assumption that virtual currencies inherently pose such risks.

## 4.2 UNIFORM REGULATION OF VIRTUAL CURRENCY BUSINESSES ACT

COMMITTEE – Already in 2014, the Uniform Law Commission discussed the need to form a new committee tasked with developing a legal framework for virtual currency businesses.[2142] The reasoning behind this was that states' actions at the time – namely merely declaring their money services business licensing rules applicable to virtual currency service providers – did not fully address "*the rights and duties of the parties to a transaction*".[2143] However, at the same time it was remarked by the Commission that regulation should not go "*beyond a balance that will enhance opportunities for widespread adoptions of virtual currencies and for additional innovations in the payments space by companies currently working on virtual currency products and applications across state borders*".[2144] By October

2139 A bill to direct the Under Secretary of Homeland Security for Intelligence and Analysis to develop and disseminate a threat assessment regarding terrorist use of virtual currency, *H.R. 2433*, 115th Cong. (2017), section 2(a).

2140 *Ibid.*, section 2(b)(2).

2141 Carlisle, D. (2017) "Cryptocurrencies and Terrorist Financing: A Risk, But Hold the Panic", *Royal United Services Institute Commentary*, 2 March; Goldman, Z. K., Maruyama, E., Rosenberg, E., Saravalle, E., Solomon-Strauss, J. (2017) *Terrorist Use of Virtual Currencies: Containing the Potential Threat*, Washington, D.C.: Center for a New American Security, 36; HM Treasury (2015) "UK national risk assessment of money laundering and terrorist financing", *gov.uk*, 82–85; Redman, J. (2017) "U.S. Government to Research Role of Virtual Currencies in Terrorism", *Bitcoin.com*, 18 May; Brito, J. (2017) "It's time to assess the potential for terrorist use of cryptocurrencies", *Coin Center*, 16 May.

2142 Miller, F. H., Hughes, S. J. (2014) "Final Study Committee on Alternative and Mobile Payment Systems Report", *uniformlaws.org*, 1–2; Comizio, V. G. (2016) "Virtual Currencies: Growing Regulatory Framework and Challenges in the Emerging Fintech Ecosystem", *Fried Frank*, 16–18.

2143 *Ibid.*, 5.

2144 *Ibid.*, 7.

2015, the work of the committee had produced a first draft.[2145] In July 2017, the Uniform Law Commission formally approved the Uniform Regulation of Virtual Currency Businesses Act.[2146] This opens the path for states to adopt the act.

Definitions – Virtual currency is defined as a "*digital representation of value used as a medium of exchange, unit of account, or store of value that is not legal tender*".[2147] Compared to the definition established for the purposes of this research, the Uniform Act puts a greater emphasis on the functions of money. However, as noted in chapter III, not all functions of money can equally be fulfilled by all virtual currencies. The definition furthermore excludes transactions where value is granted as part of an affinity or rewards program and which value cannot be redeemed for legal tender, bank credit, or virtual currency, as well as virtual currencies used within games.[2148] A virtual currency business activity can comprise any of three activities: (A) exchanging, transferring, or storing virtual currency, or engaging in virtual currency administration; (B) holding electronic precious metals or electronic certificates of precious metals, including the issuing of shares or electronic certificates representing interests in precious metals; or (C) exchanging one or more virtual currencies used within games for virtual currency or for legal tender or bank credit outside those games.[2149]

Control, exchange, storage, and transfer – The main activities regarding virtual currencies listed in the Uniform Act concern exchange, storage, and transfers, all centering around the issue of control. Control implies the power to unilaterally execute or prevent a virtual currency transaction, or the power to direct the management, operations, or policies of a legal person through voting power or through a contract.[2150] An exchange involves the assumption of control of virtual currency to sell, trade, or convert it for legal tender, bank credit or one or more forms of virtual currency, or *vice versa*.[2151] Storage means maintaining control of virtual currency on behalf of a resident by a person other than the resident.[2152] Finally, a transfer involves control of virtual currency to credit virtual currency to the account of another person, to move virtual currency from one account to another, or to relinquish control of virtual currency to another person.[2153]

---

2145 National Conference of Commissioners on Uniform State Laws (2015) "Draft Regulation of Virtual Currencies", *uniformlaws.org*, 56p.

2146 National Conference of Commissioners on Uniform State Laws (2017) "Uniform Regulation of Virtual Currency Businesses Act", *uniformlaws.org*, 48p (hereinafter: Uniform Regulation of Virtual Currency Businesses Act).

2147 Section 102(23)(A) Uniform Regulation of Virtual Currency Businesses Act.

2148 Section 102(23)(B) Uniform Regulation of Virtual Currency Businesses Act.

2149 Section 102(25) Uniform Regulation of Virtual Currency Businesses Act.

2150 Section 102(3) Uniform Regulation of Virtual Currency Businesses Act.

2151 Section 102(5) Uniform Regulation of Virtual Currency Businesses Act.

2152 Section 102(20) Uniform Regulation of Virtual Currency Businesses Act.

2153 Section 102(21) Uniform Regulation of Virtual Currency Businesses Act.

Scope – The Uniform Act "*governs the virtual currency business activity of a person, wherever located, that engages in or holds itself out as engaging in the activity with a resident*".[2154] However, a number of exceptions are foreseen, inter alea for the activities covered by the Electronic Fund Transfer Act, or federal or state securities and commodities laws of licensed money transmitters, foreign exchange dealers, purely technical service providers, personal or academic use of virtual currencies "*including creating, investing, buying or selling, or obtaining virtual currency as payment for the purchase or sale of goods or services*", or business activities generating less than USD 5.000 annually.[2155]

License – Virtual currency business activities must be licensed.[2156] The Uniform Act defines the information that must be provided as part of the licensing procedure.[2157] It also provides an option for reciprocal licensing, which facilitates businesses applying for licenses in multiple states.[2158] The competent state department may determine the amount of the security to be deposited by the applicant, in order to ensure its faithful performance of its duties.[2159] Additionally, applicants must maintain a certain net worth and reserves.[2160] The same department will also examine the competence, financial condition, experience and general fitness of each applicant, both at the time of first licensing and for renewals.[2161] A less stringent registration procedure is foreseen for businesses generating a volume of less than USD 35.000 annually.[2162]

Examination and enforcement – Apart from the license renewal examination, authorities can annually examine licensees and registrants.[2163] For this, licensees and registrants are subjected to recordkeeping duties.[2164] Such records must be shared with authorities, with respect to confidentiality.[2165] Interim material changes, changes in control, and mergers must be notified.[2166] In terms of enforcement, departments can revoke or suspend licenses and registrations, issue cease and desist orders, grant injunctive relief, impose conditions, or assess civic penalties.[2167]

2154 Section 103(a) Uniform Regulation of Virtual Currency Businesses Act.
2155 Section 103(b) Uniform Regulation of Virtual Currency Businesses Act.
2156 Section 201 Uniform Regulation of Virtual Currency Businesses Act.
2157 Section 203 Uniform Regulation of Virtual Currency Businesses Act.
2158 Section 204 Uniform Regulation of Virtual Currency Businesses Act.
2159 Section 206 Uniform Regulation of Virtual Currency Businesses Act.
2160 Section 209 Uniform Regulation of Virtual Currency Businesses Act.
2161 Sections 207 and 208 Uniform Regulation of Virtual Currency Businesses Act.
2162 Section 210 Uniform Regulation of Virtual Currency Businesses Act.
2163 Section 301 Uniform Regulation of Virtual Currency Businesses Act.
2164 Section 302 Uniform Regulation of Virtual Currency Businesses Act.
2165 Sections 303 and 304 Uniform Regulation of Virtual Currency Businesses Act.
2166 Sections 305 – 307 Uniform Regulation of Virtual Currency Businesses Act.
2167 Sections 401 – 407 Uniform Regulation of Virtual Currency Businesses Act.

Disclosure and policies – Departments may determine the disclosures to be made to licensees' or registrants' clients.[2168] This includes disclosure on whether the product or service is covered by insurance, whether transfers or exchanges are revocable, a description of liabilities and responsibilities, information on the date and time of transfers, whether pre-authorized transfers can be stopped, information on the right to receive evidence of a transaction, information on changes in fees, and on the fact that virtual currencies are not legal tender.[2169] Those that control assets for their clients must maintain sufficient assets to satisfy their clients' entitlements.[2170] Certain programs must be adopted, for instance regarding anti-money laundering rules, fraud-detection, informational and operational security, disaster-recovery and business-continuity, as well as to ensure legal compliance with this framework.[2171]

Positive aspects – The Uniform Act demonstrates a well-informed understanding of the broad range of virtual currencies in the market. Its definition essentially excludes closed scheme and unidirectional scheme virtual currencies and thus focuses on bidirectional scheme virtual currencies. Additionally, its definition of virtual currency business activities, coupled with the exceptions, makes that purely technical service providers – such as software developers and miners – and users utilizing virtual currencies for personal use are exempted. While some business entities in the virtual currency community will likely find the licensing provisions too onerous, it should be reminded that their business is most likely already subjected to licensing as money transmitter. What the Uniform Act then does for users that want to use virtual currencies to conduct payments, or merchants that want to accept virtual currencies as means of payment, is that the act imposes several provisions aimed at protecting those customers of virtual currency businesses, whereas the Bank Secrecy Act and similar state laws focus only on anti-money laundering obligations. Moreover, by providing for reciprocal licenses, the Uniform Act greatly facilitates virtual currency businesses to become licensed in all states that adopted this act. The Uniform Act therefore received fairly wide support from virtual currency businesses.[2172]

Negative aspects – A more controversial aspect of the Uniform Act was that its original drafts applied article 8 of the UCC. Article 8 of the UCC aims to protect customers' assets in case of insolvency of the securities intermediary. Here, it was argued by stakeholders that a permissible investments approach is more

---

2168 Section 501 Uniform Regulation of Virtual Currency Businesses Act.

2169 *Id.*

2170 Section 502 Uniform Regulation of Virtual Currency Businesses Act.

2171 Section 601 Uniform Regulation of Virtual Currency Businesses Act.

2172 X (2017) "Open Letter of Support for the Uniform Law Commission's Model Regulation of Virtual Currency Businesses Act from Members of the Virtual Currency Industry", *coincenter.org/pdf/ulcindustryletter.pdf*.

preferable.[2173] The final version of the act removes the reference to article 8 of the UCC, with the possibility of such an application being introduced by a separate act.[2174] At the same time, it could be argued that the absence of this reference could lead to other bodies of law being invoked, which may be less harmonized than the UCC.[2175] Another element that received criticism is the so-called on-ramp provision. Businesses generating less than USD 5.000 annually are exempted, those generating between USD 5.000 and USD 35.000 are subject to registration, with those generating over USD 35.000 subject to full licensing. Some advocates had called for higher thresholds, as well as for differentiation according to the type of business, although these suggestions were not implemented in the final act.[2176] Here, it could be argued that lower thresholds result in a higher degree of consumer protection.[2177]

## 4.3 CALIFORNIA

PRECURSOR[2178] – In 2014, the state of California passed an act to repeal a section of its Corporations Code that limited corporations to putting into circulation only "*the lawful money of the United States*".[2179] The goal of this repeal was to ensure that issuing alternative currencies – including virtual currencies – would not violate state law. Early 2015, following the initiative of New York[2180], the state started to consider a licensing model for virtual currency businesses through a bill popularly known as AB1326.[2181] The original bill received quite some negative feedback from advocates.[2182] Even though the bill was well on its way to being adopted in 2015

2173 Cooper, K. (2017) "Uniform Regulation for Virtual Currency Businesses: Coming to a State Near You", *CoinDesk*, 2 July.

2174 Jensen, B. (2017) "Primer on the Draft Uniform Regulation of Virtual Currency Businesses Act", *Data Privacy + Security Insider*, 6 July.

2175 Cooper, K. (2017) "Uniform Regulation for Virtual Currency Businesses: Coming to a State Near You", *CoinDesk*, 2 July.

2176 Electronic Frontier Foundation (2017) "EFF Comments on May 2017 Style Committee Meeting Draft of the ULC's Regulation of Virtual Currency Business Act", *uniformlaws.org*, 4 May; Coin Center (2017) "Letter from Peter Van Valkenburgh, Coin Center", *uniformlaws.org*, 4 May.

2177 Nation, J., Civalleri, J. (2017) "A Look At The Uniform Regulation Of Virtual Currency Businesses Act", *ETHnews.com*, 29 June.

2178 Parts of this section were first developed at: Valcke, P., Vandezande, N., Van de Velde, N. (2015) "The Evolution of Third Party Payment Providers and Cryptocurrencies Under the EU's Upcoming PSD2 and AMLD4", *SWIFT Institute Working Paper No. 2015-001,* 63–67.

2179 An act to repeal Section 107 of the Corporations Code, relating to business associations, *Cal. Assemb. B. 129* (2013–2014), Chapter 74 (Cal. Stat. 2014).

2180 See section 4.6.

2181 Bill regarding an act An act to repeal Section 107 of the Corporations Code, and to amend, repeal, and add Section 2003 of, and to add Division 11 (commencing with Section 26000) to, the Financial Code, relating to digital currency, *Cal. Assemb. B. 1326* (2015–2016), as amended in Senate on 8 August 2016 (hereinafter: AB1326).

2182 The negative feedback was spearheaded by the Electronic Frontier Foundation (EFF), who mainly seemed to advocate against regulation itself. Reitman, R. (2015) "A License to Kill

– it had already passed the state Assembly and was well under way in the Senate – it was suddenly ordered to inactive file, thus rendering the bill dormant.[2183] In 2016, the bill was revived, yet in a very different form. The following paragraph will highlight the main provisions of that last version of the bill.

AB1326 – There were several notable changes to the 2016 version of AB1326 compared to its 2015 versions. One was that the term 'virtual currency' had been changed into 'digital currency'. Another was that the bill proposed to create a temporary – until 2022 – Digital Currency Business Enrollment Program instead of a licensing system, administered by the Commissioner of Business Oversight.[2184] However, this change seemed to be a mere cosmetic change, as the requirements for enrollment were fairly similar to those for licensing under the previous versions of the bill.[2185] Enrolled businesses would have had to adhere to certain advertising and disclosure rules.[2186] Customers would have received receipts.[2187] Enrolled businesses would have had to submit certain information to the commissioner, for instance regarding their business model, revenue, and liquidity.[2188] Audit reports and annual business reports would have had to be filed as well.[2189] The legal framework would not have replaced existing anti-money laundering rules, making separate registration as money services business under the Bank Secrecy Act necessary.[2190] The commissioner would have been granted broad enforcement options, including the disenrollment of a business, or the levying of civil penalties.[2191]

Withdraw and resubmit – While the later 2015 draft did receive some praise by stakeholders for striking the right balance, the fundamental 2016 rewrite did not manage to gain support.[2192] It was withdrawn very shortly after being introduced.[2193] Early 2017, a new bill was introduced under the new legislature,

Innovation: Why A.B. 1326 – California's Bitcoin License – is Bad for Business, Innovation, and Privacy", *eff.org*, 7 August. Other advocates, such as Coin Center, were more willing to find middle ground by first opposing the early drafts of the bill, but later supporting the substantial amendments made throughout the 2015 legislative process. Brito, J. (2015) "Letter of Support for AB 1326", *coincenter.org*, 7 July.

2183 *Leginfo.legislature.ca.gov/faces/billHistoryClient.xhtml?bill_id=201520160AB1326.*

2184 AB1326 Legislative Counsel's Digest (1).

2185 Section 26010 AB1326.

2186 Sections 26020 and 26022 AB1326.

2187 Section 26024 AB1326.

2188 Section 26030(a) AB1326.

2189 Section 26030(c)-(d) AB1326.

2190 Section 26036 AB1326.

2191 Sections 26046 – 26049 AB1326.

2192 Van Valkenburgh, P., Brito, J. (2016) "New California digital currency bill is a step backwards", *coincenter.org*, 9 August; Electronic Frontier Foundation (2016) "Oppose A.B. 1326: The Digital Currency Business Enrollment Act is Draconian, Overbroad, and Will Hurt Innovation in the State", *eff.org*, 11 August.

2193 Dababneh, M. (2016) "Assemblymember Dababneh Issues Statement on the Regulation of Virtual Currency", *a45.asmdc.org*, 15 August.

known as AB1123.[2194] This bill more closely resembles the 2015 version of AB1326 that did receive support – rather than that bill's earlier drafts or its 2016 rewrite.[2195] The following paragraphs will discuss the main provisions of AB1123.

AB1123 – DEFINITIONS – The definition of virtual currencies employed in the bill refers to any type of digital unit that is used as a medium of exchange or a form of digitally stored value.[2196] It excludes virtual currencies used on gaming platforms, or as part of customer affinity or rewards programs if they cannot be redeemed for fiat currency.[2197] Virtual currency businesses are those that maintain full custody or control over virtual currencies on behalf of others.[2198] While principally these businesses must be licensed by the Commissioner of Business Oversight, the bill provides a number of exemptions.[2199]

AB1123 – LICENSING – Virtual currency businesses must be licensed or exempted.[2200] The enrollment is subject to a USD 5.000 application fee and must contain predefined information on the applicant and the virtual currency business, including financial information and ownership information.[2201] Other fees apply as well, for instance for renewal, or to apply for a license to acquire control of a licensee.[2202] Each licensee must maintain a certain amount of capital, calculated taking in account – amongst others – its assets, liquidity, risk exposure, liabilities, volume of virtual currency activities, activities in other states, and financial protection through trust accounts and bonds.[2203]

AB1123 – EXAMINATION – The commissioner can examine virtual currency businesses to verify their compliance.[2204] Licensees are required to file reports in

2194 An act to repeal Section 107 of the Corporations Code, and to add Section 2178 to, and to add Division 11 (commencing with Section 26000) to, the Financial Code, relating to currency, *Cal. Assemb. B. 1123* (2017–2018), as amended in Assembly on 30 March 2017 (hereinafter: AB1123).

2195 Van Valkenburgh, P. (2017) "California is back at it; a new (old) virtual currency licensing bill is pending in the Assembly", *coincenter.org*, 12 April.

2196 Section 26000(b) AB1123.

2197 Section 26000(b) AB1123.

2198 Section 26000(c) AB1123.

2199 US departments and agencies at federal, State or local level; money transmission via the United States Postal Service; commercial banks insured via the Federal Deposit Insurance Corporation; licensed money transmitters; merchants or consumers using virtual currencies solely for the purchase or sale of goods or services; transactions where "*the recipient of virtual currency is an agent of the payee pursuant to a preexisting written contract and delivery of the virtual currency to the agent satisfies the payor's obligation to the payee*"; virtual currency networks; developers and miners; and those providing data storage or cyber security services for licensed virtual currency businesses. Section 26004 AB1123.

2200 Section 26002 AB1123.

2201 Section 26006(a)-(b) AB1123.

2202 Section 26006(d)-(h) AB1123.

2203 Section 26008 AB1123.

2204 Section 26009 AB1123. Such examination can be held jointly with other State or federal regulators: Section 26010 AB1123.

the case of bankruptcy, receivership, when revoking or suspending their license, in case of cancellation of their bond or trust accounts, or when charged with or convicted of a felony.[2205]

AB1123 – ENFORCEMENT – A license can be surrendered voluntarily[2206], and the commissioner can make decisions, issue opinions or provide guidance on the requirements.[2207] To protect the general welfare of the public, the commissioner may exercise all powers regarding virtual currency businesses enclosed in the bill, or order those businesses to comply.[2208] Licenses can be suspended or revoked, for instance when the virtual currency business does not comply with the provisions of the bill or the commissioner's examination thereof, in case of fraud, when unsafe practices or practices that go against the public interest are conducted, or in the case of insolvency or bankruptcy.[2209] The commissioner's acts are subject to review[2210], and the licensee may request a hearing when his license has been revoked or suspended.[2211] The commissioner can also impose civil penalties.[2212] Licensees must file independently prepared audit reports and public accountant certifications for each fiscal year, as well as quarterly financial reports, unless exempted therefrom by the commissioner.[2213]

AB1123 – OTHER PROVISIONS – Virtual currency businesses must provide clear information regarding the potential risks of virtual currencies to their customers.[2214] Upon completion of virtual currency transactions, receipts containing specific information must be issued.[2215] The commissioner is given broad discretion to provide exemptions.[2216] Licensed money transmitters can request to convert their license.[2217] Provisional licenses can be issued to small businesses of less than USD 1 million in outstanding obligations.[2218]

---

2205 Section 26011 AB1123. Records must be kept for three years: Section 26012 AB1123.

2206 Section 26013 AB1123.

2207 Section 25014 AB1123. This includes informal guidance to prospective applicants: Section 26015 AB1123.

2208 Section 26016 AB1123.

2209 Section 26017 AB1123.

2210 Section 26018 AB1123.

2211 Section 26019 AB1123.

2212 Section 26020 AB1123. Other enforcement options granted to the commissioner are also maintained: Section 26022 AB1123.

2213 Section 26023 AB1123. An additional fee may be levied for the commissioner's expenses in administering this duty: Section 26024 AB1123.

2214 Section 26025 AB1123.

2215 Section 26026 AB1123.

2216 Section 26029 AB1123.

2217 Section 26031 AB1123.

2218 Section 26032 AB1123.

FINDINGS – The filing of AB1123 appears to be more of a strategic choice to keep the matter on the table, reportedly without the intention of pushing the bill forward without further discussion and amendments.[2219] While the bill appears less strict than the state of New York's so-called BitLicense framework[2220], it arguably needs more work before it could result in acceptable legislation.[2221] Moreover, with the Uniform Act[2222] adopted, it seems more sensible for a state to join that framework, rather than to continue to develop its own deviating rulebook.[2223] As a result of a period of inactivity before the end of the legislative year, the bill failed to pass.

## 4.4 DELAWARE

DELAWARE BLOCKCHAIN INITIATIVE – Already in 2016, Delaware's then governor Markell unveiled plans to bring the state's business registration process to the blockchain.[2224] Such includes leveraging blockchain technology for so-called UCC-1 filings, which are critical in the process of secured loans.[2225] As part of this initiative – publicly known as the Delaware Blockchain Initiative – a bill was introduced in the state Senate to allow corporations to administer their records in any electronic form, including in distributed databases.[2226] While only introduced in May 2017, the bill passed both the state Senate and House in June 2017, before being signed into law by the governor in July 2017.[2227]

CONSEQUENCES – At first sight, the bill seems to bring little change. Already before its adoption, Delaware corporate law allowed records to "*be kept on, or by means of, or be in the form of, any information storage device, or method provided that the records so kept can be converted into clearly legible paper form within a reasonable time*".[2228] The important innovation of the bill is that a blockchain-assisted process has now been explicitly allowed, and that it includes stock ledgers and records of stock transfers. This evolution can then result in the

2219 Mehta, P. (2017) "California Assembly Revisits Virtual Currency Legislation", *ETHNews*, 6 April.

2220 See section 4.6.

2221 Van Valkenburgh, P. (2017) "California is back at it; a new (old) virtual currency licensing bill is pending in the Assembly", *coincenter.org*, 12 April.

2222 See section 4.2.

2223 Berns, J. K., Mehta, P. D. (2016) "Is Now the Time for California to Regulate Virtual Currency Businesses?", *BernsWeiss*, 17 July.

2224 Higgins, S. (2016) "Delaware to Seek Legal Classification for Blockchain Shares", *CoinDesk*, 2 May.

2225 Tinianow, A., Smith, M., Long, C., Santori, M. (2017) "Delaware's 2017 Resolution: Make Blockchain a Reality", *CoinDesk*, 3 January.

2226 A Bill to Amend Title 8 Of The Delaware Code Relating To The General Corporation Law, *Del. SB 69* (2017), section 7.

2227 *Legiscan.com/DE/bill/SB69/2017.*

2228 8 Del.C. §224.

creation of blockchain-issued and traded stock.[2229] Thus far, however, this would be limited to private stock, as publicly blockchain-traded stock requires closer coordination with state and federal securities regulators.[2230]

## 4.5 NEW HAMPSHIRE

TAXES AND FEES – In 2015, the New Hampshire state legislature considered a bill that would have allowed citizens to pay state taxes and fees in bitcoin.[2231] More concretely, it would have allowed the state to "*identify an appropriate third party payment processor that will process bitcoin transactions at no cost to the state*", indicating that the state itself would likely still receive its dues in US dollars, with the third party receiving payments in bitcoin and converting those funds into US dollars for the state.[2232] However, the New Hampshire House subcommittee charged with the bill deemed it 'inexpedient to legislate', a sentiment later confirmed by a plenary vote which ended the bill.[2233]

MONEY TRANSMITTERS – Another bill, introduced at the same time as the previous one, aimed to regulate the licensing of money transmitters.[2234] The original text of the bill defined money transmission as "*(a) engaging in the business of selling or issuing payment instruments or stored value; or (b) receiving currency or monetary value for transmission to another location*".[2235] Monetary value was defined as a "*medium of exchange, whether or not redeemable in currency*", with currency encompassing only legal tender.[2236] However, throughout the legislative work, amendments were introduced that expanded the definition of monetary value to include convertible virtual currency.[2237] Such a convertible virtual currency, in turn, would be defined as "*a digital representation of value that: (a) can be a medium of exchange, a unit of account, and/or a store of value; (b) has an equivalent value in real currency or acts a substitute for real currency; (c) may be centralized or decentralized; and (d) can be*

2229 Del Castillo, M. (2017) "Delaware House Passes Historic Blockchain Regulation", *CoinDesk*, 1 July; Eha, B. P. (2017) "Who owns what, really? In securities, Delaware may soon clear things up", *American Banker*, 5 July; Lucking, D., O'Hanlon, C. (2017) "Delaware Passes Law Permitting Companies to Use Blockchain Technology to Issue and Track Shares", *allenovery.com*, 25 July.

2230 Eha, B. P. (2017) "Delaware blockchain measure seeks to change 'very base' of financial system", *American Banker*, 13 June.

2231 Act requiring the state treasurer to develop an implementation plan for the state to accept bitcoin as payment for taxes and fees, *NH HB 552-FN* (2015 session).

2232 *Id.*

2233 State of New Hampshire (2016) "House Record – Calendar and Journal of the 2016 Session", *House Journal*, Vol. 38, nr. 8, 16–18.

2234 Act relative to licensing of money transmitters, *NH HB 666-FN* (2015 session).

2235 *Ibid.*, 399-G:1(XV) (original text).

2236 *Ibid.*, 399-G:1(XIV) and (VII) (original text).

2237 *Ibid.*, 399-G:1(XV) (final text).

*exchanged for currency or other convertible virtual currency.*"[2238] Essentially, the bill would make everyone who exchanges virtual currency for other currency – virtual or otherwise – a money transmitter, subject to stringent licensing requirements. The bill was adopted by both the New Hampshire House and Senate and signed into law by the governor, to be applicable from 1 January 2016.[2239]

Exemption – However, early 2017 a bill was introduced with the intention of providing an exemption to certain virtual currency users.[2240] Concretely, the bill expands the money transmission definition to include "*maintaining control of virtual currency on behalf of others*".[2241] A new virtual currency definition is provided, considering virtual currency as a "*digital representation of value that can be digitally traded and functions as a medium of exchange, a unit of account, or a store of value but does not have legal tender status as recognized by the United States government*".[2242] In terms of exemption, the bill provides an exemption to "*persons conducting business using transactions conducted in whole or in part in virtual currency*".[2243] The bill passed both the House and Senate, and was signed into law by the governor on 7 June 2017.[2244]

Findings – New Hampshire's legislative history on virtual currencies is remarkable for hitting all ends of the spectrum. First, the legislature displayed reluctance in accepting virtual currencies – and particularly the cryptocurrency bitcoin. Next, it adopted stringent rules on money transmitters, indicating clearly that virtual currency transmitters can fall under the scope of anti-money laundering rules as well. As a result, at least one such a company decided to temporarily halt its business in the state in order to clarify its legal position under the new framework.[2245] Finally, the legislature takes a closer look and decides to exempt certain businesses, in order to not make the legal framework too restrictive on budding businesses engaging with virtual currencies. However, time will have to tell precisely how successful this last evolution will prove, as the text of the law does not clearly demarcate which businesses using virtual currencies would benefit from the exemption.

2238 *Ibid.*, 399-G:1(VII) (final text).
2239 Codified in New Hampshire Revised Statutes Annotated Chapter 399-G.
2240 Act exempting persons using virtual currency from registering as money transmitters, *NH HB 436* (2017 session).
2241 *Ibid.*, (1).
2242 *Ibid.*, (2).
2243 *Ibid.*, (3).
2244 Amending New Hampshire Revised Statutes Annotated Chapter 399-G.
2245 Poloniex (2016) "Services to New Hampshire residents to be temporarily suspended on October 6, 2016", *Press release* 21 September 2016.

## 4.6 NEW YORK

BITLICENSE – The state of New York was the first State to consider specific regulation of virtual currency service providers.[2246] In 2013, the State Department of Financial Services launched an inquiry regarding virtual currencies.[2247] In that inquiry, the department lauds virtual currencies for bringing technological innovation to commerce platforms, while also pointing out the risks presented by virtual currencies under their current regulatory grey area.[2248] The department therefore aimed to investigate whether virtual currency service providers should be considered as money transmitters, as regulated and licensed under state law, or whether an entirely new framework should be considered.[2249] Later, a public hearing on the matter was announced.[2250] Shortly after those hearings, it was remarked by the department that the inclusion of virtual currencies under the existing regulatory framework does not suffice to cover all of the specific characteristics of virtual currencies, and that therefore a new legal framework would need to be proposed.[2251] This was followed by a public order holding that the department considered applications for the establishment of virtual currency exchanges.[2252] In July 2014, a first proposal for a legal framework was published, which became known as the 'BitLicense' framework, together with a public comment period.[2253] In December 2014, an updated framework incorporating feedback from those public comments was presented, together with a new public comment period.[2254] In May 2015, the first virtual currency service provider

---

2246 The following paragraphs were first developed at: Valcke, P., Vandezande, N., Van de Velde, N. (2015) "The Evolution of Third Party Payment Providers and Cryptocurrencies Under the EU's Upcoming PSD2 and AMLD4", *SWIFT Institute Working Paper No. 2015-001*, 62–65.

2247 New York State Department of Financial Services (2013) "Notice of Inquiry on Virtual Currencies", *Press memo*, 12 August.

2248 *Ibid.*, 1.

2249 *Ibid.*, 1–2.

2250 New York State Department of Financial Services (2013) "Notice of Intent to Hold Hearing on Virtual Currencies, Including Potential NYDFS Issuance of a 'BitLicense'", *Press memo*, 14 November.

2251 Lawsky, B. M. (2014) "Remarks on the Regulation of Virtual Currencies", presented at the *New America Foundation*, Washington, DC, 11 February.

2252 New York State Department of Financial Services (2014) "Order pursuant to New York Banking Law§§2-b, 24, 32, 102-a, and 4001-b and Financial Services Law§§301(c) and 302(a)", *dfs.ny.gov*, 11 March.

2253 New York State Department of Financial Services (2014) "Regulation of the Conduct of Virtual Currency Businesses", *NYS Register*, 23 July, 14–16; New York State Department of Financial Services (2014) "NY DFS releases proposed BitLicense regulatory framework for virtual currency firms", *Press release*, 17 July.

2254 New York State Department of Financial Services (2014) "Superintendent Lawsky remarks on revised BitLicense framework for virtual currency regulation and trends in payments technology", *Press release*, 18 December. The actual revised text was released in February 2015. Fogg, J. K. (2015) "NYDFS Changes to Proposed BitLicense Regulations", *Virtual Currency Report*, 9 February.

was granted a state license.[2255] The final regulatory framework followed shortly thereafter.[2256]

LICENSE – The State of New York's proposed BitLicense requires virtual currency businesses or their agents to obtain a license to conduct their activities.[2257] Exemptions are possible for those chartered under New York Banking Law and approved by the superintendent, and merchants and consumers that use virtual currency solely for the purchase or sale of goods or services or for investment purposes.[2258]

DEFINITIONS – Virtual currencies are considered as "*any type of digital unit that is used as a medium of exchange or a form of digitally stored value*", regardless of whether that unit is managed centralized or decentralized, or created by computing effort.[2259] That definition does not extend to closed scheme game virtual currencies, or to virtual currencies used in customer affinity or rewards programs, or digital units used on prepaid cards.[2260] Virtual currency businesses are those that (1) transmit virtual currency or receive them for transmission – except when such a transmission is conducted for non-financial purposes and does not involve the transfer of more than a nominal amount of virtual currency, (2) store, hold or maintain custody or control of virtual currency on behalf of others, (3) buy or sell virtual currency as a customer business, (4) perform exchange services as a customer business, or (5) control, administer, or issue a virtual currency.[2261] Moreover, the development and dissemination of software does not constitute a virtual currency business activity.[2262]

APPLICATION – The license can be applied for at the superintendent and needs to include amongst others information about the business, its affiliates, and its directors and principal shareholders, an independently prepared background report, fingerprints, a financial statement, tax information, and insurance policies.[2263] When not all requirements are satisfied, a conditional license may

2255 Be it as a trust company, not a company under the intended BitLicense.

2256 New York State Department of Financial Services (2015) "NYDFS grants first charter to a New York virtual currency company", *Press release,* 7 May; New York State Department of Financial Services (2015) "NYDFS Announces Final Bitlicense Framework for Regulating Digital Currency Firms", *Speech by Benjamin M. Lawsky, Superintendent of Financial Services,* 3 June; Regulation of the Conduct of Virtual Currency Businesses, *New York State Register* 24 June 2015, nr. DFS-29-14-00015-A, 7–9, codified as 23 CRR-NY I 200.

2257 23 CRR-NY §200.3(a)-(b).

2258 23 CRR-NY §200.3(c).

2259 23 CRR-NY §200.2(p).

2260 *Id.*

2261 23 CRR-NY §200.2(q).

2262 *Id.*

2263 23 CRR-NY §200.4(a).

be awarded.[2264] The application is subject to a USD 5.000 application fee.[2265] A license can be suspended or revoked after a hearing.[2266]

Requirements – Licensees must appoint a compliance officer to oversee their compliance with the rules of this licensing framework.[2267] The superintendent may determine the amount and form of capital that must be maintained by the licensee in order to safeguard its financial integrity.[2268] To protect customer assets, licensees must maintain a surety bond or trust account in US dollars, and virtual currency held on behalf of others must be maintained in virtual currency of the same type and amount as that which is owed or obligated to such other person.[2269] New products, services or activities or material changes to existing ones must be reported.[2270] When control over a licensee's activities changes – also including mergers or acquisitions – such an event is subject to prior approval by the superintendent.[2271] All virtual currency business activities must be recorded and preserved for at least seven years in order to allow for the determination of compliance.[2272] Such records must include, amongst others, transaction amounts and dates, the names and account numbers of parties involved in those transactions, bank statements, records of meetings of the board of directors, and records regarding compliance with applicable state and federal anti-money laundering laws, rules, and regulations.[2273] The superintendent will examine virtual currency businesses at least once every two years in order to determine the financial soundness of their business, management policies, and compliance.[2274] Moreover, licensees must submit quarterly financial statements regarding their financial condition, financial projections, and compliance.[2275] Additionally, yearly audited financial statements have to be submitted, including statements regarding management's responsibilities in preparing those statements, an assessment of the licensee's compliance, and certification of the statements by an officer or director of the licensee.[2276]

Programs – To further ensure customer protection and compliance, licensees are required to maintain an anti-money laundering program, based on a risk assessment for the legal, compliance, financial, and reputational risks associated

2264 23 CRR-NY §200.4(c).
2265 23 CRR-NY §200.5.
2266 23 CRR-NY §200.6(c)-(d).
2267 23 CRR-NY §200.7.
2268 23 CRR-NY §200.8.
2269 23 CRR-NY §200.9.
2270 23 CRR-NY §200.10.
2271 23 CRR-NY §200.11.
2272 23 CRR-NY §200.12.
2273 *Id.*
2274 23 CRR-NY §200.13(a).
2275 23 CRR-NY §200.14(a).
2276 23 CRR-NY §200.14(b).

with their activities.[2277] Such a program must provide for internal procedures to maintain compliance, including independent testing thereof, provide for record-keeping, and report on transactions and suspicious activities.[2278] Also the adoption of a cybersecurity program is required, together with the appointment of a chief information security officer, in order to ensure the availability of the services, and to protect data from tampering.[2279] Furthermore, in order to ensure that emergency measures can be taken if needed, a business continuity and disaster recovery (BCDR) plan must be drafted.[2280]

Protection and redress – All advertising and marketing material must identify the licensee's status as licensed virtual currency business.[2281] Licensees must communicate to their customers about the risks involved with virtual currencies, as well as of the applicable terms and conditions.[2282] Specific anti-fraud measures must be foreseen as well.[2283] Last, an accessible complaint mechanism must be provided.[2284]

Findings – While New York's BitLicense framework has been in force for over two years now, practical experience remains limited. Shortly after the BitLicense framework entered into force, it was reported that 22 companies had applied for a license.[2285] However, by the end of 2016, only five of them had effectively become licensed under the BitLicense framework.[2286] Moreover, a whole list of virtual currency companies – including some of the largest bitcoin exchanges – announced to withdraw their business from the state.[2287] One reason provided by some of those leaving the state is the hidden cost of the licensing procedure – including hiring attorneys to put together the necessary paperwork – with some citing real costs of over USD 50.000.[2288] Also the scope and language of the BitLicense framework has gathered criticism. Even after narrowing down the scope of the very broadly phrased early drafts, some uncertainties remains, for

2277 23 CRR-NY §200.15(b).
2278 Note that this provision also imposes know-you-customer and due diligence obligations, and explicitly forbids virtual currency transactions that would obfuscate or conceal the identity of an individual customer or counterparty: 23 CRR-NY §200.15(c)-(k).
2279 23 CRR-NY §200.16.
2280 23 CRR-NY §200.17.
2281 23 CRR-NY §200.18.
2282 23 CRR-NY §200.19.
2283 23 CRR-NY §200.19(g).
2284 23 CRR-NY §200.20.
2285 Rizzo, P. (2015) "NYDFS Receives 22 Initial BitLicense Applications", *CoinDesk*, 13 August.
2286 New York State Department of Financial Services (2017) "2016 Annual Report", *dfs.ny.gov*, 5–6.
2287 Roberts, D. (2015) "Behind the "exodus" of bitcoin startups from New York", *Fortune*, 14 August.
2288 Bello Perez, Y. (2015) "The Real Cost of Applying for a New York BitLicense", *CoinDesk*, 13 August.

instance with regard to so-called multisig wallets.[2289] Also the conditional license has been criticized for being subject to the superintendent's discretion, rather than to objective criteria.[2290] Moreover, the requirement to notify new products or changes to products could disturb normal business activities, and the anti-money laundering rules were found to exceed existing state and federal rules in this regard.[2291] Finally, jurisdiction has been a critical point as well, given that service providers would have to determine whether or not their customers are located in the state of New York.[2292] The aforementioned Uniform Act[2293] addresses such concerns. For instance, the Uniform Act's on-ramp provisions allow for differentiation according to company size, and its anti-money laundering rules do not duplicate or tighten existing rules. The scope of the Uniform Act is more balanced and well-demarcated, and its reciprocal licensing significantly reduces licensing costs compared to a system where each state would have a different framework. However, at this point it remains to be seen whether the state of New York will replace its BitLicense with the framework proposed by the Uniform Act.

# 5 INTERIM CONCLUSIONS

## 5.1 FINDINGS

Chapter goals – The main goal of this chapter was to assess whether – and if so: how – virtual currencies are currently regulated at the US federal and state levels in four fields comparable to those examined in the previous chapters for the EU. These four fields are: money regulation, payment regulation, anti-money laundering regulation, and investment regulations. Moreover, currently ongoing legislative procedures were analyzed, in order to get a better view on virtual currency regulation in the US *de lege ferenda*. The findings of this chapter may provide insight on whether US legislators and regulators have found a need to regulate virtual currencies, and on what form such regulation may take – either considering virtual currencies under existing frameworks or by adopting entirely new frameworks. This subsection will first synthesize the findings of the comparative research.

---

2289 Hughes, S. J., Middlebrook, S. T. (2015) "Advancing a Framework for Regulating Cryptocurrency Payments Intermediaries", *Yale Journal on Regulation*, Vol. 32, 539–540; Brito, J., Castillo, A. (2013) *Bitcoin: A Primer for Policymakers*, Arlington: George Mason University Mercatus Center, 49–50.

2290 Brito, J., Castillo, A. (2013) *Bitcoin: A Primer for Policymakers*, Arlington: George Mason University Mercatus Center, 51.

2291 *Id.*; Hughes, S. J., Middlebrook, S. T. (2015) "Advancing a Framework for Regulating Cryptocurrency Payments Intermediaries", *Yale Journal on Regulation*, Vol. 32, 536–537 and 442.

2292 Hughes, S. J., Middlebrook, S. T. (2015) "Advancing a Framework for Regulating Cryptocurrency Payments Intermediaries", *Yale Journal on Regulation*, Vol. 32, 540–541.

2293 See section 4.2.

Money – While the US Constitution was found to limit the issuing of coins and notes, the relevant provision only applies to state and local actors. Private actors are therefore free to issue private currencies – virtual or otherwise. Counterfeiting statutes, however, require that such private currencies may not resemble the US dollar and that they may not be issued with an intent to defraud users. In the same vein, the 1862 Stamp Payments Act intends to prevent private currencies of values lower than one US dollar from competing with legal tender. In order for the Stamp Payments Act to apply to the case of virtual currencies, there must be broad circulation and the intention for the virtual currency to be used instead of legal tender. Moreover, the Stamp Payments Act targets obligations, which imply a right on the holder to be paid by the issuer. For the virtual currencies analyzed for the purposes of this research, it can then be concluded that most of the money-related provisions do not apply to them. Virtual currencies are not targeted by the Constitution or by anti-counterfeiting rules, given their non-physical nature and the fact that the schemes analyzed here have no underlying fraudulent intentions. The Stamp Payments Act does not apply to closed scheme or unidirectional scheme virtual currencies, given their limited circulation. The main bidirectional scheme virtual currencies analyzed here – cryptocurrencies – are no obligations, thus also avoiding the application of the Stamp Payments Act.

Payments – Regarding payments, the main act at the US federal level is the 1978 Electronic Fund Transfer Act, further regulated through the Federal Reserve's Regulation E. States add consumer protection measures – to certain extent comparable to the EU's payment services framework – through their implementation of the UCC. Applying those acts to virtual currencies, however, proves difficult. The Electronic Fund Transfer Act revolves around the use of an account, which can only be held by a financial institution. While the scope of the Electronic Fund Transfer Act does include providers of access devices and prepaid instruments, also the provisions on those service providers appear difficult to apply to virtual currencies, or still require intermediation by a financial institution. As a result, the federal rules in the payments field are not applicable to virtual currency service providers. Similar problems exist at the state level, through article 4A of the UCC. That article relies on the presence of a traditional financial actor – namely a bank – acting as executioner of a payment order. While the general contract principles of the UCC could apply to virtual currency transactions, the broader consumer protection framework for funds transfers of article 4A does not.

Anti-money laundering – At the US federal level, money laundering legislation is divided in two tiers. A first tier, set by the 1970 Bank Secrecy Act, sets reporting duties aimed at preventing money laundering. A second tier, set by the 1986 Money Laundering Control Act, criminalizes and sanctions money laundering. While the federal level requires registration of money services businesses – and imposes certain reporting and KYC requirements – state legislation may impose more stringent licensing requirements on these service providers. FinCEN, the federal entity responsible for enforcing the Bank Secrecy Act, has adopted further rules defining money services businesses. Moreover, FinCEN has provided guidance on the applicability of the anti-money laundering rules to virtual currencies and their service providers. FinCEN's guidance makes it clear that virtual currency exchangers and administrators could be considered as money services businesses, to the extent that they (1) accept and transmit convertible virtual currencies; or (2) buy or sell convertible virtual currencies for any reason. Users, who only use virtual currencies to purchase goods or services, or who only occasionally and not for profit exchange virtual currencies for real currencies, are not subjected to the Bank Secrecy Act. Moreover, given the need for exchange between virtual currencies and real currencies, closed and unidirectional scheme virtual currencies can be exempt. In order for the Money Laundering Control Act to apply, there must be a degree of knowledge that the property in a transaction derived from crime, and possibly from one of the specified unlawful activities listed in that act. The Money Laundering Control Act can then be applied to virtual currency transactions, insofar as they constitute money laundering. At the state level, a uniform act – the Uniform Money Services Act – can impose licensing requirements on bidirectional virtual currencies, given that they constitute a circulating medium of exchange. While this uniform act has not been widely implemented, existing state laws in the anti-money laundering field show similar provisions.

Investments – The legal framework regarding investments mainly regulates securities and commodity derivatives. In both cases, federal law imposes registration requirements for both the products and certain service providers – such as exchanges and investment advisors. Securities are defined very broadly, encompassing several instruments such as notes, stock, and investment contracts. Regarding notes, it can be held that they imply a promise to pay, which is not present for payment virtual currencies. Furthermore, payment virtual currencies do not satisfy the elements of the US Supreme Court's "family resemblance" test. Investment virtual currencies, on the other hand, could under certain circumstances satisfy that test. For stock, the US Supreme Court established the main characteristics of this type of security. Also in applying that case law, it can be argued that payment virtual currencies do not satisfy the characteristics of stock, while investment virtual currencies may – depending on their precise operationalization. Regarding investment contracts, reference can be made to another US Supreme Court case, which established the *Howey* test. Under that test, economic reality prevails over form. Applying the *Howey* test to virtual currencies, it can be concluded that closed scheme and unidirectional scheme virtual currencies cannot satisfy the test. While bidirectional scheme virtual currencies can be argued to satisfy some elements of the *Howey* test, they are unlikely to satisfy all elements. It must also be noted that lower courts are split over the element of common enterprise, indicating that the outcome can in part be determined by jurisdiction. For investment virtual currencies – again: depending on their precise operationalization – it can be concluded, as confirmed by the SEC, that these virtual currencies do satisfy all elements of the *Howey* test, and can thus be considered securities. Regarding commodity derivatives, the CFTC has made clear that virtual currencies can be regarded as commodities. However, the derivatives legal framework applies to transactions made for future delivery, meaning that it does not apply if there is actual delivery within 28 days. Such exempts the transactions normally associated with payment virtual currencies. As under EU law, it are then only be derivative contracts – having virtual currencies as underlying assets – that are caught under the scope of the derivatives legal framework. Regarding state laws, it must be said that federal law has to some extent preempted states' competence in the securities field. Nevertheless, state laws can impose additional anti-fraud measures, and can also impose additional registration requirements to those securities and commodity derivatives not fully covered by federal law.

*De lege ferenda* – Apart from applying existing legal frameworks to virtual currencies, US legislators are also actively working on new rules tailored to virtual currencies and their service providers. One of the most notable developments here is the Uniform Regulation of Virtual Currency Businesses Act. This Uniform Act aims to harmonize the regulation of these service providers across the states, for which it includes reciprocal licensing. The Uniform Act demonstrates clear and balanced language, focusing purely on bidirectional scheme virtual currencies. This Uniform Act is a remarkable improvement over similar frameworks such as that under consideration in California or that already adopted in New York, the latter of which has caused many virtual currency service providers to retract their business from the state. Thus far, most regulatory initiatives seem to confirm the application of anti-money laundering rules, with notably the state of Delaware looking at leveraging blockchain technology for stock trading.

## 5.2 NORMATIVE ASSESSMENT

Normative assessment – Having established the extent to which virtual currencies are currently regulated at the US federal and state levels in the four fields identified for the purposes of this research, this subsection will provide an interim evaluation of the desirability of the current regulatory situation according to the normative criteria established for the purposes of this research.

Legal certainty – While some uncertainty remains with regard to the applicability of existing laws in the field of payments to virtual currencies, recent interventions by regulators have clarified the applicability of laws in the fields of anti-money laundering and investments. Legislative initiatives are underway to further clarify applicability of anti-money laundering rules. Moreover, a well-established body of case law provides guidance in applying existing laws to new developments such as virtual currencies, and it is clear that US law – particularly in the field of investments – allows for a more flexible approach than what was found for EU law. While the full scope of applicability to more recent developments – particularly investment virtual currencies – has not been completely cleared up yet, the overall conclusion is that there is fairly little legal uncertainty regarding the applicability of existing US laws in these four fields to virtual currencies.

Proportionality – The applicability of existing US laws in the four fields identified here can be considered to be proportionate to the risks posed by the different types of virtual currencies. Closed scheme and unidirectional scheme virtual currencies appear exempt from these legal frameworks, and for bidirectional scheme virtual currencies only certain service providers fall within the scope of these frameworks – particularly that in the field of anti-money laundering. Developments regarding investment virtual currencies – and virtual currency derivative instruments – can be caught under the scope of regulation in the field of investments, while payment virtual currencies appear exempt from that field of regulation. Overall, regulators and legislators have thus far shown constraint and a willingness to engage with the sector in developing new legal frameworks. This restraint has resulted in legal frameworks that clearly distinguish between different types of virtual currencies, as well as between different actors engaging with virtual currencies. One notable case of regulatory overreach can be found in the state of New York, where the BitLicense framework has driven away certain virtual currency service providers.

Trust – Regulators in the US have made clear that, while some requirements of the legal frameworks analyzed here can be applied to virtual currencies, many consumer protection measures – such as deposit insurance – do not apply. This leads to a similar situation as for what was found regarding EU anti-money laundering laws. While registration requirements and certain anti-money laundering and anti-fraud measures can certainly help to deter malicious market players, such measures alone cannot provide the safeguards needed to truly raise trust in virtual currencies and their service providers. Despite the current level of regulation, users of virtual currencies – be it consumers, merchants, or investors – still do not benefit from the additional consumer protection measures of financial law. More recent initiatives, such as the Uniform Regulation of Virtual Currency Businesses Act, aim to provide broader consumer protection.

Regulatory coherence – Despite being one single country, US law in these four fields does contain a risk of regulatory incoherence, given that state laws can differ significantly from each other and from federal law. To some extent, federal law has preempted state law – for instance in the fields of money and investments – but even in those cases potential differences between state laws remain. The adoption of uniform and model codes in several fields have helped harmonization efforts, but as such codes are non-binding, they cannot enforce harmonization. Moreover, current developments show that federal and several state legislators are working on new legal frameworks aimed at virtual currencies and their service providers. Given that the provision of virtual currency services will in practice almost always be an interstate matter, a more coherent approach can be recommended. The aforementioned Uniform Regulation of Virtual Currency Businesses Act can, therefore, prove to be a welcome initiative to this end, if it receives wide adoption by the states.

Conclusion – Overall, it can be concluded that the assessment of the current regulatory position of virtual currencies and virtual currency service providers under federal and state US law in these four fields has yielded positive results. The legal frameworks analyzed here demonstrate a surprising degree of flexibility when being applied to new developments such as virtual currencies, enabled by their regulators and a substantial body of case law. Moreover, there is no strong indication of regulatory overreach, with the applicable frameworks allowing to distinguish between types of virtual currencies and service providers. However, the applicability of current legal frameworks is limited to registration, anti-money laundering, and anti-fraud measures. Significant consumer protection measures remain absent. Also the disparity between state and federal legislators in adopting new legal frameworks aimed at virtual currencies could use more attention to regulatory coherence. At the same time, it must be noted that initiatives to increase consumer protection in the field of virtual currencies and to enhance harmonization across state lines are well under way, and could provide a solution to these issues in the coming years.

# PART III

# CONCLUSION

# CHAPTER VIII
# INTEGRATION, ASSESSMENT, CONCLUSIONS, AND RECOMMENDATIONS

## 1 INTEGRATION OF RESEARCH FINDINGS

First research question – This section will summarize and integrate the findings of the previous chapters. The goal is to answer the first main research question, inquiring to what extent virtual currencies are currently regulated as money, or under the legal frameworks regarding e-money, payment services, anti-money laundering, and investment services in the EU. In doing so, the aim is to expose the gaps and incompatibilities following from the current position of virtual currencies under the legal frameworks analyzed in this research.

Typology – Before going into the analysis of whether the analyzed legal frameworks can apply to virtual currencies, it is reminded that a typology has been established for the purposes of this research. The typology is based on two financial flows: (1) the flow of legal tender or similar means of payment into virtual currency, and (2) the flow of virtual currency into legal tender or similar means of payment. As a result, three main types of virtual currencies can be distinguished. First, there are closed scheme virtual currencies, where neither financial flow is present. Second, there are unidirectional scheme virtual currencies, where only the first financial flow is present. Third, there are bidirectional scheme virtual currencies, in which both financial flows are present. Those three types serve to classify all practical examples analyzed for the purposes of this research. For bidirectional scheme virtual currencies, it is additionally remarked that they can serve both as means of payment and as means of investment. A number of risks were identified for virtual currencies, amongst which the risks posed by the relative anonymity and volatility of virtual currencies. If those risks are not properly mitigated by regulation, it can be argued that such a lack of regulation constitutes a derivative risk. Applying the risks to the typology, the conclusion is that closed scheme virtual currencies pose little, if any, risks to users, markets, investors, or service providers. Unidirectional scheme virtual currencies pose moderate risks to users and service providers, but principally do not affect investors or the market. Last, bidirectional scheme virtual currencies pose risks to all four of those actors.

Trust – Like any relationship or transaction, the use of virtual currencies requires a certain degree of trust from users in the virtual currency issuer or in the underlying system – such as the blockchain in cryptocurrencies. According to the trust balance, that degree of trust requires a corresponding degree of trustworthiness from the virtual currency issuer or ecosystem. One element found in law to operationalize trust is the figure of the trust service provider. However, at the present moment, the legal framework developed around that figure cannot apply to virtual currencies or their service providers. Recourse to raise trust in virtual currencies through law will then have to be sought in other legal domains, such as consumer law and financial law. While the application of consumer law could indeed help raise the trustworthiness of virtual currency service providers, financial law seems more suited to that task as it could address more of the risks identified under the typology.

## 1.1 VIRTUAL CURRENCIES AS MONEY

Money as a legal concept – In chapter III, it was found that legal notions of money often focus on the concept of legal tender. While also closely related assets – such as bank account balances and credit lines – could be explicitly or implicitly accepted as money[2294], it remains a narrow concept. Given that virtual currencies are – at least as of yet – not designated as legal tender, it seems difficult to consider them as money from a legal point of view. However, it is clear that such a narrow view becomes more and more untenable in an increasingly digitalized society, and limited case law has already considered virtual currencies as instruments fulfilling at least the same role as money.

Money under legal-economic thinking – Also from the point of view of legal-economic theories, it appears difficult to classify virtual currencies as money. The state theory does not accept virtual currencies, given that this theory focuses on the acceptance of a means of payment by a state, and given that thus far states do not accept payments in virtual currencies. For the same reasons, virtual currencies are not considered as money under the Institutional theory. The Societal theory is more welcoming of virtual currencies, but only when they become more generally accepted as a means of payment – which has not happened yet, or may even not be the intention of certain virtual currencies. A similar requirement applies under the amended state theory, which also requires the use

[2294] For instance, bank account balances are included in the ECB's M1 category. Longer term deposits can be considered as money under the M2 category of the money supply.

of a legal tender denomination. Both requirements disqualify virtual currencies from being considered as money under the amended state theory. Only the credit theory of money would be more welcoming of virtual currencies. In terms of functions of money, it can be held that virtual currencies could in theory fulfill the main functions of money. However, while they can serve as a medium of exchange, they are not widely accepted as such, nor may such be their intention. Regarding the unit of account function, it is clear that virtual currencies can serve as their own unit of account, although there are still opinions to the contrary due to the strong value fluctuations of particularly cryptocurrencies. Last, the volatility of certain virtual currencies, and inherent operational factors of others, may limit their use as store of value. This makes that, in practice, virtual currencies thus far only poorly fulfill the functions of money.

Outlook – Looking at different strands of economic thinking on money, it is clear that the concept of money is in constant evolution. It is therefore not unthinkable for virtual currencies to be considered as money under a future theory, or under a revision of or renewed attention for an existing theory. Given the close similarities between money and virtual currencies, and given that traditional theories on money are becoming increasingly untenable, such an evolution can even be argued to be desirable. From a legal point of view, neither EU nor US law expressly forbids the use of virtual currencies as a money-like concept. Future developments could then be more welcoming of the acceptance of virtual currencies as money. In such case, it does still need to be questioned whether virtual currencies can fully serve as money without state intervention. However, even if such theoretical shift were not to happen, the non-acceptance of virtual currencies as money – and the resulting non-applicability of legal tender laws – does not necessarily preclude the applicability of the legal frameworks that are analyzed for the purposes of this research, as those frameworks generally employ their own terminology and definitions.

## 1.2 VIRTUAL CURRENCIES UNDER E-MONEY AND PAYMENT SERVICES

Virtual currencies as e-money in the EU – In chapter IV, it was found that the current EU legal framework on e-money cannot apply to virtual currencies. This is because virtual currencies either cannot be considered as being issued upon receipt of funds, or are only accepted by their issuer or in a limited network around that issuer. However, the broad range of operational factors in virtual currencies warrants a case-by-case assessment, as particular sets of factors could result in different conclusions.

Virtual currencies and payment services in the EU – Given the focus of the EU payment services framework on service providers, the payment services legal framework cannot regulate the emission of virtual currencies. Moreover, it was found that closed scheme and unidirectional scheme virtual currency service providers do not fall under the scope of the payment services legal framework. The inclusion of bidirectional virtual currency service providers under the payment services framework is more debatable, but generally speaking it can be concluded that also here the payment services legal framework does not apply – despite minority opinions to the contrary.

Virtual currencies as means of payment in the US – Given that the notion of e-money is not regulated as such in the US, there are no legal frameworks with which a direct comparison can be made. However, it was found in chapter VII that the Electronic Fund Transfer Act and certain provisions of the Uniform Commercial Code aim to provide comparable protections to the users of means of payments as the e-money and payment services frameworks provide in the EU. Due to the focus of the relevant provisions in US law on the intervention of a traditional financial intermediary – generally not present in virtual currency transactions – there are only very limited scenarios imaginable where virtual currency service providers fall under the scope of the Electronic Fund Transfer Act or the Uniform Commercial Code.

Outlook – Having found that the EU legal framework on e-money does not apply to virtual currencies, the question is whether the e-money framework demonstrates room for the inclusion of virtual currencies. Given the underdevelopment of the e-money market and the shifting payments landscape since the original inception of the e-money legal framework, it is clear that the e-money framework is in need of a revision. If the e-money framework aimed to include virtual currencies, this would, however, require a fundamental overhaul of the e-money definition. At the same time, not all types of virtual currencies should be included under the e-money legal framework, and differentiation through exemptions or waivers is needed. The focus of the payment services framework on a predefined list of payment services opens the possibility for the inclusion of certain virtual currency service providers under the payment services legal framework. Such an inclusion does entail the complication of having to predefine those service providers that need to be regulated under the payment services legal framework, but at the same time such an approach allows for easier differentiation between those services that should and those that should not be regulated. The EBA already advocated the option of including virtual currencies under the payment services framework. In the US, the Electronic Fund Transfer Act and the Uniform Commercial Code could be amended. However, the recently adopted Uniform Regulation of Virtual Currency Businesses Act seems to have intervened in aiming to provide more consumer protection – outside of the Electronic Fund Transfer Act and the Uniform Commercial Code – for the users of virtual currencies as means of payment – if adopted by the states.

## 1.3 VIRTUAL CURRENCIES UNDER ANTI-MONEY LAUNDERING

Anti-money laundering in the EU – Up to the AMLD4, the anti-money laundering legal framework in the EU did not explicitly include virtual currencies. Given the broad focus of the anti-money laundering legal framework, it could be argued that virtual currencies could already serve as the property targeted by it. However, absent obliged entities that need to report on virtual currency money laundering activities, the inclusion of virtual currencies as the property targeted by the anti-money laundering framework would not prove of much value in practice. Meanwhile, the European legislator has intervened and amended the anti-money laundering legal framework, by explicitly including virtual currencies under its scope and by adding certain bidirectional scheme virtual currency service providers to the list of obliged entities. Those amendments clearly make the anti-money laundering legal framework applicable, at least to a few particular virtual currency service providers.

Anti-money laundering in the US – In the US, the federal regulator concerned with the anti-money laundering framework, FinCEN, has explicitly stated that the main instrument in the field of anti-money laundering rules, the Bank Secrecy Act, can apply to those accepting and transmitting bidirectional scheme virtual currencies, or those buying or selling bidirectional scheme virtual currencies. FinCEN did clarify that regular users and technical service providers would, in principle, not be caught under the scope of the anti-money laundering legal framework. The second leg of federal US anti-money laundering law, the Money Laundering Control Act, could apply as well. Also state laws – either through the adoption of the Uniform Money Services Act or through a separate framework – are in several states applicable to bidirectional scheme virtual currency service providers. Some states have amended their anti-money laundering legal frameworks to make such an application explicit, or have even adopted a completely separate framework to this end – as the state of New York did with its BitLicense.

Outlook – The result of the 2018 amendments to the AMLD4 is that the anti-money laundering legal framework is now applicable to certain virtual currency service providers. However, given the broad range of service providers, which is growing continuously, the practical result of that expansion may prove limited. Moreover, it is reminded that, in terms of risks, the inclusion under the anti-money laundering legal framework only addresses one particular risk – namely anonymity. Other risks posed by virtual currencies still need to be addressed elsewhere. In the US, laws in the anti-money laundering field at both the federal and state levels are principally applicable in their current forms. However, some states are still adopting amendments to make such an application explicit. Furthermore, at the state level the Uniform Regulation of Virtual Currency

Businesses Act aims to combine anti-money laundering rules with more consumer protection-oriented measures.

## 1.4 VIRTUAL CURRENCIES AND INVESTMENT SERVICES

Investments in the EU – As noted in chapter VI, the EU framework in the investment services field revolves around the notion of financial instruments. Financial instruments are at the core of investment services, offered by the entities regulated by the MiFID framework. Financial instruments include transferable securities, money-market instruments, units in collective investment undertakings, and a whole range of derivative instruments. Applying the investment services legal framework to virtual currencies, it can then be concluded that closed scheme and unidirectional scheme virtual currencies would not fall under the scope of the investment services framework, given their inherently limited transferability and negotiability. These two types of virtual currencies do not seem capable of serving as means of investment. Bidirectional scheme virtual currencies, by contrast, do demonstrate a certain propensity to serve as means of investment. However, a further distinction should be made between those bidirectional scheme virtual currencies primarily serving as means of payment, and those primarily serving as means of investment. Looking at payment bidirectional virtual currencies, it was found difficult to argue that these virtual currencies could be considered as financial instruments under the MiFID framework. Payment bidirectional virtual currencies do not confer a right on their issuer – as is required of transferable securities – nor are they short-term instruments – unlike money-market instruments. However, derivative instruments having payment bidirectional virtual currencies as underlying assets are caught under the scope of the MiFID framework, given that derivative instruments are financial instruments in their own right. Looking at investment bidirectional scheme virtual currencies, it can be argued that these instruments could be considered as financial instruments under the MiFID framework, for instance when they indeed confer certain rights on their issuer. Also other related legal frameworks can in that case apply, such as the EU's prospectus regime. However, the application of the MiFID and other frameworks of course depends on the precise operationalization of the virtual currency in question, which must be assessed on a case-by-case basis.

Investments in the US – At the US federal level, securities law has been well developed through US Supreme Court case law. For notes, there is the "family resemblance" test, whereas for stock, case law has defined the typical characteristics of this particular instrument. More relevant for virtual currencies is the *Howey* test developed for investment contracts. The *Howey* test requires an investment of money in a common enterprise, leading to the expectation of profits, whereby such profits are predominantly derived from the efforts of others. Applying those four elements of the *Howey* test to virtual currencies, it can be held that closed scheme and unidirectional scheme virtual currencies clearly cannot satisfy all elements of the test. Arguably, neither would payment bidirectional scheme virtual currencies. Investment bidirectional scheme virtual currencies, on the other hand, could possibly satisfy the elements of the *Howey* test – and thus be regarded as securities – of course depending on their precise operationalization. These conclusions have been confirmed by the SEC. In terms of commodities, the CFTC has held that virtual currencies could constitute commodities, insofar as there is indeed future delivery. State laws in the securities and commodities field are largely preempted by federal law, but certain provisions could still apply.

Outlook – The conclusion regarding the EU MiFID framework is that it does in its current state not apply to closed scheme, unidirectional scheme, or to payment bidirectional scheme virtual currencies. However, derivative instruments having any of those virtual currencies as underlying assets can be considered as financial instruments in their own right. One notable exception can be found in Germany, where the national legislator has added a financial instrument – units of account similar to foreign currencies – to the list provided by the European legislator. As a result, the German MiFID implementation applies to the service providers of payment bidirectional scheme virtual currencies, but only in the German market. Such a deviation by a Member State could then provide an idea of how the MiFID legal framework could be amended to include virtual currencies, if so desired. Regarding investment bidirectional scheme virtual currencies, it can be argued that these virtual currencies could under certain circumstances already fall under the scope of financial instruments as covered by the MiFID framework. Also here, derivative instruments qualify as well. The US legal framework in the securities and commodities field demonstrates a significant level of flexibility, owing to US Supreme Court case law. The tests developed by the court can apply to new developments regarding virtual currencies, as confirmed by regulators in the securities and commodities field, thus negating the need for immediate legislative intervention. This finding leads to a similar conclusion as for the EU legal framework, namely that the securities and commodities legal framework could apply to investment bidirectional scheme virtual currencies and derivatives – depending of course on operational factors – while closed scheme, unidirectional scheme and payment bidirectional scheme virtual currencies are not covered by the securities and commodities legal framework.

## 1.5 FINDINGS

Applicability – The main conclusion to be drawn with regard to the first research question is that in the EU currently only the anti-money laundering framework can with certainty apply to virtual currencies. This application is due to a recent legislative amendment, which aims to mitigate the anonymity risk posed by virtual currencies. Virtual currency derivatives do fall under the scope of the MiFID framework. For investment virtual currencies, it can be argued that they could fall under the scope of the MiFID framework, although thus far such an argument has not been tested yet in practice. If the argument holds, it would mitigate the risks posed by these virtual currencies to investors. The US demonstrates greater flexibility, with the legal frameworks on anti-money laundering and investment services being applicable in their current form, owing to tests developed in case law and interpretations by regulators.

Potential amendments – The other analyzed legal frameworks – concerning e-money and payment services – could be made applicable through legislative amendments. However, such an application requires a number of policy decisions. First, it needs to be assessed how to move forward with the e-money legal framework, given the drastically changing landscape in the e-money field. Such an assessment serves to determine whether virtual currencies could be placed under the e-money legal framework. A second option sees virtual currencies placed under the payment services framework, but such an inclusion requires prior assessment of the precise service providers that need to be regulated. Third, if virtual currencies end up in the payment services framework, a demarcation must be made with the MiFID framework, as a single service cannot be both a payment service and an investment service.

## 2 IN NEED OF REGULATION?

Second research question – Having answered the question to which extent virtual currencies are covered by the current EU legal frameworks regarding e-money, payment services, anti-money laundering, and investment services, the focus now turns to the second main research question formulated for the purposes of this research. That question addresses the more normative matter of whether virtual currencies should be regulated under any of the aforementioned legal frameworks. Additionally, this section questions whether regulation of virtual currencies should be the subject of a separate legal framework, or whether it can be integrated into the existing analyzed legal frameworks.

Approach – First, this section brings together the findings of the preliminary normative assessments conducted in chapters IV, V, and VI, and compares them with the findings of the functional comparison conducted in chapter VII. This analysis will assess the need for regulation of virtual currencies in the EU against the normative criteria of this research. Second, a number of additional observations are taken into account in answering the second research question. For instance, this section assesses what the objectives of the relevant legal frameworks are, and how regulation of virtual currencies could fit those objectives. The results of this section will feed into the final conclusion to this research, formulated in section 3 of this chapter.

## 2.1 PRELIMINARY ASSESSMENTS

### *2.1.1 E-money and payment services*

LEGAL CERTAINTY – In terms of legal certainty, we found that the current situation has resulted in different approaches between Member States. This is undesirable in a field of maximum harmonization, which relies on a passporting system. Therefore, we propose to remedy the current situation of uncertainty regarding the (non-)application of the legal frameworks of e-money and payment services to virtual currencies and their service providers should be remediated. Also in the US legal uncertainty remains regarding the applicability of the corresponding legal frameworks. However, at the state level a recent Uniform Act aims to at least partially alleviate this problem.

PROPORTIONALITY – In terms of proportionality, it can be held that applying either of the e-money or payment services frameworks to all virtual currencies would be disproportionate to the risks they pose. A more differentiated risk-based approach is therefore recommended. Similar conclusions can be drawn for the US, where the full applicability of the relevant legal frameworks is disproportionate to the risks posed by certain virtual currencies.

TRUST – The lack of legal certainty regarding the applicability of the frameworks of e-money and payment services to virtual currencies and their service providers does not encourage trust by users of virtual currencies. Under the present situation, stakeholders participate in virtual currency schemes fully at their own risk. In the US, the non-applicability of these legal frameworks results in a similar lack of consumer protection safeguards. Recent initiatives, such as the Uniform Act, aim to provide a solution.

REGULATORY COHERENCE – Last, the current situation of legal uncertainty has been shown to result in undesirable consequences for regulatory coherence as well. The different approaches followed by some EU Member States could cause issues with regard to the passporting system used under the e-money and payment services legal frameworks. A more unified stance in these two fields is therefore recommended. In the US, the matter is mainly regulated through federal law, and state laws have been harmonized through a widely adopted Uniform Act. As a result, there is currently little regulatory incoherence in this field in the US.

### *2.1.2 Anti-money laundering*

Legal certainty – The recent legislative amendments to the EU anti-money laundering framework have provided more legal certainty with regard to the applicability of the anti-money laundering framework to virtual currency service providers. In the US, the federal regulator has clarified the application of the existing legal framework in the anti-money laundering field to virtual currency services. Also at the state level, the corresponding frameworks can mostly apply, either in their current form or through amendments. As a result, there remains little uncertainty regarding the application of anti-money laundering laws.

Proportionality – Given that the anti-money laundering legal framework addresses only the anonymity risk of virtual currencies, it could be feared that the imposition of this legal framework on virtual currency service providers would be disproportionate to the risks it can mitigate. However, as the situation under EU law currently stands, there is little argument in favor of treating virtual currencies differently than similar instruments. Moreover, the risk-based approach of the EU's anti-money laundering framework allows for a lighter treatment of virtual currencies posing lesser risks. In the US, the general approach is to distinguish according to the risks posed by virtual currencies. Only one case was noted – New York's BitLicense – where a framework was developed that appears to go beyond the risks posed by virtual currencies.

Trust – The argument that regulation of virtual currency service providers under the anti-money laundering framework could potentially have adverse effects regarding trust – by creating the illusion that such regulation also imposes consumer protection and prudential safeguards, which is not the case – is, in our opinion, overblown. However, arguments can be made in favor of seeking more consumer protection and prudential safeguards elsewhere. A similar situation exists in the US.

Regulatory coherence – While there was little disagreement regarding the (non-)applicability of the EU's anti-money laundering legal framework before the 2018 legislative amendments, the recent regulatory action can still be supported as at least ensuring regulatory coherence across the EU. In the US, the anti-money laundering field shows little harmonization across state lines. As a result, while the laws in most states are fairly similar, they could prescribe very different licensing requirements and procedures. A recent Uniform Act aims to provide for more coherence, as well as for reciprocal licensing.

### *2.1.3 Investment services*

Legal certainty – At the moment, there is no legal uncertainty remaining regarding the application of the EU's MiFID framework to payment virtual currencies. A notable exception in Germany constitutes purely additional national legislation. In the US, case law has provided the tests needed to assess the applicability of the corresponding legal frameworks. Moreover, federal regulators have provided further clarification. While this clarification does not answer all remaining questions, there is little legal uncertainty regarding the applicability of the securities and commodities frameworks to virtual currencies.

Proportionality – Given the broad range of operational and conduct of business requirements imposed by the MiFID legal framework, it could be recommended to follow a more differentiated and risk-based approach. Inclusion of all virtual currencies under the MiFID framework, regardless of the risks they pose, seems disproportionate. The tests developed by US case law in order to assess the applicability of the securities legal framework to virtual currencies allow for such a differentiation. They ensure that only those virtual currencies posing particular risks would be caught under the scope of existing securities and commodities laws.

Trust – Given the rising use of virtual currencies for investment purposes, inclusion of certain virtual currencies under the EU's MiFID framework could help increase user and investor trust. Moreover, the requirements imposed by the MiFID framework could raise the trustworthiness of virtual currency investment service providers. In the US, the federal framework in the field of securities and commodities traditionally primarily imposed registration requirements. Broader consumer protection measures would have to be sought elsewhere, or in state laws. In recent years, however, more consumer protection measures have been implemented.

Regulatory coherence – While there is little disparity between the approaches followed by the Member States in the MiFID field, the German deviation regarding payment virtual currencies could result in difficulties for the passporting system underlying the MiFID legal framework. Especially when combined with the finding that some Member States want to regulate the same services under the e-money or payment services frameworks, it is clear that a more coherent EU-wide stance is needed. In the US, the field of securities and commodities is mainly preempted by federal law. As a result, state laws show less incoherence, providing mainly additional requirements.

### *2.1.4 Findings*

Legal certainty – From the previous analysis, it can be concluded that a level of legal uncertainty in the EU exists regarding the applicability of the e-money and payment services frameworks to virtual currencies and their service providers. In the US, case law and guidance by regulators has ameliorated the situation in the latter field. For the EU, it could then be concluded that similar guidance is needed, with the possibility of additional legislative intervention in the fields of e-money and payment services.

PROPORTIONALITY – It is clear that a differentiated and risk-based approach is needed, to ensure that only the virtual currencies posing particular risks would be regulated according to those risks. Blanket regulation of all types of virtual currencies would be disproportionate to their respective risks. Thus far, such a differentiation indeed appears to be part of the approach followed by both EU and US legislators.

TRUST – In terms of trust, the main issue is that currently there is little consumer protection to augment the trust of virtual currency users. The current situation in the EU is comparable to that in the US. The application of the MiFID framework to investment virtual currencies could prove an example of how to raise trustworthiness, as that framework also provides for broader investor protection measures. Similar protection can be envisioned for payment virtual currency users – for instance through application of the payment services framework.

REGULATORY COHERENCE – In the EU, some incoherence has been noted regarding the application of the e-money and payment services frameworks. Given that these fields aim for maximum harmonization and rely on a passporting system, it is recommended that a more unified position be adopted in this regard. In the US, some incoherence can be noted between the states, although Uniform Acts aim to alleviate that concern.

## 2.2 REGULATORY NEED

NORMATIVE FINDINGS – The normative analysis conducted in the previous subsection revealed that there is at least a need of further regulatory guidance regarding the applicability of some of the analyzed legal frameworks to virtual currencies and their service providers. Such guidance needs to clarify remaining issues of legal uncertainty, and ensure more regulatory coherence across the EU regarding the application of the analyzed legal frameworks. Moreover, it could be argued that – according to the normative criteria established for the purposes of this research – additional legislative initiatives could further strengthen the position of virtual currencies from the viewpoints of legal certainty and trust. However, such initiatives have to be proportionate to the risks posed by the types of virtual currencies included in their scope.

ADDITIONAL OBSERVATIONS – However, before concluding on the need for regulatory intervention in the field of virtual currencies, this subsection will present a few additional observations that should be taken into account. These observations became apparent throughout this research, and touch upon the pertinence of the risks posed by virtual currencies, the changing virtual currency landscape, and the normative underpinnings of the analyzed legal frameworks.

### 2.2.1 *Risk pertinence*

Markets risks – In the risk analysis conducted in chapter I, one of the stakeholder risks that were identified concerns market risks. These include money laundering risks, a risk to price stability, a risk to payment systems' stability, and a reputational risk to central banks. While these risks had to be taken into account for further consideration – to ensure that all stakeholder risks would be treated equally and that thus no preliminary preference is given to any particular risk – it should also be noted that the importance of market risks should not be overblown.

Anti-money laundering – While the money laundering risk has indeed become one of the main drivers behind legislative interventions in both the EU and the US, it has been repeatedly shown throughout this research that there are thus far little indications that virtual currencies are indeed being used for money laundering purposes on a significant scale. The policy goals behind such legislative intervention are understandable – namely to ensure that anti-money laundering frameworks can be applied to all kinds of assets derived from crime, including virtual currencies, and assets derived from crime and subsequently invested in virtual currencies – but also demonstrate the limits of legislative intervention and the need to take into account proportionality. After all, if virtual currencies are indeed not being widely used for money laundering purposes, the imposition of the anti-money laundering legal framework on a broad range of virtual currency service providers could more easily become disproportionate to the risk it aims to address.

Stability and reputational risks – The other market risks identified in chapter I can be argued to be even more contentious. As the ECB already stated in identifying them, those risks could only materialize when virtual currencies gain wide adoption. Even though the virtual currency market – and particularly the market in cryptocurrencies – has grown rather explosively in the last few years, it appears virtual currencies are still nowhere near reaching enough traction for such market risks to actually materialize. Similar concerns were voiced by the ECB – and its predecessor, the EMI – during the legislative procedure leading up to the EMD1, but also the e-money market never reached the necessary growth for market risks to materialize. As a result, it can be concluded that, while market risks are important and should be given consideration, the low risk of their materialization makes that they should not be given precedence over the other stakeholder risks that were identified.

### 2.2.2 *Changing virtual currency landscape*

Risk shift – At the same time, it should also be noted that the gravity of risks to the other stakeholders identified in chapter I may have shifted over time. This is due to a number of substantial evolutions in the virtual currency landscape that became noticeable during the course of this research. The following paragraphs will highlight two main evolutions: the shift away from closed scheme virtual currencies, and the rise of investment bidirectional scheme virtual currencies.

From closed to unidirectional – As noted in chapter I, closed scheme virtual currencies are mainly used within virtual worlds such as video games. However, more and more developers are implementing so-called micro-transactions in their games, thus effectively moving away from purely closed scheme virtual currencies to unidirectional scheme virtual currencies. As noted in the risk analysis conducted in chapter I, this evolution raises the risks associated with in-game virtual currencies. However, given that these virtual currencies can, in principle, still only be used within the virtual world in which they were issued, the overall risk could still be argued to remain lower than that of unidirectional virtual currencies that can be spent in a broader network, such as certain loyalty scheme virtual currencies.

Cryptocurrencies – As has become clear throughout this research, cryptocurrencies form the main focal point of bidirectional virtual currencies. This was already the case at the onset of this research, and their importance has only grown since then. However, during the course of this research, one important evolution became apparent. While cryptocurrencies were initially propagated as being foremost a means of payment – with investments in cryptocurrencies due to their value fluctuations being more of a fringe phenomenon – cryptocurrencies can now serve a whole range of uses, with payments more and more taking a backseat role. Three main purposes can be identified: payments, investments, and utility.

Cryptocurrencies as payment – Regarding cryptocurrencies as means of payment, it must be concluded that the big breakthrough of cryptocurrencies has thus far not yet materialized. Bitcoin – which remains the top cryptocurrency – is only accepted by a few of the world's leading online merchants, and this number is reported to even be shrinking.[2295] Some of the reasons for this lack of payment use and acceptance are fairly straightforward.

First, with the value of bitcoin rising sharply in 2017, users may opt to hold their bitcoins, rather than to spend them. Such holding, naturally, decreases the use of bitcoin in payment transactions. In turn, if less users are willing to pay in bitcoin, less merchants will be compelled to accept payments in bitcoin.

Second, there is the much-debated scaling issue of bitcoin. With a block-size limit of 1 megabyte, the Bitcoin system can effectively only process a few

2295 Katz, L. (2017) "Bitcoin Acceptance Among Retailers Is Low and Getting Lower", *Bloomberg Technology*, 12 July; Chaparro, F. (2017) "MORGAN STANLEY: 'Bitcoin acceptance is virtually zero and shrinking'", *Business Insider UK*, 12 July.

transactions per second.[2296] That limitation has already resulted in congestions, with an early 2017 report of over 100.000 unconfirmed transactions waiting in queue for hours.[2297] While such a congestion does mean that the number of bitcoin transactions has increased, it at the same time demonstrates that bitcoin is not a particularly suitable method for (near-)instantaneous confirmation and/or settlement. Over the course of 2017, a few proposals were formulated to alleviate the congestion issue. One is the implementation of Segregated Witness (SegWit), which changes the way in which some of the block data is calculated, thus effectively allowing more transactions to be processed per block.[2298] The SegWit solution became active in August 2017.[2299] Another proposal, SegWit2x, additionally increases the maximum block-size.[2300] However, given that the SegWit2x proposal did initially not gain wide support, it would have to be implemented as a hard fork – thus essentially creating a new cryptocurrency.[2301] Such a hard fork was planned to occur in November 2017[2302], but was called off due to lack of consensus.[2303] A similar hard fork was already performed in August 2017 as well, creating Bitcoin Cash with a block-size limit of 8 megabyte.[2304] Initially, it was thought that Bitcoin Cash could take the reins as the main cryptocurrency for payment use, but thus far uptake remains fairly limited. Another hard fork was performed in October 2017, creating Bitcoin Gold.[2305] The main purpose of Bitcoin Gold is to make mining feasible on regular consumer hardware again.[2306]

Third, as miners can choose which transactions they process, they naturally select those transactions awarding them the largest fees. Transactions offering little to no reward to miners are pushed to the back of the queue, or may be abandoned altogether. This freedom of choice, coupled with the congestion caused by the scaling issues, resulted in a sharp rise in average bitcoin transaction fees. In June 2017, it was reported that average fees of around USD 3–4 were required to

2296 In theory, a new block is mined approximately every 10 minutes. A block contains between 1200 and 2200 transactions on average. *blockchain.info/charts/n-transactions-per-block?timespan=1year.*

2297 Redman, J. (2017) "Bitcoin's Transaction Queue Sets a New Record", *bitcoin.com*, 23 February.

2298 Van Wirdum, A. (2015) "Segregated Witness, Part 1: How a Clever Hack Could Significantly Increase Bitcoin's Potential", *Bitcoin Magazine,* 19 December.

2299 Hertig, A. (2017) "It's Official: Segregated Witness Will Activate on Bitcoin", *CoinDesk*, 8 August.

2300 Song, J. (2017) "Segwit2x: What you need to know about the 2x Hard Fork (aka 2MB non-Segwit Transaction Capacity per block/8MB Total Block Size Hard Fork)", *Medium*, 26 June.

2301 Hertig, A. (2017) "Full Steam Ahead? Segwit2x Reaffirms Bitcoin Hard Fork Plan", *CoinDesk*, 9 August.

2302 Van Wirdum, A. (2017) "A Bitcoin Beginner's Guide to Surviving the Bgold and SegWit2x Forks", *Bitcoin Magazine,* 13 October.

2303 Hertig, A. (2017) "2x Called Off: Bitcoin Hard Fork Suspended for Lack of Consensus", *CoinDesk*, 8 November.

2304 *Coinmarketcap.com/currencies/bitcoin-cash.*

2305 Van Wirdum, A. (2017) "A Bitcoin Beginner's Guide to Surviving the Bgold and SegWit2x Forks", *Bitcoin Magazine,* 13 October.

2306 *Btcgpu.org.*

ensure transaction confirmation, rising to about USD 20 in November 2017.[2307] While bitcoin was originally hailed as a cheap alternative for the underbanked – who do not have access to or cannot afford to participate in the traditional banking system – it is clear that the underbanked population cannot afford that kind of fees. It also makes bitcoin unsuitable for low-value transactions, as the transaction fees are prohibitive in relation to the value of the transaction.

One notable exception appears to be Japan. After a legislative change in April 2017, retailers and customers are lining up to embrace bitcoin.[2308] This case, however, must be considered as an outlier in what seems to be a general downturn for cryptocurrencies as means of payment.

Cryptocurrencies as investment – As noted, in the early days of cryptocurrencies, their use as means of investment was more of a fringe phenomenon. Their value fluctuations have always attracted investors, but it was clear that investments were not intended to be the primary use of cryptocurrencies. However, this situation has changed drastically over the last few years. With the rising value of bitcoin and its decreasing usability as a means of payment, bitcoin can now be considered as increasingly becoming a means of investment. Moreover, with the rise of new cryptocurrency constructions – such as The DAO and ICO's as covered in chapters VI and VII – it is clear that there now also exists a class of cryptocurrencies intended primarily or even solely as means of investment. Despite some regulatory activity – with, for instance, the US SEC warning about the applicability of securities laws as covered in chapter VII – the market for investment cryptocurrencies is only expected to grow.[2309]

Cryptocurrencies as utility – A final development is the use of cryptocurrencies for utilitarian purposes. The blockchain technology underlying cryptocurrencies is increasingly being used for non-financial purposes. Given that blockchain technology works as a ledger in which transactions are recorded, the use of this technology for such non-financial applications will inherently still involve the use of cryptocurrencies – or tokens.[2310] Such tokens could then serve as a mere means to operate a blockchain application, and thus serve no purpose as means of payment or as means of investment external to that particular application. In essence, while such tokens are still cryptocurrencies – and could thus theoretically be bought or sold for legal tender or similar means of payment

---

2307 Redman, J. (2017) "Rising Network Fees Are Causing Changes Within the Bitcoin Economy", *bitcoin.com*, 9 June; *bitinfocharts.com/comparison/bitcoin-transactionfees.html#3m*.

2308 Helms, K. (2017) "Major Japanese Department Store Chain Marui Accepts Bitcoin", *bitcoin.com*, 6 August.

2309 In 2017, around USD 2 billion was invested in ICO's. Higgins, S. (2017) "$200 Million In 60 Minutes: Filecoin ICO Rockets to Record Amid Tech Issues", *CoinDesk*, 10 August.

2310 Van Valkenburgh, P. (2016) "Framework for Securities Regulation of Cryptocurrencies v1", *Coin Center Report*, 4.

– their purpose and functioning is more closely related to closed scheme virtual currencies. As a result, it can be concluded that if there is no monetary flow into or out of a blockchain token, the risks associated with that token to the relevant stakeholders will be very low.

CONSEQUENCES – While the move from closed scheme virtual currencies towards more unidirectional scheme virtual currencies could be argued to change fairly little to the risks these virtual currencies pose to their stakeholders, the shifting cryptocurrency landscape does bring about consequences. The most obvious consequence of the rising use of cryptocurrencies for investment purposes is that the scale on which risks to investors could materialize is increasing. Not only is the total amount of assets invested in cryptocurrencies growing rapidly, individual investors are also likely to hold more investment cryptocurrency assets for a longer duration than is the case for payment cryptocurrencies. When using cryptocurrencies for payments, individual users are less likely to hold significant amounts of these assets for a longer period of time – mainly due to the risk of value depreciation. Likewise, merchants accepting cryptocurrencies as means of payment are likely to exchange them into more traditional assets as soon as possible.[2311] While it remains outside of the scope of this research to make a policy-oriented value judgment on which of the four stakeholder risks should be accorded precedence over the others, these findings do allow to conclude that some risks – and then particularly user risks and to an increasing degree also investor risks – are becoming more prominent.

### *2.2.3 Objectives of financial law frameworks*

OBJECTIVES AND NEEDS – Before concluding on the need to regulate virtual currency developments and their service providers, it must first be assessed what the precise objectives are of the financial law frameworks analyzed in this research, and what those objectives contribute when regulating virtual currencies and their service providers. This analysis will help to identify what the precise regulatory needs are that these legal frameworks aim to address, and to compare whether a similar need exists for virtual currencies and their service providers.

E-MONEY – As noted in chapter IV, the core objective of the EU's e-money framework was to harmonize the prudential supervision of these service providers "*to the extent necessary for ensuring their sound and prudent operation and their financial integrity in particular*".[2312] The need for a separate legal framework was justified by the consideration that e-money issuance does not

[2311] Or they may even avoid holding cryptocurrency assets at all, by using a third party who accepts the cryptocurrencies for them and exchanges these values.

[2312] Recital 5 EMD1.

constitute a deposit-taking activity.[2313] To respond to the risks – particularly to the "*stability of the financial system and the smooth operation of payments systems*" – posed by e-money, a more targeted yet less stringent prudential supervisory regime was deemed necessary.[2314] However, some provisions were made more stringent, in order to allow for a level playing field.[2315] This latter objective also became the guiding objective under the EMD2.[2316] To this effect, the e-money legal framework was aligned with that of the PSD1.[2317] While retaining the reasoning of the EMD1, consumer protection is called upon in the EMD2 as justification for the directive's capital requirements.[2318] In terms of the virtual currency stakeholders identified for the purposes of this research, it can then be concluded that the e-money legal framework – like all financial regulation to a certain degree – addresses risks to the market and to users.

Payment services – Given the alignment of the e-money framework with the payment services framework, it is no surprise that both legal frameworks cite similar objectives. As a result, also the payment services legal framework mainly serves market and consumer protection. While existing consumer law frameworks remain applicable, the payment services framework further clarifies a number of elements, such as information requirements.[2319] The PSD2 confirms the objectives of systemic protection and consumer protection.[2320] Also in this framework the focus is therefore put on market and user risks.

Anti-money laundering – The primary objective of the EU's anti-money laundering legislation is to address risks to the "*integrity, stability and reputation of the financial sector, and* [to] *the internal market of the Union*".[2321] Consumer and investor risks are only secondarily cited in relation to regulatory technical standards.[2322] Also the proposed amendments to the AMLD4 do not more explicitly focus on consumer or investor protection. With regard to the identified stakeholders, it can then be concluded that the anti-money laundering legal framework focuses primarily on market risks. However, it must be noted that the risk of anonymity – addressed by the amendments to the AMLD4 – also affects users of virtual currencies. To some extent, the anti-money laundering legal framework thus also addresses user risks.

2313 Recital 7 EMD1.
2314 Recitals 11 and 14 EMD1.
2315 Recital 12 EMD1.
2316 Recital 4 EMD2.
2317 Recital 9 EMD2.
2318 Recital 11 EMD2.
2319 Recital 22 PSD1.
2320 Recitals 4 and 6–7 PSD2.
2321 Recital 1 AMLD4.
2322 Recital 61 AMLD4.

Markets in Financial Instruments – The main objective of the MiFID1 was to offer harmonized investor protection.[2323] This objective was confirmed in the MiFID2.[2324] Secondarily, the directive called for a "*comprehensive regulatory regime governing the execution of transactions in financial instruments* [...] *so as to ensure a high quality of execution of investor transactions and to uphold the integrity and overall efficiency of the financial system*".[2325] Also this objective was confirmed in the MiFID2.[2326] With regard to the identified stakeholders, the MiFID legal framework therefore addresses market and investor risks.

Objectives and virtual currency risks – The most obvious finding of this overview is that all of the analyzed legal frameworks to some extent address market risks as one of their core objectives. User risks would be addressed by the e-money and payment services frameworks, and to lesser extent by the anti-money laundering framework due to its handling of the anonymity risk. Investor risks, in turn, would only be addressed by the MiFID framework. However, with regard to virtual currencies and their service providers, it is reminded that it was observed earlier that the market risks appear to be less pertinent. In order to address the user risks posed by payment virtual currencies, an inclusion in the payment services framework could then be considered.[2327] In turn, to address the investor risks posed by investment virtual currencies, an expansion of the MiFID framework could be considered.

### *2.2.4 Desirability of regulation*

Desirability of regulation – The risk assessment conducted in chapter I made it clear that there are particular risks posed to the four stakeholders identified with regard to virtual currencies and virtual currency services. The observations made earlier added that the risk to the market may be less pertinent than it appears, and that the risk to investors is growing due to the expanding use of virtual currencies for investment purposes. In this regard, it could then be concluded that there is a certain need for regulation in order to address those risks, and that inclusion of virtual currencies under the corresponding legal frameworks – payment services for payment virtual currencies, and MiFID for investment virtual currencies – could fulfill that need. However, at the same time, it can also be questioned whether

2323 Recitals 2 and 71 MiFID1.

2324 Recitals 3, 4 and 70 MiFID2.

2325 Recitals 5 and 48 MiFID1.

2326 Recitals 5, 7 and 13 MiFID2.

2327 Given that the review of the EMD2 is still pending, and given that the e-money legal framework is already expected to be integrated into the payment services framework, it is advisable – if virtual currencies would be integrated into either of these frameworks – to combine the integration of e-money and virtual currencies into the payment services framework. By doing so, it can be ensured that all elements of the resulting framework – payment services, e-money, and virtual currencies – can be properly attuned to each other.

virtual currency stakeholders have a particular desire for regulation. Particularly within the community developed around cryptocurrencies, there appears to be a resistance to regulatory intervention. A few observations can be made in that regard.

Law as insurance – A first observation is that the effects of a legal framework are not always visible at all times. In some cases, a legal framework acts as a form of insurance: it may seem unnecessary as long as things go well, but may come very much in handy when things go wrong. This also applies to the analyzed legal frameworks. While some effects are immediately perceivable – such as the information duties imposed on service providers – other effects aim to protect stakeholders against unwanted outcomes. So while the application of these legal frameworks may at first seem unnecessary to stakeholders as long as everything goes well, it has already been established that those same stakeholders are likely to invoke protection of the legal frameworks they eschewed before when they need it. One example is the bankruptcy of the then largest bitcoin exchange Mt. Gox. In 2014, the exchange reported that a large number of the bitcoins it held on behalf of its customers were stolen.[2328] It subsequently halted all withdrawals and later began liquidation proceedings.[2329] Customers who lost their funds started filing complaints, resulting in at least one class action lawsuit.[2330] Thus far, however, no creditors have been able to retrieve funds.[2331] If this cryptocurrency exchange were regulated under the payment services framework, it would have been bound to more stringent safeguarding requirements, insulating customers' funds against other creditors in the case of insolvency, or a central counterparty could have absorbed the counterparty credit risk.[2332] Similarly, complaints were allegedly made to the US SEC on the legality of The DAO, after users' funds were breached.[2333] Such cases demonstrate how legal frameworks could have helped protecting stakeholders, even if that protection at first did not seem necessary.

Understanding the law – A second observation is that those opposing regulation do not always appear to have a firm understanding of how regulation really works. One element that often seems to be misunderstood is that of jurisdiction. Already before the US SEC's report on The DAO – and the effects thereof for ICO's – several cryptocurrency-related businesses were incorporating

2328 Abrams, R., Goldstein, M., Tabuchi, H. (2014) "Erosion of Faith Was Death Knell for Mt. Gox", *New York Times*, 28 February.

2329 Byford, S. (2014) "Mt. Gox abandons rebuilding plans and files for liquidation: WSJ", *The Verge*, 16 April.

2330 Rizzo, P. (2016) "US Judge Rules Mt Gox Class Action Can Continue Against Mizuho Bank", *CoinDesk*, 15 March.

2331 Wong, J. I. (2017) "Bitcoin's soaring price means bankrupt Mt. Gox may soon be able to pay its creditors", *Quartz*, 13 June.

2332 See article 10 PSD2.

2333 Redman, J. (2017) "White Hacker Group to Claim $4.4 Million in Controversial DAO Refund", *Bitcoin.com*, 10 April.

themselves outside the US, for instance in Switzerland and Singapore, apparently believing that this move allows them to evade US law.[2334] Similarly, the Uniform Regulation of Virtual Currency Businesses Act has been criticized by holding that a difference in state laws encourage businesses to seek out more welcoming states.[2335] However, if you are offering your services to US residents, or – if you are already located in the US – to residents of another US state, you will be subject to the legislation applicable in the jurisdiction in which you are offering your services. A Switzerland-based ICO-offering to US citizens can become subject to US securities law on the basis of long-arm jurisdiction. A New Jersey-based company offering virtual currency services in the state of New York will be caught under that state's BitLicense. While there have been calls to simply exclude US citizens from investing in an ICO, the relative anonymity may complicate the practical implementation of such an action.[2336] Moreover, as other countries are investigating such regulation as well, similar rules will likely soon apply all over the world.

Need for protection – Another element that appears to be often misunderstood is how the avoidance of legal frameworks further diminishes the protection offered to stakeholders.[2337] The prime example is The DAO, which was promoted as being a virtual company without incorporation in any jurisdiction. In The DAO, the – at least to some extent willful – avoidance of company law results in there not being a legal entity. The result of such an action is that all parties involved – from the promoters to the investors – could be held jointly and severally liable for the duties of The DAO.[2338] This, of course, exposes participants to liabilities far greater than merely their own investment. Another point, following from the potential classification of investment virtual currencies as securities, is that also re-selling such virtual currencies on a secondary market can become subject to securities law. Also here, the current avoidance of the securities legal framework by most investment virtual currency service providers puts investors at additional risk, as they may be unaware of the precise legal consequences stemming from their participation. These cases demonstrate that the rights and protections offered by the relevant legal frameworks should, at the very least, apply in full, and not be diminished.

---

2334 Wilson, F. (2017) "Jurisdictional Competition", *avc.com*, 9 July.

2335 McElroy, W. (2017) "De Facto Federal Legislation of Cryptocurrency is Nigh", *Bitcoin.com*, 11 July.

2336 Popper, N. (2017) "Despite S.E.C. Warning, Wave of Initial Coin Offerings Grows", *New York Times*, 7 August.

2337 Note how this is a distinct case from a legal framework not being applicable. If, for instance, the EU payment services framework is not applicable to a bitcoin exchange, this service provider is not willfully avoiding the additional protection this framework would offer. Other legal frameworks – such as contract law – may still be applicable, yet may offer lesser protection. A further problem, which is what is being discussed here, rises when that service provider actively avoids legal frameworks that would be applicable.

2338 Palley, S. D. (2016) "How to Sue A Decentralized Autonomous Organization", *CoinDesk*, 20 March.

Old wine or new paradigm? – Another argument used against the regulation of virtual currencies – and then particularly against the regulation of cryptocurrencies – is that they represent a new form of finance, and are thus not suitable for placement within existing legal frameworks. Bitcoin has in this regard even been referred to as a new paradigm in finance.[2339] In this sense, the rise of virtual currencies is closely related to the broader phenomenon of so-called 'fintech', whereby more technology-oriented companies develop services or products similar to those offered by the more traditional firms operating under financial law frameworks. Particularly within the banking sector, there are complaints about having to compete with these kind of companies that are often not bound to the same stringent regulatory frameworks.[2340] However, as a discussion of the broader issues regarding fintech is beyond the scope of this research, only the particularities of virtual currencies will be discussed. While it is certainly true that cryptocurrencies in themselves are quite different from what came before them, the services and products developed around them do not necessarily appear all that novel. Most of the virtual currency services currently on the market closely resemble traditional e-money services, payment services, or investment services. Also the more complex financial services developed around virtual currencies mostly seem to utilize existing methods.[2341] Referring back to the alternative classification system discussed in chapter I, the matryoshka model, it can be held that virtual currency services – at least those regarding payments – can indeed be placed within such classification, next to the more traditional means and services of payment. Taking into account the previous subsection then, it is reminded that the European legislator decided to regulate those traditional e-money and payment services. Some of the objectives of that regulation include market protection, consumer protection, as well as the desire to create a level playing field. Given these regulatory objectives, it then becomes difficult to justify that services so similar to those identified for regulation by legislators evade regulation simply through their use of virtual currencies. In other words, if virtual currency services cannot truly be called a new paradigm, it becomes hard to argue why they should be treated differently from the traditional services upon which they are based and with whom they compete. It could even be argued that the risks posed by virtual currency services – a new and therefore volatile market – are higher than those posed by more experienced traditional financial service providers, which would only strengthen the case for more, rather than less, regulation.[2342]

---

2339 X (2017) "Beyond Bitcoin – A New Paradigm For Regulation", *diacle.com*, 28 April; Rees, M. (2014) "Bitcoin to Earth: Don't Look Now, but your Paradigm is Shifting", *Bitcoin Magazine*, 22 July.

2340 Febelfin (2017) "Succesvolle editie van Febelfin Connect – Speech Johan Thijs", *febelfin.be*, 20 March.

2341 Levine, M. (2017) "Bitcoin Exchange Had Too Many Bitcoins", *Bloomberg*, 2 August.

2342 D'Ippolito, E., Musitelli, M., Sciarrone Alibrandi, A. (2016) "Protecting Crowdfunders: Is a MiFID-Mimicking Approach Appropriate?", *European Company Law*, Vol. 13, 29.

# 3 CONCLUSION

First research question – The first, more analytical, research question posed in this research asked whether the current EU legal frameworks regarding e-money, payment services, anti-money laundering, and investment services can apply to virtual currencies. Here, this research has shown that currently only the EU's anti-money laundering framework can without any doubt apply to certain virtual currency service providers, because of a recent amendment by the European legislator. While arguments could be made in favor of the application of the MiFID framework to investment virtual currencies and virtual currency derivative products, that argument remains untested in practice.

Intermediate question – An intermediate research question then asked whether the analyzed legal frameworks that are not currently applicable to virtual currencies and their service providers could be made applicable to them. With regard to e-money and payment services, it can be concluded that the former framework is in need of reorientation, with likely an integration into the latter framework. Such integration could then include placing virtual currencies or particular virtual currency services under the renewed payment services framework, but such requires a policy assessment of which service providers need to be regulated. To that end, a demarcation should be made between the service providers dealing with virtual currencies that serve as means of payment – which belong more under the integrated e-money and payment services framework – and the service providers dealing with virtual currencies that serve as means of investment – which are more suited for regulation under the MiFID framework. US law was found to be more flexible in this regard – with some of the existing frameworks being applicable without legislative intervention – and also demonstrates a clear intention of regulating investment virtual currencies under securities and commodities laws.

Second research question – The second, more normative, research question was whether such amendments should be made in order to provide stakeholders with more legal certainty, in other words, whether there is a need to regulate virtual currencies or virtual currency service providers. Given the findings of the normative assessments made throughout the research and the additional observations made in the previous subsections, the conclusion is that this second research question can be answered in the positive sense. The following paragraphs will summarize the main findings and observations leading to that answer.

Normative assessments – After answering the first research question, a normative assessment of the current situation was made for each of the analyzed legal frameworks, against the criteria of legal certainty, proportionality, trust, and regulatory coherence.

Regarding legal certainty, we found that the current situation in the EU – particularly with regard to e-money and payment services – leads to uncertainty and different approaches between Member States.

Regarding proportionality, we found that a differentiated and risk-based approach would be preferred. Moreover, in the interest of legislative parsimony, regulation merely for the sake of regulating should be avoided. As a result, it can be argued that regulation under existing frameworks is preferred over the adoption of entirely separate frameworks, if such an inclusion fits the objectives of said legal frameworks. Such would help to avoid regulatory overreach, which was found in the US state of New York's BitLicense framework.

Regarding trust, we found that the current legislative framework does little to raise user trust in virtual currencies and virtual currency services. While existing consumer law frameworks do already apply, thus far they appear to not have contributed meaningfully towards raising user trust. Regulation under the analyzed economic and financial frameworks – by which the legislator intended to offer more targeted consumer protection – could then help raise trust in virtual currencies and virtual currency services. Alternatively, more warnings could be issued against the use of virtual currencies, with the intent to lower trust in them and to discourage their use. However, thus far the many warnings issued by regulators worldwide have not managed to prevent the rising adoption of virtual currencies for both payment and investment uses. As a result, if the use of virtual currencies is to be discouraged, a more forceful option needs to be explored.

Regarding regulatory coherence, it can be noted that the current divergences by certain Member States results in incoherence, and could endanger the maximum harmonization and passporting system envisioned by these legal frameworks. Regulation as proposed here could then provide a more unified EU stance on this matter, in line with developments in the US.

Observations regarding need – A first observation regarding the need for regulation concerns the shifting virtual currencies landscape – and particularly the evolution of cryptocurrencies. While originally all cryptocurrencies served mainly payment-related purposes, there is now a clear branch of cryptocurrencies that serves primarily or even solely as means of investment. Moreover, the use of cryptocurrencies as means of payment appears to be diminishing on the whole. One result of that shift towards investments is that the investor risks, and to a lesser extent user risks as a whole, relating to virtual currencies are becoming more pertinent, whereas other risks – particularly market risks – appear less pertinent. A second observation relates to the objectives of the analyzed legal frameworks. The main finding is that user risks are addressed by the e-money and payment services frameworks – and to lesser extent by the anti-money laundering framework – and that investor risks are addressed by the MiFID framework. Given the close similarities between virtual currency services and the services targeted by those frameworks, and given the clear intention of the legislator to address the presented risks, it becomes difficult to argue why the users of virtual currency services would deserve a lesser degree of protection than users of traditional e-money, payment, or investment services.[2343] Such a difference in treatment, based merely on the underlying asset being a virtual currency rather than more established money, seems inadequately justified.

Observations regarding desirability – While it is acknowledged that there is a certain resistance to the regulation of virtual currencies – and particularly cryptocurrencies – much of such a resistance stems from a lack of understanding of how the analyzed legal frameworks operate. First, the analyzed legal frameworks protect stakeholders against undesired outcomes. A few examples provided in section 2.2.4 of this chapter indicated that stakeholders in such an event do actually want and need that protection. Second, basic legal concepts such as "jurisdiction" are often misunderstood. Avoiding a certain jurisdiction by establishing a company in another jurisdiction while still offering services in that first jurisdiction is a futile, yet common, endeavor. Arguments against regulation should not be accorded much value if they are found to be based on a fundamental misunderstanding of such regulation. Third, the willful avoidance of legal frameworks reduces the protection of the stakeholders involved, and exposes them to significant liabilities. Last, while virtual currencies are fairly novel – and particularly cryptocurrencies – the services developed around them appear to closely mimic traditional financial services. Again, it can then be considered strange that stakeholders in virtual currency services – which are arguably even more prone to risks than traditional financial services – are offered less protection. As a result, most objections against virtual currency regulation seem somewhat shortsighted, stemming from a lack of understanding of how the analyzed legal frameworks operate, or how they protect stakeholders.

Outlook – It should be acknowledged that the research undertaken is by no means an endpoint, but merely a first step in what promises to be the long story of the burgeoning virtual currency market. Therefore, a few indications can be made towards future research. First, the virtual currency market has already significantly developed and changed while conducting this research. As it is still a fairly nascent market – cryptocurrencies, for instance, are barely a decade old – there are undoubtedly more developments to come. Further follow-up of the matter is therefore needed. Even in the US, where the analyzed legal frameworks were found to be further developed than in the EU, there are still several Rumsfeldian 'known unknowns' remaining. Second, the technology behind cryptocurrencies, blockchain, is moving beyond pure currency-based services and is now being used for an endless range of

[2343] D'Ippolito, E., Musitelli, M., Sciarrone Alibrandi, A. (2016) "Protecting Crowdfunders: Is a MiFID-Mimicking Approach Appropriate?", *European Company Law*, Vol. 13, 27–31.

financial and non-financial applications. That broad range of applications also elicits legal questions stemming from other fields of law, involving *inter alea* matters of data protection, contracts, and electronic evidence. Involvement of legal experts beyond financial law will therefore be needed to follow up on how blockchain technology develops. Last, as was already mentioned before, the rise of virtual currencies can be framed within the broader development of so-called fintech. The entrance of technology-oriented companies in the financial sector has already stirred quite some controversy, and will continue to do so. The fundamental question to be addressed is how financial law – with its classic tripartite of banks, insurances, and securities – should handle the influx of market players increasingly unsuited for classification under its core pillars. Cross-sectoral regulation, for instance, could result in less need to regulate each innovation.[2344]

Final thoughts – The final conclusion of this research can therefore be a recommendation towards the regulation of payment virtual currencies under the EU's payment services framework, and a regulation of investment virtual currencies under the EU's MiFID framework. Such would provide for more legal certainty to all stakeholders than is currently the case, and ensures a more unified stance within the EU in line with international regulatory developments in the field of virtual currencies. For the sake of legislative parsimony, regulation under a separate framework should be avoided, as it risks duplicating existing frameworks or could end up imposing more stringent burdens on virtual currency service providers than is the case for traditional financial service providers, or *vice versa*. For the sake of proportionality, a differentiated approach should be followed. Such could allow for the exclusion or less burdensome treatment of virtual currencies posing lesser or no risks – such as closed scheme virtual currencies and unidirectional scheme virtual currencies – while focusing on the increasing risks posed by others – particularly the rising investor and user risks of payment bidirectional scheme virtual currencies and investment virtual currencies. While there will indeed be some resistance to regulation – particularly from within the cryptocurrency community – it can be argued that regulation, albeit properly attuned regulation, is a necessary step in the maturation process of virtual currencies. If virtual currencies are truly to become a payment or investment means for everyone, they will have to stop teetering on the edge between legality and illegality, and make the risks involved more palatable to a broader audience.

[2344] Research into cross-sectoral regulation is currently being conducted as part of a project funded by the Research Foundation Flanders (FWO), among other things in view of the challenges raised by FinTech: Veerle Colaert, Wim Decock, *Regulating Finance in a Cross-sectoral world*, G067617N. See also: Colaert, V. (2017) "Building Blocks of Investor Protection: All-Embracing Regulation Tightens Its Grip", *ssrn.com/abstract=2943985*.

# 4 RECOMMENDATIONS

## 4.1 MERCHANTS AND USERS OF VIRTUAL CURRENCIES

Use at own risk – The general recommendation to merchants and users of virtual currencies is to exert caution in using them. The use of virtual currencies, particularly cryptocurrencies, involves a number of risks, and currently their merchants and users are not offered specific financial law protection. However, recommendations are formulated for legislators and regulators as well, which aim to make the use of virtual currencies safer for merchants and users.

No payment protection – Those conducting and accepting payments in virtual currencies should be aware that, under the current analyzed legal frameworks, they are not offered specific financial law protection. If virtual currency funds are held at a service provider, potential security issues or bankruptcy of that service provider could result in a loss of funds. Moreover, given the value fluctuations of bidirectional virtual currencies, holding virtual currency assets can be a risk.

Investor beware – Those investing in virtual currencies under the current analyzed legal frameworks must realize that they are not offered specific investor protection by financial law. They can therefore only rely on the general civil law regime. Given that the use of virtual currencies as means of investment is a new development, with those investments made almost solely in startup companies, the investor risks of such investments are significant. Moreover, it must be understood what the legal qualification of the investment is. For instance, if an investment is made in an entity that is not legally incorporated with limited liability, investors risk being held accountable for more than just their investment.

## 4.2 VIRTUAL CURRENCY SERVICE PROVIDERS AND ISSUERS

Know your legal position – Virtual currency service providers and issuers should know their precise position under the analyzed legal frameworks. While it was concluded that these frameworks will in most cases not be applicable to virtual currency services, various operational factors may lead to a different outcome. A case-by-case assessment must therefore be maintained.

Understand the uses of the virtual currency – Virtual currency service providers should clearly understand the applications for which the virtual currencies they handle can be used. These uses – be it for payment purposes, for investment purposes, or for mere utilitarian purposes – indicate which legal framework those virtual currency services operate under. It can also help to avoid regulatory burdens. If a virtual currency can only serve utilitarian uses – without ulterior motives of profit – then it should not be subjected to securities law.

Understand the law – Apart from knowing which legal frameworks a particular service is operating under, service providers should also understand those legal frameworks and the jurisdiction in which they apply. This means that it should be understood that providing services in a particular jurisdiction may result in the applicability of the legal frameworks of that jurisdiction. Such understanding is needed as a first step in these service providers being legally compliant in offering their services, which can help reduce their own liabilities, as well as those of their users.

## 4.3 LEGISLATORS AND REGULATORS

Integrate e-money and payment services – A first more general recommendation that can be made towards legislators, is to find a new direction for the EU's e-money framework. It is clear that the e-money legal framework is in need of reorientation, as currently the need for the e-money framework and the distinction between the e-money framework and the payment services framework is becoming increasingly unclear. At the least, the legal framework on e-money should be integrated into the payment services framework. Furthermore, if there is a future for e-money regulation in the EU, virtual currencies need to be integrated into the e-money notion.

Understand different virtual currencies – The worst approach to virtual currency regulation is to simply throw all virtual currencies in the same regulatory basket. This research has shown that the risks posed by virtual currencies can vary greatly between the different types of virtual currencies. Moreover, a distinction must be made between virtual currencies primarily serving payment purposes, investment purposes, or utilitarian purposes. The virtual currency types must be reflected in regulation, with those virtual currencies posing little to no risk being exempted from financial law regulation, or subject to lesser burdens.

Payment virtual currencies as payment services – The main conclusion of this research is that the services developed around bidirectional virtual currencies that primarily serve as means of payment should become regulated as payment services, in order to address the user risks posed by these virtual currency services. Such provides more legal certainty than is currently the case, which in turn could help foster user trust in these virtual currency services where traditional legal frameworks that are currently applicable do not. Furthermore, it ensures a more unified EU-wide approach, and thus delineate payment virtual currency services from classification under the MiFID framework.

INVESTMENT VIRTUAL CURRENCIES AS FINANCIAL INSTRUMENTS – Last, it can be recommended to include bidirectional virtual currencies serving primarily as means of investment as financial instruments under the EU's Markets in Financial Instruments framework. Such serves to mitigate the user risks, and more importantly the rising investor risks. Moreover, it provides for more legal certainty and ensure a unified EU-wide approach, in line with international developments in this regard.

# BIBLIOGRAPHY

## 1 LEGISLATION

### 1.1 EUROPEAN UNION

Treaty on the Functioning of the European Union (TFEU).

#### *1.1.1 Regulations*

Regulation (EU) 2015/751 of the European Parliament and of the Council of 29 April 2015 on interchange fees for card-based payment transactions, *OJ* L 123 of 19 May 2015, 1–15.
Regulation (EU) No 1286/2014 of the European Parliament and of the Council of 26 November 2014 on key information documents for packaged retail and insurance-based investment products (PRIIPs), *OJ* L 352 of 9 December 2014, 1–23.
Regulation 910/2014 of the European Parliament and of the Council of 23 July 2014 on electronic identification and trust services for electronic transactions in the internal market and repealing Directive 1999/93/EC, *OJ* L 257 of 28 August 2014, 73–114.
Regulation (EU) No 600/2014 of the European Parliament and of the Council of 15 May 2014 on markets in financial instruments and amending Regulation (EU) No 648/2012, *OJ* L 173 of 12 June 2014, 84–148.
Regulation (EU) No 248/2014 of the European Parliament and of the Council of 26 February 2014 amending Regulation (EU) No 260/2012 as regards the migration to Union-wide credit transfers and direct debits, *OJ* L 84 of 20 March 2014, 1–3.
Regulation (EU) No 575/2013 of the European Parliament and of the Council of 26 June 2013 on prudential requirements for credit institutions and investment firms and amending Regulation (EU) No 648/2012, *OJ* L 176 of 27 June 2013, 1–337.
Regulation (EU) No 260/2012 of the European Parliament and of the Council of 14 March 2012 establishing technical and business requirements for credit transfers and direct debits in euro and amending Regulation (EC) No 924/2009, *OJ* L 94 of 30 March 2012, 22–37.
Regulation (EC) No 924/2009 of the European Parliament and of the Council of 16 September 2009 on cross-border payments in the Community and repealing Regulation (EC) No 2560/2001, *OJ* L 266 of 9 October 2009, 11–18.
Regulation (EC) No 1137/2008 of the European Parliament and of the Council of 22 October 2008 adapting a number of instruments subject to the procedure laid down in Article 251 of the Treaty to Council Decision 1999/468/EC, with regard to the regulatory procedure with scrutiny – Adaptation to the regulatory procedure with scrutiny – Part One, OJ L 311 of 21 November 2008, 1–54.

Commission Regulation (EC) No 1287/2006 of 10 August 2006 implementing Directive 2004/39/EC of the European Parliament and of the Council as regards record-keeping obligations for investment firms, transaction reporting, market transparency, admission of financial instruments to trading, and defined terms for the purposes of that Directive, OJ L 241 of 2 September 2006, 1–25.

Regulation (EC) No 2560/2001 of the European Parliament and of the Council of 19 December 2001 on cross-border payments in euro, OJ L 344 of 28 December 2001, 13–16.

Council Regulation (EC) No 974/98 of 3 May 1998 on the introduction of the euro, OJ L 139 of 11 May 1998, 1–5.

Council Regulation 2185/96 of 11 November 1996 concerning on-the-spot checks and inspections carried out by the Commission in order to protect the European Communities' financial interests against fraud and other irregularities, OJ L 292 of 15 November 1996, 2–5.

### *1.1.2 Directives*

Directive 2015/2366 of the European Parliament and of the Council of 25 November 2015 on payment services in the internal market, amending Directives 2002/65/EC, 2009/110/EC and 2013/36/EU and Regulation (EU) No 1093/2010, and repealing Directive 2007/64/EC, *OJ* L 337 of 23 December 2015, 35–127.

Directive 2015/1535 of the European Parliament and of the Council of 9 September 2015 laying down a procedure for the provision of information in the field of technical regulations and of rules on Information Society services (codification), *OJ* L 241 of 17 September 2015, 1–15.

Directive 2015/849 of the European Parliament and of the Council of 20 May 2015 on the prevention of the use of the financial system for the purposes of money laundering or terrorist financing, amending Regulation (EU) No 648/2012 of the European Parliament and of the Council, and repealing Directive 2005/60/EC of the European Parliament and of the Council and Commission Directive 2006/70/EC, *OJ* L 141 of 5 June 2015, 73–117.

Directive 2014/65/EU of the European Parliament and of the Council of 15 May 2014 on markets in financial instruments and amending Directive 2002/92/EC and Directive 2011/61/EU, *OJ* L 173 of 12 June 2014, 349–496.

Directive 2014/62/EU of the European Parliament and of the Council of 15 May 2014 on the protection of the euro and other currencies against counterfeiting by criminal law, and replacing Council Framework Decision 2000/383/JHA, *OJ* L 151 of 21 May 2014, 1–8.

Directive 2013/36/EU of the European Parliament and of the Council of 26 June 2013 on access to the activity of credit institutions and the prudential supervision of credit institutions and investment firms, amending Directive 2002/87/EC and repealing Directives 2006/48/EC and 2006/49/EC, *OJ* L 176 of 27 June 2013; or Directive 2004/39/EC of the European Parliament and of the Council of 21 April 2004 on markets in financial instruments amending Council Directives 85/611/EEC and 93/6/EEC and Directive 2000/12/EC of the European Parliament and of the Council and repealing Council Directive 93/22/EEC, *OJ* L 145 of 30 April 2004, 105–203.

Directive 2011/83/EU of the European Parliament and of the Council of 25 October 2011 on consumer rights, amending Council Directive 93/13/EEC and Directive 1999/44/EC of the European Parliament and of the Council and repealing Council Directive 85/577/EEC and Directive 97/7/EC of the European Parliament and of the Council, *OJ* L 304 of 22 November 2011, 64–88.

Directive 2011/61/EU of the European Parliament and of the Council on Alternative Investment Fund Managers and amending Directives 2003/41/EC and 2009/65/EC and Regulations (EC) No 1060/2009 and (EU) No 1095/2010, *OJ* L 174 of 1 July 2011, 1–73.

Directive 2009/110/EC of the European Parliament and of the Council of 16 September 2009 on the taking up, pursuit and prudential supervision of the business of electronic money institutions amending Directives 2005/60/EC and 2006/48/EC and repealing Directive 2000/46/EC, *OJ* L 267 of 10 October 2009, 7–17.

Directive 2009/65/EC of the European Parliament and of the Council of 13 July 2009 on the coordination of laws, regulations and administrative provisions relating to undertakings for collective investment in transferable securities (UCITS), *OJ* L 302 of 17 November 2009, 32–96.

Directive 2008/20/EC of the European Parliament and of the Council of 11 March 2008 amending Directive 2005/60/EC on the prevention of the use of the financial system for the purpose of money laundering and terrorist financing, as regards the implementing powers conferred on the Commission, *OJ* L 76 of 19 March 2008, 46–47.

Directive 2007/64/EC of the European Parliament and of the Council of 13 November 2007 on payment services in the internal market amending Directives 97/7/EC, 2002/65/EC, 2005/60/EC and 2006/48/EC and repealing Directive 97/5/EC, OJ L 319 of 5 December 2007, 1–36.

Directive 2007/44/EC of the European Parliament and of the Council of 5 September 2007 amending Council Directive 92/49/EEC and Directives 2002/83/EC, 2004/39/EC, 2005/68/EC and 2006/48/EC as regards procedural rules and evaluation criteria for the prudential assessment of acquisitions and increase of holdings in the financial sector, *OJ* L 247 of 21 September 2007, 1–16.

Directive 2006/112/EC of the Council of 28 November 2006 on the common system of value added tax, *OJ* L 347 of 11 December 2006, 1–118.

Commission Directive 2006/73/EC of 10 August 2006 implementing Directive 2004/39/EC of the European Parliament and of the Council as regards organisational requirements and operating conditions for investment firms and defined terms for the purposes of that Directive, *OJ* L 241 of 2 September 2006, 26–58.

Commission Directive 2006/70/EC of 1 August 2006 laying down implementing measures for Directive 2005/60/EC of the European Parliament and of the Council as regards the definition of politically exposed person and the technical criteria for simplified customer due diligence procedures and for exemption on grounds of a financial activity conducted on an occasional or very limited basis, *OJ* L 214 of 04 August 2006, 29–34.

Directive 2006/48/EC of the European Parliament and of the Council of 14 June 2006 relating to the taking up and pursuit of the business of credit institutions (recast), *OJ* L 177 of 30 June 2006, 1–200.

Directive 2006/31/EC of the European Parliament and of the Council of 5 April 2006 amending directive 2004/39/EC on markets in financial instruments, as regards certain deadlines, *OJ* L 114 of 27 April 2006, 60–63.

Directive 2005/60/EC of the European Parliament and of the Council of 26 October 2005 on the prevention of the use of the financial system for the purpose of money laundering and terrorist financing, *OJ* L 309 of 25 November 2005, 15–36.

Directive 2005/29/EC of the European Parliament and of the Council of 11 May 2005 concerning unfair business-to-consumer commercial practices in the internal market and amending Council Directive 84/450/EEC, Directives 97/7/EC, 98/27/EC and 2002/65/EC of the European Parliament and of the Council and Regulation (EC) No 2006/2004 of the European Parliament and of the Council, *OJ* L 149 of 11 June 2005, 22–39.

Directive 2004/109/EC of the European Parliament and of the Council of 15 December 2004 on the harmonisation of transparency requirements in relation to information about issuers whose securities are admitted to trading on a regulated market and amending Directive 2001/34/EC, *OJ* L 390 of 31 December 2004, 38–57.

Directive 2004/39/EC of the European Parliament and of the Council of 21 April 2004 on markets in financial instruments amending Council Directives 85/611/EEC and 93/6/EEC and Directive 2000/12/EC of the European Parliament and of the Council and repealing Council Directive 93/22/EEC, *OJ* L 145 of 30 April 2004, Directive 2003/71/EC of the European Parliament and of the Council of 4 November 2003 on the prospectus to be published when securities are offered to the public or admitted to trading and amending Directive 2001/34/EC, *OJ* L 345 of 31 December 2003, 1–44.

Directive 2003/71/EC of the European Parliament and of the Council of 4 November 2003 on the prospectus to be published when securities are offered to the public or admitted to trading and amending Directive 2001/34/EC, *OJ* L 345 of 31 December 2003, 64–89.

Directive 2003/6/EC of the European Parliament and of the Council of 28 January 2003 on insider dealing and market manipulation (market abuse), *OJ* L 96 of 12 April 2003, 16–25.

Directive 2002/65/EC of the European Parliament and of the Council of 23 September 2002 concerning the distance marketing of consumer financial services and amending Council Directive 90/619/EEC and Directives 97/7/EC and 98/27/EC, *OJ* L 271 of 9 October 2002, 16–24.

Directive 2001/97/EC of the European Parliament and of the Council of 4 December 2001 amending Council Directive 91/308/EEC on prevention of the use of the financial system for the purpose of money laundering, *OJ* L 344 of 28 December 2001, 76–82.

Directive 2000/46/EC of the European Parliament and of the Council of 18 September 2000 on the taking up, pursuit of and prudential supervision of the business of electronic money institutions, *OJ* L 275 of 27 December 2000, 39–43.

Directive 2000/31/EC of the European Parliament and of the Council of 8 June 2000 on certain legal aspects of information society services, in particular electronic commerce, in the Internal Market ('Directive on electronic commerce'), *OJ* L 178 of 17 July 2000, 1–16.

Directive 2000/28/EC of the European Parliament and of the Council of 18 September 2000 amending Directive 2000/12/EC relating to the taking up and pursuit of the business of credit institutions, *OJ* L 275 of 27 October 2000, 37–38. Directive 2000/12/EC of the European Parliament and of the Council of 20 March 2000 relating to the taking up and pursuit of the business of credit institutions, *OJ* L 126 of 26 May 2000, 1–59.

Directive 1999/93/EC of the European Parliament and of the Council of 13 December 1999 on a Community framework for electronic signatures, *OJ* L 13 of 19 January 2000, 12–20.

Directive 98/34/EC of the European Parliament and of the Council of 22 June 1998 laying down a procedure for the provision of information in the field of technical standards and regulations as amended by Directive 98/48/EC of the European Parliament and of the Council of 20 July 1998, *OJ* L 204 of 21 July 1998, 37–48.

Directive 97/7/EC of the European Parliament and of the Council of 20 May 1997 on the protection of consumers in respect of distance contracts, *OJ* L 144 of 4 June 1997, 19–27.

Directive 97/5/EC of the European Parliament and of the Council of 27 January 1997 on cross-border credit transfers, *OJ* L 043 of 14 February 1997, 25–30.

Council Directive 93/22/EEC of 10 May 1993 on investment services in the securities field, *OJ* L 141 of 11 June 1993, 27–46.

Council Directive 91/308/EEC of 10 June 1991 on prevention of the use of the financial system for the purpose of money laundering, *OJ* L 166 of 28 June 1991, 77–82.

Second Council Directive 89/646/EEC of 15 December 1989 on the coordination of laws, regulations and administrative provisions relating to the taking up and pursuit of the business of credit institutions and amending Directive 77/780/EEC, *OJ* L 386 of 30 December 1989, 1–13.

First Council Directive 77/780/EEC of 12 December 1977 on the coordination of the laws, regulations and administrative provisions relating to the taking up and pursuit of the business of credit institutions, *OJ* L 322 of 17 December 1977, 30–37.

### *1.1.3 Decisions*

Council Decision 2005/511/JHA of 12 July 2005 on protecting the euro against counterfeiting, by designating Europol as the Central Office for combating euro counterfeiting, *OJ* L 185 of 16 July 2005, 35–36.

Council Framework Decision 2005/212/JHA of 24 February 2005 on Confiscation of Crime-Related Proceeds, Instrumentalities and Property, *OJ* L68 of 15 March 2005, 49–51.

Council Decision 2002/187/JHA of 28 February 2002 setting up Eurojust with a view to reinforcing the fight against serious crime, *OJ* L 63 of 6 March 2002, 1–13.

Council Framework Decision 2001/500/JHA of 26 June 2001 on money laundering, the identification, tracing, freezing, seizing and confiscation of instrumentalities and the proceeds of crime, *OJ* L 182 of 5 July 2001, 1–2.

Council Decision 2000/642/JHA of 17 October 2000 concerning arrangements for cooperation between financial intelligence units of the Member States in respect of exchanging information, *OJ* L 271 of 24 October 2000, 4–6.

Commission Decision 1999/352/EC of 28 April 1999 establishing the European Anti-fraud Office (OLAF), *OJ* L 136 of 31 May 2001, 20–22.

### *1.1.4 Other*

Interinstitutional Agreement between the European Parliament, the Council and the Commission on budgetary discipline and sound financial management, *OJ* C 139 of 14 June 2006, 1–17.

Commission Recommendation of 22 March 2010 on the scope and effects of legal tender of euro banknotes and coins, *OJ* L 83 of 30 March 2010, 70–71.

Council Resolution of 14 April 1975 on a preliminary programme of the European Economic Community for a consumer protection and information policy, *OJ* C 092 of 25 April 1975, 1–16.

### *1.1.5 Preparatory works*

Council of the European Union (1999) "Common Position (EC) No 8/2000 adopted by the Council on 29 November 1999 with a view to adopting a Directive 2000/.../EC of the European Parliament and of the Council of ... on the taking-up, pursuit of and prudential supervision of the business of electronic money institutions", OJ C 26 of 28 January 2000, 1–11.

Council of the European Union (2000) " Position commune arrêtée par le Conseil en vue de l'adoption de la directive du Parlement européen et du Conseil modifiant la directive 91/308/CEE relative à la prévention de l'utilisation du système financier aux fins du blanchiment de capitaux", 12469/00.

Council of the European Union (2000) "2273rd Council meeting Fisheries at Luxembourg, 16 June 2000", ST 9407 2000 ADD 1.

Council of the European Union (2006) "Proposal for a Directive of the European Parliament and of the Council on payment services in the internal market", 15384/06.

Council of the European Union (2007) "2823rd meeting of the Council of the European Union (General Affairs and External Relations)", 13911/07.

Council of the European Union (2007) "Proposal for a Directive of the European Parliament and of the Council on payment services in the internal market", 7666/07.

Council of the European Union (2007) "Proposal for a Directive of the European Parliament and of the Council on payment services in the internal market", 7665/1/07 REV 1.

Council of the European Union (2007) "Proposal for a Directive of the European Parliament and of the Council on payment services in the internal market", 6634/07.

Council of the European Union (2009) "Directive of the European Parliament and of the Council on the taking up, pursuit and prudential supervision of the business of electronic money institutions amending Directives 2005/60/EC and 2006/48/EC and repealing Directive 2000/46/EC", PE-CONS 3666/09.

Council of the European Union (2009) "Proposal for a Directive of the European Parliament and of the Council of on the taking up, pursuit and prudential supervision of the business of electronic money institutions, amending Directives 2005/60/EC and 2006/48/EC and repealing Directive 2000/46/EC – Letter to European Parliament", 7760/09.

Council of the European Union (2014) "Proposal for a directive of the European Parliament and of the Council on payment services in the internal market and amending Directives 2002/65/EC, 2013/36/EU and 2009/110/EC and repealing Directive 2007/64/EC – Presidency compromise", 16154/14.

Council of the European Union (2014) "Proposal for a directive of the European Parliament and of the Council on payment services in the internal market and amending Directives 2002/65/EC, 2013/36/EU and 2009/110/EC and repealing Directive 2007/64/EC – Approval of a negotiating mandate", 16155/14.

Council of the European Union (2015) "3356th meeting of the Council of the European Union (Economic and Financial Affairs)", 16699/14 ADD 1.

Council of the European Union (2015) "3425th meeting of the Council of the European Union (Agriculture and Fisheries)", 14167/15.

Council of the European Union (2015) "Position of the Council at first reading with a view to the adoption of a Directive of the European Parliament and of the Council on the prevention of the use of the financial system for the purposes of money laundering or terrorist financing, amending Regulation (EU) No 648/2012 of the European Parliament and of the Council, and repealing Directive 2005/60/EC of the European Parliament and of the Council and Commission Directive 2006/70/EC – Adopted by the Council on 20 April 2015", 5933/4/15 REV 4.

Council of the European Union (2015) "Proposal for a directive of the European Parliament and of the Council on payment services in the internal market and amending Directives 2002/65/EC, 2013/36/EU and 2009/110/EC and repealing Directive 2007/64/EC – Confirmation of the final compromise text with a view to agreement", 9337/15.

Council of the European Union (2015) "Proposal for a regulation of the European Parliament and of the Council on information accompanying transfers of funds Proposal for a directive of the European Parliament and of the Council on the prevention of the use of the financial system for the purpose of money laundering and terrorist financing – Declarations by Member States", 5116/15 ADD 3 REV 4.

Council of the European Union (2016) "Proposal for a directive of the European Parliament and of the Council amending Directive (EU) 2015/849 on the prevention of the use of the financial system for the purposes of money laundering or terrorist financing and amending Directive 2009/101/EC = Presidency compromise text", 13872/16.

Council of the European Union (2016) "Proposal for a directive of the European Parliament and of the Council amending Directive (EU) 2015/849 on the prevention of the use of the financial system for the purposes of money laundering or terrorist financing and amending Directive 2009/101/EC = Negotiating mandate", 15605/16, 20–21.

European Central Bank (1999) "Opinion of the European Central Bank of 18 January 1999 at the request of the Council of the European Union under Article 105(4) of the Treaty establishing the European Community and Article 4(a) of the Statute of the European System of Central Banks and of the European Central Bank on 1. a Commission proposal for a European Parliament and Council Directive on the taking up, the pursuit and the prudential supervision of the business of electronic money institutions, and 2. a Commission proposal for a European Parliament and Council Directive amending Directive 77/780/EEC on the coordination of laws, regulations and administrative provisions relating to the taking up and pursuit of the business of credit institutions", OJ C 189 of 6 July 1999.

European Central Bank (1999) "Opinion of the European Central Bank of 18 January 1999 at the request of the Council of the European Union under Article 105(4) of the Treaty establishing the European Community and Article 4(a) of the Statute of the European System of Central Banks and of the European Central Bank on 1. a Commission proposal for a European Parliament and Council Directive on the taking up, the pursuit and the prudential supervision of the business of electronic money institutions, and 2. a Commission proposal for a European Parliament and Council Directive amending Directive 77/780/EEC on the coordination of laws, regulations and administrative provisions relating to the taking up and pursuit of the business of credit institutions", OJ C 189 of 6 July 1999, 7–10.

European Central Bank (2006) "Opinion of the European Central Bank of 26 April 2006 on a proposal for a directive on payment services in the internal market (ECB/2006/21)", OJ C 109 of 9 May 2006, 10–30.

European Central Bank (2008) "Opinion of the European Central Bank of 5 December 2008 on a proposal for a Directive on the taking up, pursuit and prudential supervision of the business of electronic money institutions", OJ C 30 of 9 February 2009, 1–9.

European Central Bank (2012) "Opinion of the European Central Bank of 22 March 2012 on: (i) a proposal for a directive on markets in financial instruments repealing Directive 2004/39/EC of the European Parliament and of the Council; (ii) a proposal for a regulation on markets in financial instruments and amending Regulation (EMIR) on OTC derivatives, central counterparties and trade repositories; (iii) a proposal for a directive on criminal sanctions for insider dealing and market manipulation; and (iv) a proposal for a regulation on insider dealing and market manipulation (market abuse)" OJ C 161 of 7 June 2012, 3–22.

European Central Bank (2013) "Opinion of 17 May 2013 on a proposal for a directive on the prevention of the use of the financial system for the purpose of money laundering and terrorist financing and on a proposal for a regulation on information accompanying transfers of funds", CON/2013/32.

European Central Bank (2014) "Opinion of 5 February 2014 on a proposal for a directive of the European Parliament and of the Council on payment services in the internal market and amending Directives 2002/65/EC, 2013/36/EU and 2009/110/EC and repealing Directive 2007/64/EC (CON/2014/9)", OJ C 224 of 15 July 2014, 1–25.

European Central Bank (2016) "Opinion of 12 October 2016 on a proposal for a directive of the European Parliament and of the Council amending Directive (EU) 2015/849 on the prevention of the use of the financial system for the purposes of money laundering or terrorist financing and amending Directive 2009/101/EC", ecb.europa.eu.

European Commission (1990) "Amendment to the proposal for a Council Directive on prevention of use of the financial system for the purpose of money laundering", COM(90) 593 final.

European Commission (1991) "Re-examined proposal for a Council directive on prevention of use of the financial system for the purpose of money laundering", COM(91) 182 final.

European Commission (1995) "First Commission's report on the implementation of the Money Laundering Directive (91/308/EEC) to be submitted to the European Parliament and to the Council", COM(95) 54 final.

European Commission (1997) "Communication on a European Initiative in Electronic Commerce", COM(1997) 0157.

European Commission (1998) "Explanatory memorandum – what is electronic money?", COM(1998) 461.

European Commission (1998) "Proposal for a European Parliament and Council Directive on the taking up, the pursuit and the prudential supervision of the business of electronic money institutions (COM(1998) 461)", OJ C 317 of 15 October 1998, 7–11.

European Commission (1998) "Proposal for a European Parliament and Council Directive amending Directive 77/780/EEC on the coordination of laws, regulations and administrative provisions relating to the taking up and pursuit of the business of credit institutions (COM(1998) 461)", OJ C 317 of 15 October 1998, 12.

European Commission (1998) "Second Commission report to the European Parliament and the Council on the implementation of the Money Laundering Directive", COM(1998) 401 final.

European Commission (1999) "Proposal for a European Parliament and Council Directive amending Council Directive 91/308/EEC of 10 June 1991 on prevention of the use of the financial system for the purpose of money laundering", COM(1999) 352 final.

European Commission (2000) "Communication from the Commission to the Council and the European Parliament on Retail Payments in the Internal Market", COM(2000)36.

European Commission (2000) "Communication to the European Parliament pursuant to the second subparagraph of Article 251 (2) of the EC-Treaty concerning the Common Position adopted by the Council with a view to the adoption of a European Parliament and Council Directive on the taking up, the pursuit and the prudential supervision of the business of electronic money institutions and a European Parliament and Council Directive amending Directive 77/780/EEC on the co-ordination of laws, regulations and administrative provisions relating to the taking up and pursuit of the business of credit institutions", SEC(2000) 0069.

European Commission (2000) "Opinion of the Commission pursuant to Article 251 (2) (c) of the EC Treaty, on the European Parliament's amendments to the Council's common position regarding the proposal for a Directive of the European Parliament and of the Council on the taking up, the pursuit and the prudential supervision of the business of electronic money institutions and for a Directive of the European Parliament and of the Council amending Directive 77/780/EEC on the co-ordination of laws, regulations and administrative provisions relating to the taking up and pursuit of the business of credit institutions", COM(2000) 0333.

European Commission (2001) "Opinion of the Commission pursuant to Article 251 (2) (c) of the EC Treaty, on the European Parliament's amendments to the Council's common position regarding the proposal for a Directive of the European Parliament and of the Council amending Council Directive 91/308/EEC on prevention of the use of the financial system for the purpose of money laundering", COM/2001/0330 final.

European Commission (2002) "Proposal for a Directive of the European Parliament and of the Council on investment services and regulated markets, and amending Council Directives 85/611/EEC, Council Directive 93/6/EEC and European Parliament and Council Directive 2000/12/EC", COM(2002) 625 final.

European Commission (2003) "Communication concerning a New Legal Framework for Payments in the Internal Market", COM(2003) 718 final.
European Commission (2004) "Proposal for a Directive of the European Parliament and of the Council on the prevention of the use of the financial system for the purpose of money laundering, including terrorist financing", COM/2004/0448 final.
European Commission (2005) "Implementing the Community Lisbon programme: Proposal for a directive of the European Parliament and of the Council on payment services in the internal market and amending Directives 97/7/EC, 2000/12/EC and 2002/65/EC", *COM(2005) 603 final.*
European Commission (2006) "Commission Staff working document on the Review of the E-Money Directive (2000/46/EC)", *SEC(2006) 1049.*
European Commission (2008) "Draft Commission Staff working document – Accompanying document to the proposal for a Directive of the European Parliament and of the Council amending Directive 2000/46/EC on the taking up, pursuit of and prudential supervision of the business of electronic money institutions – Impact Assessment", *SEC(2008)2573.*
European Commission (2008) "proposal for a Directive of the European Parliament and of the Council of on the taking up, pursuit and prudential supervision of the business of electronic money institutions, amending Directives 2005/60/EC and 2006/48/EC and repealing Directive 2000/46/EC ", *COM/2008/0627.*
European Commission (2009) "Commission Communication on the action taken on opinions and resolutions adopted by Parliament at the April 2009 I and II part-sessions", *SP(2009)3507.*
European Commission (2011) "Proposal for a regulation of the European Parliament and of the Council on markets in financial instruments and amending Regulation [EMIR] on OTC derivatives, central counterparties and trade repositories", *COM(2011) 652 final.*
European Commission (2011) "Proposal for a directive of the European Parliament and of the Council on markets in financial instruments repealing Directive 2004/39/EC of the European Parliament and of the Council", *COM(2011) 656 final.*
European Commission (2012) "Commission proposal for a regulation of the European Parliament and of the Council of 4 June 2012 on electronic identification and trust services for electronic transactions in the internal market", *COM(2012) 238 final.*
European Commission (2012) "Staff working document of 7 June 2012 impact assessment accompanying the document proposal for a regulation of the European Parliament and of the Council on electronic identification and trust services for electronic transactions in the internal market", *SWD(2012) 135 final.*
European Commission (2013) "Proposal for a Directive of the European Parliament and of the Council on the prevention of the use of the financial system for the purpose of money laundering and terrorist financing", *COM(2013) 45 final.*
European Commission (2013) "Proposal for a directive of the European Parliament and of the Council on payment services in the internal market and amending Directives 2002/65/EC, 2013/36/EU and 2009/110/EC and repealing Directive 2007/64/EC", *COM(2013) 0547.*
European Commission (2013) "Proposal for a regulation of the European Parliament and of the Council on interchange fees for card-based payment transactions", *COM(2013) 0550.*

European Commission (2013) "Report on the application of Directive 2007/64/EC on payment services in the internal market and on Regulation 924/2009 on cross-border payments in the Community", *COM(2013) 549 final.*

European Commission (2015) "Communication pursuant to Article 294(6) of the Treaty on the Functioning of the European Union concerning the position of the Council on the adoption of a Directive of the European Parliament and of the Council on the prevention of the use of the financial system for the purpose of money laundering and terrorist financing", *COM(2015) 188 final.*

European Commission (2016) "Commission presents Action Plan to strengthen the fight against terrorist financing", *IP/16/202.*

European Commission (2016) "Communication from the Commission to the European Parliament and the Council on an Action Plan for strengthening the fight against terrorist financing", *COM(2016) 50 final.*

European Commission (2016) "Impact assessment accompanying the document Proposal for a Directive of the European Parliament and the Council amending Directive (EU) 2015/849 on the prevention of the use of the financial system for the purposes of money laundering or terrorist financing and amending Directive 2009/101/EC", *SWD(2016) 223 final.*

European Commission (2016) "Proposal for a Directive of the European Parliament and of the Council amending Directive (EU) 2015/849 on the prevention of the use of the financial system for the purposes of money laundering or terrorist financing and amending Directive 2009/101/EC", *COM(2016) 450 final.*

European Data Protection Supervisor (2012) "Opinion of the European Data Protection Supervisor on the Commission proposals for a Directive of the European Parliament and of the Council on markets in financial instruments repealing Directive 2004/39/EC of the European Parliament and of the Council, and for a Regulation of the European Parliament and of the Council on markets in financial instruments and amending Regulation on OTC derivatives, central counterparties and trade repositories", *OJ* C 147 of 25 May 2012, 10.

European Data Protection Supervisor (2013) "Executive summary of the Opinion on a proposal for a Directive of the European Parliament and of the Council on the prevention of the use of the financial system for the purpose of money laundering and terrorist financing, and a proposal for a Regulation of the European Parliament and of the Council on information on the payer accompanying transfers of funds", *OJ* C 32 of 4 February 2014, 9–12.

European Economic and Social Committee (1990) "Opinion on the proposal for a Council Directive on prevention of the use of the financial system for the purpose of money laundering (90/C 332/26)", *OJ* C 332 of 31 December 1990.

European Economic and Social Committee (2000) "Opinion of the Economic and Social Committee on the 'Proposal for a European Parliament and Council Directive amending Council Directive 91/308/EEC of 10 June 1991 on prevention of the use of the financial system for the purpose of money laundering'", *OJ* C 75 of 15 March 2000.

European Economic and Social Committee (2005) "Opinion of the European Economic and Social Committee on a directive of the European Parliament and of the Council on the prevention of the use of the financial system for the purpose of money laundering, including terrorist financing", *OJ* C 267 of 27 October 2005, 30–35.

European Economic and Social Committee (2006) "Opinion of the European Economic and Social Committee on Implementing the Community Lisbon programme: Proposal for a Directive of the European Parliament and of the Council on payment services in the internal market and amending Directives 97/7/EC, 2000/12/EC and 2002/65/EC COM(2005) 603 final – 2005/0245 (COD)", *INT/301*.

European Economic and Social Committee (2009) "Opinion of the European Economic and Social Committee on the Proposal for a directive of the European Parliament and of the Council on the taking up, pursuit and prudential supervision of the business of electronic money institutions, amending Directives 2005/60/EC and 2006/48/EC and repealing Directive 2000/46/EC", *OJ* C 218 of 11 September 2009.

European Economic and Social Committee (2012) "Opinion of the European Economic and Social Committee on the 'Proposal for a Regulation of the European Parliament and of the Council on markets in financial instruments and amending Regulation (EMIR) on OTC derivatives, central counterparties and trade repositories'", *OJ* C 143 of 22 May 2012, 77.

European Economic and Social Committee (2013) "Opinion of 23 May 2013 on the Proposal for a Regulation of the European Parliament and of the Council on information accompanying transfers of funds COM(2013) 44 final – 2013/0024 (COD) and the Proposal for a Directive of the European Parliament and of the Council on the prevention of the use of the financial system for the purpose of money laundering and terrorist financing COM(2013) 45 final – 2013/0025 (COD)", *ECO/344*.

European Economic and Social Committee (2013) "Opinion of the European Economic and Social Committee on the Proposal for a Regulation of the European Parliament and of the Council on interchange fees for card-based payment transactions COM(2013) 550 final – 2013/0265 (COD) and the Proposal for a Directive of the European Parliament and of the Council on payment services in the internal market and amending Directives 2002/65/EC, 2013/36/EU and 2009/110/EC and repealing Directive 2007/64/EC COM(2013) 547 final – 2013/0264 (COD)", *INT/711*.

European Parliament (1990) "Resolution on proposal for a Council directive on prevention of use of the financial system for the purpose of money laundering", *OJ* C of 24 December 1990, 257–264.

European Parliament (1991) "Decision on the common position established by the Council with a view to the adoption of a Council directive on prevention of use of the financial system for the purpose of money laundering", *OJ* C 129 of 20 May 1991, 90–92.

European Parliament (1999) "Legislative resolution embodying Parliament's opinion on the proposal for a European Parliament and Council Directive on the taking up, the pursuit and the prudential supervision of the business of electronic money institutions (COM(98)0461 C4–0531/98 98/0252(COD))", *OJ* C 219 of 30 July 1999.

European Parliament (1999) "Report on the proposal for a European Parliament and Council Directive on the taking up, the pursuit and the prudential supervision of the business of electronic money institutions (COM(98)0461 – C4–0531/98 – 98/0252(COD)) and on the proposal for a European Parliament and Council Directive amending Directive 77/780/EEC on the coordination of laws, regulations and administrative provisions relating to the taking up and pursuit of the business of credit institutions (COM(98)0461 – C4–0532/98 – 98/0253(COD))", *A4–0156/99*.

European Parliament (2000) "Committee on Economic and Monetary Affairs Recommendation for second reading on the Council common position for adopting a European Parliament and Council directive on the taking up, the pursuit and the prudential supervision of the business of electronic money institutions (12004/2/1999 – C5-0306/1999 – 1998/0252(COD)) and on the Council common position for adopting a European Parliament and Council directive amending Directive 77/780/EEC on the co-ordination of laws, regulations and administrative provisions relating to the taking up and pursuit of the business of credit institutions (12005/1/1999 – C5-0307/1999 – 1998/0253(COD))", *A5-0080/2000.*

European Parliament (2000) "Position adopted at second reading on 11 April 2000 with a view to the adoption of European Parliament and Council Directive 2000/.../EC on the taking up, pursuit of and prudential supervision of the business of electronic money institutions (1998/0252(COD) – PE2)", *OJ* C 40 of 7 February 2001, 35–36.

European Parliament (2001) "Recommendation for second reading on the common position adopted by the Council on 30 November 2000 with a view to the adoption of a Directive of the European Parliament and of the Council amending Council Directive 91/308/EEC on prevention of the use of the financial system for the purpose of money laundering", *A5-0090/2001.*

European Parliament (2007) "Minutes of the sitting of Tuesday 24 April 2007", *PE 387.045.*

European Parliament (2009) "Debates Friday 24 April 2009 – CRE 24/04/2009 – 3", *A6-0056/2009.*

European Parliament (2009) "Position of the European Parliament adopted at first reading on 24 April 2009 with a view to the adoption of Directive 2009/.../EC of the European Parliament and of the Council on the taking up, pursuit and prudential supervision of the business of electronic money institutions amending Directives 2005/60/EC and 2006/48/EC and repealing Directive 2000/46/EC", *EP-PE_TC1-COD(2008)0190.*

European Parliament (2009) "Report on the proposal for a directive of the European Parliament and of the Council on the taking up, pursuit and prudential supervision of the business of electronic money institutions, amending Directives 2005/60/EC and 2006/48/EC and repealing Directive 2000/46/EC", *A6-0056/2009.*

European Parliament (2012) "Debates of 25 October 2012", *CRE 25/10/2012 – 17.*

European Parliament (2012) "Results of Votes of 26 October 2012", *PV 26/10/2012 – 6.7 & 6.8.*

European Parliament (2012) "Results of Votes of 15 April 2014", *PV 15/04/2014 – 17.7 & 17.8.*

European Parliament (2014) "Committee on Economic and Monetary Affairs and Committee on Civil Liberties, Justice and Home Affairs: Report on the proposal for a directive of the European Parliament and of the Council on the prevention of the use of the financial system for the purpose of money laundering and terrorist financing (COM(2013)0045) – C7-0032/2013 – 2013/0025(COD))", *A7-0150/2014.*

European Parliament (2014) "Minutes of the sitting of Thursday 3 April 2014", *PE 533.119.*

European Parliament (2015) "Committee on Economic and Monetary Affairs and Committee on Civil Liberties, Justice and Home Affairs: Draft Recommendation for second reading on the Council position at first reading with a view to the adoption of a directive of the European Parliament and of the Council on the prevention of the use of the financial system for the purposes of money laundering or terrorist financing, amending Regulation (EU) No 648/2012 of the European Parliament and of the Council, and repealing Directive 2005/60/EC of the European Parliament and of the Council and Commission Directive 2006/70/EC (05933/3/2015 - C8-0109/2015 - 2013/0025(COD))", *PE554.948*.

European Parliament (2016) "Opinion of the Committee on Development for the Committee on Economic and Monetary Affairs and the Committee on Civil Liberties, Justice and Home Affairs on the proposal for a directive of the European Parliament and of the Council amending Directive (EU) 2015/849 on the prevention of the use of the financial system for the purposes of money laundering or terrorist financing and amending Directive 2009/101/EC (COM(2016)0450 - C8-0265/2016 - 2016/0208(COD))", *PE594.116*.

European Parliament (2016) "Opinion of the Committee on International Trade for the Committee on Economic and Monetary Affairs and the Committee on Civil Liberties, Justice and Home Affairs on the proposal for a directive of the European Parliament and of the Council amending Directive (EU) 2015/849 on the prevention of the use of the financial system for the purposes of money laundering or terrorist financing and amending Directive 2009/101/EC (COM(2016)0450 - C8-0265/2016 - 2016/0208(COD))", *PE594.132*.

European Parliament (2016) "Opinion of the Committee on Legal Affairs for the Committee on Economic and Monetary Affairs and the Committee on Civil Liberties, Justice and Home Affairs on the proposal for a directive of the European Parliament and of the Council amending Directive (EU) 2015/849 on the prevention of the use of the financial system for the purposes of money laundering or terrorist financing and amending Directive 2009/101/EC (COM(2016)0450 - C8-0265/2016 - 2016/0208(COD))", PE594.003.

European Parliament (2017) "Report on the proposal for a directive of the European Parliament and of the Council amending Directive (EU) 2015/849 on the prevention of the use of the financial system for the purposes of money laundering or terrorist financing and amending Directive 2009/101/EC (COM(2016)0450 - C8-0265/2016 - 2016/0208(COD))", PE593.836.

European Parliament Committee on Economic and Monetary Affairs (2014) "Report on the proposal for a directive of the European Parliament and of the Council on payment services in the internal market and amending Directives 2002/65/EC, 2013/36/EU and 2009/110/EC and repealing Directive 2007/64/EC (COM(2013)0547 - C7-0230/2013 - 2013/0264(COD))", A7-0169/2014.

European Parliament Committee on Economic and Monetary Affairs (2015) "Supplementary report on the proposal for a directive of the European Parliament and of the Council on payment services in the internal market and amending Directives 2002/65/EC, 2013/36/EU and 2009/110/EC and repealing Directive 2007/64/EC (COM(2013)0547 - C7-0230/2013 - 2013/0264(COD))", A8-0266/2015.

## 1.2 BELGIUM

Belgian Act of 18 December 2016 regulating the recognition and demarcation of crowdfunding and holding diverse provisions regarding finances, *Belgian State Gazette* 20 December 2016.

Act of 27 November 2012 amending the act of 21 December 2009 concerning the statute of payment institutions, access to the profession of payment service provider and access to payment systems and of other acts relating to the statute of payment institutions and institutions for electronic money and of the credit institutions of the professional credit, *Belgian State Gazette* 30 November 2012.

Act of 15 May 2007 establishing a legal framework for certain providers of trust services, *Belgian State Gazette* 17 July 2007.

Act of 16 June 2006 on the public offering of investment instruments and the admission of investment instruments on a regulated market, *Belgian State Gazette* 21 June 2006.

Belgian Act of 2 August 2002 concerning the supervision on the financial sector and financial services, *Belgian State Gazette* 4 September 2002.

Act of 4 December 1990 on financial transactions and the financial market, *Belgian State Gazette* 22 December 1990.

Royal Decree of 24 April 2014 approving the regulation of the Financial Services and Markets Authority concerning the commercialization prohibition of certain financial products to non-professional clients, *Belgian State Gazette* 20 May 2014.

Royal Decree of 27 December 1994 concerning the currency exchange offices and the currency trade, *Belgian State Gazette* 18 January 1995.

Royal Decree nr. 56 of 10 November 1967 promoting the use of scriptural money, *Belgian State Gazette* 14 November 1967.

## 1.3 FRANCE

Loi n° 2007-211 du 19 février 2007 instituant la fiducie, *JORF* n°44 of 21 February 2007, 3052 *et seq.*

## 1.4 GERMANY

Bundesgesetzbuch (BGB).

Kreditwesengesetz in der Fassung der Bekanntmachung vom 9. September 1998 (BGBl. I S. 2776), das durch Artikel 1 des Gesetzes vom 15. Juli 2014 (BGBl. I S. 934) geändert worden ist (Kreditwesengesetz - KWG)).

## 1.5 THE NETHERLANDS

New Dutch Civil Code.

## 1.6 UNITED KINGDOM

The Electronic Money Regulations 2011, S.I. 2011 No. 99.

Money Laundering Regulations 2007, 2007 No. 2157.

## 1.7 UNITED STATES

### *1.7.1 Federal*

US Constitution
7 U.S.C. §1–2.
15 U.S.C. §77–78.
15 U.S.C. §1693.
18 U.S.C. §485.
18 U.S.C. §1960.
31 U.S.C. §5103.
31 U.S.C. §5330.
Dodd–Frank Wall Street Reform and Consumer Protection Act of 2010, Pub. L. 111–203.
Credit CARD Act of 2009, Pub. L. 111–24.
Sarbanes–Oxley Act of 2002, Pub. L. 107–204.
Commodity Futures Modernization Act of 2000, Pub. L. 106–554.
Money Laundering Control Act of 1986, 18 U.S.C. §1956–1957.
Electronic Fund Transfer Act of 1978, 15 U.S.C. §§1693–1700.
Consumer Credit Protection Act of 1978, 15 U.S.C. §§1601–1700.
Commodity Futures Trading Commission Act of 1974, Pub. L. 93–463.
Bank Secrecy Act of 1970, Pub. L. 91–508.
Commodity Exchange Act of 1936, Pub. L. 74–675.
Securities Exchange Act of 1934, Pub. L. 73–291.
Securities Act of 1933, Pub. L. 73–22.
Grain Futures Act of 1922, Pub. L. 67–331.
Clayton Antitrust Act of 1914, Pub. L. 63–212.
Sherman Antitrust Act of 1890, 15 U.S.C. ch.1.
Stamp Payments Act 1862, 12 Stat. 592, ch. 196.
Regulation E, 12 C.F.R. §205 (amended 1981).
12 C.F.R. §1005.
31 C.F.R. §1010.
A bill to improve the prohibitions on money laundering, and for other purposes, *S. 1241*, 115th Cong. (2017).
A bill to direct the Under Secretary of Homeland Security for Intelligence and Analysis to develop and disseminate a threat assessment regarding terrorist use of virtual currency, *H.R. 2433*, 115th Cong. (2017), section 2(a).

### *1.7.2 Model and Uniform Acts*

Model State Commodity Code.
Uniform Commercial Code.
Uniform Money Services Act.
Uniform Regulation of Virtual Currency Businesses Act.
Uniform Securities Act.

#### *1.7.3 California*

Chapter 74 (Cal. Stat. 2014).
California Money Transmission Act, Cal. Fin. Code §2003.
An act to repeal Section 107 of the Corporations Code, and to add Section 2178 to, and to add Division 11 (commencing with Section 26000) to, the Financial Code, relating to currency, *Cal. Assemb. B. 1123* (2017–2018), as amended in Assembly on 30 March 2017.
An act to repeal Section 107 of the Corporations Code, and to amend, repeal, and add Section 2003 of, and to add Division 11 (commencing with Section 26000) to, the Financial Code, relating to digital currency, *Cal. Assemb. B. 1326* (2015–2016), as amended in Senate on 8 August 2016.
An act to repeal Section 107 of the Corporations Code, relating to business associations, *Cal. Assemb. B. 129* (2013–2014).

#### *1.7.4 Delaware*

A Bill to Amend Title 8 Of The Delaware Code Relating To The General Corporation Law, *Del. SB 69* (2017).

#### *1.7.5 New Hampshire*

New Hampshire Revised Statutes Annotated Chapter 399-G.
Act exempting persons using virtual currency from registering as money transmitters, *NH HB 436* (2017 session).
Act relative to licensing of money transmitters, NH HB 666-FN (2015 session).
Act requiring the state treasurer to develop an implementation plan for the state to accept bitcoin as payment for taxes and fees, NH HB 552-FN (2015 session).

#### *1.7.6 New York*

23 CRR-NY I 200.

#### *1.7.7 Virginia*

Va. Code §6.2–1900.

### 1.8 UNITED NATIONS

United Nations Convention against Illicit Traffic in Narcotic Drugs and Psychotropic Substances, Vienna, 20 December 1988.

## 1.9 COUNCIL OF EUROPE

Convention Nr. 141 on Laundering, Search, Seizure and Confiscation of the Proceeds from Crime, Strasbourg, 08 November 1990.

# 2 CASE LAW

## 2.1 EUROPEAN UNION

CJEU, Banif Plus Bank Zrt. *v.* Márton Lantos, Mártonné Lantos, *C-312/14.*
CJEU, Skatteverket *v* David Hedqvist, C-264/14.
CJEU, T-Mobile Austria GmbH *v* Verein für Konsumenteninformation, C-616/11.
CJEU, Genil 48 SL, Comercial Hostelera de Grandes Vinos SL *v.* Bankinter SA, Banco Bilbao Vizcaya Argentaria SA, C-604/11.
CJEU, Commissioners for Her Majesty's Revenue and Customs *v* Loyalty Management UK Ltd and Baxi Group Ltd, C-53/09 and C-55/09.

## 2.2 BELGIUM

RvS 9 September 2008, nr. 186134.

## 2.3 CANADA

Reference Re Alberta Statutes [1938] SCR 100.

## 2.4 FRANCE

Court of Appeals Paris, 26 September 2013, nr. 12/00161.
Court of Appeals Paris, 26 August 2011, nr. 11/15269.
Commercial Court Créteil, 6 December 2011, nr. RG 2011F00771.

## 2.5 THE NETHERLANDS

HR 11 December 1959, Eelman/Hin, *NJ* 1960, 230.

## 2.6 UNITED KINGDOM

Supreme Court, Revenue and Customs v Aimia Coalition Loyalty UK Ltd, [2013] UKSC 15 (13 March 2013).

Abdi v Secretary of State for the Home Department [2005] EWCA Civ 1363, at 68 (22 November 2005).
Council of Civil Service Unions v Minister for the Civil Service, [1984] UKHL 9, at 410 (22 November 1984).
Schmidt & Anor v Secretary of State for Home Affairs [1968] EWCA Civ 1 (19 December 1968).
Associated Provincial Picture Houses v Wednesbury Corporation, [1947] 1 KB 223 (10 November 1947).
Moss *v* Hancock, [1899] 2 Q.B. 111.

## 2.7 UNITED STATES

### *2.7.1 US Supreme Court*

SEC *v.* Edwards, 540 U.S. 389 (2004).
Spectrum Sports, Inc. *v.* McQuillan, 506 U.S. 447 (1993).
Reves *v.* Ernst & Young, 494 U.S. 56 (1990).
Landreth Timber Co. *v.* Landreth, 471 U.S. 681 (1985).
Marine Bank *v.* Weaver, 455 U.S. 551 (1982).
Teamsters *v.* Daniel, 439 U.S. 551 (1979).
United Housing Foundation, Inc. *v.* Forman, 421 U.S. 837 (1975).
Tcherepnin *v.* Knight, 389 U. S. 332 (1967).
Securities and Exchange Commission *v.* W. J. Howey Co., 328 U.S. 293 (1946).
SEC v. C.M. Joiner Leasing Corp., 320 U.S. 344 (1943).
Board of Trade of City of Chicago v. Olsen, 262 U.S. 1 (1923).
Hill v. Wallace, 259 U.S. 44 (1922).
United States v. United States Steel Corp., 251 U.S. 417 (1920).
Hall v. Geiger-Jones Co., 242 U.S. 539 (1917).
United States v. American Tobacco Company, 221 U.S. 106 (1911).
Standard Oil Co. of New Jersey v. United States, 221 U.S. 1 (1911).
Legal Tender Cases, 110 U.S. 421 (1884).
United States v. Van Auken, 96 U.S 366 (1878).
Briscoe v. Bank of Commonwealth of Kentucky, 36 U.S. 257 (1837).
Craig v. State of Missouri, 29 U.S. 410 (1830).

### *2.7.2 Federal courts*

United States *v.* Elfgeeh, 515 F.3d 100 (2d Cir. 2008).
SEC *v.* Merchant Capital, L.L.C., 483 F.3d 747 ($11^{th}$ Cir. 2007).
CFTC *v.* Zelener, 373 F.3d 861 ($7^{th}$ Cir. 2004).
SEC *v.* Eurobond, Exchange Ltd., 13 F.3d 1334 ($9^{th}$ Cir. 1994).
Wals *v.* Fox Hills Dev. Corp., 24 F.3d 1016 ($7^{th}$ Cir. 1994).
United States *v.* Schnabel, 939 F.2d 197 ($4^{th}$ Cir. 1991).
Board of Trade of City of Chicago *v.* SEC, 677 F. 2d 1137 ($7^{th}$ Cir. 1982).
Aldrich *v.* McCulloch Prop. Inc., 627 F.2d 1036 ($10^{th}$ Cir. 1980).

Noa *v.* Key Futures, Inc., 638 F.2d. 77 (9th Cir. 1980).
Curran *v.* Merrill, Lynch, 622 F.2d 216 (6th Cir. 1980).
Hirk *v.* Agri-Research Council, Inc., 561 F.2d 96 (7th Cir. 1977).
Hector *v.* Wiens, 533 F.2d 429 (9th Cir. 1976).
El Khadem *v.* Equity Sec. Corp., 494 F.2d 1224 (9th Cir. 1974).
SEC *v.* Continental Commodities Corp., 497 F.2d 516 (5th Cir. 1974).
SEC *v.* Glenn W. Turner Enterprises, Inc., 474 F.2d 476 (9th Cir. 1973).

### *2.7.3 State courts*

SEC *v.* Traffic Monsoon et al., 2:16-cv-00832-JNP (D. Utah, filed 26 July 2016).
Sync Labs LLC *v.* Fusion Mfg., 2013 WL 4776018 (DC New Jersey 2013).
SEC *v.* Trendon T. Shavers and Bitcoin Savings and Trust, 4:13-CV-416 (Texas, 6 August 2013).
In re Bender, 844 N.E.2d 170 (Ind. App., 2006).
Faulkner *v.* Bost, 137 S.W.3d 254 (Tex. App.-Tyler, 2004).
Moore *v.* Moore, 111 S.W.3d 530 (Mo. App. S.D., 2003).
Jewish Community Ass'n of Casper *v.* Community First Nat. Bank, 6 P.3d 1264 (Wyo., 2000).
In re S & D Foods, Inc., 144 B.R. 121 (Bkrtcy. D. Colo., 1992).
All Seasons Resorts *v.* Abrams, 68 NY 2d 81 (CA New York 1986).
Scott *v.* Vandor, 671 S.W.2d 79 (Tex. App. Houston 1st Dist. 1984).
Sandusky Land, Ltd. *v.* Uniplan Groups, Inc., 400 F. Supp. 440 (N.D. Ohio 1975).
Silver Hills Country Club *v.* Sobieski, 155 Cal.2d 811 (SC California 1961).
United States *v.* Gellman, 44 F. Supp. 360 (D. Minn. 1942).
United States *v.* Monongahela Bridge Co., 26 F. Cas. 1292 (W.D. Pa. 1863).

### *2.7.4 CFTC*

In re BFXNA, Inc. d/b/a BITFINEX, *CFTC Docket No. 16-19* (2016).
In re Coinflip, Inc., d/b/a/ Derivabit, et al., *CFTC Docket No. 15-29* (2015).

# 3 LITERATURE

## 3.1 BOOKS, BOOK CHAPTERS AND THESES

Alter, C. (2010) *Droit bancaire général*, Brussels: Larcier.
Aristotle (1999) *Politics, translated by Benjamin Jowett*, Kitchener: Batoche Books.
Axelrod, R. (1988) "The Evolution of Cooperation", In: Gromyko, A., Hellman, M. (Eds.) *Breakthrough: Emerging New Thinking*, New York City: Walker and Co.
Bal, A. (2014) "Taxation of virtual currency", *PhD Thesis Leiden University.*
Barber, B. (1983) *The logic and limits of trust*, New Brunswick: Rutgers University Press.
Berger, P. E., Landuyt, S. (2012) "Toepassingsgebied van de wet betalingsdiensten en de wet betalingsinstellingen", In: Instituut Financieel Recht (Ed.), *Financiële regulering in de kering*, Antwerpen: Intersentia.

Bergstra, J.A., Weijland, P. (2014) "Bitcoin: a Money-like Informational Commodity", *University of Amsterdam Theory of Computer Science Electronic Report Series TCS1402.*

Birch, D. G. W., McEvoy, N. A. (1997) "Electronic cash-technology will denationalise money", In: Hirschfeld, R. (Ed.) Financial Cryptography, LNCS 1318, Berlin: Springer.

Biryukov, A., Khovratovich, D., Pustogarov, I. (2014) "Deanonymisation of Clients in Bitcoin P2P Network", Presented at *ACM Conference on Computer and Communications Security,* 3 November 2014, Scottsdale, Arizona.

Bloomenthal, H. S., Wolff, S. (2017) *Securities Law Handbook,* New York City: Thomson Reuters.

Blouin, F. X., Rosenberg, W. G. (2011) *Processing the past: contesting authority in history and the archives,* New York: Oxford University Press.

Boddaert, C. (2009) "Pand op een levende bankrekening", In: Cattaruzza, J., Kupers, W., Peeters, I. (Eds.) *Liber Amicorum Achilles Cuypers,* Brussel: Larcier.

Boedts, T. (2014) "Kunnen crowdfunding en virtuele munten innoveren zonder bijkomende regulering?" in: IBJ (Ed.) L'innovation, source de droit. Le droit, source d'innovation / Innovatie, bron van recht. Recht, bron van innovatie, Brussels: Bruylant.

Boehm, F., Pesch, P. (2014) "Bitcoin: A First Legal Analysis With Reference to German and US-American Law", In: Böhme, R., Brenner, M., Moore, T., Smith, M. (Eds.) Financial Cryptography and Data Security, FC 2014 Workshops, LNCS 8438, Berlin: Springer.

Bonneau, T. (2016) "Analyse critique de la contribution de la CJUE à l'ascension juridique du bitcoin", In: De Loustal, J. (Ed.) Liber Amicorum Blanche Sousi: L'Europe bancaire, financière et monétaire, Paris: Revue Banque Edition.

Bonneau, T., Drummond, F. (2010) Droit des Marchés Financiers, Paris: Economica.

Bowlby, J. (1969) Attachment and Loss: Vol. 1 Attachment, New York City: Basic Books.

Brito, J., Castillo, A. (2013) Bitcoin: A Primer for Policymakers, Arlington: George Mason University Mercatus Center.

Byttebier, K., Wera, T. (2011) "Het toepassingsgebied van de wet van 10 december 2009 betreffende de betalingsdiensten (samen)ge(s)teld", In: Feron, B. (Ed.) Betalingsdiensten: de nieuwe regeling onder de loep genomen / Services de paiement: la nouvelle réglementation passée au crible, Antwerpen: Intersentia.

Castelfranchi, C. (2006) "Why We Need a Non-reductionist Approach to Trust", In: Stølen, K., Winsborough, W. H., Martinelli, F., Massacci, F. (Eds.) iTrust 2006, Berlin: Springer.

Cauffman, C. (2005) De verbindende eenzijdige belofte, Antwerpen: Intersentia.

Chaaben, M. (2016) Le Financement participatif, Saint-Denis: Connaissances et Savoirs.

Clower, R. W. (1986) Money and Markets: Essays by Robert W. Clower edited by Donald A. Walker, Cambridge: University Press.

Colaert, V. (2010) "De meerlagige rechtsverhouding financiële dienstverlener – belegger", KU Leuven Faculty of Law PhD thesis.

Colaert, V. (2011) De rechtsverhouding financiële dienstverlener-belegger, Brugge: die Keure.

Cook, K. S., Hardin, R., Levi, M. (2005) Cooperation Without Trust? New York: Russell Sage Foundation.

Cornelis, L. (2000) Algemene theorie van de verbintenis, Antwerpen: Intersentia.

Cruickshank, C. (1998) "Is there a Need to Harmonise Conduct of Business Rules?", In Ferrarini, G. (Ed.) European Securities Markets: The Investment Services Directive and Beyond, London: Kluwer Law International.

Dasgupta, P. (2000) "Trust as a Commodity", In: Gambetta, D. (ed.) Trust: Making and Breaking Cooperative Relations, Oxford: Basil Blackwell.

Davies, G. (2002) A History of Money, Cardiff: University of Wales Press.

De Boeck, A. (2009) "De precontractuele aansprakelijkheid anno 2010", In: Stijns, S., Samoy, I., De Boeck, A. (Eds.) Verbintenissenrecht, Brugge: die Keure.

De Cock, D., Wolf, C., Preneel, B. (2006) "The Belgian Electronic Identity Card (Overview)", In: Dittmann, J. (Ed.) Sicherheit 2005, Sicherheit - Schutz und Zuverlässigkeit, Beiträge der 3rd Jahrestagung des Fachbereichs Sicherheit der Gesellschaft für Informatik e.v. (GI), Lecture Notes in Informatics (LNI) LNI P-77, Bonn: Köllen Verlag.

De Roover, R. (1999) The rise and decline of the Medici bank 1397 – 1494, Washington D.C.: Beard Books.

De Vauplane, H. (2015) "Bitcoin et monnaies virtuelles: entre réglementation et essai de définition juridique", In. Daems, H., De Meuleneere, I., Houssa, C., Ragheno, N. (Eds.) Digital Finance / La finance numérique, Antwerpen: Intersentia.

Defoe, D. (1726) The political history of the Devil, London: T. Warner.

Della Faille D'huysse, P. (2008) La modernisation des marchés financiers, Limal: Anthemis.

Desan, C. (2016) "Money as a Legal Institution", In: Fox, D., Ernst, W. (Eds.) Money in the Western Legal Tradition: Middle Ages to Bretton Woods, Oxford: Oxford University Press.

Dilke, O. A. W. (1987) Reading the Past: Mathematics and measurement, London: British Museum Publications.Dodd, N. (2014) The Social Life of Money, Princeton: University Press.

Dowd, K. (2014) New Private Monies, London: The Institute of Economic Affairs.

Dumortier, J. (2004) "Legal status of qualified electronic signatures in Europe", In: Paulus, S., Pohlmann, N., Reimer, H. (Eds.) ISSE 2004-Securing Electronic Business Processes, Wiesbaden: Vieweg.

Dumortier, J. (2010) ICT-Recht, Leuven: Acco.

Dumortier, J., Vandezande, N. (2014) "Legal evidence in a digital context: will signatures disappear?", In: Savin, A., Trzaskowski, J. (eds.) Research Handbook on EU Internet Law, Cheltenham: Edward Elgar.

Duranti, L. (1998) Diplomatics: New Uses for an Old Science, Lanham: Scarecrow Press.

Elderfield, M. (2007) A practitioner's guide to MiFID, Surrey: City & Financial Publishing.

Erikson, E. H. (1959) Identity and the lifecycle, New York City: International Universities Press.

Ernoult, J., Hemetsberger, W., Schoppmann, H., Wengler, C. (2008) European Banking and Financial Services Law (3rd edition), Brussels: Larcier.

European Commission (2015) Consumer Conditions Scoreboard: Consumers at home in the Single Market (2015 edition), Luxembourg: Publications Office of the European Union.

Falcone, R., Castelfranchi, C. (2001) "The Socio-cognitive Dynamics of Trust: Does Trust Create Trust?", In: Falcone, R., Singh, M., Tan, Y.-H. (Eds.) Trust in Cyber-societies: Integrating the Human and Artificial Perspectives, Berlin: Springer.

FATF (2012) Recommendations – International Standards on Combatting Money Laundering and the Financing of Terrorism & Proliferation, Paris: FATF.

FATF (2016) FATF Recommendations 2012 – International Standards on Combating Money Laundering and the Financing of Terrorism & Proliferation (2016 update), Paris: FATF.

Feron, B. (1999) "La gestion de fortune en droit belge", In: Thévenoz, L. (Ed.) Aspects juridiques de la gestion de fortune, Brussel: Bruylant.

Fischer, R., Müller, C. (2016) "§32 Erlaubnis", In: Boos, K.-H., Fischer, R., Schulte-Mattler, H. (Eds.) Kommentar zu Kreditwesengesetz, VO (EU) Nr. 575/2013 (CRR) und Ausführungsvorschriften – Band I (5. Auflage), München: Verlag C. H. Beck.

Fogg, B. J., Tseng, H. (1999) "The elements of computer credibility", In: Williams, M., Altom, M. (Eds.) Proceedings of the SIGCHI conference on Human Factors in Computing Systems (CHI '99), New York: ACM.

Franklin, B. (1907) The writings of Benjamin Franklin Volume X (1789–1790), London: Macmillan and Co.

Frevert, U. (2017) "Vertrauen in der moralischen Ökonomie des Teilens und Tauschens", In: Lehmann, K.-D., Ebert, J., Ströhl, A., Blaumer, N. (Eds.) Teilen und Tauschen, Frankfurt: Wallstein.

Frevert, U. (2016) "The History of Emotions", In: Feldman Barrett, L., Lewis, M., Haviland-Jones, J. M. (Eds.) Handbook of Emotions, Fourth Edition, New York: Guilford Press.

Friedman, M. (1994) Money mischief: Episodes in monetary history, Orlando: Harcourt

Fukuyama, F. (1995) Trust: The Social Virtues and the Creation of Prosperity, New York: Free Press.

Gambetta, D. (1988) "Can We Trust Trust?", In: Gambetta, D. (ed.) Trust: Making and Breaking Cooperative Relations, Oxford: Basil Blackwell.

Gambetta, D. (2000) "Foreword", In: Gambetta, D. (ed.) Trust: Making and Breaking Cooperative Relations, electronic edition, Oxford: Basil Blackwell.

Gans, J.S., Halaburda, H. (2014) "Some Economics of Private Digital Currency ", In: Goldfarb, A., Greenstein, S., Tucker, C. (Eds.) Economic Analysis of the Digital Economy, Chicago: University Press.

Geva, B. (2011) The Payment Order of Antiquity and the Middle Ages: A Legal History, London: Hart Publishing.

Ginossar, S. (1960) Droit réel, propriété et créance: élaboration d'un système rationnel des droits patrimoniaux, Paris: Librairie Générale de Droit et de Jurisprudence.

Glaser, R. (2009) Geldwäsche (§261 StGB) durch Rechtsanwälte und Steuerberater bei der Honorarannahme, München: Herbert Utz Verlag.

Goldman, Z. K., Maruyama, E., Rosenberg, E., Saravalle, E., Solomon-Strauss, J. (2017) Terrorist Use of Virtual Currencies: Containing the Potential Threat, Washington, D.C.: Center for a New American Security.

Good, D. (2000) "Individuals, Interpersonal Relations, and Trust", In: Gambetta, D. (ed.) Trust: Making and Breaking Cooperative Relations, Oxford: Basil Blackwell.

Graeber, D. (2011) Debt: The First 5,000 Years, Brooklyn: Melville House.

Green, J. (1995) "Risk, rationality and misfortune: towards a sociology of accidents", PhD Thesis United Medical and Dental Schools of Guy's and St. Thomas's Hospitals.

Grushack, J. (2014) "Currency 3.0: examining digital crypto currency markets", Master thesis Union College.

Hardin, R. (2004) Trust and Trustworthiness, New York City: Russell Sage Foundation.

Harper, R. F. (1904) The Code of Hammurabi, King of Babylon, Chicago: University of Chicago Press.

Harwood, W. T. (2012) "The Logic of Trust", PhD Thesis University of York.

Hayek, F. A. (1990) Denationalisation of Money: The Argument Refined, Lancing: The Institute of Economic Affairs.

Helmholz, R., Zimmermann, R. (1998) Itinera Fiduciae: Trust and Treuhand in Historical Perspective, Berlin: Duncker & Humblot.

Herrmann, C. (2010) Währungshoheit, Währungsverfassung und subjektive Rechte, Frankfurt: Mohr Siebeck.

Houmb, S. H., Ray, I., Ray, I. (2006) "Estimating the Relative Trustworthiness of Information Sources in Security Solution Evaluation", In: Stølen, K., Winsborough, W. H., Martinelli, F., Massacci, F. (Eds.) iTrust 2006, Berlin: Springer.

Ingham, G. (2000) "'Babylonian Madness': On the historical and sociological origins of money", In: Smithin, J. (Ed.) What is Money?, London: Routledge.

Jay, A. (2014) "Second Life, Second Remedies", In: Lakhani, A. (Ed.) Commercial Transactions in the Virtual World, Hong Kong: City University Press.

Jevons, W.S. (1876) Money and the Mechanisms of Exchange, New York: D. Appleton and Co.

Jones, K. (1998) "Trust", In: Craig, E. (ed.) Routledge Encyclopedia of Philosophy, Abingdon: Taylor & Francis.

Jones, K. (2001) "Trust: Philosophical Aspects", In: Smelser, N., Bates, P. (eds.) International Encyclopedia of the Social and Behavioral Sciences, Amsterdam: Elsevier Science.

Jøsang, A. (1996) "The right type of trust for distributed systems", In: Haigh, T., Hosmer, H. (Eds.) Proceedings of the 1996 New Security Paradigms Workshop (NSPW), New York: ACM.

Jøsang, A., Keser, C., Dimitrakos, T. (2005) "Can we manage trust?", In: Herrmann, P., Issarny, V., Shiu, S. (Eds.) Trust Management: Proceedings of the third international iTrust conference 2005, Berlin: Springer.

Jøsang, A., Van Laenen, F., Knapskog, S.J., Vandewalle, J. (1997) "How to trust systems", In: Yngström, L., Carlsen, J. (Eds.) Information Security in Research and Business, Proceedings of the IFIP TC11 13$^{th}$ International Conference on Information Security (SEC '97), London: Chapman & Hall.

Kaiser, C. (2016) "The Classification of Virtual Currencies and Mobile Payments in Terms of the Old and New European Anti-Money Laundering Frameworks", In: Gimigliano, G. (Ed.) Bitcoin and Mobile Payments: Constructing a European Union Framework, London: Palgrave - Macmillan.

Keynes, J. M. (1930) A Treatise on Money, New York City: Harcourt, Brace and Co.

Kim, H. (2001) "Archaic Coinage as Evidence for the Use of Money", In: Meadows, A., Shipton, K. (Eds.) Money and Its Uses in the Ancient Greek World, Oxford: Oxford University Press.

Knapp, G. F. (1905) Staatliche Theorie des Geldes, Leipzig: Duncker & Humblot.
Knapp, G. F. (1924) The State Theory of Money, London: Macmillan & Co.
Kokkola, T. (2009) The payment system: payments, securities and derivates, and the roles of the Eurosystem, Frankfurt: European Central Bank.
Krueger, M. (2002) "E-money regulation in the EU", In: Pringle, R., Robinson, M. (Eds.), E-Money and Payment Systems Review, London: Centralbanking.
Kühl, K. (2016) "StGB §261 Geldwäsche; Verschleierung unrechtmäßig erlangter Vermögenswerte", In: Kühl, K, Heger, M. (Eds.) Strafgesetzbuch Kommentar (28. Auflage), München: Verlag C.H. Beck.
Kuhlmann, D., Gehring, R. A. (2003) "Trusted Platforms, DRM and Beyond", In: Becker, E., Buhse, W., Günnewig, D., Rump, N. (Eds.) Digital Rights Management: Technological, Economic, Legal and Political Aspects, Berlin: Springer.
Künnapas, K. (2016) "From Bitcoin to Smart Contracts: Legal Revolution or Evolution from the Perspective of de lege ferenda?", In: Kerikmäe, T., Rull, A. (Eds.), The Future of Law and eTechnologies, Cham: Springer.
Kurke, L. (1999) Coins, Bodies, Games, and Gold: The Politics of Meaning in Archaic Greece, Princeton: University Press.
Lebrun, J. (1992) "La législation financière 1981–1991", In: Horsmans, G. (Ed.) Le nouveau droit des marchés financiers, Brussels: Larcier.
Lecocq, P. (2012) Manuel de droit des biens – Tome 1, Brussels: Larcier.
Lehdonvirta, V., Ernkvist, M. (2011) Knowledge Map of the Virtual Economy, Washington, DC: InfoDev/World Bank.
Lerner, T. (2013) Mobile Payment, Wiesbaden: Springer.
Levi, M. (2001) "Trust, sociology of", In: Smelser, N., Bates, P. (eds.) International Encyclopedia of the Social and Behavioral Sciences, Amsterdam: Elsevier Science.
Lieverse, K. (2017) "The Scope of MiFID II", In: Busch, D., Ferrarini, G. (Eds.) Regulation of the EU Financial Markets: MiFID II and MiFIR, Oxford: University Press.
Long, J. C., Kaufman, M. J., Wunderlich, J. M. (2017) Blue Sky Law, New York City: Thomson Reuters.
Low, S. K. (2002) "Singapore Electronic Legal Tender (SELT) – A Proposed Concept", In: OECD (Ed.) The Future of Money, Paris: OECD.
Luhmann, N. (1979) Trust and Power, New York: John Wiley & Sons Ltd.
Mann, F. A. (1992) The Legal Aspect of Money – Fifth Edition, Oxford: Clarendon Press.
Marsh, S. P. (1994) "Formalising Trust as a Computational Concept", University of Sterling PhD thesis.
Martin, F. (2013) Money: the Unauthorised Biography, London: The Bodley Head.
Mavromati, D. (2008) The law of payment services in the EU: the EC directive on payment services in the internal market, Alphen aan den Rijn: Kluwer law international.
McKnight, D. H., Chervany, N. L. (2001) "Trust and Distrust Definitions: One Bite at a Time", In: Falcone, R., Singh, M., Tan, Y.-H. (Eds.) Trust in Cyber-societies, LNAI 2246, Berlin: Springer.
McLeod, C. (2011) "Trust", In: Zalta, E. (ed.) *The Stanford Encyclopedia of Philosophy*, plato.stanford.edu.
Meehan, J. (2003) "Towards an archival concept of evidence", *Master thesis School of Library, Archival and Information Studies University of British Columbia.*

Menezes, A. J., Van Oorschot, P. C., Vanstone, S. A. (2001) *Handbook of Applied Cryptography*, Boca Raton: CRC Press.

Michaels, R. (2006) "The Functional Method of Comparative Law", In: Reimann, M., Zimmermann, R. (eds.) *The Oxford Handbook of Comparative Law*, Oxford: University Press.

Mill, J. S., Laughlin, J. L. (1885) *Principles of political economy – Abridged, with Critical, Bibliographical, and Explanatory Notes, and a Sketch of the History of Political Economy*, New York City: D. Appleton and Co.

Minjauw, H., Vandendriessche, J. (2008) "Titel VI. Het bewijsrecht in burgerlijke zaken", in: Roodhooft, R. (Ed.), *Bestendig Handboek Verbintenissenrecht*, Mechelen: Kluwer.

Minsky, H. P. (2008) *Stabilizing an unstable economy*, New York City: McGraw-Hill.

Mishkin, F. S. (2004) *The Economics of Money, Banking and Financial Markets – Seventh Edition*, Boston: Pearson.

Misztal, B. A. (1996) *Trust in Modern Societies: The Search for the Bases of Social Order*, Cambridge, MA: Polity Press.

Möllering, G. (2006) *Trust: Reason, Routine, Reflexivity*, Amsterdam: Elsevier.

Moloney, N. (2014) *EU securities and financial markets regulation*, Oxford: University Press.

Moloney, N. (2015) "Financial Markets Regulation", In: Chalmers D., Arnull A. (Eds.) *The Oxford Handbook of European Union Law*, Oxford: University Press.

Mougenot, D. (2002) *Droit des obligations: la preuve*, Brussel: Larcier.

Nussbaum, A. (1939) *Money in the Law*, Chicago: Foundation Press.

O'Neill, O. (2002) *A Question of Trust*, Cambridge: University Press.

OECD (2002) *The Future of Money*, Paris: OECD Publications Service.

Ólafsson, Í. (2014) "Is bitcoin money? An analysis from the Austrian school of economic thought", *Thesis University of Iceland Department of Economics*.

Peacock, M. (2013) *Introducing Money*, Abingdon: Routledge.

Poullet, Y. (1996) "Les transactions commerciales et industrielles par voie électronique: de quelques réflexions autour du droit de la preuve", In: X, *Le droit des affaires en évolution: le juriste face à l'invasion informatique*, Brussels: Bruylant.

Proctor, C., Kleiner, C., Mohs, F. (2012) *Mann on the legal aspect of money [6th edition]*, Oxford: Oxford University Press.

Quirin, T., Fritsch, L., Husseiki, R. (2010) *Ergänzende und alternative Techniken zu Trusted Computing (TC-Erg./-A.) – Teil 1*, Bonn: Bundesamtes für Sicherheit in der Informationstechnik (BSI).

Renner, K. (2001) *The Institutions of Private Law and their Social Functions*, Abingdon: Routledge.

Rogers, J.S. (1995) *The early history of the law of bills and notes: a study of the origins of Anglo-American commercial law*, Cambridge: Cambridge University press.

Rolland, A.-S. (2016) "Virtual currencies: how will the EU face this challenge?", *Thesis KU Leuven Faculty of Law*.

Roth, M. T. (1995) *Law Collections from Mesopotamia and Asia Minor*, Atlanta: Scholars Press.

Rothbard, M. (1978) "Austrian Definitions of the Supply of Money", In: Spadaro, L. (ed.) *New Directions in Austrian Economics*, Kansas City: Sheed Andrews and McMeel.

Rothbard, M. N. (2010) *What Has Government Done to Our Money?*, Auburn: Ludwig von Mises Institute.

Rüfner, T. (2016) "Money in the Roman Law Texts", In: Fox, D., Ernst, W. (Eds.) *Money in the Western Legal Tradition: Middle Ages to Bretton Woods*, Oxford: Oxford University Press.

Ruhmannseder, F. (2016) "StGB §261 Geldwäsche; Verschleierung unrechtmäßig erlangter Vermögenswerte", In: von Heintschel-Heinegg, B. (Ed.) Beck'scher Online Kommentar StGB (32. Edition), München: Verlag C.H. Beck.

Sáinz de Vicuña, A. (2010) "An Institutional Theory of Money", In: Giovanoli, M., Devos, D. (Eds.) International Monetary and Financial Law: The Global Crisis, Oxford: University Press.

Sawyer, M. (2003) "Money: Means of Payment or Store of Wealth?", In: Rochon, L.-P., Rossi, S. (Eds.) *Modern Theories of Money: The Nature and Role of Money* in Capitalist Economies, Cheltenham: Edward Elgar.

Schmidt, W., Krause, J. (2010) "§261", In: Laufhütte, H. W., Rissing-van Saan, R., Tiedemann, K. (Eds.) Strafgesetzbuch Leipziger Kommentar (12. Auflage), Berlin: Walter de Gruyter.

Schrans, G., Steennot, R. (2003) Algemeen deel van het financieel recht, Antwerpen: Intersentia.

Scholten, A. A. (2017) Juridische aspecten van contant geld, Zutphen: Paris.

Schulz, T. (2014) "Creating Universal Designed and Trustworthy Objects for the Internet of Things", In: Zaphiris, P., Ioannou, A. (Eds.) *Learning and Collaboration Technologies 2014, Part II*, Berlin: Springer.

Schumpeter, J. A. (1926) "G. F. Knapp", *The Economic Journal*, Vol. 36, 512–514.

Schumpeter, J. A. (1954) *History of Economic Analysis*, Abingdon: Routledge.

Selldahl, S. (2013) "Virtual currencies - Real opportunities?", *Master thesis KTH Industrial Engineering and Management.*

Semenova, A. (2011) "The Origins of Money: Evaluating Chartalist and Metallist theories in the context of ancient Greece and Mesopotamia", *University of Missouri - Kansas City PhD Thesis.*

Smith, A. (1776) *An Inquiry into the Nature and Causes of the Wealth of Nations*, London: W. Strahan and T. Cadell.

Solomon, L. D. (1996) *Rethinking Our Centralized Money System: The Case for a System of Local Currencies,* Westport: Praeger Publishers.

Steennot, R. (2008) "Informatieverplichtingen als beschermingstechniek bij de verwerving van beleggingsdiensten door consumenten", In: Instituut Financieel Recht (Ed.) *Van alle markten - Liber Amicorum Eddy Wymeersch*, Antwerpen: Intersentia.

Steennot, R. (2011) "Art. 1 - 81 Artikelsgewijze commentaar Wet betalingsdiensten", In: Wymeersch, E., Stuyck, J., Steennot, R., Vanhees, H., *Financieel recht. Artikelsgewijze commentaar met overzicht van rechtspraak en rechtsleer*, Mechelen: Kluwer.

Steennot, R. (2011) "Betalingsdiensten", In: Steennot, R., Stuyck, J., Vanhees, H., Wymeersch, E. (Eds.) *Overzicht Financieel Recht: Artikelsgewijze commentaren,* Mechelen: Kluwer.

Steennot, R. (2011) *Giraal en elektronisch betalingsverkeer*, Mechelen: Kluwer.

Steennot, R. (2012) "Betaling", In: Dirix, E., Van Oevelen, A. (Eds.) *Bijzondere Overeenkomsten: Artikelsgewijze commentaren,* Mechelen: Kluwer.

Stern, B. (1998) *Dissolution, Continuation and Succession in Eastern Europe*, The Hague: Kluwer Law International.

Storme, M. E., Helsen, F. (forthcoming) "The function of private property and its future", In: Lauroba, E., Tarabal, J. (Eds.) El derecho de la propiedad en la construcción del Derecho privado europeo: índices, sistemas adquisitivos y objetos / El dret de la proprietat en la construccio del dret privat europeu / The right of ownership in the construction of European private law, Barcelona: Tirant lo Blanch.

Surda, P. (2012) "Economics of Bitcoin: is Bitcoin an alternative to fiat currencies and gold?", Thesis WU Vienna University of Economics and Business.

Swedberg, R. (2000) Max Weber and the Idea of Economic Sociology, Princeton: University Press.

Sztompka, P. (2001) "Trust: Cultural Concerns", In: Smelser, N., Bates, P. (eds.) International Encyclopedia of the Social and Behavioral Sciences, Amsterdam: Elsevier Science.

Terryn, E. (2008) Bedenktijden in het consumentenrecht, Antwerp: Intersentia.

Tilleman, B., Verbeke, A.-L., Sagaert, V. (2007) Vermogensrecht in kort bestek, Antwerpen: Intersentia.

Tridimas, T. (1999) "Proportionality in Community Law: Searching for the Appropriate Standard of Scrutiny", In: Ellis, E. (ed.) The Principle of Proportionality in the Laws of Europe, Oxford: Hart Publishing.

Trzaskowski, J., Savin, A., Lundqvist, B., Lindskoug, P. (2015) Introduction to EU Internet Law, Copenhagen, Ex Tuto.

Unger, B. (2013) "Money Laundering Regulation: from Al Capone to Al Qaeda", In: Unger, B., Van Der Linde, D. (Eds.) Research Handbook on Money Laundering, Cheltenham: Edward Elgar.

Van Dyck, T. (2009) "De geharmoniseerde prospectusplicht: Kritische analyse van de geharmoniseerde prospectusplicht in de Prospectusrichtlijn 2003/71/EG en haar omzettingswetten in België, Nederland, Frankrijk, het Verenigd Koninkrijk en Duitsland", Thesis KU Leuven Faculty of Law.

Vande Lanotte, J., Dujardin, J., Van Damme, M. (2009) De bronnen van het administratief recht, Mechelen: Wolters Kluwer.

Vandezande, N., Van de Velde, N. (2017) "Juridische aspecten van crowdfunding in België", In: Storme, M.E., Helsen, F. (Eds.) Innovatie en disruptie in het economisch recht, Antwerpen: Intersentia.

Vardi, N. (2011) The Integration of European Financial Markets: The regulation of monetary obligations, Abingdon: Routledge.

Vardi, N. (2016) "Bit by Bit: Assessing the Legal Nature of Virtual Currencies", in: Gimigliano, G. (Ed.) Bitcoin and Mobile Payments: Constructing a European Union Framework, London: Macmillan Publishers.

Verhaeghe, L. (2013) "PingPing en PayPal: Juridisch kader, rechten en plichten", Thesis UGent Faculty of Law.

Vermaere, K. (2016) "Artikel 2, 1° 'financieel instrument'", In: Berger, P., Cerfontaine, J., Colaert, V., Lannoy, H. (Eds.) Economisch recht Deel 8: Financiële Markten en Diensten, Brussel: Larcier.

Von Mises, L. (1953) *The Theory of Money and Credit*, New Haven: Yale University Press.

Von Reden, S. (1995) *Exchange in Ancient Greece*, London: Duckworth.

Von Savigny, F. C. (1851) *Das Obligationenrecht als Theil des heutigen Römischen Rechts I*, Berlin: Veit & Co.

Warner, J. (2014) "The future of Community Currencies: physical cash or solely electronic?", In: Deutsche Bundesbank (Ed.) *International Cash Conference 2014: The usage, costs and benefits of cash – revisited*, Frankfurt am Main: Deutsche Bundesbank.

Weber, M. (1978) *Economy and Society*, Berkeley: University of California Press.

Wéry, P., Gobert, D., Kerzmann, L. (2003) "La preuve", In: Coipel, M., Wéry, P., Durant, I., Cruquenaire, A. (Eds.) *Guide juridique de l'entreprise*, Brussel: Kluwer.

Wray, L. R. (2012) *Modern Money Theory: A Primer on Macroeconomics for Sovereign Monetary Systems*, New York City: Palgrave Macmillan.

Yamagishi, T. (2011) *Trust: The Evolutionary Game of Mind and Society*, Tokyo: Springer.

Yuthayotin, S. (2015) *Access to Justice in Transnational B2C E-Commerce: A Multidimensional Analysis of Consumer Protection Mechanisms*, Berlin: Springer.

Zazzaro, A. (2003) "How Heterodox is the Heterodoxy of Monetary Circuit Theory? The Nature of Money and the Microeconomics of the Circuit", In: Rochon, L.-P., Rossi, S (Eds.) *The Nature and Role of Money in Capitalist Economies*, Cheltenham: Edward Elgar.

Zerver, A. (2015) "Vertrauen in historischer Perspektive", In: Endreß, M., Lichtblau, K., Moebius, S. (Eds.) *Zyklos 2: Jahrbuch für Theorie und Geschichte der Soziologie*, Wiesbaden: Springer.

Zimmermann, R. (2004) "Roman Law and the Harmonization of Private Law in Europe", In: Hartkamp, A., Hesselink, M., Hondius, E., Joustra, C., du Perron, E., Veldman, M. (Eds.) *Towards a European Civil Code – Third edition*, Nijmegen: Kluwer.

## 3.2 PAPERS AND REPORTS

ACPR (2014) "Position de l'ACPR relative aux opérations sur Bitcoins en France Position", *2014-P-01*.

Ahamad, S., Nair, M., Varghese, B. (2013) "A Survey on Crypto Currencies", *Proc. of Int. Conf. on Advances in Computer Science, AETACS*, 42–48.

Akindemowo, O.E. (1998) "The Fading Rustle, Chink and Jingle: Electronic Value and the Concept of Money", *University of New South Wales Law Journal*, Vol. 21, 466–488.

Alberts, J. E., Fry, B. (2016) "Is Bitcoin a Security?", *Boston University Journal of Science & Technology Law*, Vol. 21.1, 1–21.

Allen, J. M. (1985) "Kicking the Bucket Shop: The Model State Commodity Code as the Latest Weapon in the State Administrator's Anti-Fraud Arsenal", *Washington & Lee Law Review*, Vol. 42, 889–911.

Anderson, C., Butler, C., Kirch, A., et al. (1997) "Exploring Digital Cash", *courses.ischool.berkeley.edu/i204/f97/GroupE*.

Andolfatto, D., Nosal, E. (2001) "A simple model of money and banking", *Economic Review – Federal Reserve Bank of Cleveland*, Vol. 37, 20–28.

Andreoni, J. (2005) "Trust, Reciprocity, and Contract Enforcement: Experiments on Satisfaction Guaranteed", *econ.ucsd.edu/~jandreon/WorkingPapers/verify.pdf*.

Arrow, K. (1972) "Gifts and Exchanges", *Philosophy & Public Affairs*, Vol. 1, 343–362.

Article 29 Working Party (2004) "Working Document on Trusted Computing Platforms and in particular on the work done by the Trusted Computing Group (TCG group)", *WP 86*.

Athanassiou, P. (2006) "When is e-money not e-money? Reflections on the revision of the E-money Directive", *Euredia*, nr. 2006/3-4, 321-355.

Athanassiou, P., Mas-Guix, N. (2008) "Electronic money institutions", *ECB Legal Working Paper Series nr.7.*

Aubin, C. (2002) "Du franc à l'euro", *sceco.univ-poitiers.fr/hfranc/index.htm.*

Back, A. (1997) "A partial hash collision based postage scheme", *hashcash.org/papers/announce.txt.*

Baier, A. (1986) "Trust and antitrust", Ethics, Vol. 96, 231-260.

Bailey, T. (2006) "On trust and philosophy", *open.edu.*

Baker & McKenzie (2015) "Research project regarding payment services, bank group regulations and others, for Japan Financial Services Agency – Final report – Europe", *fsa.go.jp.*

Bal, A. (2013) "Stateless Virtual Money in the Tax System", *European Taxation*, 351-356.

Bangassaa, K., Sub, C., Joseph, N. L. (2012) "Selectivity and timing performance of UK investment trusts", *Int. Fin. Markets, Inst. and Money*, Vol. 22, 1149-1175.

Bank for International Settlements (1996) "Security of electronic money", *www.bis.org.*

Banque de France (2013) "Les dangers liés au développement des monnaies virtuelles: l'exemple du bitcoin", *Focus*, nr. 10.

Barber, S., Boyen, X., Shi, E., Uzun, E. (2012) "Bitter to Better – How to Make Bitcoin a Better Currency", *Financial Cryptography (FC 2012), volume 7397 of Lecture Notes in Computer Science*, 399-414.

Basel Committee on Banking Supervision (1998) "Prevention of criminal use of the banking system for the purpose of money-laundering", *bis.org.*

Basu, K. (2014) "Ponzis: the science and mystique of a class of financial frauds", *World Bank Policy Research Working Paper WPS6967.*

Baukema, J. (2014) "Virtuele valuta: (toezichtrechtelijke) stand van zaken", *Tijdschrift voor Financieel Recht*, nr. 9, 376-380.

Bayern, S. (2014) "Dynamic Common Law and Technological Change: The Classification of Bitcoin", *Wash. & Lee L. Rev.*, Vol. 71, 22-34.

Bayern, S. (2014) "Of Bitcoins, independently wealthy software, and the zero-member LLC", *Northwestern University law Review Online*, Vol. 108, 1485-1500.

Bell, S. (2001) "The role of the state and the hierarchy of money", *Cambridge Journal of Economics*, Vol. 25, 149-163.

Bleyen, V.-A., Van Hove, L., Hartmann, M. (2010) "Classifying Payment Instruments: A Matryoshka Approach", *Communications & Strategies*, Nr. 79, 73-94.

Bollen, R. (2013) "The Legal Status of Online Currencies: Are Bitcoins the Future?", *Journal of Banking and Finance Law and Practice*, vol. 24, 272-293.

Bond Pearce (2013) "Review of payment services (and e-money) requirements – a development to watch...", *bondpearce.com.*

Bonneau, T. (2014) "Une société qui utilise un compte bancaire sur lequel transitent des bitcoins est-elle un prestataire de service de paiement?", *La Semaine Juridique Entreprise et Affaires*, nr. 8, 1091.

Brandl, H., Rosteck, T. (2004) "Technik, Implementierung und Anwendung des Trusted Computing Group-Standards", *Datenschutz und Datensicherheit*, Vol. 28, 529-538.

Bretherton, I. (1992) "The origins of Attachment Theory: John Bowlby and Mary Ainsworth", *Developmental Psychology*, Vol. 28, 759-775.

Breugelmans, E., Bijmolt, T.HA., Zhang, J., Basso, L.J., Dorotic, M., Kopalle, P., Minnam, A., Mijnlieff, W.J., Wünderlich, N.V. (2014) "Advancing Research on Loyalty Programs: A Future Research Agenda", *Marketing Letters*, 127–139.

Brito, J., Shadab, H., Castillo, A. (2014) "Bitcoin Financial Regulations: Securities, Derivatives, Prediction Markets, and Gambling", *Columbia Science & Technology Law Review*, Vol. 16, 144–221.

Bryans, D. (2014) "Bitcoin and Money Laundering: Mining for an Effective Solution", *Indiana Law Journal*, Vol. 89, 441–472.

Bureau of Consumer Financial Protection (2016) "Prepaid Accounts under the Electronic Fund Transfer Act (Regulation E) and the Truth In Lending Act (Regulation Z)", *4810-AM-P.*

Cahn, E. S. (1999) "Time dollars, work and community: from `why?' to `why not?'", *Futures*, Vol. 31, 499–509.

Carnevale, D. G., Wechsler, B. (1992) "Trust in the public sector: Individual and organizational determinants", *Administration & Society*, Vol. 23, 471–494.

Cassar, C. (2015) "Virtual Currencies: Risks and regulations in Malta and Other Jurisdictions", *elsa.org.*

Castronova, E. (2001) "Virtual Worlds: A First-Hand Account of Market and Society on the Cyberian Frontier", *The Gruter Institute Working Papers on Law, Economics, and Evolutionary Biology*, Vol. 2, Nr. 1, 1–66.

Castronova, E. (2002) "On Virtual Economies", *CESifo Working Paper Series No. 752.*

Castronova, E. (2008) "Effects of botting on World of Warcraft – expert report filed for US District Court of Arizona case CV06-02555-PHX-DGC", *virtuallyblind.com/2008/03/23/mdy-blizzard-motions.*

Castronova, E. (2014) "Digital Value Transfer Systems", *Washington & Lee Law Revue Online*, Vol. 71, 14–21.

Catala, P. (1966) "La transformation du patrimoine dans le droit civil moderne", Revue trimestrielle du droit civil, Vol. 64, 185–215.

CESR (2002) "A European Regime of Investor Protection: The Harmonisation of Conduct of Business Rules", CESR/01-014d.

CESR (2002) "A European Regime of Investor Protection: The Professional and Counterparty Regime", CESR/02-098b.

Chaum, D. (1983) "Blind signatures for untraceable payments", Advances in Cryptology Proceedings of Crypto, Vol. 82, 199–203.

Claxton, N. (2011) "Progress, Privacy, and Preemption: A Study of the Regulatory History of Stored-Value Cards in the United States and the European Union", Ariz. J. Int'l & Comp. L., vol. 28, 501–538.

Cohen, M. R. (1933) "The Basis of Contract", *Harvard Law Review*, Vol. 46, 578–580.

Coin Center (2016) "A Securities Law Framework for Blockchain Tokens", *coincenter.org.*

Colaert, V., Van Dyck, T. (2008) "MiFID en de gedragsregels: Een nieuw juridisch kader voor beleggingsdiensten", *Tijdschrift voor Belgisch Handelsrecht*, nr. 3, 226–279.

Coleman, K. G. (2001) "Android arete: Toward a virtue ethic for computational agents", *Ethics and Information Technology*, Vol. 3, 247–265.

Collins, B., Mansell, R. (Eds.) (2004) "Cyber Trust and Crime Prevention: A Synthesis of the State-of-the-Art Science Reviews", *UK Department for Business, Information and Skills Foresight Project.*

Comizio, V. G. (2016) "Virtual Currencies: Growing Regulatory Framework and Challenges in the Emerging Fintech Ecosystem", *Fried Frank.*

Congressional Research Service (2014) "Bitcoin: Questions, Answers, and Analysis of Legal Issues", *crs.gov.*

Cook, T. (1997) "What is past is prologue", Archivaria, Vol. 43, 17–63.

Corritore, C., Krachera, B., Wiedenbeck, S. (2003) "On-line trust: concepts, evolving themes, a model", *Int. J. Human-Computer Studies*, Vol. 58, 737–758.

Courtland, R. (2012) "Virtual currency gets real: Will Facebook Credits and other social scrip challenge government-backed currencies?", *IEEE Spectrum.*

Crédot, F., Samin, T. (2012) "Clôture du compte en raison des activités exercées par le titulaire", *Revue de Droit bancaire et financier*, nr. 1-2012.

D'Ippolito, E., Musitelli, M., Sciarrone Alibrandi, A. (2016) "Protecting Crowdfunders: Is a MiFID-Mimicking Approach Appropriate?", *European Company Law*, Vol. 13, 27–37.

Dai, W. (1998) "B-money", *weidai.com/bmoney.txt.*

De Boer, E.R., Gudmundsson, S.V. (2012) "30 years of frequent flyer programs", *Journal of Air Transport Management*, Vol. 24, 18–24.

De Boer, J. (2012) "De trust naar Curaçaos recht", *Weekblad voor Privaatrecht, Notariaat en Registratie*, Vol. 143, 287–291.

De Filippi, P. (2014) "Bitcoin: a regulatory nightmare to a libertarian dream", *Internet Policy Review*, vol. 3, nr. 2, DOI: 10.14763/2014.2.286.

De Poorter, I. (2011) "De wet betreffende de betalingsdiensten leidt tot een betere bescherming van de consument", *Rechtskundig Weekblad*, nr. 32, 1330–1344.

De Prez, P., Timmermans, V. (2013) "Een doorstart voor het elektronisch geld? Analyse van de nieuwe regelgeving", *Bank en Financieel Recht*, nr. 2013/I, 3–25.

De Staercke, J. (2002) "Algemene beginselen van behoorlijk burgerschap: Naar een wederkerig bestuursrecht?", *Jura Falconis*, Vol. 38, 505–535.

De Witte, C. (2007) "Kan Trust in België een nuttig instrument zijn voor vermogensplanning?", *Jura Falconis*, Vol. 43, 539–558.

Decoster, S., Lewalle, C. (2014) "Le Crowdfunding: réglementation applicable, enjeux et perspectives", *Forum Financier, Revue Bancaire et Financière*, nr. 6, 455–467.

Desan, C. (2010) "Coin Reconsidered: The Political Alchemy of Commodity Money", *Theoretical Inquiries in Law*, Vol. 11, 361–409.

Desan, C. (2013) "Creation Stories: Myths About the Origins of Money", *Harvard Law School Public Law & Legal Theory Working Paper Series Paper No. 13-20.*

Deutscher Bundestag, *Schriftliche Fragen*, 17/14530, 41.

Digital Policy Alliance (2013) "Position Paper on the proposed review of the Payment Services Directive", *dpalliance.org.uk.*

Dion, D. (2013) "I'll gladly trade you two bits on Tuesday for a byte today: Bitcoin, regulating fraud in the e-conomy of hacker-cash", *Journal of Law, Technology & Policy*, 165–201.

DLA Piper (2009) "EU study on the Legal analysis of a Single Market for the Information Society – New rules for a new age?", *ec.europa.eu.*

DNB (2014) "Virtual currencies are not a viable alternative", *dnb.nl.*

Döbelt, S., Busch, M., Hochleitner, C. (2012) "uTRUSTit – Defining, Understanding, Explaining TRUST within the uTRUSTit Project", *utrustit.eu.*

Donnelly, M. (2016) "Payments in the digital market: Evaluating the contribution of Payment Services Directive II", *Computer Law & Security Review*, Vol. 32, 827–839.

Duisenberg, W.F. (1995) "Toespraak ter gelegenheid van de introductie van de chipknip in Arnhem", 26 October 1995, *www.simonl.org/docs/readeremdnb.pdf.*

Dumortier, J., Somers, G. (2007) "De wet van 15 mei 2007 tot vaststelling van een juridisch kader voor sommige verleners van vertrouwensdiensten: een eerste verkenning", *T.B.H.*, 649–659.

Dumortier, J., Van Den Eynde, S. (2001) "De juridische erkenning van de elektronische handtekening", *Computerrecht*, 185–194.

Dumortier, J., Vandezande, N. (2011) "uTRUSTit D7.1 – Legal Requirements for Trust in the IoT", *utrustit.eu*.

Dumortier, J., Vandezande, N. (2012) "Trust in the proposed EU regulation on trust services?", *Computer Law & Security Review*, Vol. 28, 568–576.

Duranti, L. (2001) "The impact of digital technology on archival science", *Archival Science*, Vol. 1, 39–55.

Duranti, L. (Ed.) (2002) "The Long-term Preservation of Authentic Electronic Records: Findings of the InterPARES Project – Authenticity Task Force Report", www.interpares.org/book/interpares_book_d_part1.pdf.

Duranti, L. (2009) "From Digital Diplomatics to Digital Records Forensics", Archivaria, Vol. 68, 39–66.

Dutton, W. H., Shepherd, A. (2004) "Confidence and risk on the Internet1", UK Department for Business, Information and Skills Foresight Project.

ECOLEF (2013) "The Economic and Legal Effectiveness of Anti-Money Laundering and Combating Terrorist Financing Policy", www2.econ.uu.nl/users/unger.

Effross, W.A. (1997) "Putting the Cards before the Purse: Distinctions, Differences, and Dilemmas in the Regulation of Stored Value Card Systems", University of Missouri-Kansas City Law Review, Vol. 65, 319–398.

ESMA (2015) "Call for evidence: Investment using virtual currency or distributed ledger technology", ESMA/2015/532.

European Banking Authority (2014) "EBA Opinion on 'virtual currencies'", eba.europa.eu, EBA/Op/2014/08.

European Banking Authority (2016) "Opinion of the European Banking Authority on the EU Commission's proposal to bring Virtual Currencies into the scope of Directive (EU) 2015/849 (4AMLD)", EBA-Op-2016-07.

European Central Bank (1998) "Report on Electronic Money", ecb.europa.eu.

European Central Bank (2004) "E-payments without frontiers", Issues paper for the ECB Conference on 10 November 2004.

Schmiedel, H., Kostova, G. L., Ruttenberg, W. (2012) "The Social and Private Costs of Retail Payment Instruments: A European Perspective", ECB Occasional Paper No. 137.

European Central Bank (2012) "Virtual Currency Schemes", ecb.europa.eu.

European Central Bank (2015) "Virtual Currency Schemes – a further analysis", ecb.europa.eu.

European Commission (1985) "White Paper on Completing the Internal Market", COM(85) 310 final.

European Commission (1995) "Communication on Priorities for Consumer Policy 1996–1998", COM(95) 519 final.

European Commission (2000) "Payment systems: Commission pledges to use full powers to create a Single Payment Area", IP/00/1283.

European Commission (2002) "Working document on a possible legal framework for the Single Payment Area in the Internal Market", MARKT/208/2001 – Rev. 1.

European Commission (2004) "Consultation paper of DG Internal Market – Application of the E-money Directive to mobile operators", ec.europa.eu.

European Commission (2005) "Application of the E-money Directive to mobile operators – Summary of replies to the Consultation paper of DG Internal Market", ec.europa.eu.

European Commission (2005) "Application of the E-money Directive to mobile operators – Guidance Note from the Commission Services", *ec.europa.eu.*

European Commission (2005) "Questionnaire on the Electronic Money Directive (2000/46/EC)", *ec.europa.eu.*

European Commission (2006) "Consultative paper on SEPA Incentives", *ec.europa.eu.*

European Commission (2006) "Report of 15 March 2006 on the operation of Directive 1999/93/EC on a Community framework for electronic signatures", *COM(2006) 120 final.*

European Commission (2008) "Your questions on MiFID", *ec.europa.eu.*

European Commission (2009) "Communication on Implementing the framework for financial markets: action plan", *COM(1999) 232 final.*

European Commission (2010) "Communication from the Commission to the European Parliament, the Council, the European Economic and Social Committee and the Committee of the Regions of 26 August 2010, A Digital Agenda for Europe", *COM(2010) 245 final/2.*

European Commission (2010) "Report of the Euro Legal Tender Expert Group (ELTEG) on the definition, scope and effects of legal tender of euro banknotes and coins", ec.europa.eu.

European Commission (2011) "Your questions on PSD", ec.europa.eu/internal_market/payments/docs/framework/transposition/faq_en.pdf.

European Commission (2012) "Green Paper of 11 January 2012 Towards an integrated European market for card, internet and mobile payments", COM(2011) 941 final.

European Commission (2013) "Europe's digital challenge", ec.europa.eu.

European Commission (2013) "Frequently Asked Questions: Anti-Money Laundering", MEMO 13/64.

European Commission (2014) "In-app purchases: Joint action by the European Commission and Member States is leading to better protection for consumers in online games", IP/14/187.

European Commission (2015) "Consumer Conditions in the EU Getting up to speed with the digital age", ec.europa.eu.

European Commission (2018) "FinTech Action plan: For a more competitive and innovative European financial sector", COM(2018) 109 final.

European Monetary Institute (1998) "Annual Report 1997", *ecb.europa.eu.*

European Payments Council (2006) "'Making SEPA a Reality' – Implementing the Single Euro Payments Area", *EPC066-06.*

European Telecommunications Standards Institute (1997) "Telecommunications Security; Trusted Third Parties (TTP); Requirements for TTP Services", *EG 201 057.*

Europol (2016) "Changes in modus operandi of Islamic State terrorist attacks", *europol.europa.eu.*

EUROSMART (2000) "A White Paper: The Euro in the Electronic Purse - Interoperability issues of smartcard based e-payments in Europe", *it.uc3m.es/~celeste/docencia/emaster/e-cash.pdf.*

Evanschitzky, H., Ramaseshan, B., Woisetschläger, D.M., Richelsen, V., Blut, M., Backhaus, C. (2012) "Consequences of customer loyalty to the loyalty program and to the company", *Journal of the Academy of Marketing Science*, Vol. 40, 625–638.

Eyal, I., Gün Sirer, E. (2014) "Majority is not Enough: Bitcoin Mining is Vulnerable", Presented at the 18th International Conference on Financial Cryptography and Data Security (FC), Barbados, March 2014, *diyhpl.us/~bryan/papers2/paperbot/Majority%20is%20not%20Enough:%20Bitcoin%20Mining%20is%20Vulnerable.pdf.*

Farmer, P. H. Jr. (2014) "Speculative Tech: The Bitcoin Legal Quagmire & the Need for Legal Innovation", *Journal of Business & Technology Law*, Vol. 9, 85–106.

FATF (2014) "Virtual Currencies: Key Definitions and Potential AML/CFT Risks", *fatf-gafi.org.*

Federal Reserve Board (1997) "Remarks by Chairman Alan Greenspan: Government regulation and derivative contracts", presented at the *Financial Markets Conference of the Federal Reserve Bank of Atlanta*, Coral Gables, Florida, 21 February.

Feigin, P. A. (2011) "The Model State Commodity Code in 2011 and new CFTC jurisdiction - Whither the states? Can "new dogs" learn "old tricks"?", *Banking & Financial Services Policy Report*, Vol. 31, 1–9.

Felsenthal, D., Old, G., Kalbag, M. (2016) "CFTC Bitfinex Enforcement Action", *Clifford Chance.*

Financial Action Task Force (2014) "Virtual Currencies: Key Definitions and Potential AML/CFT Risks", *fatf-gafi.org.*

Financial Conduct Authority (2013) "The FCA's role under the Electronic Money Regulations 2011 - Our approach (draft version)", *fca.gov.uk.*

Financial Services Authority (2011) "Implementation of the second Electronic Money Directive: supplement to HM Treasury's consultation - Feedback on CP10/25 and part of CP10/24, and final rules", *Policy Statement PS11/2.*

FinCEN (2013) "Application of FinCEN's Regulations to Persons Administering, Exchanging, or Using Virtual Currencies", *FIN-2013-G001.*

Finck, M. (2017) "Blockchain Regulation", *Max Planck Institute for Innovation and Competition Research Paper No. 17-13.*

Finney, H. (2004) "RPOW - Reusable Proofs of Work", *cryptome.org/rpow.htm.*

Fischer-Dieskau, S., Wilke, D. (2006) "Electronically signed documents: legal requirements and measures for their long-term conservation", *Digital Evidence and Electronic Signature Law Review*, Vol. 3, 38–42.

Fransens, D., Dedryvere, M. (2003) "De juridische draagwijdte van het begrip elektronisch geld: is de lading groter dan de vlag (Deel II)", *Tijdschrift Financieel Recht*, nr. 2003/4, 549–567.

Frevert, U. (2009) "Does Trust Have a History?", *Max Weber Lecture Series MWP-LS 2009/01.*

Frew, L., Folsom, R., van Wingerden, S. (2015) "Legal and regulatory issues relating to virtual currencies", *Butterworths Journal of International Banking and Financial Law*, Vol. 7, 1–5.

Froomkin, A.M. (1996) "Flood control on the information ocean: living with anonymity, digital cash, and distributed databases", *Journal of Law & Commerce*, Vol. 15, 395–507.
FSMA (2012) "Reglementair kader voor crowdfunding", *fsma.be.*
Fullenkamp, C., Nsouli, S.M. (2004) "Six Puzzles in Electronic Money and Banking", *IMF Working Paper WP/04/19.*
GAO (2013) "Virtual Economies and Currencies", *GAO-13-516.*
Geens, H. (2004) "De grondslagen van de culpa in contrahendo", *Jura Falconis*, Vol. 40, 433–460.
Gencer, A. E., Basu, S., Eyal, I., van Renesse, R., Gün Sirer, E. (2018) "Decentralization in Bitcoin and Ethereum Networks", *arxiv.org/pdf/1801.03998.pdf.*
Geva, B. (2009) "Payment Transactions under the EU Payment Services Directive: A U.S. Comparative Perspective", *Penn St. Int'l L. Rev.*, vol. 27, 713–755.
Geva, B. (2009) "The harmonization of payment services law in Europe and uniform and federal funds transfer legislation in the USA: which is a better model for reform?", *Euredia,* 2009/4, 713–755.
Geva, B. (2016) "Disintermediating electronic payments: digital cash and virtual currencies", *Journal of International Banking Law and Regulation*, Vol. 31, 661–674.
Gobert, D. (2004) "Commerce électronique: vers un cadre juridique général pour les tiers de confiance", *Revue du Droit des Technologies de l'information,* nr. 18, 33–34.
Goddard, R. D. (2003) "Relational Networks, Social Trust, and Norms: A Social Capital Perspective on Students' Chances of Academic Success", *Educational Evaluation and Policy Analysis,* Vol. 25, 59–74.
Godschalk, H. (2001) "Genesis of the EU-Directive on Electronic Money Institutions", *EPSO Newsletter* 7.
Godschalk, H., Krueger, M. (2000) "Why e-money still fails – chances of e-money within a competitive payment instrument market", presented at the *Third Berlin Internet Economics Workshop*, Berlin, May 26–27.
González, A.G. (2004) "PayPal: The legal status of C2C payment systems", *Computer Law & Security Review*, Vol. 20, 293–299.
Goodhart, C. A. E. (1998) "The two concepts of money: implications for the analysis of optimal currency areas", *European Journal of Political Economy*, Vol. 14, 407–432.
Gordon, J. D. (2011) "Defining a Common Enterprise in Investment Contracts", *Ohio State Law Journal*, Vol. 72, 59–94.
Gorzelak, K. (2008) "The legal nature of emission allowances following the creation of a Union Registry and adoption of MiFID II – are they transferable securities now?", *Capital Markets Law Journal,* Vol. 9, 373–387.
Grabowski, M., Sanborn, S. D. (2003) "Human performance and embedded intelligent technology in safety-critical systems", *Int. J. Human-Computer Studies*, Vol. 58, 637–670.
Graham, F. D. (1940) "The Primary Functions of Money and their Consummation in Monetary Policy", *The American Economic Review*, Vol. 30, 1–16.
Graux, H. (2011) "Rethinking the E-Signatures Directive: On laws, trust services, and the Digital Single Market", *Digital Evidence and Electronic Signature Law Review*, Vol. 8, 9–24.
Greenlee, P., Reitman, D. (2005) "Distinguishing Competitive and Exclusionary Uses of Loyalty Discounts", *Antitrust Bulletin*, Vol. 50, 441–463.

Grierson, P. (1978) "The origins of money", *Research in Economic Anthropology*, Vol. 1, 1–35.

Grinberg, R. (2012) "Bitcoin: An Innovative Alternative Digital Currency", *Hastings Sci. & Tech. L.J.*, vol. 4, 159–208.

Guerra, G., Zizzo, D., Dutton, W., Peltu, M. (2003) "Economics of Trust in the Information Economy: Issues of Identity, Privacy and Security", *Oxford Internet Institute, Research Report No. 1.*

Guiso, L., Sapienza, P., Zingales, L. (2005) "Trusting the stock market", *The Journal of Finance*, Vol. 63, 2557–2600.

Guo, J., Chow, A. (2008) "Virtual Money Systems: A Phenomenal Analysis", *Proceedings of the IEEE Joint Conference on E-Commerce Technology (CEC'08) and Enterprise Computing, E-Commerce and E-Services (EEE'08)*, 267–272.

Gürkaynak, G., Yilmaz, I. (2015) "Regulating payment services and electronic money: A comparative regulatory approach with a specific focus on Turkish legislation", *Computer Law & Security Review*, Vol. 31, 401–411.

Halpin, R., Moore, R. (2009) "Developments in electronic money regulation - the Electronic Money Directive: A better deal for e-money issuers?", Computer Law & Security Review, vol. 25, 563–568.

Hansen, M. (2004) "A Double-Edged Blade", Datenschutz und Datensicherheit, 525–528.

Hansmann, H., Mattei, U. (1998) "The functions of trust law: a comparative legal and economic analysis", N.Y.U. L. Rev., Vol. 73, 434–479.

Harper, J. (2014) "Removing Impediments to Bitcoin's Success: A Risk Management Study", Bitcoin Foundation Research Brief 1.

Heeks, R. (2010) "Understanding "Gold Farming" and Real-Money Trading as the Intersection of Real and Virtual Economies", Journal of Virtual Worlds Research, Vol. 2, 3–27.

Heller, D. (2017) "Do Digital Currencies Pose a Threat to Sovereign Currencies and Central Banks?", PIIE Policy Brief 17–13.

Hess, M., Weiss Voigt, A. (2014) "E-money, e- and m-payments according to Swiss law", clearit.ch.

Hills, A. (2006) "Kantian trust", open.edu.

HM Government (2013) "UK Government Information Economy Strategy", gov.uk, BIS/13/611.

HM Treasury (2015) "Digital currencies: response to the call for information", gov.uk/government/uploads/system/uploads/attachment_data/file/414040/digital_currencies_response_to_call_for_information_final_changes.pdf.

HM Treasury (2015) "UK national risk assessment of money laundering and terrorist financing", gov.uk.

HM Treasury, Baldwin, H. (2015), "UK to lead on big data research, says Harriett Baldwin", speech delivered to the Alan Turing Institute for Data Science, 14 October, London, www.gov.uk/government/speeches/uk-to-lead-on-big-data-research-says-harriett-baldwin.

Hoffman, C.D. (1998) "Encrypted Digital Cash Transfers: Why Traditional Money Laundering Controls May Fail without Uniform Cryptography Regulations", Fordham International Law Journal, Vol. 21, 836–860.

Hornák, Z., Nyilas, I., Petró, D., Schrammel, J., Wolkerstorfer, P., Ellensohn, L., Geven, A., Kristjansdottir, K., Fritsch, L., Schultz, T., Abie, H., Pürzel, F., Wittstock, V. (2010) "uTRUSTit D.3.1 - Technology and Standard Report", utrustit.eu.

Horsburgh, H. J. N. (1960) "The Ethics of Trust", The Philosophical Quarterly, Vol. 10, 343–354.

Houben, R. (2015) "Bitcoin: there are two sides to every coin", Tijdschrift voor Belgisch Handelsrecht, nr. 2, 139–159.

Houben, R. (2016) "The CJEU's view of whether Bitcoins are a currency: a Belgian perspective", International Company and Commercial Law Review, Vol. 27, 61–64.

Huang, H., Keser, C., Leland, J., Shachat, J. (2003) "Trust, the Internet, and the digital divide", IBM Systems Journal, Vol. 42, 507–518.

Hughes, S. J., Middlebrook, S. T. (2015) "Advancing a Framework for Regulating Cryptocurrency Payments Intermediaries", Yale Journal on Regulation, Vol. 32, 495–559.

Hutson, E. (2005) "The early managed fund industry: Investment trusts in 19th century Britain", International Review of Financial Analysis, Vol. 14, 439–454.

IDABC (2009) "Study on Mutual Recognition of eSignatures: update of Country Profiles - Estonian Country Report", ec.europa.eu.

Ingenico (2012) "White Paper: Electronic payment architecture and trends in Europe", ingenico.com.

Innes, M. A. (1913) "What is Money?", Banking Law Journal, Vol. 30, 377–408.

IRS (2014) "IRS Virtual Currency Guidance: Virtual Currency Is Treated as Property for U.S. Federal Tax Purposes; General Rules for Property Transactions Apply", irs.gov.

IRS (2014) "Virtual currency guidance", irs.gov, Notice 2014-21.

Irwin, A., Slay, J., Choo, K.K., Liu, L. (2013) "Are the financial transactions conducted inside virtual environments truly anonymous? An experimental research from an Australian perspective", Journal of Money Laundering Control, Vol. 16, 93–98.

Irwin, D., Chase, J., Grit, L., Yumerefendi, A. (2005) "Self-recharging virtual currency", *P2PECON '05 Proceedings of the 2005 ACM SIGCOMM workshop on Economics of peer-to-peer systems*, 93–98.

Iwamura, M., Kitamura, Y., Matsumoto, T. (2014) "Is Bitcoin the Only Cryptocurrency in the Town? Economics of Cryptocurrency and Friedrich A. Hayek", *Hitotsubashi University Institute of Economic Research Discussion Paper 602.*

J.P. Morgan (2015) "What is an investment trust?", *am.jpmorgan.co.uk.*

Jacob, J., Brinkerhoff, M., Jovic, E., Wheatley, G. (2004) "The Social and Cultural Capital of Community Currency: An Ithaca HOURS Case Study Survey", *International Journal of Community Currency Research*, Vol. 8, 42–56.

Jacobs, A., Nakata, K. (2010) "Evolving the social business: a look at stages of growth for Web 2.0 integration with business activities", presented at *First Interdisciplinary Workshop on Communication for Sustainable Communities (IWCSC '10)*, 26 September 2010, S.Carlos, Brazil.

Jacobs, E. (2011) "Bitcoin: A Bit Too Far?", *Journal of Internet Banking and Commerce,* vol. 16, 1–4.

Jacquemin, H. (2010) "Les paiements électroniques dans les contrats à distance depuis la loi du 10 décembre 2009", Revue du Droit des Technologies de l'Information, nr. 41, 5–21.

Jalava, J. (2001) "Trust or confidence?", presented at the 5th Conference of the European Sociological Association, 'Visions and Divisions', 28 August – 1 September 2001, Helsinki, Finland.

James, H.S. (2002) "The trust paradox: a survey of economic inquiries into the nature of trust and trustworthiness", Journal of Economic Behavior & Organization, Vol. 47, 291–307.

Janowski, P. (2015) "Study on the impact of Directive 2009/110/EC on the taking up, pursuit and prudential supervision of the business of electronic money institutions", circabc.europa.eu.

Johnson, B., Laszka, A., Grossklags, J., Vasek, M., Moore, T. (2014) "Game-Theoretic Analysis of DDoS Attacks Against Bitcoin Mining Pools", presented at Financial Crypto 14, 1st Workshop on Bitcoin Research, Barbados, 7 March 2014, fc14.ifca.ai/bitcoin/program.html.

Jones, A. J. I. (2002) "On the concept of Trust", Decision Support Systems, Vol. 33, 225–232.

Jones, K. (1996) "Trust as an Affective Attitude", Ethics, Vol. 107, 4–25.

Jones, S., Wilikens, M., Morris, P., Masera, M. (2000) "Trust Requirements in E-Business: A conceptual framework for understanding the needs and concerns of different stakeholders", Communications of the ACM, Vol. 43, 81–87.

Kaplanov, N. (2012) "Nerdy Money: Bitcoin, the Private Digital Currency, and the Case Against its Regulation", Loyola Consumer Law Review, Vol. 25, 111–174.

Karlstrøm, H. (2014) "Do libertarians dream of electric coins? The material embeddedness of Bitcoin", Distinktion: Scandinavian Journal of Social Theory, Vol. 15, 23–36.

Keynes, J. M. (1937) "The General Theory of Employment", *The Quarterly Journal of Economics*, Vol. 51, 209–223.

Khan, A. (1999) "The evolution of money: a story of constitutional nullification", *University of Cincinnati Law Review*, Vol. 67, 393–443.

Kien-Meng Ly, M. (2014) "Coining Bitcoin's 'legal-bits': examining the regulatory framework for Bitcoin and virtual currencies", *Harvard Journal of Law & Technology*, vol. 27, nr. 2, 587–608.

Kiran, M., Stannett, M. (2014) "Bitcoin Risk Analysis", *nemode.ac.uk*.

Kiss, J. (2009) "International Payments Law Reform: Introduction of Global Code of Payments", *Banking and Finance Law Review*, Vol. 25, 405–434.

Kiyotaki, N., Wright, R. (1989) "On Money as a Medium of Exchange", *Journal of Political Economy*, Vol. 97, 927–954.

Knack, S., Keefer, P. (1997) "Does Social Capital Have an Economic Payoff? A Cross-Country Investigation", *The Quarterly Journal of Economics*, Vol. 112, 1251–1288.

Kohlbach, M. (2004) "Making Sense of Electronic Money", *Journal of Information, Law and Technology*, 1–19.

Kohn, M. (1999) "Bills of exchange and the money market to 1600", *Dartmouth College Department of Economics*, Working Paper 99–04.

Kroll, J., Davey, I., Felten, E. (2013) "The Economics of Bitcoin Mining, or Bitcoin in the Presence of Adversaries", Presented at *The Twelfth Workshop on the Economics of Information Security (WEIS 2013)*, Washington, DC, 11–12 June.

Krueger, M. (2001) "Offshore E-money Issuers and Monetary Policy", *First Monday*, Vol. 6, nr. 10.

Kubát, M. (2015) "Virtual currency bitcoin in the scope of money definition and store of value", *Procedia Economics and Finance*, Vol. 30, 409–416.

Labbozzetta, C. (2007) "A Principled Approach to Reward Loyalty: An Argument for Code of Conduct Principles to Remedy the Contractual Unfairness and Legislative Confusion in Loyalty Programs", *Macquarie Journal of Business Law*, Vol. 4, 123–138.

Langbein, J. H. (1995) "The contractarian basis of the law of trusts", *Yale Law Journal*, Vol. 105, 625–675.

Lauwers, Y., Vanweddingen, I. (2008) "Toepassingsgebied Richtlijn betreffende betalingsdiensten in de interne markt", *Bank en Financieel Recht*, nr. 2008/VI, 372–386.

Lauzon, E. D. (2002) "Annotation: What are "Contracts of Sale of a Commodity for Future Delivery" Within Meaning of Commodity Exchange Act (7 U.S.CA. §§1 et seq.)", *182 A.L.R. Fed. 559.*

Laverdet, C. (2014) "Bitcoin: par ici la cryptomonnaie!", *Revue Lamy Droit de l'Immatériel*, nr. 100, 90–93.

Law Library of Congress (2014) "Regulation of Bitcoin in Selected Jurisdictions", *loc.gov.*

Lawsky, B. M. (2014) "Remarks on the Regulation of Virtual Currencies", presented at the *New America Foundation*, Washington, DC, 11 February.

Lee, B.C., Longe-Akindemowo, O. (1998) "Regulatory Issues in Electronic Money: A Legal-Economics Analysis", Department of Economics, University of Wollongong Working Paper 98–2.

Lehdonvirta, V. (2009) "Virtual item sales as a revenue model: identifying attributes that drive purchase decisions", Electron Commer Res, Vol. 9, 97–113.

Lehdonvirta, V. (2010) "Virtual Worlds Don't Exist: Questioning the Dichotomous Approach in MMO Studies", Game Studies, Vol. 10, nr. 1.

Lelieveldt, S. (1997) "How to regulate electronic cash: an overview of regulatory issues and strategies", The American University Law Review, vol. 46, 1163–1175.

Lelieveldt, S. (2001) "Why is the Electronic Money-Directive Significant?", EPSO Newsletter 7.

Lelieveldt, S. (2006) "Impact of the E-Money Directive – Its application to 'hybrid' operators issuing e-money", presented at the E-Money Directive (2000/46/EC) – Round Table Meeting, Brussels, 8 March 2006.

Lewis, J. D., Weigert, A. (2012) "The Social Dynamics of Trust: Theoretical and Empirical Research, 1985-2012", Social Forces, Vol. 91, 25–31.

Lewis, J. D., Weigert, A. (1985) "Trust as a social reality", Social Forces, Vol. 63, 967–985.

Loiseau, G. (2011) "Biens meubles par détermination de la loi ou meubles incorporels", JurisClasseur Code Civil – art. 527–532, Fasc. 20.

London Economics (2013) "Study on the impact of directive 2007/64/EC on payment services in the internal market and on the application of regulation (EC) No. 924/2009 on cross-border payments in the Community", MARKT/2011/120/H3/ST/OP.

Luther, W. (2013) "Cryptocurrencies, Network Effects, and Switching Costs", George Mason University Mercatus Center Working Paper 13–17.

Luxembourg Stock Exchange (2016) "Luxembourg Stock Exchange introduces blockchain into reporting service", bourse.lu.

Macneil, H. (1994) “Archival Theory and Practice: Between Two Paradigms”, Archivaria, Vol. 37, 6–20.

Macy, M., Skvoretz, J. (1998) “The Evolution of Trust and Cooperation between Strangers: A Computational Model”, American Sociological Review, Vol. 63, 638–660.

Malaguti, M. C. (2009) “The Payment Services Directive: Pitfalls between the Acquis Communautaire and National Implementation”, CEPS-ECRI Research Report No. 9.

Malekzadem, J. (2010) “Beslag op domeinnamen. Een eerste verkenning”, Rechtskundig Weekblad, Vol. 73, 1498–1506.

Mansour, Y. (2014) “Regulating payments for M-Content: The positive impact of the deregulation”, International Review of Law, Vol. 9, 1–12.

Marshall, R. (2015) “Bitcoin: Where Two Worlds Collide”, Bond Law Review, Vol. 27, 89–112.

Matravers, M. (2006) “Hume on trust”, *open.edu*.

Maurer, B. (1998) “Cyberspatial Sovereignties: Offshore Finance, Digital Cash, and the Limits of Liberalism”, Indiana Journal of Global Legal Studies, Vol. 4, 493–519.

May, M. (2004) “From consultant to courtier”, *Consulting to Management*, Vol. 15, 17–34.

May, T.C. (1994) “Cyphernomicon”, *spinnaker.com/crypt/cyphernomicon/CP-FAQ*.

Mayer, R. C., Davis, J. H., Schoorman, F. D. (1995) “An Integrative Model of Organizational Trust”, *The Academy of Management Review*, Vol. 20, 709–734.

Mbiti, I., Weil, D. (2013) "The Home Economics of E-Money: Velocity, Cash Management, and Discount Rates of M-Pesa Users", *American Economic Review*, Vol. 103, 369–374.

McKnight, D. H., Choudhury, V., Kacmar, C. (2002) “The impact of initial consumer trust on intentions to transact with a web site: a trust building model”, *Journal of Strategic Information Systems*, Vol. 11, 297–323.

Menger, K. (1892) “On the Origin of Money”, *The Economic Journal*, Vol. 2, 239–255.

Mersch, Y. (2014) “Efficient retail payments: key in strengthening the competitiveness and growth potential of the EU”, Speech at the ECB/Banca d’Italia Workshop on Interchange Fees, Rome 24 March 2014, *ecb.europa.eu*.

Middlebrook, S. T., Hughes, S. J. (2014) "Regulating Cryptocurrencies in the United States: Current Issues and Future Directions", *William Mitchell Law Review*, Vol. 40, 813–848.

Miller, F. H., Hughes, S. J. (2014) “Final Study Committee on Alternative and Mobile Payment Systems Report”, *uniformlaws.org*.

Möllering, G. (2013) “Trust without knowledge? Comment on Hardin, ‘Government without trust’”, *Journal of Trust Research*, Vol. 3, 53–58.

Möllering, G. (2001) “The Nature of Trust: From Georg Simmel to a Theory of Expectation, Interpretation and Suspension”, *Sociology*, Vol 35, 403–420.

Munro, J.H. (2003) “The Medieval Origins of the Financial Revolution: Usury, Rentes, and Negotiability”, *The International History Review*, vol. 25, nr. 3, 505–562.

Nakamoto, S. (2008) “Bitcoin: a peer-to-peer electronic cash system”, *bitcoin.org/Bitcoin.pdf*.

National Conference of Commissioners on Uniform State Laws (2015) “Draft Regulation of Virtual Currencies”, *uniformlaws.org*.

National Conference of Commissioners on Uniform State Laws (2017) “Uniform Regulation of Virtual Currency Businesses Act”, *uniformlaws.org*.

Navas Navarro, S. (2015) “Un mercado financiero floreciente: el del dinero virtual no regulado (Especial atención a los BITCOINS)”, *Revista CESCO de Derecho de Consumo*, Nr. 13/2015, 79–114.

New York State Department of Financial Services (2017) "2016 Annual Report", *dfs.ny.gov.*

Newman, S., Sutter, G. (2002) "Electronic Payments – the smart card: Smart cards, e-payments, & law – Part II", *Computer Law & Security Report*, Vol. 18, 307–313.

Nikolova, N., Möllering, G., Reihlen, M. (2015) "Trusting as a 'Leap of Faith': Trust-building practices in client–consultant relationships", Scandinavian Journal of Management, Vol. 31, 232–245.

O'Hara, K., Shadbolt, N. (2004) "Knowledge technologies and the semantic web", UK Department for Business, Information and Skills Foresight Project.

OECD (2012) "Report on Consumer Protection in Online and Mobile Payments", OECD Digital Economy Papers, No. 204.

Okano, Y. (2016) "Virtual currencies: issues remain after Payment Services Act amended", Iakyara, Vol. 243, 1–5.

Oliphant, H. (1920) "The Theory of Money in the Law of Commercial Instruments", The Yale Law Journal, Vol. 29, 606–624.

Pacifici, E. (2015) "Making PayPal pay: Regulation E and its application to alternative payment services", Duke Law & Technology Review, Vol. 13, 89–115.

Pacione, M. (1997) "Local Exchange Trading Systems as a Response to the Globalisation of Capitalism", Urban Studies, Vol. 34, 1179–1199.

Papagiannidis, S., Bourlakis, M., Li, F. (2008) "Making real money in virtual worlds: MMORPGs and emerging business opportunities, challenges and ethical implications in metaverses", Technological Forecasting & Social Change, Vol. 75, 610–622.

Papilloud, C., Haesler, A. (2014) "The veil of economy: electronic money and the pyramidal structure of societies", Distinktion: Scandinavian Journal of Social Theory, Vol. 15, 54–68.

Parliamentary Office of Science & Technology (2014) "POSTNote: Alternative Currencies", POST-PN-475.

Patton, M. A., Jøsang, A. (2004) "Technologies for Trust in Electronic Commerce", Electronic Commerce Research, Vol. 4, 9–21.

Payment Systems Market Expert Group (2012) "Minutes of the meeting of 27 March 2012, Brussels", ec.europa.eu.

Payment Systems Market Expert Group (2013) "Minutes of the meeting of 24 October 2013, Brussels", ec.europa.eu.

Payment Systems Market Expert Group (2014) "Minutes of the meeting of 22 October 2014, Brussels", PSMEG 008/14.

Payment Systems Market Expert Group (2015) "Minutes of the meeting of 28 April 2015", PSMEG/005/15.

Payments Committee (2012) "Summary Record of the Eighth meeting of the Payments Committee of 17 October 2012", ec.europa.eu, PC/013/12.

Payments Committee (2012) "Summary Record of the Sixth meeting of the Payments Committee of 21 March 2012", PC/005/12.

Payments Council (2012) "Minutes of the Seventh meeting of the Payments Committee, Monday, 9 July 2012", PC/010/12.

Peck, M. (2012) "The cryptoanarchists' answer to cash", *IEEE Spectrum*, June 2012, 51–56.

Peeters, J., Van Dyck, T. (2006) "De prospectusplicht in de prospectuswet van 16 juni 2006", Bank- en Financieel Recht, nr. 2006/IV, 199–249.

Périnet-Marquet, H. (2010) "Regard sur les nouveaux biens", La Semaine Juridique Edition Générale, nr. 44, doctr. 1100.

Pflaum, I., Hateley, E. (2014) "A bit of a problem: National and extraterritorial regulation of virtual currency in the age of financial disintermediation", Georgetown Journal of International Law, Vol. 45, 1169–1215.

Pixley, J. (1999) "Impersonal Trust in Global Mediating Organizations", Sociological Perspectives, Vol. 42, 647–671.

Plassaras, N. (2014) "Regulating digital currencies: bringing Bitcoin within the reach of the IMF", Chicago Journal of International law, Vol. 14, 377–407.

Pollitt, M. (2002) "The Economics of Trust, Norms and Networks", Business Ethics: A European Review, Vol. 11, 119–128.

Price, C. (2006) "Trust in Plato's Republic", open.edu.

Raab, C. (2004) "The future of privacy protection", UK Department for Business, Information and Skills Foresight Project.

Ramchurn, S. D., Jennings, N. R. (2004) "Trust in agent-based software", *UK Department for Business, Information and Skills Foresight Project.*

Reed, C. (2010) "How to Make Bad Law: Lessons from Cyberspace", *The Modern Law Review*, vol. 73, nr. 6, 903–932.

Richet, J.-L. (2013) "Laundering Money Online: a review of cybercriminals' methods", presented at Tools and Resources for Anti-Corruption Knowledge, United Nations Office on Drugs and Crime (UNODC), 1 June.

Riegelsberger, J., Sasse, M. A., McCarthy, J. D. (2003) "The researcher's dilemma: evaluating trust in computer-mediated communication", *Int. J. Human-Computer Studies*, Vol. 58, 759–781.

Riegelsberger, J., Sasse, M. A., McCarthy, J. D. (2005) "The mechanics of trust: A framework for research and design", *Int. J. Human-Computer Studies,* Vol. 62, 381–422.

Ross, S. (2012) "Digital Preservation, Archival Science and Methodological Foundations for Digital Libraries", New Review of Information Networking, Vol. 17, 43–68,

Roth, F. (2009) "The Effect of the Financial Crisis on Systemic Trust", Intereconomics, Vol. 44, 203–208.

Royer, S. (2016) "Bitcoins in het Belgische strafrecht en strafprocesrecht", Rechtskundig Weekblad, 483–501.

Sagaert, V. (2005) "Het goederenrecht als open systeem van verbintenissen? Poging tot een nieuwe kwalificatie van de vermogensrechten", Tijdschrift voor Privaatrecht, Vol. 42, 983–1080.

Salomon, M., Soudoplatoff S. (2010) "Why Virtual-World Economies Matter", Journal of Virtual Worlds Research, Vol. 2, 3–14.

Sardoni, C. (2015) "The functions of money and the demand for liquidity", Università di Roma Sapienza Dipartimento di Scienze Sociali ed Economice Working Paper 3/2015.

Sasse, M. A. (2004) "Usability and trust in information systems", UK Department for Business, Information and Skills Foresight Project.

Sciarrone Alibrandi, A. (2009) "Rights and Obligations of Users and Providers of Payment Services", Euredia, 635–638.

Schapper, P. R., Rivolta, M., Veiga Malta, J. (2006) "Risk and law in authentication", Digital Evidence Journal, Vol. 3, 10–16.

Schröder, M. (2014) "Bitcoin: Virtuelle Währung - reelle Problemstellungen", JurPC Web-Dok. 104/2014.

Schudelaro, A. (2003) "To Be or Not to Be Electronic Money, That's the Question", Information & Communications Technology Law, Vol. 12, 49–55.

Securities and Exchange Commission (2014) "SEC Charges Bitcoin Entrepreneur With Offering Unregistered Securities", sec.gov.

Securities and Exchange Commission (2017) "Report of Investigation Pursuant to Section 21(a) of the Securities Exchange Act of 1934: The DAO", SEC release 81207.

Seligman, A. B. (1998) "Trust and Sociability: On the Limits of Confidence and Role Expectations", American Journal of Economics and Sociology, Vol. 57, 391–404.

Semenova, A., Wray, R. (2015) "The Rise of Money and Class Society: The Contributions of John F. Henry", Levy Institute Working Paper 832.

Shaker, L. (2006) "In Google we trust: Information integrity in the digital age", First Monday, Vol. 11, nr. 4.

Shapiro, S. P. (1987) "The Social Control of Impersonal Trust", American Journal of Sociology, Vol. 93, 623–658.

Shcherbak, S. (2014) "How should Bitcoin be regulated?", European Journal of Legal Studies, Vol. 7, 41–83.

Shelton, A.K. (2010) "Defining the lines between virtual and real world purchases: Second Life sells, but who's buying?", *Computers in Human Behavior*, Vol. 26, 1223–1227.

Shim, G., Lee, S., Kim, Y. (2008) "How investor behavioral factors influence investment satisfaction, trust in investment company, and reinvestment intention", *Journal of Business Research*, Vol. 61, 47–55.

Shubik, M. (2014) "Simecs, Ithaca Hours, Berkshares, Bitcoins and Walmarts", *Cowley Foundation Discussion Paper 1947.*

Sillence, E., Briggs, P., Harris, P., Fishwick, L. (2006) "A framework for understanding trust factors in web-based health advice", *Int. J. Human-Computer Studies*, Vol. 64, 697–713.

Simon, P. (1999) "La position de la profession sur la monnaie électronique", *Revue d'économie financière*, nr. 53, 37–38.

Smith, B. W., Wilson, R. J. (1997) "How Best to Guide the Evolution of Electronic Currency Law", *American University Law Review*, Vol. 46, 1105–1130.

Smith, C. (2005) "Understanding Trust and Confidence: Two Paradigms and their Significance for Health and Social Care", *Journal of Applied Philosophy*, Vol. 22, 299–316.

Smith, D. (2012) "More Money, More Problems: The Bitcoin Virtual Currency and the Legal Problems that Face It", *Case Western Reserve Journal of Law Technology & The Internet*, vol. 3, 427–442.

Smits, R. (2008) "The Changing Payments Landscape of Europe: Issues of Regulation and Competition", *Yearbook of European Law*, Vol. 27, 405–444.

Sonderegger, D. (2015) "Regulatory and Economic Perplexity: Bitcoin Needs Just a Bit of Regulation", Washington University Journal of Law & Policy, Vol. 47, 175–216.

Spaas, T., Van Roey, M. (2015) "Quo vadis Bitcoin?", Computerrecht, nr.84, 113–124.

Springael, B. (2014) "Bitcoins: het virtuele goud?", Tijdschrift voor Financieel Recht, nr. 468, 759–763.

State of New Hampshire (2016) "House Record - Calendar and Journal of the 2016 Session", House Journal, Vol. 38, nr. 8.

Steennot, R. (2010) "Girale en elektronische betalingen: nieuwe wettelijke regeling", Nieuw Juridisch Weekblad, nr. 226, 518–537.

Stokes, R. (2012) "Virtual money laundering: the case of Bitcoin and the Linden dollar", Information & Communications Technology Law, vol. 21, nr. 3, 221–236.

Storme, M. E. (1998) "Van trust gespeend? *Trusts* en fiduciaire figuren in het Belgisch privaatrecht", *Tijdschrift voor Privaatrecht*, Vol. 35, 703–814.

Storme, M. E. (2001) "De invoering van de elektronische handtekening in ons bewijsrecht - een inkadering van en commentaar bij de nieuwe wetsbepalingen", *Rechtskundig Weekblad*, 1505–1525.

Surda, P. (2014) "The Origin, Classification and Utility of Bitcoin", *papers.ssrn.com/sol3/papers.cfm?abstract_id=2436823.*

Szabo, N. (2005) "Bit gold", *unenumerated.blogspot.com/2005/12/bit-gold.html.*

Taylor, H. A. (1987) "Transformation in the Archives: Technological Adjustment or paradigm Shift?", *Archivaria*, Vol. 25, 12–28.

Thayer, J. B. (1887) "Legal Tender", *Harvard Law Review*, Vol. 1, 73–97.

The Clearing House, Independent Community Bankers of America (2014) "Virtual currency: risks and regulation", *theclearinghouse.org.*

The Evaluation Partnership ltd. (2006) "Evaluation of the E-money Directive (2000/46/EC) - final report", *ec.europa.eu.*

Thompson, S. L. (2009) "Securities Regulation in a Virtual World", *UCLA Entertainment Law Review*, Vol. 16, 89–117.

Thorpe, C., Hammer, J., Camp, J., Callas, J., Bond, M. (2007) "Virtual Economies: Threats and Risks", *Proceedings of Financial Cryptography and Data Security '07*, Trinidad and Tobago, 12–15 February 2007.

TIPIK (2011) "Directive 2007/64/EC - General report on the transposition by the Member States", *ec.europa.eu.*

TIPIK (2012) "Conformity Assessment of Directive 2007/64/EC, Poland", *ec.europa.eu.*

Toms, S., Zdrowski, M., Hall, R. (2015) "Virtual currencies: Mining the possibilities", *allenovery.com.*

Tonkiss, F. (2009) "Trust, Confidence and Economic Crisis", *Intereconomics,* Vol. 44, 196–202.

Trautman, L. (2014) "Virtual Currencies: Bitcoin & What Now after Liberty Reserve, Silk Road, and Mt. Gox?", *Richmond Journal of Law and Technology*, vol. 20, 1–108.

Tu, K. V., Meredith, M. W. (2015) "Rethinking Virtual Currency Regulation in the Bitcoin Age", *Washington Law Review*, Vol. 90, 271–347.

Tucker, G. (1997) "Some Legal Issues Relating to Digital Cash on the Information Highway", *Journal of Law and Information Science*, Vol. 8, 46–67.

Turpin, J. (2014) "Bitcoin: the economic case for a global virtual currency operating in an unexplored legal framework", *Indiana Journal of Global Legal Studies,* Vol. 21, 335–368.

Twomey, P. (2013) "Halting a shift in the paradigm: the need for bitcoin regulation", *Trinity College Law Review,* Vol. 16, 67–90.

Tymoigne, E., Wray, L. R. (2005) "Money: An Alternative Story", *CFEPS Working Paper 45.*

US Mint (2014) "2014 Biennial Report to the Congress", *usmint.gov*.

US Senate Banking Committee (2013) "The Present and Future Impact of Virtual Currency – Testimony of Mercedes Kelley Tunstall", *banking.senate.gov*.

US Senate Committee on Banking, Housing and Urban Affairs (2013) "The present and future impact of virtual currency – hearing of 19 November 2013", *banking.senate.gov*.

US Senate Committee on Homeland Security and Governmental Affairs (2013) "Beyond Silk Road: Potential Risks, Threats and Promises of Virtual Currencies – Testimony of Edward Lowery III", *hsgac.senate.gov*.

US Senate Committee on Homeland Security and Governmental Affairs (2013) "Beyond Silk Road: Potential Risks, Threats and Promises of Virtual Currencies – Hearing of 18 November 2013", *hsgac.senate.gov*.

US Senate Committee on Homeland Security and Governmental Affairs (2013) "Beyond Silk Road: Potential Risks, Threats and Promises of Virtual Currencies – Testimony of Jennifer Shasky Calvery", *hsgac.senate.gov*.

Valcke, P., Vandezande, N. and Van de Velde, N. (2015) "The Evolution of Third Party Payment Providers and Cryptocurrencies Under the EU's Upcoming PSD2 and AMLD4", *SWIFT Institute Working Paper 2015-001*.

Van den Eynde, S. (2001) "DAVID – Digitale archivering: een stand van zaken vanuit Belgisch perspectief, deel I", *www.edavid.be*.

Van der Wielen, H. (1996) "Elektronisch geld in Nederland", 10 October 1996, *www.simonl.org/docs/readeremdnb.pdf*.

Van der Wielen, H. (1997) "Electronic Money: a European Perspective", presented at the Seminar on Electronic Money, hosted by the Bank of England, London 4 February 1997, www.simonl.org/docs/readeremdnb.pdf.

Van Eecke, P. (2009) "De elektronische handtekening in het recht", Tijdschrift voor Belgisch Handelsrecht, 322–354.

Van Hove, L. (1999) "Electronic purses, interoperability and the Internet", First Monday, Vol. 4.

Van Hove, L. (2004) "Electronic purses in Euroland: why do penetration and usage rates differ?", SUERF Studies 2004/4.

Van Hove, L. (2005) "Making electronic money legal tender: pros & cons", Free University of Brussels Working Paper.

Van Rhee, C. H. (2000) "Trusts, Trust-like Concepts and Ius Commune", European Review of Private Law, Vol. 3, 453–462.

Van Valkenburgh, P. (2016) "Framework for Securities Regulation of Cryptocurrencies v1", Coin Center Report.

Van Valkenburgh, P. (2017) "The Bank Secrecy Act, Cryptocurrencies, and New Tokens: What is Known and What Remains Ambiguous", Coin Center Report.

Vandenabeele, V. (2002) "De elektronische handtekening: rechten en plichten van de certificatiedienstverlener, de certificaathouder en de vertrouwende derde", T.B.B.R., 609–615.

Vandevoorde, W. (2011) "De Belgische omzetting van Richtlijn 2007/64/EG betreffende betalingsdiensten in de interne markt. Een overzicht.", Tijdschrift Financieel Recht, nr. 2011/3, 2–85.

Vandezande, N. (2014) "Between Bitcoins and mobile payments: will the European Commission's new proposal provide more legal certainty?", International Journal of Law and Information Technology, vol. 22, 295–310.

Vandezande, N. (2015) "Originality in the Belgian Civil Code and the influence of digitalization", papers.ssrn.com/sol3/papers.cfm?abstract_id=2660222.
Vandezande, N. (2017) "Virtual currencies under EU anti-money laundering law", Computer Law and Security Review, Vol. 33, 341–353.
Vandoolaeghe, A. (2010) "De Wet Betalingsdiensten op de korrel genomen", Droit de la Consommation - Consumentenrecht, nr. 89, 62–103.
Vanuxem S. (2010) "Les choses saisies par la propriété. De la chose-objet aux choses-milieux", Revue interdisciplinaire d'études juridiques, Vol. 64, 123–182.
Vereecken, M. (2000) "Electronic Money: EU Legislative Framework", European Business Law Review, Vol. 11, 417–434.
Vereecken, M. (2001) "A Harmonised EU Legal Framework for Electronic Money", EPSO Newsletter 7.
Wandhöfer, R. (2012) "The 2012 Payment Services Directive Review: Too Much too Soon?", EPC Newsletter.
Weber, R. (2001) "The European E-Money Directive: Background, Problems, and Prospects", Y.B. Int'l Fin. & Econ. L., Vol. 5, 293–309.
Weber, R., Darbellay, A. (2010) "Legal issues in mobile banking", Journal of Banking Regulation, Vol. 11, 129–145.
Williams, C. C. (1996) "The New Barter Economy: An Appraisal of Local Exchange and Trading Systems (LETS)", Journal of Public Policy, Vol. 16, 85–101.
Williams, J.C. (2012) "Cash Is Dead! Long Live Cash!", Federal Reserve Bank of San Francisco 2012 Annual Report.
Wilusz, D. (2011) "Legal determinants of electronic money systems development in European Union", Prawny i ekonomiczny przegląd prawa gospodarczego, vol. 2, 125–134.
Wolff, J. (2006) "Trust and the state of nature", open.edu.
Woolard, C. (2016), "UK FinTech: Regulating for innovation", speech delivered at the FinTech: Regulating for innovation event, 22 February, London, www.fca.org.uk/news/uk-fintech-regulating-for-innovation.
Working Group on EU Payment Systems (1994) "Report to the Council of The European Monetary Institute on Prepaid Cards", ecb.europa.eu.
Wray, L. R. (2000) "The Neo-Chartalist Approach to Money", CFEPS Working Paper 10.
Wray, L. R. (2014) "From the State Theory of Money to Modern Money Theory: An Alternative to Economic Orthodoxy", Levy Economics Institute Working Paper 792.
X (2017) "Open Letter of Support for the Uniform Law Commission's Model Regulation of Virtual Currency Businesses Act from Members of the Virtual Currency Industry", coincenter.org/pdf/ulcindustryletter.pdf.
Yamaguchi, H. (2004) "An Analysis of Virtual Currencies in Online Games", ssrn.com/abstract=544422.
Yeo, G. (2013) "Trust and context in cyberspace", Archives and Records, Vol. 34, 217–225.
Yermack, D. (2013) "Is Bitcoin a Real Currency? An economic appraisal", NBER Working Paper No. 19747.
Zähres, M. (2012) "E-money – Niche market that might be expanding", Deutsche Bank Research Banking & Technology Snapshot, www.dbresearch.com.
Zaltman, G., Moorman, C. (1988) "The importance of personal trust in the use of research", Journal of Advertising Research, 16–24.

Zarifis, A., Efthymiou, L., Cheng, X., Demetriou, S. (2014) "Consumer Trust in Digital Currency Enabled Transactions", Business Information Systems Workshops Lecture Notes in Business Information Processing, Vol. 183, 241–254.

Zhang, J., Breugelmans, E. (2012) "The impact of an item-Based loyalty Program on Consumer Purchase Behavior", Journal of Marketing Research, Vol. 49, 50–65.

## 3.3 PERIODICALS AND BLOGS

Abrams, R., Goldstein, M., Tabuchi, H. (2014) "Erosion Of Faith Was Death Knell For Mt. Gox", *New York Times*, 28 February.

Agrawal, N. (2016) "Is Your Crypto-Crowdsale A Security?", *Coincenter*, 18 July.

Backman, M. (2014) "Home Depot: 56 Million Cards Exposed In Breach", *Cnn Money*, 18 September.

Bafin (2017) "Ims International Marketing Services Gmbh: Account Freezing And Winding-Down Of Unauthorised Money Remittance Business", *Bafin.de*, 10 April.

Bafin (2017) "Onecoin Ltd (Dubai), Onelife Network Ltd (Belize) Und One Network Services Ltd (Sofia/Bulgaria): Bafin Issues Cease And Desist Orders Holding The Companies To Stop Own Funds Trading In "Onecoins" In Germany", *Bafin.de*, 27 April.

Bafin (2017) "Onecoin Ltd, Dubai: Prohibition Of Involvement In Unauthorised Money Remittance Business", *Bafin.de*, 18 April.

Bank Of America Merril Lynch (2013) "Bitcoin: A First Assessment", *Bank Of America*, 5 December.

Barnato, K. (2016) "Will Terror Attacks End Bitcoin Free-For-All In Europe?", *Cnbc*, 2 May.

Batteh, K. (2016) "Why The Cftc Bitfinex Enforcement Actually Benefits Bitcoin Exchanges", *Coindesk*, 6 June.

Bello Perez, Y. (2015) "The Real Cost Of Applying For A New York Bitlicense", *Coindesk*, 13 August.

Berns, J. K., Mehta, P. D. (2016) "Is Now The Time For California To Regulate Virtual Currency Businesses?", *Bernsweiss*, 17 July.

Bradbury, D. (2014) "Is Bitcoin A Digital Currency Or A Virtual One?", *Coindesk.com*, 19 March.

Brito, J. (2015) "Letter Of Support For Ab 1326", Coincenter.org, 7 July.

Brito, J. (2017) "Congress's New Anti-Money Laundering Bill Likely Duplicates Existing Law On Digital Currency", *Coin Center*, 23 June.

Brito, J. (2017) "It's Time To Assess The Potential For Terrorist Use Of Cryptocurrencies", *Coin Center*, 16 May.

Britton, N. (2015) "Closed-End Funds Struggle In Flat Market, Outperform Over 10 Years", *Morningstar*, 10 September.

Buterin, V. (2013) "Bootstrapping A Decentralized Autonomous Corporation: Part I", *Bitcoin Magazine*, 19 September.

Byford, S. (2014) "Mt. Gox abandons rebuilding plans and files for liquidation: WSJ", *The Verge*, 16 April.

Byrne, P. (2016) "#THEDAO: Broken, but worth fixing", *prestonbyrne.com*, 17 May.

Carlisle, D. (2017) "Cryptocurrencies and Terrorist Financing: A Risk, But Hold the Panic", *Royal United Services Institute Commentary*, 2 March.

CFTC (2017) "CFTC Grants SEF Registration to LedgerX LLC", *Press release pr7584-17*, 6 July.

Chaparro, F. (2017) "MORGAN STANLEY: 'Bitcoin acceptance is virtually zero and shrinking'", *Business Insider UK*, 12 July.

Chen, T. (2013) "Six Reasons Why Card-Linked Offers Are Replacing Daily Deals In 2013", *Forbes*, 2 April.

Clifford, S. (2010) "Aisle by Aisle, an App That Pushes Bargain", *New York Times*, 17 August.

Coin Center (2017) "Letter from Peter Van Valkenburgh, Coin Center", *uniformlaws.org*, 4 May.

Commission de Surveillance du Secteur Financier (2014) "Virtual Currencies", *Press release* 14 February.

Cooper, K. (2017) "Uniform Regulation for Virtual Currency Businesses: Coming to a State Near You", *CoinDesk*, 2 July.

Cuen, L. (2017) "Bitcoin News: US Lawmakers Want Travelers To Declare Cryptocurrency Assets At Border", *International Business Times*, 19 June.

Dababneh, M. (2016) "Assemblymember Dababneh Issues Statement on the Regulation of Virtual Currency", a45.asmdc.org, 15 August.

De Vauplane, H. (2015) "La fascination autour du Bitcoin et des "monnaies virtuelles": comment les définir?", Alternatives Economiques, 7 November.

De Voogd, O. (2016) "Estonia vs Bitcoin saga: Requesting EC Start Infringement Proceedings Against Estonia", steemit.com, 16 September.

Del Castillo, M. (2016) "Bitcoin Developers Warn Ethereum Fork Sets Unsettling Precedent", CoinDesk, 22 July.

Del Castillo, M. (2017) "Bitcoin Options Firm LedgerX Crosses Key Launch Hurdle", CoinDesk, 23 January.

Del Castillo, M. (2017) "Delaware House Passes Historic Blockchain Regulation", CoinDesk, 1 July.

Eha, B. P. (2017) "Delaware blockchain measure seeks to change 'very base' of financial system", American Banker, 13 June.

Eha, B. P. (2017) "Who owns what, really? In securities, Delaware may soon clear things up", American Banker, 5 July.

Electronic Frontier Foundation (2016) "Oppose A.B. 1326: The Digital Currency Business Enrollment Act is Draconian, Overbroad, and Will Hurt Innovation in the State", eff.org, 11 August.

Electronic Frontier Foundation (2017) "EFF Comments on May 2017 Style Committee Meeting Draft of the ULC's Regulation of Virtual Currency Business Act", uniformlaws.org, 4 May.

European Central Bank (2000) "Issues arising from the emergence of electronic money", ECB Monthly Bulletin, November.

European Central Bank (2013) "Payment statistics for 2012", Press release 10 September.

Febelfin (2017) "Succesvolle editie van Febelfin Connect – Speech Johan Thijs", febelfin.be, 20 March.

Federal Bureau of Investigation (2011) "Defendant Convicted of Minting His Own Currency", Press release 18 March.
Fildes, J. (2006) "BBC starts to rock online world", bbc.co.uk, 12 May.
Finley, K. (2016) "A $50 Million Hack Just Showed That the DAO Was All Too Human", Wired, 18 June.
Fogg, J. K. (2015) "NYDFS Changes to Proposed BitLicense Regulations", Virtual Currency Report, 9 February.
Godschalk, H. (2013) "Can an overseer overlook some basics? – The ECB on e-money and virtual currencies", DGC Magazine, 11 August.
Godschalk, H., Krueger, M., Strauch, C. (2013) "The ECB on e-money and virtual currencies: Does the regulator know the regulations?", PaySys SEPA Newsletter July.
Greenberg, A. (2013) "FBI Says It's Seized $28.5 Million In Bitcoins From Ross Ulbricht, Alleged Owner Of Silk Road", Forbes, 25 October.
Guarascio, F. (2014) "Financiers snipe at draft EU law against money laundering", Euractiv, 20 February.
Helms, K. (2017) "Major Japanese Department Store Chain Marui Accepts Bitcoin", bitcoin.com, 6 August.
Hern, A. (2015) "Nasdaq bets on bitcoin's blockchain as the future of finance", *The Guardian,* 13 May.
Hertig, A. (2016) "Ethereum's Two Ethereums Explained", *CoinDesk*, 28 July.
Hertig, A. (2017) "Full Steam Ahead? Segwit2x Reaffirms Bitcoin Hard Fork Plan", *CoinDesk*, 9 August.
Hertig, A. (2017) "It's Official: Segregated Witness Will Activate on Bitcoin", *CoinDesk*, 8 August.
Hertig, A. (2017) "Rebranding The DAO: The Contentious Blockchain Concept is Back", *CoinDesk*, 20 February.
Higgins, S. (2016) "CFTC Grants Full Registration to Bitcoin Swaps Trading Platform", *CoinDesk*, 26 May.
Higgins, S. (2016) "Delaware to Seek Legal Classification for Blockchain Shares", *CoinDesk*, 2 May.
Higgins, S. (2017) "$200 Million In 60 Minutes: Filecoin ICO Rockets to Record Amid Tech Issues", *CoinDesk,* 10 August.
Higgins, S. (2017) "Forfeit Your Bitcoin? Congressional Bill Draws Fire Over Border Check Rules", *CoinDesk*, 19 June.
Higgins, S. (2017) "SEC Denies SolidX Bitcoin ETF Proposal", *CoinDesk*, 28 March.
Higgins, S. (2017) "SEC Rejects Winklevoss Bitcoin ETF Bid", *CoinDesk*, 10 March.
Hinkes, A. (2016) "The Law of The DAO", *CoinDesk*, 19 May.
Jensen, B. (2017) "Primer on the Draft Uniform Regulation of Virtual Currency Businesses Act", *Data Privacy + Security Insider*, 6 July.
Katz, L. (2017) "Bitcoin Acceptance Among Retailers Is Low and Getting Lower", *Bloomberg Technology,* 12 July.
Krebs, B. (2015) "Data Breach at Health Insurer Anthem Could Impact Millions", *krebsonsecurity.com,* 4 February.
Krugman, P. (2013) "Bitcoin Is Evil", *New York Times*, 28 December.
Lee, T. B. (2016) "Ethereum, explained: why Bitcoin's stranger cousin is now worth $1 billion", *Vox,* 24 May.

Levine, M. (2014) "Bitcoin Banking Will Be Boring", *Bloomberg*, 17 July.
Levine, M. (2017) "Bitcoin Exchange Had Too Many Bitcoins", *Bloomberg*, 2 August.
Lucking, D., O'Hanlon, C. (2017) "Delaware Passes Law Permitting Companies to Use Blockchain Technology to Issue and Track Shares", *allenovery.com*, 25 July.
Macheel, T. (2016) "The DAO Might Be Groundbreaking, But Is It Legal?", *American Banker*, 19 May.
Mather, J. (2013) "Ponzi logic: debunking Gary North", *The Libertarian Standard*, 1 December.
McElroy, W. (2017) "De Facto Federal Legislation of Cryptocurrency is Nigh", *Bitcoin.com*, 11 July.
McElroy, W. (2017) "Prepare For SB1241's Pit Bull Assault on Bitcoin Freedom", *Bitcoin.com*, 7 June.
McMillan, R. Metz, C. (2013) "The rise and fall of the world's largest bitcoin exchange", *Wired*, 6 November.
Mehta, P. (2017) "California Assembly Revisits Virtual Currency Legislation", *ETHNews*, 6 April.
Metz, C. (2015) "Bitcoin May Never Make It to Wall Street, But Its Tech Will", *Wired*, 12 May.
Milian, M. (2012) "Aaron Emigh: Rewarding Shoppers With a Silent Signal", *Bloomberg*, 30 August.
Münzer, J. (2013) "Bitcoins: Aufsichtliche Bewertung und Risiken für Nutzer", *www.bafin.de*, 19 December.
Münzer, J. (2014) "Bitcoins: Supervisory assessment and risks to users", *BaFin Expert Articles*, 17 February.
Murphy, R. (2010) "The fractional-reserve banking question", *Mises Daily*, 14 June.
Nation, J., Civalleri, J. (2017) "A Look At The Uniform Regulation Of Virtual Currency Businesses Act", *ETHnews.com*, 29 June.
New York State Department of Financial Services (2013) "Notice of Inquiry on Virtual Currencies", *Press memo*, 12 August.
New York State Department of Financial Services (2013) "Notice of Intent to Hold Hearing on Virtual Currencies, Including Potential NYDFS Issuance of a 'BitLicense'", *Press memo*, 14 November.
New York State Department of Financial Services (2014) "NY DFS releases proposed BitLicense regulatory framework for virtual currency firms", *Press release*, 17 July.
New York State Department of Financial Services (2014) "Order pursuant to New York Banking Law§§2-b, 24, 32, 102-a, and 4001-b and Financial Services Law§§301(c) and 302(a)", *dfs.ny.gov*, 11 March.
New York State Department of Financial Services (2014) "Regulation of the Conduct of Virtual Currency Businesses", *NYS Register*, 23 July.
New York State Department of Financial Services (2014) "Superintendent Lawsky remarks on revised BitLicense framework for virtual currency regulation and trends in payments technology", *Press release*, 18 December.
New York State Department of Financial Services (2015) "NYDFS Announces Final Bitlicense Framework for Regulating Digital Currency Firms", *Speech by Benjamin M. Lawsky, Superintendent of Financial Services*, 3 June.

New York State Department of Financial Services (2015) "NYDFS grants first charter to a New York virtual currency company", *Press release,* 7 May.
Orcutt, M. (2015) "Is Bitcoin Stalling?", *MIT Technology Review,* 18 February.
Padovano, C. (2016) "Yes, Crypto-token Crowdsales Can Be Classified As Securities. Here's Why:", *decentralizedlegal.com,* 15 August.
Palley, S. D. (2016) "How to Sue A Decentralized Autonomous Organization", *CoinDesk,* 20 March.
Perez, S. (2014) "Target's Data Breach Gets Worse: 70 Million Customers Had Info Stolen, Including Names, Emails And Phones", *TechCrunch,* 10 January.
Pitta, J. (1999) "Requiem for a Bright Idea", *Forbes,* 1 November.
Poloniex (2016) "Services to New Hampshire residents to be temporarily suspended on October 6, 2016", *Press release* 21 September.
Popper, N. (2016) "A Hacking of More Than $50 Million Dashes Hopes in the World of Virtual Currency", *New York Times,* 17 June.
Popper, N. (2016) "Ethereum, a Virtual Currency, Enables Transactions That Rival Bitcoin's", *New York Times,* 27 March.
Popper, N. (2017) "Despite S.E.C. Warning, Wave of Initial Coin Offerings Grows", *New York Times,* 7 August.
Posner, E. (2013) "Fool's Gold", *Slate,* 11 April.
Quinn, B., Arthur, C. (2011) "PlayStation Network hackers access data of 77 million users", *The Guardian,* 26 April.
R.A. (2014) "Bitcoin's deflation problem", *The Economist,* 3 April.
Redman, J. (2017) "Bitcoin's Transaction Queue Sets a New Record", *bitcoin.com,* 23 February.
Redman, J. (2017) "Rising Network Fees Are Causing Changes Within the Bitcoin Economy", *bitcoin.com,* 9 June.
Redman, J. (2017) "U.S. Government to Research Role of Virtual Currencies in Terrorism", *Bitcoin.com,* 18 May.
Redman, J. (2017) "White Hacker Group to Claim $4.4 Million in Controversial DAO Refund", *Bitcoin.com,* 10 April.
Rees, M. (2014) "Bitcoin to Earth: Don't Look Now, but your Paradigm is Shifting", *Bitcoin Magazine,* 22 July.
Reitman, R. (2015) "A License to Kill Innovation: Why A.B. 1326 – California's Bitcoin License – is Bad for Business, Innovation, and Privacy", eff.org, 7 August.
Rizzo, P. (2014) "BTC Price Declines Following False Report of Bitcoin Ban in China", *coindesk.com,* 21 March.
Rizzo, P. (2015) "NYDFS Receives 22 Initial BitLicense Applications", *CoinDesk,* 13 August.
Rizzo, P. (2016) "Petition Pushes CFTC to Clarify Rules on Blockchain 'Delivery'", *CoinDesk,* 20 July.
Rizzo, P. (2016) "US Judge Rules Mt Gox Class Action Can Continue Against Mizuho Bank", *CoinDesk,* 15 March.
Roberts, D. (2015) "Behind the "exodus" of bitcoin startups from New York", *Fortune,* 14 August.
Rowell, D.M. (2010) "A History of US Airline Deregulation – Part 4: 1979 – 2010: The Effects of Deregulation – Lower Fares, More Travel, Frequent Flier Programs", *The Travel Insider,* 13 August.

Sankowski, M. (2013) "Bitcoins, Fractional Reserve Banking, and Private Currencies", *monetaryrealism.com*, 2 May.

Santori, M. (2016) "Appcoin Law: ICOs the Right Way", *CoinDesk*, 15 October.

Shadab, H. B. (2014) "Regulating Bitcoin and Block Chain Derivatives", *Written statement to the Commodity Futures Trading Commission Global Markets Advisory Committee 'Digital Currency Introduction – Bitcoin'*, 9 October.

Simonite, T. (2011) "What Bitcoin Is, and Why It Matters", *MIT Technology Review*, 25 May.

Song, J. (2017) "Segwit2x: What you need to know about the 2x Hard Fork (aka 2MB non-Segwit Transaction Capacity per block/8MB Total Block Size Hard Fork)", *Medium*, 26 June.

Stanley, A. (2017) "Investment Firm Blockchain Capital is Launching a $10 Million ICO", *CoinDesk*, 16 March.

Stiglitz, J. (2008) "The fruit of hypocrisy", *The Guardian*, 16 September.

Summers, J. (2013) "FastCash4Bitcoins Suspends Sales", *Bitcoin Magazine*, 3 June.

SuperData Research (2014) "2014 Digital Games Year in Review", *superdataresearch.com*, 3 December.

Swiss Federal Council (2014) "Report on virtual currencies in response to the Schwaab (13.3687) and Weibel (13.4070) postulates", *news.admin.ch*, 25 June.

Talbot, D. (2008) "Second Life Closes Banks", *MIT Technology Review*, 10 January.

Tinianow, A., Smith, M., Long, C., Santori, M. (2017) "Delaware's 2017 Resolution: Make Blockchain a Reality", *CoinDesk*, 3 January.

Todd, M. (2010) "The Murky Waters of State Commodity Laws", *Securities and Investment Blog – Cosgrove Law Group*, 27 July.

Torpey, K. (2017) "Are crypto 'tokens' securities by another name?", *American Banker*, 9 March.

Trugman, J. (2014) "Welcome to 21st-century Ponzi scheme: Bitcoin", *New York Post*, 15 February.

Ummelas, O., Seputyte, M. (2014) "Bitcoin 'Ponzi' Concern Sparks Warning From Estonia Bank", *Bloomberg*, 31 January.

S Department of Justice (2008) "Digital Currency Business E-Gold Pleads Guilty to Money Laundering and Illegal Money Transmitting Charges", *Press* release 21 July.

US Department of Justice (2014) "Chief Technology Officer of Liberty Reserve Sentenced to Five Years in Prison", Press release 14–1393, 12 December.

US Department of the Treasury (2013) "Treasury Identifies Virtual Currency Provider Liberty Reserve as a Financial Institution of Primary Money Laundering Concern under USA Patriot Act Section 311", Press release, 28 May.

Van Valkenburgh, P. (2017) "California is back at it; a new (old) virtual currency licensing bill is pending in the Assembly", coincenter.org, 12 April.

Van Valkenburgh, P., Brito, J. (2016) "New California digital currency bill is a step backwards", coincenter.org, 9 August.

Van Wirdum, A. (2015) "Segregated Witness, Part 1: How a Clever Hack Could Significantly Increase Bitcoin's Potential", Bitcoin Magazine, 19 December.

Vandezande, N. (2014) "Internet Income? IRS Decides Bitcoins are Taxable Property, not Money", LSE Media Policy Project blog, 31 March.

Vandezande, N. (2014) "Searching for more legal certainty in bitcoins and mobile payments", Oxford University Press Blog, 23 April.

Vandezande, N. (2015) "The legislative future of virtual currencies", LSE Media Policy Project blog, 19 January.
Vandezande, N. (2016) "Bitcoin: a new currency in Japan?", KU Leuven CiTiP Blog, 4 April.
Vandezande, N. (2016) "European Parliament to join regulatory debate on virtual currencies", KU Leuven CiTiP Blog, 24 May.
Vandezande, N. (2016) "Bitcoin will have to 'know-its-customer'", KU Leuven CiTiP Blog, 14 July.
Vandezande, N. (2016) "Bitcoin exchanges no payment service providers, but do they want to be?", KU Leuven CiTiP Blog, 2 November.
Vandezande, N. (2017) "Bitcoin takes a ride on the Chinese rollercoaster", KU Leuven CiTiP Blog, 24 January.
Vandezande, N. (2017) "Virtual currency law is Zen for Yen", Policy Forum, 20 April.
Vandezande, N. (2017) "SEC dropping the mic: token sales can be subject to securities law", KU Leuven CiTiP Blog, 28 July.
Wagner, A. (2014) "Digital vs. Virtual Currencies", Bitcoin Magazine, 22 August.
Wallace, B. (2011) "The rise and fall of bitcoin", Wired, 23 November.
Waters, R. (2016) "Automated company raises equivalent of $120M in digital currency", Financial Times, 17 May.
Wilson, F. (2017) "Jurisdictional Competition", avc.com, 9 July.
Wong, G. (2006) "Educators explore 'Second Life' online", CNN, 14 November.
Wong, J. I. (2017) "Bitcoin's soaring price means bankrupt Mt. Gox may soon be able to pay its creditors", Quartz, 13 June.
X (2016) "The DAO of accrue", The Economist, 19 May.
X (2017) "Beyond Bitcoin – A New Paradigm For Regulation", diacle.com, 28 April.

## KU Leuven Centre for IT & IP Law

The KU Leuven Centre for IT & IP Law Series brings together the results of research activities of the Centre for IT & IP Law. The central research themes of the series concern the legal and ethical aspects of information technology, innovation and intellectual property.

Each book in the series focuses on the essential developments in the current legal framework, necessitated by the rapid evolution of technology in various fields, such as government, media, health care, informatics, digital economy, banking, transport and culture. The research is characterised by an interdisciplinary approach, constantly cross-fertilising legal, technical, economic, ethical and socio-cultural perspectives.

Books are published in English, Dutch and/or French.

www.ingramcontent.com/pod-product-compliance
Ingram Content Group UK Ltd.
Pitfield, Milton Keynes, MK11 3LW, UK
UKHW011353270325
1699IPUK00005B/17

9 781780 686752